Beyond National Sovereignty: International Communication in the 1990s

THE COMMUNICATION AND INFORMATION SCIENCE SERIES
Series Editor: BRENDA DERVIN, The Ohio State University

Subseries:
Progress in Communication Sciences: Brant R. Burleson
Interpersonal Communication: Donald J. Cegala
Organizational Communication: George Barnett
Mass Communication/Telecommunication Systems: Lee B. Becker
User-Based Communication/Information System Design: Michael S. Nilan
Cross-Cultural/Cross-National Communication and Social Change: Josep Rota
International Communication, Peace and Development: Majid Tehranian
Critical Cultural Studies in Communication: Leslie T. Good
Feminist Scholarship in Communication: Lana Rakow
Rhetorical Theory and Criticism: Stephen H. Browne
Communication Pedagogy and Practice: Gerald M. Phillips
Communication: The Human Context: Lee Thayer

Beyond National Sovereignty: International Communication in the 1990s

edited by

Kaarle Nordenstreng

and

Herbert I. Schiller

Ablex Publishing Corporation
Norwood, New Jersey

Library of Congress Cataloging-in-Publication Data

Beyond national sovereignty: international communication in the 1990s
    / [edited by] Kaarle Nordenstreng, Herbert Schiller.
        p.   cm.
    Rev. ed. of: National sovereignty and international communication.
    © 1979.
    Includes indexes.
    ISBN 0-89391-959-4. — ISBN 0-89391-960-8 (pbk.)
    1. Communication, International.   2. Communication—International co-
operation.   3. Sovereignty.   I. Nordenstreng, Kaarle.
II. Schiller, Herbert I., 1919-   . III. National sovereignty and international
communication.
P96.I5B49   1992
302.2—dc20   92-29949
                                                                  CIP

Ablex Publishing Corporation
355 Chestnut Street
Norwood, New Jersey 07648

Contents

V

PART VI POSTSCRIPTS

Contributors

Laurien Alexandre, Dean of Academic Affairs at the Antioch University Southern California, Marina de Rey

Oliver Boyd-Barrett, Professor at the School of Education, The Open University, Milton Keynes, England

William Drake, Assistant Professor of Communications at the University of California, San Diego

Richard Falk, Professor of Political Science at Princeton University, Princeton, New Jersey

Andre Gunder Frank, Professor of Development Studies and Social Sciences at the University of Amsterdam, The Netherlands

Johan Galtung, Professor of Peace Studies at the University of Hawaii, Honolulu (Founder and Director of the International Peace Research Institute, Oslo, 1959-69)

Cees Hamelink, Professor of International Communication at the University of Amsterdam and at the Institute of Social Studies, The Hague, The Netherlands (President of the International Association for Mass Communication Research, 1990–94)

Edward Herman, Professor Emeritus at University of Philadelphia, Pennsylvania

Ullamaija Kivikuru, Senior Lecturer of Communications at the University of Helsinki, Finland

John A. Lent, Professor of Communication at Temple University and Director of Third World Media Associates, Philadelphia

Eileen Mahoney, Associate Professor of Communication at the George Washington University, Washington, D.C.

Jesús Martín-Barbero, Founder and Research Professor of the School of Communication Sciences at Universidad del Valle, Cali, Colombia

Robert G. Meadow, Adjunct Professor at the Annenberg School of Communications, University of Southern California and President of Decision Research, Los Angeles

Vincent Mosco, Professor of Journalism at Carleton University, Ottawa, Canada

Hamid Mowlana, Professor of International Relations and Director of International Communication Program at the American University, Washington, D.C. (President-Elect of the International Association for Mass Communication Research)

Kaarle Nordenstreng, Professor of Journalism and Mass Communication at the University of Tampere, Finland

Omar Souki Oliveira, Associate Professor of Telecommunications at Universidade Federal des Minas Gerais, Brazil

Chakravarthi Raghavan, Chief Editor of Third World Network, Geneva, Switzerland

Dan Schiller, Professor of Communication at the University of California, San Diego

Herbert I. Schiller, Professor Emeritus of Communication at the University of California, San Diego, Visiting Professor, New York University, 1993

Leonard R. Sussman, Senior Scholar in International Communications, Freedom House, New York

Immanuel Wallerstein, Professor of Sociology and Director of the Fernand Braudel Center at the State University of New York in Binghamton

Preface

Fifteen years ago the newly appointed series editor of Ablex Publishing Corporation, Melvin Voigt, offered us the possibility of editing a book on international communication. We accepted the challenge, and in 1979 *National Sovereignty and International Communication* was published—the first in what has grown into an impressive list of books on communication.

The first edition went out of print in the mid-1980s, and we were asked by Walter J. Johnson, Ablex's publisher, to prepare a revised edition. We agreed in principle but hesitated for quite some time. It was difficult to decide what to retain from the original and what to add to a new version. Given the rapidly and massively changing international arena, and the accummulating scholarship in the field, the task was daunting. It invited a revision, but at the same time it left us with a dilemma of trying to frame what was still a moving landscape.

Now in the early 1990s, the international scene is no less turbulent, but we felt the project could be delayed no longer—this despite the fact that the far-reaching changes in Eastern Europe have not yet run their course and the Middle East remains a region of deep and unresolved conflict. Indeed, the New World Order, which some suggest has replaced the Cold War, is hardly more than a convenient slogan to divert attention from the all-to-familiar questions of poverty and oppression, now more intense and widespread than ever.

We ended up putting together a completely new set of texts. This should not suggest that the first edition is outdated. On the contrary, most of the earlier contributions remain valid. Actually, the first edition can be regarded more usefully as a base line of relevant reference material. What is at hand in the present new volume may be seen as a successor work, offering a stock-taking of developments in the field in the 1990s.

As with the first edition, however, this volume does not attempt to provide a totally comprehensive picture of a constantly expanding field. For instance, UNESCO and the specifics of the New World Information and Communication Order (NWICO) have been mostly bypassed. There are other recent books focusing on that topic (notably Nordenstreng's *The Mass Media Declaration of UNESCO*; Preston, Herman, and Schiller's *Hope and Folly*; and Gerbner, Mowlana, and Nordenstreng's *The Global Media Debate*).

Also, even now we do not presume to offer a definitive theoretical framework for the study of international communication. Much like the original reader, this is a collection of contemporary explorations and essays on international communication issues, with the concept of national sovereignty serving as a departure point and a continuing, though problematic, theme.

The book contains 20 chapters which have been organized into five parts with a postscript by the editors.

Part I is an overview of the global scene from a general historical perspective beyond the particular aspect called communication. This is presented by outstanding analysts of global policies.

In Part II, the national media are placed in an international context, and the experience of the United States, Brazil, Finland and Tanzania are examined and a current Latin American approach to cultural imperialism is set forth.

In Part III, ongoing reginal and transnational developments are highlighted by focusing with a historical perspective on topics of news exchange, free trade zones, and digital telecommunications.

In Part IV includes an examination of the implications of two decades of debate on transborder data flow, a critical review of the use of international organizations in the field of communications, and a case study of the use of television as a propaganda instrument in foreign policy.

Finally, Part V provides some emerging perspectives on global developments in general and communication prospects in particular.

La Jolla, California, August 1992
Kaarle Nordenstreng and Herbert I. Schiller

PART I
Overview of the Global Scene

Chapter 1
No End to History!
History to No End?*

Andre Gunder Frank

The most important lesson of the East German voting is this: Economics is more important than nationalism or ideology. East Germans behaved like any "normal" democratic electorate: They voted their pocket-books...not so much "Deutschland über alles" as "Deutsche Mark über alles."—Josef Joffe, Foreign Editor, Suddeutsche Zeitung in *New York Times/Herald Tribune* March 22, 1990

MATERIALISM VS. IDEALISM: AN INTRODUCTION

The material real world has disconfirmed many ideas and undone many ideals in recent years. Ideological positions right and left have been undermined by world economic events. Among the political ideological positions disconfirmed by economic reality is Francis Fukuyama's (1989) "end of history." The course of history, which is largely driven by economic forces, shows that neither history itself, nor his and our ideas of history—even of democracy—are at an end. In

* I am grateful to Paulo Frank and Marta Fuentes for help, both in form and content.

particular, historical materialist reality in the past, present, and I fear future belies Fukuyama's underlying position that "the ideal will govern the material world in the long run." This fondly held ideal is at the base of much of the praise accorded Fukuyama's thesis about the victory of liberalism. I submit that there is no evidence, material or otherwise, that history moves to this or any other end.

Material evidence shows that world economic forces beyond anyone's control shape international and national political relations, as well as local social movements, ideological notions from left to right notwithstanding. The real competition until very recently, was not the ideological and political Cold War between the United States and the Soviet Union. The real competitive struggle takes place within the world economy and now especially among the United States, Europe, and Japan (see Frank, 1984a). The erstwhile militarily and politically defeated enemies in Japan and Germany are winning the economic and technological competition in the world economy.

The more the "superpowers" dedicate their resources, efforts, and ideologies to military and political "defense," the more defenseless do they render themselves against the real threat of world economic competition. Paul Kennedy (1987) is right in arguing that economic overextension of "defense" expenditures brings on the fall of empires. It certainly led to the undoing of "superpower" in the United States and the former Soviet Union. However, Kennedy does not go far enough in his analysis, in that he fails to address the underlying cause of economic overextension: competitive capital accumulation in a single world system. Over the past 5,000 years, competitive capital accumulation has been *the* motor force of historical development and cyclical shifts of hegemony (Frank, 1990a, 1991; Gills & Frank, 1990). Although its historical analysis would lie outside the scope of this chapter, it should be evident that the long history of the world economy, its unequal center/periphery, hegemony/rivalry, and upper/lower class structure, and its uneven cyclical development are unlikely to have suddenly ended with Fukuyama. Nor, therefore, should our ideas about history end with his.

For all these and other reasons, the artificial division of the world into American-led capitalist and Soviet-led socialist political blocs was illusory. The political block system did not reflect the reality of political economic competition or the growing division of the world into three of more economic blocs in the Americas, Europe and Asia. The emergence of such blocs was visible on the horizon as early as 1972 (Frank, 1972, reprinted in Frank, 1981). I presented evidence of this bloc formation throughout the 1980s when the world was still blinded by Cold War ideology (Frank, 1981, 1983-1984, 1986, 1988).

Blinded by this ideology, Ronald Reagan sought to reverse the course of history in an appeal to American nationalism. He was elected in 1980 on the nationalist promise "to make America Number 1 again," especially against the ideological enemy and "Evil Empire" in the former Soviet Union. However, neither ideology nor nationalism proved effective against hard economic reality. The Reagan administration made the United States into the world's greatest debtor—now wholly dependent on the inflow of Japanese and European capital—and virtually forced the country out of the competitive race in the world economy.

True, under Reagan's leadership the United States defeated the Soviet Union in the Cold War. However, the United States won this pyrrhic victory at the cost of itself losing the Cold War to noncombatant Japan and Germany. The American victory was more one for military might and increased defense spending (waged by the world's second largest planned economy at the Pentagon!). It was much less so a victory of the moral and political superiority of "free enterprise" and "democracy" over "communism." At the same time, the American preoccupation with Cold War defense allowed Germany and Japan to best the United States in the world technological economic competition. Moreover, even the U.S. Cold War success would not have been possible without the resulting Japanese and European contributions of capital exports to the U.S. These helped mask (and share the burden posed by) the threat of American bankruptcy from the twin budget and trade deficits, which were largely derived from defense expenditures. The Soviet Union's already inefficient economy faltered under the additional defense burden, and its political leadership was finally obliged to cry uncle. Ironically, as the Soviet "challenge" recedes, America turns to "Japan bashing" instead. That is the measure of success of the Reagan policy.

The immediate reason behind these developments, as I have also argued since 1972, is yet another long cyclical world crisis of capital accumulation. This crisis began in the mid 1960s. Lower profits would require drives to reduce costs of production, and these in turn would spur technological development—and competition at the same time. Thus, this crisis would radically alter the terms of the competitive race in the world economy. It would also result in the reintegration of the "Second World socialist" economies into the world market in an intermediate position between the industrially and technologically developed "First World" and the underdeveloped "Third World." For the Second World the terms of incorporation would be better than those of most of the Third World but inferior to those of the West, on which both are dependent. That was my argument in "Long Live

Transideological Enterprise! The Socialist Economies in the Capitalist International Division of Labor and West-East-South Political Economic Relations" (Frank, 1977, 1980).

The logical conclusion of these arguments and real world developments was to plead for both the economic realism and the political desirability of European union (although it would still leave Eastern Europe dependent on Western Europe). That was my argument in *The European Challenge: From Atlantic Alliance to Pan-European Entente for Peace and Jobs* (Frank, 1983-1984). Now the Cold War is over, and Germany and Japan have won. The "Common European Home" proposed by Gorbachev is already under construction.

To be sure, if the presumed Soviet enemy had been able to best Japan in world economic competition, there would have been even less reason to "democratize" the regime there than there now is in LDP-governed Japan. But as it turned out, Soviet economic failure made economic perestroika inevitable, and it in turn made political glasnost necessary. Now "the Evil Empire" has become a force for peace in the world—albeit threatening and threatened by interethnic civil war and perhaps by fascism at home, as Fukuyama also warns.

Therefore, neither history nor some of Fukuyama's own analysis of it lend support to his main thesis. Historical and contemporary reality, as well as some of his and my analysis of it, show that there is *no* end to history, neither in reality nor as an idea. There is no such governance of idea(l)s over the material world in the long run, and no such final victory of democracy. Much of what has been said and written about Fukuyama's "End of History" is without foundation, as he himself explained when he noted that he had been "so misunderstood by so many." To begin with, Fukuyama never argued that we have arrived at the end of history *itself*. Only those who believe that Armageddon is upon us claim this to be true. Of course, history will not end tomorrow, and Fukuyama knows this all too well. Indeed, like the rest of us, he writes about the present *and future* of history. We may disagree whether we are in the midst of a transition from one (kind of) history to another, and if so which. I would argue that this supposed transition or metamorphosis is highly overrated, left and right: Materialism remains alive and kicking. Fukuyama believes in idea(l)s and argues that we have arrived at the end of a certain *idea(l)* of history, because a democratic idea(l) has finally triumphed—or triumphed finally.

To pursue and settle possible agreements and disagreements, we should examine the real world in both its material and its idea(l) manifestations. Simple appeals to ideological(ly convenient) categories are not enough. Therefore, we will submit three widely held related notions to the test or reality: (a) the now almost universal belief in the "magic" of marketization/privatization or "capitalism", (b) the final "triumph" of electoral democracy (which signals Fukuyama's end of history), and (c) the widespread belief that market capitalism and political democracy are one and the same, if not inextricably linked. As will be shown, the historical record and contemporary reality prove otherwise. In fact, these three notions—and the equally ideological left/right debate about them—hamper material understanding and reasonable discussion of the real world. Unfortunately, despite his often incisive analysis, Fukuyama and his central theses also appeal to and support ideology rather than reason.

FREE MARKET CAPITALISM VS. SOCIALISM

Take capitalism, privatization, the market, world market export promotion, and competitiveness. I submit that the current privatization craze is just as economically irrational and politically ideological as was the earlier nationalization craze. It makes very little difference whether an enterprise is owned privately or publicly; for all have to compete with each other on equal terms in the world market. The only exceptions to this rule are public enterprises that are subsidized by the state budget, and private enterprises that are also subsidized from the state budget and/or are otherwise bailed out "in the public interest." Well-known examples in the United States are Detroit's Chrysler Corporation; Chicago's Continental Bank and Trust Company (at the time the eighth-largest U.S. bank); the Ohio, Maryland, California and Texas Savings & Loans; and even New York City. Moreover, in the market, public and private enterprises can both make equally good and bad investments and other management decisions. In the 1970s, (public) British Steel overinvested badly, and (private) U.S. Steel underinvested badly. In the 1980s, both closed down steel mills over the public objections of labor. So did the private steel industry in Germany under a Christian Democratic government and the public steel industry in France under a Socialist government.

I would argue that privatizing public enterprises now at bargain basement share prices that double next week on the national stock exchange is just as fraudulent a practice as nationalizing loss-making enterprises and paying for them above market value, or nationalizing profitable enterprises with little or no indemnification. This "now you see it, now you don't" game is all the more egregious in the case of enterprises in the East and the South, which are now privatized and bought up with devalued domestic currency purchased (or swapped for debt) by foreign companies or joint ventures with foreign exchange from abroad. In sum, the privatization debate is a sham; it is far less about productive efficiency than about distributive (in)justice.

Let's take the fashionable "models" of "private capitalist" export production and world market success: the East Asian Four Tiger/Dragon NICs/NIEs of South Korea, Taiwan, Hong Kong, and Singapore. To begin with, all four owe their present economic position either to political beginnings born of the Cold War (in the case of the first three) or to racial/communal problems (in the case of Singapore). As bastions of anticommunism during the Cold War, Korea, Taiwan, and Hong Kong benefited enormously from American and other economic and political support. For political reasons, the United States enforced a program of land reform on Korea, Taiwan, and Japan—resulting in an income redistribution upon which domestic markets and initial import substitution would be founded. Only then could these countries launch their export-led growth. Hong Kong and Singapore are city states that benefit from large hinterland sources of labor and capital without having to share their political and economic burdens. In Korea and Taiwan, growth was heavily dependent, and in Singapore less so, on national state intervention and Japanese foreign investment. None of these apply to Hong Kong. So the nature of this "model" and the essential "magic" of private capitalism in it is questionable at best.

Is *export*-led growth (ELG) the answer, at least after an initial period of import substitution (ISI)? The gospel preached by the World Bank, the IMF, and their many spokespersons and followers around the world would have us believe that it is. However, ELG has also been the practice, if not the model, in other far less successful countries in Asia, notably the Philippines, Malaysia, Indonesia, Thailand, and Sri Lanka. More recently the Peoples Republic of China, or at least its southern and eastern coastal provinces, have in like manner adopted a policy of ELG. Moreover, ELG was also implemented in Latin America, notably in Mexico, which started this "model" in the 1960s, and Brazil, Argentina, Chile, Peru, etc. The same can be said of a number of African countries, like Tunisia and the Ivory Coast. However, the Latin American ELG of the 1970s led to the economic disaster of the 1980s, the "lost decade" (national product and income in 1990 is significantly less than it was in 1980), and the despair of the 1990s (many countries experienced further decline in 1989, some as much as 10% and 20%).

Chile is perhaps an exception (1989 growth was 8%). The 17-year iron dictatorship of General Pinochet left the growing export economy with a healthy balance of trade and payments, albeit at the expense of an impoverished majority. The Chilean "success," however, was not founded on manufactures-based ELG. On the contrary, Chile tried and failed on that score, except for the profitable export of cluster bombs to Iraq for use in its war against Iran. Instead, Chile achieved ELG based on the use and abuse of its natural and agricultural resources. That was precisely the "development strategy" also imposed on Argentina by its also "Chicago Boy/Friedmanite monetarist" Economics Minister, Martinez de Hoz. Yet he only succeeded in laying the basis for the worst depression and highest inflation in the country's history. So what *is* the model of success or failure, and how is one or the other implemented?

Take Eastern Europe, for instance. Its economies, like their Latin American counterparts, also failed for a variety of reasons, including the Soviet model emphasis on—now outmoded—heavy industry, *and military buildup* (at a time when the East Asian NICs/NIEs concentrated their resources on high tech). In the 1980s particularly, all of the East European economies missed this high-tech train. Of course, if the East European "NICs" had become, indeed even remained, more competitive in the world market than the East Asian NICs, they would have had no revolution of 1989, Fukuyama's and our own celebration of democracy notwithstanding. Now their failure is universally attributed to socialism, and Eastern Europe now shares the Reaganomic and Thatcherist belief in the "magic of the market" as the sure fire alternative. Freeing the market and market freedom are now seen as the solution to all problems on the way to paradise. Greater inequalities of income and mushrooming unemployment are regarded as "small" costs. Moreover, few are willing to consider the costs of privatizing or reconverting East European military sectors, which may account for 25% to 50% of GNP!

So, whatever agreements or disagreements there may be about a model for success, there now seems to be universal agreement on the model of failure: *Socialism*. The "evidence" is in Eastern Europe, for all to see. But is it really? In the 1970s, the countries of Eastern Europe (and "socialist" countries everywhere) switched from ISI import substitution to "import-led growth." They then sought to fuel their growth by importing technology and capital from the West, which they intended to pay for by exporting the derivative manufactures back to the West and the world market. Actually, this import-led growth (ILG) strategy of exporting manufactures to import technology by the East Europeans NICs was only the supply constraint/scarcity economy version of the self-same ELG strategy of importing technology to export manufactures followed by the demand-constrained surplus economies of the East Asian and South American NICs. Moreover, the East Europeans continued with their export promotion to the Soviet Union and each other.

Unfortunately for them—and for the peddlers of ideological models for success—the East European NICs failed no less than the South American ones did, and a few South East Asian ones to boot. No doubt, there were domestic reasons for all these failures, as well as world economic ones. The latter, in a word, were caused by the world economy in crisis, which permitted only few successes to penetrate the protected and recessionary import markets in the West and the world generally.

The "solution" everywhere was to run up debts instead. In the 1970s, moreover, crisis-reduced domestic investment demand in the West made credit financed exports to the South and the East all the more necessary and welcome. So the banks, awash with investible money, loaned and loaned. Debts piled up in the South American and East European NICs alike, and in some South East Asian ones, like the Philippines and Indonesia, as well. This debt economy prospered until the renewed recession in 1979–1982 made the "solution" into yet another problem. The recession obliged closure or restricted access to this South/East casino and its replacement during the 1980s by Reaganomic American roulette in the U.S. casino instead (Frank, 1988).

Those who now find ideological comfort or even discomfort in the failure of "really existing socialism" and the "success" of world market export led growth would do well to make the following comparisons with "really existing capitalism":

- In the 1970s, the same export/import led growth strategies were adopted by Communist Party-led governments in the East (Poland, Romania, Hungary) and military dictatorships in the South (Argentina, Brazil, Chile).
- In the 1980s, the same debt service policies on the IMF model were adopted and implemented by Communist Party-led governments in the East (Poland, Hungary, Romania, Yugoslavia) and by military dictatorships, other authoritarian governments, *and their successor democratic governments* in the South (Argentina, Brazil, Mexico, Philippines).
- There were variations on the theme of debt service, but it is difficult to correlate, let alone explain, them by reference to the political color or ideologies of regimes or governments: The most stellar pupil of the IMF was Nicolae Ceaucescu in Romania, who actually reduced the debt until the lights went out, first for his people and then for himself. In Peru, on the other hand, the newly

elected President Alan Garcia defied the IMF and announced he would limit debt service to no more than 10% of export earnings. Actually, they were less than that before he assumed office. Then, they rose to more than 10% under his presidency. Real income fell by about half, and the novelist Vargas Llosa sought to succeed to the presidency after moving from the political center left to the extreme right. But what does that mean, if anything?

• Communist General Jaruselski in Poland and the populist Sandinistas in Nicaragua also implemented IMF style "adjustment" and "conditionality" on their people. Both did so *without* the benefit of pressure from the IMF, since Poland was not a member and Nicaragua had no access to it. In Nicaragua, there was "condicionalidad sin fondo," that is, conditionality without the Fund and without any bottom or end to the Sisyphean policy. Hungary had the most reformed economy and the most liberal political policy still led by a Communist Party in the Warsaw Pact. Yet Hungary paid off the early 1980s principal of its debt three times over—and meanwhile doubled the amount still owed! That is more than Poland or Brazil or Mexico, which on the average paid off the amount of debt owed only once or twice, while at the same time increasing its total only two times. No matter, the Solidarnosc government that replaced General Jaruselski and the Communist Party in Poland now benefits from IMF membership and imposes even more severe economic sacrifices on its population than its predecessors. Hungary is going to its first free election as these lines are written. Also no matter (who wins), all parties agree to follow the IMF prescriptions after the election.

So are there any "ideological" lessons to be learned from the comparisons and patterns of these economic policies—or successes and failures? Well yes, some: In the cases of Latin America and South East Asia, it is still possible to appeal to "nationalist antiimperialism," and sometimes even to "socialism," to voice and mobilize popular opposition to these political economic austerity policies. Nowhere is that now possible in Eastern Europe—since "Socialism is a failure" and the Communist parties are discredited. They engineered the domestic economic crisis in the first place and then implemented the debt service and austerity policies. And of course, they were subservient instruments of Russian imperialism. So nobody could appeal to them or their policies. On the other hand, the West represents the future. Moreover, the Western IMF and its policies were the "secret weapon" and "de facto ally" of the opposition groups. They are now in power, or making their bid for it, thanks primarily to the economic and secondarily to the political crisis, which was engendered by the implementation of these austerity "adjustment" policies with IMF support. So now there is not only no economic but also no political alternative to further austerity policies, which are tied to IMF and other Western advice and conditions.

The political irony is that "really existing socialism" failed not least because of the unsuccessful implementation of import/export led growth models and IMF style austerity policies in the East. Yet "really existing capitalism" pursued the same models and policies in the South and also failed. However, nobody in the West or East says so; and nobody in the South any longer has a plausible "socialist alternative" to offer. Why was there a "change of system" in (part of) the East in the face of failure, but none in the South in the face of the same failure? Jeanne Kirkpatrick was wrong when she said that "totalitarian" countries in the East don't change, while "authoritarian" ones in the West do. Actually, it is arguable whether in either case there was any "change of system," or an "end of history."

It is easy to sympathize with Fukuyama's chagrin at being misunderstood on this score by so many. Like his, my own careless use of words and (misplaced?) confidence in readers' good sense and fairness caused similar troubling experiences. In 1972, I wrote "dependence is dead, long live dependence" (reprinted in Frank, 1984b). My intent was not that *dependence* itself, any more than *history*, was dead and finished. Naturally, history goes on, and, as we have observed, dependence goes on with it. Certainly, both have continued a "long life" since 1972, even though, especially during the brief "success" of OPEC and other oil exporting countries, many ideologically minded or blinded people left and right claimed that dependence was really dead. So those who (mis)interpreted my statement to mean that the history of dependence was finished were at best mistaken, if not ill-intentioned. My intent was only to say that the *idea* of dependence with the implicit *ideal* of independence was dead.

The reason for this demise, as I argued in 1972, is also the same long crisis of capital accumulation in the world economy. In this crisis, "dependence theory" (which I had helped launch in the 1960s) could no longer offer any realistic economic strategy or political policy that might further non- or independence. On the contrary, I argued in 1972, the issue of the day would be how to analyze and accommodate to this world crisis of accumulation. By 1973 and 1974, I argued why accommodation to this crisis would (have to) spell economic belt tightening and political repression in much of the Third World (Frank, 1981). Of course, political economic repression would turn out to be all the more necessary in the "underdeveloped" Third World, if it also became unavoidable even in the Second "socialist" world and the First "capitalist" world. Everywhere, economic policy would have to adopt to the material exigencies of the world economy and its new crisis of capital accumulation.

In other words, the policy shortcoming of dependence theory was that no capitalist or socialist "system" can be independent, and no policy can yield independence from the world economy. For all are in one way or another dependent, or interdependent as it is now fashionable to say, even if some are more equal and dependent than others. History has demonstrated materially that even (temporary) "superpower" status or the adoption of "socialism" cannot offer non- or independence from world economic development and history. A forteriori, the "Third World" cannot escape dependence, let alone by going into debt, which is only another expression and instrument of dependence in the world system. Therefore by the mid 1980s, I concluded that "delinking" Third World countries from the "capitalist" world economy, as I had advocated in the 1960s, was no longer a realistic policy. Likewise, "liberation" through domestic "socialism" in Third World countries offers scarce alternatives. The "socialist bloc" cannot offer an alternative economic division of labor, which might support politically progressive regimes in these countries. Ironically, the "socialist system's" infrastructure offers no material support for the Marxist superstructural ideology of liberation in this world system (Frank, 1984a, 1988-1989).

In this sense, at least, there has been no end to history and no significant change in the political economic structure of the world system in which history unfolds.

ELECTORAL POLITICAL DEMOCRACY FOR ALL?

There is almost universal agreement, shared by Fukuyama, that everywhere the victor is "democracy" and its "system." With the elections and the transfer of government in Nicaragua and Chile in early 1990, democracy finally appeared everywhere in Latin America. The "revolution of 1989" and the elections in the first half of 1990 have also installed democracy in Eastern Europe, and it seems to be progressing in the former Soviet Union and recently also Mongolia, albeit alas not yet in China, Burma, and some other countries. Many hope for some of the same in much of Africa. Hardly anyone, and least of all the present writer, would today fail to welcome any outbreak of democracy. Fukuyama hails it as the "end of the evolution of human thought about such principles" of human governance. *That* is what he meant by his reference to "the end of history." However, history has taught that it is always dangerous to announce or pronounce the end of anything—and certainly of evolution. I for one cannot join Fukuyama on *that* daring pronouncement. We should ask ourselves—and him— just *what* democracy we have arrived at. Perhaps he—and we—are indeed talking more about idea(l)s than about reality in the material world.

Does democracy ultimately mean the expression and implementation of Abraham Lincoln's famous "will by the people, of the people, and for the people"? Is it the democratic "ideal [that] will govern the material world"? Where and how then does a democratic electorate, or its elected government, govern the material world or even economic policy regarding it?

In the West, in the mid 1970s James Callaghan and Jimmy Carter were both elected on social democratic Keynesian economic policy promises. Yet both abandoned these policies and their electorates to switch to monetarist policies instead. What would become Thatcherism started when the British Labour Prime Minister Callaghan abandoned Keynesianism in 1976 (ostensibly as a condition for an IMF loan, though a Treasury official would later reveal that they wanted this policy change anyway). Then, Milton Friedman wrote a column entitled "From James to Jimmy," counseling Carter to do likewise. However, Carter did not need Friedman's advice to convince him. More weighty material reasons did; and the economic about turn by Democratic President Jimmy Carter in 1977 started what would become Reaganomics (Frank, 1980b).

Social democratic parties and governments elsewhere in North America and Western Europe did exactly the same: Pierre Trudeau in Canada, Helmut Schmidt in Germany, Francois Mitterand in France (after his forced U-turn in 1981), Felipe Gonzalez in Spain—the list could be extended. Indeed, Americans voted for Reagan, but not for Reaganomics, as all opinion surveys demonstrated. All these governments disappointed the electorates who voted for them, and turned to implement Friedman's monetarism, but they did not do so just because of the governing power of his idea(l)s. It was material economic circumstances that governed and forced governments to implement unpopular economic policies.

Was it any different in the "socialist" East before the arrival of democracy—or, for that matter, is it now, when democracy has "finally" arrived in Eastern Europe? Take Poland, for instance. Why did the governments of the Communists Gomulka and Gierek, the Communist General Jaruselski, and Solidarnosc's Prime Minister Mazowiescki *all* implement the same antipopular policies? Indeed, Solidarnosc and the

Communists proposed essentially the same weak economic reforms in 1981 before General Jaruselski imposed martial law on December 13. Then, he lacked the political power to impose even the Solidarnosc-sponsored reforms, because he was governing with martial law instead of the people's will represented by Solidarnosc! Where and what is the democratic expression of that will now that Solidarnosc *is* in power (or rather in government) and is forcing even more drastic antipopular economic belt tightening on the population than the previous government? The same question might be asked of the governments, democratically elected or not, in Hungary, Yugoslavia, and elsewhere.

The Third World is, of course the clearest case of the failure of electoral popular democracy to govern the material world or to implement its own economic policy. Where is the democratic governance over the material world or even of economic policy by, of, and for the people of Argentina in the elected governments of Mrs. Peron, the Junta generals from Videla to Galtieri, and the elected presidents Alfonsin and then Menem? All of the them implemented one unpopular economic austerity policy or another. All failed to satisfy both the consumer desires of the people and the producer development of the nation/country/state. After an already decade-and-a-half-long crisis, in 1989 national income declined by another 10% and the people's income declined by 50%. In recent years, the share of wages and salaries declined from 50% to 20% of national income. Now the populist Peronist President Menem is imposing even more austere economic policies than his predecessor Alfonsin did.

In Peru, under the democratically elected APRISTA President Alan Garcia, national income declined 20% in 1989 and the people's income probably by more than 50%. Is that the "democratic" governance over the material world by, of, and for the people? In Central America, the economic crisis has ravaged the economies of all countries about equally, irrespective of democracy in Costa Rica, more or less veiled military power behind the thrones of the elected presidents in El Salvador and Guatemala, or "Marxist" "socialism" in Nicaragua, which implemented "condicionalidad sin fondo" of its own accord, as observed above. Of course, the U.S.-sponsored Contra war helped shoot up the rate of inflation beyond 30,000% a year anyway.

Why did and do *all* these governments follow essentially the *same* economic policies in the face of the same material economic circumstances? They all did so, because they *had to*. That is, they all *had to* do, not what "the people" wanted, but what economic circumstances demanded. However, not simply the "national" economy and its wealth or poverty constraints on the exercise of the popular will was determinant for the policy "choices" that were and are made. It was and is first and foremost the *dependence within the world economy* that sets out the narrow margins of "democratic" choice and policy. So is there really a "democratic" end (of evolution) of "history"? Or does the electorate only choose the political leaders on each of a hundred-odd "sovereign" national houseboats, which float on an ocean of changing economic currents and recurrent storm crises, over which governments have no control whatsoever? Even the steward and/or the passengers who might have rearranged the chairs on the deck of the Titanic had more "democratic" powers of self determinant choice by, of, and for the people. However, on the Titanic 80% of fourth-class passengers died, 60% of third class, 40% of second class, 20% of first class. The rich and powerful at least have a "democratic" first choice, both on the Titanic and elsewhere. Money talks louder than idea(l)s.

Little wonder—or is it?—that the East Germans, like any normal electorate, voted with the pocketbook. But to how much avail? Similarly, the Nicaraguans were presented with a choice between continuation of conscription and the war (threatened by Bush against the Sandinistas) and money (offered by Bush to Chamorro). The Nicaraguan people chose money and peace. Let us hope that the winning side now delivers the peace and money it promised. The Panamanian "elected" and American installed President Endara went on a lenten fast/hunger strike in the attempt to get the money he says he was promised for his people. For first due to the embargo and then to the invasion, Panamanians now suffer from 50% unemployment.

The people of the German *Democratic* Republic did indeed vote "Deutschemark uber alles." The grass roots democratic social movement Neues Forum probably contributed more than anyone else to bringing down The Wall and bringing on the elections. However, they were soon thanklessly shoved aside by the move to unification, by the elections, and by the voters. It should have come as no surprise, especially after the election n Nicaragua, that East Germans would first abandon Neues Forum and then the Social Democrats (who were still leading in opinion surveys a couple of weeks before the election). The people voted—freely and democratically—for Helmut Kohl, who had unscrupulously offered them the fastest way to the most Deutschemarks.

Indeed, after the wall came down, a large majority of East Germans—like Neues Forum—still favored independence. Reunification only became *the* issue of immediacy on both sides of the border after two-to-three thousand East Germans daily started to vote with their feet, or their Trabant cars, for the Deutschemark on the other side. Even the exchange of East German marks for West German ones—and the conundrum of at what rate to exchange them—only became an issue because the pressure of the East Germans' economic demands threatened a fait accompli beyond anybody's control. In a word—of our epigraph—"economics is more important than nationalism or ideology" in the whole process of the reunification of Germany (and of Europe).

Had the East German economy not faltered in the 1980s, both absolutely and relative to that of West Germany, there would have been little movement for "democratic" opposition to the regime. The wall and then the regime itself would not have come down, East Germany itself would not have been doomed, and its people would not have voted with their feet and ballots for the speediest possible reunification with the Deutschemark. Of course, all this should be, and now fortunately is, the democratic right of the people of East and all Germany.

When Fukuyama says that "we have to recognize that an important revolution is under way in the world, and in that revolution, ideas count," we should exercise a bit more care than he does to recognize just what ideas that may be and why they count. It is an ideological coverup to claim that what is happening in Germany and elsewhere is done first and foremost in the good ideological name of democracy or even secondarily in the bad ideological name of nationalism. Both ideologies serve to cover up both rank materialist motives and real material forces. In this regard as well, Fukuyama's thesis cannot stand up to the evidence—or even to much of his own analysis.

Fukuyama himself correctly observes that, "as communism recedes from Eastern Europe, it is fascinating to watch the recrudescence of longstanding nationalist conflicts." Indeed, though there is some reason to doubt that it is "communism" that recedes and to fear that the "fascination" may turn into terror. One brand of nationalism is recrudescing all over already, that of being German. This sudden rediscovery of "our German identity" is not limited to West and East Germany. In Poland, Czechoslovakia, Romania, Hungary, and the former Soviet Union, all sorts of people, many of whom can hardly speak German, are now finding it economically attractive to rediscover their German identity. Heaven only knows, and God forbid, what nationalist conflicts this new identity crisis may soon conjure up in Central and Eastern Europe. Before they go any further, these German identities may express themselves through ethnic parties in democratic elections. We can only hope that democratic channels will be enough to accommodate them. Of course, German Chancellor Kohl's attempt to avoid committing Germany to respect the Oder-Neisse border with Poland, in the East for fear of losing right-wing German nationalist votes in the West, offers little hope on that score.

There is indeed recrudescent nationalism in the former Soviet Union and Eastern Europe. The Balkans are threatened with balkanization, which in living memory has already led or contributed to two

World Wars. Even brief inspection shows that immediately behind all this nationalism and ideology lurks the more important economics of it all (see Frank, 1990b).

The expanding and deepening economic crisis in Eastern Europe and the former Soviet Union has contributed materially to the desire and ability of social (and also ethnic/nationalist) movements to mobilize so many people for farreaching political ends. The course and (mis)management of the economic crisis has generated shifts in positions of dominance or privilege and dependency or exploitation. These shifts affect countries, sectors, and different social, including gender, and ethnic groups within the former Soviet Union and Eastern Europe. All of these economic changes and pressures generated or fuelled social discontent, demands, and mobilization, which find expression in revitalized social (and ethnic/nationalist) movements. It is well known that economically based resentment is fed by the loss of "accustomed" absolute standards of living as a whole or in particular items *and* by related shifts in economic welfare among population groups. Most economic crises are polarizing and further enrich, relatively if not also absolutely, the better off. The same crises also further impoverish, both relatively and absolutely, those who were already worse off, including and especially women.

Both the privileged and the underprivileged are mobilized to action by these developments. The less privileged mobilize to defend their livelihood against abuse from "the system" and against those who benefit from it through corruption or otherwise. Among ethnic groups, these include Turks in Bulgaria, Hungarians in Romania, Gypsies and others in Hungary, Albanians in Serbia, Serbians in Yugoslavia, Slovakians in Czechoslovakia, and Romanians, Azerbaijanis and a host of others in the former Soviet Union and especially in its Central Asia. The latter, among other problems, are plagued by recent increases of unemployment, which now exceeds 25% of the labor force. Is it any wonder that these young people of such diverse ethnicities and nationalities are moved to participate in nationalist and other ethnic demonstrations?

The privileged also develop resentments against the "system," which forces those who are better off to "carry" or "subsidize" at their own "expense" their "good for nothing," "lazy" poorer neighbors. Moreover, all too often the more privileged are attracted to greener pastures beyond their socialist/capitalist/national borders. Among these are many Russians, Armenians, and others in the former Soviet Union, and especially the economically more developed Lithuanians, Latvians, and Estonians. The latter sought and obtained independence from the former Soviet Union, which they perceive as hindering their own further economic development. Among the more privileged regions and groups are also the Slovenians and to a lesser extent the Croatians in Yugoslavia, and of course the East Germans, who turned toward the economic magnet in the West.

The population at large also mobilizes, or at least is more readily mobilizable, in support of demands that arise out of increasing economically based resentments. Such demands often find political expression in ethnic/nationalist platforms. Recent economic(ally based) resentments throughout Eastern Europe and the former Soviet Union are indisputably a major factor in generating (and accounting for) the widespread popular mobilization through social (and ethnic/ nationalist) movements. Antisemitism is also rearing its ugly head again all over Central and Eastern Europe.

With regard to these movements, Fukuyama correctly signals the danger of a fascist potential in the former Soviet Union, where the Pamyat Russian nationalists are gaining force, and in Serbia under the leadership of Premier Slobodan Milosevic. He also correctly points to growing rightist antiforeign sentiments in Western Europe, organized in political parties like Le Pen's in France and the former SS man Schongruber's Republicans in Germany. We would do well to recall that, last time around, fascism in Europe grew out of the world economic crisis. Moreover, in Germany fascism was additionally furthered by *The Economic Consequences of the Peace* of Versailles, as John Maynard Keynes entitled his book about the costs of the war reparations debt imposed on Germany. Now the debt in Eastern Europe, not to mention Latin America, threatens renewed social upheavals and dangers to democracy. What is strangely missing in Fukuyama's rendition of this newly developing Shakespearean tragedy à la Hamlet is the materially obvious economic Prince of Denmark.

FREEDOM OF THE MARKET = DEMOCRATIC FREEDOM?

Most curious of all, perhaps, is the now fashionable identification of free market "capitalism" and electoral political "democracy" as though they were inseparable if not indistinguishable.

The "successes" of the East Asian NICs and Japan have scarcely been associated with much electoral democracy. Japan has had elections, but the LDP has been unalterably dominant almost as long as the PRI in Mexico. Moreover, the LDP and PRI factions do not reflect alternatives of political choice as much as of personal leadership. South Korea, Taiwan, and Singapore have "prospered" under completely authoritarian regimes, which are only now beginning to yield in response to economic success. In Hong Kong, of course, there has been and still is no question or discussion of any kind of political democracy by either the near mainland Chinese or the distant insular British. The Hong Kong Chinese, per contra, demand democratic self-determination with their feet, if not with their voices and votes.

In the West, that is, in North America, Western Europe, and more recently in parts of Southern Europe and Oceania, political social democracy has been much less the cause than the effect of economic success in the capitalist market—and importantly so in the *world* capitalist market. These countries in the West have been able to afford the precious luxury of electoral political democracy only where and when the basis of their economic wealth afforded it to them. It is of course delicate and controversial to point out that, without a regime of West/South relations based on "imperialism" and "colonialism" in the past and "unequal exchange" to this day, the West would not have been able to gain and maintain its basic economic wealth, income, social democracy—and therewith also political democracy. Unfortunately for them, the "socialist" countries in the East were only very moderately able to benefit from such inflows of income from the South. The reasons for this failure have less to do with the inadequacies of socialist planning at home than with their inadequate insertion in the world market abroad. As for the dependent South, it has long suffered economically, socially, and politically from the support that it affords to economic development and political democracy in the West.

There is little material basis if any to expect significant improvements in these economic–political relationships in the world economy in the foreseeable future. On the contrary, material development in the world economy is likely to make matters worse in the short and medium/long run. As long as the debt burden continues and even mounts in the near future, the debt-ridden economies in the South will continue to suffer and the debt will continue to threaten their democracies. Alas, the same is true of the new or aspiring, but still debt-ridden, democracies of Poland, Hungary, Yugoslavia, and elsewhere in Eastern Europe. Any financial arrangement à la IMF, or even the commercial terms for the proposed new European Bank for Reconstruction and Development, can inevitably only maintain and aggravate these burdens and dangers. Such policies would extend the same burdens dangers on to other parts of Central and Eastern Europe and perhaps the Baltic Republics.

In the medium run, parts of Central Europe (East Germany, Bohemia, Hungary, Slovenia) may well be incorporated into the Common European Home, but in a dependent position at the back of the ground floor where they will compete with the recently already incorporated parts of Southern Europe. Other parts of Eastern Europe (in Poland, Romania, Bulgaria, Serbia, perhaps Slovakia) are more likely to be relegated to the basement, where they are likely to be less "Europeanized" than "Latin Americanized" or even to suffer "Lebanonization." Poland is already experiencing Latin Americanization; and Kosovo, Transylvania, and the Transcaucasus are already threatened with Lebanonization.

World economic material and labor-saving long-run development is furthering marginalization of ever larger parts of the Third World along the African way. However, industrial and agricultural progress and decline in the West are also marginalizing growing parts of its population into racial, ethnic, and other drug- and crime-ridden ghettoes. Now that massive unemployment and increased regional differentiation and social polarization is also coming to the East, it too is threatened by the same kind of economic, social, and political marginalization. Indeed, in Southern parts of Yugoslavia and the former Soviet Union, not to mention Western and other parts of China, this marginalization is already making its mark. Fukuyama does as well to ring the political alarm bell here, as he does to ring praises of democracy there. However, he might as well have also drawn attention to the material economic basis of both democracy and alarm.

Like money of course, electoral democracy appears very desirable, especially when one does not have any. Then it is easy to appreciate the coming of elections among multiple parties and a freer press to debate political and other options, etc. This is particularly the case in the "socialist" East, where oppressive Communist Party bureaucracies and foreign domination have hamstrung economic development and political expression. The return of electoral democracy is also welcome in those parts of the South, in the Americas and Southeast Asia, where military or other authoritarian regimes have run the economy into the ground and into a hole of debt. The human cost has been, first, tens of thousands of assassinations, disappearances, and torture, and then increased hunger, disease, infant mortality, crime, etc. A whole generation suffers from tragically reduced life opportunities. It should not be necessary to point out that all this has been quantitatively and qualitatively worse in the (capitalist) South than in the "socialist" East. However, the new democracies offer little hope to reverse this human tragedy.

In the face of this material world history, some people may well wish now to associate democracy with the free market and/or capitalism. In the East, most people associate capitalism with promises of a bright future. In the South, however, capitalism is associated with bitter

experience past and present. In some countries, the dismal state of the
economy again threatens the democratic state. Unfortunately, the
Poles are already experiencing the same bitter fruits of market/
democracy (cum debt) as the Argentinians, Brazilians, and Filipinos
have in recent years.

So it is hardly the case that market and democracy, or economic and
political freedom, always go together. In fact, the opposite could be
argued equally well. In an electoral democracy, it is one man (now,
fortunately, one person), one vote. In the market, it is one dollar, one
vote. That is, many dollars, many votes; no dollars, no vote. Indeed,
those who have or can earn only few or no dollars at home are
marginalized not only from voting economically, but tend to be also
excluded from voting politically. It is no accident that the most
marginalized poor vote the least in elections. In the United States they
are 50%, and the homeless have no residence and therefore not even
the right to vote.

Similarly, those who have no or earn only few dollars abroad, but
only pesos or zlotys at home, are also marginalized both economically
and politically in the world system, unless they now have marks or
yen. The yearly "economic" (really political) summits of the Group of
Seven (G 7) offers a vivid illustration of this principle. They illustrate
it all the more so, since the G 5 only admit Canada and Italy into their
circle by traditional noblesse oblige. Moreover, the charmed circle of
real decision makers is limited to the G 3 governments or central
banks of only the United States, Germany, and Japan, with even those
of Britain and France on the outside looking in. There is also a wider
sort of consultatory circle of 24 OECD industrialized countries with
some voice but no vote. In the political economic councils of the world
outside the UN General Assembly's talking chamber, the rest of
(wo)mankind, however, who live in the "third" and "second" worlds in
the South and East, have no real voice or vote.

What is worse, the market not only excludes the already dollarless
from this political influence at home and abroad. The operation of the
market is also generally polarizing to make the rich richer and the
poor poorer—and thus even more marginalized. The Bible tells us that
this is not a recent fact of life, when it observes that, "to those that
hath, shall be given; and from those that hath not, shall be taken,"
even the little economic and political vote that they have. Of course,
the market like a lottery does offer the opportunity to some, and the
illusion to many, to win a better position in it, mostly through the
exercise of some temporary monopoly power, legal or illegal, moral or
immoral. *That* opportunity is what makes the market—and the
lottery—so attractive to so many, including the losers. The latter,

however also have one other political option to press their case to be heard: they can and do mobilize themselves through social movements to exercise another form of democracy.

Thus, electoral democracy is not the be all and end all—even of democracy, let alone of history or its idea. Another increasingly important part of democracy are the nonparty social movements, particularly in civil society, or what may be called participatory "civil democracy" (Fuentes & Frank, 1989; Frank & Fuentes, 1990).

In the absence of political democracy in the East, people had massive recourse to civil democratic social movements to lay the basis for electoral party democracy in the first place. All the New, Civic, and other Forum movements in the GDR, Czechoslovakia, and Hungary sought to maintain their identity and independence from the new political parties. Yet all these movements were soon overwhelmed by the electoral process and the imperatives of running the state. Perhaps the blessings of multiple political parties (Hungary already has 50 of them!), elections, and parliaments appear so important, after so many years without them, that people tend to neglect the equally important other processes and institutions of civil democracy.

It remains to be seen, however, whether Fukuyama's summum bonum of electoral and parliamentary democracy can offer more opportunities for popular self-determination than this participatory civil democracy did. It can be argued that the new de jure electoral and parliamentary state institutions de facto serve effectively to *disen*-franchise people in Eastern Europe again after their massive exercise of participatory democracy. How much democratic self-determination, contra Fukuyama, can these institutions guarantee and afford the people, especially if their economies are Third World-ized?

Therefore, it would be tragic now to abandon the conquest of this civil democracy to the blessings of the exercise only of political democracy through political parties, which contest elections for a government to run the state (as best it can under the external and domestic economic constraints).

For in the West and the South, civil democracy increasingly complements political democracy everywhere, precisely because of the limitations of the electoral process organized through political parties. Social movements arise and mobilize people for a myriad of economic, social, cultural, and political causes and demands of the population, which elections and the government cannot provide or do not offer without the popular pressure exercised through this civil democracy. Indeed, it is again the economic crisis, especially in the South, that obliges people to organize and mobilize themselves in grass roots social movements. These movements promote participant democracy and alternative production and distribution to defend livelihood and identity against the ravages of the economy and the neglect or domination by the state. Of course, as observed above, it was also first and foremost the economic crisis in Eastern Europe and the Soviet Union that fuelled the social movements to demand and achieve some economic perestroika and political glasnost there. The need for the same or other social movements acting in and through civil society will also remain after the installation of elected governments based on political parties.

At the same time, such social movements in civil society, no less and often more than political parties in government, will also represent regional and ethnic or nationalist interests and demands. The best we can hope for is that each will recognize the others' equal right to existence within the political institutions of the state and the international community of states. The worst we can fear, along with Fukuyama, is that ethnic, nationalist, and chauvinist groups will go into renewed armed battle with each other in another process of balkanization, which threatens us all.

A CONCLUSION WITHOUT ISM

Fukuyama is not alone in suffering from the (ill-intentioned?) misinterpretation of his writings, and my conclusions from the above run the risk of further misinterpretation. For most interpretations of recent events, particularly in Eastern Europe, fall into two ideological categories (or traps?). The majority are "anti-Marxist" and revel in the "obvious victory of capitalism and freedom." The minority try to defend "Marxism" and "Socialism" from guilt by association. They argue that only "Stalinism" failed in the debacle of "really existing socialism," which was *not really socialism* and does not represent true Marxism. The two camps loudly disagree about the content of their different ideologies, but they quietly agree on the importance of ideology itself. My interpretation is in a third category and suggests both camps put too much faith in ideology itself and that therefore neither ideological camp is drawing its conclusions from the real material evidence.

Neither Marxist nor Anti-Marxist idea(l)s do or should govern. The evidence suggests that, contrary to Fukuyama and many of his commentators, the material world governs in the long run, and mostly in the short run, too. That is why, no matter what our idea(l)s may be, we should analyze reality in order to change it. Actually, Fukuyama has done much more of that than he has been given credit for. In offering my own conclusion, I can only appeal to the reader to examine the evidence and divest himself or herself as much as possible of dark or rose-colored glasses and ideological blinders. Let us give credit where credit is due to real successes and analysis, and withhold credit where it is not due—to ideal-isms.

Yet, my declaration in 1972 that I am "neither a Marxist, nor an anti-Marxist" any more than I am pro- and anti-Newtonian (Frank, 1984, chap. 24) also led to apparently deliberate misinterpretations, analogous to those from which Fukuyama suffers. Marxists had long since criticized me for not being one of them and then said, "Aha, he finally admits this failure himself," so he must be an enemy of Marxism and good conscience. Anti-Marxists said, "Aha, he admits that he is *not anti*, so he is not one of us" and must be an enemy of science and good fellowship. Yet all I was trying to say is that I try to follow the (Marxist?) Chinese maxim, "seek truth from facts" and the American (anti-Marxist) one to "tell it as it is."

Following this procedure, one conclusion emerges at least tentatively from this materialist comparative examination of recent and past—including several-millennia-old—material and ideal reality: Ideal categories and isms, like communism, socialism, but equally so capitalism (or earlier feudalism), and even Fukuyama's liberalism, serve more to obfuscate than to enlighten. Would it not be better to discard these largely ideological categories and labels? They offer ideological self-satisfaction, but they impede and obscure the analysis of the material real world economic development and the real rather than ideal alternative choices it offers yesterday, today, and tomorrow. To call the world system structure and/or process of political economic competition "capitalist" adds little to our understanding of the real world system or how it operates, past, present, and future. Use of these labels also adds nothing to anyone's ability to improve his or her competitive position in the world system or any part of it. The world political economic system obliges all to compete still today and likely tomorrow, as it has for millennia past. The bottom line has been the ability to compete effectively. Some do and are in the black, albeit only temporarily; and most can't and are in the red, most of the time. As in any race, there are few winners and many losers.

There is no concluding end. No economic, political, social, or cultural "model" or "ism" offers a guarantee for success, let alone for long, and never forever. No such model marks the end of history. People will continue to dance on the material stage of history. Some may wish to do so to Fukuyama's ideological tune, and others to different national, ethnic, religious, political and other ideologies—many of which in turn are also very materially based. Either way, there is no end to history! Is history also to no end?

REFERENCES

Frank, A.G. (1980a). Long live transideological enterprise! The socialist economies in the capitalist international division of labor.

Frank, A.G. (1980b). *Crisis: In the world economy*. New York: Holmes & Meier and London: Heinemann.

Frank, A.G. (1981). *Reflections on the economic crisis*. New York: Monthly Review Press and London: Hutchinson.

Frank, A.G. (1983-1984). *The european challenge*. Nottingham, UK: Spokesman Press (1983) and Westbury, CT: Lawrence Hill (1984).

Frank, A.G. (1984a). Political ironies in the world economy. *Studies in political economy, 15*. [Reprinted in T. Boswell & A. Bergesen (Eds.), *America's changing role in the world-system* (pp. 25-55). New York: Praeger, 1987.)

Frank, A.G. (1984b). *Critique and anti-critique*. New York: Praeger and London: Macmillan Press.

Frank, A.G. (1986). Is the Reagan Recovery real or the calm before the storm? *Economic and Political Weekly, XXI* (21 & 22).

Frank, A.G. (1988). American roulette in the globonomic casino: Retrospect and prospect on the world economic crisis today. In P. Zaremblca (Ed.), *Research in political economy* (Vol. 11, p. 3-43).

Frank, A.G. (1988-1989). The Socialist countries in the world economy: The east-south dimension. In Lelio Basso International Foundation (Ed.), *Theory and practice of liberation at the end of the XXth century* (pp. 307-328). Brusells: Bruylant, (Also in B.H. Schulz & W.H. Hansen (Eds.), *The Soviet bloc and the Third World: The political economy of east-south relations*, Boulder, Co: Westview Press, 1989.)

Frank, A.G. (1990a). A theoretical introduction to five thousand years of world system history. *Review, XIII*, 155-248.

Frank, A.G. (1990b). "East European revolution of 1989: Lessons for democratic social movements (and socialists?) *Economic and Political Weekly*, February 3, 1990, and *Third World Quarterly, XII* (2), April 1990. (Also in *The future of socialism: Perspectives from the Left* (William K. Tabb, Ed., pp. 87-105). New York: Monthly Review Press, 1990).

Frank, A.G. (1991). A Plea for World system history. *Journal of World History, 2*(1), 1-28.

Frank, A.G. & Fuentes, M. (1990). Social movements in world history. In S. Amin, G. Arrighi, A.G. Frank, & I. Wallerstein (Eds.), *Transforming the revolution. Social movements and the world-system*. New York: Monthly Review Press.

Fuentes, M., & Frank, A.G. (1989). Ten theses on social movements *World Development, XVII*, 2.

Fukuyama, F. (1989). The end of history" and "End of history: So misunderstood by so many. The original article was published in *The National Interest*, excerpted by the author in the *Washington Post* and *International Herald Tribune*, and versions of it were translated and reprinted worldwide. Fukuyama's answer to his critics was similarly publicized, including an excerpt in the *IHT* December 15, 1989. *El Pais* in Madrid, for instance, devoted a special 16-page Sunday supplement to the 4 pages of the reply and half a dozen of the countless comments from around the world.

Gills, K., & Frank, A.G. (1990). The cumulation of accumulation. Theses and research agenda for 5000 years of world system history. In C. Chase-Dunn & T. Hall (Eds.), *Precapitalist core/periphery systems*. Boulder, CO: Westview Press.

Kennedy, P. (1987). *The rise and fall of the great powers*. New York: Random House.

Chapter 2
Geopolitical Transformations and the 21st-Century World Economy

Johan Galtung

INTRODUCTION: THE GEOPOLITICAL
BACKGROUND

It looks as if the transition from Yalta to Malta certainly was a giant step, not toward peace but to the New World Order. The question is what that means. Although there is no conclusive evidence, we may have good reasons to believe that, whereas at Yalta they divided Europe, at Malta they divided the whole world, or most of it.[1] More particularly, four major zones, spheres of interest or regions can be described as follows:

I. *United States will have hegemony over the Western Hemisphere and the Middle East*, with an inner periphery in Canada–Mexico and Israel, and an outer periphery in the rest.

II. *The European Community will have hegemony over most countries in Central and Eastern Europe, and the 68 countries of the ACP (African–Caribbean–Pacific) system established by the Yaounde-Lome conventions from 1964 onward,*[2] with an inner periphery in the former (some with associate status) and an outer periphery in the latter: the most globally encompassing empire in history. Confederate EC is now

28

moving toward a federal European Union with common finance, foreign, and defense policies, making the structure irreversible by using majority rule, not consensus. There will be expansion of membership. Inner center: Germany, France and England, and basically trilingual.

III. *Japan will have hegemony over East-Southeast Asia.* This might mean an inner periphery of the two parts of Korea (South and North), the three parts of China (PR China, Hong Kong, and Taiwan) and Vietnam (The Buddhist-Confucian countries) and an outer periphery of the ASEAN countries, the four socialist and ex-socialist countries Mongolia, Burma and Laos and Cambodia, and then Australia/New Zealand and the other Pacific Islands, including Hawaii. In short, the old Great East Asian Co-Prosperity Sphere;[3] the *dai-to-a-kyoeiken*. The Japanese sphere has the largest population by far. So far the signs are that the sphere will be based on economic rather than military power, although it is hard to tell how long that will last given pressure from other zones.

These first three zones, spheres, or regions will probably crystallize economically as the Dollar-zone, the ECU/DM-zone, and the Yen-zone, respectively. The next four regions will for the foreseeable future not be in the possession of what could be called world currencies (in plural), and may have to lean toward one of two of the three mentioned. Which one(s) will be a source of conflict of major geoeconomic and -political significance.

IV. *The former Soviet Union will have hegemony over itself.* This may mean a center in Russia with White Russia, possibly also with Eastern Ukraina (orthodox) and Northern Kazakhstan (with heavy Russian population)[4], and a periphery consisting of the rest of the Commonwealth of Independent States (CIS). Like for the Western Hemisphere, however, "hegemony" is incompatible with "sovereignty" for the republics. To foresee the structure that will emerge is impossible at this stage, but many ties, at the very least economic, will remain. And it is very difficult to believe that this vast structure will not also have a center, and by implication a periphery, whether run the Gorbachev way, by the Party–Army–KGB troika in some new way, by capitalists/free marketeery or by neofascists.

By *a hegemonial system*, then, is meant the following:

- the right and duty of military intervention by the hegemon in case of "instability" threatening their sphere of interest;
- the duty to punish disobedient client states and individuals as individual and general prevention, including court processes;

- intervention by "gentlemen's agreement," also on behalf of other hegemons, so criticism will be soft and short lasting on an "I-don't-undercut-you-if-you-don't-undercut-me" basis;
- economic preponderance on an "I-don't-try-to-outcompete-you-in-your-region-if-you-don't-try-to-outcompete-me-in-mine" basis;
- cultural regionalism guaranteeing some cultural homogeneity;
- political regionalism, meaning regional organizations for basic decision making controlled by the hegemon (and not by the United Nations), possibly with cross-representation of other hegemons, the political region defining the territory of "self-defense"[5];
- hegemons in deep trouble may be assisted by other hegemons;
- the final arbiter, the primus inter pares, the hegemon of the hegemons, is the United States, not the United Nations, settling conflicts among hegemons and assisting hegemons in distress.

This "Malta system" of international feudalism has already been put to a test, with the U.S. intervening in Panama and leading the "coalition" against Iraq, and the former Soviet Union intervening in the trans-Caucasian and Baltic republics, eliciting only muted critique from other hegemons. When France and the former Soviet Union tried to soften/avoid the Gulf War, the argument "if-you-don't-support-me-I-might-work-against-you-when-you-are-in-trouble" no doubt carried much weight. New Caledonia, the Baltic States! The EC tried to take on a softer operation in Yugoslavia. And Japan has not yet taken on any military hegemonial role using economic power: "better buying Pearl Harbor than bombing Pearl Harbor."

The Malta system needs completion with more world regions:

V. *China will have hegemony over itself.* China has usually exercised this, except for two or three periods of disgrace, the last being from the 1840s till the 1940s. China may have to accept that not only Korea and Vietnam but also Tibet are outside the region. It should be noted that this concept is entirely compatible with the old Confucian doctrine of *han* Chinese versus the four types of barbarians, North, East, South, and West.[6] The innermost center remains Beijing, not Shanghai.

VI. *India will have hegemony over South Asia.* This would mean an inner periphery of the other SAARC[7] countries on the subcontinent (Pakistan, Bangladesh, Sri Lanka, Nepal, Butan, and the Maldives); and an outer periphery with a heavy population of Indian nationals, such as the litoral of the Arab Sea, Bengal Bay and India Ocean, and also the Trinidad and Fiji Islands.

VII. *A coming Islamic/Arab superpower.* We are here talking about a possibility two to three generations hence, bringing one billion

Muslims and the 47 countries of the Islamic conference together, possibly with a nucleus of the Arab countries (today 200 million divided into 22 states, if we count Palestine), or with a non-Arab, Turkish nucleus of Turkey, ex-Soviet Islamic republics, and Pakistan/ Iran. It could hardly operate without a center, inner periphery, and outer periphery like the others, opening a Pandora box of problems for this region. The rivalries in the Damascus–Baghdad- –Cairo–Tehran–Istanbul pentagon of old empires have age-old history. But some day polycentric formulas like the European Community may emerge. Time will tell.[8]

It may be argued that neither the European Community nor the Islamic Conference has the necessary coherence. But what they do not have they may get, even through a race for coherence with Islamic countries catching up as the EC proceeds.

But so far it only makes sense to talk about six regions and six hegemons/superpowers, three of them global, three regional.

Needless to say, if this is anything like an adequate vision of the geopolitical map of the 21st century, then the political and military implications are tremendous. Thus, we are actually talking about a world with six superpowers, four of them veto powers in the Security Council (even EC has two vetoes). Five of them already have nuclear weapons (EC even double), and the sixth, Japan, may be heading straight for directed energy weapons (DEW) systems, such as offensive laser beams,[9] beamed directly from satellites or indirectly via geostationary mirrors. In terms of conventional arms the five major arms exporters in the world are found within four of them, and the other three are the major arms importers.[10]

And this is where the "New World Order" enters. It can be seen as an effort to manage the totality of this six/seven-polar world from Washington, D.C. If so the U.S. enters in two capacities: as the hegemon in Region I, so to speak, and as the primus inter pares, the hegemon's hegemon, with the others serving as regional deputies. The frequently encountered term *multipolar* does not catch this reality at all; it is more like six/seven parallel unilateralisms organized in three layers with Washington, D.C. on top; then the hegemons, some more developed militarily than economically; and then the rest (see Table 1).

Idealistically speaking this should leave the U.S. free to focus on the Western hemisphere with occasional interventions in the highly uncrystallized Middle East, hoping that a local hegemon may be found/ created. From gambling on Iran (e.g., the Dhoffar rebellion, in Oman), Egypt, and to some extent Israel, the current approach may be to make a hegemon out of the Middle East allies in the anti-Saddam Hussein

Table 1   GEOPOLITICS I: A GUIDE TO THE "NEW WORLD ORDER" (Pax Americana)

Image A (NEW WORLD) ORDER	Image B Development	Image C Power
U.S.A.	Washington DC; WDC	Inner Center: U.S.A.
Canada	More Developed; MDC	Center: Hegemons
Latin America	Less Developed; LDC	Periphery: Inner, Outer
CENTER **The Hegemons**	**INNER PERIPHERY** **More Favored**	**OUTER PERIPHERY** **Less Favored**
I. U.S.A.	Canada-Mexico	Central, South America
	Israel, Gulf Corporation	Middle East
II. EC/EU	Eastern Europe	
	(EC-associates?)	ACP system
		Yaounde-Lome
III. Japan	South Korea + North Korea	Mongolia, Burma
	China + Taiwan + Hong Kong	Indo-China, Laos,
	Vietnam	Cambodia
	Australia/N.Z.	ASEAN
		Pacific Islands
IV. CIS/Moscow	Russian Republics	The rest
V. China/Beijing	Russian Republics	
	han provinces	The rest
VI. India/Delhi	SAARC system	litorals, islands
VII. Islamic core	Mashreq or Turkey +	Maghreb
World Directorate	World Middle Class	World Proletariat

war so that a major part of the Islamic world can also be administered through deputies.

This may be what they hope, but hardly what will happen. The New World Order is more like a nightmare, collapsing everywhere even before it is born. To see this, let us try a concrete listing of the conflict formations as they are today, leaving aside tomorrow. In so doing it should be pointed out that the regions have a certain cultural homogeneity, at least where center/inner periphery are concerned: I and II are Judeo-Christian, III and V are Buddhist/Confucian, IV is Orthodox, VI is Hindu, and VII is Muslim.

In short, a dangerous, familiar world with well-known conflicts (see Table 2). To refer to it as a *new world order* is correct only in one sense: it is more peaked, with the superhegemon, the U.S., on top. In the longer run this may increase the chance that all six will turn against the U.S., making the future position of the European Community/ Union even more important.

Table 2   GEOPOLITICS II: A CONFLICT MAP FOR A SEVEN-POLAR WORLD

- Unipolar conflicts, inside the spheres of interest, with the hegemon using "peacekeeping forces" in the inner and "rapid deployment forces" in the outer periphery, against revolts;
- Bipolar conflicts, between two hegemons over jurisdiction: like US/ EU over Caribbean-Pacific and possibly Latin America; US/Japan over Southeast Asia and US/Japan/EU over the Pacific; US/CIS over certain weapons; US/other hegemons in the Middle East (Egypt, Libya, Iran, Iraq, and successors to Iraq, Israel); EU/CIS over Baltic republics and German and Polish east borders; EU/Japan over how to divide Soviet Union; EU/India over litorals and islands; EU/ Islam over migrants; Japan/CIS over the Kuriles; Japan/China over oil; CIS/China over East Siberia; CIS/Islam over Central Asia; China/India over border areas; China/Islam over non-Han China; India/Islam over Kashmir and Muslims in India.
- Multipolar conflicts with more than two hegemons, organized: US/ EU + Japan or US + EU/Japan + CIS + China + India + Islam economically, or Christianity/Islam, Occident/Orient civiliza-tionally. Ominous.
- Coalitions of hegemons, e.g., the "North", as in the Gulf war with four hegemons cooperating (and one abstaining) to control the outer periphery of one region, thereby reinforcing hegemony. Veto power guarantees no UN action against loyal client states.
- Coalitions of peripheries, e.g., under the slogan "clients all over the world unite; you have only your hegemons to lose." But costs are higher and resources smaller than for the Center, the "South" exists only as a set of outer peripheries, and the Third World is a myth. Moreover, the New World Order power is military rather than economic, reflecting the declining economy of the U.S. And veto power guarantees no UN action against hegemon states.

GEOECONOMIC IMPLICATIONS OF THE GEOPOLITICAL ORDER.

First, some points about world economics in general before we make use of this geopolitical vision, with military and cultural aspects, and before looking at the six or seven regions. Surprisingly little is known about the world, *geo, gaia*, as one economic system. Liberal economics is the economics of countries (national economics, *Vol-*

kswirtschaftslehre in German—VWL) or the economics of enterprises (business administration; *Betriebswirtschaftslehre* in German—BWL); and their relations. Marxist-Leninist economics is the economics of class relations, within and among societies, and is more global. Liberal economics focuses on growth, Marxist economics on distribution. Both are necessary, neither of them sufficient to answer the key question: how is the world doing, seen as one country, one enterprise, one class? Four areas will be touched upon: world trade profile, world currency exchange, world arms race, and world debt burden.

World trade is reported to increase 12%–13% annually, with the increase increasing,[11] in other words with acceleration. Is that good or bad? For the traders it sounds rather good, even very good, since their profits depend on volume. The question is whether world trade (W) in the sense of interregional trade is at the expense of intraregional (R) trade (e.g., within South), which might be at the expense of intranational trade (N), which in turn might be at the expense of local (L) self-reliance. There is no reason to assume that $L + N + R + W$ is constant, if for no other reason because of the increasing numbers of producers and consumers. But the *world trade profile* does matter. All four should be healthy, vigorous. International trade $(R + W)$ at the expense of autonomous L and N development might be very cancerous[12] and very vulnerable, for instance to wars.

The daily international trade volume is estimated at about $10 billion.[13] But the volume of *world currency exchange* was reported to be $200 billion per day, or 20 times what would be warranted by the trade volume if we assume for the product flow across borders a money flow in the opposite direction. Of course, that flow does not have to change denomination; it could be kept in dollars. And some rumors (CNN, January 1991) speak of $500 billion as the volume of daily currency transactions.

In that case the proportion would be about 50:1, indicative of a very strong imbalance of finance economy over real economy. This, in turn, may be indicative of some very basic instability in the system, with finance traders hedging and speculating, launching and withdrawing all the time. Sooner or later that world bubble will probably burst.

One reason for this may be precisely the current multiple unipolar organization of the world. Compared to the Bretton-Woods system, and the position of the U.S. in general and the dollar in particular right after the Second World War, with Germany and Japan in ruins, there is no doubt that the current world economic landscape has a more multipeaked topography. The potential for heavy conflicts is tremendous, as pointed out above. At the same time, and the Gulf War will increasingly bear witness to this, military articulation of conflicts imply unbearable costs to destroyers and destroyed alike, per time unit. The destructive capacity tends to zero as it gets depleted ("running out of ordnance"), and the destruction tends to unity as it gets completed ("running out of targets"). The question is what comes first. But even with the latter first and a clear relation between destruction and capitulation, the costs are tremendous. In short, the military may be undermining itself, like any cure so much worse than the disease.

We might then speculate that conflict relations within and between the spheres of interest will increasingly be articulated with economic rather than military means, a word-pair not to be confused with constructive/destructive. A military arms race does not necessarily end with a war (confrontations may be avoided, for instance[14]); and a market race, complete with bankruptcies, debt and IMF conditionality, may take considerable tolls when the economy is measured in terms of human development (e.g., child mortality) in all layers of society, not in terms of GNP only. If war is politics by other means, then economic relations might also be war by other means. Depending on how the race is conducted, the number of victims may easily exceed even that of a cruel war, and certainly that of a nonbelligerent arms race. Thus, the annual toll of children from malnutrition is 16 million; that of the Second World War was (only) 8 million.

The cost–benefits are usually negative for the arms race, except when there are profits from arms sale, from the war itself, and from massive reconstruction; and positive for the market race, except when the economy is no longer growing, under recession–depresson conditions. But the exceptions may be the rule and may also coincide in one country, like the U.S. (and the U.K.), with massive construction following massive destruction.[15]

In other words, the market race in a broad sense may take over in a post-Cold War war, but only partly and not necessarily leading to less violence. Moreover, the market race leads to conflicts that cannot be solved through market mechanisms alone, and that in turn may lead to war. The conflict between Kuwait and Iraq over war debts, oil prices, and the use of the Rumaylah oil fields is an important example: Saddam Hussein wanted, and to some extent negotiated, adjustments the market could not offer, did not get them and went to war instead, probably partly out of anger, partly to enrich Iraq, partly to have withdrawal as a "bargaining chip."[16] Another example would be the relation between Japan and the U.S. with pure market principles leading to unacceptable consequences in both countries, such as ever-increasing Japanese market shares in key branches, including sensitive real estate, and increasing U.S. political interference into the socioeconomic culture of Japan. Both parties currently negotiate adjustments to market principles, but mainly in vain.

This is where the *world arms race*, at the annual rate of far above $1 trillion, becomes a triple back-up system to the market race. When conflicts, including those generated by the market system, abound, the market for arms will prosper. Most of those arms will sooner or later be used one way or the other to threaten, kill, and destroy; only extremely few are destroyed or preserved for posterity in museums. The rest is rather obvious: destruction of targets is followed by reconstruction, destruction of means of destruction by rearmament. The circle feeds itself.

But the hegemons cannot go on killing and destroying endlessly within their own spheres of interest without incurring heavy resistance. Moreover, peace keeping and rapid deployment do not come cheaply these days, and not all wars are short and decisive, meaning acceptable to the violence senders.

Other ways of keeping peripheries at bay have to be found, the most obvious being the *world debt burden*, which for the Third World ($1,340 billion according to the World Bank at the end of 1990) and the U.S. alone exceeds $2 trillion. The U.S. debt, like Australia's gross debt of $3 billion is much higher than Brazil's and Mexico's per capita, do not appear on such lists, but on the very useful *Asiaweek* barometer.

Wise people used to say that small debts are a burden to the debtor, big debts to the creditor. Economically, yes; but that is a very narrow perspective on debts. The basic point is not the quantity of debt service, bound to be low given the "performance" of most indebted countries (the basic reason why they are indebted anyhow). Much more basic is the quality, how the debt is serviced. There is a world market demand for raw materials and commodities, meaning that repayment will be in products, keeping the indebted countries at the lower half of the degree of processing axis. This will increase the supply and lower the prices (Fisher's law[17]), possibly increasing the demand and freezing world division of labor. At the same time finely tuned refusal to give new credit, or to withdraw credit (by selling bonds, for instance) is a mechanism of political control that may substitute for military intervention.[18]

In short, geoeconomics is geopolitics with other means, and vice versa. To be peace-productive, market behavior has to be ethically conscious[19], a set of conditions very far from satisfied today. More concretely, there is a limit to how much speculation and giant debts the world financial markets can take, and how much arms trade the world can take. Moral barriers against excessive speculation, seeking and granting credit (both sides of the equation) and trade with means of destruction, could be imagined, some of it even backed up by international law backed up by sanctions. But the effects of such deals are likely to be far away from the wrongdoer, meaning that there is little or no moral community and sentiment (Adam Smith) to draw upon.

And the same goes for the first of the four factors, the world trade profile. The macrolevels, W and R, attract the macrocorporations in search of macrotrade with macroprofits. And the local and national levels are sapped of their energy, leading to giant population dislocations and ecoimbalances.

GEOECONOMICS AS REGIONAL ECONOMICS: AN OVERVIEW

With the world divided into six or seven geopolitical regions, the next focus would be on how these regions will behave economically in the coming decade, the 1990s, starting with the center, then looking at the relation to the inner and the outer peripheries.

To do this some factors indicative of how an economy is performing are needed—a very controversial area indeed. Here three such factors will be used:

- Q/P, the ratio between the quality of the product offered and the price, both quality and price being taken in the broad sense;
- C/N, the degree of processing in a product, goods or services, from the raw, *le cru*, nature (N, raw material, the simplest human faculties) to the processed, *le cuit*, with culture (C, the form imparted to the raw materials in industrial processing, or to the human faculties through education of any kind);
- F/R, the synchrony between the (rate of growth) of the finance economy of financial assets and the (rate of growth) of the real economy of (other) goods and services. Inflation is asynchrony.

The basic point is to keep all three factors within bounds. At zero or very low levels we have an economy of nature-given products and skills, exchanged in a real, barter economy (which is where price enters). Then there is a "take-off," attending to quality (e.g., long-term reliability), processing, and more sophisticated economic systems with various types of financial assets. At the far end would be an economy in financial assets only, at an incredibly high level of sophistication and quality, but obviously made for King Midas rather than for human beings.

Here are some predictions for the six/seven regions:

1. *The economic decline of the United States will continue*, with some minor upswings always greeted with the same official optimism, because all three indicators above are in bad shape at the same time. Relative to the competitors, there is production at ever lower levels of processing. There is also insufficient attention given to the quality/price ratio and the old adage that "the bitterness of poor quality remains longer than the sweetness of a low price." These two secular trends are partly due to the militarization of the U.S. economy (with every second engineer working for the Pentagon[20] and low level of spinoffs (among other reasons because of the secrecy clauses); partly due to the "postindustrial" move toward the finance economy and away from the real economy (bad F/R ratio), leading to inflation, stock exchange crashes, and speculation (often criminal, usually immoral) instead of production to get in the black every quarter; and partly due to the deskilling of the working class through destruction of trade unions, bad education, and the terrible quality of highly addictive U.S. television.

The only major exception (see Michael Porter's "clusters of excellence"[21]) would be arms, increasingly higher in high-tech sophistication, which should not be confused with military efficiency or efficacy. These arms could, as mentioned, improve the GNP in three ways: as arms trade, as mercenary service to be paid for like any other service, and as means of destruction, paving the way (literally speaking) for profitable reconstruction when the destruction is completed.[22] The ideal solution would be to do all three in an area rich enough to pay the bill for the arms, for the war itself, and for reconstruction. The Gulf area satisfied all three, with deficit financing from the outside, of course; Indochina, none of them.[23]

The U.S. is by far the most indebted country in the world today, at least six times the level of no. 2, Brazil (but then the U.S. has little more than twice the population). With the U.S. currency value curve looking like a typhoid fever chart, the credibility of the U.S. dollar will continue its downward slope, and the U.S. will probably either have to print money or abrogate loans unless some new products sufficiently high on Q/P and even C/N can be found, meaning with the same added value and market attractiveness as arms. Printing money will produce inflation and devaluation. Abrogation will legitimize retaliation.

In either case *the dollar as world currency will probably not survive the 1990s.* An ECU–yen combination is the likely alternative, given the economic dynamism of regions II and III, or possibly a dollar–ECU–yen combination. The U.S. will then squeeze the Western Hemisphere, including Canada, and the Middle East instead, tolerating no deviation from U.S. economic dominance, currently using the "war against drugs" as cover. The wars against Panama and Iraq are indicative of what this means.

2. *The general European Union upward economic trend in almost all fields of economic performance will continue*, except for workers' salaries, where the 1993 inner market may imply a leveling downwards, "social dumping."[24] Europe, and not only EC/EU, have monitored Q/P, C/N, and F/R carefully. Western Europe still has an adequate educational system both at the elite and the general population levels, even if U.S.-style TV (favoring visual, not sequential mental processes, with no borderline between information and entertainment, very short sequences, and idiotizing commercials) will ultimately take their toll. At the same time a "Latin Americanization" of Central/Eastern Europe has already set in, helped by local elites[25] and the aversion against any market scepticism. Cheap but well-schooled labor will be amply available in this great area of exploitation next door. This will lead to violence, which in turn may be profitable.

3. *Japan will continue its upward surge, but not alone.* It should be noted that the periphery of Japan, inner and outer, is by far the largest in the world. The implication is of key global importance: Japan can slow down and even reverse the policy of keeping the U.S. afloat as a market, having a reserve market to fall back upon. A Unified Japan–Unified Korea–Unified China/Vietnam (The Buddhist–Confucian counties) Common Market, linking Japan and its inner periphery, with Japan as "inner center," is probably in the cards, depending on Korean unification.[26] We are then talking of a region with 1,340 million human beings, and not only the 340 million in the European Community after German partial unification.[27]

There have been some guesses that Western Europe and/or Eastern Europe–former Soviet Union would be the Japanese alternatives to the U.S., and there is, of course, some truth to this. But the Japanese are cautious and prefer gambling on several horses. They know that the EC/EU area may also be closing, that Eastern Europe and ex-Soviet Union are heading for considerable problems similar to other Third World-type economies, and that the sphere of Buddhist–Confucian countries is more hard working. Thus, the Greater East Asian Co-Prosperity Sphere may be realized 50 years after its official demise, with economic means, as current Japanese investment patterns seem to indicate.[28]

Bridging regions II and III, and a bad omen for the U.S., is Japanese–German cooperation with Mitsubishi Heavy Industries and MBB Daimler-Benz up front.[29] Space + Arms = Space Arms, to balance the Star Wars of the U.S.? For both this means access to the highest technology of the other region, a policy attempted by the U.S. in Japan, but then too high-handedly. Spinoffs for their peripheries would have to be in it lest the "inner centers" become isolated. A German–Japanese axis has to be firmly rooted.

4. *The economic decline of the former Soviet Union will continue.* The key factor is neither the problems of the Stalinist system, although they were considerable, nor the problems of the transition to a "market economy," although they are close to insurmountable, but the nature of the system they are getting in return for the old. The term *market economy* masks the basic difference between center and periphery capitalism, some of the key characteristics of the latter being a very low level of C/N (although at that level possibly a high Q/P due to the simplicity of the product, and the cheap availability of the production factors); elites negotiating within the discourse and on the terms set by the center; increasing distance between elite and people in the periphery; unemployment, and increasing misery for a high proportion of the latter. To make this system work, command capitalism is needed, that is, neofascism. Significant reactions against the inequities of the market system will be brutally repressed, as in Latin America and China in 1989.

A likely scenario, after the former Soviet Union has arrived at some agreement with Japan[30] over at least two of the South Kurile Islands, would be massive investment by a German–Japanese economic alliance (see 3 above), dividing ex-Soviet Union economically at the Urals, declaring the Second World War finished. The historic motivation for doing so would be very clear: to undo the trauma of defeat.

Given the enormous natural resources and supply of labor at relatively high levels of education and health, the former Soviet Union should grow in spite of capital and management deficits, given the size of their science and technology establishment.[31] However, a positive feedback is needed, not only for speculators but for the population at large. And that feedback is today negative and may continue to be so for the people at large.[32]

5. *China will continue being China, with a low-level impact on the world economy except indirectly as a part of the enormous Japanese region.* But, as such, China will make itself felt. The factor profile is less positive than for the former Soviet Union, being less well endowed with natural resources and labor at adequate levels of health and education. But capital can flow into the country from overseas Chinese. The Buddhist–Confucian culture and structure should make for management patterns similar to those of the Japanese. There is a tradition of being hard working. But the most essential problem for

China is to achieve more balanced growth, between classes, genders, and regions of the country.[33]

6. *India will be more of a military than an economic challenge, and a periphery for Regions I, II and III*, like the others using "peacekeeping forces" for the inner and "rapid deployment forces" for the outer peripheries.[34] India may become good at C/N with its high-level science and technology establishment, but hardly at Q/P. There may even be some carryover from the British tradition of diffidence and disregard for the esthetic dimension of quality, Indian products generally looking unattractive to the world market.

7. *The Islamic/Arab region will essentially be a periphery for Regions I, II, and III.* Moreover, there is too much political-military work to be done to bring about higher levels of integration, some of it even deep inside non-Islamic countries (the eight Islamic insurgencies in the world right now: Kosovo, Lebanon, intifada in Israel/Palestine, the Central Asian former Soviet republics and Azerbaidzhan, Kashmir, India, China, Philippines). Parts of region VII are already in II and II.

And the same applies to the Third World, the South, as a whole, which will continue being exploited and probably more than before. A major reason for this is the way in which the South is being fragmented among the six or seven regions, as in the old colonial system. Major rebellions and all kinds of fundamentalisms will be the result, unless the fine recommendations of the South Commission[35] are followed, particularly increase South–South cooperation to improve Q/P, C/N, and F/N, and to lower the dependence on the North for technology and currency. But will the hegemons ever permit that?

In short, the key economic actors will remain the Judeo-Christian (particularly Protestant) and the Confucian–Buddhist (particularly mahayana) regions, meaning Nos. I, II, and III. This is essentially the OECD area from a governmental point of view (with the G7 as Executive Committee), and the Trilateral at a more individual and corporate level. To summarize:

- the economic position of the U.S. continues to deteriorate;
- the economic position of the EC/EU and the *dai-to-a* regions are continuously improving, although this applies above all to Germany and Japan, the innermost centers (see Appendix for data);
- Japan may integrate economically with its vast inner periphery;
- Germany has already expanded territorially, and may do more, with Eastern Europe and the Baltic as economic periphery[36];
- there is a Japan–Germany axis taking shape, connecting two countries with ⅕th of the gross world product, and II and III;

- what happens in the Indian and the Islamic regions points more toward political/military than economic autonomy;
- the Third World as a whole, the "South," has little coherence, divided by distance, religion/culture, race, and by being on the peripheries of different centers. The debt burden is essentially a political instrument used to preserve the status quo, or any order of interest to the creditors, as was seen clearly in the beginning of the Gulf crisis, using debt to buy UN votes.

The most dynamic factor in this picture is the U.S., to be explored in the next section. Not only the U.S. but also South America (from Rio Grande southwards) with only few exceptions, is affected,[37] and indirectly the whole world. By sinking, space is made for others. This also applies to South America relative to other Third World regions. That others stretch out for a handshake across the quickly sinking former Soviet Union and the slowly sinking U.S. should surprise nobody. But only those with long arms can do so, meaning Japan and Germany. And they might do well to remember that decline is never total, there is always something that does not decline, like military power in both cases and cultural power for the U.S. The U.S. has been more successful than any other country in producing *world* culture, generally plebeian and vulgar, but the most global there is, a major factor behind what remains of political clout.

IS THE U.S. ECONOMY MOVING INTO A DEPRESSION?

The answer given in this section will be "yes, and it has been there for some time." Concretely, that means that we are talking about more than a (normal) downswing of the business-cycle, also of more than a prolonged trough before the upward turn. We are not talking about getting in and out of a recession, but about the "d-word," depression. Moreover, we are not talking about a world-wide depression but essentially about a Western Hemisphere depression, since one basic point in the theory and practice of spheres above is the effort by the DM/ECU and Yen zones to insulate themselves from any Western Hemisphere depression, where the dollar probably will remain the international currency for a long time (with the possible exception of some of the Caribbean ACP countries in Region II that will be under difficult cross-pressure, given the Caribbean Basin Initiative).

Of course, all finance economies are linked, so there will always be stock exchange shockwaves, as for communicating vessels. Often this is misinterpreted to mean that the "world economy is one." But the ability to overcome stock exchange shocks with substantial index drops depends on the local F/R ratio, with inflation being but one way F/R can go wrong. And the real economies are less tightly coupled, some being more healthy than others in the sense of adequate Q/P and C/N, and the healthy ones may be immune to the pathologies elsewhere in the world economy.

The position taken here is that a depression is *not* a deep recession, for example, with business stagnating more than 3 years, and, consequently, low, zero, or even negative economic growth, maybe even for more than 6 years, with dramatic, quick decreases in earnings and prices (including of real estate, gold, and money), and increases in unemployment, above 12%, into 25% and more.[38] This is certainly more than serious for those who lose their jobs and see their earnings fall more than the prices, having little or nothing to fall back upon, but conceptually only a question of degree, and politically this can all be handled as a deep or long-lasting recession, for example, with Keynesian means (in the U.S. through military Keynesianism). The difference between recession and depression, however, is qualitative, not quantitative.

At the surface depression in a developed economy is Q/P, C/N, and F/R is disarray. But deeper down the basic *characteristic of a depression is serious impairment of the endogenous ability to restore and sustain economic growth.* A recession downswing is supposed to be followed by an upswing, generated endogenously by the economy pulling its resources of any kind together. A recession may even be healthy if interpreted as a resting period for the economy, a signal that the economy was going too fast—maybe needed once every decade or so.[39] The parallel to the overworked person being forced by some disease to slow down is obvious. But in a depression the very ability to restore economic growth through one's own efforts has been damaged, if not beyond repair at least for a longer period, as with a person with an impaired immune system.

Depressions can come to an end but only exogenously, through factors outside the economic system. Wars or other catastrophes stimulating massive demand, a charismatic leader releasing new energies in the population, even "a new beginning" would be examples. Intervention by outside forces; having experts build, repair, and assemble production factors; or other countries agreeing to demand the products of the country in depression are other formulas. But acts of geoeconomic solidarity, motivated by pity for the sick, are limited by fear of effective competition after recovery, unless they are effectively integrated into some supereconomy. Given the present level of decay, it does not look as if the U.S. will easily come out on top of that one, making solidarity less risky.[40]

The "less developed countries" can be seen as being in a lasting depression, incapable of producing growth by their own means and in need of all the measures indicated above: charismatic leaders, development expertise from the outside, solidary demand, "new beginnings" of all kinds, etc. But the most effective exogenous stimulus of development, demand for products high on Q/P and C/N, is usually withheld from developing countries.[41] In addition, the concept of *depression* seems to be reserved for "more developed countries" undergoing a change from stable high to stable low growth. And exogenous stimuli may easily substitute for endogenous efforts, making them very controversial.[42]

Seen this way, any effort to answer the question has to go beyond a listing of the well-known economic indicators. We have to focus, not only on the symptoms of economic decline, but also on possible underlying economic pathologies. The focus should be on the self-healing capacity, which leads us to examine the social (and cultural, and human, and ecological, etc.) setting in which the economy is encased. Only when the economic pathologies are encased in a syndrome of social and political pathologies, with no clear self-healing capacity, would we be in a position to use the dreaded "d-word," *depression*.

But this does not define unambiguously the point of entry for an analysis of economic pathologies. Obviously, what is observed is that business stagnates, meaning that willing sellers and willing buyers do not make enough deals—not why they don't. There is a mismatch: the producer tries to sell what the buyer does not demand; the domestic or foreign consumer demands what the producer does not supply at affordable prices. The vicious circle aspect is obvious since most people are both producers and consumers, weakening each other.

One point of entry would be analysis of production factors and products. But we also need a theory of consumption factors, and the production bias of mainstream economic theory then becomes painfully evident. And, in general there is also the third in-between cluster of factors, distribution, to take into account. Thus, how can we otherwise explain the ills of the former Soviet (but not the U.S.) economy with products accumulating at the production sites, money accumulating at the consumption sites, and the connecting distributive link missing?

Having said this, the following is a simplistic but systematic check list for the diagnosis of the U.S. economy.

Production Factors

Nature: Even if we are not close to the depletion limits for important raw materials as discoveries continue to be made, we may be beyond the pollution limits. Thus, how much can the U.S. soil carry of fertilizer/pesticide and other types of pollution? How much pollution-related pathologies through air, water, food and radiation can human beings take? Is AIDS related to this?

Labor: We are essentially talking about the educational and health labor quality needed to sustain high-quantity production at high quality, meaning high Q/P. If high schools have as much as 3,000 drop-outs per day, or above one million per year[42]; if 2 million of those leaving elementary school every year are not really literate; if 15,000 hours of schooling for 18-year-olds are competing with 18,000 hours of television, communicating 18,000 murders and 340,000 idiotizing commercials; if training is increasingly in pictorial forms of understanding at the expense of sequential reasoning with words tracing causal and logical chains; if there are interruptions impeding any chain of reasoning beyond the simplistic; then where is educational quality? Especially when compared to the Japanese, who probably have the highest level of education for, say, the bottom 50% of the population in the world? If in addition 37 million U.S. citizens are without health insurance, 25% of the children live below the poverty line (50% of the Black children), and the infant mortality in the cities is at Third World level, then quality of health is obviously not achieved either, for the working class.

Capital: Credit has to be easily available, which means that financial instruments have to be bought and sold. On the other hand, if this activity is excessive, the asynchrony relative to a sluggish real economy would become evident and lead to lack of confidence because F/R is not kept within bounds. The U.S. may be suffering both from lack of credit and from an overheated finance economy at the same time, meaning insufficient credit available to the small and too much to the big economic actors. The Savings and Loan pathology (*scandal* is a too moralizing word) is a case in point: The big use the big amounts in principle available to the small and squander them; as a result the small (the taxpayers) have to pay.

Bad loans driving out the good ones is one mechanism at work here. The old U.S. institution of *walk-away* (leaving the farm, the shop, the office, the home when debts exceed their value, taking away whatever is not a permanent fixture in a big truck, even a mobile home with ample storage space) will lead to the bankruptcy of smaller banks; big speculations even lead to the bankruptcy of the bigger ones.[43]

Technology: Even if it is true that the U.S. has the highest elite education in the world, this does not necessarily translate into high C/N for marketable products. In principle "C" is what is taught in schools of engineering, faculties of natural sciences, and schools of education. But there may be heavy filtering on the way. Thus, if 50% of the engineers and the R&D are for the military, then security clauses and irrelevance for civilian use would impede transfer to the civilian market for a heavy portion of "C" and force the economy into arms trade to balance accounts. Processing of raw materials for military purposes, by engineering specialists, relegates products to corners of society where they can only recover investment through destruction or arms sales because of the threat of destruction. But processing of raw brains for education purposes, by education specialists, also tends to relegate the highly educated into corners of society, the campus or intellectual ghetto, with little spinoff into regular society. There are few spinoffs from the military to the civilian sector, and few spinoffs from gown to town, because intellectuals are largely absent from public space (media, election campaigns, major events) in the U.S.[44]

Management: The U.S. managerial culture is still very much based on the strong-man theory for the CEO, responsible for balanced books every quarter, and of course tempted to focus on finance rather than real economy for that reason. MBA training will tend to produce CEOs in money or law rather than engineering, Thus, both time pressure and *deformation professionelle* will tend to increase the pressure on the finance economy for the company to be permanently in the black. And if occasionally in the red, the standard reaction will be to cut expenses by firing competent personnel defined as redundant rather than through an overall cut in salaries combined with collective, long-term planning. When the crisis turns worse, the standard reaction will be to sacrifice the firm through bankruptcy rather than sacrifice incompetent leadership through voluntary withdrawal, public apologies, and, in extremis, suicide. In addition, the extreme differentials in salary between U.S. CEOs and the ordinary worker, so much more than in the competitor countries Japan and Germany, probably have a very demoralizing effect on the employees.[45]

Products

The persistent trend over a long period is C/N deterioration in the U.S. products for export and imports, meaning more exports of products low in degree of processing, and more import of products high in degree of processing.[46] As a communicative act this introduces a vicious circle, giving the U.S. economy a low C/N image, with wood, scrap iron, waste paper, rice, and other foodstuffs, except for sophisticated means of destruction. High C/N images introduce a virtuous circle by making others think "these people can probably make anything sophisticated," an image today associated with the Germans and the Japanese, but probably much less with the Swiss (cheap swatches are a far cry from Swiss watches) and the British (biscuits), let alone the United States.

Consumption Factors

Consumption is here analyzed in terms of two factors, Q/P (for the product) and $(W \times B)$ (demand, want by buying power).

Q/P: If we assume, *ceteris paribus*, that consumers go for a high Q/P, then any general national failure to achieve this will lead consumers to buy foreign products when available, except for people who are heavily nationalist (K-mart: buy U.S.), heavily masochist, or simply badly informed. Heavy and reasonably truthful advertising will counteract the latter two. Availability of foreign products may be reduced through tariff and nontariff barriers, which in turn may lead to reciprocation. Being similar to economic sanctions, tariff barriers may be advantageous for C/N low countries, among them parts of the U.S., forcing them to produce C/N high products for their own demand rather than the easy way out, through trade across vast C/N differentials: selling *le cru*, buying *le cuit*.

W × B: If demand is conceived of as the product of want and buying power, and want is a composite of need (N, the minimum consumption requisites for survival as human beings) and greed (G, only limited by the time available for consumption), then some simple conclusions follow from $W = N + G$.

With less buying power for basic needs, more (by definition) misery; and the more misery the lower the quality of labor as production factor. Often forgotten by those who see unemployment as useful in creating excess demand for jobs is the low quality of the workers and the high probability of "junk workers, junk work; junk work, junk products." The buying power for greed may more than compensate in total market turnover stimulated by commercial propaganda to enhance G-want, and by easily available credit (e.g., plastic cards) to enhance instant buying power.

But the more buying power available for ever more greed, the more pressure on capital, and the lower the quality of capital as production factor (e.g., because of junk bonds, "walk-away" strategies, etc.). In short, when $B \times N$ is too low (needs are left unsatisfied), labor as production factor suffers; when $B \times G$ is too high (greeds multiply and are "satisfied"), capital as production factor suffers, resulting in junk labor and junk capital; typical syndromes of under- and overdevelopment, respectively. The U.S. is a good example of a country where the two coexist, eroding labor from the bottom and capital from the top. Moreover, the two syndromes may coexist in the same person, with TV/video bought on expensive credit terms in the slums and pathological eating habits (anorexia nervosa, bulimia) also among the affluent.

Distribution Factors

Communication: In general excellent, due to the high level and easy availability of telematics (television, telephone, telefax, telex, and the possible "tele" to come for taste, smell, touch, etc., including telesex). E-mail is highly interactive. For the production factors this makes interaction over any distance possible, obviating the need for production sites that are contiguous in space and continuous in time.

Transportation: Deteriorating, as seen by the Third world level of so many streets and highways, tracks and bridges, pipes and sewers. The very slow mail system also belongs in this category, making repairs depending on spare parts problematic, increasing the demand for high quality products in the sense of reliability over time when repair across space is unavailable.

Sales points: Another word for the market place, and certainly abundantly available. They also serve as ever-present commercials for themselves and for consumption in general, increasing the frustration due to the unsatisfied needs and greeds.

In short, business stagnation and low or negative economic growth are multifaceted phenomena. There is no single point to start. Take interest rates, dollar exchange rates, or bonds as examples. Higher interest will attract capital from abroad, but will also cause even more bankruptcies in firms, farms, and families already overburdened with debts, and, through that, in banks. Lower interest rates may help all the latter, provided they apply to loans, not only to deposits (with banks pocketing the difference to compensate for both past and future deficits), but will frighten away foreign capital, even to the point of the massive withdrawals the U.S. economy cannot afford to suffer.

Higher dollar rates make exports in principle more, and imports less, expensive to the buyers; but very little follows from that alone. The principle applies conversely for lower dollar rates, and again not much follows from that alone. The dealers may fail to adjust to lower prices, pocketing the difference to compensate for past and future deficits; the products exported and imported may vary too much in demand elasticity, substitutability, and so on. Moreover, with cheaper dollars an exporter may try to switch from export to local production, buying cheaply available production and consumption factors (food, clothes, housing, health, education, entertainment, etc.). High dollar rates may lead to a trade deficit, lower dollar rates to foreign investment excess. What is worse, a trade deficit or an investment excess, in the longer run?

Another possibility is to print more dollars, the U.S. being the only country that can print the currency used to denominate international debts. The result will be inflation, meaning lower, even negative interest, leading to withdrawal of credit. Either way, manipulating rates or quantities, is likely to backfire. The same applies to defaulting on the bonds declaring them nonredeemable except in new bonds with similar conditionalities, which is close to abrogating the loan. The argument might be that the credit was extended under duress. Or no argument at all, only "try come and get it," with the arms arsenal available to this particular debtor (and not to the debtors to that country) as the *ultimo ratio*. Like defaulting on the dollar, this will undermine the dollar as *the* world currency, reducing U.S. economic action space by reducing credibility even further.

But in spite of all of this, one factor remains in the U.S. favor: the U.S. as *the* world producer of world culture, for the people and for the peoples, not necessarily for the elites. There is money to be made.[47] And there is enormous sympathy to draw upon, attracting thousands, millions to the U.S., among them the highly skilled in search of a "new beginning." Whether they will be able to replace current economic elites that have gone stale is another question. They are solidly entrenched. And they keep for themselves much of the money still to be made.

CONCLUSION: WHAT CAN BE DONE?

Even if the U.S. fails to reconquer the *ichiban* position, to improve the U.S. economy is important for the citizens' sake. Manipulating the finance economy is symptom healing at best. What is needed is healing the real economy by stimulating the necessary conditions for high C/N and high Q/P while watching F/R (which is much easier if the other two are taken care of). Proposals:

- *Reindustrialization* at a high C/N level, improving the linkage between U.S. creativity and U.S. civilian production, first with a view to producing for domestic demand, second to recreate old and create new high C/N niches on the world market;
- *Selective stops for foreign imports and investment*, not to punish them, nor to protect domestic competitors, but as a part of a "let us accept that we are behind and that we have to take on the challenge to produce at least for ourselves" package;
- *Massive change in corporate culture*, essentially learning from the Japanese more collective, less individualist and hierarchical patterns, putting real economy rather than finance economy people in charge, reducing intracompany wage differentials, treating workers better in general with much more participation;
- *Massive change in education culture*, which is less a question of changing the schools than their major competitor, idiotizing television, for example, through viewer boycott.

But what is bad for the U.S. is not necessarily bad for the world, even if what is bad for General Motors (and Ford) is also bad for the U.S.[48] Other regions, hopefully not only the centers, may be given a chance. And the U.S. may reflect. And come back, some day—hopefully, not with a vengeance.

REFERENCES

American paradox: Smart bombs, dumb VCRs; Why are makers of world's best weapons falling behind in consumer goods? (1991, March 5). *International Herald Tribune.*
Batra, R. (1985). *The great depression of 1990.* Dallas: Venus Books.
Chodos, R., & Garmaise, E. (1988). *The decline of the American economy.* Montreal/New York: Black Rose Books.
Dollar's health could improve if Gulf flares. (1990, September 24). *Wall Street Journal.*
Drucker, P.F. (1986, Spring). The changed world economics. *Foreign Affairs,* pp. 768-791.
Galtung, J. (1980). A structural theory of imperialism. In *Essays in peace research* (Vol. IV, Chap. 13). Copenhagen: Ejlers.
Galtung, J. (forthcoming). *World politics of peace and war.*
GATT. (1991, May). *Far Eastern Economic Review,* p. 57.
The leisure empire. (1990, December 24). *Time.*
Palmer, J. (1990, December 2). *Guardian Weekly.*
Porter, M.E. (1990). *The competitive advantage of nations.* New York: Free Press.

The rising tide: Japan in Asia. (1990, Winter). *The Japan Economic Journal.*
Shopping for a better world. (1991). New York: Council on Economic Priorities.

NOTES

[1] The Malta meeting took place in December 1989. No transcripts have been made available; that will still take some time. But the new empirical reality after a major political encounter may provide better evidence of the intentions than any record.

[2] A relatively concrete agenda for the transition from the EC as confederation to federation was prepared for the EC summit meeting in Rome, December 14-15, 1990, by the Italian foreign minister De Michelis, at that time chair of the EC Council of Ministers (see Palmer, 1990); and followed up in Maastricht December 10-11, 1991.

[3] Professor John Stephan, Department of History, University of Hawaii, has done extensive research into the meaning of this concept to the Japanese military government. Included, to some, was not only Hawaii, but also the Western coast of North America from Alaska/Yukon and the Pacific states to Mexico and beyond.

[4] In other words, the Solzhenitsyn plan, or something close to that. Ukraina may be subdivided along historical and confessional lines, given the possible Polish claims and the Catholic/Orthodox split; and Kazakhstan on demographic lines.

[5] The UN Charter, Art. 51, does not specify the meaning of *collective*: "Nothing in the present Charter shall impair the inherent right of individual or collective self-defense if an armed attack occurs against a member of the United Nations—". But geographical contiguity or some preexisting arrangement may be reasonable interpretations, both of them compatible with the "sphere of interest" idea, legitimizing what the superpower will do anyhow. The Gulf crisis is an interesting exercise in how legitimacy can be obtained, even bought.

[6] The idea is attributed to Confucius, who also, as a sign of his depreciation of non-Chinese, had the idea that barbarians with leaders will always remain inferior to Chinese without.

[7] The South Asian Association for Regional Cooperation can be seen as a tool by the other six to regulate Indian power, as a tool for that power, or as the former becoming the latter.

[8] The objection that the khalifats were also divided (Damascus, Baghdad, Cairo, Istambul), that there were also Persian and Mogul empires, and so on, would not impress a European too much; Western Europe has been through similar divisiveness. The Arab world may have moved from about 500 polities early this century (under the weak Ottoman configuration) to the present 22 (if Palestine is counted), figures similar to the European transition from the medieval to the Westphalian system.

[9] The solar power system, SPS, would be based on enormous space platforms with solar energy receivers and transmission to land-based antennas. But that directed energy can also be used as a weapon of mass destruction.

[10] See my *World Politics of Peace and War* (forthcoming). It is important to note that the world's leading arms exporters and importers are precisely the six/seven centers outlined here.

[11] The Internationale Wirtschaftszahlen from Institut der deustchen Wirtschaft in Koln gives world exports in 1970 at $314B and in 1989 at $3026B, corresponding to an average annual growth rate of 12.7%. GATT, quoted by the *Far Eastern Economic Review* (9 May 1991, p. 57) gives 13.5% growth for world imports and 13% growth for world exports.

[12] This conclusion presupposes a view of the world more as a system, even an organism, and less as a set of states. No organism would survive conditions of only intracellular, or only intercellular activity. That rules out the extremes, leaving a vast band of acceptable economic systems in between.

[13] The volume was $.86B per day in 1970 and $8.29 per day in 1989 according to the date mentioned in Note 11 above. (1986, p. 782) gives about $12.5B per day, with the foreign exchange transactions running 12 times that level. Is this too much? Too little? In-between? We do not even seem to have a theory, leaving alone an answer. What is needed is a comparison with the other types of trade, with the trends.

[14] The idea underlying the Nixon–Brezhnev "traffic rules" for the cold war, because both of them could inflict "unacceptable damage" to the other and had values that were not that dissimilar, one of them being not to have a war on their own territory (one of them because the country had never experienced it in recent generations, the other because it had). It is interesting, and chilling, to note how any such concept broke down in connection with the "Gulf crisis" 1990–1991. If both parties want a war, albeit for different reasons, they will probably get it.

[15] The Gulf war offers many examples of this. Both U.S. and UK contractors were in the market for the reconstruction of Kuwait (before anything like an estimate of the damage was available), as a reward for participation in the liberation. U.S. Commerce Secretary Mosbacher urged the Saudis to reconsider a major telephone contract to Alcatel (France) and L.M. Ericsson (Sweden) and start discussions with ATT. The same Mosbacher "convinced the Kuwaitis to locate their postwar recovery team in Washington rather than London or Riyadh"; partly as a result, "U.S. companies are lapping up about 70 percent of the initial wave of rebuilding contracts." The world seems to be enacting the most vulgar Marxism, with capitalism destroying capital to get new contracts, meaning that Marxism cannot be that vulgar (*International Herald Tribune*, March 11, 1991). Also see "Dollar's Health" (1990). All one has to keep in mind is that after reconstruction may come redestruction and rereconstruction.

[16] Thus, the market did not compensate Iraq for the war against Iran, even if many countries paid Iraq handsomely. Better than single shot payments for means of destruction is a stable earning capacity based on means of construction.

[17] The Yale economist Irvin Fisher had the very reasonable idea that, when many heavily indebted families sell the same goods, for example, household silver, on the market, then the price of that commodity will decrease. The analogous element for heavily indebted Third World countries would be raw materials.

[18] This mechanism is in principle available to Japan for the U.S.; whether it will be used remains to be seen. At the same time the U.S. has bases in Japan, a very explosive combination.

[19] *Shopping for a Better World* (1991) is a very important attempt along such lines. The idea is to mobilize consumers to vote with their buying power for or against products and the firms producing them, adding to economic rationality (a high Q/P ratio) other considerations: "giving to charity," "women's advancement," "advancement of minorities," "animal testing," "disclosure of information," "community outreach," "South Africa," "environment," "family benefits," "workplace issues," "military contracts," "nuclear power." In the present version customers would have to use the guide to select the products; later on, they might be guided by proper labeling on the products.

[20] A very common consideration heard from those engineers is the challenging and interesting nature of the job. To achieve destruction under difficult conditions cannot be easy. But this also offers interesting insights into the criteria for challenge conveyed by engineering schools. They could be improved upon.

[21] Porter (1990) defines *clusters of excellence* for the 10 countries in his study. They are based on such production factors as skilled labor and infrastructure, demand conditions at home for the product, the presence of supporting industries, and heavy domestic competition. Only by becoming lean and mean domestically can the companies hope to excel internationally. The present clusters of excellence for the U.S. would include software, consumer package goods, movie making, commercial airlines, and credit card services; whereas the U.S. has lost leadership in automobiles, steel, consumer electronics, machine tools, office products, consumer durables, apparel, and some telecommunications. Of the top 25 U.S. industries in terms of world export share, 15 have a heavy load on natural resources. Britain leads the field only in biscuits and auctioneering, Germany in chemicals and luxury cars (the competition between BMW and Mercedes!), Sweden for the same reason in trucks. Conspicuously missing from this list is the arms trade, imparting an air of lack of realism to the Porter study. The shadow side, not to be mentioned among gentlemen in corporate boardrooms? See "American Paradox" (1991), giving a partial answer: "—nearly 70 percent of federal research and development money went to the military, up from 50 percent a decade ago."

[22] The history of post-Gulf War economics will provide interesting insights into how the world economy is working. Thus, Kuwait, and Iraq, would have a unique chance to develop by taking on the reconstruction challenge themselves; but Kuwait will probably give that major impetus away, and Iraq will be denied that stimulus if key targets can only be repaired by foreigners.

[23] As a consequence Indochina has not been reconstructed, neither has it come in for major redestruction since 1975; a likely follow-up to reconstruction in the Gulf area.

[24] Capital, the fastest moving production factor, will under conditions of free mobility seek the cheapest labor. To keep the field equal, either expensive labor has to become less expensive (social dumping) or cheap labor less cheap (social upgrading) or both at the same time. Thus, in September 1989, 1 hour of a German worker in manufacturing industry cost DM 34.22 (DM 15.73, or 36%, being social security contributions) as against DM 18.15 for workers in Spain (social security 37%) and DM 6.80 for workers in Portugal (social security 35%). Obviously the European Community is in for some major dumping or upgrading.

[25] *Der Spiegel* has run an almost continuous series on this since the Wall came down November 1989. The massive demand for Western-produced goods was one of the factors that brought down the socialist regimes; the supply is then made available directly from Western suppliers more than by building new production facilities. In the former DDR subsidies make it possible for the consumers to buy, thereby affecting consumer tastes for a long period to come. In the other countries only a very limited segment of the population is able to buy, and the dealers will sell at the prices they are willing to pay. Vaclav Klaus, the Chicago School-oriented Czech finance minister, seemed to think they have to learn market economics and bring prices down to get more buyers. The objection would be that these businessmen understand market economics better than a finance minister, and also know something about the layers in society. The financial upper class is a guaranteed clientele; better aim for that one since they may not be available if the prices become "cheap" (Giffin goods). In that case they shop abroad for prestige goods.

[26] As unification can only be as a confederation of equals under the present circumstances it cannot be "under the leadership of President Kim Il-Sung." Either he must give up that or disappear from the scene. Then the road may be open.

[27] *Partial* because four areas, two of them parts of Kaiser Germany (the areas in Poland and the enclave in Russia; Pommern, Schlesien, and Ost-Preussen) and two of Nazi Germany (Sudeten in Czechoslovakia and Austria) are still outside. To know what

that means in concrete terms, we may have to wait for a new political generation to come into power in Germany. The present generation has made its deal: the integration or takeover of former DDR.

[28] *The Japan Economic Journal* had a special supplement, *The Rising Tide: Japan in Asia* (Winter 1990) with some interesting data. Thus, in the area comprised by China, the four Tigers, the ASEAN countries and Australia/New Zealand 4,593 Japanese companies employ 981,499 workers, backed by an expatriate Japanese community of 100,000, including dependents. The investment in 1990 will be in the range of $8–10 billion, "perhaps double U.S. investment." The total investment, $36 billion, is only 20% of Japan's international investment, and still behind the U.S. Actually, even "Tiger" investment in ASEAN (except for Singapore) is higher than Japanese investment in the same region. Japanese trade grew from $61.8 billion in 1982 to $126.4 billion in 1989, with Japanese exports 40% higher than the imports, creating the usual trade deficit problem. In 1990 4.6 million Japanese traveled in the region, spending each one $200 per day. But the cultural impact is negligible, unlike in the U.S.: in the *karaoke* bars "the locals who frequent them sing their own nation's popular songs, not Japanese tunes."

One persistent pattern in the Japanese strategy is to move in where others move out. Investment by Japanese manufacturing firms jumped 24.1% in 1989 from the previous year, coming second only to the U.S., and Japan is supposed to become no. 1 in Hong Kong for 1990. Investment by British manufacturers declined in 1989, for the first time in a decade (*Japan Economic Journal*, December 22, 1990). In the same vein Japan is posed to move into Vietnam en masse the moment the U.S. embargo is lifted. Major companies have sales offices already, assembly plants are being planned (Toyota), and soon (*International Herald Tribune*, January 3, 1991). This is in direct continuation of Japan's ASEAN policy, since the three former Indochinese countries will probably sooner or later become members of an expanded 10-member ASEAN, together with Myanmar (Burma). To this we could add Japanese interest in the other (partly former) socialist countries in the region, North Korea and Mongolia. Relations are quickly improving, mainly based on raw materials and cheap labor.

[29] Following the Big Two are other heavy examples of Japanese–German cooperation: Itoh-Klockner, Meiji Mutual Life-Dresdner Bank, and Hoechst, Bosch, and Siemens have set up cooperation with a wide range of Japanese firms, including Matsushita, Mitsubishi, Asahi and Fujitsu (*International Herald Tribune*, November 26, 1990). And Daimler-Benz, of course, does not intend only to cooperate with Mitsubishi. The chairman of Daimler-Benz, Edzard Reuter mentions cars as integrated systems, defense and aerospace as fields of cooperation. The basis for cooperation seems rather solid, for more details about economic profiles, see Appendix.

[30] The former Soviet attitude seems to be that the islands have no military significance, and their economic importance is at most proportionate to their (insignificant) size. However, they are a part of the *corpus mysticum* that is Japan, and not only for the extreme right. To get them back is to restore the wholeness of that body, of the sun goddess in a sense. Thus, if the Soviet Union asks for a quid in return for that giant quo, they will probably get it. If they ask for nothing, however, they might get much more. The political issue is theological more than military or economic.

[31] Of course, the best known part is the Soviet military machine, particularly the advanced bombers and the missiles, and the space capability. Even if obtained at the expense of (all?) other branches of industry, such as mass production of an adequate passenger car, this certainly shows a potential for first rate high tech capability.

[32] It is very hard to see how a "market economy" can include, at an adequate level of consumption, the entire 290 million strong population, in the foreseeable future. To organize a Latin American type economy with 20%–30% integrated into a Western run

world economy, a "¹/₃ society," should take only some years. But at that point the process may well come to a stop.

³³ China's economic development after the new economic policies (*dengism*) were launched in the early 1980s has been extremely lopsided. The policy of economic zones along the coast (opposite Macao, Hong Kong, and Taiwan) created regional imbalances and is now backfiring, since Beijing has been unable to transfer wealth to the poorer landlocked regions. "To fight back, many inland regions have set up trade barriers, hoarded raw materials in scarce supply, and diverted goods slotted for the state to the free market" (*Business Week*, December 24, 1990). Classwise, the basic factor is probably that dengism generated capital by giving farmers close to the cities access to the city market, then stimulated investment in millions of "township enterprises" and the formation of a merchant class. There was nothing in this policy for bureaucrats–intelligentsia, the students, or the workers, or for people in cities in general, who responded through corruption or the revolt of May-June 1989. But China is now taken off the black list due to "constructive behavior" in the Security Council in the Gulf Crisis.

³⁴ The rapid deployment force in the Maldives and the peacekeeping force in Sri Lanka are, in the view of this author, merely portents of things to come.

³⁵ Like in the U.S., Latin American fundamentalism seems to be evangelical/ Protestant, if we do not include liberation theology, and very much linked to business interests. This might set into motion entrepreneurial capitalism, and may also be extremely ruthless, with El Salvador, Guatemala and Honduras, and Brazil as examples. In all four the Protestants may be in the majority early in the third millennium (*Der Spiegel*, No. 47, 1990).

³⁶ If the area around Konigsberg/Kaliningrad becomes an independent Baltic republic partly populated by Volga Germans, then the corridor problem, from present Germany through present Poland, will certainly emerge again. But that corridor would also have obvious economic advantages. Geoeconomics easily becomes geopolitics, and vice versa. Will Europe handle the problem better now than in the 1930s?

³⁷ Some recent data from Brazil during the decade of the brutal conditions of the International Monetary Fund may serve as examples of this. The top 10% increased their share of personal income from 47% in 1981 to 53% in 1989 (the top 1% from 13% to 17%); the bottom 50% decreased their share from 13% to 10% (the bottom 10% from 0.9% to 0.6%) (*istoe-senhor* November 21, 1990). Of course, this is not catastrophic if at the same time there is economic growth. There is not: income per capita will decrease 6% in 1990, the worst since the −6.6% registered in 1981 (*Gazeta Mercantil*, November 30, 1990). Most decrease is in industry, then agriculture, then the services.

³⁸ See the theory of depression in Batra (1985, chap. 6, pp. 113-132). The approach chosen in this chapter, however, differs from Batra's, who also makes a distinction between the economic surface and the social core of these cyclical phenomena. Interestingly, *Business Week* (August 13, 1990) also went against the trend, seeing considerable problems ahead. Right they were.

³⁹ Like the type A executive, subconsciously longing for a slight coronary that may offer him a reason acceptable to others, and to himself, to slow down a little. Moreover, there is a surprise element leading to some shakeup, reshuffling.

⁴⁰ Thus, it is hard to see the U.S. fitted into a supereconomy with such rules as are currently being planned for the European Community/Union, not only a currency mechanism but a Central Bank and common currency, meaning that member countries no longer have independent fiscal policies. But being neither a supereconomy nor a subeconomy in the future, there is still ample space, given the size of the U.S. economy, for it to be one among others in a setting of multipolarity, as argued here. This is also the thesis in a major work by Chodos and Garmaise (1988); see particularly pp. 197ff.).

However, multipolarity does not exclude hegemony as the authors seem to think. The Bush administration (1988) is trying to build a North American Free Trade Area of 360 million people and $6 trillion product and beyond that an area for the whole Western Hemisphere.

[41] If it is exogenous, how can it be reproduced when needed again? What positive externalities are lost by giving the role as stimulus, and the enormous challenges that go with it, to the exogenous sector, for example, to an "expert"?

[42] The figures given here are fairly typical of what is reported almost daily in U.S. newspapers. The public image the U.S. public has of its own system is probably a very important factor behind the deep pessimism of the public.

[43] That speculation is, in turn, related to concentration of wealth, where the Reagan years up to the October 1987 crash brought about wealth at the disposal of the top 1% very similar to the figures before the crash of October 1929, well above 30%. It should be noted that the depression came 4 years later. How bad the F/R ratio has become can be seen from some figures taken from *Monthly Review* of June 1990. Only 15% of the investment in the period 1983–1988 was in the productive sectors agriculture, mining, industry, and transportation, the other 85% being in trade, banking, insurance, and the real estate market. As a result the capital value of the productive sector was worth less than the capital value of banking, insurance, and real estate in 1989. At the same time the pathological state of U.S. banking, including the link between Salomon Brothers, Inc. and the U.S. Treasury, is a major factor in creating the instability in the dollar value incompatible with the position as world currency. To sign a contract in dollars becomes too risky.

[44] The famous book by Russell Jacoby, *The Last intellectuals* (New York: Basic Books, 1987) makes this point very well: the disappearance of intellectuals from the public U.S. scene and the take-over by junk/pop intellectuals of the journalist/columnist variety.

[45] The implicit comparison is, of course, with Japanese management culture. Both pictures may be somewhat overdrawn, but even with some correction these are differences of major significance.

[46] Dr. K. Schwartzman of the Department of Sociology at the University of Arizona, using the trade composition index (TCI) developed by the present author (see Galtung, 1980) comparing the U.S., Brazil, Mexico, and Portugal, has shown how the U.S. is deteriorating and the others improving after the Second world war.

[47] See "The Leisure Empire" (1990): "American entertainment rang up some 300 billion dollars in sales last year, of which an estimated 20% came from abroad. By the year 2000, half of the revenues from American movies and records will be earned in foreign countries."

[48] Thus, General Motors Corp. and Ford Motor Co. had a combined loss of 2.1 billion dollars in the red for the fourth quarter of 1990 alone (*The Wall Street Journal*, February 15-16, 1991). IBM third-quarter 1991 was about 80% below the same quarter the year before. The flagships going down?

APPENDIX: GERMANY, U.S., AND JAPAN COMPARED ON ECONOMIC INDICATORS
(SOURCE: *INTERNATIONALE WIRTSCHAFTSZAHLEN,* 1991; IDW, KOLN)*

	GERMANY	UNITED STATES	JAPAN
Life expectancy 1985-89, m-f	71.8-78.4	71.4-78.7	75.2-80.9
Life expectancy gain, 1970	4.4-4.6	4.3-3.6	5.9-6.2
Employment % 1989, p-s-t	4-40-56	2.9-26.9-70.2	7.9-34-58
Unemployment % of Labor force	5.5	5.3	2.3
Youth (>25) unemployment, %	17.3	36.9	25.4
Hours of work/workeryear	1610	1996	2142
Lost days disputes/workeryear	5	170	5
Self-employment rate, %	11.2	9.0	24.2
% GDP growth per employee 1989	2.7	1.0	2.9
% CPI change 1988/89	2.8	4.8	2.3
Private consumption 1988, %GDP	54.8	66.5	57.5
Investment 1988, %GDP	19.9	17.1	30.6
Value added industry, 1988, %	41.4	28.5	39.7
Taxes and soc. sec. 1988, % GDP	37.4	29.8	31.3
Costs of soc. sec. 1988, % GDP	24.3	13.8	12.0
Workerhours costs in industry, $	19	14.4	15.8
% Shareholders equity, industry	27.1	42.7	29.4
Trade Balance 1970, $B	4.3	0.5	0.4
Trade Balance 1989, $B	71.5	− 128.9	64.2
Current account	44.4B	− 99.3B	35.8B
Current account balance 1970	0.87	2.3	1.97
Current account balance 1989	55.4	− 110.0	57.2
as % of GDP, for 1989	4.4	− 2.0	2.0
Food, % export-% import	4.6-9.6	10.1-5.3	0.6-14.7
Min. Fuels, % export-% import	1.2-7.6	2.8-11.1	0.-20.4
Tools, vehicles, %exp.-%imp.	48.7-30.5	42.6-43.5	69.8-14.2
Share, world export, 1989, %	11.4	12.1	9.1
Share, world import, 1989, %	8.6	15.5	6.7
Difference export-import	2.8	− 3.4	2.4
Real exchange rates, 1989	120.4	67.3	128.6
Research and development, %GDP	2.9	2.8	2.9
Worker: CEO income differential (BUSINESS WEEK)	1:23	1:80	1:17
Foreign net debt (ASIAWEEK)	Credit	$664B	Credit

*Some comments may be in order. One general impression is the similarity between Germany and Japan on the one hand and how they differ from the U.S. on the other, essentially reflecting growth vs. decline. Thus, the U.S. has very high proportion in the tertiary sector, very high youth unemployment (possibly not because they are young but because the phenomenon is more recent), very high number of labor disputes, a negative difference between GDP and CPI growth, the highest private consumption and the lowest investment, the lowest gross value added in industry, the lowest labor costs but then also the highest shareholder equity. On the world scene the U.S. has negative trade and current account balances, although (still) only 2% of GDP. The U.S. is a net exporter of foodstuffs and importer of machine tools/vehicles; with the other two it is the other way around, but then the U.S. is a net importer and the other two net exporters. On September 1, 1990, the CBS "60 Minutes" reported that, after the Second World War, 95% of products consumed in the U.S. were made in the U.S.; that figure is now 4%.

One interesting figure outside this pattern is the highest self-employment: by far Japan (24.2%), among them the countless small shops and firms tied together in primary relations (sociologically speaking).

At the end there are two lines often referred to, one from the domestic and one from the international scene. The difference between the pay differentials between the ordinary worker and the CEO (with the United Airlines ratio being 1:1200) is significant given that, in 1990, CEO pay rose 7% and corporate profits declined 7%; in the U.S. (see also *Wall Street Journal*, June 4, 1991). But the relation to Germany and Japan being in the black and the U.S. deeply in the red, paying as much as 27% of each federal (not social security) revenue dollar in interest, is hardly simple, given that U.S. CEOs had been benefiting from high differentials long before the U.S. became a net debtor.

Chapter 3
Geopolitical Strategies of the U.S. in a Post-American World

Immanuel Wallerstein

On Christmas Day, 1991, President George Bush spoke to the nation on the occasion of Gorbachev's resignation. He spoke of a U.S. "victory" in the Cold War. But was it a victory? And if it was, what kind of geopolitical strategy is available for the U.S. in a world where there is no "cold war"?

The U.S. has been since 1945 the single most powerful state in the interstate system and its hegemonic power. Its central strategic aim was to maintain and enhance that hegemonic power. But to state the objective this way and so obviously is to tell us little about its translation into more concrete geopolitical objectives, of which there were four.

The primary objective was "to contain the U.S.S.R.," seen (in Reagan's memorable expression) as the "evil empire." This was proclaimed to be the primordial objective, and the other three objectives were seen as essential adjuncts to the pursuit of this primary one. The other three objectives were to maintain the unity of the "free world," to ensure a steady, nonradical political and economic evolution of the Third World, and to maintain a unified home front in the United States committed to the U.S. hegemonic role.

The United States has had considerably more difficulty in pursuing each of these objectives than it has admitted publicly or even to itself. This is particularly true of the latter three, presumably secondary, objectives. The U.S. homefront has been rattled by internal social turmoil which exploded once in the late 1960s and is threatening to explode once again in the 1990s. The Third World has always been more contentious than the U.S. hoped, from the Chinese Revolution to the Vietnamese war to a Cuban regime thumbing its nose at the U.S., and from the Iranian seizure of the U.S. embassy to the Persian Gulf War. Japan and the NATO allies have become major economic threats to the United States' well-being. But up to 1989, all the difficulties at home, in the Third World, and with O.E.C.D. countries were limited in their impact by the ability of the negotiators to brandish the ideological menace of Communism and thereby to maintain the legitimacy and practical reality of the U.S. "leadership" in the world political arena.

The Soviet "menace" to the world system has always been over-stated, both by U.S. and Soviet officials and ideologists. The conflicts have always been carefully orchestrated and contained and operated within rules that did not seriously threaten U.S. hegemony in the post-1945 world. But nonetheless, the conflicts have seemed real enough to most people that it kept most of them from doing things that would threaten the stability of the Cold War.

Stability is the key term. The Cold War ensured a relatively stable world order, which of course is an inversion of what the propaganda would have had us believe. The very belief in an unstable world order was an essential part of the package of rendering it in reality quite stable.

Today, the Cold War is no more. The U.S.S.R. has ceased to exist, and Russia and the east European states are no longer "communist." What this means is not victory for the U.S. but defeat, since the Cold War was the single most important pillar of U.S. geopolitical strategy. Without it, the U.S. lacks the strength to play a hegemonic role.

It is first of all no longer the preeminent center of world production. Japan and western Europe have not only caught up to the U.S., but are steadily improving their position relative to the United States. There is absolutely no reason to expect that this will be less true as we go into the 21st century.

The financial position of the U.S. state is even worse. The catastrophic wastage of the Reagan years (the military Keynesianism, the redistribution of the U.S. rich, and the massive financial speculative activity ultimately at the cost of the U.S. taxpayer) have saddled the U.S. with a massive debt. The size of the debt will make it particularly difficult for the U.S. (more than for western Europe or Japan) to deal with the current world depression, and hence, make the U.S. still less competitive.

Ideologically, the U.S. will find that, without anti-Communism, it stands for very little. Classical 19th-century liberalism—political reformism plus market-oriented economies—has little genuine appeal anymore, despite the upsurge of their use of slogans. Human rights does have an appeal, but it is hardly a slogan that will strengthen U.S. hegemony, since it will be used as much against its interests as for it.

The U.S. has two major strong points left, and each is threatened. One is its military force. The U.S. is still spectacularly stronger than any other state. But it will be impossible to keep this up much longer. There is no ideological justification for it, and the cost has become unsupportable. The U.S. military will undergo considerable retrenchment in the next decade. It is doubtful that U.S. forces will continue to be stationed outside the U.S.

The second continuing strong point is the U.S. research capacity, which is still greater than that of any other country. But it is doubly threatened on the one hand by the constant advance in the research capacity of Japan and western Europe, and on the other hand by the financial cutbacks currently being suffered by U.S. educational institutions. It may take 30 years to erode U.S. advantage here entirely, but it is eroding.

Of course, all the negatives have been true at least since the late 1960s, but their impact has been slowed down hitherto by the ability of the U.S. to brandish Cold War slogans. Now that it can no longer do this, its relative decline will precipitate.

Furthermore, there are new dangers ahead. They are primarily of three different kinds. The first comes from the other O.E.C.D. states. When the new Kondratieff–A-phase starts, after we come out of the current depression (which has not at all reached yet its bottom point), the U.S. is faced with the prospect of being left far behind in the triangular Japan–E.C.–U.S. race to obtain relative monopolies in the new leading products.

The second danger comes from the Third World. Faced with still further marginalization in the 50 years ahead, and no longer having any reason to believe in the credible possibility of "national development" within the capitalist world economy, the Third World will turn increasingly to what I think of as the Ayatollah Khomeini and the Saddam Hussein options. The first is the assertion of total otherness in a very militant form. The second is the attempt to create direct military challenges to the O.E.C.D. states. Both these threats were contained with considerable difficulty in the last decade. They will become greater, not lesser, threats in the years ahead, abetted by the unstoppable proliferation of nuclear weapons.

The third danger comes from the prospect of internal social warfare within the United States itself. And the O.E.C.D. states are faced with the same reality: the widening economic and demographic polarization between North and South has created a South-North migratory flux which, whatever the legal barriers, will mean an enormous growth in the O.E.C.D. countries of the "Third World within" in the coming decades. While this will be true of all O.E.C.D. countries, it will result in the highest relative numbers in the U.S. (for historical reasons). Given the economic difficulties the U.S. will be facing, this is a formula for acute internal social conflict.

Given this somber situation, what can the United States do? That is, what kind of geopolitical strategy is it likely to follow? The most urgent problem to resolve will be the stanching of the relative economic decline. In a triangular race for competitive advantage (Japan–E.C.–U.S.), the optimal strategy for the weakest of the three (the U.S.) will be to make an alliance with one of the other two. It seems to me far more likely that we shall see a Japan–U.S. alliance than an E.C.–U.S. alliance. While the cultural links between the U.S. and Europe are clearly closer than between the U.S. and Japan, this will actually work against a Europe–U.S. tie. European unity is being forged today, can only be forged, against the U.S. It is the only way Europe can reassert itself culturally. Japan has no such problem. It is and will remain culturally quite distinct from the U.S.

Secondly, Europe doesn't need the U.S. military strength as much as Japan does. The major military problem is the political legacy of the Second World War. The remilitarization of both Germany and Japan continues to raise political problems both internally for each and externally for the countries which were on the other side. Perhaps this will be forgotten in 20–30 years, but this is not yet the case. But Germany has the possibility of legitimating a remilitarization as part of Europe. Japan has no such cover, and thus needs the U.S.

Thirdly, traditionally and for obvious reasons, sea(-air) powers join forces against land-based hinterlands. While this is perhaps less important than in previous centuries, it still plays a role in the thinking of military strategists.

Thus, it seems to me likely that there will emerge an alliance, both political and economic, of Japan and the U.S., with the U.S. as the junior economic partner (whose strength would be heavily on the R & D side), but as the partner who would continue to offer the bulk of the military effort. Of course, the alliance would not be easy to forge, and that might not arouse popular enthusiasm on either side, but it would not be the first *mariage de convenance* known to history.

The second problem would be the restless Third World. The most urgent tactical need for the O.E.C.D. countries would be to divide the countries of the Third World. Towards this end, Japan and the U.S. will concentrate on including China in the benefits of their new condominium. China outside would be a major menace. China inside would be a major asset. It would be a large new market. More important, it would be a large new reservoir of cheaper labor. And China has both military and political strengths not to be underestimated. Europe's counterpart would be Russia, and for the very same reasons.

Once China and Russia were included inside the new arrangement, the O.E.C.D. countries would not really need to include any other Third World countries. They could not really handle the inclusion of any more, since each "inclusion" comes at some economic price. Of course, there might be minor exceptions—either because of geopolitical or cultural propinquity (parts of eastern Europe, Korea, etc.), or because of some special economic value of particular distant enclaves. But by and large, the rest of the Third World will be economically ignored.

The ignored zones will not appreciate this and will begin to look into the Ayatollah Khomeini and Saddam Hussen options. The U.S. will seek to keep them in check by bluster, by noise, and by shows of military force. But I cannot see how these will be particularly efficacious. And, to the degree they are not, U.S. isolationism will grow, rendering the potential for intervention still less. In short, the U.S. has no plausible geopolitical strategy to handle the unrest of the Third World in the 30–50 years to come.

The third geopolitical problem will be its internal unity. The U.S.S.R. has disintegrated, though few would have predicted it 10 years ago. It is not beyond the realm of possibility that the United States will become the arena of disintegrative shocks in the decade or two ahead. The United States had one civil war from which it took 100 years to recover. It could have a second, with less obvious internal geographical lines and therefore one less easy to handle. There is nothing inevitable about such disintegration, but it would require a major political turnaround to make it unlikely. It would require quite simply a shift in the direction of greater internal equality, both economically and racially.

Anyone who knows the U.S. well knows both that this would not be easy and that it would not be impossible. Indeed, I would wager that one of the key political battles within the world system over the next 20-odd years will be the internal social battle in the U.S., a battle over the identity and the soul of the American people. When and if the U.S. resolves its deep internal fissures, it will have come up on the other side of its pseudo-victory in the Cold War.

Chapter 4
The New World Order: A View from the South

Chakravarthi Raghavan

Humankind has entered the last decade of this second millennium after Christ with a bang—with a billion-dollar-a-day "transfer of technology" from the North to a country of the South (Iraq)—the Gulf War and its aftermath heralding a New World Order!

And even before the dust and smoke in the wake of Operation Desert Storm and liberation of Kuwait from Iraq could settle down has come the collapse of the Soviet Union as a central State entity and integrated economy stretching from Europe to the Far East.

U.S. President George Bush, who spoke of the New World Order, did not spell out its contours, though he spoke of it in terms of the 1990s as the American decade, and an American 21st Century with ever-rising standards of living for Americans, and of the U.S.–West European NATO alliance extending its horizons to maintain order and safeguard vital common (economic) interests in the South. But some U.S. newspaper columnists (William Safire and Charles Krauthamer) spelled it out as *Pax Americana*.

These developments came even as the world polity was in the grip of some contradictory forces and processes—the growing interdependence among nations and sectors of the world economy; the attempts of the U.S. and the major industrialized countries to use this to knit the world economy (the sum total of several national economies) into a single global economy through the instrumentality of the Transnational Corporations (TNCs); the end of the Cold War and the collapse of the centrally planned command economies in central and eastern Europe; and the growing concerns among the public (of the North) over planetary issues like environment and problems of survival and "development" in the South.

Towards the end of the 1980s, the Cold War and the East–West ideological divide that had plagued the world after the Second World War had come to an end in Europe—symbolized by the tearing down of the Berlin wall in 1989, and the subsequent unification of the two Germanies—holding out some hopes of a transition to a more peaceful world and prospects of a "peace dividend," diversion of resources from armaments to peaceful purposes to meet unmet needs of humanity.

But the end of the Cold War also brought to the fore existing rivalries and differences among the United States, Europe (and in particular the 12-member European Community, which was trying to grow beyond its role of a customs union and a trading bloc into an economic and political Power), and Japan in the Far East—fuelling neomercantalist tendencies (Ernst, 1989, cited in Raghavan, 1990, pp. 39–40) and spurring attempts to form contending regional economic coalitions and blocs.

The initial euphoria with which the collapse of central planning in Europe was greeted, both in the West and the East, soon gave way to somber realization that the transition from centrally planned and command economies to market-oriented ones (for which there is no historical experience to draw upon or learn from) could be long, uncertain and not smooth; that moves towards democracy would have to contend against the feudal, fascist, and ethnic rivalries that had prevailed in most of the region in the interwar years and had merely been pushed underground, and not eradicated by the postwar Communist rule in these countries; and that the Soviet Union (with its superpower nuclear arsenals and weapons) could be wracked by internal conflicts and disintegrate into many constituent units.

Vast, revolutionary advances in communications and transport had already brought the world closer and increased the growing interdependence—among and between nations and various parts of the world economy. There were forces at work to use this interdependence to knit closely together the world's nations into one global economy.

> The primary agent of globalization is the transnational enterprise. The primary driving force is the revolution in information and communications technology....In a globalizing world, competition among transnational enterprises in sophisticated products and services...is also competition among systems....For the global corporation competing in

the international economy, it means competing under the same set of rules—that is the same set of domestic rules in different countries. (Ostrey, 1990, p. 4; see also UNCTC, 1991, pp. 81–82)

In other words, the TNCs—with their interlinked interests in commodities, manufacture, banking, and finance, and hold on technology through patents and cross-licensing—are trying to change the postwar international systems, based on national sovereignty of States, into a single transnational system of production, distribution, trade, consumption, and "culture"—a *Transnational World Order* (TWO) where national sovereignty would give way to the interests of the TNCs and world capital, and the countries of the South would be pushed back, in economic terms, to their colonial era existence of maintaining law and order and protecting the interests of the foreign investors against their own peoples.

Side by side, there has been the growing consciousness among people, more so in the rich, satiated North, that for all the economic indicators of well-being, the quality of life itself has been deteriorating. With this consciousness came the search for new paths for protecting the environment and moving towards sustainable development.

DESERT STORM AND IMPLOSION IN THE SOVIET UNION

The New World Order that came with "Desert Storm" seemed to be an edifice sought to be built on desert sands.

In August 1991—a year after Iraq's invasion and annexation of Kuwait, and its defeat in the Gulf War and restoration of Kuwait's sovereignty (and continuing efforts to establish some kind of 'order' in the entire region)—came the almost overnight collapse of Communist power and the Soviet Union as a State. It is too early to predict the final outcome—whether the Soviet Union and its control over the constituent republics would give way to a new Russian- (and white European-)dominated confederation, an "empire of sorts" 'à la that of the czars or some other configuration, and what its effect (in the short to medium term) would be on the Asian republics of the former Soviet Union and their Muslim population, and their interactions with the countries and peoples to their south and east—in an arc running from the Asian part of Turkey across Arabia, Iran, and South Asia to China. In the short to medium term it appears already to be having unsettling effects in Europe (in terms of the European Community's efforts to integrate itself and forge links with the rest of the European countries) and in Asia and Far East.

History does not of course start or stop at particular points of time, but is a continuum.

But if one is tempted not take an *ahistorical* view, so to say looking at current history in the making as at a frame in a movie film, the question could be asked, When did this "New World Order" begin? It is not academic. For on its answer might depend answers to questions about the stability of this New World Order or its duration.

Did it begin on January 16, 1991, when the U.S. and Europe began their war against Iraq? Or did it all begin when Michail Gorbachev proclaimed his *perestroika* and *glasnost* and the Soviets began to work in tandem with the U.S., as a junior partner, or from the day in 1989 when the Berlin wall came down and the "market" god became the only true God, vanquishing the Satan of central planning?

Or was it merely a clearer manifestation of the postwar order or the even earlier position of the U.S. as the new imperial center and *Pax Americana*, despite its being checkmated for a while by Soviet power under Stalin and his successors? Did the Gulf war signify the rise of a *Pax Americana* or the pyrotechnics of a falling one (Kennedy, 1987)?

Whatever the answers, the Gulf War and its aftermath, and the breakup of the Soviet Union, raise a number of questions about what are usually called North–South relations.

NEW ORDER AND NORTH–SOUTH RELATIONS

Since the 1950s, the term *North* has been used to describe the group of industrialized nations (more or less equal in terms of economic and social development) joined together in the Paris-based Organization for Economic Cooperation and Development (OECD), and some integrated even more in trading blocs (like the European Community), with some homogeneity of interests and culture (except perhaps for Japan) and ways of thinking.

The terms *South* and *Third World* have been applied to the group of newly independent and underdeveloped nations of Africa, Asia, and Latin America (which gained independence a century ago but are very dependent economically) and the Caribbean.[1]

But in a unipolar world—the New World Order and *Pax Americana*, with the U.S. perhaps an unchallengeable military superpower but living as a nation beyond its means (by borrowing abroad) though still able to demand and get others like Germany and Japan to pay for its wars—the concept of a North has come to be questioned.

So has been the concept of the South and whether it is useful to talk of North–South relations, and what kind of North–South relations could be envisaged for the 1990s and into the next century.

Through the 1980s there had been challenges to the very concept of the South. In various international fora there was a constant refrain about the heterogeneity of the countries of the South—implying, and sometimes explicitly stated, that not only can no one speak on behalf of the South, but that the South should have no single view. The countries of the South, in the Group of 77, apparently have no legitimacy or right to evolve a common view and choose a single voice to speak for them.

The only legitimate groupings, in this view, are "interest group-ings"—the Cairns[2] group of so-called "nonsubsidizing agricultural exporting nations," with Australia as its leader, is often cited as example—of the countries of the North and the South, led naturally by one of their Northern constituents.

There was not much challenge to the concept of a North in dealing with countries of the South. In these dealings the industrialized countries grouped in the Organization for Economic Cooperation and Development (OECD) coordinate and function as a bloc, taking posi-tions on the basis of a lowest common denominator. After the tearing down of the Berlin wall and abandonment of their Marxist ideology and central planning, the former East European socialists want to join this North, but have not so far been admitted to the club. But they, too, more vehemently perhaps as new converts have espoused the Northern view against the South.

North–South relations do not stand in isolation—and even the world order, old or new, is not "free-standing," but part of the totality of global political, economic, and other relationships, even relationships within and among nations and peoples. They have a past, a present, and perhaps a future, too.

THE COLONIAL PAST

They are rooted in the past—of European colonization of other lands and peoples—of the Europeans who went to the Americas and under the theory of "discovery" claimed and took over the land occupied by the native American, and decimated them and their cultures—and created the colonies in North and South America, and engaged in the "trade in men"—the abduction of Africans and their transportation and sale across the seas into slavery, and the concomitant decimation of their civilizations in coastal areas—that went with it.

Even as they were colonizing the Americas, the Europeans (then in their preindustrial, mercantilist phase), trying to "trade" for spice and cotton textiles and silk with India and the Far East, also committed piracy—as when Vasco da Gama and his associates from Portugal stopped an Arab dhow plying in the Arabian sea from the Gulf to Southwest India, looted its goods, and sunk the boat with all the crew. This was justified by Portuguese historian Barros under the doctrine that the "common right to navigate all seas" recognized in Europe "does not extend beyond Europe and therefore the Portuguese as Lords of the Sea are justified in confiscating the goods of all those who navigate the sea without their permission" (Panikkar, 1953, pp. 42–43).

This doctrine, of one law for the White colonial rulers and another for the non-White ruled, prevailed in the entire colonial era, as European metropolitan powers brought Asia and Africa under their colonial rule, used force, waged wars, reached agreements and broke them (all in defiance of then prevalent international law and doctrines of "just war"), in Britain's "opium wars" against China (for the right to sell and trade opium to the people of China to enable British traders to buy Chinese silks and other commodities, rather than pay in gold) and U.S. Admiral Perry's expedition to open up Japan for trade (Raghavan, 1990, pp. 40–43, 72–74).

These doctrines (already being asserted again in the efforts to change the rules of international economic relations) seem to be staging a comeback with the New World Order across a wide front of relations of the U.S. and Europe with the countries of the South.

The initial colonization phase (of the 16th and 18th centuries) was followed by the imperial phase of North–South relations— qualitatively different from that under the old empires because of the advent of industrial capitalism in Europe and its capital accumulation process, beginning in Britain as the dominant center, and later spreading to Europe and North America.

THE NEW CENTER AND DECOLONIZATION

The two wars in Europe in this century ended Europe's ability to hold or expand its imperial role and, at the end of World War II, the U.S. emerged as the dominant or imperial center.

Even before, U.S. capital was looking for markets abroad—and between the two wars, had come up against the reality of imperial preferences (British, French, etc., in their colonies, the Japanese attempts in Korea and China) and the British and French stranglehold on information flows, which were seen as obstructing U.S. trade and economic interests—with Kent Cooper of the Associated Press criticizing the British and French domination of information flows through Reuters and Havas (news agencies) and making demands for change through the doctrine of Free Flow of Information, which presaged Third World complaints in the 1970s and 1980s over U.S. and European domination of information and calls for a New International Information Order.

Thus before and during World War II, the Americans became supporters of freedom struggles in countries like India and in other areas. Both this tradition and U.S. capital's economic interests became an element in the U.S. push, in the postwar order, to break up the Empires (with some covert support in some colonies to armed struggles) and their system of imperial preferences (in trade and for capital from the metropolis).

The threat of Stalin and Soviet-sponsored Communist regimes in East Europe helped the U.S. launch both the Marshall Plan and NATO, firmly linking Western Europe with the U.S. The Marshall Plan helped U.S. corporations to expand into Europe.

With NATO, and the web of alliances around it, aimed at encircling the Soviet Union and China, the U.S. followed some contradictory policies—opposing liberation movements and siding with European "empires" (in Indo-China and Southern Africa) where the alternative was seen as "communists," and remaining neutral or supportive where it was thought the bourgeoisie would emerge as the postcolonial rulers—as in South and South-East Asia and parts of Africa.

All these contradictory forces helped the ongoing freedom struggles in Africa and Asia, and led to the wave of postwar decolonization, starting with India, which had become ungovernable, and economically unprofitable, for the British by the early 1930s, who handed over power in 1947 after partitioning the subcontinent. Liberation came thereafter to several parts of Asia and later of Africa, with the British giving up their empire and colonies more easily than the French and other European metropolitan powers.

But the newly liberated countries by and large did not follow either the *laissez faire* capitalist or socialist central planning path, and sought to find other alternatives, and what are now called North--South relations shaped up in this background.

Politically, most of them refused to take sides, and thus came into being the Non-Aligned Movement. But the same countries that refused to become part of these alliances not only joined the United

Nations, where they were sovereign equals and where the East–West relations gave them the illusion of room for manoeuvre, but flocked to join the IMF and the World Bank, the international instruments of world capitalism, where they were unequals.

For a while, until perhaps the mid-60s, the developing countries and their leaders seriously believed that, with political independence, they only had to work hard to catch up with their former masters. They found themselves faced with some handicaps, and this led to their demanding, and to some extent being granted, special help and privileges—aid, bilateral and multilateral, financial and technical, and trade preferences, and some minor reforms of the rules.

The Latin Americans, who had been "free" of colonial rule more than a century earlier and, in the post-1945 situation, identified themselves culturally as Europeans and as somewhat superior to the Afro-Asians in economic terms, by the mid-'60s realized their equal dependency and came together with the Afro-Asians at UNCTAD-I (1964) to constitute the Group of 77 for furthering efforts at economic decolonization of their countries (for a brief survey of the group and its first 20 years, see Raghavan, 1984, pp. 27–36).

But gradually the countries of the South realized that they were trapped into a system out of which there was no escape, and that they were condemned always to the bottom of the pyramid. At best they were like a mouse on the treadmill, constantly running merely to stay in the same place, but often not even succeeding in that and falling behind. They began groping around for an escape hatch.

THE NEW INTERNATIONAL ECONOMIC ORDER

The postwar economic order based on the Bretton Woods monetary and financial system collapsed in 1971, with the U.S. unilateral decision to end the dollar–gold convertibility obligation, and subsequent efforts to restore it have been mere patchwork and not added up to a system. The decision of the Arab Petroleum Exporting Countries in 1973 to seize control of their oil wealth and set prices acted as a catalyst and galvanized the South to unitedly demand changes in the system—the New International Economic Order and various other 'orders' that were bruited about in the 1970s, when many in the South thought things could be changed by rhetoric.

Then followed nearly a decade of UN-sponsored sectoral conferences and meetings, and discussions within the various fora, on ways to implement some of the objectives of the NIEO declaration, but which did not make any progress, leading to the moves for so-called global negotiations in the UN General Assembly, accepted in principle in 1979 but never launched because of differences on "details."

In retrospect at least, it is clear that the North, in accepting these declarations by consensus, was acting in bad faith and had no intention of working towards them. It merely regrouped itself, played for time by endless talks and forum games, frustrating, at practical levels, even the efforts of the South to organize itself or strive for mutual cooperation.

THE EFFORT AT ROLLBACK

Then came the Reagan-Thatcher era, the conflict in the North itself between financial and industrial capital, when the capitalist centers and the custodians of the interests of speculative finance capital like the U.S. Federal Reserve (during the Carter Presidency itself) and some other central banks, decided to strike back and did so through the international monetary and financial system and high interest rates—resulting in a crashing of commodity prices accentuating the adverse terms of trade facing commodity producers, the debt crisis, and the adjustment forced on the South by the IMF and World Bank.

Along with adjustment came the effort to roll back the South to its prewar colonial frontiers in terms of economic relations and structure—through trade and the GATT and the Uruguay Round.[3]

The GATT (General Agreement on Tariffs and Trade) came into being in 1948 as a "temporary" arrangement—a provisional treaty—pending the entry into force of the Havana Charter and its International Trade Organization (ITO) which, with the two Bretton Woods institutions (The International Monetary Fund and the International Bank for Reconstruction and Development), had been envisaged as the economic pillars of the post-1945 world order.

Learning from the experiences of the interwar years in Europe and North America (the beggar-my-neighbor policies of protection), the Havana Charter provided a multilateral framework of rules and principles and disciplines to govern international trade, applicable to policies and actions of governments and states as well as of private operators and enterprises. Its institutional framework, the ITO, would have enabled further evolution of this framework as also for a gradual process of international trade liberalization and competition, but remained aborted.

Side by side with the Havana charter negotiations, the European allies and the United States and a few of the then independent or near-independent states, had agreed to exchange tariff concessions to stimulate their mutual trade. Pending ratifications of the Havana Charter, these concessions, with some other trade policy provisions (of the Havana Charter) to insure that tariff concessions were not negated in other ways, were incorporated into a provisional agreement (an executive agreement among governments not needing ratifications) to enter into force immediately.

But the U.S. Congress turned down the Havana Charter (because it would take away U.S. sovereignty and Congressional authority to legislate on trade policy), and GATT has remained in force now for 40 years as a provisional treaty, a "contract" among governments, without the trappings and authority of an international organization set up by a treaty. Legally GATT has no secretariat: the secretariat of the Interim Committee for the ITO (under the Havana Charter), set up by the UN, has provided the legal cover for the GATT's secretariat, which "services" the "contract" and carries out duties assigned to it from time to time by the Contracting Parties through collective decisions at their annual meetings or at the GATT Council, which functions in between the annual meetings.

For a while, until at least the mid-1950s, there had been hope that the U.S. might reconsider its position. But when it became clear it would not, governments used the GATT machinery for exchanging trade concessions among themselves and liberalizing trade through a multilateral process—extending to all signatories, under the Most Favored Nation treatment principle enshrined in Article I of the GATT, any trade concessions that two or more contracting parties exchange among themselves directly or through multilateral trade negotiations. There have been seven rounds of multilateral trade negotiations so far under GATT auspices, which, as the name signifies, dealt with trade concessions for goods crossing the border—both conditions under which they could cross (the tariff and nontariff barriers the state imposed or could) and the equality of treatment (compared to domestic products) they would enjoy *after* the "foreign goods" cross the border.

THE STICK AND CARROT APPROACH

But the Uruguay Round negotiations launched at Punta del Este in 1986 are qualitatively different from the earlier rounds of trade negotiations. Though called multilateral trade negotiations, they are not really about traditional trade (exchange of goods across international borders) but about restructuring the world economy into a transnational system, and an effort to insure for the TNCs—the instruments being used to knit the world into a global economy and insure the perpetual capital accumulation for the benefit of the center—freedom to operate without any interference from governments of the South.

It has sought to bring on to the negotiating agenda issues that are not strictly "trade" but involve issues of production, distribution, and consumption within countries—issues such as *services* (for which as yet there is no agreed definition except that they are not *goods*), Trade-related Investment Measures (TRIMS) relating to rights of foreign investors and limitations on rights of sovereign states to regulate their activities, the so-called Trade-Related Intellectual Property Rights (TRIPS), as also *agriculture*, which for various reasons had never been fully governed by GATT disciplines, and rewrite GATT rules to legitimize institutional discrimination against the South and enable cross-retaliatory trade sanctions.

The reason why this "restructuring" effort was sought through "trade," and the GATT's negotiating process, was the tremendous advantage that the U.S. and the other rich nations have in this negotiating arena.

Firstly, trade (with communication) is the biggest interface of nations with others, and Third World nations, struggling to sell abroad and earn foreign exchange to import necessities and investment goods and intermediate inputs for their development programmes, are most vulnerable on this front. One can, by not seeking their resources, at least for a while, defy the IMF and the World Bank and escape their influence and conditionalities (for opening up the domestic economy to foreign investments and exchanges). But it is difficult for any country to close its frontiers and shut itself off from trade with the outside world. Very large continental economies, with considerable domestic reorganization and repression (political, economic, and social), could perhaps do this for a time, but not the vast majority of the Third World nations.

Even now, the IMF and World Bank, particularly the latter, though contributing only to about 5% of Third World investment for development, exercise an enormous influence on the economic policies of these countries, including the area of trade policy. However, while the Bank is able to hold out a carrot, it is unable to wield the stick, which the trading system and its retaliation provisions provide. One of the efforts in the Uruguay Round is to enable the three to combine forces in influencing trade and economic policy in the countries of the South.

Secondly, among the fora dealing with economic issues, the Third World countries are weakest inside GATT, in terms of collective organization and bargaining. Though based on consensus decision making, and though developing countries now account for nearly two-thirds of the membership and could prevail in any vote, the GATT negotiations and decision-making processes are totally non-transparent and controlled by the North. The GATT's so called *green room* process (so named after the wall-paper decor of the GATT Director-General's conference room in Geneva, where such meetings take place)—informal meetings of a small group of negotiators, under the chairmanship of the Director-General and at his "invitation" to hammer out accords on difficult issues—enable the powerful to easily coerce the few individual countries of the South (who do not negotiate or bargain collectively inside GATT). A constant refrain (from the officials and the major trading nations) in GATT is that it is a "contract" among individual "contracting parties" with varying interests, and that there are no North–South differences but only differing trading interests[4]—though this does not seem to prevent the North from consulting and coordinating among themselves within the OECD or the various informal groupings, including the annual summits of the Group of Seven leading industrialized countries.[5]

Third World countries were literally dragged into these negotiations intended by the major industrialized countries to lay down new rules of the game governing, not only international economic relations, but also how countries are to organize and run their domestic economies, creating in effect a global *laissez faire* state.

After 4 years of intense technical preparations and discussions, and negotiations, what was intended to have been the final ministerial-level meeting to conclude the Round ended in total failure at Brussels in December 1990.[6]

While the negotiations "broke down" because of differences over agriculture support policies—between Europe (and Japan), on the one side, and the U.S. and some other agricultural exporting countries in the Cairns group (named after the place in Australia where the first meeting was held) on the other—in reality there were considerable other differences among industrialized countries, and between them and the developing countries, on almost every issue. The negotiations were restarted in January 1991, without setting any formal deadline. Still various target dates in 1991 were informally set but missed. At end of December 1991, the GATT Director-General produced a text of his own, the Draft Final Act (DFA), in the hope it would be taken as a package and accepted, and the agreement signed and sealed by mid-April of 1992, to enable the ratification processes to be completed and agreement brought into force on January 1, 1993. As of April 1992, this hope too has evaporated and the outlook is clouded and uncertain.

Side by side arose a consciousness among peoples in the affluent North that, though their incomes and standards of living were increasing, the quality of life was decreasing, and that ecology and environment do not observe frontiers and ignore East–West and North–South divides. This gave rise to the Green and other ecological movements in the North.

Thus parallel to the push for a global *laissez faire* transnational system, this environment consciousness resulted in the report of the World Commission on Environment and Development, popularly known as the Bruntland Report after its chair Mrs. Gro Harlem Bruntland of Norway, and the calls for environment and sustainable development.

Unable to ignore these, the governments of the North have "embraced" the "green issues" and have attempted to co-opt the environmental movement into this global *laissez faire* market philosophy. These two forces are being brought together—whether in confrontation or cooperation remains to be seen—through the 1992 UN Conference on Environment and Development (UNCED), the "Earth Summit" in Rio de Janeiro, Brazil.

TWO, NWO, AND ECOLOGY

We have thus some different strands and contradictory processes at work on the international scene.

First, there is this New World Order (NWO) of George Bush and his commentators, and while there is no challenge to U.S. power, especially since the collapse of Soviet power, its stability even in the Gulf does not seem assured. If the Gulf war is any indication, it will be a New World Order and *Pax Americana* based on the economic muscle and sinews of other industrial and economic powers, Germany and Japan, with the U.S. not even a technology leader, but dependent on them for technological inputs and financial largess and support.

The situation of the U.S. is not very different from that of Britain, which, before World War I and more so in the interwar years, found it was technologically and financially unable to maintain *Pax Brittanica* against the challenges from Germany in Europe, and began to drag in the United States on its side.

Second, there are the earlier attempts to create a Transnational World Order (TWO) through the Uruguay Round, originally set to be concluded in 1990 but which could not be and have been extended and with moving, but missed, deadlines, the last being by mid-April of 1992. As of mid-April 1992, the conclusion of the Round still remains in the realm of hope and clouded by many uncertainties—both political and economic.

Its conclusion appears to be dependent on domestic forces and their conflicting interests within the U.S. and on whether the U.S., the European Community and Japan overcome their neomercantalist rivalries and serious trade and economic differences and join forces against the South (as they did against Iraq in the Gulf War over oil) to force through a New Economic Order favoring the TNCs on intellectual property, investments, and services.

Or will the three, unable to overcome their neomercantalist rivalries, stake out spheres of economic influence and control in the South (in a new version of the earlier colonial era)? There are some signs of the latter:

The United States has already entered into a Free Trade Area (FTA) agreement with Canada, and a North American Free Trade Area (NAFTA) agreement is being negotiated among Canada, Mexico, and the U.S. It has also launched the "Enterprise for Americas Initiative" (EAI), which envisages free trade agreements with Latin American and Caribbean countries willing to join the U.S. in a free trade area involving goods, services, and investments. On the face of it, this would result in a huge free trade area for the entire Western Hemisphere. However, a scrutiny of the negotiations and agreement with Canada, the stipulation in NAFTA negotiations that the accord would be separate from the U.S.–Canada agreement (and thus not having to extend to Mexico the benefits of the bilateral privileges for each in the FTA) suggest that the proposed EAI would also appear to involve, not plurilateral negotiations with all Latin American countries wishing to join, but a series of bilateral negotiations and agreements. The overall result would be that the U.S. would be able to trade freely with each of its partners, but that the partners would not be trading freely among themselves (for some recent developments and analysis, see UN Conference on Trade and Development, 1991, pp. 69–71).

The overall result of this "hub (U.S.)-and-spokes (individual trading partner)" arrangement would be a throwback to the old imperial rule, where the rules of the metropolitan country were applied to the colonies.

The EC has proposed association agreements—with the European Free Trade Arrangement (EFTA) countries, central and east Europeans (in European Economic Zone), and expansion (on its terms) of existing and future ones with the Mediterranean countries as well as its arrangements with African-Caribbean-Pacific (ACP) countries under the Lome Pact, involving free or preferential trading privileges for all these and the EC countries, but with decision making vested with the EC member states—would again introduce a gradation of rights and a variation of the imperial rule.

Japan, whose main exports are to Europe and the U.S., is mulling its options—whether to form a hub-and-spokes arrangement with the countries of Asia while simultaneously pursuing its agreements with the U.S. and Europe.

These suggest that the new "regional trading blocs" will not be building blocs for freer multilateral trade, but trading blocs around two or three poles, with the TNCs established in all these three poles providing the integrating element (UNCTC, 1991, pp. 31–82)—in line with their own global profit maximization and capital accumulation priorities rather than priorities of sovereign countries and their public welfare or even a global public welfare determined by States.

But whatever way these conflicts are resolved, the New Transnational World (Economic) Order and the increased marginalization of the peoples of the South, with these economies integrated into the "global" economy in a new colonial-era type of relations, would be an inherently unstable order.

Third, there is the movement for environment and sustainable development, which has drawn in a lot of nongovernmental participation and public awareness and concern and orchestration, but is still very inchoate in terms of its ability to prevail.

The first two trends and goals can be compatible. Bush's NWO and the Gulf War could be seen as an inevitable result or extension of the drive for a TWO and the U.S. assertion and use (under S.301 of the U.S. Omnibus Trade and Competitiveness Act of 1986) of unilateral and illegal trade sanctions to gain economic demands on others.

The objective of ever-rising standards of living for the American people into the 21st century, which has been promised under the New World Order but can't be achieved by the actuality of U.S. economic position or pressures it can mount, can and are being sought to be enmeshed with the NWO and enforced on the periphery through threats of trade sanctions and military power. But this could come into conflict with the economic objectives of the other two trading blocs— Japan and the European Community, and the wider Europe.

Another complication, at least for the short to medium term, is the attempt of the east and central European former Marxist regimes, now joined by the constituent republics of the former Soviet Union, all seeking to establish market regimes, a transition which it is now realized would be neither short nor easy but a long-drawn-out and turbulent process needing massive aid and trade opportunities to make the change.

But the third process for the environment and sustainable development goal is not, though it is being sought to be enmeshed into the
NWO and the TWO. The very institutions and their economic models
and policies that have resulted in the ecological and development
crisis—the growing impoverishment of the South and degradation of
the environment, and the threat to the world's ecology—and the
economic systems based on greed and avarice and global profit maximization and accumulation by the TNCs, are sought to be entrusted
with the evolution and management of the New Environment Order!

EQUITABLE ECO-ORDER OR GLOBAL DISORDER?

The public worries and concerns are sought to be distracted and
diffused by the adoption at the 1992 UNCED Summit of an "Earth
Charter" (a vague declaration of "ethical principles" of behavior) and
an Agenda 21 or some vague goals and objectives and programmes (no
specifics or commitments) for further discussions and negotiations in
the future, some "free-standing" international instruments to stop
deforestation (meaning tropical deforestation), some vaguer instruments on global warming and climate change (without any real
obligations for cutbacks of carbon emissions or energy consumption
and other wasteful ways in the North), and use of trade and other
instruments (with talk too in the U.S. of ecology being a security
issue) to enforce them.

Some of the principles and ideas for the Earth Charter and Agenda
21 seem to be an attempt to reverse some of the post-1945 principles of
international law and national sovereignty (incorporated in some UN
General Assembly Declarations like those on natural resources or the
Charter of Rights and Duties of States), and perhaps provide some
legitimacy for future exercise of military and economic sanctions
against the recalcitrant or independent-minded Third World States.

But it will not include questions like changes in lifestyles and
cutbacks on consumption patterns in the North or for its citizens
making any sacrifices, but controls on the South to reduce or abandon
the yearnings of its people for a better life, adopting instead lifestyles
and development models for the benefit of humanity, and converting
the resources of the South (forests and genetic resources—biological
diversity) into "global commons," while the real global commons
(atmosphere and space and oceans, etc.) are begin deregulated and
privatized to become the private property of the TNCs. It won't even

provide for a greater say for the South in setting some of these goals and in decision making, or influence in their implementation.

The emerging pattern is already being seen in the South as environmental colonialism.

As the former Secretary-General of UNCTAD, Dr. Gamani Corea, has said, the overall outcome would be that, since the planet cannot bear the effects of the poor trying to be rich, and the South aiming to achieve the standards of the North, the South should abjure development and adopt Gandhian simplicity of life ("Rich Must," 1991, p. 16).

However ethically desirable a Gandhian life-style may be, the marvels of modern communication, the TV and audio-visual services, including films and videos (whose scope as a trade in service are sought to be extended and expanded in the Uruguay Round), bring to the poor around the world images of how the rich, and even the poor within the rich nations, live.

The poor do imitate the rich, and are bound to exert pressures on their governments, in these days of democratic governance, or even in nondemocratic ones, for such a life-style.

Gandhi succeeded in getting India to follow his ideas in his lifetime. But he never preached what he did not practice—on himself and his family. After his death, when his followers failed to practice what they preached, they lost their following.

Those in the North preaching this environment/sustainable development gospel would need to first practice it in their own lives and countries before they can hope to get it accepted and practiced in the South.

But there are no signs this may happen.

Miracles may still take place. But unless there is such a miracle and a radical change, the North will use its coercive power to force development models and economic structures on the South to enable the North to continue its way of life. But that will be an inherently unstable order and will very soon put an end to the NWO and TWO in global disorder, as Gamani Corea put it, long before global warming.

Those pushing for a NWO or a TWO to maintain themselves in perpetuity might do well to ponder some eternal truths.

There is a story in the Indian epic *Mahabharat* where Yama (who in Hindu mythology is the Lord of Death, eternal Time) asks his spiritual son Yudhishitira, the eldest of the Pandava heroes, "What is the greatest wonder of the world?" Yudhishitira replies: "Every day, men see creatures depart to Yama's abode, and yet those who remain seek to live forever. This verily is the greatest wonder."

REFERENCES

Ernst, D. (1989 April). *Technology, global economic security and latecomer industrialization—an agenda for the 1990s.* Paper for UNCTAD/UNDP Round Table on technology and trade policy [UNCTAD Secretariat, mimeo].

Kennedy, P. (1987). *The rise and fall of great powers.* New York.

Ostrey, S. (1990, April 19). Help the three systems sing in harmony. *International Herald Tribune,* p. 4.

Panikkar, K.M. (1953). *Asia and Western dominance.* London.

Raghavan, D. (1984). Third World comes of age and faces new challenges. In *IFDA Dossier No. 43.* Switzerland.

Raghavan, C. (1990). *Recolonization: GATT, Uruguay Round and the Third World.* Penang/London.

Rich must change life-styles. (1991). *Third World Resurgence,* No. 10, p. 16.

UNCTAD. (1991). *Trade and development report.* Geneva/New York.

UNCTC (UN Centre for Transnational Corporations). (1991). *The triad in foreign direct investment* (pp. 81–82).

The Uruguay Round in a blackhole. (1991). *Third World Economics,* No. 24.

NOTES

[1] The term *third world* entered the development terminology in the 1960s, derived from the French *troisiéme etat*—to signify those who had no control over their destiny (unlike the king and the nobility and church of those days)—and thus independent of the East–West or market vs. central planning theologies and relationships.

[2] Named after the town in Australia where they first met, it consists of: Argentina, Australia, Brazil, Canada, Chile, Colombia, Hungary, Indonesia, Malaysia, New Zealand, the Philippines, Thailand, and Uruguay.

[3] For a detailed account and fuller understanding of the GATT and the Uruguay Round and linked processes, see Raghavan (1990).

[4] In the beginning, when it broached the subject, the U.S. had talked of a new North–South trade round, of the industrialized countries exchanging trade concessions with the newly industrializing countries, and in return for their own concessions to the NICs forcing them to open up their markets to other Third World countries. But very soon this North–South dimension dropped out of the U.S. terminology.

[5] United States, United Kingdom, Germany, France, Japan, Canada, and Italy.

[6] For report on the Brussels meeting, see *Third World Economics,* 7-8 (1990), pp. 5–12.

PART II
National Media In
International Context

Chapter 5
The Externalities Effects of Commercial and Public Broadcasting

Edward S. Herman

The balance between commercial and public broadcasting in the West shifted steadily, and perhaps decisively, in favor of the former from the 1970s into the early 1990s. Public broadcasting has been "under siege" from commercial interests and conservative governments throughout this period (Etzioni-Halevy, 1987), with the tempo of attack stepped up in the 1980s. Public broadcasting monopolies have been broken in Belgium, France, Italy, Norway, Portugal, Spain, Switzerland, and elsewhere, and commercial broadcasters have been rapidly enlarging their domains, encroaching on public system advertising, putting public broadcasters' funding by the state under further pressure by reducing their audience shares, and forcing them to alter their programs to compete for audiences. In the United States, public broadcasting, already marginalized, has been subjected to further financial pressures and politicization.

The internationalization of communications and the mass media has contributed substantially to the shift in balance. The enlargement of markets in Europe and worldwide, actual and in prospect, has produced an explosion of national and cross-border mergers, the integration of production and distribution facilities in a search for economies of scale, and defensive and aggressive maneuvering for position and power. Transnational transmissions by satellite have brought in commercial programs outside of national control, have put pressure on local public systems, and created a sense of inevitability of deregulation and commercialization. The conservative drift of politics over the past decade or so, which has fueled the deregulation process, has also enhanced the political power of commercial media entrepreneurs and shifted the ideological balance from any public service emphasis to the free market and commercial imperatives.

Although many democratic and progressive critics of the media have been harsh on public broadcasting, most of them have looked upon its decline as a distinctly adverse and threatening development. The most common view is that, while public broadcasting has never realized its potential, it has nevertheless contributed modestly to a public sphere of debate and critical discourse and has provided information and viewpoints essential to the citizenship role. By contrast, commercial broadcasting is viewed as an entertainment vehicle that tends to marginalize the public sphere in direct proportion to its increasing dominance and profitability.[1]

In this chapter, after a brief account of the changing balance between commercial and public broadcasting and the reasons for this shift, the main focus is on the economic theory of "externalities" and "public goods" and their application to broadcasting. It will be seen that theory itself suggests that commercial systems will tend systematically to ignore the public goods aspects of broadcasting and are likely to produce negative externalities. It will be shown that this "market failure" is substantial and consequential. Furthermore, we shall see that in a mature commercial system like that of the United States, broadcasters' power insulates these market failures from serious public debate and makes them virtually uncorrectable through political processes. Finally, the extent and implications of the internationalization of market systems of broadcasting will be discussed.

THE DECLINE OF PUBLIC BROADCASTING
IN THE WEST

Public broadcasting has been in decline in the West for the past several decades, at different rates and with some interruptions in the various states. The pace has been determined in part by the degree of initial grip of public broadcasting—its relative importance, the cultural traditions in which it evolved, and legal and institutional protections of its status. It has been affected also by the power and commitment to dismantle of its commercial rivals and political enemies.

An important distinction should be made between the U.S. and other Western experience. Public broadcasting was marginalized early in the United States; with the defeat of an amendment to the Communications Act of 1934 that would have reserved 25% of broadcasting space for educational and nonprofit operations, the triumph of commercial broadcasting was confirmed, and its power was steadily enlarged thereafter.[2] A small place was carved out for educational and other nonprofit broadcasting in the 1950s and after, but federal sponsorship and funding of public broadcasting did not come about till 1967, and one of the functions of public broadcasting was to relieve commercial broadcasting of a public service programming obligation that it did not want and was sloughing off. Even in the small niche reserved for it, public broadcasting has been a steady target of conservative attack for its excessive preoccupation with public affairs, and was subjected to a further financial crunch and politicization in the Reagan era. The marginalized position of public broadcasting in the United States is indicated by the fact that its total revenue is approximately one-fiftieth of that of the three major networks taken together.[3]

With the increasing profitability and strength of commercial broadcasting in the United States, and the gradual erosion and then virtual liquidation of political/administrative regulation of broadcasters activities in the 1980s,[4] this country constitutes what we may call a "mature" commercial system, and should display the full flower of accomplishments and failings of commercial broadcasting. It is certainly not clear that all other countries will reach this mature state, but a number of them are moving rapidly in this direction, and the U.S. experience shows that cultural and political barriers that appeared formidable can be swept aside in a surprisingly short time by a unified and powerful advertising and broadcasting fraternity (see below). Furthermore, the market processes at work on an international scale are tending to weaken public systems and integrate all open economies into a global broadcasting regime (see below).

In contrast with the United States, in other countries of the West public broadcasting was initially a dominant or important part of broadcasting. In a large majority of instances, state broadcasting was given monopoly status, with varying degrees of autonomy of the broadcasting agency and programming inputs from the private sector. This granting of monopoly rights was often done to allow the government and dominant political parties to control or at least contain this powerful new instrument. But in most cases there was also an explicit recognition of the public service capabilities of broadcasting—its power to educate, enlighten, and help make better citizens, as well as to entertain—and this was incorporated into charters and ideologies of state-sponsored broadcasting entities. They were legally obligated to serve a varied fare (not just entertainment, or whatever best served the interest of the broadcaster), to reach minorities as well as the largest adult audience, to serve children's special needs, and to provide universal service.

These public service objectives have surely not invariably been realized in practice, and the real world performance of public broadcasting has been spotty. In states with authoritarian rule for many years like Spain, Portugal, and Greece, broadcasting was a blatantly propagandistic instrument of the ruling elite group; but even in countries like France, Italy, and Belgium, the inability of the public broadcasting service to free itself from ongoing political intervention and control greatly limited the service capability of public broadcasting.[5] In a majority of democratic states, however, public broadcasting has realized its public service potential to at least a modest degree, or better.[6]

In cases where public broadcasting has been institutionalized for an extended time period in moderately favorable circumstances, as in Great Britain, its public service performance has been greatly superior to that of broadcasting institutions in a country like the United States with an overwhelmingly dominant commercial sector.[7] The British public service tradition has also profoundly affected commercial broadcasting in that country, where the commercial system was obligated by contract with the state to meet public service responsibilities that U.S. broadcasters have been able to increasingly ignore. The result has been that, in Great Britain, in contrast with the United States, commercial TV has competed with the BBC in public service performance, as well as in attention to large audiences. This condition may be coming to an end, however, following the auctioning off of the commercial TV franchises in "the great TV lottery" of 1990–1991, with the heavy debts of successful bidders, new entrants, and related new instabilities and market pressures making the erosion of public service highly likely.[8]

Public broadcasting is still powerful in Western Europe, Canada, and Japan. A declaration of public service broadcasters attending a European Broadcasters Union (EBU) symposium in Brussels in 1989 pointed out that European public service broadcasters reach 475 million viewers, broadcast 155,000 hours of programs per year, 85% of which are produced in Europe (Declaration, 1989, p. 15). But in country after country in Europe public broadcasters are losing market share: sometimes by the selling off of public broadcasting facilities by the state (France), more often by the granting of new channels to commercial interests (Spain, Belgium, prospectively in Sweden[9]), or the bypassing of traditional networks by cable or satellite transmission (Holland, Switzerland). In some countries, like Italy, France, and Belgium, public broadcasting has gone quickly from dominance to minority status. In others, like West Germany and Switzerland, it has maintained its dominance, but with a slowly eroding market share. In Great Britain, it has temporarily stabilized its position with approximately half the terrestrial broadcasting market, but it faces threats from satellite-cable systems and, even more importantly, funding shortfalls and the increasing market pressures from the auctioning and restructuring of ITV.

With commercial interests providing increasing amounts of "free" broadcasting, it has become harder to justify stable, let alone increasing, license fees for the service with a shrinking (even if still large) audience.[10] Commercial broadcasting interests and conservative politicians are pleased to defund their competition (for broadcasters) and source of unwanted public discourse (for conservative politicians). The combination has tended to freeze or (more often) reduce in real terms public broadcasting funding. This has made it difficult for public broadcasters to improve their product quality in competition with their commercial rivals,[11] who have used their increasing ad revenues to enhance the stability of their programs.[12] This provides the basis for a cumulative process of public broadcasting decline and commercial broadcasting growth, familiar in the newspaper business.[13]

The other funding option for public broadcasting is advertising. In many cases Western European public broadcasting already relied to some extent on advertising, although frequently with a ceiling level and on a bloc basis, not giving the advertiser discretion to choose programs as in the United States. When solicited under competitive conditions, public broadcasting's use of advertising as a funding source quickly erodes its public service aims, as audience size and advertiser interest becomes controlling. Thus, Spanish public broadcasting, which relies almost exclusively on advertising, approximates commercial broadcasting in its programming (Bustamente, 1989, pp. 72-75), and RAI, the Italian public system, under intense competition with the Berlusconi empire, has also substantially lost its public service character.[14] This is in part the design of conservative political enemies of public broadcasting in the United States and elsewhere—to neutralize this potential public arena by subjecting it to commercial discipline.[15]

Public broadcasting requires public subsidies to realize its full benefits. These were obtainable, even if on a frequently niggardly basis, when public broadcasting was the only available broadcasting medium and/or when a combination of political interest, limited commercial options, and a public service tradition were joined to sustain public broadcasting. In the 1970s and onward, conditions changed in a manner unfavorable to public broadcasting. The maturation of television made the commercial exploitation of TV audiences by advertisers a magnet to media entrepreneurs, advertisers, and the advertising industry. Technological changes made cable and satellite broadcasting economically feasible, thereby weakening the "scarcity of channels" argument for regulation, and allowing a circumvention of traditional broadcasting channels. This process was hard to oppose or limit in an age of deregulation. These developments contributed to an aura of inevitability and resignation to the commercialization of broadcasting. The decline of social democracy and spread of conservative governments in the West was a related and corollary development, important in paving the way for commercial interests and the deliberate weakening and partial dismantling of public broadcasting systems. This was consistent with conservative political agendas as well as deregulation ideologies, as public service broadcasting has long been distrusted by conservatives, who have discovered that "unfree" broadcasting allows more debate and dissent on public issues than the "free" variety.

EXTERNAL EFFECTS OF COMMERCIAL AND PUBLIC BROADCASTING

The economic profession has increasingly recognized that the market can produce satisfactory results only if there are limited externalities associated with the production and consumption of particular products. By definition, *externalities* are effects that the market does not take into account; they are "externalized" by producers and consumers.[16] Sometimes this is done knowingly, because costly actions would be required to control or eliminate them. In other cases, they occur because the external effects cannot be controlled or separated out for market assessment. Well-known traditional external effects like factory smoke became institutionalized in an era when little attention was given to such social costs and where means of control were not yet available. As the social costs have become more apparent and pressing, a struggle has ensued between the polluters and society, the former striving to preserve their right to externalize costs, the latter trying to force the polluters to reduce or eliminate the externalized burden or pay for its impact on others. But where such burdens are externalized, economists classify this as a case of "market failure."

It is important to recognize that externalities may be positive as well as negative in effects. A beautiful flower garden available to neighbors to view and smell offers a positive external effect, just as polluting smoke, or a loud transistor radio on the beach, create negative effects. A public school system yields positive externalities of a more complex sort, in that a literate and scientifically educated population will be more productive and creative than one less well trained, with resultant gains to society beyond those of the individuals taken separately. A good school system may also make for a more politically aware populace and a better working democratic order. The market does not take into account such indirect and second order benefits. But these have long been recognized as providing a rationale for government subsidy of schools in the face of another potential market failure.

Education fits the concept of a "public good," in that it is "endowed with the public interest" by virtue of the significant positive externalities associated with it. This is also one rationale for government subsidization of basic research, where again the private market "fails" if its investment level is lower than it would be if it took account of the benefits to "other firms" and the society as a whole from such fundamental inquiry.[17]

In a more refined view of *public goods*, they are defined as those whose outputs are nonexclusive and nonexhaustive, so that one individual's use does not limit the use of the good by others (Mishan, 1982, pp. 146-163). The standard examples are national defense and public parks (when use levels are not high). According to conventional economic reasoning, in the case of pure public goods the marginal (or incremental) cost of providing the good to any particular individual is zero, and therefore the price should be zero (Bator, 1958, pp. 351-379). The free market will therefore fail in the case of a public good, because it will have no incentive to produce anything at a zero price.

Broadcasting has long been recognized as having public good properties, in both of the scenes just described. It has a capacity for political and technical education and enlightenment comparable to that of formal schooling; that is, there is a potential for the production of large positive externalities, which were recognized in the early euphoric years of radio, and even as late as 1946 in the FCC's statement on *The Public Service Responsibilities of Broadcast Licensees*.[18] Broadcast signals also have the second and more formal characteristic of a public good, as one person's reception of a signal does not reduce that of others. This means that the optimal price for this service to the recipient of the signal is zero, and the market is likely to fail.

Before the advent of cable and scrambling devices for broadcast signals, it was not possible to charge recipients of signals for their broadcast benefits. There could be a license imposed for the use of receivers, but this would have to be state imposed and implied a public and noncommercial service. Public broadcasting could also be funded by direct subsidies from the state. As is well known, the commercial route into broadcasting has been advertising, which is attracted by broadcasters in exchange for the advertisers' right to solicit large signal-receiving audiences, who would get the programs plus advertising at no direct charge.

The externalities effects of this mode of financing, and of the fundamentally commercial and profit-making incentives of the ownership and control of broadcasting stations, clearly tend to be adverse from a theoretical standpoint. It is true that the signals are offered at a zero price, so that the market failure in the production/sale of public goods arising from positive pricing is not applicable. However, the output offered is one where the most advantageous pricing of *advertisements* is achieved, not the best output as seen by the recipients of signals. The actual outputs thus fall short of the optimal public goods output (Noll, Peck, & McGowan, 1973, pp. 33-42).

The commercial imperative also has profound effects on the composition of broadcasting output. The force of competition and stress on the rate of return on capital, which comes to prevail in a free market, will compel firms to focus with increasing intensity on enlarging audience size and improving its "quality," as these will determine advertising rates. A recent audience decline for NBC's morning "Today Show," moving it a full rating point behind ABC's "Good Morning America," is reportedly the basis of a $280,000 a day advertising income differential between the shows.[19] Managements that fail to respond to market opportunities of this magnitude will be under pressure from owners and may be ousted by internal processes or takeovers. There will be no room for soft-headed "socially responsible" managers in a mature system, and in the United States the three major networks have in fact been taken over by strictly market-driven corporate owners.[20] The resultant subordination of all other considerations to the quest for advertiser support has been impressive,[21] and as Erik Barnouw has said, "The preemption of the schedule for commercial ends has put lethal pressure on other values and interests" (Barnouw, 1978, p. 95).

The output compositional effect of the commercial quest for large audiences and advertiser support should be a steady shift toward noncontroversial materials that will divert, excite, and entertain. Positive externalities have no place in a mature commercial system, except where media firms occasionally program for public service with public relations benefits in mind.[22] We would therefore expect the evolution of commercial broadcasting to be characterized by the gradual sloughing off of these less profitable areas as profit-making opportunities appear in the niches earlier reserved for "public service."

Public broadcasting, by contrast, is likely to give substantial weight to positive externalities. This is because, as described earlier, the broadcasting media were from the beginning recognized as potentially valuable tools of education and citizenship training, capable of universal outreach and service to both mass audiences and minorities, and public broadcasting took on early responsibility for realizing this potential. Most important, public broadcasting has not been driven by the profit motive or funded primarily by advertising, so that its functional role has not been incompatible with its funding source or institutional linkage, as the market-linked and profit-oriented commercial systems have been. It should be noted, however, that insofar as public broadcasting is forced to compete with growing commercial systems for a mass audience, with limited funding, there should be an erosion of original purpose and quality (see above).

Broadcasting also has a potential for generating negative externalities. These may not be easy to pinpoint as they can be matters of spiritual discomfort, insecurity, and the encouragement of bad habits and aggressive behavior. To some extent, they are the negative counterparts of the foregone positive externalities (ignorance, insecurity, and isolation versus knowledge and improved ability to act and participate). And to some extent they are the negative aspects of the positive pleasures received from standard entertainment packages. Sometimes the question of sign of the externality is debatable. If spy-adventure thrillers with strong political overtones integrate the listening-watching audience into the spirit of an arms race and imperial aggression, this patriotic togetherness would be regarded as good by imperial policy makers, but as a dangerous, irrational mobilization of bias by others.

We would expect a mature commercial system, with ongoing competitive pressures, and with a main eye on audience size, to produce significant negative externalities. Sex and violence have been long-standing commercial formulas for attracting large audiences, and they can be offered at low cost.[23] Public broadcasting systems are not as audience-size driven, and we would therefore not anticipate the associated negative externalities as a major problem in a mature public broadcasting environment.

This analysis of the likely externalities performance of commercial and public broadcasting ignores the question of whether commercial broadcasting might not produce a larger *total* output than public broadcasting and therefore better satisfy consumers' demands. According to this line of thought, public broadcasting is an instrument of elite and minority audience service and tends to neglect programming attractive to mass audiences. Commercial broadcasting is needed to realize the value of broadcasting as an entertainment vehicle and to quickly enlarge the total output of the industry. If this were true, the benefits of public broadcasting's cultivation of outputs with substantial positive externalities and limited generation of negative externalities would be offset by a major deficiency and gap in its outreach.

This argument is not easy to evaluate, as public broadcasting has often been designed for educational and political services, and elite and minority audiences, leaving it to commercial broadcasters to provide entertainment. Public broadcasting systems have also often been chronically underfunded, and have simply not been assigned the function of providing popular and mass market service. If we ask what a "mature" public broadcasting system would look like if designed to achieve both entertainment and public interest aims, there doesn't appear to be any reason "in principle" why public broadcasting wouldn't satisfy mass audiences as well as other needs.[24] However, this "principle" assumes that democratic capitalism works in an unbiased fashion, and that large public goods benefits to the majority of ordinary citizens will be readily funded out of tax revenues. Unfortunately, experience under Western governments in recent decades shows that, while they are remarkably open-handed in using tax monies for producing weapons under a system of "military Keynesianism," they are extremely grudging in funding the needs of the civil society. This bias tends to be exacerbated in the area of broadcasting as many of the benefits attainable under public systems are prospective, indirect, and general, and in some cases (like the United States), not having been offered and withdrawn, are not missed. Furthermore, the growing power of commercial broadcasters provides a further and decisive addition to the normal reluctance of western governments to serve nonsecurity state demands and needs.

EMPIRICAL EVIDENCE ON EXTERNALITIES EFFECTS

The empirical evidence on externalities effects generally supports the theoretical analysis just described, but many of the suggested effects are hard to measure and the evidence is necessarily spotty and tentative. Some of the evidence I will summarize briefly is also indirect: the programming characteristics themselves from which effects may be plausibly inferred, but where the effects remain to be proved. I will also focus disproportionately on the U.S. experience, partly on the ground that this is a mature commercial system, so that the dynamics, evolution, and results of commercialization should be most clearly evident there.

Positive Externalities Foregone or Realized

In accord with theoretical expectation, commercial incentives have caused commercial broadcasting to strive to capture a mass audience with entertainment programs. Furthermore, neither U.S. nor Western European experience supports the view that proliferating channels via cable and satellite would alter this situation: economic forces have caused the smaller rivals of the established networks to offer light entertainment fare similar to that of the dominant firms, and frequently with fewer nonentertainment deviations.[25]

Public affairs programming. Public affairs programming refers to talks, discussions, and other forms of extended presentations dealing with local, national, and international issues.[26] It is distinguished from "news," which is about current affairs, and often does not address issues at all. Public affairs per se represents broadcasting's contribution to a public forum and discussion and debate about issues, and public affairs programming is an important measure of broadcasting performance in an area where it can contribute positive externalities.

As commercial broadcasting has consolidated its position in the United States, and ad-supported programs have displaced "sustaining" programs, public affairs programming has declined in quantity and quality. As Dominick and Pearce showed in their 1976 survey of trends in TV programming, "as profit increased, diversity went down," so that by 1974, "three categories—action/adventure, movies, and general drama—accounted for 81 percent of prime time, sending the diversity index to its lowest value ever." What they call "reality programming"—news, public affairs, and interview-talk shows—has "generally declined," displaced by "entertainment" (Dominick & Pearce, 1976, pp. 76-77).

Between 1976 and 1984, the FCC had a programming guideline that it theoretically applied to broadcasters in evaluating license renewals, called the 5-5-10 rule.[27] The rule required that, between 6 A.M. and midnight, broadcasters offer at least 5% informational programming (public affairs plus news), 5% local programming, and 10% nonentertainment programming. The FCC has never asked broadcasters to provide a minimal quantity of straight public affairs programming, so that the informational programming standard could be met by 5% of programming time with "happy hour" local news.

The FCC standard of 1976 was fixed so that broadcasters could easily meet it at that time; in other words, it simply accepted the existing programming structure as satisfactory, and gave broadcasters room for further deterioration before running into the guidelines.[28] Richard Bunce, using programming data from *TV Guide*, found that, by 1970, public affairs programming by TV stations had already fallen to 2%. Stations were still able to meet a 5% quite nicely, as their news programs amounted to 9.2% of programming (Bunce, 1976, p. 27). The situation remained essentially unchanged over the next 18 years: James Donahue, also using the *TV Guide* as a source of data, found that total public affairs programming in 1988 by commercial broadcasters was 2.2% of program time between 6 A.M. and midnight (Bunce, 1976, p. 7). These levels are extremely low and far below those provided by public broadcasters in Europe or by commercial TV in Great Britain.[29]

Bunce pointed out that the shrinkage of public affairs programming to its 2% level took place at a time when the profitability of television was reaching dramatically high levels. By 1970 the profits of major station owners was in the range of 30%–50% of revenue, and much more on invested capital. Bunce estimated that, for the period 1960–1972, the ratio of pretax income to depreciated tangible investments for the broadcast networks never fell below 100% a year (Bunce, 1976, pp. 96-98). These staggering profits did not alleviate broadcaster pressure for further profits, because the workings of the market cause profits to be capitalized into higher stock values, which become the basis of calculation of rates of return for both old and new owners. Thus in 1984 the FCC lifted its requirement that broadcasters keep program logs and make them available for public inspection because of the terrible financial "burden" this imposed on broadcasters (FCC, 1984). This action by the FCC was also a logical corollary to the FCC's 1984 decision terminating any programming limits on the broadcasters, based on an expressed confidence and faith that the market would produce any programs the consumer demanded.[30]

Experience in the United States also suggests that the maturity of commercial broadcasting brings with it a decline in variety of viewpoints and increased protectiveness of establishment interests. A telling illustration is the handling of the Vietnam war in the United States, where, as Erik Barnouw notes, "The Vietnam escalation of 1965–67 found commercial network television hewing fairly steadily to the administration line. Newscasts often seemed to be pipelines for government rationales and declarations.... Though a groundswell of opposition to the war was building at home and throughout much of the world, network television seemed at pains to insulate viewers from its impact....Much sponsored entertainment was jingoistic" (Barnouw, 1978, pp. 62-63). The U.S. networks not only made none of the seriously critical documentaries on the war, during the early war years they barred access to outside documentaries. As Barnouw points out "this policy constituted de facto national censorship, though privately operated" (Barnouw, 1978, p. 138).

But while the mass protest against the war rarely found any outlets in commercial TV, it "began to find occasional expression in NET programming in such series as *Black Journal*, NET *Journal*, *The Creative Person*, and—explosively—in the film *Inside North Vietnam*, a British documentarist's report on his 1967 visit to 'the enemy'" (Barnouw, 1978, p. 63). This pattern helps explain why Presidents Johnson and Nixon fought to rein in public broadcasting, with Nixon quite openly seeking to force it to deemphasize public affairs (see Note 15). The commercial systems did this naturally.

In depth news presentations reached their pinnacle with Edward R. Murrow's "See It Now" programs in the mid-1950s. There was a resurgence of news documentaries in the early 1960s, in the wake of the quiz scandals of 1959, but subsequently the decline continued, despite occasional notable productions. Sponsors don't like controversy and depth—in entertainment as well as nonfiction.[31] When environmental issues first became of national concern, NBC nevertheless dropped the environmental series "In Which We Live" for want of sponsorship, although the major companies were all busily putting up commercials and other materials on the environment. Their materials, however, reassured, and did not explore the issue in depth and with any balance, as the NBC series did (Barnouw, 1978, p. 135). More recently, a program with Barbara Walters on the abortion issue was unable to obtain sponsors, who openly rejected participation for fear of controversy (Lipman, 1989). The commercial networks usually anticipate advertiser attitudes in their programming decisions, and even in their policies toward advertisements.[32]

Fear of "fairness doctrine" requirements of balance also made serious programs that took a stand on an issue a threat to broadcasters; and watering them down to obviate challenges for lack of balance made them lifeless. Documentaries, appealing to sponsors and creating no enemies, would be about travel, dining, dogs, flower shows, lifestyles of the rich, and personalities past and present. In short, under the system of commercial sponsorship, the documentary was reduced to "a small and largely neutralized fragment of network television, one that can scarcely rival the formative influence of 'entertainment' and 'commercials'" (Barnouw, 1978, p. 139). The form survived mainly in an aborted quasi-entertainment form called *pop doc*, specializing in brief vignettes, with a focus on individual villains, pursued by superstar entertainers, and settling "for relatively superficial triumphs" (Barnouw, 1978, p. 138). Other public affairs programs, like discussion panels, were placed in weekend ghetto slots, and consisted mainly of unthreatening panels asking unchallenging questions of officials. In the years before the death of the Fairness Doctrine, the "public service" obligation was met largely by public service announcements cleared through the Advertising Council, which provided a further means for the broadcasters to establish a record of public service without addressing any serious issue.

The evidence from Western Europe is similar. Public broadcasting systems offer wider ranges of choice and significantly more national news, discussion programs, documentaries, cultural, and minority programs than commercial systems in the United States or in-country (Blumler et al., 1986, pp. 348-350). The spread of commercial systems within Europe has not increased diversity and in fact threatens it through its effects on the public service capabilities of public broadcasters. The first commercial broadcast channel in Italy offered literally zero news and public affairs programming, and Murdoch's Sky Channel provided 95.6% entertainment and sport, and under 1% information (Pragnall, 1987, p. 6). French commercial TV has been notable for "the lack of variety...the tendency of the stations to align their programming on each other; the excessive screening of films and the neglect of the documentary; and...the haziness of the frontier between the commercial and the program."[33] In Finland, the commercial network MTV's public affairs programming fell from 23.8% of its air time to 11% between 1979–1980 and 1983–1984; the public system's public affairs programming fell from 49.5% to 44.1% (Sarkkinen, 1986, p. 11). In the Netherlands, still subject to only modest commercial threat, informational programs on public broadcasting rose from 28% to 41% of air time between 1973 and 1986, youth and children's programming grew from 6% to 14% (Bekkers, 1987, p. 32).

Qualitative as well as quantitative measures of public affairs and cultural programming also tend to favor public broadcasting. As Sepstrup points out, commercial systems must seek a transnational common denominator and regularly "stay away from challenging the cultural and political mainstream" (Sepstrup, 1989, p. 35). Blumler et al. (1986, p. 353) point out that under systems where audience maximization is the sole criterion, "a narrowing of program range ensues and considerations of quality become vulnerable." Using a peer system measure of quality—prizes for TV shows awarded in major international competitions—they show that Britain has done outstandingly well, whereas the United States has done only marginally better than the distinctly smaller Sweden (p. 353).

THE DEGRADATION AND PLUTOCRATIZATION OF POLITICS

It is easy to exaggerate the quality of political life in the pre-TV era, but the maturing of commercial TV in the United States has had several significant negative effects on the political process. First, TV time in the United States must be purchased from the commercial broadcasters. This has made the quest for political office extremely expensive, as this powerful communications instrument has become a campaign imperative. Thomas Patterson notes that "it is no coincidence that the 1964 presidential campaign was both the first to use advertisements heavily and the first in which overall campaign spending skyrocketed" (Patterson, 1982, pp. 33-34). This has reduced the democratic character of U.S. political life by increasingly limiting the quest and attainment of office to the wealthy and those willing to serve the wealthy. Extending the franchise increased democratization in the United States; the escalating requirements of electoral finance in the regime of commercial broadcasting has reversed this trend, in the process reducing the diversity of debate and political options.

Second, the commercialization of broadcasting in the United States has further weakened its democratic political character by centralizing and nationalizing politics, and, as Benjamin notes, delocalizing it, "because appeals made in one place or to one group may be immediately communicated regionally or nationally. Thus the distributive politics of particular appeals to particular groups can no longer be made by candidates without their first calculating the possible effects on other groups in their electoral coalitions" (Benjamin, 1982, p. 5). The individual is more isolated, political participation tends to be reduced, the idea of collective social action is weakened.

Third, the cost and importance of TV has put a premium on well-produced and carefully packaged "spots" that provide effective imagery. Lasting 30 or 60 seconds, these spots are essentially advertisements that depend on images, formulas and style. In this format, issues are downgraded. Just as programming and ads have tended to merge, with public affairs sharply downgraded, so are politics and ads merging, with issues carefully evaded and obfuscated. As Barnouw notes, the U.S. candidate for major political office "no longer plans campaign speeches; he plans and produces 'commercials'" (Barnouw, 1978, p. 76).

TV news coverage of elections is also constricted in time and oriented to photo opportunities and entertainment values (personalities, drama, horse-racing). Frank Mankiewicz and Joel Swerdlow point out that genuine intelligent discussion is avoided as "bad television," and, with 1 minute and 15 seconds allotted each candidate on the evening news (an extra 30 seconds on "in-depth" presentations), issues are ruled out. They are also ruled out by the networks' failure to investigate and report controversy that bites. George McGovern's charge in 1972 that the Nixon administration was seriously corrupt was true, but Nixon did not have to confront the charge on TV until well after the election (Mankiewicz & Swerdlow, 1979, pp. 104-105).

CHILDREN'S PROGRAMMING

Broadcasting offers a potentially major and efficient vehicle for educating and entertaining children. Children, however, are not very important buyers of goods, especially small children, and are therefore of only moderate interest to advertisers. The positive social benefits of quality radio and TV to children are externalities, and U.S. experience demonstrates that they will be ignored or marginalized by commercial broadcasters.

As in the case of public affairs programming, the U.S. commercial system eventually ghettoized children's programming, with Saturday and Sunday morning fare that was largely cartoon entertainment. Between 1955 and 1970, weekday programming for children on network affiliated TV stations in New York City fell from 33 to 5 hours (Palmer, 1988, p. 22). Only on Saturday did the children continue to get substantial time, but not with any new or nonentertainment programs. A major FCC study of children's TV published in 1979 concluded that children are "drastically underserved" (quoted in Palmer, 1988, p. 5).

The abuses on children's programs had reached such severity in the 1960s that a number of citizens groups were formed to fight the commercial system. One, Action for Children's Television (ACT), formed in 1968, lodged a protest with the FCC in 1970. Their petition requested that the FCC require that an hour of commercial time each weekday be programmed for school-age children, and a half hour for preschoolers. The FCC's response was a 1974 Policy Statement, which acknowledged that children had a special status and that broadcasters had a responsibility to serve them. It noted that advertising on children's programs, heavy in volume and pressing sugary products, should be limited, and that the employment of hosts to make sales pitches to children should be curbed. It also suggested that children's programming should be enlarged, should educate and inform, not just entertain, and should not be confined to the schedule's "graveyards." This was, as usual, left to the voluntary actions of the broadcasters. Although the situation did not improve in the interim, on December 22, 1983, the Reagan-era FCC, in a notable decision, finally dealt definitively with the ACT petition of 14 years before, concluding that broadcasters had *no* responsibility to children.

The situation as regards children's programming deteriorated further after 1983; the well-regarded weekday series "Captain Kangaroo" was dropped from CBS's weekly schedule, which terminated all regularly scheduled weekday programs on the commercial networks (Palmer, 1988, p. 24). The most notable feature of the past decade in children's television has been the literal integration of product advertising and programming. According to Peggy Charren, the head of ACT, there are more than 65 series that have been developed to sell children a bill of goods, including Hasbro Bradley's GI Joes, Transformers, Wuzzles, and, My Little Pony; Mattel's He-Man and the Masters of the Universe; She-Ra: Princess of Power; Kenner's Care Bears, etc. She notes that "TV programs based on merchandise—so-called 'program-length commercials'—are a phenomenon unique to children's television." There is no distinction made between programming and advertising, and advertisers "retain editorial control of the shows, making sure that every component of a particular toy-line is included in each episode" (Charren, 1987, p. 9). ACT filed petitions in October 1983 and June 1984 urging the FCC to prohibit programs that are commercials and arrangements whereby stations get kickbacks in profits from the sale of products bearing the names of programs or their characters. These petitions were rejected by the FCC in April 1985.

Public broadcasting in the United States has been left with the burden of addressing the weekday broadcasting needs of 40 million children, and any weekend fare of substance. But there is no national policy or regular funding for such programs on public broadcasting channels. They are funded individually and on an ad hoc basis, even when they are of proven excellence. In Japan, where commercial networks are predominant and offer mainly animated cartoons for children, public television is allocated substantial resources for children's programming, and Japanese children "receive both in-school instruction programs, and lighter, often broadly informational and educational programming for at-home viewing" (Palmer, 1988, p. 48).

In Great Britain, BBC has long attended to children's broadcasting needs with a mix of forms ranging from animated cartoons to news, drama and documentaries. British commercial television is also held to a BBC level of obligation to children's programming by agreement, and schedules the same amount of program time for children as BBC. In 1985, for example, the ITV stations were required to carry each week "(in hours: minutes): 7:25 of children's drama and entertainment; 3:31 of children's informative programs; 2:32 of pre-school education; and 6:55 of school instructional programs" (Palmer, 1988, p. 49).

In Holland, youth-children oriented programs increased from 6% of broadcasting time in 1973 to 14% in 1986 (Bekkers, 1989). In West Germany, the public networks have Children and Young People's Departments and they devote substantial resources to programming addressed to children's needs at various stages of development. Starting in 1989, West German public network Zweites Deutsches Fernsehen (ZDF) has had a regular news program for children (Muller, 1990). As the head of ZDF's children's department has said, "Children's programming has become a trademark of public service television" (Schacter, 1989, p. 22).

In the United States, commercial broadcasting, although immensely profitable, has sloughed off its responsibilities to children, and this has not been compensated for by public broadcasting. The poor performance of U.S. school children is often noted in the mass media, and is sometimes attributed in part to the underfunding of schools, but the foregone potential of TV broadcasting is never mentioned.[34]

NEGATIVE EXTERNALITIES

While the failure of commercial broadcasting to produce public affairs, cultural, and children's programs that promise important positive externalities has been subject to only modest study and even less publicity, its exploitation of the audience-enlarging vehicles of sex and violence has aroused important elements of the mainstream and has received greater attention. The aggressive use of themes of sex and violence, often in combination, can produce externalities in the form of distorted human and sexual attitudes, insecurity, and reduced ability to function in a social order, and aggressive and violent behavior.

TV violence builds audiences. It therefore makes its way onto the screen increasingly under the pressure of commercial imperatives. As Mankiewicz and Swerdlow have pointed out, violent programs "are viewed by lots of people," and lots of money is made, so that "when the do-gooders complain about violence, network spokesmen can point to this remunerative cycle and say that they are only 'giving the public what it wants'" (Mankiewicz & Swerdlow, 1979, p. 45). The level of violence produced in the mature U.S. system is impressive. Mankiewicz and Swerdlow contend that, before he or she is 15 years old, an average American child will have witnessed between 11 and 13 thousand acts of violence. And, "If one wishes to see fifty-four acts of violence one can watch all the plays of Shakespeare, or one can watch three evenings (sometimes only two) of prime-time television" (p. 6).

Professor George Gerbner and his associates in the United States have compiled an annual television program Violence Profile and Violence Index since 1967. Gerbner has found a remarkable stability in, and high absolute level of violence on, prime-time U.S. programs over the entire 22 years of the project. On average seven of 10 prime-time programs use violence, and the rate of violent acts runs between five and six per hour. Some half of prime-time dramatic characters engage in violence and about 10% in killing, as they have since 1967. Children's weekend programming "remains saturated with violence," with more than 25 acts of violence per hour, as it has for 22 years. Children's daytime weekend programs tend to be three to six times more violent than prime-time programs designed for adults. Since deregulation, violence on children's programs has increased markedly (Gerbner & Signorielli, 1990).

Violence programming has grown in Western Europe, along with the new surge of commercialization, and in direct relation to the shift to action-adventure and movies. With the proliferation of commercial channels and the high costs of original programming, there has been a heavy demand for mainly foreign movies and series to fill the program gap.[35] Sepstrup points out that the great increase in buying of U.S. movies and serials is not based on a special preference for U.S. products, it is grounded in commercialization (Sepstrup, 1989). With market-based imperatives in place, violence as an important ingredient of programming follows. In reference to their transnational study of TV violence, Huesmann and Eron point out that, "of the violent programs evaluated in the first wave of the study in Finland, Poland, and Israel, about 60% had been imported from the United States" (Huesmann & Eron, 1986, p. 47).

While there has been little dispute that commercial broadcasting has been associated with a large diet of violence, there are ongoing debates over the effects of violent programs. There are problems of causality: does alienation and aggression come from watching violence on TV, or do alienated and violence-prone people tend to watch programs that express their world view? Is TV violence an incitement and stimulus to violence or a catharsis? Despite continuing debate, the overwhelming consensus of experts and studies over several decades, covering a number of countries and supported by a variety of models of behavior and controlled experiments, is that TV violence makes a significant contribution to real world violence by desensitizing, making people insecure and fearful, and habituating, modeling, and sometimes inciting people to violence (Gerbner & Signorielli, 1990; Huesmann & Eron, 1986; Mankiewicz & Swerdlow, 1979; Barlow & Hill, 1985; National Institute of Mental Health, 1982).

COMMERCIAL BROADCASTING AND ANTIDEMOCRATIC POWER

The threat of a centralized, monolithic, state-controlled broadcasting system is well understood and feared in the West. What is little recognized or understood is the centralizing, ideologically monolithic, and self-protecting properties of an increasingly powerful commercial broadcasting system. State-controlled broadcasting has always been constrained in democratic political systems by the need to accommodate multiparty systems and interests, which tend to produce some degree of autonomy, and make the public system vulnerable to political change. There is always the background threat of the unleashing of commercial competition.

Commercial systems are, in principle, subject to the possibility of increasing state control and competition from public broadcasting. But U.S. experience suggests that, once a commercial system is firmly in place, it becomes difficult to challenge, and as its economic power increases so does its ability to keep threats at bay and gradually to remove all obstacles to uncompensated commercial exploitation of the public airwaves. There is competition between members of a commercial system, but it is for large audiences through offering entertainment fare under the constraint of advertisers, and, as has been stressed here, it ignores externalities as a matter of structural necessity and the force of competition.

In the United States, dominance of the commercial radio broadcasting networks had been essentially achieved by 1934. Church, labor, civil liberties, educational, and public interest forces were decisively beaten with the passage of the Communications Act of 1934 and defeat of the Wagner-Hatfield amendment, which sought to reserve 25% of broadcast channels to noncommercial operations. Even at that early date, the broadcasters' resources, influence on strategically placed politicians and civil servants, and attempt to identify commercial broadcasting with freedom and democracy were effective. Newspaper opposition was muted and gradually transformed into solidarity with the broadcasters by encouraging newspaper owners to acquire network affiliated stations, and by appeals to the threat of political control over the media. In the end, the bulk of the press supported the broadcasters. The primary manifestation of this support, and of the broadcasters own power to control debate, is that the Wagner-Hatfield amendment and the entire question of how broadcasting should be owned, controlled, and regulated, was simply not discussed. As Robert McChesney notes (McChesney, 1990, p. 41):

> Given the clear contrast between the political strength and financial wherewithal of the radio lobby and that of the opposition movement [which favored the Wagner-Hatfield amendment], the reformers obviously needed extensive (and preferably sympathetic) print coverage. Unfortunately, what little coverage the press offered was heavily oriented toward presenting the position of the commercial broadcasters. This delighted the radio lobby.

Shortly after the 1934 defeat, any organized opposition to commercial broadcasting collapsed, and from that time onward it has been subject to no serious threat of structural change or effective regulation. Regulation of advertising and programming steadily eroded in the face of broadcaster demands, until the final collapse of even nominal standards in the Reagan era. As one illustration of the power of the industry to fend off virtually any threats, in the liberal environment of 1963 the FCC leadership decided to try to impose a formal restraint on commercial advertising, but only to the extent of making as the regulatory standard the limits suggested by the broadcasters' own trade association. This enraged the industry, which went quickly to work on Congress, and the FCC quickly backed down (Krasnow, Longley, & Terry, 1982, pp. 194-196).

An equally dramatic case occurred in 1977, in the midst of another one of the periodic outbursts of protest at the extent of violence on TV. Congressional committees have regularly gone through ritual hearings on this topic, leading to the conclusion that the industry, while to be congratulated on its progress, needed to do more, voluntarily. In 1977, however, an unusually aggressive and naive House subcommittee actually drafted a report calling for investigation of the structure of the television broadcasting industry, as a necessary step to attacking the violence problem at its source! As George Gerbner describes the sequel (Gerbner, 1984, p. 170):

When the draft mentioning industry structure was leaked to the networks, all hell broke loose. Members of the subcommittee told me that they had never before been subject to such relentless lobbying and pressure. Campaign contributors were contacted. The report was delayed for months. The subcommittee staffer who wrote the draft was summarily fired. The day before the final vote was to be taken, a new version drafted by a broadcast lobbyist was substituted. It ignored the evidence of the hearings and gutted the report, shifting the source of the problem from network structure to the parents of America. When the network-dictated draft came to a vote, members of the full committee (including those who had never attended hearings) were mobilized, and the watered-down version won by one vote.

As a final illustration of the commercial broadcasting industry's self-protective power, let me refer once again to the case of children's television. The country claims to revere children, and child abuse is given frequent and indignant attention. But although the erosion of children's programming, and the commercial exploitation of the residual ghettoized programs, occurred as the commercial networks were making record-breaking profits, and although substantial numbers of adults have been angered by this programming, it has taken place without audible outcry. The FCC has been pressed hard to do something about the situation by organized groups like ACT, but the mass media have not allowed this matter to become a serious issue. When, after the 13-year delay in dealing with the ACT petition, the FCC decided in December 1983 that commercial broadcasters had no obligation to serve children, this decision was not even mentioned in the *New York Times*. In fact, during the years 1979–1989, although many important petitions were submitted by ACT and decisions were made by the FCC that bore significantly on the commercial broadcasters neglect and abuse of children,[36] the *New York Times, Washington Post*, and *Los Angeles Times* had neither a front page article nor an editorial on the subject.[37] The dominant members of the press, most of them with substantial broadcasting interests of their own, simply refused to make the huge failure of commercial broadcasters in children's programming a serious issue.

It is also enlightening to see how the principles of broadcasting responsibility were gradually amended to accommodate broadcaster interests, without discussion or debate. From the time of the Communications Act of 1934, and even earlier, it was accepted even by the broadcasters that their important privilege of rights to public air channels was in exchange for and contingent upon their serving "the public convenience, interest and necessity." In the 1934 hearings, the

National Association of Broadcasters acknowledged that it is the "manifest duty" of the FCC to assure an "adequate public service," which "necessarily includes broadcasting of a considerable proportion of programs devoted to education, religion, labor, agricultural and similar activities concerned with human betterment."[38] The 1946 FCC report stated that the "broadcasters" themselves recognize the importance of public affairs programming (see the quote in Note 18), and the report asserts that "sustaining programs" are the "balance wheel" whereby "the imbalance of a station's or network's program structure, which might otherwise result from commercial decisions concerning program structure, can be redressed" (FCC, 1946, p. 12). It even quotes CBS's Frank Stanton to the same effect. The report refers to the sustaining programs as an "irreplaceable" part of broadcasting, and public service performance in the interest of "all substantial groups among the hearing public" as a fundamental standard and test in approving and renewing licenses (FCC, 1946, p. 10).

As advertised programs displaced sustaining programs, and the "balance wheel" disappeared, what gave way was any public interest standard. The industry defense was in terms of "free speech" and the Alice-in-Wonderland principle that if the audience watches the public interest is served.[39] But the industry hardly needed a defense: raw power allowed the public interest standard to erode quietly, the issues undiscussed in any open debate, even as regards the enormous abuses and neglect in children's programming.

INTERNATIONALIZATION AND EXTERNALIZATION

The last several decades have witnessed the increasing and accelerating integration of broadcasting into a global market. This has occurred through a variety of routes. Among the most important have been the cross border acquisition of interests in and control of program production and rights, cable, and broadcasting facilities; the sale or rental of program stocks (movies, syndicated programs), technology and equipment; and the establishment and operation of satellite transmission facilities.[40] The attempt to establish positions in the EEC countries in anticipation of the 1992 unification, and in the rapidly globalizing market as a whole, with both production and distribution facilities has led to a scramble to integrate vertically as well as to establish a cross border presence. These are a function of technological development, market growth, and the opening of economic borders, which have created profit opportunities that media entrepreneurs have hastened to exploit.

These developments have tended to increase the strength of commercial broadcasting and reduce that of public systems. Commercial systems have led the way across borders, as they have tried to reach new audiences and spread the overhead costs of domestic programs. The threat posed to public systems by some of these developments have perhaps been exaggerated—cross-border transmissions by satellite, for example, have been a commercial failure thus far[41]—but the forces at work are multileveled, and public broadcasting systems are vulnerable. The crossing of borders by satellite and cable has put more pressure on states dominated by public systems to allow commercial broadcasting and to increase advertising on public channels.[42] Some public broadcasters have followed, and joined forces with commercial interests in various joint venture and syndicate operations, in an attempt to maintain cost competitiveness and protect their market shares.

The new commercial systems in Western Europe have been crassly commercial, with the public service component of their broadcasts at negligible levels and their entertainment mainly low-grade foreign made movies and the like. They engage in what is referred to as *cream skimming*, trying to capture a segment of the mass audience with minimal cost while assuming no public service responsibilities whatsoever.[43]

In terms of the framework used here, the services of the new commercial operations yield no positive externalities, but do produce some negative externalities. And as they skim away some of the audience of public broadcasters, the latter are put under financial pressure, as described earlier, and tend to wither by financial stringency and inability to compete, or seek and obtain commercial funding and transform themselves into commercial broadcasters in outlook and priorities. In the process, the externalities benefits made available by a mature and tolerably independent public broadcasting system erode, and the contributions that broadcasting can make to children, education more broadly, and to the democratic polity diminish.

The strength and momentum of the forces of the market in the last decade of the 20th century are formidable. It therefore seems likely that the U.S. pattern of commercial hegemony over broadcasting will be gradually extended over the entire globe, although we may anticipate a strong residual presence of public broadcasting in some countries. In the short term this triumph of the market should contribute to more effective management of a "strong state" devoted to pursuing the interests of the business class. Its long-run implications are more obscure.

REFERENCES

Bagdikian, B. (1987). *The media monopoly*. Boston: Beacon
Barlow, G., & Hill, A. (1985). *Video violence and children*. New York: St. Martin's.
Barnouw, E. (1978). *The sponsor*. New York: Oxford.
Bator, F. (1958). The anatomy of market failure. Quarterly *Journal of Economics, 72*, 351-379.
Baughman, J. (1985). *Television's guardians: The FCC and the politics of programming 1958-1967*. Knoxville, TN: University of Tennessee Press.
Bekkers, W. (1987). The Dutch public broadcasting services in a multi-channel landscape. *EBU Review, 38*, 32.
Benjamin, G. (1982). Television and Election Strategy. In G. Benjamin (Ed.), *The communications revolution in politics*. New York: Academy of Political Science.
Bernhard, N. (1991). *"Ready, willing, able": Network television news and the federal government, 1947-1960*. Unpublished doctoral dissertation, University of Pennsylvania.
Blumler, J., Bynin, M., & Nossiter, T. (1986). Broadcasting finance and programme quality: An international review. *European Journal of Communication, 1*, 343-364.
Bonney, B. (1983). Australian broadcasting, professionalism and national reconciliation. *Media Culture & Society, 5*, 263-274.
Britain proposes overhaul of broadcasting system. (1989). *Broadcasting, 117*, 40.
Burgelman, J-C. (1989). Political parties and their impact on public service broadcasting in Belgium. *Media Culture & Society, 11*, 167-193.
Bunce, R. (1976). *Television in the corporate interest*. New York: Praeger.
Burton, J. (1991). Swedes award commercial TV license. *Financial Times*, p. 2.
Bustamente, E. (1989). TV and public service in Spain: a difficult encounter. *Media Culture & Society, 11*, 72-75.
Cardiff, D. (1983). Time, money and culture: BBC programme finances 1927-1939. *Media Culture & Society, 5*, 373-393.
Carter, B. (1990, February 26). NBC losing money race. *New York Times*, pp. D-1, D-2.
Charren, P. (1987, Spring). TV justice for children. *The Connecticut College Alumni Magazine*, p. 9.
Cole, B., & Oettinger, M. (1978). *Reluctant regulators*. Reading, MA: Addison-Wesley.
Collins, R. (1989). The language of advantage: Satellite TV in Western Europe. *Media Culture & Society, 11*, 351-71

Dominick, J., & Pearce, M. (1976). Trends in network prime-time programming, 1953-74. *Journal of Communication, 26*, 70-80.

Donahue, J. (1989). *Shortchanging the viewers: broadcasters neglect of public interest programming.* Washington, DC: Essential Information.

Elliot, P. (1982). Intellectuals, the 'information society' and the disappearance of the public sphere. *Media Culture & Society, 4*, 243-253

Etzioni-Halevy, E. (1987). *National broadcasting under siege.* Basingstoke, Hampshire: Macmillan.

Falkenberg, H. (1983). No future? A few thoughts on public broadcasting in the Federal Republic of Germany, Spring 1983. *Media Culture & Society, 5*, 235-45.

Federal Communications Commission. (1946). *The public service responsibilities of broadcast licensees.* Washington, DC: FCC.

Federal Communications Commission. (1984). Report and Order. 98 FCC 2d 1106.

Gerbner, G. (1984). Science or ritual dance? A revisionist view of television violence effects research. *Journal of Communication, 34*, 164-173.

Gerbner, G., & Signorielli, N. (1990, January). *Violence profile 1967 through 1988-89: enduring patterns.* [Mimeo].

Goldman, K. (1989, October 30). Blurred lines: TV network news is making recreation a form of recreation. *Wall Street Journal*, p. 1.

Graham, G. (1989, June 28). Never mind the quality. *Financial Times*, p. 8.

Hayes, T., & Abernathy, W. (1980). Managing our way to economic decline. *Harvard Business Review*, pp. 67-76.

Herman, E., & Chomsky, N. (1988). *Manufacturing consent.* New York: Pantheon.

Hodgson, P. (1989). Public service value—passport to the future. *EBU Review, 40*, 19.

Huesmann, L., & Eron, L. (1986). *Television and the aggressive child: A cross-national comparison.* Hillsdale, NJ: Erlbaum.

Kahn, A. (1971). *The economics of regulation* (Vol. 2)., New York: John Wiley.

Kleinstuber, H., McQuail, D., & Siune, K. (Eds.). (1986). *Electronic media and politics in western Europe.* Frankfurt: Campus Verlag.

Krasnow, E., Longley, L., & Terry, H. (1982). *The politics of broadcast regulation.* New York: St. Martin's Press.

Landro, L. (1990, April 3). Film satirizing and industry plays to a touchy audience. *Wall Street Journal*, pp. B-1, B-6.

Lipman, J. (1988, August 15). Advertiser-produced TV shows return. *Wall Street Journal*, p. 17.

Lipman, J. (1989, June 16). Barbara Walters radio special on abortion shunned by sponsors. *Wall Street Journal*, p. B-1.

Mankiewicz, F., & Swerdlow, J. (1979). *Remote control.* New York: Ballantine.

McChesney, R. (1990). The battle for the U.S. airwaves, 1928-1935. *Journal of Communication, 40*, 29-57.

Mishan, E. (1983). *What political economy is all about.* Cambridge, UK: Cambridge University Press.

Muller, S. (1990). Logo—the ZDF's news programme for children. *EBU Review*, *71*, 15-16.

Murdock, G., & Golding, P. (1989). Information poverty and political inequality: Citizenship in the age of privatized communications. *Journal of Communication, 39*, 180-195.

National Association of Broadcasters. (1983). *Final Report on Local Commercial Stations*. NAB Television Programming Study, Appendix B. Washington, DC: NAB.

National Institute of Mental Health. (1982). *Television and behavior: Ten years of scientific progress and implications for the eighties. Vol. 2: Technical reviews*. Washington, DC: U.S. Department of Health and Public Services.

Noll, R., Peck M., & McGowan, J. (1973). *Economic aspects of television regulation*. Washington, DC: Brookings Institution.

Palmer, E. (1988). *Television & America's children: A crisis of neglect*. New York: Oxford University Press.

Patterson, T. (1982). Television and Election Strategy. In G. Benjamin (Ed.), *The communications revolution in politics*. New York: Academy of Political Science.

Pragnell, A. (1987). *Television in Europe: Quality and values in time of change* (Media Monograph No. 5). Manchester, UK: European Institute for Media.

Raboy, M. (1983). Media and politics in Socialist France. *Media Culture & Society, 5*, 303-320.

Sarkkinen, R. (1986). *Structure of TV programming in Finland* (Yle. Rep/No. 34). Helsinki: Planning and Research Dept.

Sassoon, D. (1985). Political and market forces in Italian broadcasting. In R. Kuhn (Ed.), *Broadcasting and politics in Western Europe*. London: Frank Cass.

Scannell, P. (1989). Public service broadcasting and modern public life. *Media Culture & Society, 11*, 135-167.

Schacter, M. (1989). Children need good television. *EBU Review, 40*, 22.

Scitovsky, T. (1971). *Welfare and competition*. Homewood, IL: Richard D. Irwin.

Sepstrup, P. (1989). Implications of current developments in West European broadcasting. *Media Culture & Society, 11*, 29-54.

Snoddy, R. (1991a, July 26-27). The great TV lottery. *Financial Times*, p. 8.

Snoddy, R. (1991b, October 17). Auction to bring shake-up in British commercial TV. *Financial Times*, p. 9.

Snoddy, R. (1991c, October 17). Sharp picture emerges of TV in the 1990s. *Financial Times*, p. 11.

Snoddy, R. (1991d, October 18). UK Commercial Broadcasting Auction: Thatcher 'mystified' by decision. *Financial Times*, p. 10.

Snoddy, R. (1992e, February 8-9). Battle for the soul of ITV. *Financial Times*, p. 7.

Tunstall, J. (1986). Great Britain. In H. Kleinssteuber, D. McQuail, & K. Siune (Eds.), *Electronic media and politics in Western Europe*. Frankfurt: Campus Verlag.

Vionnet, M-C. (1990). Save children's television! *EBU Review, 41*, 19.

Waterman, D. (1986). The failure of cultural programming on cable TV: an economic interpretation. *Journal of Communication, 36*, 92-107.

Wirth, M., & Wollert, J. (1978). Public interest programming: FCC standards and station performance. *Journalism Quarterly, 55*, 554-561.

Wirth, M., & Wollert, J. (1982). Deregulation of commercial TV in the USA. *Telecommunications Policy, 6*, 155-163.

NOTES

[1] See Elliott (1982), Bonney (1983), Murdock and Golding, (1989), Barnouw, (1978), pp. 113-152, 179-182), Sepstrup (1989), and Scannell (1989). Scannell believes that the contribution of public broadcasting to the public sphere is more than modest.

[2] For a good account of this early history of the consolidation of commercial broadcaster power, see McChesney (1990).

[3] This is based on a comparison of the total advertising revenue of the three networks in 1988 with the total revenue of PBS for that year. It may also be noted that public broadcasting's revenue base is more uncertain and volatile than that of commercial broadcasters. From its inception till now it has depended on a combination of foundation grants, government allocations on a year-by-year or at most 3-year basis, and, increasingly, corporate funding.

[4] In the Reagan era, the term of the franchises of broadcasters was increased and challenges to renewals were essentially eliminated; controls on advertising and programming, already slight, were also removed; and the Fairness Doctrine, also previously fairly nominal in providing a right of reply, was formally terminated. For an analysis and history of the paralysis of the FCC, see Baughman (1985); see also Cole and Dettinger (1978).

[5] On Belgium, see Burgelman (1989); on France, Raboy (1983); on Italy, Sassoon (1985).

[6] This would apply to the United States, Great Britain, Japan, West Germany, Holland, Denmark, Norway, Sweden, Finland, Switzerland, Australia, and Canada.

[7] See below, under Empirical Evidence of Externalities Performance, for data and citations.

[8] See the excellent series of news articles on this process by Raymond Snoddy in the London *Financial Times*, including Snoddy (1991a, 1991b, 1991c, 1991d, 1992).

[9] Early in 1991, the ruling Social Democrats of Sweden agreed to support the introduction of a land-based commercial television station. There were already three private satellite TV channels broadcasting in Sweden. Controlling interest in the new land-based channel was granted in November 1991 to Kinnevik and the Wallenberg investment company Patricia, over the protest of the Swedish Price and Competition Office, which did not like the fact that Kinnevik already owned one of the satellite channels. See Burton (1991).

[10] In the United States, also, the introduction of commercial channels devoted to cultural materials formerly the exclusive province of PBS—Arts and Entertainment channel, and Discovery (focusing on nature and science)—has further weakened the case for public subsidies to public broadcasting.

[11] In Belgium, the public stations not only lost their monopoly, but they are not allowed to take advertising, they are required by law to produce certain programs, and their budget was cut. As Vionnet asks: "How do you fix a good meal when your hands have been cut?" (Vionnet, 1990, p. 20).

[12] Patricia Hodgson, head of policy and planning of BBC, pointed out in 1989 that the BBC license fee "brings in at the moment approximately two thirds of the cash available to commercial television." What is more, the license fee is linked to the Retail Price Index only till April 1991, after which its real value will fall with inflation (Hodgson, 1989, p. 19).

[13] For a description of this process, which has made most U.S. cities into one newspaper towns, see Bagdikian (1987, pp. 122-125).

[14] Jay Blumler, Malcolm Bynin and T.J. Nossiter (1986, p. 357) quote the president of RAI as stating that "any public service working in a competitive environment cannot help defending and enlarging its market share as a *top priority*", and the head of one of France's public channels is quoted as urging his colleagues to adopt "the mental attitude of the private sector."

[15] See Herman and Chomsky (1988, pp. 14-17), Barnouw (1978, pp. 58-68). Commercial interests and their funding preferences, along with the perceived need to neutralize right wing threats to public funding, has caused public television in the United States to feature William Buckley, Jr., long celebratory programs on free enterprise with Ben Wattenberg and Milton Friedman, and aggressive, right wing-dominated public affairs panels in the commercial TV mode.

[16] "The distinguishing feature of externalities is that they are economic relations that do not or cannot go through the market, thus causing people to receive benefits free and incur costs or endure discomforts without compensation" (Scitovsky, 1971, p. 269).

[17] It goes without saying that the market also fails if competitive and security market pressures cause managers to take a very short-term view of the firm's interest (Hayes & Abernathy, 1980).

[18] According to the FCC, "American broadcasters have always recognized that broadcasting is not merely a means of entertainment, but also an unequaled medium for the dissemination of news, information, and opinion, and for the discussion of public issues" (1946, p. 39). This alleged recognition has had no influence on behavior and performance of the broadcasters, and in the long run, very little on the FCC. See below.

[19] ABC could charge $10,000 more per 30-second commercial, which multiplied by 28 commercials shown during the program yields the $280,000 excess (Carter, 1990).

[20] In the first half of the 1980s, NBC was taken over by General Electric Corporation, a huge multinational important in weapons and nuclear reactor manufacture; ABC was acquired by Capital Cities, a media conglomerate famous for its bottom-line focus; and control of CBS was assumed by Laurence Tisch of Loews, a large conglomerate in the cigarette, hotel, and other businesses. A fourth network emerging in the 1980s, Fox, is controlled by Rupert Murdoch, owner of a global media empire not known for its socially forward looking policies.

[21] Both CBS and NBC have resorted to joint marketing arrangements with retail chains like K-Mart and Sears in the late 1980s in order to bolster viewership. All of the networks have accepted advertiser-produced programs, that allow an advertiser to "showcase its ads," which the *Wall Street Journal* refers to as "a giant step backward" (Lipman, 1988). On the abuses in children's TV, see below under "Children's Programming."

[22] A quiz program scandal in 1959, in which a popular show was found to have been "fixed," led to a tremendous outcry, hearings, etc., and a temporary jump in public interest programming by the networks (see Baughman, 1985, pp. 36, 39, 49).

[23] A recent news report notes that entertainment shows tend to cost twice as much as "tabloid TV," news shows that merge news and entertainment, often using reenactments. A pathbreaking show of this character on Rupert Murdoch's Fox Broadcasting, called "A Current Affair," "has a particular penchant for grisly murders and stories having to do with sex" (Goldman, 1989, p. 1).

[24] The major successful systems have had to be prodded in some areas to supply popular fare, but in other cases they have been more innovative in popular programming than commercial systems (see Falkenberg, 1983, pp. 236-238). On the gradual enlargement of BBC's agenda, and reasons for its lags and eventual responses, see Cardiff (1983, pp. 373-393), Tunstall (1986, pp. 110-134).

[25] A study by Jim Donahue of the public affairs programming of U.S. stations and networks shows that, in 1988, 90% of the new Fox network's affiliated stations failed to meet a 5% standard for information programming that the FCC applied as a guideline between 1973 and 1984 (when the guideline was abandoned). None of the three major networks' affiliated stations failed to meet this standard in 1988 (Donahue, 1989, p. 8). For an explanation in terms of demand and cost factors of the failure of "narrow-casting" to fill the gaps left by the majors, see Waterman (1986, pp. 92-107).

[26] The definition by the FCC, in its Form 303-A, includes "programs dealing with local, state, regional, national or international issues or problems, including but not limited to talks, commentaries, discussions, speeches, editorials, political programs, documentaries, mini-documentaries, panels, roundtables and vignettes, and extended coverage (whether live or recorded) of public events or proceedings, such as local council meetings, congressional hearings and the like."

[27] I say theoretically, because there appears to have been no case where the FCC refused a license renewal for failure to meet this standard, although numerous broadcast stations failed to meet it.

[28] Michael O. Wirth and James A. Wollert (1978, p. 561) wrote that, initially, "the average station already significantly exceeds any 5-5-10 standard"; but 2 years later, still having failed to evaluate the adequacy of the initial standard, Wirth and Wollert say that, as in 1976, stations are "doing an adequate job in fulfilling their public interest responsibilities" (Wirth & Wollert, 1982, pp. 158-159).

In the field of banking, capital regulation has proved consistent with a steady decline in bank capital deposit ratios. The rules have been adjusted to the demands of the market, except in times of crisis and numerous bank failures, at which point the regulators impose capital rules that bite. The bank regulators are deemed to be at least partially responsible for bank failures, so that their historic inability in non-crisis periods to impose effective capital minima is revealing. The FCC has no similarly urgent stake in effective minima for public affairs programming.

[29] In their sample of three weekday evenings in 1985, Blumler et al. (1986, p. 350) found that, for national news + current affairs + documentaries + children's programs, ITV, the commercial system in Britain, used 26% of its broadcast time, whereas the three major U.S. networks used 8%. The Dutch broadcasting system had 14% of its time allocated to children's programs alone (Bekkers, 1987, p. 32).

Of course, in the United States, public broadcasting has filled some of the gap left by the commercial systems. But its outreach is not as great as the majors—its audience share is lower than comparable programs offered by the commercial networks would attain, and its programs suffer from underfunding.

[30] This decision of course eliminated the 5-5-10 rule. It was based in part on an National Association of Broadcasters study that showed that a weighted average of a broadcaster sample of programs was well above the floors. To the FCC, this proved that the market was doing its job and regulation was not needed. The study, however, failed to assess the trend, the relation of the regulatory floor to the average at earlier dates, and, most important, the criteria of a *proper* floor. It also failed to discuss public affairs separately from news (NAB, 1983).

[31] The Blumler et al. (1986, p. 358) "international review" yielded the "unexpected" finding that "various 'political' pressures could even seep into a thoroughly market-oriented broadcasting system through advertisers' sensitive, blame-shunning pores." In

a study of network TV news, 1947-1960, Nancy Bernhard (1991) stresses the great effect of sponsorship in constraining news choices.

[32] CBS and NBC recently refused to accept advertising for the movie "Crazy People," which mentions and satirizes major advertising firms by name, on the ground of their offensiveness to the named advertisers (Landro, 1990).

[33] Statement of Gabriel de Broglie, the departing head of the national supervisory organization CNCL, in January 1989, quoted in Graham (1989).

[34] On the press treatment of children's TV and other broadcasting matters, see "Commercial Broadcasting and Antidemocratic Power" below.

[35] This is an important reason for the surge in cross-border and vertical mergers in the communications business, as the value, and importance to broadcasters of gaining access to, old stocks of movies and TV series, and ongoing production of such programs, have risen sharply.

[36] A five-volume FCC report on children's TV, released in October 1979, was never mentioned by the *New York Times*, nor did it find newsworthy the FCC decision in April 1985 rejecting two ACT petitions calling for the curbing of specific abuses in the commercialization of children's TV.

[37] Only the *Christian Science Monitor* took this issue seriously enough to editorialize on it—this paper had two editorials on the subject.

[38] Quoted from an NAB statement submitted to hearings on the Communications Act of 1934, in FCC (1946, p. 10).

[39] From Alice-in-Wonderland: "I do," Alice hastily replied: "at least—at least I mean what I say—that's the same thing, you know."

"Not the same thing a bit!" said the Hatter. "Why, you might just as well say that 'I see what I eat' is the same as 'I eat what I see'!"

"You might just as well say," added the March Hare, "that 'I like what I get' is the same thing as 'I get what I like'!"

[40] Murdoch combines under one corporate umbrella broadcasting facilities in two countries (Australia and the United States), major newspapers in three countries, and a satellite broadcasting channel emanating from Great Britain (among other interests). Berlusconi's system encompasses ownership interests in Spain, France, West Germany, and Yugoslavia, as well as in Italy.

[41] This has been a result, in part, of weak signals and "breaking in" problems, but the language/culture barrier has proven to be more formidable than anticipated, and the future of such transmissions is uncertain. See Collins (1989).

[42] Domestic media entrepreneurs can argue that commercial broadcasting from abroad is encroaching at home and taking advertising money that should be available to residents; and domestic nonmedia companies resent the fact that advertisers from abroad can now make pitches through TV in their market that they cannot make through domestic TV. These arguments have been pressed in both Denmark and Sweden. See Kleinsteuber (1986, pp. 39, 289).

[43] The term *cream skimming* was developed in U.S. regulatory economics to describe the phenomenon of unregulated firms coming into profitable regulated markets only, reducing their profitability to regulated firms and thus reducing the willingness of regulated firms to serve markets that were unprofitable. The concept has applicability to unregulated markets as well (Kahn, 1971, pp. 7-11, 221-246).

Chapter 6
Brazilian Soaps Outshine Hollywood: Is Cultural Imperialism Fading Out?

Omar Souki Oliveira

HOME-GROWN VERSUS CANNED

One evening in 1973, IBOPE, the Brazilian polling institute, detected a most unusual phenomenon: All persons interviewed in Rio de Janeiro and São Paulo, joint population of more than 25 million, were watching the same television program, "Selva de Pedra" (Jungle of Concrete) (Ramos, 1986, p. 53). This was the highest rating ever achieved by any television program before, and still remains as an unmatched feat.

"Selva de Pedra," a Brazilian soap opera, is a good example of the most successful television genre in Latin America, the *telenovela*. Shown for 9 months, it tells the story of an ambitious young man, who leaves the Brazilian countryside and goes to Rio in search of a better life. There he stumbles upon wealthy women who aid him in a frantic process of upward mobility. The story ends with the hero and his favorite lover celebrating the joys of life, and sailing away in a newly acquired yacht (Costa, Simoẽs, & Kehl, 1986).

This particular *telenovela* was produced by TV Globo, Brazil's major network, and the fourth largest in the world. By 1973, Brazilian soaps, produced by Globo and three other networks (Manchete, SBT, and

Bandeirantes), had already pushed the American "canned" programs to less popular hours (Costa et al., 1986, p. 290). Since then, U.S. imports have been mostly used as fillers. In order to reduce costs, and still remain an average of 20 hours on the air, Brazilian networks show inexpensive U.S. programs, such as morning cartoons and late night feature films. But prime time is dominated by *telenovelas*.

The Brazilian situation apparently contradicts research data that show the United States overwhelming the Third World with television programs (Varis, 1974, 1984). In the 1970s, some countries in Latin America, such as Argentina, Brazil, Cuba, Mexico, Peru, and Venezuela, demonstrated that they not only could produce their own television shows, but were also able to export them to several other nations, including the industrialized West. Thus some Western authors have been provided ammunition for their arguments against the notion of media imperialism (Rogers & Antola, 1985; Straubhaar, 1983, 1989, 1991; Tracy, 1988). Brazil is often presented as an example of a country that, as it were, fought back cultural intrusion and won the battle.

Indeed, there is quantitative evidence that this appears to be the case. Empirical support for the tendency is provided by the audience hours index (Straubhaar, 1983). This measurement is acquired by multiplying a program's length (in hours) by its audience, as provided by IBOPE. In 1963, the audience hours index for the *telenovelas* was 2% versus 25% for U.S. series. But the situation changed in 1977: as *telenovelas* leaped to 22%, U.S. series declined to 17% (Straubhaar, 1983, p. 66). In 1984, Rogers and Antola (1985, p. 32), using the same index, found that *telenovelas* reached 24% of audience hours, while U.S. series and feature films shrunk to a mere 8%. They also showed that, between 1972 and 1982, the percentage of imported programs in Brazil dropped from 60% to 39% (Rogers & Antola, 1985, p. 25).

Recently, I interviewed a sample of 166 business students, at the UFMG, Federal University in Brazil, about their appreciation of a variety of U.S. television programs such as "Fantasy Island," "All in the Family," "The A-Team," "Kojak," "Dallas," "I Love You," "Miami Vice," "Jimmy Swaggart," "Bill Cosby," "Bozo," "Great American Hero," "Thundercats," "The Lucy Show," and "Hill Street Blues." They were asked to evaluate the programs on a 1 to 10 scale, with 1 meaning very low appreciation and 10 very high. The average score across all 14 shows was 1.60. "Miami Vice" received the highest average rating: a mere 3.00. Students were also asked about their degree of agreement, on the same scale, with 1 indicating very low agreement and 10 very high, with two statements. The first said that Brazilian television should show more U.S. movies, and the second that Brazilian radio stations should play more U.S. music. The average scores were, respectively, 2.61 and 2.43. Hence, the interviewed students showed very low appreciation for U.S. cultural products, and didn't seem to want more of them in the Brazilian media (Oliveira, 1989, p. 16).

When in direct confrontation, Brazilian soaps are usually favored over Hollywood productions, even if the *telenovela* is broadcast by a less popular network. Globo has traditionally been the leader, attracting between 60% and 80% of the audience at any particular time (Tracy, 1988, p. 17). But on April 26, 1990, TV Manchete showed an episode of its new production, "Pantanal," against "The Untouchables," a U.S. feature film for which Globo paid $200,000. The audience ratings for these programs in Saó Paulo were, respectively, 29% and 27%, and in Rio, 51% and 30% ("A guerra," 1990, p. S-2). So in the two major television markets in Brazil the *telenovela* defeated a famous Hollywood production shown by the leading network.

The great popularity of the genre is not restricted to the domestic markets. In 1975, Globo discovered Portugal, with "Gabriela," an adaptation from a novel named *Gabriela, Clove and Cinnamon* written by Jorge Amado, a best-selling writer in Brazil. It portrays the adventures of a young country woman raised in the cacao farms during the 1920s, within a context of tremendous social turmoil, due to the sudden increase of wealth drawn from chocolate exports. For the first time in Portugal, a *telenovela* was broadcast daily to the entire nation (Marques de Melo, 1988, p. 40). Not only was the *telenovela* exported but also its main actress. The show's leading character is played by Sonia Braga, now a familiar name to U.S. audiences due to her roles in feature films such as "The Milagro Bean Field War," "The Kiss of the Spider Woman," and "Moonlight Over Parador."

The wide acclaim *Gabriela* received in Portugal encouraged additional incursions abroad. Currently, Globo exports to 128 countries, among them Cuba, China, the former Soviet Union, and what had been East Germany (Marques de Melo, 1988, p. 39). Its productions outnumber those of any other station in the world (Tracy, 1988, p. 17).

"Escrava Isaura" (Slave Girl Isaura), another of Globo's remarkable international successes, has been commercialized in more than 30 countries. "Escrava Isaura," drawn from a famous literary work written by Bernardo Guimarães, described the agony of a slave girl in the hands of a domineering master (Fernandes, 1987, p. 205). This particular program has been especially popular in socialist and ex-socialist countries. For example, in Cuba, Fidel Castro complained that he could not schedule meetings during the show. His advisors, as well as most of the Cuban audience, followed every episode with great interest. In Poland, ratings reached 85%, the highest ever achieved by any kind of program, surpassing international soccer matches and the traditionally popular evening news. In China, "Escrava Isaura" captured an estimated audience of 450 million viewers. The identification the Chinese had with the slave girl, played by Lucelia Santos, was so remarkable that, when the actress went to China in 1985, more than five thousand people went to Beijing's international airport to welcome her. Further, the book from which the program was derived was translated into Spanish and Chinese, and each edition sold, respectively, 250 thousand copies in Cuba, and 300 thousand in China (Marques de Melo, 1988, p. 44).

A seemingly obvious conclusion from the foregoing is that the days of cultural imperialism are numbered. In fact, it has been suggested that U.S. influence on Brazilian television programs has been "Brazilianized almost beyond recognition" (Straubhaar, 1983, p. 77); and that Latin America *telenovelas* shown in the U.S. Spanish networks are an example of some sort of "reverse media imperialism" (Rogers & Antola, 1985, p. 33). Moreover, it is believed that "in Brazil one sees a television devoted to national culture" (Tracy, 1988, p. 17), and that the impact of U.S. television has been exaggerated (p. 9).

Despite the quantitative support for these views, they are still considered rather superficial by several observers. Sinclair (1990, pp. 349–350) remarks that the major influence of programs imported from the West has never been so much their foreign source, but "the institutionalization of a model" that asks for "whatever programmes might attract the size and kind of audiences" required by advertisers. And for many Latin American scholars, the *telenovela* phenomenon is far from representing a reaction against an imported worldview. On the contrary, it examplifies the creolization of U.S. cultural products. It is the spiced up Third World copy of Western values, norms, patterns of behavior, and models of social relations (Beltrań & Cardona, 1982; Costa et al., 1986; Fischer, 1984; Pignatari, 1984; Quiroz & Cano, 1988; Ramos, 1986; Sodré, 1984).

As we will see, there is more to Brazilian television than meets the eye. Although "Gabriela" and "Escrava Isaura" may justify the notion that U.S. media domination in Brazil has been exaggerated, these two programs represent more the exception than the rule. The overwhelming majority of Brazilian soaps have the same purpose as their U.S. counterparts, that is, to sell products. Since *telenovelas* concentrate their stories on a glamorized version of "Brazilian reality," they have better chances of capturing larger domestic audiences than imported shows. They do so, but not to raise levels of cultural awareness or to promote consciousness about the country's needs. Thus, from a qualitative perspective, and an in-depth study of the genre and its role within Brazilian society, we may draw conclusions that are just the opposite of those suggested by some Western scholars.

Of course, Brazilian soaps have a number of specific qualities related to the plot and have introduced significant technical innovations. Yet, their commercial interests tend to override all other concerns, just as with U.S. shows.

Here we present an invitation to switch the level of discussion from quantitative analyses to deeper layers of inquiry, which would include the study of the repressive context under which the genre bloomed, its pacifying tendencies, and its consistent use as an effective purveyor of domestic and transnational products.

THRIVING WITH REPRESSION

The recent history of television in Brazil can be confused with the unfolding of a repressive government (Pereira & Miranda, 1983, p. 19). Since its establishment in 1969, 5 years after the armed forces took power, Globo became, so to say, the official network. It received special treatment from the military who, besides investing heavily in the telecommunications infrastructure, gave the network most of the government's large advertising accounts. The generals used television to legitimize their oppressive rule; therefore, government alone became the largest advertiser in the nation (Mattos 1984).

Thus, Globo had plenty of resources, further boosted by an initial contract with Time-Life, to spend on managerial modernization and technical refinements. The network's growth moved hand in hand with the so-called "Brazilian economic miracle." But as we will see later, both Globo's images and the "miracle" have more to do with imagination than reality.

Among the military's strategic priorities was the unification of the vast territory, which is approximately the size of continental United States, and bringing together a population of roughly then 120 million people (now 150 million) (Oliveira, 1991, pp. 120–121). Microwave towers were built every 60 kilometers linking the major Brazilian cities so that television signals could come closer to every corner of the land. Globo's financial strength allowed it to rent half the available links all the time (Costa et al., 1986, p. 191). And in 1986 the station received another gift from the military. Instead of terrestrial links, domestic television could. use a $210 million transmission system composed of two Canadian-built satellites (Turner, 1988, p. 71). Globo benefitted the most. In fact, the network's frenetic mobility could only be surpassed by its own *telenovela* characters.

Why was the military so generous with Globo? The answer is simple: It needed an anesthesia to be applied to the masses along with one of the most brutal regimes in the entire Brazilian history. After usurping power from a democratically elected president, the generals reduced wages and activated an income concentration process that took from the poor and gave to the rich.

According to Furtado (1981, p. 42), the economic model imposed upon the Brazilian population had a strong antisocial character, which benefited upper and middle classes and further deteriorated the living conditions of lower sectors. Between 1960 and 1980, the wealthiest 10% of Brazilian society increased its earnings from 39.6% to 50.9% of the total, while the poorest half saw its participation slashed from 17.4% to 12.6% (Suplicy, 1987, p. A-22). Annual per capita income decreased steadily, and continued dropping even after the military finally left government in 1985. Between 1983 and 1988 it dropped from $1,473 to $1,142 ("Consumo," 1989, p. 11).

Although the military encouraged the modernization of production, helping increase the industrial output, approximatley half of the Brazilian population was totally excluded from the benefits (Furtado, 1981, p. 59). Moreover, it was under the generals' heels that the real buying power of the minimum wage accelerated its tragic decline; in 1959, it was the equivalent of $300 per month; in 1986, $100; and today, $50 (Occhiuso, 1990, p. 18).

In no other country are social differences so drastic: 50% of Brazilian families have per capita earnings of less than $26 a month, and live in permanent poverty. Due to the high levels of urbanization (70%), poverty is concentrated in the cities. More than half of the urban dwellings lack electricity, more than 71% have no running water, and more than 79% have no refrigerators. The wealthiest 1% of the population holds as much of the total earnings as the poorest half (Jaguaribe, Valle e Silva, Abreu, De Aívila, & Fritsch, 1989, p. 18).

Dissidence and opposition were swiftly crushed by the military, and the media were forbidden to broadcast any news that could directly or indirectly accuse the government of wrongdoing (Oliveira, 1991, pp. 122–125; Quintão, 1987, p. 160). Precisely, in 1969, when Globo formed its network, the Brazilian dictatorship was considered one of the most cruel in the world (Ramos, 1986, p. 24).

Under these circumstances Globo's *telenovelas* thrived. They portrayed lives filled with personal success and upward mobility that somehow transferred to the realm of dreams whatever quarrels the masses had with the government. So conflict was resolved through bright images of happiness while the gloomy reality could be forgotten during the evening hours. In sum, television world was called "Brazilian reality," so that the horrors of daily life could be swallowed.

THE MASSIVE PACIFIER

A couple of years after its installation, color was added to Globo's images, and the ideology of development prevailed through the steady diffusion of the "Brazilian economic miracle" (Costa et al., 1986, p. 291). Concern with sleekness and strong emphasis on the "Brazilian reality" counteracted the presence of U.S. imports. Higino Corsetti, the dictatorship's Minister of Communication, pointed out that Globo was the only network able to follow the government guidelines related to the transmission of high-quality programs in the areas of entertainment, information, and education. In addition, Corsetti said that the best of Brazilian television was the *telenovela* (Costa et al., 1986, p. 290). No wonder, since its inception, the genre has been performing the "much needed" role of a massive pacifier to most, while selling durable goods to the wealthy few.

As a tranquilizer for the people, Brazilian soaps are faithful to their origins. In the end of the 17th century, autocratic governments in England and France forbade the performance of outdoor theaters, because they were "too distasteful and uneducated." But official theaters were reserved for the aristocrats only. As soon as the prohibition was lifted in France, in 1806, the melodrama, one of the forefathers of the *telenovela*, bloomed. Outdoor representations were mostly a public catharsis, which ridiculed the elites and exorcized the inner frustrations of hungry masses. Their major characteristics were, not words, but action and strong emotions. In a sense, it went head on against the subdued nature of the classical theater, represented indoors. It was made for the common and illiterate people to help them deal with repression. The major themes were fear, enthusiasm, sorrow, and laughter, all exaggerated, to which corresponded four types of situations: horrifying, exciting, tender, and comic. These were lived by four types of characters: the Traitor, the Hero, the Victim, and the Joker. The combination of these factors helped the audience forget its sorrows and, at least psychologically, overcome oppression (Barbero, 1988, p. 148).

In 1967, at the height of political persecution in Brazil, Marques de Melo (1973, p. 252) interviewed 135 housewives in São Paulo. He found that the *telenovela* gave those women a chance to escape from "day-today bitterness and find a different life." Television opened for them a window into a world of mystery, suspense, love and passion, in which everything ends up well. The bad are punished, the good ones rewarded...While watching the *telenovela* episodes people forget their real problems." In short, viewers had a chance to live vicariously and experience some illusory happiness. This is exactly what the melo-drama did approximately 200 years ago.

There are technical differences, though. The modern Brazilian melodrama shown on television mixes a variety of themes. Instead of concentrating on a single story or the discussion of social conflict within a fixed situation, the *telenovela* attempts to imitate real life dealing with problems the audience faces. The viewers' social or psychological concerns, in essence, determine the story. In fact, Globo conducts systematic audience surveys to check consumer preferences, expectations, and overall behavior. If a program's ratings suddenly shrink, Globo's interviewers are immediately out on the streets of Rio and São Paulo verifying what went wrong. Moreover, during the productions there is a professional called *continuista* who checks all the details, such as hairdos, dresses, and attire, so that nobody is seen on the screen wearing something incongruous with the previous episode. In general, viewers not only notice occasional slips, they call the station and complain (Marques de Melo, 1988, pp. 30, 50).

Reality is often confused with fiction. One of the common tricks to achieve such an effect is the inclusion of whatever dates are being celebrated, or important real-life events. For instance, Christmas or Carnival celebrations are usually included in the *telenovela* that is being broadcast at those times of the year, since these are important dates for the population.

More recently, with the opening of the political system, even heated discussions about social issues can be found in the Brazilian soaps. One of the rare occasions in which the military censored a *telenovela* arose precisely because of political insinuations. The broadcasting of "Roque Santeiro" had to wait 10 years, until 1986, when it was finally allowed out. The story is just the opposite of many others. The hero, in this case, returns to his home village, and finds generalized corrupt-ion and political manipulation. The plot develops as he tries to correct these vices, which were "coincidentally" most dominant during the military years. "Roque Santeiro" was shown while the country was mobilized, tired of oppression, demanding political openness and democracy. The program received consistently high ratings, never dropping below the 80% mark (Aldrichi, 1986).

During the showing of a *telenovela*, viewers' worries are solved in the best possible way. The characters end up better off than when they started their seemingly unsolvable ordeals. One is left with the illusion that there is some possibility of fairness within the status quo. The general direction offered by the *telenovela* is that the uneducated/ nonconsumer will become educated/consumer. The genre creates a general belief in progress, even among the marginalized sectors of society, who want to move up and think it possible. Actually, this fast and easy upward mobility from the bottom of the social scale to its highest peaks is one of the major traits of *telenovela* heros (Costa et al., p. 171).

Although the stories have a lot to do with real life, solutions are far-fetched. The systematic happy ending just doesn't happen in real life, especially in a country plagued by unemployment, inflation, income disparities, generalized poverty, and violence.

The Brazilian rural/urban exodus was intensified in the 1960s. Since then, poor rural workers continuously come to already over-crowded cities in search of food and shelter, a movement characterized as runaway urbanization. While in 1950, roughly 60% of Brazilians lived in rural areas, the situation was reversed in less than 40 years. Now only 30% live in the countryside (Jaguaribe et al., 1989, p. 18). This process includes the tremendous growth in urban slums throughout the territory. Most families, upon arriving in the city, cannot find jobs for the breadwinner or schools for the children. Instead of improving, their living conditions often deteriorate even further (but, of course, *telenovela* characters have much better luck).

In reality, this migration breeds stress in society as a whole. The uprooted individual feels lost in the big city. There are new demands and rules unheard of in the village. The sense of loneliness prevails within a nation that was hurriedly and haphazardly "modernized." Those involved see their set of values and beliefs suddenly smashed and replaced by cold and businesslike relationships that have nothing to do with their more traditional ways. In the city, if a job is secured, they are merely anonymous workers who can be replaced at any moment. There are no values attached to one's personal history, and those who arrive in the urban areas envy the few who were able to make it (Costa et al., 1986, p. 287).

Others don't stop at envying. As they see starving wives and children, they are left with little option other than stealing from the wealthier. The dramatic increases in the crime rate, especially in Rio and São Paulo, illustrate this tendency. The devastating effects of authoritarian rule linger and violence has increased. Security in the big city has become a paranoia of upper classes, who live in con-dominiums protected by private police and electronic gadgetry (Barreto 1981, p. 41). Currently, there are seven times more assassinations of children in Brazil than in Lebanon, a nation at war (Dimenstein, 1990, p. 14).

Someone has to try to make sense out of this madness. *Telenovela* characters come to rescue the viewer from psychological confusion. Daily socializing with these fictional beings was transformed into a national addiction in the 1970s, when most people preferred to stay home than venture out in the streets at night (Marques de Melo, 1988, p. 27). There were two main reasons for this choice. Political repression was generalized, and wages were steadily losing their buying power. Home was the safest place, and television the cheapest entertainment.

But in the process of distracting a scared audience, the glowing medium has also been "smartly" used to fill the pockets of national and transnational corporations.

THE MAGIC PRODUCT PEDDLING DEVICE

The irony of Brazilian television is that, although the images reach the entire nation, only approximately 20% of the audience may ever achieve the levels of consumption and social mobility shown in the stories. The percentage is indeed very small, but enough to suit the commercial purposes of local and foreign enterprises (Pietrocolla, 1987, pp. 46–47). Twenty percent out of a total of 150 million corresponds to the size of some of the wealthiest markets in the West, such as Canada or Scandinavia.

However, the remaining 80%, who cannot partake of television's abundance, are left with the impression that prosperity may some day be attainable. So instead of distributing wealth and real consumption power, the medium in general, and the *telenovela* in particular, become a "large supermarket chain which distributes symbolic goods...it also distributes income symbolically, and at an imaginary level materializes the dreams and promises of the Brazilian 'Miracle'" (Costa et al., 1986, p. 173).

For those who are not able to break the limitations of poverty, *telenovelas* provide the chance to experience the daily emotions of belonging to a different world. Real boundaries are overcome by fantasy (Fischer, 1984, p. 46), and the habituation once born out of sheer escapist necessities becomes a conditioned reflex, which is wisely manipulated by expert merchandisers.

In fact, a closer look at a Brazilian *telenovela* gives the observant viewer the impression of being in a Turkish bazaar. Everything within sight is for sale. The couch where the characters sit, the suits they wear, the Scotch they drink, the paintings on the walls, light fixtures, carpets, lamps, and so on, all are being advertised. In addition, labels in the kitchen are purposely shown displaying the brand name of pans, stoves, and appliances characters prefer. When the hero goes outside, it is time to promote sunglasses, cars, stores, and even banks. This procedure is labeled *merchandising*.

Yet, such practice is not a privilege of Brazilian television. It was introduced elsewhere with great success. In the 1960s, a Peruvian soap called "Simplemente Maria" (Simply Mary) described the good fortune of a slum girl who underwent the usual metamorphosis. Her skills as a seamstress transformed her from an exploited maid into a respected fashion designer. But there was a secret to her glory: the use of a Singer sewing machine. Wherever ,the program was shown in Latin America, "the sales of Singer sewing machines skyrocketed (and, in fact, Singer ads often appeared before, during, and after broadcasts of the *telenovela*)" (Rogers & Antola, 1985, p. 30).

Merchandising is officially permitted in Brazil and works wonders for both stations and advertisers. There isn't the slightest attempt to disguise commercial television's ultimate purpose. The medium has been transformed into wall-to-wall advertising (in country where 88% of the population is either illiterate or precariously educated) ("O drama," 1983, p. 86).

Brazil occupies the 80th position in the world ranking of educational investments, and the seventh in advertising expenditures (Barreto, 1981, p. 16). The lion's share goes to Globo. It is estimated that the station devours three fourths of all television advertising expenditures in Brazil, which is the equivalent of half a billion U.S. dollars a year. The network prices are among the highest in the world: an average of $500 per second (Marques de Melo, 1988, p. 22).

But it works. One of the characters in "Roque Santeiro" was disturbed by a sexually appealing billboard advertising Hope (a brand name for women's underwear). In a few months time, Hope's national sales, of 120 thousand pieces per month, doubled ("Merchandising," 1988, p. F-1).

An advertising agency, Apoio Comunicacão, links Globo with its merchandising clients. Apoio's director, Jorge Adib, says there are two types of products advertised within *telenovelas*: those which are an integral part of the scene and important to its coherence; and those that are not necessary, but may be included for the purposes of bringing in extra cash. According to Adib, there have been "some" excesses, though. In 1983, "Louco Amor" (Crazy Love) taught house-wives the use of frozen food, but the excessive showing of the freezer's brand name, Prosdoćimo, was overbearing. "It was an aesthetic mistake but the client was immensely happy," he said (Ramos, 1986, p. 82).

Indeed, the procedure has been abused. Banco Itaú, one of the largest private banks in Brazil, was advertised by six *telenovelas* between 1983 and 1985. A number of episodes showed characters who benefited from the bank's services and special checks. One situation, however, was particularly blatant: A peasant from northeastern Brazil, one of the poorest regions in the planet, was taught how to use electronic banking upon arriving in São Paulo (Ramos, 1986, p. 92).

At times the plot is changed to accommodate merchandising needs. In 1987, there was a serious radiation accident in Goiânia, a city near Brasilia. Naturally, the accident not only had a negative impact on tourism, but also on the commercialization of goods produced in the region. Sales dropped 40%. The bad image seemed stuck to the city until, in 1989, a slight change in "O Salvador da Patria" (The Fatherland's Savior) included Goiânia in one of Clotilde's (the main character) travels. The role was played by Maite Proenca, who received extra fees for this institutional merchandising. In Proenca's words, "Adib and I agreed on extra pay, normal, as if it were a beer merchandising" (Apolinaŕio, 1989, p. E-1).

In "Gabriela" one of the village bars only served Antartica, a beer and soft drink trade mark. But Coca-Cola counterattacked in another show, "Duas Vidas" (Two Lives), where the main character just drank Coke. Likewise, Volkswagen, General Motors, Levi's jeans, and so on, are all advertised inside and outside *telenovelas*. As late as 1982, "Elas Por Elas" (An Eye for an Eye) provided an interesting example of a *telenovela* that took the term "soap opera" literally. It displayed a sample of Vale Quanto Pesa, a popular bathing soap, as the only clue to a mysterious bathroom murder (Ramos, 1986, p. 81).

This product-peddling bias should be expected, though. Within industrial societies of the advanced North or dependent South, the logic of consumption molds cultural manifestations, which address the needs of the productive system (Oliveira, 1991a, pp. 51–53; Sodre; 1984, p. 125). As the cultural counterpart of national and transnational production units, Globo's main role is to homogenize and unify consumer behavior (Oliveira, 1991a, 1991b). At one time, it had to import most of its commodities and even had a foreign partner. Today, in order to keep a tighter grip on its markets, it has redesigned the assembly line. The output has little resemblance to original items, and for this very reason sells more. Compared to the commercial voracity of Brazilian soaps, U.S. imports look relatively tame.

CULTURAL IMPOSITION FROM WITHIN

The fact that Brazil has replaced U.S. programs with high-quality *telenovelas* should not be underestimated. It represents an important and significant trend, and deserves the attention it has gotten. But, does it mean that cultural imperialism as such is fading out?

Not really; *Telenovelas*'s historical purpose has been to adapt and dramatize capitalistic notions to fit the Latin American taste. Through the portrayal of success stories, they convey the idea of social harmony and possibilities of easy upward mobility to impoverished masses. Television reflects the strong cultural and economic dependency ties that link Latin America with industrialized nations, and its programming has a notable absence of themes that would address the real needs and aspirations of Latin Americans (Oliveira, 1991b, pp. 211–212; Quiroz & Cano, 1988, pp. 189–190).

Since real buying power is just found in minute middle and upper classes, the rest of the population may also engage in heavy shopping, but only through television images (Oliveira, 1988, p. 24). According to Ramos (1986, p. 54), the structure of reality inbedded in the *telenovela* themes and subthemes is alien to most Brazilians. it promotes the culture from the Rio and São Paulo elites who live far removed from the rest of the country. The lifestyles of these people resemble more those of wealthy Americans than the daily ordeal of the average Brazilian. The diversity presented in Globo's programs, in general, reflects the differences found within a selected group, who has strong consumption habits. But from the point of the dominant classes "it is necessary to educate the new consumption markets, and create new habits for rural and urban populations" (Costa et al., 1986, p. 287).

Other forms of human manifestation, representing the wide variety of cultures found in Brazil, such as Afro-Brazilian traditions, Indian rituals and legends, Northeastern costumes, German, Italian and Japanese settlements, southern gaucho heritage, and so on, are seldom if ever, portrayed by *telenovelas*. The domain of the genre is restricted to the needs of those who can buy; therefore, it emphasizes lifestyles that suit the industrial mode of production, and denies space to autonomous cultural manifestations (Oliveira, 1986, pp. 141–144; Sodré, 1983, pp. 125–126).

The dominant classes define what is good and what isn't. Social change is then unthinkable outside the limits prestablished by the genre which now shapes the national conscience. And the audience has been conditioned to watch. The first step was suggestion. Repeated over and over, it became persuasion, and with time, persuasion has turned into imposition (Ramos, 1986, p. 56).

In most Brazilian soaps, the American lifestyle portrayed by Hollywood productions reappears with a "brazilianized" face. Now we don't see wealthy Anglo-Saxons anymore, but rich white Brazilians enjoying standards of living that would make any middle-class American envious.

The Rio and São Paulo elite culture should not be confused with the rest of Brazil, though. If it is considered as an example of the cultural diversity found in the immense land, this would inevitably lead to distorted conclusions. Brazilian *telenovelas* may represent a quantitative change form the overwhelming importation of U.S. programs that occurred during the 1950s and 1960s. But viewed from a more qualitative perspective the *telenovela* phenomenon isn't as revolutionary as suggested by Rogers and Antola (1985), Straubhaar (1983, 1989, 1991), and Tracy (1988). And as we've tried to demonstrate, Brazilian television may be as far from being "devoted to national culture" (Tracy, 1988, p. 17) as once imported shows were.

In short, Brazilian soaps are the new guardians of the status quo. They do have their own well-groomed characteristics, but haven't been able to evade the demands of the power structure from which they derive. Glamorous as they are, even outshining Hollywood, their role within Brazilian society isn't different from that of U.S. imports. Unfortunately, the refinements applied to the genre were to enhance not diversity, but domination.

REFERENCES

A guerra do video. (1990, May 9). *Estado de Minas*, p. s-2.

Adrichi, V. (1986). *VideoBrasil*. São Paulo: MPM.

Apolinário, S. (1989, May 14). Goiañia usa novela contra estigma do césio. *Folha de São Paulo*, p. E-1.

Barbero, J. M. (1988). Matrices culturales de la telenovela. *Culturas Contemporaneas, 2*, 137–162.

Barreto, R. M. (1981). *Análise transacional da propaganda*. São Pualo: Summus.

Beltrán, L. R. (1978). TV etchings in the minds of Latin Americans: Conservatism, materialism, and conformism. *Gazette, 26*(1), 61–85.

Beltrán, L. R., & Cardona, E. F. (1982). *Comunicacão dominada*. Rio de Janeiro: Paz & Terra.

Consumo 'per capita' caiu 22, 47% em 5 anos. (1989, February 15). *Estado de Minas*, p. 11.

Costa, A. H., Simões, I. F., & Kehl, M. R. (1986). *Um país no ar*. São Paulo: Brasiliense.

Dimenstein, G. (1990). *A Guerra dos meninos*. São Paulo: Brasiliense.

Fernandes, I. (1987). *Telenovela brasileira*. São Paulo: Brasiliense.

Fischer, R. M. B. (1984). *O mito na sala de jantar*. Porto Alegre: Movimento.

Furtado, C. (1981). *O Brasil pós-milagre*. Rio de Janeiro: Paz & Terra.

Jaguaribe, H., Valle e Silva, N., Abreu, M. P., De Ávila, F. B., & Fritsch, W. (1989). *Brasil: reforma ou caos*. Rio de janeiro: Paz & Terra.

Marques de Melo, J. (1973). *Communicacão social: teoria o pesquisa* (3rd ed.). Petrópolis: Vozes.

Marques de Melo, J. (1988). *As telenovelas da globo*. São paulo: Summus.

Mattos, S. (1984). Advertising and government influences: the case of Brazil. *Comunication Research, 11*(2), 203–220.

Merchandising faz da novela 'balcão'. (1988, October 23). *Folha de São Paulo*, p. F-1.

Occhiuso, J. (1990, April 20). Olho no ciclone. *IstoéSenhor*, pp. 12–18.

O drama da educacão. (1983, November 16). *Veja*, pp. 86–89.

Oliveira, O. S. (1986). Satellite TV and dependency: An empirical approach. *Gazette, 38*, 127–145.

Oliveira, O. S. (1988). Brazilian media usage as a test of dependency theory. *Canadian Journal of Communication, 13*, 16–27.

Oliveira, O. S. (1989, July 9). Pesquisa detalha nossa dependência cultural. *Estado de Minas*, p. 16.

Oliveira, O. S. (1991a). *Genocídio cultural*. Sao Paulo: Paulinas.

Oliveira, O. S. (1991b). Mass media, culture and communications in Brazil: The heritage of dependency. In G. Sussman & J. Lent (Eds.), *Transnational communications: Wiring the Third World* (pp. 200–213). Newbury Park, CA; Sage.

Pereira, A. M. P., & Miranda, R. (1983). *Televisáo*. São paulo: Brasiliense.

Pignatari, D. (1984). *A signagem da televisáo* (2nd ed.). São Paulo: Brasiliense.

Pietrocolla, L. (1987). *Sociedade de consumo*. São Paulo: Global.

Quintão, A. (1987). *O jornalismo econômico no Brasil depois de 1964*. Rio de Janeiro: Agir.

Quiroz, M. T., & Cano, A. M. (1988). Los antecedentes y condiciones de la producción de telenovelas en el Peru. *Culturas Contemporaneas, 4–5*, 187–222.

Ramos, R. (1986). *Grã-finos na Globo: cultura e merchandising nas novelas*. Petrópolis: Vozes.

Rogers, E., & Antola, L. (1985). *Telenovelas*: A Latin American success story. *Journal of Communication, 35* (4), 24–35.

Sinclair, J. (1990). Neither West nor Third World: The Mexican television industry within the NWICO debate. *Media, Culture and Society, 12*, 343–360.

Sodré, M. (1984). *O monopolio da fala*. Petrópolis: Vozes.

Straubhaar, J. (1983). O declínio da influência americana na televisão brasileira. *Comunicacáo & Sociedade, 9*, 61–77.

Straubhaar, J. (1989, May). *Change in assymetrical interdependence in culture: The brazilianization of television in Brazil*. Paper presented at the International Communication Association Conference, San Francisco.

Straubhaar, J. (1991). Beyond media imperialism: Assymetrical interdependence and cultural proximity. *Critical Studies in Mass Communication,* *8,* 39–59.

Suplicy, E. M. (1987, June 1). Brasil, campeáo de desigualdades. *Folha de Sáo Paulo,* p. A-22.

Tracy, M. (1988, March). Popular culture and the economics of global television. *InterMedia,* pp. 9–25.

Turner, R. (1988). Callers hang on for new lines. *South, 90,* 71.

Varis, T. (1974). Global traffic in television. *Journal of Communication, 24,* 102–109

Varis, T. (1984). The international flow of television programs. *Journal of Communication, 34,* 143–152.

Chapter 7
Modernity, Nationalism, and Communication in Latin America*

Jesús Martín Barbero

Nationalism, now more crucial than ever and perhaps more difficult than any other problem, today in Latin America is burdened with a double ambiguity. The first is the ambiguity of the diverse, eccentric nature of the constitution of the national states of the region (see Lechner, 1981). The second is the ambiguity cast by a critical theory that refuses to see what emerges from the process of transnationalization—a new phase of capitalism characterized, not only by economic change, but by political change in the nature and function of the national state (see Roncagliolo, 1982). And, consequently, the change in direction of dependency—"an open struggle for independence with a geographically defined colonial power is very different from a struggle for identity within a extended translational system, intricately interrelated and interpenetrated" (Canclini, 1983, p. 24).

The pressures of an economic crisis, whose most dramatic expression is the social effects of a foreign debt making certain national situations almost ungovernable, and the dangerous operation of internal cultural devaluation, converge on this reconfigured national space.

---

*Adaptation of a chapter from the author's book, *Communication, Culture and Hegemony: From Media to Mediations*, Sage, 1993, translated by Elisabeth Fox.

Certain intellectual circles' acknowledgment of the backward, provincial, and authoritarian dimensions of national culture in relation to the worldwide dimensions of the culture industry could legitimize the transnationalization driven by capitalism. "The uneasiness of national culture disappears against the backdrop of the culture industry" (Schwarz, 1986, p. 17), freeing itself in this way from the logic of a culture that presents itself without contradictions, at ease with itself! It is, nevertheless, precisely in the recognition and acceptance of the uneasiness of nationality that the possibility lies of a nationalism, that, conscious of its historical contradictions, can become a strategy to resist the new forms of domination and a creative space open to the challenges of the new processes of communication.

REFLEX MODERNIZATION AND STATE NATIONALISM

Beginning in the 1920s, most Latin American countries reorganized their economies and readjusted their political structures, launching industrialization based on the substitution of imports, the formation of an internal market, and a growing number of jobs for which state intervention in transportation and communication infrastructure was crucial. Although national industrialization responded to the demands of the international market, it differed in each country as a result of the varying degrees of success of the "national projects" undertaken by the bourgeoisie since the mid-19th century.

There is much debate over the possibility of speaking of a "national bourgeoisie" in Latin America during these years and their role in the formation of the nation state. As Malcolm Deas asked, "How could there have been national politics and a national economy without the articulation of class interests at a national level?" (Deas, 1983, p. 150) Naturally, there were differences in the scope and ability of the different national bourgeoisie, for example, between Brazil and Ecuador. These differences, however, were not so much among the Darwinist concepts that directed modernization and national development as among their results. The counties, however, shared similar phenomena of urban growth and erosion of traditional society.

The explosive urbanization of Latin America was the result of population growth and migration from the countryside. In some countries, for example, Argentina, huge waves of immigration from Europe constituted another factor in urbanization. Societies began to form mass societies, in confrontation with "normal" society, with its segregation of classes and social groups. Although not necessarily a national bourgeoisie, the appearance of the "new bourgeoisie" (Romero, 1983, p. 268) controlling both politics and the economy had a significant effect on both. It was not only economic pressure that allowed this to occur; it was also the desire to integrate the countries into the life style of the "modern countries." Only modernization, it was felt, already defined as an urbanized, European world, could pull the countries out of their morass. It was acceptable, therefore, to ignore the backwards parts of the country and everything that stood in the way of progress. It not, the existence of the nation itself was endangered.

The new bourgeoisie profited from modernization, fulfilling the creoles' old dream of a "National project," while giving it a new meaning.[1] With the national project the creole class assumed national attributes and became "national." "The national project was a lengthy undertaking in which the creole class constructed the State and the Nation" (Palacios, 1983, p. 16). The project faltered and failed in the 19th century, but was used later as the foundation of an internal power base, the new project of construction of the modern nation.

A new nationalism was born, based on the idea of a national culture, the synthesis of different cultural realities, and a political unity bringing together cultural, ethnic, and regional differences. The nation absorbed the people, the masses, "transforming the multiplicity of desires of the diverse cultures in a single desire, to participate in a feeling of nationhood" (Novaes, 1983, p. 10). To work for the nation was to work for unification, overcoming the fragmentation that generated the regional and federal wars of the 19th century. Unification made possible communication—roads, railways, telegraphs, telephones, and broadcasting among the regions and, especially, from the regions to the center, the capital.

There were two schools of thought in this effort, although they shared many basic elements. One school identified national progress with the progress of the class that directed industrialization. The other, present in those countries with the cultural and social formation Darcy Ribeiro has called "pueblos testimonio" (Ribeiro, 1977, p. 155 ff.), attempted to fuse the new nation with that other, earlier nation coming "from below." The goal of the first school of thought was to industrialize and join the civilized nations; in the second school there was a tension between the need to industrialize and an awareness of their uniqueness as a nation. This tension was present in Peru at the end of the 1920s in the debate that brought the "national problem" and the "Indian problem"—the projects of Haya de la Torre and José Carlos Mariátegui, respectively—into open confrontation (on this debate, see Albavera et al., 1981).

All over Latin America, the modernization that directed the changes and gave meaning to the new nationalism was more a movement of economic and cultural change than a reinforcement of independence. Squeff, in reference to Brazilian nationalism, affirmed, "We were able to modernize only by translating our raw material into an expression that was accepted abroad" (Squeff & Wisnik, 1983, p. 55). Cultural policies depended on economic policies. More than expanding the internal market, the countries internalized foreign models and requirements. Latin America wanted to be a nation in order to finally acquire an identity, but, in order to achieve this identity, it had to adopt the theory of modernization of the hegemonic countries, only then could the efforts and achievements of the countries receive validation. The logic of development was none other than this and its key was the modernizing nationalism of the 1930s, its previous and indispensable stage.

In order to modernize, the political structure needed a centralized state. It was impossible to conceive of national unity without strengthening the center and organizing the country around one point that consolidated decision making. In some countries, centralism justified the establishment of the basic mechanism of a nonexistent public administration—national accounts, the organization of taxes, a public registrar.[2] In other countries where a public administration already existed, centralism meant the unification and standardization of diverse culture epochs, habits and expressions. Heterogeneity suffered a drastic reduction throughout the region as profound cultural differences were lost in or projected onto the nation a whole. Those countries without profound cultural differences and heritages took relatively minor cultural differences and turned them into folklore to sell to tourists in curiosity shops. The absorption and "folklorization" or national diversity were not just functional strategies of a centrist policy. In certain periods, as is seen in the "indigenist novel," there were also ways of demonstrating the "consciousness of the new country,"[3] and affirming a still-forming national identity.

In addition to centralization, the other component of the nationalism of the 1930s was the protagonist role of the state. (We return to this point in greater detail in our discussion of populism.) In some countries, for example, Mexico, the protagonism of the state was so strong that it made the state the hegemonic agent par excellence (Zermeño, 1972). The Mexican State was strengthened by the permanent "plebeian volcano," the country's internal and external wars, and the constant erosion of the power of the upper classes, requiring a strong state and resulting in a paradox of overpolitization and desocialization. In Chile, the protagonism of the state at the expense of the institutions and class organizations of civil society resulted in the atomization of politics and an instrumentalist conception of democracy.[4] Industrialization was first and foremost the task of the state. "The spirit of entrepreneurship, in capitalist countries defining a series of characteristics of the industrial bourgeoisie, in Latin America, especially during the most important periods, was a characteristic of the State. *The State took the place of a social class, unsuccessfully called into action, and became the Nation.* The State supported the political and economic access of the masses to the benefits of industrialization" (Galeano, 1972, p. 370; emphasis in original).

The same thing happened to culture. For Vasconcelos in Mexico the Revolution was more than the historical eruption of the masses; it was an opportunity to civilize the masses under the direction of the state, the great educator. His concept was contained in murals "exalting the armies of Zapata and the international proletariat but painted on the walls of government buildings" (Monsivais, 1981, p. 35). The muralist added peasant armies and international working classes to the humanist and culturalist project of Vasconcelos, but "The State dictated the rules of the country; the State monopolized the historical sentiments of artistic and cultural patrimony" (p. 38).

Paradoxically, the growth of the Mexican State was a "conquest by the people," a popular revolution against creoles, private corporations and foreign threats. This paradox explains the force of national culture in Mexico, the strength of what culture meant even after it had been abandoned by the state and tuned over to the culture industry. Even then, what was "national" was not merely what the state identified and encouraged, it was the way the masses felt the social legitimacy of their aspirations. No other Latin American country had as marked a sense of nationalism as Mexico. The Mexican Revolution gave the Mexican State a popular representability beyond any formal representation. The absence of a revolution in other Latin American countries, even those with a strong state, explains why national culture was so disconnected from real culture and why the concerns of the state for culture appeared, and still appear, merely rhetorical.

NATIONALIZATION OF THE MASSES AND TRANSFORMATIONS OF THE POPULAR

If the 1930s were important years in Latin America because of the processes of industrialization and modernization of economic structures, in politics they were as or more important because of the "eruption" of the masses in the cities. As cities grew, aided by the exodus from the countryside, the crisis of hegemony, the result of the absence of a hegemonic class, encouraged many states to seek legitimacy in the masses. It was impossible to remain in power without taking up the defense of the demand of the urban masses. Populism's claim to legitimacy was the defense of popular aspirations. More than a strategy from a position of power, it was an organization of power that gave form to the agreement between the masses and the state. The ambiguity of the agreement was the result both of the vacuum of power filled by state—with the resulting paternalistic authoritarianism—and the political reformism the masses represented. Not wishing to attribute to populism a false efficacy, or to reduce the masses to a passive and easily manipulative state—which was not the case—it is important to explain the meaning of the social presence of the masses and of the massification they materialized.

Migration and the new sources and types of employment in the cities nurtured hybrids and new forms of popular classes. "There was an explosion of the people. It was impossible to measure how much was the result of their larger numbers and how much was the result of the decision of many to make themselves known and their presence felt" (Romero, 1983, p. 318). The crisis of the 1930s brought about an offensive by the rural areas on the cities and a reorganization of social groups. There was a quantitative and qualitative change in the poplar classes as a result of a mass that could no longer be defined within the traditional social structure and that "dismantled the traditional forms of participation and representation" (Faleto, 1982, p. 109). The masses changed the whole of urban society, its way of life and thinking and, eventually, the face of the city itself.

The urban masses swelled the size of the popular classes and created a new form of popular existence: "The disappearance of the popular world as the place of the Other, the forces of negation of the capitalist forms of production" (Sunkel, 1985, p. 16). The insertion of the popular classes in a "mass society" pushed the popular movement toward a new strategy of alliances. The new social experience fashioned a new vision, a new concept less openly confrontational. "It was a vision of a society that could be reformed gradually, of a society that could become more just" (Gutierrez & Romero, 1981, p. 8).

For some time the masses were marginal. In comparison with "normal" society, the masses were heterogeneous and mestizos. The inferiority complex suffered by the recent immigrants from rural areas—who had to learn how to take a bus, find their way around the city, get working papers—was compounded by the disdain felt for them by the old society; a disdain that hid fear more than repugnance. More than an assault, the masses meant the impossibility of maintaining the rigid organization of differences and hierarchies that had held society together. The aggression of the masses was nonviolent yet equally dangerous—it was not the rising up of a class but the freeing of an uncontrollable energy. It was a "proletarian downpour" (Romero, 1982, p. 54). That did not find its political insertion in the political parties or in the traditional organizations of the working class, but whose expressions of violence revealed the force of which it was capable.

The presence of the masses in the city slowly acquired more specific characteristics. The sheer numbers meant a housing shortage, a transportation problem, a new way of living the city, walking the streets, behaving. Slums sprang up, and traditional ways of life disappeared; the city began to lose its center. The rich countered the dispersion of the poor—the favelas, villas miserias, callampas—by moving further out, forming their own circles around the city. The masses continued to invade everywhere. Ignoring the rules, and the threat their presence represented, their most secret desire was to gain access to urban service: jobs, health care, education, entertainment. They were unable to gain access, however without the massification of the services themselves. The revolution of expectations drove home the paradox—subversion lay in integration. Massification was the integration of the popular classes in society and society's goods and services that until then had been the privilege of the elites. Society could not accept this change without a profound transformation. The transformation occurred, but not the one revolutionaries expected, and, therefore, many thought nothing had changed.

Massification affected everyone, but not all felt and experienced it in the same way. The upper classes quickly learned to separate the demands of the masses—with their measure of political threat and their potential for economic growth—from the supply end of massification, the mass-produced material and cultural goods "without style" for which they felt only disdain. Massification was especially painful for the middle classes, the petit bourgeoisie, who, as much as they desired, could not distance themselves from the masses. Massification "threatened their dream of interiorization that was their characteristic, their jealously guarded individuality and their condition as persons that could be differentiated" (Romero, 1983, p. 374).

Massification brought more advantages than disadvantages for the popular classes—massification promised material survival as well as cultural access and ascent—although the masses were the most defenseless against the new conditions and situations. The new mass culture began as a culture not only directed at the masses but a culture where the masses found—in music, stories, radio, films—some of their fundamental views of the world and forms of expression and feelings.

Jose Luis Romero is responsible for the most original name for mass culture, *alluvial folklore*, and for a finely nuanced sociological and phenomenological characterization of this culture in Latin America (Romero, 1982, p. 67). Romero, as Benjamin, views mass culture from the perspective of experiences that gain access to forms of expression rather than from the perspective of manipulation. In his analysis of the culture of the mestizo, Romero found something close to what had interested Arquedas: hybrids and reelaboration, the destruction of the myth of cultural purity and the acknowledgement without disdain of the movement from folklore to popular in relation to the use in traditional music or radio and modern instruments (Arquedas, 1977, p. 124). Mass culture is the hybrid of foreign and national, of popular informality and bourgeois concern with success, of two classic types: those who try to look rich without the means to do so, "Who imitate the eternal forms that characterize this type," and the opposite, the impudent types from the slums and the underworld. It is essentially an urban culture that compensates its open materialism—what matters is what has economic value and social success—with a superabundance of feelings and passions.

Official policies from the left and the right looked with suspicion upon the masses and mass culture. The right was defensive; the masses threatened their established social privileges and destroyed sacred cultural borders. The left considered the masses a dead weight, a proletariat without class awareness or vocation for struggle. Mass culture did not fit with their cultural scheme; it threatened it. Only for the populists did the presence of the urban masses in politics constitute a "class experience that nationalized the masses and gave them citizenship" (Portantiero, 1981, p. 234). This implies that, if as a state project, populism could be politically overcome, as a "phase of political constitution of the popular sectors" it was fundamental. Historical memory sometimes tricks the analyst, showing in this case, that the relationship between the underclasses and the people is not always clear. There is a space of conflict that does not coincide entirely with the relationships of class and production. It is a different and specific contradiction located at the level of "social formations" that puts the people in conflict with those in power (Laclau, 1978, p. 122) in a "popular democratic" struggle characterized by the historical strength of popular tradition in contrast with the discontinuity of class structure.

The peculiarities of the way in which the Latin American masses made themselves present in society were ultimately the result of the double appeal that motivated the masses from the time of the urban explosion: the class appeal that is only perceived by a minority and the popular-national appeal that reached the majorities. Could this mass mobilization have been merely a manipulation of the people by the state with the aid of the mass media? Today, we know this was not the case. Populism's appeal to the "popular classes" contained elements of manipulation—higher salaries, the right to organize, etc.—that, projected onto the mass media, structured the appeal to the constitution of workers as citizens of a national society. Here, with all its ambiguity, lay the effectiveness of the appeal to popular traditions and the construction of a national culture. Here as well lay the specific role of the mass media like films and radio that constructed their discourse for the proposal of a national imaginary and sentiment on the basis of the continuity of the imaginary of the masses with a narrative and scenic memory and on popular iconography.

POPULISM AND MASS MEDIA IN THE CONSTITUTION OF A NATIONAL IMAGINARY

The discontinuities between the state and the nation, and the twisted and torturous path by which the masses burst in on and became part of Latin American politics, require a profound change in perspective in the history of the mass media. The social and political demands of the underclasses made themselves heard by the whole of society through the national-popular movements. The national-popular movement was acknowledged by the majorities, however, through a discourse directed at the masses. With some exceptions, historians of the mass media have only studied the economic structure and the ideological content of the mass media; few have studied the mediations through which the mass media acquired institutional form and cultural depth. Studies move between attributing the dynamics of all cultural change to the media and reducing the media to passive instruments in the hands of class interests with almost as much autonomy as a Kantian subject.

But, if the cultural and political mediations have not been present in the history of the mass media, it is probably because most of the history written about Latin America leaves out culture or reduces it to fine arts and literature. In the same way, the political history of Latin America consists of great moments and important figures and almost never the events and cultures of the popular classes. An English historian, for example, raised the following questions about Colombian history: "What was the popular impact of independence? What do we know about the political practices of the illiterate? What do we know about informal communication in politics or how local ideas about national politics are formed?" (Deas, 1983, p. 151).

The study of this cultural space, however, does not suggest introducing an entirely separate new topic but focusing on that space where the social meaning of economic and political processes for a society are articulated and formed. This would entail writing the history of the mass media from the perspective of cultural processes as articulator of communication practices—hegemonic and popular—within social movements. Some studies have begun to work from this perspective. Their findings allow us to begin to understand some of the mediations from which, historically, technologies become the communication media.

In the analysis of mediations and social movements, it becomes apparent that it is necessary to distinguish between two stages in the development of the media and the constitution of mass culture in Latin America. In the first stage, from the 1930s to the end of the 1950s, the efficacy and social significance of the media resided in the manners of appropriation and acknowledgement of the media and of themselves through the media, by the popular masses, rather than in the industrial organization and ideological content of the media. Of course, economics and ideology were important to how the media functioned. The significance of the economic structure and ideology of the media, however, lay outside the media in the conflict that motivated and structured the social movements—the conflict between the state and masses, and its "compromised" solution in nationalist populism and in populist nationalism. During this first stage, the decisive role of the mass media was their ability to convey the summons of populism, turning the masses into the people and the people into the nation.

The summons came from the state, but it was only successful to the extent that the masses perceived in it some of their basic demands and forms of expression. The function of the caudillos and the mass media was to rephrase the masses' demands and expressions. This was not only the case of those countries that experienced the "drama" of populism but also of countries that in other forms and with other names and rhythms went through the crisis of hegemony, the birth of nationhood and the entrance to modernity. The cinema in most countries, and radio in all countries, gave the people of the different regions and provinces their first taste of the nation.[5] This function of the media is acknowledged, although unfortunately only in the conclusions, in a history of Colombian radio. "Before the appearance and growth of radio, the country was a patchwork of regions, each separate and isolated. Before 1940 Colombia could very well call itself a country of countries rather than a Nation. Hyperbole aside, radio allowed the country to experience an invisible national unity, a cultural identity shared simultaneously by the coast, Antioquea, Pasto, Santander and Bogota" (Pareja, 1984, p. 177). This observation puts us on the trail of another dimension of massification—transforming the political "idea" of nationhood into the daily experience and sensation of nationhood.

National building is not only an economic question of the unification of national markets, internal trade and exports. A country is unified by its schools and communication media more than by its highways and railroads. The national project is a political and cultural project that, in the case of populism, would find its language in the "new" discourse, the popular-massive discourse, made possible by the media. Radio allowed the passage of the still predominant rural cultures to the new urban culture, making possible their entrance into modernity without completely losing certain features of their traditional identity, introducing features of their oral culture—organized on the basis of a symbolic-expressive rationality—in an urban culture beginning to organize itself on the basis of instrumental rationality. During these years radio nurtured an idea of the national that did not deactivate the sense of belonging to a region. The experience of nationality at this time was a peculiar experience, that of discovering that you are an inhabitant of a country that is shared with other regions, although the destruction of this plurality was already beginning. The cinema would construct a nation by theatricalizing it, giving it a face, gestures, voices and images (Monsivais, 1976). In cinema, Monsivais observed, Mexicans learned how to be Mexicans. What for many years had been synonymous with vulgarity appeared as an element configuring the "national character." Seeing themselves in the movies legitimized their features and gestures as part of the national culture with all that this contained of chauvinism, but also as a creator of a new urban-national identity.

At the end of the 1950s populism entered in crisis; its now radical social demands required its transformation into a revolution and, not able to survive without becoming more radical, its cycle ended. In its place appeared development. The idea of modernization in populism was a political project, in development it was an economic project that would be served by the reforms both of the state and of society. During populism, the state was the visible incarnation of the social contract, now the state would become a technical and neutral entity carrying out the demands of development (Lechner, 1981, p. 306). Maintaining their rhetoric of "public service," the mass media as well as education and culture gradually would be privatized. The function of the state and the meaning of mass would change. During populism the mass referred to the social presence of the masses, to the presence of the masses filling the streets and overflowing the hospitals and schools; now mass would refer to the *media* and would be confused with communication. This is the message of the Organization of the American States: the best indicator of the level of development of these countries is the development of their communication media. Communication became a measure of development: "without communication there is no development," a development measured in the number of newspaper copies, radio sets, and televisions. We can now answer the question about the meaning of the media in the new project. If during the birth of a national culture radio and film were to a certain degree receptive to the culture diversity of the countries, with the arrival of television we witnessed the start of a new model driven by the tendency to *form a single public* (Sodré, 1981). It is a model that tends towards the unification of demand by means of an imaginary of consumption that is not longer national but explicitly and shamelessly *transnational*. This implies a single model of development for all the countries and for the whole country, a model in which differences become obstacles. There is a second key mechanism on which the model that dominates television is organized, the tendency to *confuse reality with the present*. The mechanism of contemporalization, of submission of all the times and temporalities that make up Latin America into one single time, the present, the only time that measures productivity. Television confronts the different and anachronic times that run through the cultural reality of these countries, reshaping and sealing off memories and unifying forms of speech and gestures as a basic condition of development.

TRANSNATIONAL COMMUNICATION AND TRANSFORMATIONS IN THE FIELD OF CULTURE

We began our reflection by analyzing the political and cultural contradiction of what is meant by national. We are going to conclude it by referring to the change that in the last years has affected the meaning of the history on which the national state is based.[6] The role of the transnational actor is no longer only that of economic pressure— with its negative effect on national behavior—but in the *desocializing rationality* of the state and the legitimization of the dissolution of the public. An "abstract" state, divorced from society by the concealment of its social origins, is confronted with a civil society identified with private interests whose best expression is the market. From here we can see in transnationalization the key dynamic that, with its requirement of adaptation and technological renovation, will permit these countries to overcome their crisis—the jump seems logical.

In this way, for Latin America—trapped by a foreign debt suffocating its economies, deteriorating social conditions, and making any government unstable—this is the solution, overcoming the out-of-date policies of sovereignty to adjust to the times of transnational temporality. It is a time in which the state is no longer a guarantee of the interests of the collectivity, or the nation as a political subject, and has become the manager of a transnational project. The new structures and recomposition of the collective identities that the transnational process is producing show that what is at stake is the sense of history. Here the new communication technologies are not merely instrumental, they have a role in the restructuring of the state on the basis of a paradoxical logic, making the state strong in its possibilities and tendencies toward control and making it weak by disconnecting it from its public functions. Mastering the economic crisis, by closely linking itself to the process of privatization, reveals the deepest tendency of capitalism to prevail over the "old" idea of a public space. We can therefore not be surprised when Richeri (1985) observes that the media themselves are losing their communicative identity; their relation to the social movements is no longer their capacity to mediate[7] but their technological development as a new space of industrial reconversion and a new time of realization of capital.

The neoconservative project that has attempted a solution to the crisis since the beginning of the 1970s is organized around economic proposals—the suppression of the rights of organized labor, privatization, and the restriction of public expenditures—that cannot be carried out without also undertaking policies to reorganize the field of culture, including political culture. By attempting to substitute the state as the agent of hegemony, the new policies make private initiative appear to be the true defender of freedom of creation and the only link between national cultures and the international culture that has become the model and guide of renovation. The center of society has moved from politics to the marketplace.[8] This has brought about an upheaval, a reconstitution of identities and of the system of acknowledgement and symbolic differentiation of classes and social groups. It is here that the new dynamics of culture tie in with the transformations in communication. How can the readjustment of hegemony that these changes bring about be conceived without ignoring its agents, the complexities of the process, or the contradictions that mobilize it?

The first step is to abandon the concept of transnationalization that reduces communication to a set of strategies for cultural domination and that ignores the ways in which hegemony operates, in other words, by "giving new meaning to the knowledge and habits of each community and subordinating them to a complex transnational system (Canclini, 1985). This implies rethinking the interaction between the hegemonic messages and the perceptive codes of each community, the different experience that through fragmentation and readjustments constantly remakes and recreates cultural heterogeneity. More than in terms of homogenization, transnationalization should be conceived of as the dislocation of the centers that articulate the universe of each culture. This dislocation is carried out by means of processes that insert the rationality of the modernizing project—secularization and specialization of the symbolic worlds—in a movement of segmentation and integration of the world economy (Brunner, 1987). While the sources of production of culture are moved away from the community toward specialized bodies, the community's forms of life are gradually remodeled and replaced by patterns of consumption separated from the "creative nucleus" that constitutes, according to Ricoeur, the vital core of each culture (Ricoeur, 1964, p. 286).

Subordinated and mixed with this process, the different cultural logics of the communities form new identities and reconstitute the meaning of national and local. The proposals of the culture industry are reformed and changed not only by the "nationalization" brought about by the local industries in which the insertion of their own is usually a mixture of humor and resentment, but also through the "ability of the communities to transform what they see in something else and experience it in a different way" (Monsivais, 1988, p. 76).

REFERENCES

Albavera, F.S., et al. (1981). *Problems nacional: Cultura y clases sociales.* Lima: DESCO.

Arquedas, J.M. (1977). *Formación de una cultura nacional indoamericana.* Mexico: Siglo XXI.

Braslavsky, C., & Tedesco, J.C. (Coordinators). (1982). *Tendencias históricas de la educación popular como expresiones de los proyectos políticos de los estados latinoamericanos.* Mexico.

Brunner, J.J. (1985). *Notas sobre cultura popular, industria cultural y modernidad.* Santiago, Chile: Flasco.

Canclini, N.G. (1983). Las políticas culturales en América Latina. *Chasqui,* No. 7, 24.

Candido, A. (1972). Literatura y subdesarrollo. *América Latina en su literatura.* Mexico: Siglo XX1.

Celis, C.U. (1984). *Los anõs veinte en Colombia ideologia y cultura.* Bogota.

Deas, M. (1983). Las presencia de la política nacional en la vida provinciana de Colombia (M. Palacios, Coord.). *La unidad nacional en América Latina.* Mexico: El Colegio de Mexico.

Faleto, E. (1982). *En América Latina: Desarrollo y perspectivas democráticas.* Costa Rica: Flasco.

Galeano, E. (1972). *Las venas abiertas de América Latina.* La Habana: Casa.

Garreton, M.A. (1983). *La cuestión nacional.* Santiago, Chile: ILET.

Gutierrez, L.H., & Romero, L.A. (1981). *Buenos Aires, 1920–1945: Una propuesta para el estudio de la cultura de los sectores populares* [Mimeo]. Buenos Aires, Argentina.

Laclau, E. (1978). *Política e ideologia en la teoria marxista.* Madrid: Siglo XXI.

Lechner, N. (Ed.). (1981). *Estado y política en América Latina.* Mexico: Siglo XXI.

Mattelart, A.M. (1986). *Penser les medias.* Paris: La Decourverte.

Monsivais, C. (1976). *Notas sobre la cultura mexicana en el Siglo XX.* Mexico: Historia General de México, Tomo 4, El Colegio de México.

Monsivais, C. (1981). Notas sobre el Estados, la cultura nacional y las culturas populares en México. *Cuadernos politicos,* No. 30, 25.

Monsivais, C. (1988). Interview. *Dia-logos de la comunicación,* No. 19, 76.

Novaes, A. (1983). *O nacional e o popular na cultura brasileira.* Sao Paulo: Brasiliense.

Palacios,, M. (1983). América Latina: Travesias hacía la nación moderna. *La unidad nacional en A.L.*

Pareja, R. (1984). *Historia de la radio en Colombia.* Bogotá, Colombia: S. de C.S.

Portantiero, J.C. (1981). *Lo nacional-popular y la alternative democrática en América Latina.* Lima, Peru: DESCO.

Ribeiro, D. (1977). *Las Américas y la civilización.* Mexico: Extemporaneos.

Richeri, G. (1985). Nuevas tecnologias e investigación sobre la comunicación de masas. In M. de Moragas (Ed.), *Sociología de la comunicación de masas.* Barcelona: Gustavo Gili.

Ricoeur, P. (1964). Civilisation universelle et cultures nationales. *Historic et verite.* Paris: Du Seuil.

Romero, J.L. (1982). *Las ideologias de la cultura nacional.* Buenos Aires: CEDAL.

Romero, J.L. (1983). *Latinoamérica: Las ciudades y las ideas.* Mexico: Siglo XXI.

Roncagliolo, R. (1982). *Comunicación transnacional: Conflicto político y cultural.* Lima Peru: Desco.

Schwarz, R. (1986). Nacional por sustración. *Punto de vista,* No. 28, 17.

Serrano, M.M. (1986). *La produción social de la comunicación.* Madrid: Alianza.

Sodré, M. (1981). *O monopolio de fala: Funcao e linguagen de televisao no Brasil.* Petrópolis: Vozes.

Squeff, E., & Wisnik, J.M. (1983). *O nacional e o popular na cultura brasileira - musica.* Sao Paulo: Brasiliense.

Sunkel, G. (1985). *Razón y pasión en la prensa popular*. Santiago, Chile: ILET.
Zermeño, S. (1972). *Estado y político en América Latina*. Mexico: Siglo XXI.

NOTES

[1] See on the origins of their project using Guatemala as an example, *La Patria Criollo*, Costa Rica, 1972.

[2] This was the case of Colombia (1984).

[3] The expression comes from Candido (1972, p. 335).

[4] This is the conclusion reached by Garreton (1983) in his analysis of the crisis of 1973.

[5] The media built on the groundwork laid by the education system in the provision of this daily experience of nationhood. A key text that provides a framework for this process and some specific national case studies is C. Braslavsky and J.C. Tedesco.

[6] Here we are basing ourselves on the analysis of Mattelart (1986, p. 165).

[7] On *mediation* as a theory of communication, see Serrano (1986).

[8] On the implications of this move for the field of culture, see J.J. Brunner (1985).

Chapter 8
Peripheral Mass Communication: Rich In Contradictions

Ullamaija Kivikuru

Finland is one of the dozen richest countries in the world, and the population of five million accordingly enjoys all the mass communication privileges of a post industrialized society: More than a hundred newspapers with a total circulation of some 2.3 million, a thousand and odd journals and magazines, a three-channel national television network, a four-channel national radio system, some tens of private local radio stations and cable companies, also carrying several satellite programs. There are thousands of book titles published annually, and the information rights of the Swedish-speaking minority are well protected. Since the beginning of the century, Finland has been among the first in Europe to adopt media novelties, starting with cinema and records, ending with cable and video.

Tanzania is one of the world's poorest countries. In this republic composed of mainland Tanzania and the island of Zanzibar, there are so far only two national daily papers with a combined circulation of less than 200,000 for the 22 million population. Radio is the main medium, but not all of its three services can be heard all over the country. There are 30–40 irregularly published journals, and private newspapers have emerged quite recently. A unique characteristic of Tanzania is rural papers—regional educational publications attached to literacy education. Television covers only Zanzibar, cinemas are found only in the biggest towns, but video has in recent years entered the media view of the affluent urban population. Some 85% of the population live in rural areas having access only to radio services. The media system of the country can be described by such epithets as scarce, urban, and highly educational.

Given such a striking difference, it seems unjustified to compare the two media systems, in short, *media vehicles* (Boyd-Barrett, 1977, pp. 120–125). Still, I am going to do exactly this and even suggest that in regards to media contents, poor Tanzania is in many ways better off than rich Finland. The two media systems reflect different stages and different tragedies in cultural peripheralism.

Peripheralism refers here to societies or cultures reflecting a real or perceived *dependence* position. Crucial for an *underdog* culture is a distinction between "us" and "them". Hence, a sense of *boundary* is a life-or-death question for any periphery. Further, a cultural periphery could be assumed to indicate more distinctly than core societies various dimensions and layers of locality in order to increase *internal cohesion*. What is meant by *locality* here is concrete or intellectual proximity: real or perceived common cultural denominators.

It is exactly the peripheral status that justifies discussing the two very different media vehicles here: rich, northern Finland, still carrying a vague peripheral legacy, and Tanzania, representing a more traditional *underdog* society.

In the following I am going to present four theses on these two media vehicles. More precisely, I set out my theses one by one, supporting my claims with empirical data. In the final pages I discuss the matter more generally.

THESIS ONE: GENUINE LOCALITY DWELLS IN SCARCITY

In many aspects, but not all, *the scant mass communication of Tanzania represents a higher degree of genuine locality and relevance than the abundant media system of Finland.* The main projection of Tanzanian mass communication is directed towards its own society and the "superstate" (Galtung, 1980, p. 267), in this case sub-Saharan Africa, which the periphery identifies itself with and takes its strength from. With the assistance of interpersonal communication, mass communication operates as a *"buffer zone" in nation building*, adding to the urban-oriented media system "hand-woven" elements originating from networks of traditional communication established centuries ago.

The present conventional mass communication system in Tanzania simultaneously reflects deliberate nation building and haphazard, inconsistent media practice. For the time being, Tanzanian news production is highly dependent on exogenously produced material, while the entertainment field is much more domestically oriented than the Finnish one (Table 1). Still, the weak news vehicle is today able to refocus the media content, though this is done in quite a crude way, via exclusion, ignoring considerable parts of the world, above all developments in Europe and North America. Just after independence, this was not the case. The Tanzanian media content reflected directly the biases of the international news-gathering networks. For example, Tanzania focused on Europe and the United States in the 1960s. Today the focus is distinctly on Black Africa. There are domestically and regionally operating mediations, either formal gates or informal systems of news priorities, which affect selection of media content and cause reorientation (Table 2).

However, the buffer-zone effect tends to weaken in those sectors of mass communication experiencing rapid growth. Entertainment media, film and video especially, have adopted an extremely commercial course in the country. Obviously, the present political liberalization will strengthen the private media considerably. Hence, the buffer zone could be only temporary, but presently it supports the weak existing mass communication and "patches" it. For example, Tanzanian mass communication is more urban-oriented than the Finnish, but locality

Table 1.   Foreign Material in Finnish & Tanzanian Mass Media, 1987

Medium	Finland	Tanzania
Newspaper	28	34
Radio news & current	45	50
Radio, all progr.	50–60	10
TV news & current	45	55(Z)
TV, all progr.	48	80–85 Z)
Cable	90	–
Video	90	100
Magazine	35–40	15–20
Book	16	50–55
Film	93	95–99
Local papers	3–5	3ND5
Foreign media		
–radio		100
–satellite	100	

Note: Crude figures, % of volume

Table 2.   Foreign News Projection, Tanzania, 1967–87

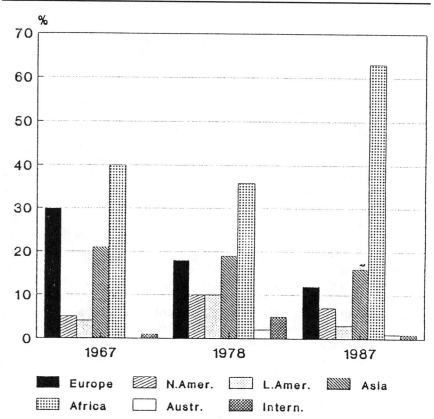

1967: 4 papers
1978: 2 papers
1987: 2 radio stations, 3 papers

is brought into the system partly via so-called traditional communication and orality embedded in it, partly via various mass organizations introduced by the present political order and carrying some key communication functions.

Oral communication operates as a fairly effective buffer zone. In fact, rituals, horns and drums, as well as narrations and *ngonjera* debates at the evening fire, carry an analogical function as the more recent layers of interpersonal communication: village meetings, branches of women's and youth organizations, or cooperatives which form the backbone of the economic life at the local level. The role of all these, as well as various local religious organizations, is to socialize an individual, to place him or her in the community.

There is no need to idealize these forms of interpersonal communication, however. *Only very few forms of oral communication are as such truly democratic and two-way by character*: The dominant social order is embedded even in the most colloquial gossiping at the marketplace or at the well. Still, oral communication does possess the potential for variation according to situational needs. This is a characteristic built in orality, and it feeds concrete locality into mass communication allowing adjustment of message substance according to individual needs, even in cases of communication following the one-way mode.

At the moment, the potential of the multiparty system is discussed not only among politicians, urban intellectuals, and the national media, but also among ordinary villagers on the slopes of Mount Kilimanjaro, 600 kilometers from Dar es Salaam and outside the direct reach of any mass media other than radio. In village offices and village meetings, the multiparty option is brought up. Radio has operated as a catalyst in these processes. Similarly, the multiparty system is debated in the Swahili daily in a localized media format: in *mashairi* poetry produced by ordinary members of the audience.

Though weak, the Tanzanian media vehicle is obviously able to adapt to issues found relevant by the ordinary people. The local opinion might also differ from the dominant opinion of the conventional media vehicle (Kivikuru, forthcoming). For example, the media have been leaning towards the multiparty option, while the dominant opinion in villages tends to be the opposite:

> Personally I prefer single party. Since we got independence in 1961 until today we've never faced any problems. Perhaps there are a few leaders who we can say are giving CCM (the revolutionary party) a bad image. But when it comes to human rights, I think we are doing well. Just look at Kenya, there has been a lot of chaos there, many people have died in demonstrations. Even those in opposition are not united there. Factions are what lead to fights between tribes and bring about a state of war in the country. You find a group of people fighting against another. Like the bandits in Mozambique. If the leadership is good, the one party system is good. if the leadership is bad, the people would opt for multi party. (Young male villager, Moivaro, Arusha region, in an in-depth interview)

> Chama Cha Mapinduzi (the revolutionary party) has brought peace to this country. Other nations with many parties are always fighting against each other. Look at South Africa, even before they get independence the parties have started fighting against one another. Why should we ask for problems? (Male teacher, Soni village, Tanga region, in an in-depth interview)

Why is the rural population concerned about the potential of political changes? Could this be interpreted as general interest in politics, partly instigated by the media? Partly perhaps, but the main reason is probably a personal concern about something that might look like uncertainty or insecurity about the future in a country which has been politically stable throughout its independence. The local administration is based on the single-party system, and so are the channels to central administration. In short, the news interest is closely linked with personal well-being.

In any case, the media vehicle in Tanzania is able to service people with information both on the multiparty issue, as well as on another theme, reflecting the African superstate orientation: interest in what is happening in South Africa. A considerable proportion of ordinary people in the same Northern villages were able, with only a 2–3 days' delay, to memorize details about the South African government's secret support to *Inkatha*. Many villagers also expressed concern about the double standard of the South African government. The news reached them, and they were able to form opinions based on it.

Naturally, this kind of behavior applies only to very few issues which have been on the ideological agenda for years and which are not only fed to the community by the media, but also by individual experiences of, say, racial inequality.

On the other hand, the oversized media apparatus of Finland tends to offer a wide spectrum of what could be called *surrogate rather than true locality*: Name and place-dropping plus personalization in news transmission, expressions of such commonly experienced feelings as love, hate, and jealousy in popular entertainment are redundantly presented by the mass media. It is entertainment especially that emerges as dominated by exogenously produced material and by endogenous material characterized by components of "reduced" locality such as generally shared emotions rather than historically particular and complex processes.

In news transmission, the view of the world is definitely more sophisticated and modified via domestic editing and selection in Finland than in Tanzania, though the agenda in Finland is still set by the transnational news agencies: The Finnish media report on issues brought to the news agenda by the international networks in news transmission. The present dominant orientation towards Europe, both Eastern and Western Europe, is a reflection of the changed focus of the international networks, though a considerable proportion of news material is produced at home by Finnish journalists. In fact, domestic gates tend to amplify rather than reduce, for example, the bias towards the industrialized world in news substance—*Reuters, AFP,* and *AP* devoted proportionally more space to the developing world than the dominant journalism does in Finland today. In the 1960s, Finnish media devoted more space to developments in Africa than today; this cannot be interpreted as an expression of genuine interest only, but also as a reflection of concern over decolonialization highlighted by the then-dominant international news agency supply (Table 3).

In a periphery, links between the media and the power structure are also close in a system which is predominantly based on private ownership. In Finland, the media system turned its focus distinctly to Europe in the mid-1980s at the cost, above all, of the developing world. This could be interpreted partly as a reflection of an all-European

Table 3. Foreign News Projection, Finland, 1961–87

1961: 16 dailies
1971, 1980,1987: TV, radio, 10 dailies

tendency, but the Finnish media reflect the trend in a classic peripheral manner: via projection to elite countries, via preference for political and economic elites, and elite authorities (Galtung & Ruge, 1973, p. 69). Simultaneously, this also indicates the close links between the media and the politicoeconomic power structure in a periphery, disregarding ownership form. The most recent example of this comes from Finland. Since the late 1980s, the whole media apparatus has turned towards the European community, but almost entirely via neutral news argumentation. First during the final stages of the political debate on the Finnish relationship to the European Community, opinionated journalism started to flourish to a larger extent. Obviously, the media system volunteered to give the political system some breathing space in its difficult task of forming a decision on the EC.

THESIS TWO: MAINSTREAM KILLS CORPUS

A desire to identify with the all-European superstate instead of any peripheral entity is manifested in the dominant form of Finnish mass communication. The sense of boundary, characteristic to "traditional" peripheralism, seems to weaken in the old periphery's mass communication content. However, the rich cultural spectrum of the European continent is hardly reflected in the Finnish media content. Instead, the Finnish media focus predominantly on the mainstream of European culture.

Wealthy Finland is in a far better position to foster peripheral autonomy than poor Tanzania, but the *mass media culture supports mainstreaming with the core culture and indifference to genuine locality and spontaneous creativity, especially in areas considered societally less essential, such as entertainment.* The proportion of domestically produced material in Finnish mass communication decreases steadily, though not radically fast. More and more assembly line produced transnational mass communication is imported, because even a rich periphery cannot afford to produce the enormous volume of media content needed for the oversized mass media vehicle of the Nordic country.

The most recent mass media, video and cable (see Table 1), depend most heavily on exogenous and transnational material, while the proportion of translations in book publishing is quite modest. Thus, the old medium, the book, is able to defend itself in locality questions quite well. Further, the Finnish media culture is becoming more and more one-sided: The proportion of Anglo-American material is grow-

ing especially in entertainment and feature-type ("non-news") categories, while the traditionally strong position of Sweden as a source is
weakening. Above all, this indicates that not even the richest cultural
peripheries are able to release themselves from the domination of big
production powers (Tables 4–7).

In television, film, and book publishing, as well as news transmission, sources of exogenous material are more diversified in Finland
than in Tanzania, but are still strongly dominated by material from
the Anglo-American world or, more precisely, material produced by
transnational or semi-transnational corporations operating predominantly in English. Interesting novelties representing the spontaneous

Table 4.   Top Projections of Non-News, Finland, April 1987

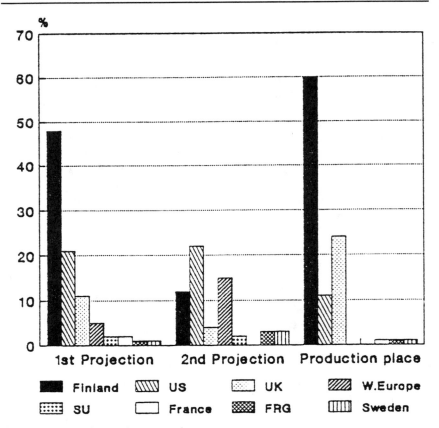

TV & 7 magazines, frequencies:
primary projections & origin

Table 5.   Origin of Literature Translations into Finnish, 1987

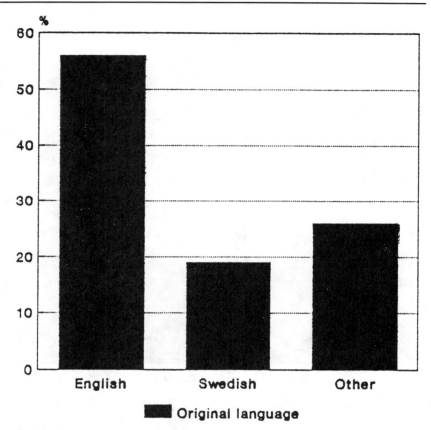

N = 8,700 titles, proportion of
translations 16 %

cultural production of, say, Denmark might not appear at all in the
Finnish media, if the big core media organizations in Central Europe
or the United States pay no attention to such novelties.

Further, cultural ties seem to be more persistently reflected in the
mass media than politicoeconomic ones. Though the Finnish media
have over the years devoted somewhat more attention to phenomena in
their gigantic nextdoor neighbor, the former Soviet Union, than most
European countries, the coverage given to it has been modest. Above
all, "soft" material from the former Soviet Union is still rare, though
its proportion has grown since the late 1980s. Again, it was not

Table 6.   Origins of Films Shown in Cinema Theatres, Finland, 1987

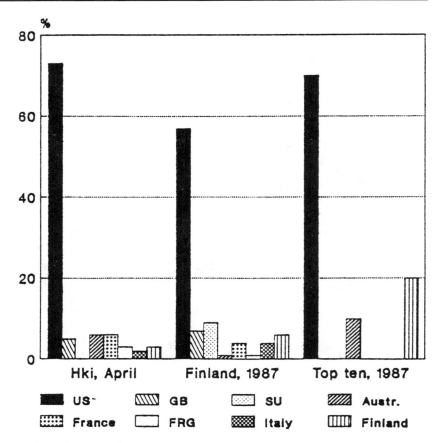

Based on frequencies

Finnish mass media which "discovered" the neighbor but, rather, the international news machinery became strongly interested in the political and societal changes there, and this change in news criteria was reflected in Finland also.

In fact, spontaneity, creativity, and genuine locality in the sense of togetherness and two-way communication are more frequently expressed outside than inside the conventional mass media in Finland: in amateur theater, pop concerts, and summer festivals.

In a way, this could be interpreted in more general terms as an embedded request for orality and two-way communication among

Table 7.   Origin of Pop Music Records, Finland, 1987

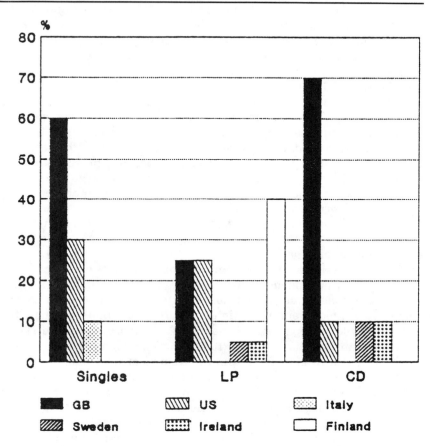

Based on Top Ten lists of sales

media users. *If mass communication content becomes too manufac-tured, too print- or assemblyline-oriented, the audience create spon-taneous channels of their own*—at least the most active components of the audience such as the young do. Could this be seen as a postmodern quest for *corpus*, the immediate, organized intimacy that is an inher-ent characteristic of oral communication?

Corpus indicates that no sharp distinction between senders and receivers is made in the communication act: the relationship is close and intimate, and the sender/initiator has general societal authority, not specific communication authority as such. This means that the communication process does not demand a high standard of professionalism. Though a *corpus* communication act requires organization, stiffness, and formality, it is conditioned by custom and tradition, not the communication practice as in conventional mass communication. Orality indicates a unique sense of time and, consequently, a specific form of causality: "Ancient things remain in the ear" as a Ghanaian proverb says (Kivikuru, 1990, pp. 49–50, 434–443).

However, news transmission seems to remain outside popular quests for corpus. Despite minor fluctuations, the news vehicle, once established, emerges as quite stiff and conservative, the distinction between the-knowledgeable-who-send and the ignorant-who-receive is marked; causalities follow conventional logic, and presentation formats are highly standardized. But this is true, to a large extent, also in Tanzania. This may mean that the basic problem adheres to the standardized format of news and, above all, its tight link to timeliness.

In short, the evidence from the two peripheries suggests that mass communication actually reinforces asymmetrical interdependence with two different cores.

The professional core is found abroad, in the big cultural centers. This dependence links peripheral mass communication to the international and transnational transmission networks. A rich periphery is able to enter multiple networks, but simultaneously this entrance links the peripheral media vehicle more and more closely with the transnational system. However, even a rich periphery rarely uses its wealth to gain from innovative pioneer developments in the field of international mass communication. Most often, mainstream networks are favored. The relationship is cruder in a poor periphery, hardly able to acquire enough basic services from abroad. A poor periphery has to go for the cheapest services, which often appear also as the most commercial and least interested in giving much attention to the needs of such peripheries. However, internal mechanisms in a poor periphery are more capable of controlling the gate for foreign influences, while the "oversized" media giant of wealthy peripheries is no longer easy to regulate with media policies.

The power core is endogenous, found within the periphery itself. This linkage transforms peripheral mass communication into one ideologically more alert than in the core and disregards the ownership structure, which naturally affects the media vehicle somewhat. The link to the power core appears more distinct in times of friction and political reorientation, especially the link with the professional core is nevertheless experienced more strongly by professionals, producing an obvious reluctance to acknowledge the existence of an established interdependence with the power structure.

This double interdependence obviously protects the media vehicle from oversized biases in either direction, but it also simultaneously makes the whole system stiff and inflexible, resistant to rapid changes. This linkage consequently prevents strengthening of cultural autonomy in rich peripheries such as Finland: Even *if the local power structure lacks potential and/or the will to control operations of the media vehicle, asymmetry in relation to the professional core drives the vehicle to similarity and increased synergy in content options.*

THESIS THREE: MEDIA PROFESSIONALISM BRINGS CONTRADICTIONS

My third thesis reads as follows: *Media professionalism appears frequently as a significant "killer" of genuine peripheral media culture, creativity, and innovativeness*, both in the rich North and poor South. In relation to core culture, media professionalism eagerly agrees to *modeling* endogenous cultural production according to exogenous patterns. The inverted pyramid structure of news is apparent also in African rural papers, though the intellectual atmosphere of Tanzanian villages can hardly be assessed as supporting the economic, squeezed, time-saving pyramid format. In Finland, "domestic" format novelties in television entertainment appear frequently. When scrutinized properly, they appear as modeled formats, though produced locally. Theodore L. Glasser has described the phenomenon quite accurately:

> Professionalism implies standardization and homogeneity; it accounts not for differences among journalists but for what journalists have in common. Professionalism effectively denies cultural differences by having us understand them as, to borrow a phase from Clifford Geertz, "ignorable differences, mere unlikeness." (Glasser, 1991)

Furthermore, because of the time-bound character of mass communication, any media vehicle tends to prefer routinized practices. The combined effect of the "ideology" of professionalism, the encouragement of an unquestioned adoption of core journalistic practices, and the tendency to routinized solutions means reinforcements of the *status quo* and resistance to change. In weak peripheral cultures, this characteristic is less marked than in wealthy ones, which are in principle more apt to multiplicity and variation in cultural production. It seems probable that peripheral mass communication also tends to attach itself to the mainstream of core journalism rather than to its *avant-garde* forms. Thus, the tendency toward professional uniformity accelerates in an underdog culture.

Simultaneously, however, media professionalism also offers tools for cultural self-defense and spontaneous forms of authentic cultural production. Through increased and acknowledged professionalism, journalists are able to increase their integrity in relation to the power structure. Professionalism gives due credibility to this form of cultural production and, indirectly, the whole field of culture gains more operational space.

In other words, *media professionalism is a deeply contradictory concept.* It might be worth reconsidering the reflections of Peter Golding (1977) and Oliver Boyd-Barrett (1977) at the early stage of the Great Media Debate. Could it be that the determining factors reinforcing media mainstreaming, stereotyping, and dependence are not found in hardware imbalances, but in the software side, in the minds of the professionals identifying rather with their colleagues in the core than with their fellow citizens? Naturally, the hardware and the software are interlinked, but the software side deserves due attention. Media professionals, more than many other intellectuals, seem to volunteer in *cultural bridgeheading*: Elite groups in a periphery share the interests and values of the core culture, disregarding their suitability in the peripheral circumstances. Elements of cultural familiarity and locality could simply be added in stereotyped transnational contents via domesticated forms of cultural production such as modeling (Galtung, 1971, pp. 81–117).

The tendency toward professional mainstreaming appears more frequently in a wealthy industrialized periphery such as Finland, because cultural professions in general are distinct and specialized there. Further, the whole media apparatus and the professionals running it are assessed as more significant by the societal set-up. In Tanzania, media professionalism adopts quite crude forms of modeling. Modeling favors more sophisticated forms of operation in Finland, but the strength of modeling as such has not decreased.

In summary, media practice and journalistic culture appear as crucial qualities affecting mass communication content as well as media infrastructures and media policies, but these two components of professionalism have been minimized or totally ignored in the debate on imbalances and biases in recent years. Media professionalism emerges as a phenomenon giving support to *Anthony Giddens's* elaborations on societal practice as a complex compilation of convergent individual subjects and infrastructures conditioned by context, time, and locality (Giddens, 1984, p. 2).

The understanding of media professionalism as one of the key elements reinforcing the *status quo* in mass communication links the media vehicle in a natural way with both locality and the particular history of the society the vehicle is operating in; difficulties in bringing about changes become more easily explicable.

THESIS FOUR: MEDIA VEHICLE CARRIES LEGACIES OVER TIME

It can therefore be hypothesized that *mass communication frequently operates as a conservative societal force: All changes other than nonrestricted growth of media volume take place slowly, and the particular legacies of the past could be read in the forms and operations of the media vehicle*, even in cases where deliberate communication policies have been designed to change the situation. The vehicle easily adapts to rapid growth if no regulation is exercised, limiting the potential to control the operation of the vehicle in other sectors of the vehicle.

Even such simple quantitative data as lists of most favored news projections of the two peripheries (Table 8) give evidence of the tie to history. The "preference spheres" of Finland and Tanzania are different, reflecting both peripheral introversion and simple geographical proximity and the particular history of each country.

Introversion is expressed in the high level of interest given to the periphery itself in relation to other nations, proximity being preferen-

Table 8.   Top Foreign News Projections, Finland and Tanzania 1987

Finland	Tanzania
United States	Tanzania
Finland	South Africa
Soviet Union	Kenya
United Kingdom	United States
Sweden	Zambia
FRG	Zimbabwe
France	SriLanka
Japan	Algeria
Italy	Uganda
Israel	Soviet Union
Chile	India
South Africa	United Kingdom

Note: All media, text, based on frequencies.

tially given to nextdoor neighbors. In the case of Finland, various layers of cultural history are reflected in such features as the stable preference status given to the former Soviet Union and Sweden plus the Federal Republic of Germany, but above all in the deliberate overall turn towards the West—this was an ideological decision made as early as the 19th century. Today it is reflected in cultural preferences which are in clear contradiction to mere geographical proximity: The Anglo-American sphere is preferred because it is interpreted as representing western values in a superior way. Similarly, in the case of Tanzania, prominence in news attention given to former British colonies in Africa cannot be explained by geographical proximity alone. It is also the shared past that increases news interest. On the other hand, newly attained independence adds controversial flavor to the attention given to the United Kingdom: The former colonial masters are part of Tanzanian history and so deserve due media attention ranging from politics to sports. Simultaneously, however, the bitterness of this historical link is frequently reflected; the United Kingdom remains on the outer sphere of news attention only (Table 8).

In the case of Tanzania, the entertainment market expresses a much higher level of cultural introversion than in Finland. This in turn increases the volume of concrete locality in the Tanzanian media vehicle, while the situation in Finland is the opposite. It is the entertainment section that most frequently prefers surrogate forms of locality, indefinite by origin.

Thus, each peripheral media vehicle seems to carry features of its unique history with it; *affluence and deliberate media policies do have their effect, but the legacy of history remains strong.* In Finland, the present media vehicle is based on the press that was established in the 18th century, when the country still was part of Sweden. In Tanzania a similar characteristic can be found in the dominant journalistic culture. So far, Tanzanian journalism has been characterized by such epithets as formal, authority-oriented, and top-down. The same features characterized the *gazeti journalism* in the colonial period. Though media policies have been changed, the professional ideology seems quite persistent.

Similarly, the structure of, say, *Radio Tanzania Dar es Salaam* greatly resembles the *BBC*. On the other hand, nonrestricted growth tends to lead to an even more asymmetrical development. In Finland, the hunt for media novelties has neither much to do with the basic functions of mass media nor freedom of expression. The population is offered a multilayer network of mass media offering predominantly identical content preferences: The media vehicle tends to establish, on top of each other, formats following the same pattern. In Tanzania, rapid growth of film and video markets could be interpreted as a reflection of a growing hunger for entertainment. This has led to a situation where the cheapest possible material is acquired to supply the need. After a while the function of, say, video may be viewed in light of past experiences: Video is simply seen as a means to bring "modern," exogenously produced entertainment to urban populations.

In sum, special attention should be given to the historical nature of the communication vehicle. Previous layers of infrastructures, policies, and practices affect newly designed policies. It is natural, then, to accept that colonial or peripheral practices lag in disappearing from the media vehicle. But do they disappear from the production of cultural meanings as well? People are structured into certain social positions given the historic development of institutions, but due attention should be allowed for the individual meaning formation as well.

MISINTERPRETED IMBALANCE?

The cases of Finland and Tanzania do not fit well into the standard explanations given by research into mass communication flows, or, to be more exact, the mainstream research of this sector originating in the 1970s. A distinct *pendulum movement characterizes the debate on international mass communication flows.* In the late 1960s and the 1970s, the great concern was the North/South imbalance and what was called "transnationalization of culture": Americanization, homogenization, and cultural imperialism (e.g., Sunkel & Fuenzalida, 1979). In the 1980s, the scientific discussion has been dominated by conceptualization of a global culture. This conceptualization has not been interested in homogenization, but signs and levels of *quasi* and true cosmopolitanism, diversity, and richness in various discourses (Featherstone, 1990, p. 2). This kind of polarization could prove fruitful in scientific discourse, but in actual fact, it has not turned out that way so far.

For example, some interesting thoughts about *popularity* and democracy have been expressed (Schiller, 1989), but not elaborated further. Maybe imbalance and transnationalization, after all, represent a slight improvement from the standpoint of the popular masses. Mass communication respecting national borders has only rarely been democratic by nature, and total exclusion from information flows could hardly be propagated as an ideal condition, either.

Further, the thrilling new *reception research* has only recently touched on dependence thinking (e.g., Mattelart & Mattelart, 1990). If one goes to the basics the perception of the receiver in dependence research represents a crude form of the old bullet theory: When exposed to large volumes of transnationalized mass communication, people are assumed to reject their endogenous culture and adopt a new one without hesitation. There is quite a long way toward the concept of active audiences!

In fact, the discussion about the acknowledged North/South imbalance of information has still explicitly concentrated on quantities. No doubt the Great Media Debate started with reflections on quality of media content on the South, but it transferred quite soon to demands for action to construct and improve media structures in the developing world. Such a course of discussion easily leads to oversimplifications.

The first doubtful implication is that *with increased quantities, the quality of existing mass communication in the South is also going to improve, that is, become more versatile and pluralistic.* This standpoint could no doubt be defended if elaborated accordingly, but there is no automatic equation between volume and multiplicity as the case of Finland demonstrates. With a range of various mass communication forms available, the spectrum of media contents could be assumed to increase, but knowing the well-documented tendency toward main-streaming of contents and formats in the North (e.g., Altheide, 1985), the bulk of media content could be characterized as standardized rather than varied. In its straightforward form, the implication appears quite inconsistent with the mainstreaming and transna-tionalization thesis, claiming without elaboration that a large volume automatically brings substantial variations.

The second and perhaps more crucial implication is that *mass communication appears as a simple ahistorical compilation of media structures and deliberate communication policy actions,* ignoring the cultural dimension which has been repeatedly elaborated in the writings of the "third generation" development communication re-search (e.g., Jayaweera, 1987; Servaes, 1986; Wang & Dissanayake, 1984; Hartman et al., 1989).

According to the second implication, imbalances of information can be "rectified" simply with money, training and human will. Tragic evidence on the actual practice in the South cannot be explained only by reference to a lack of resources. Obviously, new elements introduced to southern media vehicles have strengthened nation-level mass com-munication, but also weakened existing mass communication net-works such as oral media in Tanzania. Southern peripheries may have been brought into the international interdependence system in the news sphere, but the biases of that interdependence have become sharper than ever.

Imbalances should not be sought only in the South. The intriguing and complex character of asymmetrical interdependence, as reflected in such a specific field as mass communication, may be more distinctly detected in the media vehicles of affluent northern peripheries. Multiplicity in channels reinforces growth of volume, while true multiplicity and relevance of content could actually be weaker than in the South.

Evidence has been found in several peripheries that people under asymmetrical cultural interdependence tend to favor more culturally proximate material in mass communication if there is a choice (e.g., Straubhaar, 1991, pp. 50–55). The problem lies in the fact that peripheral media vehicles tend to develop into a direction without offering a choice. the media vehicle prefers to produce new versions of books, films, or television series which have been popular earlier domestically, and to import material from a few well-known sources via a few well-known channels. In short, the system tends to operate against its own interests.

This type of argumentation is too particularistic to be covered by theoretical formulations only and too elaborate to be proved simply via figures and percentages as perceived imbalances of media volume and projection. The third implication consequently concerns methodology: *Research on imbalances and dependencies has so far been dominated by either highly theoretical considerations or compilations of quantitative data.* This dichotomy is not very fruitful in the case of peripheral mass communication, because the complexity of the phenomenon and its history-bound particularity requires a combination of both theory and data.

PLACING THE NATION, WRITING THE NATION?

Though recent research has indicated tendency to label geographical locality as a somewhat old-fashioned concept in the modern world of mobile populations with fluctuating origins, an implicit linkage between locality and nationality is still easily found in texts advocating global culture. Despite all fashionable talk about global culture, homemade mass communication seems to be preferred, because it is valued for its cultural identity. The world is still characterized by competing ethnonational cultures rather than a wider pan-nationalism.

Endogenously produced material is still considered as offering more "identification poles" (Desaulniers, 1987, p. 122) for receivers: Receivers in Finland and Tanzania are supposed to feel more at home with events, individuals, and processes which mass communication presents as manifestations of physical proximity. Accordingly, quantitative content analysis has been assessed as a practical tool, able to indicate proportions of domestic and foreign media content in the form of crude but clear-cut percentages. If the proportion of domestic material is identifiably low, there is room for concern about national culture being endangered.

The locality connection is, however, far more complex. As Homi Bhabha has said, no modern community is any longer purely horizontal, based only on geographical closeness. Simultaneously, no modern community lacks the horizontal locality totally (Bhabha, 1990b, pp. 296–299). Raymond Williams elaborated on the same equation via two interrelated concepts, *native* and *nation*:

> "Nation" as a term is radically connected with "native". We are *born* into relationships which are typically settled in a place. This form of primary and "placeable" bonding is of quite fundamental human and natural importance.
>
> Yet the jump from that to anything like the modern nation-state is entirely artificial. (Williams, 1983, p. 5)

The basic function of locality could be considered simply as promoting either *societal competence* or *societal motivation*. Societal competence stands for legitimation of societal frames and generates ideology (stress on cohesion building), while increased motivation might also mean venturing to break the established frames in search of new relevant forms of societal activity (stresses on cohesion breaking).

Consequently, the basis for selecting locality elements varies for situational and historical reasons. If there is a societal need for strengthening the sense of boundary—in short, *a need for strengthening vertical ties in cultural activity* as in the case of Finland considering membership of the European Community—a combination of abstract and concrete identification poles is used for legitimization of the planned action. These elements are linked into consistent *causal relationships and manifested in cultural products* such as journalistic work. Journalism molds the material into agendas and legalized forms of argumentation ("Our agriculture is going to lose much, but in order to save the Finnish folk home, we have to join the European Community"). A bonding strategy is developed to alert members of the society to the significance of togetherness ("We have to go through this as a unified nation"). Hence, a vertical activity cannot exist without a horizontal dimension. People must feel that the cause is theirs, and worth the labor and sacrifice.

In forms of *horizontal cultural activity, the contradictory elements of locality dominate.* People in Tanzanian villages most want information about and cooperation with their neighbor villages, but they also want to be better than their neighbors, in farming as well as in *ngoma* dancing or production of a village paper. Sophisticated distinctions in, say, "their *ngoma*" and "our *ngoma*" are elaborated and debated.

Cultural identity advocates creativity, participation, and variation of cultural activity, but this dimension does not exist without a dose of verticality and cohesion: Multiplicity requires a base of uniformity to depart from. In the case of Tanzanian indigenous culture, the existence of verticality can be detected in, say, the fact that it is the generally acknowledged *ngoma* that villagers are eager to compete in, while there is a noticeable reluctance to talk about *kibukis* (bad spirits), which also are a very vivid part of the indigenous culture, but not favored by the present societal system.

Hence, a prerequisite for cohesive national culture and national identity is *cultural identity, standing for spontaneity, creativity, and variety. National culture and cultural identity are interrelated, but they operate also as each other's opposites.* This also makes understandable the close connection between peripheral culture and peripheral power structure. Quite understandably, the power structure prefers the dimension of national culture and its cohesion-building elements. The form of ownership of the media vehicle plays a role here, but private media obviously also assess cohesion as a useful tool, a prerequisite for smooth societal operations.

MISINTERPRETED FREEDOM?

The two examples of peripheries indicate here two different phases of cultural identity seeking. Both media systems tend to lean towards professional mainstreaming and societal competence rather than creativity and true participation. I see the origin of the problem basically in *the imbalance between intellectual resources and disproportionate growth of the media vehicle*—a clear misinterpretation of freedom of expression. Sheer increase in the volume is assessed as an indication of increased freedom of expression.

In Finland, there is no specific societal need to emphasize cultural identity for the time being. Multilayer tendencies to stress uniformity embedded in the society allow space for only occasional outbursts of cultural identity. The middle-of-the-road culture dominates the picture. A sense of cohesion and order is exaggerated by both decision makers and professionals, and the infrastructures are a manifestation of the same exaggeration. The sheer size of the media vehicle requires controlled, fluent operation.

In Tanzania, national identity is still strongly stressed, however, and the "natural" societal environment offers a fairly good basis for nation making: slight tribal differences, one dominant language, and fairly stable political system.

It is predominantly in the name of national pride that, for example, pressures to introduce television have been brought to hear. In Africa, there are only two other countries (Botswana, Malawi) without television, so that Tanzanian nation building is disgraced by not having one, though on a practical level, the decision is going to mean increased international content and a decrease in resources available for domestic production of any form of mass communication. The ongoing liberalization of cultural policies is probably going to lead to occasional outbursts of national culture: haphazard, inconsistent demands for control and cohesion. The majority of mass communication will flow quite capriciously, without proper organization. For the time being, this capriciousness is an "insurance policy" against too much emphasis on cohesion building, but with a rapid expansion of conventional mass communication in sight, similar demands for order and fluency as in Finland might strengthen.

The Tanzanian case is tragic. There is a fairly solid intellectual basis for versatile cultural activities such as mass communication. There is more political operation space than ever before for versatile mass communication. There is a distinct need for expansion of mass media, especially in the fast-growing urban centers. The technology to link even the remote villages in modern mass communication networks does exist, and there are at least foreign funds available to acquire that technology. Still, what is actually happening in the country is not the expansion of true, spontaneous intellectual mobility, but the opening ceremony for a port for products from the discount racks of transnational mass communication industries.

A periphery is in principle privileged because peripheries yield more easily than metropolises, what Agnes Heller calls *"cultural surplus"* (Heller, 1988). Quite naturally, a passion for cultural surplus; that is, creativity, spontaneity, and relevance, starts from a position of inferiority rather than of superiority. However, the *basic operational form of a cultural periphery is reaction*: reaction to the core, reaction to domestic power policies, and delayed and cautious action, if any. This verticality of intellectual activity influences the specified field of mass communication quite crudely, most frequently via a phenomenon which is misleadingly interpreted as *professionalism*. In true professionalism, there is always space for continuous struggle against routines and criticism of dominant practices. This contradiction between creativity and routines restricts the scope of peripheral mass communication, more so if the societal system is well organized and structured as in affluent peripheries.

In the journalistic practice, the locality turns into poles of cultural identification, and they express themselves in hierarchies of taste and ways of life, composing finally what is called "Europeanness" and "Finnishness," or "Africaness" and "Tanzanianness," for example. An individual finds himself in a discursive relationship with these manifestations of "accepted" locality mediated by the cultural institutions and the mass media. The media operate as "value harbors" freezing manifestations of locality into stereotyped meanings. Identity exists only if people under its umbrella feel it to be so and accept these interpretations of meanings.

The mechanism of establishing cultural identification poles is in principle very similar to the realms of national and cultural identity; only the emphasis varies. Cultural identity allows multiplicity and contradiction, while national identity stands for cohesion and order. Quite naturally, mass communication, because of its tight link to timeliness, routines, and organized production and distribution, respects national identify more.

Does all this then simply mean that there is no space for true locality, true motivation and participation in conventional mass communication in peripheries? Is mass communication actually only a trick through which the citizens are put into their proper places; given a shared history and present, an accepted set of tools to cope with an accepted set of accepted problems?

If one analyses the mass communication vehicle alone, one could be tempted to answer "yes." From this limited scope, mass communication at best appears as a catalyst for genuine thinking and creativity taking place outside the media vehicle and, at worst, it emerges as a misleader or a tool for oppression and passivity.

But a vehicle is useless without passengers. It is the receivers who actually create the function for the media. They are the ones who bring flexibility, disorder, and even anarchy into the operation of the communication vehicle, however fixed its routines seem to be. As Karol Jakubowicz (1988) has stated, the majority of people are happy with their role as mere receiver, they do not demand the right to communicate as such. Still, they are active in their relationship with the media; they are far from an obedient mass. They ignore, they select, they compare media substance with their immediate surroundings; they might dance around the identification poles, but they make the melodies for the dance themselves. They are tolerant, but if the identification poles appear repeatedly outdated or irrelevant, they desert the vehicle. The power of the popular taste is real.

It is easy to agree in principle with the above argument, but we fail to see the depth of its implications. Quite frequently a discourse on mass communication turns into a cliché formula if the sophisticated surface is swept away; Big Brother still wants to inform, educate, and entertain the helpless, passive receivers. Big Brother might be indigenous or exogenous, but his mind tends to remain the same. Media research should finally accept the intellectual challenge to rid itself of that cliché.

We should, however, try to catch the real implications. We should realize that Big Brother is not only a straightforward evil, easy to point a finger at, such as a restrictive political system or endless poverty, but something trickier, more devious: the media vehicle itself. The Big Brother element is built into the media system and the concept of professionalism in such a hideous way that it is difficult to grasp.

Still, we should make an attempt. The broad frame of my argument here is based on a study done a couple of years ago. Its title suggests my line of thought on peripheral mass communication: "Tinned Novelties or Creative Culture?" The more I have thought about the issue since the completion of study, the more convinced I have become that if Big Brother in the media vehicle is not revealed, more and more emphasis will be placed in media substance on the first part of the phrase and, above all, the first word. Just tins.

REFERENCES

Altheide, D. (1985). *Media power*. Beverly Hills: Sage.

Bhabha, H. (1990a). Introduction: Narrating the nation. In H. Bhabha (Ed.), *Nation and narration* (pp. 1–7). London/New York: Routledge.

Bhabha, H. (1990b). DissemiNation: Time, narrative, and the margins of the modern nation. In H. Bhabha (Ed.), *Nation and narration* (pp. 291–322). London/New York: Routledge.

Boyd-Barrett, O. (1977). Media imperialism: Towards an international framework for the analysis of media systems. In J. Curran, M. Gurewitch, & J. Woollacott (Eds.), *Mass communication and society* (pp. 116–135). London: Arnold and Open University Press.

Brennan, T. (1990). The national longing for form. In H. Bhabha (Ed.), *Nation and narration* (pp. 44–70). London/New York: Routledge.

Burgelmann, J.-C., (1988, June 24–28). *Structuring cultural identity by forecasting a policy on communication technology: The need of a complementary politico-sociological approach.* Paper presented at the 16th Conference of International Association for Mass Communication Research (IAMCR), Barcelona, Spain.

Desaulniers, J.-P. (1987). What does Canada want? L'histoire sans lecon. *Media, Culture and Society, 9*, 149–157.

Featherstone, M. (1990). Global culture: An introduction. In M. Featherstone (Ed.), *Global culture: Nationalism, globalization and modernity* (pp. 1–14). London/Newbury Park/New Delhi: Sage.

Galtung, J. (1971). A structural theory of imperialism. *Journal of Peace Research, 7*, 81–117.

Galtung, J. (1980). *The true worlds. A transnational perspective.* New York: The Free Press.

Galtung, J., & Ruge, M. H. (1973). Structuring and selecting news. In S. Cohen & J. Young (Eds.), *The manufacture of news. Deviance, social problems and the mass media* (pp. 62–72).

Giddens, A. (1984). *Yhteiskuntateorian keskeisiä ongelmia: Toiminnan, rakenteen ja ristiriidan käsitteet yhteiskunta-analyysissä (Core problems of societal theory: Concepts of action, structure and contradiction in societal analysis).* Keuruu: Otava.

Glasser, T. L., (1990, August 10). *Professional knowledge and the ideals of a liberal education: Taking diversity seriously.* Paper presented at the AEJ Convention, Boston.

Golding, P. (1977). Media professionalism in the Third World: The transfer of ideology. In J. Curran & M. Gurewitch & J. Woolacott (Eds.), *Mass communication and society* (pp. 291–308). London: Arnold and Open University Press.

Hartman, P., Patil, B.R., & Dighe, A. (Eds.). (1989). *The mass media and village life: An Indian study.* New Delhi/Newbury Park/ London: Sage.

Heller, A. (1988). L'Europe, un epilogue? *Lettre Internationale.*

Jakubowicz, K. (1988). *The New information and communication technologies and democratization of communication.* Paper presented at the 16th IAMCR conference Barcelona.

Jayaweera, N. (1987). Rethinking development communication: A holistic view. In N. Jayaweera & S. Amunugama (Eds.), *Rethinking development communication* (pp. 76–94). Singapore: AMIC.

Kivikuru, U. (1990). *Tinned novelties or creative culture? A study on the role of mass communication in peripheral nations.* Publication 1F/10/90. Helsinki, Finland: University of Helsinki, Department of Communication.

Kivikuru, U. (forthcoming). *The changing media view of Tanzanian villages.* Helsinki, Finland: Finnish National Commission for Unesco Series.

Mattelart, A., & Mattelart, M. (1990). *The carnival of images.* New York: Bergin & Garvey.

Schiller, H. (1989, April 11–13). *Farewell to cultural sovereignty.* Paper presented at a conference on "Television, Entertainment and National culture—The Canada-U.S. Dilemma in a Broader Perspective." Quebec, Canada.

Servaes, J. (1986). Cultural identity and the mass media in the Third World. *Third Channel, II,* 299–316.

Straubhaar, J. (1991). Beyond media imperialism: Assymetrical interdependence and cultural proximity. *Critical Studies in Mass Communication, 8*(1), 39–59.

Wang, G., & Dissanayake, W. (Eds.). (1984). *Continuity and change in communication systems. An Asian perspective.* Norwood, NJ: Ablex.

Williams, R. (1983). *The year 2000.* New York: Pantheon.

Part III
Regional and Transnational Developments

Chapter 9
NWICO Strategies and Media Imperialism: The Case of Regional News Exchange

Oliver Boyd-Barrett, with the collaboration of Daya Kishan Thussu

MEDIA IMPERIALISM REVISITED

In the context of writing about media in cross-cultural contexts for an Open University course in 1977, I defined *media imperialism* as "the process whereby the ownership, structure, distribution or content of the media in any one country are singly or together subject to substantial external pressures from the media interests of any other country or countries without proportionate reciprocation of influence by the country so affected (Boyd-Barrett, 1977, p. 117).

Part of my intention at the time was to concentrate attention on media rather than on culture or political economy, because I felt that what was most needed was a much more substantial empirical base of information and analysis of international media, before further attempts were made to integrate them into broader theoretical frameworks. I was reacting to an ongoing debate about the transnational media that I perceived to be overrhetorical and founded too much on assertion rather than substance.

A significant limitation of my definition, if taken on its own, was that it appeared to focus the field of investigation on the interaction of influences among media systems, and to marginalize the direct influence of nonmedia interests on media systems. It also appeared to exclude consideration of the diversity of audiences and audience interpretations. By specifically talking in terms of "country," my definition may also have seemed to accept, unintentionally, a framework of nation states as the only meaningful units of analysis, when of course the phenomenon it addressed could also be interrogated through alternative concepts such as center-periphery or metropolitan-rural. My choice of words, finally, with reference to "external pressures," perhaps suggested an inclination to the "conspiracy" rather than the "cultural absorption" approach to media imperialism.

Many of these qualifications were in fact present in my discussion about media imperialism across a number of publications, within one of which I had proffered my provisional definition. Thus, many of the doubts signposted 14 years later by Sreberny-Mohammadi (1991) were in fact recognized almost from the beginning of the debate, for example, concerns to do with the cultural complexity of the "victim" countries; recognition that media imperialism was not just about media relations between rich and poor countries but about relations between some of the rich countries themselves; the scope for national governments to control media imports; scepticism about the assumed "purity" of "traditional" cultures many of which had for long been "contaminated"; scepticism also about the absence of anything positive in the literature about cross-cultural media influence to set against all its alleged negative consequences; acknowledgment of important centers of media production and exportation in the Third World and which were run very much along capitalist lines; and recognition of the complexity and multiplicity of audience "readings."

I believe my original definition did serve a purpose, nevertheless. It suggested, and was meant to suggest, that here was a phenomenon to do with inequality of available media services, one which could usefully be addressed on its own terms, as well as in combination with broader terms such as *cultural imperialism* or *neoimperialism* (I had linked the concept of "media imperialism" to classical Marxist and neo-Marxist accounts of imperialism elsewhere—see Boyd-Barrett, 1977b). The definition did indicate by implication that media imperialism may be a matter of degree, and that it might differentially affect different elements of media systems.

I adopted this approach some time later (Boyd-Barrett, 1981–1982), when I stated that "the issue of Western media penetration of other countries requires analysis of a very wide range of variables or dimensions" and then proceeded to identify the dimensions involved in an analysis of the major Western-based international news agencies. I suggested likely variables for each key dimension and assessed the available evidence in relation to these variables. The three key dimensions concerned (a) the extent to which the media in a country are dependent upon services imported from and provided by the major news agencies, (b) the extent to which the nondomestic activities of the major news agencies are affected by factors in the control of national governments or other indigenous powers within a client area, and (c) the extent to which the content of the major news services can be said culturally, politically, morally, or in any other way to be "alien" to their clienteles.

Here and elsewhere (e.g., Boyd-Barrett, 1981–1982), I attached considerable weight to the significance of indigenous media and nonmedia attempts to promote local alternatives to the transnationals and in other ways to reduce their likely influence. In this I was influenced by a variety of considerations.

There were those chapters in Tunstall's influential *The Media Are American* (Tunstall, 1977), which recounted the development of independent or semi-independent media production and export centers in the Third World. Might not such centers in time become a great deal more influential? Secondly, there was the "great UNESCO debate" itself, the debate of the New World Information and Communication Order, and the initiatives to which it contributed in the world of news flow, most notably the establishment of the Non-Aligned News Agencies Pool as well as various regional news exchanges. These experiences again suggested that strong forces were at work in the LDCs, which could at least contain the influence of Western media systems and perhaps even push back the market territory they controlled. Finally, I was influenced by the psychology of the time, the political psychology of a pre-Thatcherite U.K. in seemingly terminal industrial decline, accelerated by OPEC control of the price of oil, and requiring IMF rescue, a climate in which it sounded merely arrogant to continue talking so self-assuredly about differences between "first" and "third" worlds. Contributing to that psychological climate was the role of a post-Vietnam U.S.A. involved eternally and uncomfortably in Middle Eastern and other Third World imbroglios that seemed only to highlight the relative powerlessness of that nuclear "superpower."

News Exchange Mechanisms (NEMs)

Given this background and the centrality of "news flow" issues in many debates about media imperialism, it was appropriate that I should be given a chance to put to the test my hypothesis of regionally generated resistance to domination by Western transnational corporations—in the context of news agencies and one decade further on. The main conclusion that I draw from this opportunity is that, while there may have been a proliferation of news-exchange initiatives, and that some positive benefits have been derived from these, the overall importance of the Western transnationals has not been reduced. This conclusion is drawn, not so much from an analysis of the transnationals themselves, but from an analysis of the structural and other weaknesses which seriously cripple the development of NEMs. Some of these weaknesses are perhaps intrinsic to the particular ways in which certain NEMs have been organized, and which perhaps can be remedied, but other weaknesses are an inevitable reflection of the deep and continuing economic inequalities between economically powerful and economically weak societies. It is ironic that with the discrediting of Marxist-Leninism as a basis for political action in the 1990s, it is precisely the 1970s framework of political economy that may have offered the soundest prognosis of international news markets.

I was invited to write the final version of a UNESCO study of recently established international and regional news exchanges, based on reports around the world by field officers and consultants. It was intended that these would contribute to future collaboration between UNESCO and emerging information networks in the Third World. A version of this report is published by John Libbey (London) (Boyd-Barrett & Thassu, 1992). NEMs covered in the survey included both international news exchange mechanisms such as the Non-Aligned New Agencies Pool (NANAP), Broadcasting Organisations of the Non-Aligned Countries (BONAC), Inter Press Service (IPS), and regional exchange mechanisms including Pan-African News Agency (PANA), Union of National Radio and Television Organisations of Africa (URTNA), Asia-Pacific News network (ANN), Asia-Pacific Broadcasting Union Television News Exchange (ASIAVISION), Pacific News Exchange (PACNEWS), Latin American Special Information Services (ALASEI), Latin American and Caribbean Broadcasting Union (ULCRA), and Caribbean News Agency (CANA), and others.

The surveys examined the objectives, organization, ownership, services, and clients of the various agencies and exchange mechanisms. An evaluation of the achievements and limitations of the news exchange mechanisms was undertaken to identify ways in which performance could be improved. The reports from the NEMs were analysed in a comparative framework. The surveys were based on existing studies, reports and other available material. Limited original research was undertaken.

CONTEXT

The NWICO Debate

What was the origin of NEMs and in particular of the NEMs covered in the UNESCO survey? The need to identify and correct the imbalance in the existing patterns of global information flows led to considerable debate in the 1970s within UNESCO, the Non-Aligned Movement and other international arenas. UNESCO itself had acted as catalyst to such a debate from the time of its 1953 publication, *The Flow of News*, and through its support of many bilateral news exchange arrangements between national news agencies. In its 1970s resuscitation, the debate addressed the need to accomplish a change from vertical (North-South) to horizontal (South-South) communication flows in international news. The first-ever instrument devoted by UNESCO to this end was the Media Declaration adopted in 1978. The NWICO debate culminated in the creation of an international commission on information and communication headed by Sean MacBride, and this endorsed the need for a NWICO in its 1980 report, *Many Voices One World* (International Commission, 1980). These developments contributed to an alleged 'politicization' of UNESCO, forming the pretext for the withdrawal of the U.S. and U.K. from UNESCO in 1984 and 1985. A further outcome was the creation within UNESCO of the International Programme for Development of Communications (IPDC), employing an essentially technocratic approach to communication development in the Third World. This program has supported international news exchange mechanisms such as the Broadcasting Organization of the Non-Aligned Countries (BONAC).

The Global News System

The emergence of NEMs from among the LDCs may be seen as an explicit attempt to break from an entrenched pattern of news dependency. The global news system has a long-established history that reaches back to the mid-19th century. The system involves a complex pattern of unequal exchange relationships between large transnational agencies and regional and national agencies. Thus the patterns of news flow are linked to the politics and economics of Western-based transnationals (Boyd-Barrett, 1980; Smith, 1980).

In the existing global news system, there remains a quantitative North-South imbalance between the volume of news and information flowing from the developed to the developing world and the volume of flow in the opposite direction. Most of the world news flow emanates from major transnational agencies (these include the "big four" news agencies—AP, UPI, Reuters, and AFP—and the world's largest television news enterprises, Visnews and WTN; but there are many other actors, many of them Western-based, which include national agencies such as Germany's DPA or Japan's Kyodo, as well as the "supplemental" services of established media such as the BBC Monitoring Service, the New York Times News Service, etc.). These agencies also exercise considerable influence on the news agendas of client media, in both developed and developing worlds.

The Major News Agencies: News Coverage

The impetus to the development of NEMs was accelerated by, and would not have occurred without, the considerable dissatisfaction expressed in several LDC forums concerning the services of the major Western-based international news agencies. The academic research in this area gives partial but not complete support for many of the complaints that have been expressed. There are two broad kinds of academic evidence in the assessment of the coverage of major news agencies (see discussions in Boyd-Barrett, 1980, 1981–1982, 1986): (a) large-scale quantitative surveys over one or more agency wires, and (b) more qualitative case-studies of the coverage of particular countries, issues or topics.

The literature identifies several causes of alleged "qualitative" bias although these are by no means unique either to the major news agencies or to media of the developed world, nor are they consistently present in all agency news reporting all of the time. These causes can be summarized as deriving from an interrelated cluster of variables that include (a) constraints imposed by working practices, (b) ideologies of news, (c) political and social ideologies, (d) the influence of the foreign policy objectives of the governments of those countries in which the transnationals have their major base, (e) an incipient "star system" in news agency reporting, and last but not least, and working in rather a contrary direction to the above, (f) a caution not to offend, manifested in the downplaying of aspects of domestic political coverage of countries in the region to which a given news wire is directed or in excessive dependence on local news media as sources. The latter phenomenon may result from the concern of the transnationals to maintain as wide a net of correspondents across as many capitals as possible, avoiding expulsion from any country until such time as expulsion is inevitable if the agency is to maintain credibility with its important western clients or members. Caution may sometimes be calculated to safeguard useful sources of revenue where these are threatened. The Third World generally is not regarded as a significant *direct* source of revenue, but ability to furnish news *about* the Third World for markets in the developed world has significant implications for revenue.

Research literature has identified the origins of several aspects of "quantitative" or structural bias in the wires of the transnational agencies. These include (a) aspects of geographical bias: news wires privilege news of the region (to which a given wire is directed) first and foremost, followed by news of either Western Europe or North America, followed by news of other Third World regions and the Second World; (b) aspects of topic bias: the major agencies privilege stories of international and domestic politics, economics, military, and defense. They give relatively little attention to such categories as culture, social services, trade unions, education, religion, and so on; (c) aspects of source bias: elite sources are privileged, and in particular government sources; (d) capital city/big city bias; (e) linguistic bias (English, French, Spanish, German, and Arabic are the most favored languages).

The Development of Models of News Exchange in the Third World

A review of accounts prior to the UNESCO survey of systematic news exchange involving Third World news media yields evidence of at least four major models of operation, based on NANAP, PANA, CANA and IPS. (A useful bibliography which contains many of the sources drawn upon for this subsection is included in Boyd-Barrett, 1986; Mowlana, 1985.)

NANAP is a cooperative of national news agencies within which, at least until the 1990 civil war, the Yugoslav news agency Tanjug played a pivotal role in coordinating regional news centers. Its news is oriented to the interests of the nonaligned world with a news agenda different from that of the major transnational agencies. Reported problems include insufficiency of independent reporting, variability in the quality of contributed news, variability in levels of participation of different member agencies, excessive protocol news, inappropriate selection and writing for the needs of international markets, difficulties in developing a substantial client base, and political control over or ownership of some contributing national news agencies.

The focus of *PANA* is more restricted—namely, to a particular continent, Africa. PANA was set up under the auspices of the Organization of African Unity, and is therefore answerable to an intergovernmental agency. It depends to a considerable extent on the cooperation of African national news agencies, but has its own headquarters and own journalistic staff, some of whom are coopted from news agencies of member countries on a rotating basis. It thus generates many stories for itself in addition to those which are contributed by member agencies. Within the limits of its constitution, there is a certain amount of cosmetic editing of contributed news which helps to adjust the content of its news wires to the needs and circumstances of the regional continental market served by the agency. PANA has a very distinct African focus. There is evidence to suggest that it is a major source of news about Africa for the Nigerian News Agency and possibly for other African agencies (Musa, 1990). But it may have much less visibility in retail press and broadcast media (Malam, 1991). Reported problems include political influence with respect to contributed news and the agency's answerability to the OAU's political machine; shortage of resource and of state-of-the-art technology (too many agency news stories arrive in garbled form in the offices of member agencies); considerable variability among members in contributions of subscription revenue or of editorial content. PANA has not been able to generate substantial revenue from outside Africa.

CANA is a cooperatively owned regional news agency. It brings together private and government-owned media, mainly in the English-speaking Caribbean, with private interests predominating, and with a mission to foster a Caribbean identity as well as to improve the gathering and dissemination of Caribbean news. Evidence suggests that, since the break from complete dependence of Caribbean media on Reuters for their supply of regionwide stories, there has been a significant increase in the quantity and quality of regional coverage. The agency is still tied to Reuters insofar as Reuters continues to be a major source of international news to Caribbean media through CANA, and in the sense that CANA acts as a news-gathering agent for Reuters. Critics may argue that this places a question mark over CANA's independence in the dissemination of regional news for international markets, and that it also places a question mark over Reuters's independence in its coverage of the region (this arrangement with CANA is similar to arrangements Reuters has with some other national news agencies). Cana services primarily represent the English-speaking Caribbean. There have been worries about the firmness of its independence from inter-island and intra-island tensions across the region as a whole. CANA has generated more revenue than many regional news initiatives, and has been able to show a surplus in some recent years, although it also benefits from aid from donor organizations. The distinctive features of CANA, therefore, are the dominance of private media interests and the relationship with Reuters.

Inter-Press Service is a cooperative of journalists that has established a very clear alternative news agenda, one which is process-oriented and geared to issues relevant to the LDCs. More than other agencies of the new generation of regional news agencies, IPS has established a very considerable, independent body of journalists around the world, as well as a sophisticated communications network. It provides a range of services, which include news services but also include telecommunications services and consultancy support. It has not been able to depend on revenue from news markets, but has developed contracts with UN agencies for a wide number of different services, as well as with other regional news agencies for the supply of communications support. Its news service still tends to privilege Latin American news, and IPS is not considered to be a particularly relevant source of news for media in parts of the Third World other than Latin America.

NEWS EXCHANGE MECHANISMS (NEMS): THE UNESCO SURVEY

The UNESCO survey very usefully builds on and largely confirms the scattered information hitherto available (summarized in part in the previous section), but across a much wider range of different NEMs at a particular point in time, namely the late 1980s. What follows is a very brief summary of the detailed report, now published by John Libbey.

Achievements

In terms of the quantity of information available, certainly, the NEMs have added to both interregional and intra-LDC information flow. While NEMs have not been able to substitute for the major transnational news agencies they have supplemented such information with a LDC orientation, sometimes inflected with a radical redefinition of news as process, and contributing to an increasing horizontal communication and information exchange. The development of NEMs therefore has contributed to a growing awareness of, and sophistication in, discussion about the problems of global news flow.

Agencies like IPS have helped to change the way news is defined, gathered and presented. With its emphasis on processes rather than spot news, IPS has challenged the style of conventional news agency journalism by evolving a developmental journalism. More than other agencies of the new generation of regional news agencies, IPS has established a very considerable, independent body of journalists around the world, as well as a sophisticated communications network. It has provided invaluable service to UN agencies and various non-governmental and developmental organizations worldwide. In Latin America IPS is well established as a credible news agency with a clear Third World focus.

NEMs have also contributed to improved scientific, technical and commercial information exchange among the LDCs. Agencies like PACNEWS, CANA, and ANEX may well have helped promote a sense of regional identity through better and wider news and information exchange. One such sign is the improvement in coverage of African issues in African media since the advent of PANA. Before PANA there was no link between the existing national news agencies in Africa. But today a network of African news agencies with PANA as coordinator has emerged, disseminating news gathered, processed, and written from an African perspective. NEMs have also given prominence to liberation movements. WAFA (PLO) through NANAP, and ZIANA (Namibia/ANC) through PANA, have been able to publicize their causes. Since most of the NEMs are devised to lessen the dependence on Western news sources, they also keep alive various issues raised during the NWICO debate.

There are likely to be significant if intangible gains for the member countries or agencies of NEMs that result from the cooperation process itself. There is also the promise that, through cooperative strategies, NEMs will bring more effective pressure to bear towards much-needed reductions in telecommunication rates than is often possible for members acting singly.

Constraints

Most NEMs have to operate under severe financial constraints. Many members and subscribers do not pay their dues or fees regularly. The erratic dependability of member fees, and of the donations of national and international bodies, is often recognized as constituting an insecure economic environment, one that makes it difficult to plan ahead and to develop.

The indifference of many LDC governments towards the NEMs with which they are associated is a handicap. Not much of their copy is used by clients even in the South, and there are very few subscribers in the North.

There are serious problems of transmission and the quality of reception is often poor. Satellite communication is expensive. Tariffs charged by PTTs are exorbitant. NEMS cannot match the speed of transnational agencies: The news is transmitted and received on teleprinters, and not many LDC news exchange mechanisms are computerised.

Considerable disparities of professionalism or of technical infrastructure among members can lead to the domination of one or a few of the member countries within the region covered by an NEM. Western cultural influence can still be substantial, even where the intention is that it should be reduced. For example, the European Broadcasting Union dominates ASIAVISION, Radio Australia dominates PACNEWS; CANA takes international news from Reuters.

There is a problem of language. Many journalists contributing to NEMs do not have the language skills necessary or appropriate for the range of language services provided. Working in major *linguas francas* such as English or French as second languages has implications for the competitiveness of services. The domination of European languages (mainly English, French, and Spanish), which are also often the languages of LDC elites, also contributes to a metropolis-oriented journalism. The NEMs themselves, like their member organizations and agencies, are typically based in capital cities and often have very limited reach into the vast rural hinterlands.

General expectations of media in many LDCs do not always contribute to the operation of NEMs. There is scant regard for democratic ideas in many LDCs. A weak polity, economy, and exploitative society insure that the ruling elite can manipulate media to further its own ends. Thus the media are susceptible to power corruption, and may not be receptive to radical journalism. These factors help to explain the excessive use of so-called protocol news in the NANAP.

Political, religious, cultural, and linguistic differences among LDCs may also affect news copy. Political interference in the working of the news exchange mechanisms is also not uncommon. There are problems of political control. The involvement of governments as dominant actors in the ownership and management of news exchange mechanisms means that NEMs are extremely sensitive to issues of political contention and regional disputes. Involvement of governments also reduces the attraction of NEM news services to the wealthy news media of the developed world, which attribute high value to editorial independence.

There is limited interregional exchange. IPS has poor coverage in Asia, while the NANAP is less prominent in Latin America. The organizational structures of several news exchange mechanisms need sharper articulation.

Information about usage of NEM copy in media or other client organizations is very incomplete, but what there is suggests that usage is in many instances disappointing, reflecting some of the difficulties already discussed. This is especially true for usage in media outside the regions covered by the NEMs, and in the important media markets of the western world where the potential for revenue is highest. Radicalization of news as process is a further impediment to sales in these markets; and the strongest features which might commend NEM series (such as direct representation of LDC sources or points of view) are sometimes already present in established western provision as in the digests of the BBC's monitoring service.

Implications for Media Imperialism

It is clear that many, if not most, factors contributing to the weaknesses of NEMs reflect deep structural imbalances between the developed industrial countries and the LDCs. The poverty of those countries reduces the ability of their governments to prioritize attention to media; there is relatively little advertising revenue to sustain independent operations.

NEMs fashioned on the model of collaborative intergovernmental structures, even when supported by donor organizations, appear cumbersome, susceptible to various political, bureaucratic, and financial barriers to their ability to sustain strong competition in the face of the Western transnationals. IPS has demonstrated an important alternative model that is formally independent of governments and intergovernmental organizations in their roles as owners, but still dependent on such organizations in their roles as clients. This dependence on governments or intergovernmental organizations for either patronage or revenue does not enhance the market prospects for sales of news services to news media in the affluent developed countries, whose own news needs are met by the Western transnationals anyway, and which distrust the involvement of government bodies in the operations of NEMs. Alternative routes to self-sufficiency, through the establishment of financial news operations, for example, and possibly in collaboration with Reuters, may deserve more attention from a pragmatic point of view, but they also suggest constraints on the potential for radical journalism.

The integration of many LDC governments and intergovernmental organizations into the prevailing international political and economic order may carry with it the implication that there is less than wholehearted commitment on the part of such organizations to NWICO philosophy on which many NEMs are formally based. Financial restraints, problems of journalism recruitment and training, difficulties of access to sources, further reduce the ability of NEMs to deliver services that adequately adopt NWICO objectives.

Taken as a whole, therefore, the NEMs do not appear to have had a significant impact on the structures of media imperialism over the past two decades. The broad implication, then, is that the existence of local centers of news gathering and dissemination does not in and of itself indicate a weakening in the market hold of the major Western transnationals. It may be true that the identity of the leading transnationals is changing (e.g., with the inclusion of new players such as CNN), perhaps becoming more diverse, but this diversity is still confined to a few powerful countries of the world, and the patterns of global dependency are unaltered by changes in the identities of particular players.

To put it somewhat differently, there is little or no evidence that the NEMs have demonstrated that they are anywhere near a position where they can mount a credible challenge to the continuing dominance of the major transnationals. These continue to enjoy substantial market advantages arising from their long-established global communications networks; access to the cheapest and most efficient communications systems; strategies of market diversification which are spinoffs from such networks; economies of scale; vertical integration of the transnationals with the media industries of the most affluent markets which they serve; and other cultural, political, and linguistic affinities with these affluent markets.

It has been argued recently (Gurevitch, 1991) that the development of global electronic journalism, building on cooperative sharing arrangements between organizations like Eurovision and Asiavision, has set a new trend towards greater egalitarianism in news flow and the primacy of (polysemic) video over print. We believe this view does not give due weight to the continuing importance of newsfilm agencies such as Visnews or WTN as contributors to the television news-exchange cooperatives, or to the very uneven patterns of contributions among members within or between cooperatives. Gurevitch considerably underestimates the continuing importance of the major transnational wire services for television, radio, news agency and newspaper clients, as these services provide a breadth of news coverage that is not matched by the newsfilm agencies, and a depth of coverage that enables television newsreaders, for example, to "fix" and interpret the newsfilm they receive from other sources. He overlooks the interlocking relationships between transnational print and newsfilm agencies (e.g., part ownership of Visnews by Reuters) that further reduce the real "diversity" of sources in global news. In short, apparent increases in diversity of sources and form often disguise considerably more significant continuities in patterns of concentration and inequality, the identification of which is still a significant outcome of media imperialism theory.

REFERENCES

ACCE Institute for Communication Development and Research. (1989). *An evaluation study of the functioning and impact of URTNA's Programme Exchange Mechanisms within the general context of interprofessional cooperation and international exchange.* UNESCO Commissioned Paper, Nairobi.

Alfonzo, A. (1989). *Description and evaluation of the principal information mechanisms, systems and agencies for integration and cooperation in Latin America.* UNESCO commissioned report.

Amunugama, A. (1981). News exchanges among Asian countries. *Media Asia,* 8 (2), 66–69.

Ansah, P. (1984). The Pan-African News Agency: A preliminary assessment. *Media Development,* 4, 34–37.

Asian Institute for Development Communication (AIDCOM). (n.d.). *Ongoing news exchange mechanisms among news agencies of Asia.* Kuala Lumpur.

Beric, I., & Miljkovic, V. (1989). *Functioning and impact of the non-aligned news agencies pool* (Evaluation Survey, Draft Report). Zagreb: Institute for Development and International Relations.

Boyd-Barrett, O. (1977a). Media imperialism: Towards an international framework for the analysis of media systems. In J. Curra, (Ed.),. *Mass communication and society,* London: Edward Arnold.

Boyd-Barrett, O. (1977b). *Mass communication in cross-cultural contexts* (Unit 5 of Open University course DE353, Mass Communication and Society). Milton Keynes, UK: Open University Press.

Boyd-Barrett, O. (1980). *The International news agencies.* London: Constable.

Boyd-Barrett, O. (1981–1982). Western news Agencies and the 'media imperialism' debate: What kind of data-base. *Journal of International Affairs,* 35(2), 247–260.

Boyd-Barrett, O. (1986). News agencies: Political constraints and market opportunities—the case of the 'Big 4.' In T. Varis & Kivikuri (Eds.), *Approaches to International Communication* (pp. 67–94). Helsinki: Finnish National Commission for UNESCO.

Boyd-Barrett, O., & Thussu, D. K. (1992). *Contraflow in global news.* UNESCO/John Libbey.

Culek, Z. P. (1990). *The south-south news flow: A case study on the performance of the non-aligned news agencies pool.* Zagreb: Institute for Development and International Relations.

Culek, Z. P. (Ed.). (1989). *Functioning and impact of the broadcasting organisation of the non-aligned countries* (Evaluation Survey, Draft Report). Zagreb: Institute for Development and International Relations.

Giffard, C. (1984, Autumn). Interpress service: News from the third World. *Journal of Communication, 34*(4), 41–59.

Gladstone, W. (1989). The Caribbean News Agency (CANA) and Caribvision/ Caribscope (CBU). Survey Commissioned by Unesco.

Gurevitch, M. (1991). The globalization of electronic journalism. In J. Curran & M. Gurevitch (Eds.), *Mass media and society* (pp. 178–193). Sevenoaks, UK: Edward Arnold.

Hamelink, C. (Coordinator). (1989). Inter Press Service Report of an in-depth evaluation, the Hague.

Harris, P. (1981). News dependence and structural changes. In J. Richstad & M. H. Anderson (Ed.), *Crisis in international news: Policies and prospects* (pp. 357–358). New York. Columbia University Press.

International Commission for the Study of Communication Problems. (1980). *Many voices, one world.* Paris: UNESCO.

Jakubowicz, K. (1985). Third World news cooperation schemes in building a new international communication order: Do they stand a chance? *Gazette, 36*(2), 81–93.

Kirat, M., & Weaver, D. (1985). Foreign news coverage in three wire services: A study of AP, UPI, and the Non-Aligned News Agencies Pool. *Gazette, 35,* 31–47.

Malam, M. (1991). *Study of Pan-African news agency.* Report of Doctoral Study in Progress, City University Graduate Seminars.

Mankekar, D. R. (1981). *Whose freedom? Whose order? A plea for a new international information order by Third World.* New Delhi.

Masmoudi, M. (1979, Spring). New international information order. *Journal of Communication,* pp. 172–195.

Mowlana, H. (1985). *International flow of information: A global report and analysis* (UNESCO Reports and Papers on Mass Communication). Paris: UNESCO.

Musa, M. (1990). *Confronting Western news hegemony: A case study of news agency of Nigeria.* Doctoral thesis, University of Leicester.

OANA. (1986). OANA Newsletter of Organisation of Asia-Pacific News Agencies, Silver Jubilee 1961–1986, New Delhi.

PANA. (1990). *Evaluation of the activities of the pan-African News Agency (PANA) Dakar.* UNESCO Commissioned Report.

Pavlic, B., & Hamelink, C. J. (1985). *The new international economic order: Links between economics and communications.* Paris: UNESCO.

PTI, IIMC, UNESCO. (1984, April 25–27). Seminar on improving news pool performance. Reports: Recommendations: Documents.

Resolution ⁴/₁₉ in Records of the UNESCO General Conference Twenty First Session, Belgrade. (1980, September 23-October 28). Resolutions Paris, Vol. 1.

Roach, C. (1990). The movement for a new world information and communication order: A second wave? *Media Culture and Society, 12,* 283–307.

Samarajiwa, R. (1984). Third World entry to the world market in news: Problems and possible solutions. *Media, Culture and Society, 6,* 119–136.

Savio, R., & Harris, P. (1980). Inter press service: The NIIO in practice. *Media Development, 27,* 38–42./

Schramn, W., & Atwood, L. E. (1981). Circulation of news in the Third World: A study of Asia Hong Kong. Chinese University Press.

Smith, A. (1980). *Geopolitics of information.* London. Faber.

Sreberny-Mohammadi, A. (1991) The global and the local in international communications. In J. Curran & M. Gurevitch (Eds.), *Mass media and society* (pp. 118–138) Sevenoaks, UK: Edward Arnold.

Sullivan, G., & Valbuena, V. T. (1990). *A content analysis and evaluation of the Pacific News Exchange (PACNEWS)* (UNESCO report). Singapore: Asian Mass communication Research and Information Centre,

Tunstall, J. (1977). *The media are American.* London: Constable.

UNESCO Doc. COM/MD/38. (1977). San Jose Declaration and Recommendations, UNESCO, Paris.

Weaver, D. H., & Wilhoit, G. C. (1983). Foreign news coverage in two U.S. wire services: An update. *Journal of Communication; 33,* 132–148.

Chapter 10
Free Trade in Communication: Building a World Business Order*

Vincent Mosco

WHOSE NEW WORLD ORDER?

In 1989 the United States and Canada signed the first trade agreement in history that extends free trade in goods to the service and
investment sectors, including communication. This is particularly
significant because, as a General Agreement on Tariffs and Trade
(GATT) report concludes, service industries are taking up an increasing share of world trade. According to the study, total trade in services
reached $560 billion in 1988, equaling the combined total of trade in
food and fuel. Services such as banking, telecommunications, management consulting, and accounting make up 40% of total world trade
(Greenspons, 1989). With 11.2 % of world services exports, the United
States leads the world. The Free Trade Agreement (FTA) is particularly significant for the United States because it serves as a model
to the 96-nation GATT membership that has been debating the issue
of trade in services. As a report of the Washington Center for Strategic
Studies notes, "Having established a bilateral framework for free

* The research reported on here was supported in part by a grant from the Faculty of
Graduate Studies and Research, Carleton University.

trade, the Americans and Canadians should be in a stronger position to tackle complex trade-in-services negotiations" (Dizard, 1989, p. 5). As for Canada, it appears to be the weaker partner in this relationship. For it has just agreed to eliminate most opportunities to manage its own trade in services and concluded that agreement with the leading exporter of services in the world.

Moreover, Canada ventures into this new economic territory without setting up a supranational political body that would address the wider, social, political, and cultural problems that can result from an agreement of this significance. Such problems are left with the diminished powers of national states and the enhanced powers of the markets and the multinational firms that manage them. Though Canada sought some form of binational governmental protection, the U.S. balked. As a result, the FTA provides for a binational panel to determine only if existing (mainly U.S.) trade laws are applied correctly.

Recognizing the broad significance of the free trade deal, then President Reagan hailed it as "a new economic constitution for North America" (Warnock, 1988, p. 9). Though he opposed the agreement, the Attorney General of Canada's largest province agreed with Reagan's assessment, arguing that, "like a constitution, the scope of the agreement is all embracing. It touches on virtually all aspects of governmental activity." He concludes that the FTA "imposes new constraints on what Canadian governments can do for people in the future, and the erosion of our ability to govern ourselves will be difficult to reverse" (Cameron, 1988, p. 241).

This chapter examines what makes the Free Trade Agreement a new constitution for North America. In doing so, it identifies how the Agreement promotes major changes in Canadian political culture and in its political institutions. Notwithstanding the claims of economists and constitutional lawyers who see it as a simple treaty to eliminate tariffs, one can argue that the FTA is a constitutional document because it deepens and extends the post-World War II process of reconstituting the Canadian cultural and political landscape.

The significance of the agreement extends beyond the realm of Canada-U.S. relations, because it serves as a U.S. model to forge and manage the global economy. Meetings began in 1990 to integrate Mexico into what would become "a North American common market from the Arctic to the Yucatan, embracing 350 million" (Farnsworth, 1990). Canada agreed to formally join the U.S. and Mexico in continent-wide deliberations in 1991. In August 1992 the three nations reached an accord that, subject to the ratification of their respective governments, would apply most of the tenets of the Canada–U.S.

accord to Mexico. This raises the concern that liberalized services trade principles would eliminate many of the supports that governments in Europe, Latin America, and elsewhere have relied on to implement national communication and information policies.

The Canada–U.S. Free Trade Agreement is therefore a significant document in international communications policy because it embodies the principles of President Bush's New World Order, or what is, in essence, the U.S.-led response to the Third World call for a New World Information and Communication Order. The U.S. version would secure private business control over the global production and distribution of culture and communication.

FREE TRADE AND CANADA'S POLITICAL CULTURE

The FTA was the subject of heated political debate in Canada, culminating in the fall of 1989 when it became the sole issue in a bitterly fought national election campaign. Much of the ferocity grew from the concern that the Agreement would accelerate the demise of Canada's fragile cultural industries. Already overwhelmed with American magazines, movies, and television programs, Canadians, feared the critics, would lose those last remaining policy protections in the industry central to maintaining national sovereignty (Crean, 1988).

This is an important issue, and it receives some treatment below. However, before addressing the question of cultural industries, it is necessary to examine the broader cultural significance of the Agreement. The FTA is more than a treaty that applies to cultural industries, because its provisions promote major changes in Canadian political culture, particularly by advancing the process of harmonizing Canada's political values with the neo-Conservative agenda of the Reagan-Bush era. In essence, the agreement is not just *about* culture, it *is* culture. Specifically, the FTA is arguably the most significant cultural product, among the many, that the U.S. has shipped across the border since it replaced Britain as Canada's principle trading partner. This can be demonstrated with an analysis of the FTA's "Objectives and Scope," its treatment of culture, and its use of the term *monopoly*.

At the beginning of the document, "Article 102: Objectives and Scope" describes what amounts to a Bill of Rights for Transnational Business. The five objectives of the FTA include eliminating barriers to goods and services trade, facilitating fair competition, liberalizing investment within the trade area, establishing effective joint admin istrative procedures, and laying a foundation to expand the agreement for future bilateral and multilateral arrangements.

The second of this two-page "Objectives and Scope" section strengthens these economistic goals by giving them precedence over principles contained in other agreements and over the wishes of states, provinces, and local governments. According to Article 104, "In the event of any inconsistency between the provisions of this Agreement and such other agreements, the provisions of this Agreement shall prevail to the extent of the inconsistency, except as otherwise provided in the Agreement." This is particularly important, because there is no reference here to the need to affirm and protect the institutions in each country that provide for the safety, health, education, social welfare and cultural expression of their respective citizens. In other words, what amounts to a Bill of Rights for Transnational Business has become the chief defining document for North America.

Furthermore, Article 103 binds the Parties "to ensure that all necessary measures (defined as "any law, regulation, procedure, requirement or practice") are taken in order to give effect to its provisions, including their observance, except as otherwise provided in this Agreement, by state, provincial and local governments." The U.S. political culture is centralist, so that state and local government involvement in national policy is minimal and most Americans would not expect that these levels of government would be directly involved in the national trade policy process. This is not the case, however, for Canada, where provincial power is embedded in its federalist system. Though specific governments have realized these tendencies in different ways, this provision places U.S. political values in the forefront of the FTA, not as an assertion of *national* governmental authority but rather to establish the precedence of *continental* governance over national, regional, or local power where the latter conflicts with the continental business objectives of the agreement.

The FTA extends this principle of business dominance by redefining the very concept of culture to be a marketable commodity. In fact, it does so in the very section that ostensibly protects cultural industries! Supporters of the Agreement cite Article 2005 (1): "Cultural industries are exempt from the provisions of this Agreement." But just one clause down, in Article 2005 (2), the Agreement qualifies the exemption by permitting a Party to take "measures of equivalent commercial effect in response to actions that would have been inconsistent with this Agreement." In other words, if one Party believes that the other is unfairly subsidizing an industry, including culture, it can retaliate by raising duties in some other area. Rather than exempt culture, the FTA makes it a specific target of retaliation. More importantly, by including culture in a section that permits retaliation to equivalent *commercial* effect, as Duncan Cameron observes, "Canada has accepted the American definition of culture: a commodity to be bought and sold for profit" (Cameron, 1988, p. xvi). If you agree to permit commercial retaliation against cultural subsidies, then you have agreed to define culture as a commodity. In this way, another prominent feature of American capitalism has entered the founding document of continentalism.

Finally, the FTA accepts the American cultural redefinition of a Canadian crown corporation by replacing the latter with the American term of opprobrium, the monopoly. Canada has built its communications system on a foundation of crown corporations or public enterprises empowered to advance national or provincial goals. At the national level, the CBC, the National Film Board, Telefilm Canada, and others have promoted Canadian cultural values that extend well beyond the commodity sphere. Before it was privatized, the crown corporation Teleglobe promoted Canada's national goals in international telecommunication. When Bell Canada did not believe that the company could profit from providing telephone service to the three prairie provinces, provincial crown corporations were established to serve the region and, to this day, provide arguably the least expensive and most universally accessible telephone service on the continent (Babe, 1990).

In addition to expanding the commodification of culture, the FTA redefines the crown corporation, Canada's traditionally accepted means to pursue public policy goals. Canadians who benefited from national crown corporations now face monopolies whose activities must be constrained. These specific constraints are described below. What is important to understand here is that the document accepts the U.S. government's negative view of a major institution of Canadian political culture.

In sum, the very language of the agreement, its deeply layered textual politics, reconstitutes the Canada–U.S. relationship by, among other things, identifying the preeminence of the commercial rights of international business, redefining culture as a marketable commodity, and redefining an instrument of public policy, the crown corporation, to be a monopoly, which, by definition, restricts the free trade goals of the agreement.

FREE TRADE AND THE POLITICS OF COMMUNICATION POLICY

The foregoing offered evidence of the FTA's cultural significance. The following examines specific mechanisms of the deal that demonstrate the ways this cultural significance can be used to change communications policy in Canada and lay the groundwork for a U.S. version of a global free-trade regime in communication and information services.

Cultural Industries

The trade agreement can affect Canadian culture in another fundamental way. In addition to strengthening the conception of culture as a commercial commodity, the deal places the cultural commodity squarely within the sphere of products open to retaliation against what a party can claim to be unfair subsidization.

Concretely, let us assume that this or some future Canadian government were to take steps to support its film industry, perhaps, as it has promised in the past, by asserting some national control over distribution to improve opportunities for Canadian film makers. The agreement provides the U.S. with the treaty right to penalize Canada by imposing a duty on Canadian products, *"to equivalent commercial effect."* Presumably, since there is no specific mechanism for determining that effect, the aggrieved party would determine the specific dollar amount and announce its action. It would be up to the party charged to protest the action, take it to the agreement's dispute settlement board, or deny the grievance and take its own counter measures.

This is far from an unlikely prospect. In April 1989, the U.S. charged that Canadian law and practice unfairly restricts foreign investment in the broadcasting and cable television industries (*Ottawa Citizen*, April 29, 1989). Moreover the U.S. Department of Commerce is on record expecting changes in Canadian cultural policy. According to the FTA "Summary of Provisions" issued by the Department's Office of Canada, "for its part, Canada has agreed that the U.S. can respond to actions taken by Canada that would be inconsistent with the FTA if cultural industries were covered. This should encourage the adoption of nondiscriminatory policies by Canada" (U.S. Department of Commerce, 1987, p. 7). For the U.S. Department of Commerce, "nondiscriminatory policies" are those that would eliminate Canadian government actions to develop national communication and cultural institutions. For the U.S. government, the only nondiscriminatory policy is no national communication policy.

A May 1989 report of the Washington, D.C., Center for Strategic and International Studies is more specific. According to the report, the long-term U.S. goal "is to modify or eliminate Canadian regulatory rules that require television stations to devote 60% of their program-

ming during the day, and 50% in prime time, to Canadian material"
(Dizard, 1989, p. 18). The White House has specifically stated that it
would retaliate against what it sees as "cultural protectionism." It
warns that any policy to

> legislate, proclaim, or take other action having the force in effect of law,
> either directly or indirectly, which impedes the production, distribution,
> sale or exhibition of film, television programs, video recording would
> provoke U.S. trade retaliation. (de Kerckhove, 1989, p. 21)

In March 1991 the U.S. offered additional evidence that it does not
recognize a Canadian right to protect its cultural industries. Re-
sponding to congressional calls to retaliate against such protection,
U.S. Trade Representative Carla Hills referred to the cultural industries exemption as nothing more than an agreement to disagree, and
asserted that, even in the cultural domain, "we reserve our rights to
bring cases against Canada" (*Ottawa Citizen*, March 13, 1991, p. E6).
    In essence, for the first time the U.S. has the power of a treaty to
back its claim to the right of retaliation against Canadian attempts to
preserve and build on its national culture.
    In addition to diminishing Canada's ability to protect its culture,
there are other provisions of the agreement that, though less significant, suggest that the cultural "exemption" is more of a rhetorical
device than a policy guideline. These include Canadian agreement to
provide copyright law protection for retransmission of American
copyrighted programming. This means, for example, that Canadian
cable companies will have to pay copyright holders for the use of any
signals that they transmit. Though the federal regulator, the Canadian
Radio-television and Telecommunications Commission (CRTC), determined in May 1990 that the cable companies themselves would have to
bear the cost, the association representing Canadian cable companies
was quick to point out that, "in the long term as a cost of doing
business, the subscriber is going to pay for it" (Partridge, 1990).
Furthermore, Canada agreed to eliminate postal rate differentials for
U.S. publications with a significant Canadian circulation, and to end
the requirement that prohibited advertising companies from taking
an income tax deduction for expenses incurred on material not printed
in Canada. By January 1990 the Canadian federal government had
jettisoned a promised $220 million program of subsidies to Canadian
magazines and replaced it with one that provides $110 million for less
specific purposes. The executive director of the Canadian Magazine
Publishers' Association sees this as a "result of Canada's continuing
vulnerability to pressures from the U.S." (Godfrey, 1990). Additionally,

both parties agreed to eliminate tariffs on printed matter and recordings.

The copyright provisions are especially significant, because they mesh with provisions of the 1988 Canadian Copyright Act to establish reciprocity in cultural production. Since Canada imports far more than it exports in the cultural sphere, this means a substantial increase in the payments from the Canadian cultural sector to foreign producers. Babe estimates a $100 million net outflow. As a result, though the Copyright Act revisions claim to increase the flow of resources to Canadian cultural creators, reciprocity provisions, according to Parker, "make it quite probable that 'free trade in culture' will actually shrink the size of the fund available for Canadian creators and cultural production, and intensify Canadian dependence on foreign (mainly U.S) production" (Parker, 1988, p. 33).

Communication Regulation

The *national treatment* provision of the agreement requires that each country treat businesses of the other in the same way that it treats its own (Article 105 and 1402). In the communications sphere this means that the CRTC must treat AT&T, or some other non-Canadian firm doing business in Canada, in the same way that it treats Bell Canada.

Moreover, neither party is permitted to set rules regarding the "establishment of a commercial presence" within the country as a prerequisite to providing a service. Consequently, national treatment must be offered to firms whose link to the country is purely electronic. As a result, Canadian service workers will compete with Americans who are paid lower wages and receive fewer benefits, in part because American workers have lower rates of unionization.

Canadian service workers will also have to compete more often with workers from Third World nations, whose low-wage labor U.S. companies use to process data and perform other low-level information services. This concern is heightened by the prospects of incorporating Mexico into a continent wide free-trade area. This provision is not lost on the analysts from the Washington Center for Strategic Studies. As they understand it, the agreement "clearly permits the direct provision of computer services on both a network or a stand-alone basis. This is a potentially important point for cross-border activities of all of manufacturing and services sectors covered in the agreement" (Dizard, 1989, p. 14). Given the prospects of a U.S.–Mexico trade agreement, Canadian analysts fear that U.S. companies will use Mexico as a low wage base for exports to Canada and elsewhere. Though the

Canada-U.S. agreement contains standard "rules of origin" language that is supposed to prevent this sort of activity, many analysts argue that the rules often do not work as intended. One of these, the president of the Business Council of British Columbia, concludes that

> if the United States and Mexico were to succeed in reaching a new trade agreement, Canada could probably expect more sourcing by U.S. companies of components made in Mexico; as a result, more Mexican intermediate goods would find their way into our market. (Matkin, 1990)

Concern about such a development has led to the formation of a coalition among Canadian, American, and Mexican groups who began to work together in 1989 to fight continent wide free trade. The coalition sees this as "part of a hemispheric strategy promoted by U.S. multinational business interests and their Canadian allies to integrate markets, gain free access to raw materials and energy inputs and pit worker against worker in a destructive competition for jobs" (Diebel, 1989, p. A4).

Third World nations recognize the dangers of national treatment provisions for the retention of some control over their domestic economies, particularly in the media sector. According to Martin Khor Kok Peng, vice president of the Malaysian-based Third World Network, with a national treatment clause, "media companies...in the United States or Australia may be given the freedom to set up media companies or to buy out media companies in the Third World, including television and the print media, and therefore control the cultures of Third World countries" (Weissman, 1991, p. 338).

Telecommunications

The national treatment provision takes on particular importance when it is applied to the opening of free trade in "enhanced" telecommunications and information services.

Over the years governments have struggled with legal definitions of *telecommunications services* in order to make pricing, service, and access distinctions. These have included distinctions among technologies (is it primarily telephone or computing?) and among types of services (is it simply message transmission, or does it incorporate message manipulation?) In essence, these are convenient fictions that facilitate certain particular policy interests (Mosco, 1990).

One distinction that many governments accept separates *basic* from *enhanced* telecommunications services. Though policy makers and regulators disagree about precisely what constitutes a *basic service*, in general the *basic* category applies to the traditional use of the telephone to send and receive voice messages. An *enhanced service* is one, like electronic mail, in which a computer intervenes to reconfigure the message.

Like most distinctions made in this field, this one is difficult to establish in practice. All new telephone equipment contains microprocessors that reconfigure messages to make transmission and switching more efficient. In practice, Canadian regulators define *basic services* more broadly than do their U.S. counterparts. This is important because a provision of the agreement (Annex 1404, Section C, Article 6) specifically exempts the provision of basic facilities and services. Consequently, basic telephone service, including local and long distance voice communication, is afforded some protection.

Nevertheless, telephone networks are carrying an increasing amount of enhanced services, such as data, video, and other electronic information products. The Canadian government identifies enhanced services as the fastest growing telecommunications market in Canada, estimating annual expansion at 63% (Canada, Communications Canada, 1987, p. 47). This results from business demand for more services and the growing digitization of networks. The FTA explicitly opens free trade in enhanced service (Annex 1408) and requires the CRTC to treat American companies, whether or not they set up offices in Canada, as if they were Canadian (Article 1402 (7)). Consequently, one can expect that U.S. companies, such as AT&T, will pursue the Canadian enhanced services market. There has been considerable discussion in Canadian circles that Rogers Communications, Inc., the largest cable television company and major partner in the company Unitel, which is proposing to develop a competitive long-distance telephone network, is looking for "a major strategic partner from abroad" (Partridge, 1991).

This will cut into the market share of Bell Canada and other Canadian telecommunications providers that look to the enhanced market for future growth. Consequently, Canadian basic service providers plan to petition the CRTC for substantial rate increases to permit them to compete more effectively with American firms. The Canadian Government acknowledges that "small business and residential subscribers might suffer" as a result of these developments and that competitive pressures "could have a major impact on the prices charged for local telephone services" (Canada, Communications Canada, 1987, p. 55). Hence, in practice, the basic service exemption is likely to prove as weak as the cultural industries exemption, and Canadian basic telephone subscribers will literally pay the price.

In addition to this, we are beginning to see evidence that the Canadian Government supports broadening the definition of an enhanced service. The government has promoted the case of one Canadian company, Call-Net, which claims that its minor addition to a basic service qualifies the company as an enhanced service provider. As a result, Call-net has argued that Bell Canada should be required to lease it the lines necessary to provide service to its Toronto area customers. The CRTC resisted this argument but relented after several federal government demands for reconsideration. Now, under the national treatment principle, Canadian regulators must permit AT&T, MCI, or any of the U.S. regional telephone companies (each of which is larger than Bell Canada) to offer the same service in Canada.

In the latter part of 1989, the Canadian Government took additional steps toward opening competition in the telecommunications market. Acting on a Supreme Court of Canada ruling, the federal government asserted jurisdiction over provincially regulated telephone systems. Several of these provincial jurisdictions, particularly those whose telephone systems are under provincial ownership, fearing local rate hikes, have balked at competitive entry. This action sends a clear signal that the federal government will not tolerate objections to opening telecom markets.

The federal government has also encouraged a major telecommunications firm, Unitel (changed from CNCP in May 1990), to enter the long distance telecommunications market. This company, once limited to the national telegraph business, has received a major boost from Rogers Communications, whose media empire includes cable television (the leading franchise holder in Canada), Cantel (one of two Canadian cellular phone systems), communications satellite, and pay-per view television services. Rogers bought a 41% share of the company and plans to promote its entry into telecommunications markets. Bell Canada has already predicted major local rate increases if CNCP-Rogers is permitted to enter the long distance telecom market (Tasse, 1989). One can anticipate that such approval would also stimulate already strong interest from U.S. telecom firms.

Finally, the federal government has introduced legislation that would increase its control over the CRTC by giving the government the right to provide the CRTC with policy guidance in addition to its current power to ask the CRTC to reconsider regulatory decisions. Concretely, this would help ensure that the regulator, which overturned a CNCP bid to compete in 1985, would enjoy less freedom to oppose the government's procompetitive, protrade policies.

Crown Corporations

FTA controls on the operation of crown corporations limit Canada's ability to respond to the expansion of American communications firms across the border. The cultural section of this chapter noted the linguistic shift that the FTA produced in this area. Canada's crown corporations have become *monopolies*. In addition to this act of renaming, the FTA restricts a nation's power to use these organizations, whether private or public, for national development. Article 2012 provides a broad definition of *monopoly*: "any entity, including any consortium, that, in any relevant market in the territory of a Party, is the sole provider of a good or a covered service."

The provisions governing monopolies begin, as do the provisions on cultural industries and telecommunications services, with the appearance of a gain for Canada. Recall how the FTA appears to exempt cultural industries and basic telecommunications services. Similarly, article 2010 states that "nothing in this Agreement shall prevent a Party from maintaining or designating a monopoly." This is followed by what amounts to a set of restrictions so severe as to make it unlikely that Canada will ever again be able to establish crown corporations. Article 2010(2) stipulates that, before designating a monopoly, a Party must notify and consult with the other and provide assurances that the monopoly will not impair the agreement by doing what are essentially all the things that governments create monopolies to do. The monopoly is forbidden from operating in such a fashion that permits it to be anticompetitive, nationalistic, or subsidize one of its services, like first class mail, basic telephone, or basic cable television services, out of revenues from other services (Article 2010 (3)). In essence, one is permitted to establish a crown corporation provided that it does not behave like one. Furthermore, since such a measure would be the equivalent of a direct or indirect nationalization, Article 1605 stipulates that the Party establishing a "public monopoly" would be required to pay "prompt, adequate and effective compensation at fair market value" to *potential* corporate or individual victims of the other party. It is doubtful, for example that the CBC would have been created under these conditions. Inspired by this spirit of opposition to crown corporations, the Canadian government has cut back on the budgets and the powers of several of its crown corporations including the CBC and has privatized others including Teleglobe

Canada, the designated provider of international telecommunication services.

Moreover, these provisions essentially preclude some future government from, for example, establishing the 21st-century version of the CBC: a crown organization that would provide a national data, information, and entertainment highway for all Canadians. Such an entity would, by definition, have to violate the treaty in order to meet its goals. This severely restricts the opportunity for a Canadian government, unless it chooses to risk the consequences of scrapping the treaty, to set a national policy in mass media and information that differs from or challenges, in any substantial fashion, the policy of the United States.

The New World Order In Communication

If we call Third World policies in international communication an effort to build a New World Communication and Information Order, then the FTA is one among a number of steps toward the creation of a Western version of a New World Order. But like many "new and improved" products in a world of advertising illusions, the "New" New Order presents little that is actually new. Rather, it deepens and extends patterns of the Old Information Order for an electronic age. Concretely, changes in the communications industry, in what is to be gained and in who has entered the industry help to explain the interest in this "New" Order and also help to account for the Free Trade Agreement.

Much of the literature on why Canada moved toward free trade with the United States concludes that the economic crisis of the 1970s and early 1980s led the government and business to conclude that Canada could not succeed with a national economic strategy but must explicitly link its economy with that of the U.S. Such a policy was considered to be the only realistic alternative to long-term economic stagnation (Warnock, 1988; Westell, 1984). The near economic depression of the early years of this decade convinced policy makers that Canadian economic growth required stronger trading ties with the United States, particularly because the U.S. led the world in the production and distribution of what many believed to be the key resource of future growth: information. Analysts have argued that information and related service sectors are rapidly replacing their industrial counterparts, and that nations need to master their information resources in order to establish or maintain a strong position in the global economy.

The stakes in information have grown as business and government recognize that information is a direct source of capital accumulation because it is a profitable commodity. Moreover, information systems are indirect sources of accumulation, because they serve as instruments of managerial control necessary to build and operate global systems of production, distribution, and consumption. The drive to turn resources, including information, into profitable commodities and instruments of control, has historically been central to the development of capitalism. However, the extension of this process to the information area was limited by technical and political forces.

Technical constraints limited the ability to measure what constitutes an information product and to monitor information transactions. Political resistance was constituted in public opposition to encroachments on universality built into the entitlement notion of information as a public good. The technical obstacles are being overcome by the development of digital technology which applies a common code to measure information and monitor its use efficiently and effectively. Moreover, the global integration of processing, distribution and display technologies makes it possible to connect and thereby control business operations globally and locally. Such control extends to effective command of international markets in finance, labor, raw materials, and consumers.

Public opposition is increasingly overcome by the pressures of large business and government information users who have become active participants in international and domestic policy debates in order to meet their needs for cost-effective networks. These new players have succeeded in reorganizing a policy process that was traditionally structured to support the needs of large service providers, such as telephone companies (with a guaranteed annual return on capital), their unionized employees (with well-paid, secure jobs), and residential subscribers (with low cost, universal service). As information has gone from being an incidental cost of doing business to a strategic source of profit and control, large users have promoted such policies as deregulation, privatization, and free trade. In Canada, they have done so through individual businesses such as the Royal Bank. More frequently, the interests of multinational users are given focus and force through the work of such lobbying groups as the Communications Competition Coalition, a group of Canada's largest companies, the Canadian Business Telecommunications Association and the Information Technology Association of Canada.

The FTA both reflects and constitutes the needs of these transnational businesses. Politically, the Canadian Government is particularly dependent on FTA provisions in the communications sector because its efforts to meet the needs of large users through domestic policy changes have encountered considerable opposition, particularly to deregulatory efforts in the telecommunications sector. In 1985, a coalition of trade unions, consumer organizations, and social welfare institutions helped to block the government's effort to permit competitive entry in the public telecommunications market. The FTA, with all the power and legitimacy of a bilateral treaty, is an important instrument to realize deregulatory goals and foreclose nationalist alternatives that would promote universality, access, and Canadian control over its communications industry. A U.S. report on the FTA recognizes that one of the major accomplishments for U.S. business interests is that the deal "implies a commitment that current restrictions on both sides of the border will not be expanded" (Dizard, 1989, p. 5). These "restrictions" would include low-cost universal telephone service, Canadian broadcast content regulations, government support for film production and distributions, and rules that insist on national processing of banking and other sensitive data.

The European Community Alternative

In contrast to the North American FTA the European Community has taken a different approach, albeit within the framework of a market model. Owing in part to the greater parity of its memebers, the EC is establishing a "social charter" as well as an economic union Such a continental charter is to provide some protection for public institutions, including public education, social welfare, occupational health and safety, and national culture (Greenhouse, 1989). Indeed, it is particularly ironic for Canadians to observe the EC proposing to institute quotas on media imports that are strikingly similar to those pioneered by Canadian policy makers in the pre-FTA era. For example, to regulate the flow of U.S.-made television programs, which reached US $1 billion in 1989, the European Community proposes to limit future imports to 50% of all programming on European TV and supplement this with restrictions on the amount and type of advertising sponsorship, a regulation that would curtail U.S. ad penetration (Greenhouse, 1989).

As Canadians can well understand, there is no guarantee that controls will improve the quality of European television. Though a leading West German television executive sees this as "a combat for our own culture," the director of the European Institute for the Media worries that "there is a danger that the European rubbish will be no better than the American rubbish" (Greenhouse, 1989). These debates will undoubtedly persist beyond 1992. The interesting point from a contemporary policy perspective is that the package of EC-wide regulations, the European Social Charter represents an alternative model to the FTA for organizing the global information economy. As one commentator concludes, "To the extent that the U.S.-Canada Free Trade area impinges on Canadian sovereignty, it cedes political sovereignty to market forces. The EC, in sharp contrast, doesn't cede sovereignty to the market so much as elevate sovereignty to a supranational body, and one that happens to believe in industrial policies, trade unionism, a welfare state, and other elements of a 1940s-style mixed economy" (Kuttner, 1989, p. 18). This analyst puts his finger on what North American supporters of the FTA fear when they use terms such as *Fortress Europe* or *creating new barriers.* They are concerned about the development of even the most minimal of a social democratic alternative to a world information order forged and managed by transnational business (Crawford, 1988).

CONCLUSION

Whatever challenge the EC poses to the Canada-U.S model, the EC alternative does underscore the quite radical step that the FTA represents. The Agreement is the basis for the Canada–U.S.–Mexico deal. That accord, which the parties reached in August 1992, applies all of principles that the FTA incorporated for the cultural industries and telecommunications. It is also being used as a model for the multilateral GATT trading process.

More fundamentally, the Agreement is arguably the first constitution to guarantee the fundamental rights of multinational business. In essence, the FTA puts the weight of a treaty behind the view that the rights of business to pursue commerce and set social and public policy take precedence over the political rights of national citizens and their national governments. This marks a significant step toward creating a world business communication and information order, a cornerstone of The New World Order.

REFERENCES

Babe, R. (1990). *Telecommunications in Canada: Technology, industry, and government.* Toronto: University of Toronto Press.

Cameron, D. (1988). *The free trade deal.* Toronto: Lorimer.

Canada. (1987). *The Canada-U.S. Free Trade Agreement.* Ottawa: The Department of External Affairs.

Canada, Communications Canada. (1987). *Communications for the twenty-first century*. Ottawa: Communications Canada.

Crawford, M. H. (1988). *EC '92: The making of a common market in telecommunications*. Incidental paper, Harvard University Program on Information Resources Policy.

Crean, S. (1988). Reading between the lines: Culture and the free trade agreement. In D. Cameron (Ed.), *The free trade deal* (pp. 223–237).

de Kerckhove, D. (1989), October). Control of the collective mind: Free trade and Canada's cultural industries. *Canadian Forum*, pp. 20–23.

Diebel, L. (1989, June 25). Pressure mounting for free trade pact to include Mexico. *The Toronto Star*, pp. A1, A4.

Dizard, W. (1989). *Telecommunications services in the U.S.-Canadian Free Trade Agreement: Where do we go from here*. Washington, DC: Center for Strategic and International Studies.

Farnsworth, C. H. (1990, March 28). U.S. sees rapid movement on Mexican free-trade talks. *The New York Times*.

Godfrey, S. (1990), January 20). Is culture truly excluded from free trade? *The Globe and Mail*.

Greenhouse, S. (1989, June 25). Workers want protection from the promises of 1992. *The New York Times*.

Greenspons, (Ed.). (1989, September 15). Service industries driving growth, GATT report says. *Report on Business*.

Kuttner, R. (1989, April 17). Bloc that trade: The second marriage of Keynes and Adam Smith. *The New Republic*, pp. 16–19.

Matkin, J. (1990, May 7). Will Canada lose its FTA advantage? *Report on Business*.

Mosco, V. (1990). *Transforming telecommunications in Canada*. Ottawa: Canadian Centre for Policy Alternatives.

Parker, I. (1988, February-march). The free trade challenge. *Canadian Forum*, pp. 29–35.

Partridge, J. (1990, May 17). TV viewers will foot bill for royalties, Lobbyist says. *Report on Business*.

Partridge, J. (1991, March 9). Rogers lifts ban on foreign ownership. *Report on Business*.

Tasse, R. (1989, March 9). If there is to be telecommunications competition, make it genuine. *The Report on Business*.

U.S., Department of Commerce. (1987). *Canada-U.S Free Trade Agreement: Summary of Provisions*. Washington, DC: International Trade Commission.

Warnock, J. W. (1988). *Free trade and the New Right agenda*. Vancouver: New Star Books.

Weissman, R. (1991, March 18). Prelude to a new colonialism: The real purpose of GATT. *The Nation*, pp. 336–338.

Westell, A. (1984, November-December). Economic integration with the United States. *International Perspectives*, pp. 5–26.

Winsor, H. (1989, November 3). CRTC head assails new broadcast act. *The Globe and Mail*.

Chapter 11
A Private View of the Digital World*

Dan Schiller and RosaLinda Fregoso

A long-standing movement toward digitization of global communications infrastructures in the 1980s began a period of rapid acceleration. Existing analog telephone facilities began to be progressively replaced by faster, more flexible and powerful digital systems. This transformation, however, was not only technical, but also institutional—both in its sources and in its implications. Furthermore, it emanated, not from a closely bounded information processing and transport sector, but from the shifting international economy as a whole.

The technical foundations of this process lay in the early postwar era, in the innovation of a common language of microelectronics for both computing and, somewhat later, telecommunications. Computer companies and their major business customers then began to foray into telecommunications networking to distribute data and processing power as and where they needed (IBM and GE experimented with microwave transmission of business data as early as 1944) (Brock,

*An earlier version of this chapter, written by Dan Schiller, appeared as "Pathways to Digitization in International Telecommunications," 1986, *Social Science and Policy Research* (Seoul), *8* (2), 287-304. Schiller and Fregoso shared the task of updating it, with Schiller concentrating on the modernization process and Fregoso on privatization in the less developed countries. Fregoso conceptualized and drafted the section on Latin America, which Schiller integrated into the final version published here.

1981, p. 182). Telephone companies, on the other hand, began to computerize switching (circuit allocation) to serve growing urban customer bases with greater efficiency. More recently, the telephone group also began to press for authority to introduce "enhanced" information services reliant upon computer software, so as to stimulate usage of underutilized telephone plants.[1]

Into the 1980s, although innovation of digital networks was rapidly accelerating, national telecommunications infrastructures (public switched telephone networks or PSNs) remained wedded, as they had for a century, to analog technologies. Only an unprecedentedly massive and costly upgrade could give rise to encompassing software-controlled digital systems. Digital switches were being developed, however, that would provide controlling hubs around which systems integrating diverse message streams for voice, data, and images could be constructed. These switches could be coupled to digitized transmission media, making increased use of satellites and optical fibers, to furnish unprecedented information-carrying capability.[2] In the most advanced developed market economies, accordingly, the digitization process began to accelerate; between one-quarter and one-half of all their central office telephone switches had been digitized by the late 1980s (Gitlin, 1989, p. 63; U.S. Congress, 1990, p. 329). To complete the modernization process, expenditures of tens, perhaps even hundreds, of billions of dollars were projected (U.S. Congress, 1990, p. 329).

Not only was modernization of existing analog telecommunications plant hugely expensive, however. It also both built upon and generated profound political-economic conflict over the terms of entry into the "information societies" it would undergird.

DIGITAL VISIONS IN CONFLICT

In most countries, telecommunications had long been the province of government ministries of posts, telephones, and telegraphs (PTTs); in the United States, though it remained privately owned, extensive exit, entry, and price regulation by the Federal Communications Commission imposed broad public accountability obligations on the telephone industry. Data processing, however, was more strictly a private business, largely free of government regulation and the public-interest concept from which it descended. Should merging computer–communications systems evolve mainly out of the public switched telephone network? Or, should digitization occur in some significant part outside the domain of the PSN, and inside that of the computer industry and its major corporate customers? Technical convergence toward software-controlled digital systems repeatedly prompted the question, "What length must a cable be before it ceases to be part of the computer and becomes a communications circuit?" (U.S. Federal Communications Commission, 1968, p. 3).

This question became increasingly urgent and multifaceted, as the range of affected interests expanded during the 1960s and 1970s, and as the implications of telecommunications modernization became more sharply drawn. Efforts to digitize telecommunications infrastructures, meanwhile, developed, not from a single firmly fixed reference point, but from dynamic, divergent, and often only half-articulated strategies. Two divergent designs proved especially significant in the global struggle to shape the modernization process.

The first model was an extension of years of private network-building effort by major corporate users of telecommunications and computers. As their need for telecommunications skyrocketed in postwar decades, corporations typically had come to rely on separate systems for voice, data, image, and video communications. These evolving networks, it should be stressed, were configured to accommodate specific applications. Their institutional functions, technical capabilities, and geographic and organizational access points were determined first and foremost by private need. It was not long, however, before corporate telecommunications managers began to recognize that their increasingly fragmented in-house networks were both unwieldy and expensive. Disparate power sources, diverse transmission media, incompatible equipment, and resultant difficulties in planning, coordination, and training inspired such companies to seek means of *integrating* their sprawling communications systems to achieve greater control at lower cost. Their demand for *multifunctional* networks correspondingly began to intensify.[3] In turn, efforts accelerated to develop the *digital* networks, which were best equipped to handle combinations of voice, data, and image signals, and which could grow in scope and function to support a widening array of transnational corporate activities.[4]

The first design for digitization, accordingly, may be thought of as offering an in-house transnational corporate plan for digitization. It emanated from the demand side of the telecommunications industry, and it centered on creating digital networks both *within* corporations (whose internal communications typically comprised a majority of total corporate telecommunications expenditures), and *between* major companies and their suppliers, distributors, and customers. Nothing about the digitization process, therefore, altered these companies' established commitment to *carefully bounded, special-purpose private systems*. Quite the contrary, digitization only confirmed their consistently expansionary ambitions for communications. Corporate users thus continued to insist on their need for intra- and intercorporate networks; now, however, they insisted that these should be *digital, multifunctional* (integrated) systems.

A second model for digitization, initially in substantial opposition to the first, emanated mainly from the institutional complex surrounding the *public* telephone network. It originated in the late 1970s as a design by the *suppliers'* side of the telecommunications services industry for ubiquitous integrated systems within and between subscribing nation-states. *Integrated services digital networks* (ISDNs)—the name they gave this model—in fact began to emerge from established domestic telephone networks through a series of evolutionary stages. With projected arrival of what was termed *broadband ISDN,* around which intense planning began to occur in the later 1980s, video and highspeed data applications also were planned for ISDN inclusion.

Access to these multifunctional ISDNs would be more comprehensive than that accorded by the in-house model, for ISDN was planned to evolve out of domestic public telecommunications infrastructures. ISDN thus would initiate a progressive reconstruction of entire PSNs in digital form, centralized at both planning and operational levels under the aegis of either the traditional telephone industry (in the U.S.), or the domestic telecommunications ministry or PTT (in Western Europe). In theory, at least, ISDN would eventuate in worldwide connectivity for voice, data, and image communications, and would allow identical ("portable") terminals and standardized service applications across borders.[5] The patchwork of disparate networks in use within and between major corporations, proponents of the ISDN model hoped, thereby would be reduced, and subscribing companies would abandon their characteristically fragmented voice, data, and image networks and migrate to centralized ISDNs. Expanding corporate demand for multifunctional digital systems thus would be served by a limited set of coordinated, relatively encompassing ISDNs, linked internationally and offering generic services and standardized access.

ISDNs attained limited operational reality by the early 1990s in several of the developed market economies. In Japan, Nippon Telegraph and Telephone Corporation had gained 6,100 contracts for its ISDN telephone service, which was available in 215 Japanese cities by March 1990. In the United States, ISDN commercial services were also available, while European policymakers looked, perhaps too optimistically, to opening a commercial, pan-European ISDN by 1992 (Poe, 1990, pp. 47, 50-51; Bushaus, 1990, pp. 45, 48; Gilhooly, 1990, pp. 46, 49, 51).

Business users wondered, despite these developments and the fanfare that accompanied them, how quickly would ISDN actually furnish ubiquitous, compatible, end-to-end digital service? Would the projected technical capacities of ISDN prove flexible enough to attract corporations insisting on highly specialized applications? Who would pay for the colossal modernization effort required to digitize the national telecommunications infrastructures (PSNs)—for which ISDN was a spearhead? And on what terms would large business users be allowed to interconnect their existing private networks with the new digital systems.[6] To put a point on it, (as did Phillips, 1988, pp. 311-317) to what extent would ISDNs' deliberate protection of past public telecommunications investment be purchased at business users' expense? These questions became yet more complex—and divisive—when placed, as we shall see they had to be, in an international context.

Though often concealed behind fiercely technical discussions, contention therefore erupted over who would supply and pay for telecommunications modernization—and over the terms, the technical specifications, the pace, and the geographic range of the modernization process. Only through a further historical analysis will we be in a position to comprehend the nature and likely outcome of this conflict.

THREE STAGES OF PRIVATIZATION

Planning for the technical metamorphosis of telecommunications was intertwined with—and increasingly defined by—what became a worldwide tendency toward "privatization" or "liberalization" of information technology systems and services. Apparent for over 30 years by 1990, the privatization trend may be analyzed in three stages or periods—each of which built upon and extended the achievements of its predecessor(s).

The first period of privatization commenced in the late 1950s within the United States. Preeminent in the world economy as a consequence of the destruction caused by the Second World War, U.S. companies were expanding rapidly in both domestic and overseas markets. In sectors ranging from oil exploration to automobile production to retail sales, these corporations made increasingly heavy use of telecommunications to expand markets and increase the efficiency of their administration, distribution, and production. As they became aware of their growing dependence on telecommunications, they organized to lobby government authorities for specific, far-reaching change in the rules governing domestic telecommunications provision.

From the beginning, their objectives were radically at variance with those of AT&T and the other telephone companies, which collectively comprised the U.S. public switched telecommunications network. As early as 1957, major business users were demanding—as the Automobile Manufacturers Association put it—"the same latitude in the use and implementation of our communications facilities that we enjoy in the use and implementation of the many thousand of other tools, facilities and services necessary to the conduct of our business" (FCC, 1957, pp. 850-851; quoted in Schiller, 1982a, p. 11). Instead of continuing to be the province of a monopoly supplier with extensive public accountability obligations, telecommunications should be progressively integrated with computing as a private matter. Diminished costs, customized applications, security of planning against unpredictable rate increases or service availability problems, even investment tax credits: all were incentives for escalating bypass of the public switched telephone network. But by far the most vital corporate advantage to be derived was usually left unstated: *maximization of private control both of information systems and the data coursing through them.*

With striking consistency, regulators affirmed business users' demands (Schiller, 1982a, supplies a more complete discussion). Private microwave networks, an early object of regulatory change demanded by such users, were authorized by the FCC, and microwave frequencies were allocated to noncommon carriers. Limited initially mainly to pipelines, utilities, and railroads, these private networks eventually burgeoned through diverse sectors. By 1982, they were in use in many industries and collectively depended on some 15,000 microwave relays—while the domestic common carriers themselves operated fewer than 9,000 relays (Schiller, 1982b, pp. 84-96). Private satellite networks some years later extended this same development to another powerful new medium, while competitive telecommunications companies, such as MCI, also were authorized. Attachment of "foreign terminals" of many kinds, including especially computers and private branch exchanges, was also liberalized dramatically. This led to emergence of a multibillion-dollar "interconnect" industry to supply an enormous range of specialized instrumentation. The regulatory boundary between telecommunications and data processing was likewise repeatedly redrawn, to accommodate and enlarge private control of information systems. With the break-up of AT&T, which resulted in the largest corporate reorganization in history, the corporation at the core of the U.S. public telephone network was itself transformed into a staunch advocate of privatization.[7]

Seeking a variety of competitive advantages, managers of print-based production chains embraced the newly deregulated telecommunications equipment and services.[8] Credit reporting and financial information companies migrated to electronic service delivery; manufacturers moved to link design more closely to production via computer networks. Even book publishers deployed computer-communications systems to facilitate tighter inventory control and to expedite distribution among publishers, wholesalers, retailers and libraries.

In consequence of these structural and policy changes, there followed a cumulative shift in the balance of power over network development, applications, and cost distribution. Publicly regulated telephone carriers lost pride of place in favor of private noncarrier businesses and competing equipment and service suppliers. By the late 1980s, the fastest-growing segment of the telecommunications services market, both domestically and for international connections, was for high-capacity private "T-1" lines. More than one-third of *all* U.S. spending on capital facilities for telecommunications was then accounted for by individuals and companies *apart from* communications common carriers (U.S. Department of Commerce, 1989, p. 29-4; Roekl, 1990, p. 29; U.S. Congress, 1990, pp. 332, 333). Private or shared special-purpose systems began to fragment what had been relatively unitary national telecommunications infrastructures (PSNs)—with deepening policy implications.

The needs of diversified transnational corporations for new telecommunications applications were themselves indeed supranational. Companies flocked to transborder delivery of data and video as well as of more traditional voice services. CBS, HBO, Citicorp, and dozens of other companies looked to transborder satellite applications to link overseas affiliates (Schiller, 1985a, pp. 106-113). Others demanded that *wide area telecommunications service* (WATS)—"800" numbers— should be extended from domestic to transnational contexts. Calls dialed "free" from overseas then might be routed automatically to sponsoring companies in the United States, diminishing the need for foreign sales offices. "There really is no longer a 'domestic market' separated from international dealings," summed up an AT&T executive in 1981: "Large customers increasingly expect to deal with their international telecommunications and data in a systematic, unified way. International systems solutions to communications needs are increasingly demanded" (quoted in Schiller, 1982a, p. 104).

Thus a second, complementary, push to "liberalize" or "privatize" or "denationalize" telecommunications—propelled by similar objectives as the first—began to take shape. By the later 1970s, business users sought to introduce new opportunities for private control of telecommunications within the domestic economies of major trading partners of the U.S. Pressure to privatize was introduced throughout the developed market economies of the OECD nations—by various U.S. Government agencies, in concert with equipment suppliers and business user groups organized by transnational corporate telecommunications managers.

The most spectacular success came in Great Britain, where the national carrier, British Telecom, was privatized, and a competitive carrier, Mercury (owned by Cable & Wireless), authorized. This permitted the U.K. to offer itself as a more hospitable site for the information system operations of major firms needing access to European markets, and put additional pressure on the continental countries to revise their telecommunications policies. Competition was also authorized, though in a somewhat different fashion, in Japan. Support for liberalized terminal attachment provisions, private networks and competitive carriers, and deregulation of merged computer–communications services, became an article of faith among elites in most of the major developed market economies (for discussion of one recent instance, see Thorngren, 1990, pp. 94-98).

Spiraling research and development costs in the telecommunications equipment industry contributed further momentum to deregulation, by making it impossible to recoup outlays for digital switches within any single national market. Subsequent generations of switches, making use of photonics, would cost even more than the estimated $1–2 billion required to produce the current generation digital central office switch. Few companies could contemplate such investments, and few had access to a sufficient number of national markets to make them profitable. Previous procurement arrangements enjoyed by preferred domestic equipment suppliers, tying them closely to the government PTTs whom they furnished, therefore came under unprecedented strain. Joint ventures across national borders began to supplant the earlier industry structure: AT&T–Philips, Ericsson–Honeywell, British Telecom–Mitel, Northern Telecom-–Daewoo, Siemens–Rolm. At the same time, restrictive government procurement codes were subjected to intensifying pressure. With varying success, both computer firms and telephone companies sought partners with whom to underwrite production of whole lines of computer and communications products; this again involved them with foreign interests.[9]

To be sure, these changes were uneven. Not infrequently they were opposed by PTT administrators and telecommunications unions. Nonetheless, decisive changes in favor of the in-house model of development began to occur in many countries, and the prospect by the early 1990s was for continuing movement in this same direction. In

Western Europe, for example, a few of these successful efforts were: the employment of antimonopoly provisions of the EEC statutes against PTTs which resisted liberalization, the EC's release of a Green Paper on Telecommunications which favored "competition" in Common Market telecommunications, and the bow by the Conference of European Postal and Telecommunications administrations to the demand of the European Council of Telecommunications Users Associations, that it embark on radical structural reform to limit the power of Europe's public monopoly carriers (Bernard, 1989, p. 313; Gilhooly, 1990, p. 64, Schiller, 1990).

At the same time, ostensibly *international* policymaking bodies active in key areas of telecommunications were opened to greater private involvement. A kind of organizational privatization was visited on the Center for Telecommunications Development, whose functions were to study and advise on telecommunications investment proposals from less developed countries. Loosely affiliated with the ITU, the Center was created in the wake of the Maitland Commission report on telecommunications and development, and seems to have been formed in significant part to "help Western manufacturers and operators expand business to the Third World." Financed largely by private money, the Center permitted explicit and direct involvement by private groups in its multilateral project deliberations. The "substantial role" private interests could play was evidenced by the composition of the Center's Advisory Board. Along with representatives from a number of national telecommunications administrations, members from the following "semiautonomous" or private firms were elected for 2-year terms at the Board's first meeting in November 1985: Teleglobe Canada, Alcatel (France), Detecon (FRG), NEC (Japan), LM Ericsson (Sweden), British Telecom (UK) and the U.S. Telecommunications Suppliers Association (Eugster, 1986, p. 381).

The developed market economies already had been heavily over-represented within the crucial standards-setting agency of the International Telecommunication Union, the CCITT. Yet the latter's bylaws also permitted private companies to attain formal standing, and thus to exert growing influence over the vital design decisions underlying any digitization scheme (Rutkowski, 1983, p. 40).

In this context, ISDN planning *itself* became a chief object of the privatization drive. Transnational business users expressed continuing concern that ISDN was little but a grandiose PTT ploy to shore up threatened European public networks. Viscerally opposed to government (PTT) involvement in a new generation of value-added information services, such users succeeded in insinuating key policy demands of their own into the planning process. In particular, they battled to modify the design of ISDN to ensure allowance of private interconnection on maximally favorable terms, and to permit place- ment of critical networking functions within private user-based equip- ment (Schiller, 1985b, pp. 105-125). Corporate users soon began to be courted by telecommunications service providers who could not afford to neglect their opinions—or their business.[10]

Thus the deregulation juggernaut began to intervene into the context and planning of ISDN. In the crucial third stage of privatiza- tion, in consequence, the two previously disparate approaches to digitized telecommunications began to find common ground. Before evaluating this unprecedentedly ambitious phase of privatization, we may take stock of the existing corporate investment in information technology that formed its foundation.

In operation by 1984 were more than 1,000 transnational computer- –communications systems, "the overwhelming majority of them estab- lished by transnational corporations from developed market economies to service their worldwide affiliate network" (United Nations Eco- nomic and Social Council, 1984). American Express, for example, was then spending over $500 million annually on telecommunications to support its global operations. "Among major international com- panies," noted an American Express vice president, "this amount is hardly atypical. In fact, for many financial services companies, com- munication is the second-largest expense after staffing costs." The annual expenditures of the top 100 telecommunications users by 1989 were estimated to range from between $1 billion at the top of the list to about $20 million at the bottom, with the average falling between $50 and $100 million.[11]

These enormous expenditures were nonetheless but a fraction of a broader metamorphosis of the entire capital base of the corporate economy. By 1984, in aggregate, corporate outlays for communications equipment, office, computing and accounting machinery, and instru- ments of every kind comprised a stunning 46% of nonresidential purchases of producer's durable equipment (in constant 1972 dollars); this proportion had increased steadily since the 1940s, but accelerated dramatically after the 1974–1975 recession (U.S. Department of Com- merce, 1985, p. 24, Table 5-7). Electronic products moved ahead of factory machinery and mobile equipment to become the largest single category of capital equipment spending (Winter, 1986, p. 6). This colossal continuing investment in private information technology systems formed the basis for the emerging "information economy," and was as encompassing and sectorally diverse as that economy itself.

One consequence of growing corporate reliance on information networks was that companies became vociferous in demanding the ability to use such networks to interconnect to other organizations (Branscomb, 1982, p. 759; and, especially, Estrin, 1985). Direct linkages between internal corporate information resources and data processing facilities, and those of suppliers, distributors, and customers, afforded a stunning range of competitive advantages—at least to those companies which were first to innovate them. By the mid-1980s, interorganization networks included systems interconnecting airlines and travel agents, banks, insurance firms and agents, research institutions, medical product suppliers and hospitals, and automobile manufacturers and parts subcontractors (Estrin, 1985, 1986).

Heightening corporate dependence on telecommunications, however, not only conferred competitive advantages in established markets, but likewise created a foundation for diversification into profitable new information services. Indeed it became increasingly difficult to distinguish between communications companies and large corporations ostensibly serving entirely different markets. Business users, in effect, increasingly became service suppliers—a trend that deepened with further innovation of digital networks.[12]

Within this context, the concerted drive to privatize telecommunications should be viewed as an effort to create a thoroughgoing global foundation for systematic corporate exploitation of information. In its third—and, in 1990, still current—phase, privatization accordingly became even more sweeping. The objective was to create truly private *trans*national systems for information processing and transport, not only across the developed market economies but also across the less developed states and, less predictably, Eastern Europe.

Attempts to open up less developed regions to private capital from the developed market economies, of course, were hardly new. However, while earlier efforts had centered on enlarging markets first for agricultural products, and then for manufactured goods, in the 1980s and 1990s the developed market economies began to take aim at information technology, and information products and services (H. Schiller, 1981).

Telecommunications privatization was widely perceived to be a critical prerequisite of this emerging shift in the international division of labor. Some of the most vigorous advocates of telecommunications privatization in this context were the World Bank,[13] the International Monetary Fund, the U.S. Agency for International Development, and the U.S. Departments of Commerce and State. During the 1980s, these influential agencies elevated the doctrine into a reigning orthodoxy, a cure-all whose application purportedly would benefit a vast range of activities from electrical power generation and water provision, to agricultural marketing boards, to health, waste disposal, education, and—of special relevance to this discussion— telecommunications. In this sweeping vision, privatization became a "creative process designed to shift whole areas of economic activity ... from the politicised, non-commercial sector to the consumer-respon- sive profit making private sector (Pirie & Young, 1986, pp. 13-14).

The enthusiasm of the World Bank, the IMF and AID for "raising LDC interest in privatization" quickly began to bear fruit. A U.S. Department of Treasury inquiry of all embassies and missions in April 1985 reported that all but 4 of nearly 60 replies indicated that divestment and privatization of state-owned industries and services were of concern to their governments. The international debt crisis, with its savage impacts across the less developed countries, doubtless contributed to this pliancy. And the U.S. Department of Commerce's National Telecommunications and Information Administration (NTIA) aggressively promoted the idea of privatization through a number of "feasibility studies" co-sponsored with interested U.S. corporations. In 1986, for instance, the NTIA was joined by ITT in a project which studied the privatization of selected telecommunication services in Jamaica. The NTIA's study of Guatemala's privatization options was co-sponsored by the International Trade Commission, AT&T, Bell South, and Puerto Rico Telephone Company. Plans to privatize part of Costa Rica's Electric and Telecommunications Au- thority (primarily its data communications activities) were formulated in 1988 with funds from the NTIA, the International Trade Commis- sion, AT&T, and Motorola (Cowan, 1986, p. 16; U.S. Department of State, 1981, p. 14).

Because telecommunications in the less-developed nations had tended to fall under the budgetary and regulatory authority of the state, and because they were often a relatively reliable revenue source, financially strapped governments were reluctant to relinquish their provision. Thus, privatization was by no means always an assured outcome. Yet even absent true privatization, what one analyst termed *gradual reform* in the direction of competition—"to make telecom- munications entities more flexible, commercial and efficient"—be- came strongly apparent in the 1980s. Internal reorganization to enhance cost-efficiency by cutting PTT employment; creation of more autonomous and, perhaps, pliant, government entities to replace full- fledged telecommunications ministries; joint ventures and manage- ment contracts with private suppliers; and permission to "major competitors and users to create alternative systems and interconnect them to the public network" were under consideration by many nations (Roth, 1986). All would increase Western information technology equipment sales while further opening up the less developed countries to the in-house model of telecommunications development.

Plans to divest national telecommunications systems to private entities also proceeded apace across the globe, from New Zealand to Puerto Rico (Kane, 1990, pp. 1, 15; Schultz, 1990, p. 2; and see below). A private teleport furnishing satellite services "to a limited number of special customers" at rates undercutting Intelsat's (the nonprofit international satellite consortium), was planned for start-up in late 1986 within the Montego Bay (Jamaica) Export Free Zone (Schultz, 1990, p. 17; see also Kokkeong, 1986). India and Taiwan exemplified a broader trend favorable to business users, in which regulation of telecommunications was separated from the state-owned enterprises providing service (Cowhey, Aronson, & Szekely, 1989). In India, the telephone operations of the major regions of Delhi and Bombay were also restructured as commercial private services (Wellenius, 1989).

Other Third World elites instituted similar policy changes. The Chilean government, for instance, authorized investment by a private Australian firm in the national telecommunications company (Wellenius, 1989). And Argentina began to privatize its public telephone company, Empresa Nacional de Telecommunicaciones (Entel), as part of a wider reform that also spun off the national airline, Aerolineas Argentinas. In early 1988, Argentina's President Alfonsin announced an agreement to sell part of Entel to Spain's Telefonica. An Argentinian law mandated, however, that the sale of state-owned enterprises required approval from both Houses of Parliament. And the nation's powerful Peronist-dominated trade union voiced strong opposition to denationalizing the telephone system (Ares, 1988a). After Alfonsin's administration conceded to the Peronists on certain "social" measures—such as discounts in phone charges for retirees and lower train fares for students and teachers—the privatization initiative received Parliamentary approval. After further postponement, 60% of Entel was sold off in two parcelled franchises—one to Spain's Telefonica, and one to the U.S. regional telephone company, Bell Atlantic. An additional 10% of Entel's stock was slated for sale to employees, with the remainder to be sold through a public offering (Ares, 1988b; Christian, 1990, p. c6; "Argentina Unveils," 1990, p. D5).

Events in Mexico offered another example of this massive policy reversal in telecommunications within the less developed countries. As the international debt crisis deepened during the 1980s, Mexican elites began to seek new sources of direct foreign investment. To this end, they offered access to strategic sectors which earlier had been placed, usually by painful and protracted effort, beyond the reach of foreign capital—such as electronic equipment and accessories, and high-tech services enterprises. Strong rhetorical backing for this policy occurred with the advent of the Salinas de Goltieri administration in Mexico, which enthusiastically accepted market forces as the pivot of development. A resultant *privatization wave,* as it was referred to by the Mexican press, washed over several state-owned enterprises, including Aeromexico.

Telefonos de Mexico (Telmex) was by far the most prominent of the privatized enterprises. Telmex had longstanding and intimate ties to foreign telecommunications companies—most importantly, ITT (whose telecommunications manufacturing operations were in the mid-1980s acquired by France's CGE-Alcatel) and Sweden's Ericsson. Telmex's monopoly dated to 1946; and, in 1958, Mexican citizens gained control of a majority of the company's equity. Only in 1973 did the Government assume majority ownership; regulation and control of Telmex were then significantly unified within the Mexican State.[14]

This difficult passage toward increased national control was halted and began to be reversed in the late 1980s. A Mexican law made public in September 1989 proposed to restructure Telmex to permit an increase in foreign ownership participation to a level of 49%, to separate regulation and control of telecommunications in Mexico, and to open service to competition.[15] Commercial interest in the prospective privatization was intense, to judge by reports that would-be investors included, at various times, not only two Mexican investment houses and the Mexican conglomerate, Grupo Alfa, but also Sweden's Ericsson, Spain's Telefonica, the U.K.'s Cable & Wireless, a Japanese telephone company, and the U. S. companies GTE, Bell South, and U.S. West.[16]

Nationalistic antiimperialism, principally directed against the U.S., was an intermittently potent sentiment in Mexico, even among elites. The 1989 law sought to ward off public opposition to growing foreign domination through a provision stipulating that 51% of the phone company's stock had to remain in Mexican hands (through a combination of state, private or employee ownership). Nonetheless, according to Cuauhtemoc Cardenas, Mexico's major opposition party leader, the potential for democratic control of Telmex was compromised by the measure. Underscoring that privatization amounted to an "acquiescence to foreign capital," Cardenas characterized the privatization wave as one more "imposition by the IMF on Mexico for solving its debt problem" (Vidal, 1989). Efforts to consolidate and finalize the terms of the Telmex privatization were concluding in June 1990 (Rohter, 1990, p. C10; Moffett, 1990a, b).

As Cardenas also observed, the major development agencies had turned to the international debt crisis as a prime lever in accomplishing global privatization. The sale of state-owned enterprises was heralded as a way to find immediate cash income (and scarce foreign exchange if divestment was to foreign investors), as well as to "settle foreign debt" by encouraging banks "to convert part of their debt owned by LDCs into equity" in newly privatized businesses (Ohashi, 1986, Tab G, p. 2; Pirie & Young, 1986, p. 13; Taylor, 1986, p. 1). If the takeover of nationalized concerns by foreign interests "is not a viable option," divestment could be made to domestic private interests. "Wherever possible," one analyst elaborated, "it is wise to give affected parties a *stake* in privatization" (Poole, 1986, Tab D, p. 12). In either case, it was agreed by such writers, direct monetary aid and technical assistance to less developed countries "should be conditioned to a greater extent on their economic policies .... When aid is given for specific development projects, private sector involvement should be urged, and in so far as possible made a condition of development aid. For example, aid to contract and operate irrigation networks, roads, or electricity generation facilities could be given on the condition that these are privately built and operated (Pirie & Young, 1986, p. 1).

This entire process was lucrative for the expanding services sector of the developed market economies. Western investment banks, management consultants, accountancy firms, and advertising agencies "should handle LDC privatization" from the initial valuation and issuance of stock to the mandatory promotional campaign needed to sell it to investors (p. 12).

The intended benefits of privatization were also explicit. Once a government enterprise was sold, the state "can no longer exert control or interference." Although the conditions of divestment might alleviate its subsequent impact *if* ameliorative provisions were written in at the outset, "(the) new management will be expected to make far reaching changes, notably in the financial structure and in operations, aimed exclusively at profitability." Put frankly, "this will eliminate the former social overhead objectives," including concerns for public employment and the more general notion of public accountability (De la Giroday, 1986, Tab P, p. 15). Equally high on the reform agenda for large business users were cost-based pricing of services and allowance of "at least limited bypass of problems of congestion and poor technical quality that may potentially plague the overall network" (Bruce, 1989, pp. 17, 18).

Privatization and specialized services for large business users were often justified, ironically, in the name of economic development. In 1988, former U.S. Secretary of State George Schultz expressed this linkage: "Modern telecommunications are no longer a luxury for developing countries. Rather, in a world increasingly dependent on the latest information, telecommunications have become a powerful engine of economic growth. A growing number of cases shows that modern telecommunications create new jobs, attract foreign investment, and provide the revenue to meet basic human needs" (Schultz, 1989, pp. 62-65). Third World elites themselves sometimes began also to claim that, if only they could transform their countries into "information societies," they might aspire to the levels of prosperity realized by the developed market economies.[17] Such claims for telecommunications as a contributor to development recalled an earlier, and equally dubious and self-serving call, in the 1950s and 1960s, for introduction of commercial mass media as a path to modernization— often by the same development agencies.

The threat of corporate capital flight was a more palpable inducement to privatization by the less developed countries. In a period of aggravated debt crisis, a second was the insistence by the United States and other developed market economies that international financial assistance for Eastern European and Latin American countries should be tied to radical political-economic policy changes— notably, conversion of state-owned industries into private corporations (Pine, 1990, pp. A1, A15; Kempster, 1990, pp. A1, A13). A third was "bypass," the threat of which was often used, just as it had been in the developed market economies, to justify privatization.

Transnational corporate bypassers characteristically exploited newly available technologies, such as satellites and cellular radio systems, as "a rapid and lost-cost alternative to upgrading crumbling local telephone networks." In countries such as Thailand and Indonesia, for example, cellular radio furnished "a quick fix"—"the fastest way to get good phone service to those who ... are willing to pay a premium" (Baker, Gelston, & Kapstein, 1990, pp. 80-81). On a transnational scale, the Intelsat system, earlier hailed by U.S. policymakers as a "triumph of U.S. foreign policy," nevertheless found itself embattled, as private entities such as PanAmSat successfully challenged its international monopoly (Schiller, 1985a; Hudson, 1990, pp. 191-192, 222-245).

A proposal by Motorola, already the world's leading provider of cellular telephone apparatus, gave another indication of the nature and scope of emerging transnational private systems. Motorola's plan was to create a $2 billion network of 77 low-orbiting satellites to provide worldwide cellular telecommunications integrating both voice and data services. The primary markets for the system, which was expected to interconnect with landline services already available in developed market economies, were areas *lacking* "state-of-the-art telephone service"—principally Third World nations and Eastern Europe.[18]

IMPLICATIONS OF PRIVATE DIGITAL NETWORKS

The historical commitment of most nations to state-run telecommunications was, by 1990, either under siege or already in ruins. What were the implications of this fact?

Significant national variation remained in telecommunications policy and operating procedures, to be sure, and additional important constraints were sometimes built into the privatization process. Mexican authorities, for example, who presented privatization as a means to renewed national economic development, insisted that the prospective purchasers of Telmex would have to undertake an expansion program ensuring 12% annual growth in telephone lines (Moffett, 1990b).

Despite such checks on unfettered private control, the inhouse, corporate model of digitization bid fair to become globally dominant. It even threatened to encompass the traditional monopoly providers of public-switched telephone service. Advocates of privatization argued that it was "the logical alternative" to bypass of entire domestic telecommunications systems by transnational companies seeking "more efficient private systems" (Cowan, 1986, p. 9). But in fact, again following the pattern set in the developed market economies, *both* privatization *and* bypass occurred. Furthermore, *privatization itself was only an especially thoroughgoing and radical means of bypassing public telephone networks*—a means that left the surviving organization(s) less encumbered with public service obligations. The constitutents of the PSN *itself*—meaning, in the United States, AT&T and even the regional Bell operating companies—were no longer behaving as publicly obligated enterprises, but rather as aggressively ambitious private businesses. The prime questions for such service vendors revolved around simple economic demand: how large a market, how fast, for switched-data (ISDN-type) services (Bushaus, 1990, p. 48)? Their best answer was to keep their strategic options open, by cultivating expanding private network markets as well. Both suppliers and users, in short, now found it profitable—and, as a result of continuing deregulation, increasingly feasible—to bypass PSNs at levels ranging from local loop all the way to global grid.

The originally crucial differences between ISDN and inhouse models over the role of the public network in the evolution to a digital world correspondingly began to narrow. As a result, in one account, "the old ideal of ISDN as the network to end all networks has faded. Increasingly, it is being seen as one of many networks—public, private, intelligent or mobile—in a multiservice environment" (Gilhooly, 1990, p. 51). This apparently benevolent pluralism, however, could not efface the rise to global prominence of the inhouse model of telecommunications.

Even by the late 1980s, this seachange was beginning to have marked impacts on a range of social and economic relationships. The decision to invest in digital telecommunications technology posed unprecedented risk because it represented a basic transformation of the network in an increasingly competitive, deregulated environment. Major investment decisions of the past, in contrast, had been taken with regulatory assurance of capital recovery (Egan & Taylor, 1990, p. 328). Important new sources of institutional instability thus began to appear in an industry that, whatever its problems, had long been protected from the most ravaging impacts of the business cycle by its public or quasipublic status. One new source of instability was overbuilding of systems by competing service suppliers on high-density routes—such as the North Atlantic axis—which was leading rapidly to excess capacity (Johnson, 1986). Imprudent acquisitions and incautious financing, likely compounded by the competitive scramble to acquire newly privatized telephone companies, were others (Schiller, 1990).

Profound social "opportunity costs" were also imposed by privatization. Given the awesome expenditures required by modernization, what assurances could be given that profit-maximizing companies would pursue policies aimed at lessening longstanding economic and informational disparities between rich and poor nations, or between the countryside and the city, or between social classes? What was the likelihood, that is, of such companies' making ability-to-pay a *less significant* prerequisite of access to telecommunications and information services? What was the chance, on the other hand, that traditionally high telecommunications industry employment and wage levels could persist in a newly competitive environment?[19]

Finally there was the crucial question of where the "intelligence" required to service, maintain, and manage digital systems, including databases shaping access to information services, would be located. The ability to centralize private control over the configuration and accessibility of network intelligence would be especially problematic for the less developed country storing "its network control and maintenance intelligence elsewhere in the network": "International boundaries will be nonexistent; databanks located within certain countries will service the entire network and contain information on all users. The intelligence required to control the network within one country may, in fact, be located in another (Thomas, 1983, pp. 33-34). Private control over network intelligence therefore could be expected to magnify opportunities for transnational companies to dictate the terms of trade across the entire range of information products and services that would be provided over their networks.

For those seeking to make a business of telecommunications and information, such considerations were outweighed by the sheer profit-making potential of their metamorphosizing industry. Those groups bypassed by digitized systems—like those who had lost out from the Industrial Revolution of the previous century—were undoubtedly of another mind.[20]

REFERENCES

Ares, C. (1988a, August 3). Los Peronistas, con mayoria en el Senado, anuncian su rechazo al proyecto argentino de Telefonica. *El Pais* (Madrid).

Ares, C. (1988b, August 6). El acuerdo entre Telefonica y la Entel argentina estara listo a finales de agosto. *El Pais* (Madrid).

Argentina unveils bids for phone firm. (1990, June 27). *Los Angeles Times,* p. D5.

Baker, S. Gelston, S., & Kapstein, J. (1990, April 16). The Third World is getting cellular fever. *Business Week,* pp. 80-81.

BBN Communications Corporation. (1981, April). *A history of the ARPANET: The first decade* (Rep. No. 4799). Prepared for Defense Advanced Research Projects Agency.

Bernard, K. E. (1989). The EC Green Paper. *Telecommunications Policy, 13,*(4), p. 313.

Borrego, J., & Mody, B. (1989). The Morelos satellite system in Mexico. *Telecommunications Policy, 13,*(3), 265-276.

Brannigan, M. (1986, March 17). Custom-made communications. *The Asian Wall Street Journal Weekly,* Section 2, 16-17.

Branscomb, L. M. (1982). Electronics and computers: An overview. *Science, 215* (4534), 755-760

Brock, G. W. (1981). *The telecommunications industry.* Cambridge, MA: Harvard University Press.

Bruce, R. R. (1989). Restructuring the telecom sector in developing countries: New options for policymakers. *IEEE Technology and Society Magazine, 8*(4), 17-18.

Bushaus, D. (1990, May 28). ISDN in the USA. *Communications Week,* pp. 45, 48

Christian, S. (1990, April 23). Argentina tries to sell its shaky phone system. *New York Times,* p. C6.

Communications Workers of America. (1990, March). *Information Industry Report.*

Contribution of the Director General, Intelsat. (1990, May 24). *Developments in the international telecommunications environment.* BG-85-15E, B/690.

Cowhey, P. F., Aronson, J. D., & Szekely, G. (1989). *Changing networks: Mexico's telecommunications options* (Monograph Series 32). San Diego: Center for U.S.–Mexican Studies, University of California.

De la Giroday, J. (1986). Development of a country privatization strategy. In M. Pirie & P. Young (Eds.), *Public and private responsibilities in privatization* (Tab P). Washington, DC: Agency for International Development.

de Mendoza, A. P. (1989). Telefonos de Mexico: Development and perspectives. In P.F. Cowhey, J. D. Aronson, & G. Szekely (Eds.), *Changing networks: Mexico's telecommunications options* (Monograph Series 32, pp. 91-99). San Diego: Center for U.S. to Mexican Studies, University of California.

Estrin, D. L. (1985). *Access to inter-organization computer networks.* Unpublished doctoral dissertation, Massachusetts Institute of Technology.

Estrin, D. (1986, April 27-30). *Interconnection of private networks: A link between industrial and telecommunications policy.* Paper presented at the 14th Annual Telecommunications Policy Research Conference, Airlie, VA. (Published in revised form; see D. Estrin, "Interconnection of private networks," *Telecommunications Policy, 11*(3), 247-258.)

Eugster, E. (1986). Report: ITU. *Telecommunications, 20* (3), 381.

Flanigan, J. (1990, March 11). Mexico's telephones mean U.S. dollars. *Los Angeles Times,* p. D1.

Freeman, H. L. (1986). International telecommunications policy: The critical choices. *Telecommunications, 20* (4), 42-46.

Gasman, L. (1986). The bypass connection. *High Technology, 6* (5), 27.

Gilhooly, D. (1990, March 19). CEPT restructures; welcomes competition. *Communications Week,* p. 64.

Gilhooly, D. (1990, May 28). Europe gets ISDN ready for 1992. *Communications Week,* pp. 46, 49, 51.

Girishankar, S. (1990, June 18). ISDN details ready. *Communications Week,* pp. 1, 46.

Gitlin, B. (1989). Europe may motivate U.S. effort. *Communications News, 26* (9), 63.

Heywood, P. (1987). Common ISDN game plan, schedule adopted by major nations of Europe. *Data Communications, 16* (2), 69-70.

Huber, P. W. (1987). *The geodesic network January 1987 Report on competition in the telephone industry.* Prepared by the Antitrust Division, U.S. Department of Justice. Washington: USGPO.

Hudson, H. E. (1990). *Communication satellites their development and impact.* New York: The Free Press.

Hungarian telecom: Catching-up with Europe. (1990). *Eastern European & Soviet Telecom Report, 1* (3), 14-15.

Irwin, M. R., & Merenda, M. J. (1989). Corporate networks, privatization and state sovereignty: Pending issues for the 1990s? *Telecommunications Policy, 13* (4), 329-336.

Johnson, L. L. (1986, November). *Excess capacity in international telecommunications: Poor traffic forecasting or what?* (Note N-2542-MF). Santa Monica: The RAND Corporation.

Kane, B. (1990). Puerto Rico: General strike demands: 'stop privatization!' *Labor Notes,* No. 134, pp. 1, 15.

Kempster, N. (1990, July 5). 24 rich nations set terms for aid to Eastern Europe. *Los Angeles Times,* pp. A1, A13.

Kleinfeld, N.R. (1986, April 27). The 'irritant' they call Perot. *New York Times,* Section 3, 1, 8-9.

Landes, D. S. (1972). *The unbound Prometheus.* Cambridge: Cambridge University Press.

Lazzareschi, C. (1990, June 26). Motorola plans global cellular telephone system. *Los Angeles Times,* pp. D1, D4.

Lynch, K. (1990, June 18). Global-mobile plan. *Communications Week,* p. 12.

Mantelman, L. (1989). Tips from Europe's ISDN pioneers. *Data Communications, 18* (6), 112.

Markoff, J. (1990, June 8). Computer project would speed data. *New York Times,* pp. A1, C6.

Mitchel, R., with Mason, T. (1986, April 14). How General Motors is bringing up Ross Perot's baby. *Business Week,* pp. 96-100.

Moffett, M. (1990a, June 1-2). Mexico to sell its 54% of phone monopoly. *Wall Street Journal Europe,* p. 4.

Moffett, M. (1990b, June 7). Mexico to privatize its telephone system. *Wall Street Journal,* p. A12.

National Research Council Computer Science and Technology Board, Commission on Physical Sciences, Mathematics, and Resources. (1988). *The national challenge in computer science and technology.* Washington, DC: National Academy Press.

Ohashi, T. M. (1986). Marketing the SOEs: Capital markets and marketing devices. In M. Pirie & P. Young (Eds.), *Public and private responsibilities in privatization* (Tab B). Washington, DC: Agency for International Development.

Phillips, K. L. (1988). ISDN in the year 2000. *Telecommunications Policy, 12* (4), 311-317.

Pine, A. (1990, July 5). Bush to propose global aid for Latin America. *Los Angeles Times,* pp. A1, A15.

Pirie, M., & Young, P. (Eds.). (1986). *Public and private responsibilities in privatization* (Tab I). Washington, DC: Agency for International Development.

Poe, R. (1990, May 28). Japan outdistances reluctant users. *Communications Week,* pp. 47, 50-51.

Poole, R. (1986). The politics of privatization. In M. Pirie & P. Young (Eds.), *Public and private responsibilities in privatization* (Tab D). Washington, DC: Agency for International Development.

Roeckl, C. (1990, June 18). DS-3 boom. *Communications Week,* p. 29.

Rohter, L. (1990, April 3). A telephone overhaul in Mexico. *New York Times,* p. C10.

Roth, G. (1986). Privatization of public services. In M. Pirie & P. Young (Eds.), *Public and private responsibilities in privatization* (Tab F). Washington, DC: Agency for International Development.

Rutkowski, A. M. (1983). The international telecommunication union and the United States. *Telecommunications, 17* (10), 40.

Schiller, D. (1982a). *Telematics and government,* Norwood, NJ: Ablex.

Schiller, D. (1982b). Business users and the telecommunications network. *Journal of Communication, 32* (4), 84-96.

Schiller, D. (1985a). Intelsat: Ultimo objetivo del unilateralismo USA. *Telos,* No. 2, 106-113.

Schiller, D. (1985b). The emerging global grid: Planning for what? *Media Culture & Society, 7,* 105-125.

Schiller, D. (1990). Las telecomunicaciones en el mercado unico europeo: La vision desde los Estados Unidos. *Telos,* 23, 79-87.

Schiller, H. I. (1981). *Who knows: Information in the age of the Fortune 500.* Norwood, NJ: Ablex.

Schultz, B. (1990, June 18). New Zealand deal. *Communications Week,* p. 2.

Schultz, G. (1989). U.S. contributions to communications development. *Department of State Bulletin, 89* (2148), 62-65.

Sotomayor, A. A. (1989, September 21). Ola privatizadora: Turno de telmex. *Excelsior* (Mexico City).

Special report the top 100 users: Buying and building better networks. (1990, May 21). *Communications Week,* pp. S1-S28.

Taylor, C. (1986). Policy environments and privatization. In M. Pirie & P. Young (Eds.), *Public and private responsibilities in privatization.* Washington, DC: Agency for International Development.

Temin, P., with Galambos, L. (1987). *The fall of the Bell System.* Cambridge: Cambridge University Press.

Thomas, Capt. J. R. (1983). Intelligence ownership: Problems ahead for the ISDN. *Telecommunications, 17* (11), 34, 33.

Thorngren, B. (1990). The Swedish road to liberalization. *Telecommunications Policy, 14* (2), 94-98.

United Nations. (1986, August). *UNCTC, Current Studies, Foreign Direct Investment in Latin America: Recent Trends, Prospects and Policy Issues.* New York: Author.

United Nations Economic and Social Council, Commission on Transnational Corporations. (1984, April 18-27). *The role of transnational corporations in transborder data flows.* 10th Session, E/C101984/14.

U.S. Congress, Office of Technology Assessment. (1990, January). *Critical connections: Communication for the future* (OTA-CIT-407). Washington, DC: USGPO.

U.S. Department of Commerce. (1986). *1986 U.S. Industrial Outlook.* Washington, DC: USGPO.

U.S. Department of Commerce. (1989). *1989 U.S. Industrial Outlook*. Washington, DC: USGPO.

US Department of Commerce. (1985). *Survey of Current Business, 65* (7).

U.S. Department of State. (1981, May). *U.S. Government and Private Sector Contributions to Communications Development*. Washington, DC: Bureau of International Communication and Information Policy.

U.S. Department of State. (1990, Spring). *Eastern Europe: Please Stand By*. Washington, DC: Advisory Committee on International Communications and Information Policy, Report of the Task Force on Telecommunications and Broadcasting in Eastern Europe.

U.S. Federal Communications Commission. (1957, March 15). *In the matter of allocation of frequencies in the bands above 890 Mc* (Comment of the Automobile Manufacturers Association, Docket 11866). Washington, DC: Author.

U.S. Federal Communications Commission. (1968, March 6). In the matter of ... the interdependence of computer and communication services and facilities ((First Computer Inquiry). Comment of the American Petroleum Institute, Docket 16979)). Washington, DC: Author.

Vidal, J. O. (1989, September 22). Pide 'no aflojar el paso' en lo economico. *Excelsior.*

Weisman, D. L. (1989). The proliferation of private networks and its implications for regulatory reform. *Federal Communications Law Journal, 41* (3), 331-367.

Wellenius, B. (1989). Las inversiones en telecomunicaciones. *Telos,* No. 17, 97-105.

Wilke, J. (1986, March 31). A 'dream' business that's just a phone call away. *Business Week,* 70.

Winter, R. E. (1986, April 30). Forecast for '86 capital outlays improves. *Wall Street Journal,* 6.

Wintsch, S. (1989). Toward a national research and education network. *MOSAIC, 20* (4), 32-42.

Wong, K. (1986, May). *High tech and Singapore's industrial development*. Unpublished manuscript, Temple University.

NOTES

[1] In the 1980s, the average television set in the U.S. was in use for over 7 hours each day; the average telephone handset for only a small fraction of this time. Call forwarding, call waiting, telebanking and "dial-it" numbers—there were 460 million "dial-it" calls for weather, sports, pornographic messages, and other services in 1985 in New York State alone—were examples of this strategy of finding new uses for telephone plant. See Wilke (1986, p. 70).

[2] With at least 250 times the information carrying capacity of twisted pair Cooper wires, and mandating reduced need for expensive amplifiers to boost attenuating signals, optical fiber technology evolved with startling rapidity. Fiber available in 1985 had 36 times the capacity of its antecedent of 1979; fiber selling at $8/meter in 1982, sold for just 50 cents/meter by 1985 (U.S. Department of Commerce, pp. 29-36).

[3] General Motors's internal corporate telecommunications system underwent an overhaul to permit interconnection of no less than 230,000 terminals through 50 digital switches. Perhaps 100 previously separate data communications networks and over 100 data centers within the company were integrated and centralized. See Mitchel, with Mason (1986, pp. 96-100); Kleinfeld (1986, Section 3: pp. 1, 8-9); Gasman (1986, p. 27).

[4] The crucial contributions to this process of evolving specialized "public data networks," beginning with the Arpanet, and extending through and beyond the National Research and Education Network, remain to be explored systematically. See BBN Communications Corporation (1981); National Research Council Computer Science and Technology Board, Commission on Physical Sciences, Mathematics, and Resources (1988); Wintsch, (1989, pp. 32-42); Markoff (1990, pp. A1, C6).

[5] In a context where disparate national standards and regulations made supranational networking a continuing problem for business users such projected compatibility itself constituted a source of support for the ISDN approach. See, for example, Heywood (1987, pp. 69-70).

[6] Here, a key point of contention became where the "intelligence" guiding the new systems—including not only programs defining network access and service availability, but also information and software program resources—was to be stored. How much of that intelligence would be located within the network and, by immediate inference, within the control of the network operator, and how much would be placed within the attached equipment of subscribing companies?

[7] Indeed it has been argued that AT&T top management recognized this necessity and sought to use it—through the terms of the divestiture—as a means of enlarging its sphere of corporate freedom. See Temin, with Galambos (1987).

[8] "More and more companies," one analyst declared, "are using networks to lock up customers and suppliers and make it difficult for allegiances to go away"; in Brannigan, (1986, Section 2: pp. 16-17). On continuing rapid growth of private corporate networks more generally, see Schiller, 1982a; Merenda (1989, pp. 329-336); Weisman (1989, pp. 331-367); Huber (1987); U.S. Congress (1990, pp. 106-142; 332-337).

[9] By the mid-1980s, for example, AT&T had paired itself in diverse ways with Philips, Olivetti, Convergent Technologies, Electronic Data Systems, Goldstar, Ricoh, and Telefonica.

[10] Telecommunications service vendors sought private means of cultivating more intimate knowledge of business users' needs through, for example, creation of ISDN user groups. See Girishankar (1990, p. 46). In France and the FRG, as well, business users, partnered with ISDN network suppliers, were chiefly responsible for inventing and developing applications (Mantelman, 1989, p. 112).

[11] See Freeman (1986), U.S. Congress (1990, p. 137). The best ongoing coverage of business user network strategies, applications, and capabilities was provided by the trade journal *Communications Week;* see, for example, "Special Report" (1990, pp. S1-S28).

[12] And, in support of a strategy aimed squarely at communications and information (and military electronics), General Motors—the classic "smokestack" corporation of the "old" industrial society—bought Hughes Aircraft for over $5 billion in 1985, and Electronic Data Systems, a leading computer-services firm, for $2.5 billion, in 1984. Within 1 year of its acquisition by GM, EDS—whose primary task was to coordinate the systems integration process mentioned above—had tripled its revenues (to about $3.4 billion in 1985), simply by taking over GM's in-house information processing. See Mitchel, Mason (1986, pp. 96-100).

[13] World Bank loans for telecommunications projects between 1986 and 1988 were nearly $769 million (U.S. Department of State, 1981, p. 1). Overall, U.S. Government expenditures for telecommunications development increased from $442 million in 1985

to $504 million in 1988. Six major agencies, including AID, the Departments of Commerce and State, and the Export-Import Bank, furnished most of this (p. 2).

[14] Even so, major blocks of Telmex stock remained in the hands of foreign parties. In early 1990 U.S. investors owned about 11% of TelMex's 4 billion shares, while the Mexican Government owned 54% (Flanigan, 1990, p. D1; Moffett, 1990a, p. 4).

[15] Vidal (1989), Flanigan (1990). Foreign private interests in telecommunications were also demonstrable in the Morelos satellite project; see Borrego and Mody (1989, pp. 265-276).

[16] Vidal (1989), Moffett (1990b, p. A12). The coming private regime in Mexican telecommunications was predictably hailed in the U.S.: "Mexican Telephones Mean U.S. Dollars," trumpeted one news account, which also noted that "a failure of the privatized economy to create jobs fast enough for the people inevitably laid off by modernizing state companies like Telmex" might induce a significant political reaction (Flanigan, 1990, pp. D1, D7).

[17] Advocates of privatization in Mexico claimed it would reignite the process of national modernization, among other things, by forcing a restructuring of Telmex. In turn, the Mexican Government sought accelerated modernization of telecommunications both to extend network development and service, and to facilitate specialized digital services for large business users. See United Nations (1986); Sotomayor (1989), de Mendoza (1989, pp. 91-99).

[18] See Lynch (1990, p. 12), Lazzareschi (1990, pp. D1, D4). This may be an aappropriate place to observe that privatization of telecommunications in some of the Eastern European countries occurred as a windfall of their embrace of the capitalist market during 1989-1990. For an indication of U.S. business interest in the resulting markets, see Advisory Committee on International Communications and Information Policy (1990).

[19] Between 1981 and 1990 employment in U.S. telecommunications services fell from 1,077,300 workers to 823,000, a drop of over 20%. In telecommunications manufacturing, where corporate freedom to shift production to foreign factories was more easily exploited, the employment impact of deregulation was even more severe. See Communications Workers of America (1990).

[20] We have borrowed and modified this sentence from Landes (1972, p. 123).

Chapter 12
Four Conundrums of Third World Communications: A Generational Analysis

John A. Lent

In a 1974 paper prepared for the International Association for Mass Communication Research (Lent, 1974), I laid out four conundrums that I felt puzzled Third World communication personnel. They were (a) making mass media economically and culturally practicable for newly emergent nations, (b) having media better serve the interests of the masses, not just elites and white collar groups, (c) resolving the conflict between press freedom and development journalism/communication, and (d) designing mass media theory and research appropriate to the Third World.

During the intervening generation, we have heard these concepts discussed thousands of times—from all possible perspectives. We heard the condemnation of some of the principles that are the foundations of these problems; we heard calls for new orders, horizontal communication, development support communication, new information technology, and privatization. In the process, we may have become confused by the never-ending discussion of these circuitous problems, recognizing that perhaps the only sure conclusion is that they indeed are conundrums.

CONUNDRUM NO. 1

Throughout much of the world, World War II was a watershed era when military and political colonialism was complemented with, or superseded by, a more pervasive cultural colonialism. Societies not in a position to afford sophisticated electronic media found themselves more and more in the clutches of cultural colonizers such as the United States, United Kingdom, and Japan. They depended on these powers to provide capital for investment in media and for their technological needs; they also relied on them for most of their media contents. They dispatched their personnel to England, the U.S., and Japan to learn how to run English, American, and Japanese media. The end result: These emerging nations had their own national media systems, but in name only.

The alternatives to this counterfeit scenario were obvious—local ownership, indigenous contents, locally trained personnel, use of native language and culture, less dependence upon outside technology. Easier said than done. In poor, emerging nations, oftentimes the only capable entity willing to provide these alternatives was the government, which in postindependence periods tended to be authoritarian. So, the options were: foreign-owned and -influenced media, at the risk of extinction of the native cultures, and government-owned and controlled media, at the risk of loss of freedom of expression and private entrepreneurship.

A third answer lurked in the background, although it never was popular among the new nations in a hurry to have the latest and best, and multinational corporations and foreign governments bent on creating dependency relationships. Simply stated, it was that a nation should not be tempted by the paraphernalia of modernity until it is sure there are elements in the society capable of keeping them indigenous and free.

It was difficult, and seemingly hypocritical, to tell newly independent countries to slow down, not to expect or want all the accoutrements of modernity which those in older, larger countries possessed. It was not easy to tell them that traditional cultural and personality strains should be preserved and built upon (see Gusfield, 1967). The lure of satellite hookups, home video, cable television, or slick Westernized programming was too appealing, and country after country sought loans or consortia linkages with foreign interests—usually the very colonial societies they had fought for their freedom.

After a generation of attention on this conundrum, has much changed? Have mass media become more economically and culturally practicable for developing nations? Has media imperialism been abated? Have alternatives to the one-way flow of news been adopted? Are Third World countries any less dependent upon the more industrialized ones for communication technology, capital, know-how, or contents?

Much has been attempted since 1974 to change media contents and flows of news and information. Various countries have moved to limit foreign content in their media, to initiate binational or regional news and feature exchanges, and to increase or upgrade indigenous media content. For example, in parts of the Caribbean and in the Philippines, radio broadcasters must play a certain percentage of local music; in many Asian societies, local media now have incentives to produce quality indigenous programming. Governments in some parts of the world initiated protectionist action to save their movie industries (by taxing, banning, censoring, and otherwise limiting foreign films and by upgrading local industries through subsidies, film festivals, training, and other benefits) and formed regional agencies to exchange television programming.

Regional and Third World news services also came into prominence, especially after 1976, when the Non-Aligned Countries Movement Newspool was launched in New Delhi, and the Caribbean News Agency in Barbados, the latter as a joint venture of government and private media. Although the pool still operates, there are conflicting reports about its effectiveness; one repeated criticism is that because the pool relies on national, government news services, much propaganda is disseminated that is not used by end receivers. Still other regional news services started up, including the Asia-Pacific News Network (ANN), Pan African News Agency (PANA), Organization of Petroleum Exporting Countries (OPEC) News Agency, ASEAN News Exchange (ANEX), and PACNEWS. All of these agencies placed "staggering financial burdens" upon national authorities, although they received international cooperation and some outside national cooperation in financial areas (Ali, 1985, pp. 67–71).

An older news agency that came into more prominence during the 1970s is Inter Press Service (IPS), established in 1964 to specialize in Third World affairs. The service has been hailed as a viable alternative to the Big Four (Associated Press, United Press International, Reuters, and Agence France Press), repeatedly accused of dominating the world news flow to the benefit of the countries of the North. IPS is inexpensive to operate, because it uses local correspondents who are paid wage scales of their countries. Other philosophies of IPS that make it more culturally practicable for Third World societies are that it emphasizes horizontal flows of news (from the masses to the masses and from South to South countries); alternative news values (the process of development news, rather than that of the bizarre, aberrational, or sudden deaths/disasters), and people's democratization (people participating in decisions that affect their lives) (Giffard, 1984; see also Hester, 1979). IPS has had a stormy relationship with certain quarters in the U.S. that have questioned its credibility and opposed its plan to connect the Third World countries via satellite.

With all this activity, how much change has taken place? Not very much, if we read the findings of researcher Tapio Varis. In a 1983 follow-up study to one conducted a decade before (Varis, 1974, 1984), which revealed the high level of television dependence upon a few industrialized countries, Varis saw no clear changes in the worldwide proportion of imported programs. As some countries lessened their dependence on shows from the big exporting countries, others increased theirs.

Varis found that the North–South countries gap still holds and that the bulk of imported programming came from the U.S., followed by Western Europe and Japan. Perhaps an encouraging sign was that, in 1983, regional exchanges were important; i.e., Arab stations received one-third of their programs from other Arab countries; Latin American, 10% from other Latin Americans (Varis, 1984). Also on the positive side, some countries (notably the most populated of China and India) remained relatively free of imported content, while others turned away Western shows considered anathema to their cultural values or national ideologies.

A 1991 journalistic survey of Asian television networks indicated the situation has changed considerably since Varis's 1984 report. U.S. television programming that enjoyed "nearly effortless domination most everywhere else" faced a tough sell in the Pacific Rim countries. U.S. industry trade groups claimed the percentage of U.S. programming ranged from five percent in China and South Korea to 15% to 20% in Malaysia and the Philippines (Mahler, 1991, p. 13-H).

Among reasons given for the diminishing use of U.S. fare were language and cultural barriers, national restrictions on content, broadcast monopolies, hard-currency restrictions, import quotas, piracy, and overwhelming competition. Much of the competition emanates from Hong Kong studios, whose thousands of hours of programming are popular throughout East and Southeast Asia. For example, one-half of all foreign programs in Thailand come from Hong Kong (Mahler, 1991, p. 13-H).

Similarly, Straubhaar, in a 1984 study, showed a decline of U.S. influence in Brazilian television. By the 1980s, broadcasters began to substitute Brazilian shows for U.S. fare during prime time. However, they bought more U.S. programs for daytime and late nighttime use where smaller audiences could not support Brazilian-produced shows (Straubhaar, 1984; see Wildman & Siwek, 1988).

What has also become more apparent is that, although foreign programs continued to dominate Third World screens, they were not necessarily the most popular. Throughout Latin America, regional or local shows usually top the ratings; the same applies to Asia. This factor confirmed the widely acknowledged belief that pricing—not popularity—is the reason imported television programs predominate in the Third World. In fact, export prices represent less than 1% of local production costs (Hoskins, Mirus, & Rozeboom, 1989, pp. 55–75). Such low export prices for shows of high production quality adds to the conundrum, making it difficult for drama producers to compete. The possible solution of implementing import quotas does not work because it leads to local cheap quiz, talk shows, and panel discussions; furthermore, with satellite and cable cross-border transmission, quotas are more untenable (see Hoskins et al., 1989, p. 72).

Certainly one factor that changed, especially during the 1980s, is the widespread introduction of other media technology—videocassettes and satellite-relayed and cable television—capable of bringing in foreign programming. Video has had a tremendous impact upon Third World film and television industries, government revenue, and people's morals and values. It is a difficult medium form to control because of the rampant pirating and smuggling and because it comes into homes independent of media systems. Cable connected to satellite is also changing viewing patterns.

With the existence of regional and alternative news services, has the flow of news changed worldwide? Sreberny-Mohammadi (1984), based on a 1979 study of 29 countries, reported the Big Four news agencies are still the second most important sources of news (after national services), that news is still defined as the exceptional event ("coups and earthquakes"), and that politics dominated the news budget. Perhaps a change is that regionalism is given prominence in news decisions; most countries play up their own regions first, then North America, and Western Europe. But the findings suggest that not much changed concerning the reporting of the Third World (other than a country's own region) and Eastern Europe; they remained invisible (Sreberny-Mohammadi, 1984).

In other attempts to screen pervasive outside influences, some Third World governments have taken steps to curb foreign advertising agencies and their messages. In some instances, they have stipulated that all broadcast commercials must use local talent, voices, and settings; other authorities, taking more drastic action, have either nationalized the transnational advertising agencies or set up their own.

But the transnational corporations in most countries prevail. They sidestep local laws with "Ali Baba" agencies that are listed in the names of locals but are actual fronts for transnationals, and they establish full-fledged regional networks aimed at providing world-wide service to major clients, thus taking away a huge chunk of the market share from local agencies.

One part of this first conundrum where the trend is much more pronounced than in the 1970s concerns the rapidly escalating dependence of Third World nations upon industrialized countries and multinational corporations for information/communication technology. Third World nations are clamoring to be part of the so-called information age, without having the capital, technology, and know-how necessary to be self-sustaining. This sounds familiar because it is the same scramble these same countries found themselves in a couple of decades ago when television and radio were promoted as their panacea. Despite a phenomenal growth between 1975 and 1985 that saw radio receivers in the Third World more than double and TV sets triple, there was not much support for the notion that these media were societal cure-alls, which was the thinking of the 1950s and 1960s.

Third World nations today are fed a full diet of information on computers and satellites and how they can solve many development problems. The results have been the generation of myths concerning the capabilities of new information technology—rather than well-thought-out national policies that look at the technology's effects upon the national economy, labor force, privacy, cultural values, and dependency relationships—and a diversion of attention from previous dialogues on development journalism, ethics, media autonomy, NWICO, freedom of information, and human values, to discussions about information hardware—its prices, uses, and possibilities.

Different from a generation ago is multinational corporations' total commitment to, and success at, selling their wares, eventually hoping to place a telephone in every home, a microcomputer in every village, and other elaborate information paraphernalia in every nook and cranny of the globe. Such information growth mania has made Third World countries more dependent upon outside forces, widened the gap between the haves and have-nots, and damaged local autonomy. In some cases, large investment in new information technology has created a further drain on the economic base of mass media, resulting in negative impacts upon newsgathering.

Another difference is the sophistication with which multinational corporations control information and communication. One tactic used is privatization. The World Bank, International Monetary Fund, and U.S. Agency for International Development have been pushing privatization as the "reigning orthodoxy" to benefit many areas, a "creative process designed to shift whole areas of economic activity...from the politicized, non-commercial sector to the consumer-responsive profit-making private sector" (Schiller, 1986).

A subtle way the major development agencies, in conjunction with multinational corporations, promote privatization is to tout it for settling international debts. Through the sale of state enterprises, immediate cash is found to settle foreign debts by encouraging banks to "convert part of their debt owed by less developed countries into equity" in newly privatized businesses. A few years ago, Dan Schiller warned that, particularly in impoverished countries, privatization of national telecommunications will allow private capital to "skew control over network intelligence" and that,

> Centralized network intelligence will vastly magnify the opportunities for transnational companies to dictate the terms of trade with the less developed nations across the whole range of information products and services that will be provided over the network. (Schiller, 1986, p. 20)

Still another difference more discernible in recent years is the tendency of some Third World countries and media operations to do what has been considered the monopoly of media in Western, more industrialized nations—exporting their media products, buying communication property abroad, and tying in with conglomerates of industrialized nations. Concerning the latter, Third World media have increasingly become affiliated with U.S., European, and Australian multinational corporations such as those of Rupert Murdoch, Dow Jones, Time-Warner, Robert Hersant, or Robert Maxwell. Additionally, some national conglomerates that Third World mass media connect to are themselves parts of multinational corporations; for example, Samsung Corporation, the world's 35th largest company, which owns South Korean newspaper, magazine, and broadcasting interests, controls a portion of Corning Corporation in the U.S.

Other national conglomerates own substantial numbers of mass media in the Third World. In India, the Birla Group, publishers of the *Hindustan Times,* has companies dealing with aluminum, automobiles, carpets, chemicals, shipping, steel, tea, and textiles; in Brazil, Sistema Globo, which has a very cozy relationship with

government, owns TV Globo (world's fourth largest television network), 43 television stations, a large radio group, the daily *O Globo*,
magazines, books, and comics.

Conglomerates own many media in Indonesia, Malaysia, the Philippines, the Caribbean, Mexico, Sri Lanka, and Singapore as well.
Indonesia's Bimantara Group, which started Rajawali Citra Televisi
Indonesia in 1988, has assets of US$1 billion and equity in 90
companies, including an assembly plant for Mercedes trucks, palm oil
plantations, insurance brokerages, animal vaccine manufacturing,
and leasing, holding, investment, transport, petroleum, plastics, food,
and telecommunications companies. A subsidiary, Settel of Los Angeles, California, deals closely with Hughes Aircraft of the U.S.

Fleet Group, a Malaysian investment arm of Fleet Holdings, has
grown to astronomical proportions, not only in mass communications,
but in many other businesses and industries. As with Indonesia's
Bimantara, Fleet Group is very closely aligned with the government.
Fleet controls New Straits Times, which owns 70% of Sistem Televis-
yen Malaysia, five dailies, three Sunday newspapers, many magazines,
book publishing firms, a food products company, and a major hotel
chain. It is composed of, or closely tied to, more than 150 companies
dealing with investment, hotels, realty, telecommunications, trading,
land development, cinemas, shipping, recreational services, drilling,
travel, car rental, construction, electronics, restaurants, credit companies, newsprint, insurance, banking, leasing, and computers, among
others.

In sum, a number of changes have occurred concerning the Third
World mass media's dependency upon foreign communication and
information suppliers. In some cases, television networks have instituted regional exchanges, sought culturally appropriate foreign
programming, and attempted more local shows, some of which have
come to the top as the most popular. Most countries now have their own
national news services, from which more news is taken than from the
Big Four agencies, and there has been an expansion of regional and
Third World news services. But looming menacingly over the indige-
nization of programming and news flows are the increasing dependence of Third World countries upon multinational corporations for
communication/information technology and the tie-ins of Third World
mass media concerns with foreign and domestic conglomerates.

CONUNDRUM NO. 2

A generation ago, much of the Third World was anxious to divest itself
of centuries-old colonial institutions and traditions, the mass media

included. Nationalist writers rightly explained that colonial news-papers in their nations were there solely to keep colonists in touch with themselves and their civilizations back in Europe or the U.S. (Fanon, 1965). They complained, again justifiably so, that the media were designed for the elite members of society, not the masses.

Governments of these newly emergent countries picked up the refrain and promised remedies. They called for changes in media organization, control, and personnel to meet the goals of a new society and to build a national consciousness under a new leadership. The result: Newspapers changed hands, ministries of information were set up, new guidelines were instituted. But what really changed?

Not much as far as the masses were concerned, for, whereas in colonial societies, media were used by elite colonialists to keep abreast of happenings in the mother country and of other colonialists, in the postindependence period, media were used by native elite and white-collar groups to communicate with other elite and white-collar groups. And as in colonial days, determining the majority and minority of a society had very little to do with statistics (see Balandier, 1966), so that media catering to urban elites were treated as the majority press, all others as a minority. Thus, the printed media especially had very little identification with the masses—the statistical majority, often not even using their language.

As said before, there were calls for change. In 1972, Kenya's foreign minister said the press had to recast the image it was portraying of the nation to give a proper share to the rural areas, to allow regular space, presented in simple language, for rural readers, and to put more reporters in the countryside. He thought the government had to abolish import duties on newsprint and ink used to serve rural regions and to provide transport to carry the newspapers there (*African Journalist*, 1972, p. 1). The London *Times* editor, speaking to a predomi-nantly Third World group, said the editorial concept that "what the government says is news is news" must be abandoned in favor of more grassroots inquiry, more interviews, more letters to the editor, more articles of dissent, more broadcasting phone-in programs (Evans, 1973), and more public access to the media generally.

Despite these soundings, an ironical characteristic of some Third World mass media was that, as the production and distribution technology was modernized, the format and contents of the product were not. High-speed, full-color offset presses printed newspapers full of dull, dated, and often unintelligible information; ultramodern broadcasting stations turned out news shows that could have been done just as well with pencil and pad. Contents did not reflect the aspirations or problems of a growing society—problems of the metrop-olis, pollution, growth for growth's sake, consumerism, or education.

Presentations were in traditional hackneyed fashion; for example, if education was to be promoted, pictures and story of a minister opening a school building were displayed, rather than serious, in-depth analysis of equalization of learning, life-long learning, learning as innovator, diversified higher learning, or learning for a good life (see Adiseshiah, 1972); if development was the story, one could expect to read or hear the words of a minister extolling the virtues of economic progress, never anything about the hazards of rapid, unplanned modernization, for example, pollution of the air, sound, water, and land.

For a brief period in the late 1970s, it seemed that changes would be made as development researchers and practitioners placed more emphasis on interpersonal communication networks and folk media, on adapting formal media to villagers' problems, on using smaller media, on reopening ancient lines of communication between Third World nations, and on reassessing the development models associated with these people. Much of this thinking and activity was put aside, however, as the high technology campaigns of the Information Age blanketed the world. Nevertheless, a residue has come down to us today through groups such as World Association of Christian Communications, Asian Social Institute, and Worldview International.

Although formal mass media are still chiefly elitist throughout the Third World, some progress has been made in the past generation to make them more accessible to a wider public. Underrepresented (and in some cases, nonrepresented) groups, especially women, but also peasants, minorities, and ethnic groups, have been analyzed pertaining to their coverage and the images reflected of them in the media. Conferences and consultancies on media and their portrayal of women have been held in Asia, Africa, and the Caribbean, with rather uniform conclusions, pointing out that women are portrayed in dichotomous terms—either as subservient, young sex objects or as caring mothers and housewives; that very little to advance the role of women is shown; and that women play a very small part in media operations. Similarly, reporting of minorities and ethnic groups has also received some attention.

In recent decades, important data were collected by field practitioners and researchers on how to communicate with rural societies. The philosophies of Freire, Díaz Bordenave, and Fuglesang, proclaiming that self-reliance, participation, a faith in people's ability to learn and change, and horizontal information flows, were treated as important characteristics in the communication process. Exciting experiments, mostly in the 1970s, with some in the 1980s, encouraged the public's participation in the design and implementation of mass communication, among them being the Sudan Rural Television Project, Costa Rica's Total Language campaign, and the United Nations Technical Cooperation among Developing Countries.

Folk and traditional communication forms were explored more vigorously with Ranganath (1976) experimenting with the capacity of Indian folk media to accept developmental messages; Kidd (see Kidd & Colletta, 1981) and Fuglesang (see Fuglesang & Chandler, 1986) looking at folk and interpersonal channels in Africa; Dissanayake (1977) assessing audience preference for traditional media in Sri Lanka; or Valbuena (1986, 1987b) documenting folk media in the Philippines. In a number of countries, folk forms were adapted for use in the mass media. Some governments and broadcasting services (e.g., Indonesia, Korea, Malaysia, Nigeria, and the Philippines) campaigned and made resources available for the preservation of folk media.

As evidence piled up that big media, such as television, had not done their job in the development process, criticisms were voiced and alternatives sought. Examples such as Zaire and Zambia were trotted out where so many of the national resources were used for the expensive infrastructure that little was left to do programs that modernized attitudes and behavior. In Nigeria, after 25 years of television, local officials and broadcasters admitted the medium had failed to meet the "challenge of accelerating the development process, contributing to the integration of society and providing the means for preserving traditional cultural values" (McLellan, 1986, p. 4). They, and others, pointed out that nothing had changed; that modern equipment—modeled after the West, cumbersome, expensive, and heavily centralized—had been introduced, but the messages were the same.

Some practitioners felt that a big medium such as television, to be used for development, had to be re-invented—combined with solar power, satellites, or low-cost video equipment, for group viewing in rural villages. One of the first large experiments in this regard was Satellite Instructional Television Experiment (SITE), set up in 1975–1976 to transmit via satellite, messages to 2,400 villages in six Indian states. Designed to supplement children's education and upgrade farmers' skills, SITE was praised by some for its hardware and chastised by others for using irrelevant programs. One complaint was that inarticulate farmers were not reflected properly in programs designed for rural elites and privileged farmers.

In parts of Africa, especially Niger and Senegal, and in Indonesia, solar-powered television receivers are in use for rural group viewing, while in many parts of the Third World, small-format video is used to allow participation by ordinary people in development projects. In the late 1980s, Sri Lanka tested the viability of its first locally operated community radio station, an experiment that has been tried in other countries. Station journalists visit nearby Sri Lankan villages and encourage people to choose topics for their own shows, form their own questions, and edit their statements.

Additional small community radio stations, using indigenous languages and talent and promoting participation, self-sufficiency, and self-reliance, have been operated in parts of Latin America (see O'Connor, 1989), in India (see Anjaneyulu, 1989), Kenya (Heath, 1986), and Liberia (Kweekeh, 1987; Foote, 1989).

Other encouraging prospects of making communication better serve the masses include utilizing interpersonal information flows, small-group dynamics, and small-media technologies. In Ciamis, Indonesia, the Integrated Rural Environmental Program established a number of development communications groups KKP that combined traditional and modern media to bring about change (Oepen, 1986, pp. 87–102); use of small group and interpersonal communication channels was widespread during the "People Power" of the Philippines in early 1986. However, Pratt (1986, p. 529) lamented that the use of traditional media among small groups in the spread of information about population control was miniscule in most of Africa.

Among examples of small media technologies have been the successful use of audio cassettes throughout Central America, blackboard newspapers in the Philippines, or mimeographed papers on the village level, as in parts of Africa. Finally, there have been growing concerns in Third World countries about the violent nature of some imported media messages. At the forefront was the "breast is best" campaign of the late 1970s, as well as others denouncing media advertising of tobacco products and other goods dumped on the Third World once they have lost their appeal in the West because of their dangerous characteristics. Newly formed consumer groups have looked into media's role in promoting violent messages, such as misleading medicinal advertisements and dangerous goods.

In conclusion, although the huckstering of new information technology smothered the emphasis on alternative means of "mass" communication innovated in the 1970s, some campaigns and experiments have rekindled the new paradigms in recent years. Among the latter were efforts to make media more accessible to underrepresented groups, to incorporate the masses in message design and implementation, to reinvent big media such as television by connecting it to solar energy and satellites, and to use small media technologies such as videocassettes, audiocassettes, blackboards, or community radio stations.

CONUNDRUM NO. 3

A generation ago, territories of the Third World were in the process of redefining the concept of press freedom inherited from colonists. Because of the transitional nature of these societies, government leaders rationalized such modifications of these press freedom concepts on the grounds that, in emerging nations, unusual powers are sometimes necessary to force decisions that will benefit the people. They asked that the mass media show restraint in criticizing government, and, at the same time, promote national goals and identities. The press was implored to accept a deliberately guided press concept until the nation was stabilized, after which time the powers that be would lessen press restrictions. The questions asked by some critics of this notion were: How long will it take for stabilization? Who will decide when that time arrives?

Although the terms *development journalism* and *deliberately guided press* were often used interchangeably in the Third World, it would seem they are contradictory. If development journalism, as Quebral (1973, pp. 25–28) claimed, pushes for awareness (not just a nonpurposive chronicling of facts) and offers alternatives, then it would follow that development journalists could better do their jobs if not threatened by restrictions when they come up with alternatives other than those of the government.

Development journalism in its original form was an honorable attempt by independent journalists to report comprehensively and accurately the development story of a nation in a way that related to and benefited the masses. However, governments, because they had the capital and resources, eventually became the sponsors of most development communication projects. In the process, oftentimes the projects were designed to boost government policies and promote cults of personality that had marginal rewards for the people. The result has been that the term has received a bad reputation, especially among Western (mainly U.S.) journalists and scholars, many of whom were not aware of the intentions of the original framers of the concept. These critics have tended to denigrate all development journalism and communication projects, whatever their purposes or origins.

One of the problems is that during the past generation, some of the organizations and individuals originally affiliated with development journalism folded or moved on to other endeavors, in the process, leaving a void filled by government funded agencies (oftentimes ministries of information), with their own brand of development communication.

It would be foolhardy to condemn all development communication projects emanating from the government as being self-serving. There seem to be exceptions, including government media programs to promote health in Bangladesh, the Philippines, Pakistan, Indonesia, and India (*Media Asia*, 1985), the development-oriented soap opera "Hum Log" on India's government-controlled Doordarshan Television (see Singhal, 1988, pp. 109–126), and the 30-minute weekly "Cock Crow at Dawn," used by Nigerian government-owned television to sell large-scale mechanized farming (see Ume-Nwagbo, 1986, pp. 155–167).

Other worthy development journalism/communication work continues today, independent of government propaganda machines. World Association of Christian Communications and Worldview International, among others, use communication skills to get messages across to the masses on nutrient, environment, consumer, and sanitation issues; independent development journalists still function in isolated pockets such as in parts of southern India, and some elitist dailies continue to carry development stories (see Lent & Vilanilam, 1979; Ogan, 1982).

The argument for or against Western (U.S.) style press freedom in the Third World has received immense attention during the past 20 years. Government officials regularly go to the lectern to claim press freedom is a foreign concept, meant to promote Western interests. They, and others, point out that, during and immediately after World War II, when U.S.-type press freedom was thought to be a panacea for the world's problems, it was used to push the U.S. political and economic systems.

Others point out that the Third World should practice Western-style press freedom because their presses traditionally were started by Western colonialists. However, it must be recalled the colonialists established presses that did the bidding of missionaries and civil servants, leaving much to be desired in the area of press freedom. If anything, the colonial heritage left in place in the Third World a set of regulations that restricted, rather than liberated, and much of the contemporary legislative control on the press of the Third World has been built into regulations left behind by the British, French, Spanish, or Americans, and since abandoned in those countries themselves.

Contemporary Third World officials back up their idea that press freedom is a luxury of the West, not affordable in their countries, by stating that this, and other political and civil rights, must take a back seat to more fundamental human rights of food, shelter, and clothing. They believe that the press must be free and responsible, and to be the latter, it must put into motion governmental plans of development. As in the West, Third World editors think their primary role is to inform; but, unlike their counterparts in the West, they see their secondary job as mobilizing for national development, not entertaining.

In discussing press freedom, analysts usually look at the obvious legislative constraints, but these pale in contrast to the threat of oligopolistic ownership of mass media. The conspicuous increase in press ownership by local governments and businesses, and by the multinational combines, certainly lends support to A. J. Liebling's much-earlier dictum that freedom of press belongs to the person who owns one. The high cost of establishing mass media has set up a self-perpetuating situation where ownership is limited to those who already have economic power. Close alliances between big media owners and businesses, industrial, and political powers mean a uniformity of ideas, continued press support of these power brokers and the status quo, and accrued benefits to the owners. The dilemma in the Third World has not yet reached the alarming state of media in the U.S., the country that has pushed its concept of press freedom worldwide and that has been used as an exemplar for the Third World. About two dozen conglomerates control most of the mass media of the U.S., where one-fifth of the wealthiest individuals are media owners.

Third World government and media personnel must be confused about different interpretations and styles of news in other parts of the world. They must recognize that the difference is fine indeed between a propagandistic "line" credited to presses of socialist countries, and the objective "approach" of Western journalism. They must be baffled as they observe situations in the U.S. where reporters are told to be politically inactive, while their publishers and editors socialize with and support powers that be. They must wonder how objective U.S. and other Western journalists are who, for convenience or security, practice "pack journalism."

In summary, because of deliberately guided and development communication principles and practices established by Third World governments, the concept of press freedom inherited from the West has been altered during the past generation. This is a laudatory turn of events. First of all, the Western-style press freedom forced upon some cultures by colonizers was never relevant or free. The very nature of the colonial press, as a vehicle for the colonialists and not nationals, inhibited its appropriateness. Second, as increasing attention is focused on the lack of independence of the Western (mainly U.S.) press, its legitimacy (much less its universality) as a model becomes more suspect.

CONUNDRUM NO. 4

As mass communication education and research took hold in the Third World, it became apparent that they were closely tied to the theory and methodology developed in the U.S. and Europe. This was understandable, and possibly unavoidable at the time, because the discipline of mass communication evolved in these areas and most Third World media researchers received their education there.

But what was difficult to fathom was why mass media developers in the Third World latched onto certain Western communication theories relating to their own cultures and held them sacrosanct. For example, Lerner's and Rogers's models of mass media and development were quoted throughout the Third World without much thought given to their applicability; Western-originated methods were as freely dispensed. Thus, one found illiterate Colombian peasants Q-sorting, Asians unaccustomed to answering questions by mail receiving long questionnaires—in English, no less.

In suggesting that mass communication theory and research be made more appropriate to the Third World, I wrote in 1974 that homogenizing indices developed in the West had to be abandoned; that one shot, "safari" research be replaced by long-term, committed, and relevant studies; and that comparative research be given a back seat to more individual systems' approaches. Has all of this been accomplished? Hardly, but some steps have been taken.

First and very important is the fact that awareness of Third World media problems has come of age. The literature shows this trend, as does the number of conferences, workshops, and symposia devoted to Third World media. Gratifying is the fact that the Third World has developed a number of media research centers with their own researchers in charge, as well as their own associations, journals, and other resources. For example, a 1956 Unesco report could not find a single African country where mass communication study had been seriously undertaken, and in the Third World, listed only Brazil, India, Cuba, El Salvador, Honduras, Indonesia, Mexico, and the Philippines as having mass communication centers (Ugboajah, 1975, p. 10). During the past generation, regional groups, as well as nation-bound institutes, have sped up their research activity. In the West, professional organizations and journals have taken more heed of the Third World and provided a forum for critical scholars who previously might not have been heard.

Before the mid-1970s, very few researchers recognized (or dared to admit) that something was amiss in how research was applied to Third World media. Now, a few books and even more articles are written and conferences are organized on these difficulties. Thus, some scholars are cautious about comparing media systems across countries, lest they have determined levels of equivalence, and about using inflexible Western social science techniques in the Third World. Governments in some cases have taken precautions that their cultures are not mined for data that are not fed back to the populations studied (Lent, 1983; see also Beltran, 1975; Pausewang, 1973). Also, during the 1970s, the old paradigms and theories concerning communication and development were challenged (Melkote, 1987), although they made a triumphant comeback in the 1980s.

But, in spite of these accomplishments, the criticism continued to trickle out in the 1980s concerning communication research about or applied to the Third World. Rita Atwood said most communication research on Latin America by U.S. researchers suffered from "ethnocentric rigidity, mercantile or imperialistic motives, and methodological inadequacy," and that U.S. mass communication publications have not paid attention to works of the many pioneering critical scholars who hailed from Latin America (Atwood & McAnany, 1986, p. 13). Hanno Hardt said "comparative and international communication research in this country (U.S.)...has been shaped by the role of the United States in creating the political realities of international politics and conducting foreign affairs after World War II" (Hardt, 1988, p. 129). He added that the past research "operated in reaction to specific events or policies, rather than as an independent intellectual enterprise committed to the development of theories of media systems in a variety of cultures" (Hardt, 1988, p. 143).

Although such criticism and awareness are laudatory, much remains to be done before research can truly be relevant to the Third World. There is still a void of empirical work on applicability of research techniques to various cultures, despite efforts by institutions such as Asian Mass Communication Information Centre (AMIC) or African Council for Communication Education (ACCE). There needs to be work done on systematically identifying research designs and paradigms, on exploring their effects upon cultures, on determining what is being criticized, and on seeing how the literature is promoting existing paradigms. In short, there are needs to subject Western-originated research techniques to rigorous testing in the Third World to determine empirically their strengths and weaknesses.

Along the same lines, there must be more internal searching for alternative theoretical and research models. AMIC helped spur work in this direction by having scholars look at mass communication theory in Asia from Chinese, Indian, Buddhist, and Islamic perspectives (see *Media Asia,* 1986). In one of the AMIC contributions, Jayaweera argued that Indians do not have to construct new paradigms of communication, as they have an "inexhaustible reservoir of alternate models within their own history."

Additionally, efforts must be increased to provide more relevant educations for future communication researchers and practitioners.

Beginning in undergraduate schools, curricula must be constructed that emphasize different values than those now in vogue. For example, in the Philippines, Flor (1987, pp. 21–22) said mass communication students are plagued with the "cult of scientism," media-centric curricula, materialistic role models in media, a profit-oriented media industry, and the adoption of Western models of communication education. In recent years, some countries have begun to send their mass communication faculty for advanced education to Third World universities and centers, for example, the Philippines, Malaysia, Cuba, or India (Valbuena, 1987a), or to a variety of places, rather than just a few universities in the U.S. This should widen the perspectives of future communication researchers.

Although, during the 1970s, attempts were made at cooperative and relevant research between Third World media centers and individuals, there are shortcomings here as well. In some countries, jealous media researchers refuse to share their data with others who might be able to apply them to the betterment of society or academia. In some cases, after valuable resources have been very generously used to sustain (in some cases, pamper) Third World educators abroad for graduate study, these people have returned home in a "me first" frame of mind, devoting much time to furthering their own financial or political—and not scholarly—interests. At other times, they return as promoters of Western models, never having learned the skills of critical thinking.

To summarize, the important changes of the past generation have been the breaking up of the U.S. monopoly of communication study, the development of regional and national media research centers in the Third World, and the questioning of the appropriateness and integrity of much Western research and theory that has been applied to the Third World. Much remains to be done. Most importantly, the scholarly world must be ever vigilant that the strong U.S. research tradition does not regain supremacy, a scenario quite possible since the U.S. research institutions and individuals command so much of the new technology that can disseminate that tradition quickly and widely.

CONCLUSION

The past generation has been productive because those involved with Third World mass media now are certainly more cognizant of the problems and the difficulty of finding suitable solutions, and because there has been a proliferation of centers and individuals committed to solving the conundrums.

What is distressing, however, is that so much of the good work of those committed to solving these dilemmas is being overshadowed by the hucksters of high technology and other machinery and techniques that have failed in the past. One can take hope in the idea that, perhaps, the common people of the world, unlike the elites, do not overestimate the powers of technology to shape their lives, and therefore, will not see them as the panaceas that they are promoted as.

REFERENCES

Adiseshiah, M. (1972, September). *Asian education in 2000*. Paper presented at Third International Conference, Modernisation in Asia, Penang, Malaysia.

The African Journalist. (1972, June). Africa's People Gap, p. 1.

Ali, S. M. (1985). International cooperation for the activation of information flow. *Media Asia, 12*(2), 67–71.

Anjaneyulu, S. K. (1989). Scaling down: Local radio in India. *Development Communication Report, 1*, 1–2.

Atwood, R., & McAnany, E. G. (1986). *Communication and Latin American society, trends in critical research, 1960–1985*. Madison: University of Wisconsin Press.

Balandier, G. (1966). The colonial situation: A theoretical approach (1951). In I. Wallerstein (Ed.), *Social change: The colonial situation*. New York: John Wiley and Sons.

Beltrán, L. R. (1975, December). Communications research in Latin America. *Intermedia*, pp. 7–10.

Dissanayake, W. (1977, Spring). New wine in old bottles: Can folk media convey modern messages? *Journal of Communication*, pp. 122–124.

Evans, H. (1973, February). *Stewardship of the mass media*. Paper presented at Press Foundation of Asia, One Asia Assembly, New Delhi.

Fanon, F. (1965). *Studies in a dying colonialism*. New York: Monthly Review Press.

Flor, A. G. (1987). Alternative visions versus realities in communication education. *Media Asia, 14*(1), 21–22.

Foote, D. (1989). Local radio for development: Haba na haba. *Development Communication Report, 1*, 3–6.

Fuglesang, A., & Chandler, D. (1986). The open-snuff box: Communication as participation. *Media Development, 2*, 2–4.

Giffard, C. A. (1984, Autumn). Inter Press Service: News from the Third World. *Journal of Communication*, pp. 41–59.

Gusfield, J. (1967). Tradition and modernity: Misplaced polarities in the study of social change. *American Journal of Sociology, 72*(4).

Hardt, H. (1988). Comparative media research: The world according to America. *Critical Studies in Mass Communication, 5*, 129–146.

Heath, C. (1986). Politics of broadcasting in Kenya—community radio suffers. *Media Development, 2,* 10–12.

Hester, A. (1979). Inter Press Service: News for and about the Third World. In J. A. Lent (Ed.), *Third World mass media: Issues, theory and research* (pp. 83–102). Williamsburg, VA.

Hoskins, C., Mirus, R., & Rozeboom, W. (1989, Spring). U.S. telvision programs in the international market: Unfair pricing? *Journal of Communication,* pp. 55–75.

Kidd, R., & Colletta, N. (1981). *Tradition for development.* Berlin: German Foundation for International Development.

Kweekeh, F. (1987, March). Radio for rural development in Liberia. *Intermedia.* pp. 27–29.

Lent, J. A. (1974, September). *Mass media in the developing world: Four conundrums.* Paper presented at IAMCR, Leipzig, Germany.

Lent, J. A. (1983, February). Western type communications research in the Third World—A critical appraisal. *Vidura,* pp. 33–38.

Lent, J. A., & Vilanilam, J. V. (1979). *The use of development news: Case studies of India, Malaysia, Thana and Thailand.* Singapore: AMIC.

Mahler, R. (1991, November 3). A tough sell in Asia: Television shows from America. *Philadelphia Inquirer.* p. 13–H.

McLellan, I. (1986). *Television for development: The African experiment.* Ottawa: International Development Research Centre.

Media Asia. (1985). Symposium on Health and Mass Media, *12*(4).

Melkote, S. (1987). Biases in development support communication. *Gazette, 40,* 39–55.

O'Connor, A. (1989). People's radio in Latin America—a new assessment. *Media Development, 2,* 47–52.

Oepen, M. (1986). Appropriate communication in community development. *Communicatio Socialis Yearbook, 5,* 87–102.

Ogan, C. (1982). Development journalism/communication: The status of the concept. *Gazette, 29*(1/2), 3–13.

Pausewang, S. (1973). *Methods end concepts of social research in a rural developing society.* Munich: Weltforum Verlag.

Pratt, C. (1986). Communication policies for population control: Nigeria in the African context. *The Journal of Modern African Studies, 24*(3), 529–537.

Quebral, N. (1973). What do we mean by development communication? *International Development Review, 2,* 25–28.

Ranganath, H. K. (1976). A probe into the traditional media: Telling the people tell themselves. *Media Asia, 3*(1), 25–28.

Schiller, D. (1986). *Pathways to digitization in international telecommunications.* Unpublished paper.

Singhal, A. (1988). Television soap operas for development in India. *Gazette, 41,* 109-121.

Sreberny-Mohammadi, A. (1984, Winter). The world of news study. *Journal of Communication,* pp. 121–132.

Straubhaar, J. (1984, April). Brazilian television: The decline of American influence. *Communications Research,* pp. 230–231.

Ugboajah, F. (1975, December). Communication research in Africa. *Intermedia.*

Ume-Nwagbo, E. N. E. (1986). 'Cock crow at dawn,' a Nigerian experiment with television drama in development communication. *Gazette, 37,* 155–167.

Valbuena, V. T. (1986). *Philippine folk media in development communication.* Singapore: AMIC.

Valbuena, V. T. (1987a, March). The American streak in ASEAN communication education—a remedia response. *Philippine Communication Journal,* pp. 13–20.

Valbuena, V. T. (1987b). *Using traditional media in environmental communication.* Singapore: AMIC.

Varis, T. (1974, Winter). Global traffic in television. *Journal of Communication,* pp. 102–109.

Varis, T. (1984, Winter). The international flow of television programs. *Journal of Communication,* pp. 143–152.

Wildman, S. S., & Siwek, S. E. (1988). *International trade in films and television programs.* Cambridge, MA: Ballinger Publishing Co. for American Enterprise Institute.

PART IV
Regulations
by Law and
Organization

Chapter 13
Territoriality and Intangibility: Transborder Data Flows and National Sovereignty*

William J. Drake

In 1978, delegates from 78 governments attending a conference of the Intergovernmental Bureau of Informatics endorsed a report warning that transborder data flows (TDF) "could place national sovereignty in jeopardy" (IBI, 1978, p. 237). In 1979, a committee of the Canadian government suggested that TDF "poses possibly the most dangerous threat to Canadian sovereignty" (Government of Canada, 1979, p. 57). Similarly, a report by the Commission of the European Community (EC) worried that foreign control of TDF and related industries threatened "a reduction in [Europe's] independence in decision-making in all walks of public and private life" (EC, 1979, p. 12). In 1982, the President of France said that the use of TDF for the "dissemination of information processed and largely controlled by a small number of dominant countries could cause the rest to lose their sovereignty" (Francois Mitterand, in Buss, 1984, p. 113). These were not isolated statements of concern. From the mid-1970s to the mid-1980s, an international debate raged over TDF—the transmission

*For their helpful comments on an earlier version of this chapter, I would like to thank the editors, and Friedrich Kratochwil, Meheroo Jussawalla, Lisa Martin, and G. Russell Pipe.

of computerized information via telecommunications and across national borders for processing, storage, and use. Many governments and independent analysts worried that the use of TDF, particularly by American-based transnational corporations (TNCs), could have negative effects on national economic, legal, and sociocultural independence. Cumulatively, these effects were said to undermine national sovereignty and justify new regulations.

Given its once fervent tone, it is rather curious that just a few years later, the TDF debate is largely dead. A broad and complex issue area has been significantly narrowed; parallels might be if international monetary policy was solely about exchange rates, trade policy only about tariffs, or environmental policy simply about ozone depletion. Whereas the TDF concept used to encompass a wide variety of issues, today only a few still receive serious governmental attention, and the principal ones—trade in services and intellectual property rights— are being addressed with an eye to promoting rather than restricting corporate TDF. Only the issue of personal privacy protection is an exception to this rule, and even here the policies thus far have presented at most minor inconveniences for most TNCs. More tellingly, the very term "TDF," with its connotations of multiple problems requiring regulations, is today invoked primarily with regard to privacy. Indeed, the mention of TDF to some policy makers can now elicit loud yawns and knowing sighs. Needless to say, using the phrase in the same sentence as "national sovereignty" is viewed as an even more archaic practice demonstrating that one is stuck in the past.

None of this would be unusual if the problems associated with TDF had been resolved through policy. But they were not: TDF was effectively removed from the international agenda before that could happen. Government and industry insiders variously offer two different explanations for this lack of action. Some cynically maintain that the entire debate was just a fad promoted by a multinational cabal of bureaucratic turf builders, greedy consultants, and ambulance chasing academics. Others take the matter more seriously and focus on the substance of the issues rather than the supposedly purely self-interested motivations of those who raised them. They point out that when the rapid growth of TDF was first identified, little was known about its precise substance, scope, and consequences. There was a dearth of hard evidence about which TNCs used what types of TDF resulting in what socioeconomic effects, so that the complexity and uncertainty surrounding the topic generated anxiety and forced people to guess about worst-case scenarios. That is true, but from here on the argument goes astray. These observers believe that in response, governments and independent analysts systematically examined the issues and came to the informed conclusion that there was still no evidence that TDF had negative effects. In their view, the TDF debate turned out to be a wild goose chase in search of a "solution without a problem," and the realization of this after years of discussion led to the collective sense of burn out that is palpable if one raises the topic with them today.

This chapter proposes an alternative explanation for the rise and premature decline of the TDF debate in general and its sovereignty dimension in particular. I will attempt to show that despite the lack of hard evidence as to how specific types of transactions eroded national interests, their general properties—their intangibility, functionally integrative, and opaque nature—led to an early recognition that TDF constituted the carving out of a private, transnational cyberspace removed from public authority. As such, governmental and independent analysts around the world attempted to define a range of potential problems associated with TDF and appropriate policy responses. But when this process gathered steam, TNCs successfully mobilized to cut off the debate and prevent the widespread adoption of new regulations. TNCs had two cards to play in this game: their material power resources, that is, control over the technology and markets and the money and connections needed to organize a multinational lobbying campaign; and immaterial power resources, that is, control over the information necessary to evaluate issues and frame the policy discourse. As a result, proregulatory policy makers and analysts had to base their arguments on extrapolations about what negative effects *could* occur in principle given the new technological capabilities without being able to prove that they actually *did* occur in practice. That was a weak position for this minority to defend, and support for their views progressively eroded among the majority of policy makers. TDF discourse was a terrain contested by a highly mobilized and clear-eyed corporate interest configuration on one side and a looser and less-certain group of analysts on the other. Their respective abilities to define reality and shape the terms of debate for everyone wavering in between were highly unequal. No wonder that many policy makers who initially leaned toward regulation now honestly profess the beliefs that they had been wrong and that, as corporate spokespersons proclaimed from the beginning, TDF regulation was "a solution in search of a problem."

The chapter is organized as follows: The first section sets the stage by exploring the concept of sovereignty and the types of economic transactions most threatening to it. The second section traces the rise of TDF and the process by which it was institutionalized on the international agenda. The third section presents an overview of the potential problems identified during the debate. The final section shows how efforts to establish new regulations dissolved in the face of uncertainty and corporate pressure and gave way to a new, pro-liberalization agenda.

NATIONAL SOVEREIGNTY AND TERRITORIALITY

Constitutional vs. Operational Sovereignty

In world historical terms, national sovereignty is a fairly recent and modernist innovation. In the medieval era, various individuals and organizations—for example, monarchies and emperors, princes and barons, feudal lords, religious groupings like the Roman Catholic church—employed different power resources to control the masses. The result was a heteronomous system of power, in which many entities exercised authority in distinct functional domains coexisting within the same territorial spaces. The notion of a "national" state with absolute and comprehensive authority over all aspects of a territorially bounded society did not exist. That began to change through a process of war and peace making in which Europe's top rulers split up the continent into mutually exclusive domains of total control. Tentatively in the Peace of Augsburg of 1555 and more clearly in the Peace of Westphalia of 1648, the monarchies involved mutually recognized and legitimated each other's authority within fixed boundaries on the understanding that it did not extend beyond them. Thus was born the interstate system, with sovereignty serving as the "constitutive principle" that specified its units and the bases upon which they were separated and stood in relation to one another (Ruggie, 1983, p. 274). Through war, imperialism, and emulation, sovereignty spread across the globe, supplanted alternative modes of organizing political space, and became the administrative anchor for even transterritorial processes in the economic and social domains.

But despite its centrality to all of world politics, the concept of sovereignty has remained contestable. Scholars, policy makers, and citizens employ it in two sharply different ways that derive from their more or less articulated baseline visions of social ontology and international relations. The first view is that sovereignty is a *constitutional* attribute of states. Sovereignty means that states are not formally subject to other sources of legitimate authority, and it entails mirror ordering principles. The external principle is horizontal: States are jurisdictionally separate and equal, enjoy the same rights and privileges, and are not bound by a higher supranational authority. The internal principle is vertical: National polities are hierarchically organized, with states at the top exercising supreme power over their societies (Hinsley, 1986; James, 1986). In this view, sovereignty is solely a legal construct: It refers only to states' entitlement to act as they choose, rather than their actual ability to do so. Moreover, sovereignty is an inalienable right which can only be taken away by force, that is, through the loss of territory in war or colonial annexation. A suggestive parallel is drawn between private property under capitalism and sovereignty in the international system. In both cases, society may impose constraints on how an actor uses her possession, but this does not negate the fact of ownership (Kratochwil, Rohrlich, & Mahajan, 1985).

Constitutional sovereignty is the foundation of traditional public international law, which positions states as its subjects. Despite recent challenges from the development of transnational and humanitarian law, which seek to directly endow individuals with certain rights, it appears to remain the most fundamental legal principle underlying world order (Falk, Kratochwil, & Mendlovitz, 1985; Fleiner-Gerster & Meyer, 1985). Constitutional sovereignty is also the central assumption of the dominant school of international relations theory in the English-speaking world—neorealism. Neorealists argue that the international system is structurally anarchic, or lacking a centralized, supranational source of authority. Consequently, authority devolves to the level of states, and it is the combination of anarchy and the distribution of state power that determines political events. In this view, sovereignty is a constant and definitive feature of the international system as long as the "deep structure" of anarchy remains intact. Changes in the secondary structure of power distribution, for example, the postwar shift from military multipolarity to bipolarity, or the (alleged) rise and fall of the British and American hegemonies, did not alter the system's constitutive principle. Ephemeral, "process-level" changes like participation in international organizations and regimes, economic imperialism or globalization, regional integration, or technological change may limit states' automony but not their structural status as separate and formally equal entities, since "the sovereignty of states has never entailed their insulation from the effects of other states' actions" (Waltz, 1979, p. 96). Neorealists castigate as intellectually sloppy and short-sighted observers who have in the past announced the "death of sovereignty" when considering some new set of constraints, for example, the consolidation of multilateralism or increasing economic interdependence, and assert that such transactions only occur in the first place because states choose to establish facilitative institutional frameworks (Krasner, 1988; Thomson & Krasner, 1989).

This conception has the advantage of cautioning skepticism during periods of change which prove to be more apparent than real, and provides a baseline for thinking about the structural continuity of the interstate system. But adherence to this static vision distracts attention from the most interesting questions about lived history. Invariant system structure so defined generates only very general constraints and compulsions on states and tells us nothing about how ruling elites interpret and act on specific challenges in different contexts. Constitutional niceties aside, process-level events often lead states to *behave* as if their sovereignty *is* in question, and this in turn redefines what it "is" and means for daily life. Defining sovereignty solely in terms of legal freedom begs the question, "free to do what?," and what states seek is control over their domestic and international environments. To explain state action, it is better to assess how elites understand, construct, and respond to constraints on their actual abilities to act as if the state is sovereign.

The second conception of sovereignty as an *operational* attribute of states allows us to do that.[1] From a social constructionist perspective, operational sovereignty means not only that states are constitutionally separate, but also that their independence must constantly be (re)established through communally recognized action. "Sovereignty is an institution, and so it exists only in virtue of certain intersubjective understandings and expectations; there is no sovereignty without an other....The sovereign state is an ongoing accomplishment of practice, not a once-and-for-all creation of norms that somehow exist apart from practice" (Wendt, 1992, pp. 412-413). Here the horizontal and vertical principles are actual state authority vs. global pressures and domestic society.

> The sovereignty of states, both internal and external, may be said to exist both at a normative level and at a factual level. On the one hand, states assert the right to supremacy over authorities within their territory and population and independence of authorities outside it; but, on the other hand, they also actually exercise, in varying degrees, such supremacy and independence in practice. An independent political community which merely claims a right to sovereignty (or is judged by others to have such a right), but cannot assert this right in practice, is not a state properly so-called. (Bull, 1977, pp. 8-9)

An underspecified notion of operational sovereignty seems common among liberal theorists who argue that transnational economic processes and interdependence limits states' freedom of action (L. Brown, 1972; Haas, 1964; Morse, 1976; Soroos, 1986; Vernon, 1971). But they fail to challenge the reified and objectivist social ontology of analysts who view social institutions as fixed ensembles of rules separate from daily practice and cognition. This leaves them open to the neorealist charge that they have merely misequated sovereignty with autonomy, making it a leaky vessel divisible into increments with some measuring higher and lower on a continuum. Over the years, liberals have treated short-term trends in transactions as harbingers of fundamental change in the international system, only to have their analyses discarded by later generations of scholars.

In contrast, critical theories such as those advocated throughout this volume recognize that it is through the ongoing practices of power relations and norm development that sovereignty is constantly constructed and contested (Rosenberg, 1990). Social structures and interpretive human action are dialectically involved in a relation of mutual constitution, so structures are what we make (of) them in time and space; they and their meanings are continuously (re)produced and transformed in daily action. Anthony Giddens's work on structuration theory highlights this duality by noting that "the structural properties of social systems are both the medium and outcome of the practices that constitute those systems" (Giddens, 1979, p. 69). And as the dual structures of anarchy and sovereignty have no existence independent of our knowledgeability, it is how social actors understand and act in and on them in specific historical contexts that gives them causal weight. If elites view sovereignty as inviolable, they may behave one way; if they do not, they may act in others that are inexplicable from a constitutionalist baseline. And there are certain economic conditions under which operational sovereignty will most clearly appear to be at bay; we now turn to those that are directly relevant to the case of TDF.

Territoriality and Intangibility

Rendering sovereignty operational requires the assertion of territorial control—the structuring of social action within a physically bounded political space. Territorial control involves at least four dominant practices, the ease of each depending on the qualitative nature of the transactions to be governed. First, states erect external *borders* around their spaces through which transnational transactions can be administratively mediated. National borders most succinctly express the concept of sovereignty in our collective memory, and states have imposed border controls throughout history. To keep out foreign armies, they deploy military power or enter into security agreements. To control the movement of people, they maintain a discriminatory passport regime and physical checkpoints such as roadblocks, immigration processing facilities, and the like. To control the flow of goods, they designate ports of entry with customs houses. As these examples suggest, external borders are more feasible for the movement of tangibles like people and goods than for intangibles like pollution, radiation, and information.

Second, states erect administrative *boundaries* within their territories. Unlike borders, these are functional spaces rather than physical places. Functional boundaries separate zones of action by superimposing vertical organization onto an otherwise fluid set of horizontal exchanges. By mapping space in this fashion, the state can then establish authoritative rules within each domain of social life. For example, the regulation of the financial, communications, legal, and related industries requires that each can be delineated from the other before a set of rules on accreditation, pricing, service quality, and so on can be devised. Obviously, the capacity to erect internal boundaries is greatest when transactions are functionally differentiated and task-specific, for example, when there is some distinctive activity that can be labeled "banking" and treated differently from another called "insurance."

Third, in the economic domain, states also impose *barriers to entry* on domestic and/or foreign firms within these sectoral boundaries. Barriers may be applied on an intraindustry (e.g., fixing the number and identity of banks) or interindustry (e.g., keeping insurance firms out of banking) basis. The capacity to erect barriers is greatest when efforts at market entry can be readily identified by the flow of goods and services and ensuing payments. And fourth, to achieve all of the above, states must be able to *monitor* transactions across and within their territories. Since it is the essential raw material of all decision making, a sufficient quantity of quality information must be accessible to policymakers. This is especially so in complex issue areas characterized by uncertainty and tradeoffs between objectives. As Michel Foucault has amply demonstrated, the state's power to create an order of things is fundamentally predicated on surveillance (Foucault, 1970). Surveillance is achieved through the administrative routinization of state involvement in all areas of domestic life, and through the internationalization of the state via external contact points in embassies, intelligence operations, multilateral institutions, and so on. Monitoring is easiest when information moves through clearly defined, numerically limited, and technically transparent channels, and when the volume, velocity, and complexity of that movement is insubstantial.

Performance of these functions involves difficult costs/benefit calculations. The erection of borders, boundaries, barriers, and monitoring mechanisms is sometimes possible even when transactions lack
tangibility, functional differentiation, and transparency. But doing so
can require Draconian measures that are subject to challenge by the
parties involved. An intangible transaction such as a cross-border
radio broadcast may be locked out, but only through an expensive and
controversial jamming policy. Similarly, information about diverse
social activities or market processes within boundaries may be difficult to obtain voluntarily, but states can in principle demand it from
social groups or companies. *The key question is whether power relations and other factors surrounding the transactions in question
facilitate their territorialization at sustainable political and economic
costs.* And in the case of TDF, states were confronted with a dual
problem: first, the rapid expansion of key economic transactions that
are intangible, functionally integrative and technically opaque, resulting in what Albert Bressand has called the "B3 complex" of
eroding borders, boundaries, and barriers; and second, the clear
likelihood that any effort to reign them into a framework of public
authority would undergo strong challenges from TNCs (Bressand,
1986). If states had viewed their sovereignty solely as a fixed constitutional attribute, they would not have worried about TDF's consequences for it. But from a social constructionist perspective, we can
understand why TDF appeared to undermine the integrity of territorial control and forced them to consider alternative responses.

FROM TERRITORIALITY TO TRANSNATIONALISM

The Transformation of Information Transfer

To understand the rise of TDF, it is necessary to begin with telecommunications. From the outset, telecommunications was usually a
creature of the state. Napoleon's government developed the semaphore
of "visual telegraphy" to coordinate his military campaigns. Upon the
creation of electronic telegraphy and telephony, most states nationalized their systems and gave both regulatory and service provision functions to Ministries of Posts, Telegraphs and Telephones
(PTTs). In the United States and parts of Canada, services were
provided by regulated private firms such as the American Telephone
and Telegraph Co (AT&T), while regulatory functions were left to state
agencies. National carriers served as monopoly providers of services
and monopsony purchasers of equipment from private manufacturers
that the state selected and protected from competition. Governments

cooperated in the International Telecommunication Union (ITU) to maintain an international regime for the standardization of systems and the regulation of services. Its purposes were to preserve sovereignty over national networks, while setting rules for international interconnection and the joint, noncompetitive provision of services.

The near universal regulatory and institutional form promoted many legitimate social, economic, and political objectives, but also constrained the development of systems and services. The rate of technical change was limited by government budgets and the necessity of amortizing investments across a range of network elements before moving to the next generation of equipment. The direction of change was skewed toward compatibility with extant domestic systems and slowly developed international standards. The diffusion of change was limited by nationalist procurement policies for equipment in the major countries and the ITU's joint service arrangements, both of which split the global markets into mutually exclusive, noncompetitive domains. These technical and institutional conditions in telecommunications *carriage* constrained the forms and flow of information *content*. They yielded a small variety of analog telegraph, telex, and telephone transmissions. Messages moved through a limited number of wired and wireless paths and internetwork gateways, and were of manageable volume and velocity. States reserved the rights under the ITU-based regime to monitor, interrupt, or terminate transmissions at the border if they deemed national security and public order to be at risk. Since PTTs and regulated private carriers were the sole or dominant providers of communications, they could erect internal boundaries and barriers to entry. Information flows, while intangible, could be easily subjected to territorial state control.

Over the past 30 years, the information control revolution has progressively reversed these conditions. Most aspects of the revolution are beyond the scope of this chapter, but three are important here. Technologically, major developments included the strategic merging of digitalized telecommunications and computers (informatics) to create *telematics,* or integrated systems for the production, movement, and application of information, and the diffusion across network terminals and switches of microelectronics and software-based intelligence functions. The variety, speed, power, accuracy, and security of systems and services increased radically, while the costs of computing and transmission fell in parallel. The global network of networks became a distributed data processing system that could be flexibly reconfigured to meet TNCs' specialized service demands. Economically, market structures underwent related changes. On the supply side, there was a significant growth in numbers and diversification in identities of the equipment manufacturers and service suppliers vying for market shares. On the demand side, TNC users in agricultural, manufacturing, and service industries became increasingly sophisticated in their needs and applications as managers redefined telecommunications as a key strategic competitive tool.

Most importantly, the political frameworks that once shaped technomarket change in accordance with state objectives also experienced a deep transformation as the locus of control shifted to the private sector. This was achieved through the internationalization of a power struggle born in the United States, where comparatively liberal systems of state/society relations and property rights and other factors gave TNCs greater control over the economy in general and communications in particular than their counterparts had attained abroad. The battle arose in the unregulated computer industry, where the government, and especially the Department of Defense (DOD), supported manufacturers through procurement, while encouraging them to spinoff products into the commercial market. Large corporate users quickly realized that the value of their computers would be greatly enhanced if these could be connected via telecommunications in order to share capabilities and facilitate companywide "rationalization." But as AT&T practices and FCC regulations limited their control, the deregulation of telecommunications became a necessary objective. Competitive manufacturers and services suppliers and large users forged links in a new interest configuration to play a key role in convincing the FCC to pursue domestic deregulation in the 1960s and 1970s (D. Schiller, 1982). This stimulated corporate innovation and markets, and allowed American-based firms to get far out in front of foreign competitors in the development and use of advanced telecommunications and TDF. Playing catch-up, TNCs from the industrialized countries began to make piecemeal demands on their PTTs for the "flexibility" to construct similar systems, and by the mid-1980s they swung fully behind the American-inspired agenda of global liberalization. As TNCs expanded their control over networks and services, first in the United States and later elsewhere, the diversification and invigoration of supply and demand structures radically accelerated the rate of technical change, redirected it toward corporate demand, and generated a diffusion pattern shaped by competitive global markets.

Although necessarily schematic, these observations provide a background for assessing the transformation of information transfer. Technical advances in networks and equipment meant that most anything processing electronic information—banks' automatic teller machines, supermarket cash registers, office work stations, automated manufacturing lines, supercomputers, and so on—could be woven into the private information fabric. Humans could interact via or with remote computers, and computers could engage in joint processes without human intervention. As new systems developed, so did services: no longer were users confined to simple analog transmissions of telephone, telegraph, and telex messages, as an increasingly diverse range of computer-enhanced offerings such as distributed data processing, online databases, videotext, teletext, store and forward messaging, videoconferencing, facsimile, file transfer, electronic and voice mail, and on and on, could move through the digital bitstream.

In parallel, institutional change meant that TNCs could construct electronic highways with increasing ease. In the 1960s, most corporate TDF moved over private circuits leased from national carriers in bulk at flat, usage-insensitive rates. Originally large firms demanded these to handle their high volumes of telephone traffic among remote offices without going through congested public-switched networks. But as liberalization began, they attained progressively greater rights to attach computerized customer-premise equipment and transform the lines into advanced information management systems. National carriers responded in the late 1970s by building public-switched data networks as an alternative, but many TNCs balked at their alleged deficiences and continued to use private lines for intracorporate TDF. And as liberalization proceeded, TNCs could interconnect their circuits into wholly private networks or attain the "virtual" equivalent from the PTTs. The interfacing of singular and centralized national public networks has been replaced by a complex, multilayered fabric of transnational interconnection among heterogeneous private and public systems. TNCs can increasingly move any form of information through whichever route they deem optimal while retaining their private control.

The cumulative effect is a radical increase in the technical, economic, and political costs of territorializing information. It is technologically difficult for states to monitor transmissions in progress and determine which is contrary to national interests. Change in the underlying carriage presents several problems. Transmission lines have become very secure with the laying of fiber optic cables, which are less easily tapped into than traditional copper cables, microwave relays, and satellite links. Many networks now employ packet switching, which breaks transmissions down into a series of units traveling independently across various pathways for reassembly at the termination point. Any monitoring would therefore have to occur at the customer/network interfaces, the electronic equivalent of posting police next to the terminals. But even to the extent that this is feasible, changes in the form of information content present further hurdles. Public network computers record the time, destination, and duration of calls, but they cannot "read" in real time contents represented in digital form and comingled with other messages in the bitstream. "A U.S. State Department cable; a news broadcast; an Olympic pole vaulter [sic]; the TV program 'I Love Lucy'; a computer software program; inventory data from Sears Roebuck in Brazil to its Chicago, Illinois headquarters, and money transferred from Citibank, Manhattan to its Sao Paulo branch are all virtually indistinguishable when converted to electronic impulses" (Theberge, in Brown, 1983, p. 79).

In addition, corporate encryption techniques have become increasingly sophisticated with the growing importance of proprietary information and trade secrets. States can demand access to the codes, but using them consistently would be a cumbersome affair. Finally, the sheer volume of transmissions moving through multiple pathways would require a fairly large-scale undertaking to track and sift through. Of course, the United States National Security Agency (NSA) is known to monitor international traffic, but does so with a huge staff, a budget estimated at more than $30 billion, and a multitude of land, sea, and air-based "platforms" or listening posts around the world. Even so, the NSA's recent veto of American participation in a corporate consortium laying fiber in Russia indicates that there may be limits to its highly secretive capabilities. Either way, an undertaking on this scale is far beyond the means of other states. This leads to the economic and the political costs, which proved more important, insofar as they prevented governments from pursuing a technical fix to the problem of surveillance in the first place.

Economically, the fact of intangibility has not changed, but the variety and significance of what is intangible has. Transactions that used to take place slowly through other media, such as arranged meetings or the postal system, now occur instantly within networks, and entirely new types of transactions have also been created therein. A significant portion of the global economy has migrated into the transnational cyberspace of private networks. TNCs in agriculture, manufacturing, and especially information-intensive services industries use TDF for many key functions, for example, product planning and development, manufacturing and production control, financial and portfolio management, accounting, marketing and distribution, and so on (UNCTC, 1982). Indeed, a leading corporate spokesperson has called TDF the "lifeblood of virtually every major economic activity" (Joan Spero of American Express in Drake, 1984, p. 304). Governments reliant on private sector decisions and business confidence for economic growth would risk grave consequences if TNCs fought their attempts at surveillance. Or such firms might simply pick up and leave for countries with more hospitable regulatory environments, or devise ways to bypass any restrictions through creative networking. And politically, while states have legal rights under the ITU to monitor, interrupt, or terminate transmissions, doing so frequently for reasons other than national security would be risking a bruising fight. In sum, as the technological, economic, and political changes of the information control revolution deepened, TDF became progressively more difficult and costly to subject to territorial control than was prerevolutionary information transfer.

Agenda Setting: International Institutionalization of the TDF Issue Area

Governments were slow to recognize the full implications of the merging of telecommunications and computers. Up to the mid-1970s, new technical possibilities in telecommunications were generally thought to pose only two challenges: supply, or how to make the emerging systems and services available to paying corporate customers; and regulation, or how to limit corporate incursions into protected network, equipment, and service markets. With underlying switched networks largely under monopoly control, few people were thinking about the wider socioeconomic consequences of corporate *usage* of the resources they were provided with. Indeed, the national carriers' mandates were limited to the provision of carriage, and did not allow routine judgments about their content. Finally, since information transfer had not been a problem previously, there was no a priori reason to suppose that computerized "conversations" posed new and different problems.

The seeds of change were laid outside the ambit of telecommunications authorities. In the late 1960s, concern was growing across the industrialized countries about the protection of personal privacy in computerized data banks (Westin & Baker, 1972). In 1970, the German state of Hesse established the first Data Protection Act setting rules on what information about citizens could be gathered and processed in computers. Parallel discussions were begun at the multilateral level in the Council of Europe (COE) and the Organization for Economic Cooperation and Development (OECD). Initially, the analyses typically examined computers on an organizationally isolated, stand-alone basis. But slowly, a new problem came into focus: corporate computers were being tied together via networks, and large quantities of personal information about citizens were being instantly transmitted across borders. The Canadian government was one of the first to inquire about the consequences; in a telecommunications policy study, it noted almost in passing that "a concentration in foreign databanks of information about Canadian individuals, transactions, and institutions might render ineffective Canadian laws dealing with such matters as personal privacy and corporate operations" (Government of Canada, 1971, p. 164). Similar observations were being made in Sweden and France, and the general question of "computer communications" was taken up in the COE and OECD. In a 1974 conference, the OECD's expert group coined the term "TDF" and raised the question of whether it "constituted a problem sufficiently important in its implications for national sovereignty for governments to propose regulatory action" (Gassman & Pipe, 1976, p. 27). The group was not ready to answer this in the affirmative, but agreed to an expanded study program on both the problem and possible policies. Thus began the wider institutionalization of TDF on government agendas.

What is significant here is that by defining the issue as "transborder" rather than "international" data flows, participants invoked an image of corporate activities unmediated by territorial control.[2] From the outset, the terms of discourse were framed as *the unenforceability of a sovereign state's policies even within its own territory, and the subjugation of nationals to foreign decision-making.* Hence, many governmental and independent analysts shared the view that, "in relation to TDF issues, the term 'sovereignty' should be used to designate the *practical ability* of a nation .... to develop and effectively implement its economic, cultural and social policies" (Knoppers, 1984, p. 85; emphasis added). Constitutional sovereignty was recognized to be irrelevant if states could not make it operational.

Over the next few years, four factors converged to broaden the issue and raise the stakes. First, the collective understanding of information's nature and significance was changing. As the information control revolution gathered steam, many policymakers and analysts became convinced that a fundamental transition was underway in global capitalism. While variously describing it as the rise of an information economy or society, post-industrial age, technotronic era, and so on, they agreed that information and related technology were becoming the essential resources in firms and markets. The question was who would control the information-intensive industries of the future and be the winners in an era when traditional sources of national wealth like the steel, shipbuilding, and textile industries were in decline? It is also important to note that the mid-1970s were a time when it briefly became acceptable in official circles to discuss TNC power (at least *sotto vocci*), as evidenced by the hearings held by

Frank Church in the United States Senate. As American-based firms were overwhelmingly its largest providers and users, the (usually unspoken) subtext of the debate abroad was that TDF seemed to represent yet another dimension of *le defi americain.*

Second, it was also becoming clear that privacy was just the tip of the iceberg. As TNCs used telecommunications and information for many purposes beyond managing their employees and customers, it stood to reason that TDF might raise other issues as well. Perhaps in an effort to downplay the privacy question, some TNCs made public information suggesting that only about 2% of their TDF pertained to individuals. The rest consisted of scientific, technical, economic, and managerial information. Further, up to 90% of TDF comprised *intra-corporate* transmissions between the home offices, branch plants, and subsidiaries of globally dispersed companies, with the remainder being *intercorporate* sales of commodified information to external customers. Rather than squelching the discussion, these revelations supported the growing sense that governments should be looking at the breadth of nonpersonal TDF and considering how its use might impact their economic, legal, and sociocultural objectives. Since telecommunications is an infrastructure underlying all economic processes, and information was becoming the key factor of production, TDF usage could have effects across the agricultural, manufacturing and services sectors. A much broader issue was being cognitively constructed, with the initial framing of "TDF vs. sovereignty" remaining as the overarching discursive framework.

Third, the debate was bursting out of the confines of governments' inner circles. TDF was a new and "hot" item on the international agenda about which policymakers knew little but yet wanted to formulate responses. That provided intellectual challenges as well as professional and monetary incentives for many independent analysts to get into the game. By the late 1970s, there was a burgeoning multinational community of academics, lawyers, consultants, journalists, and industry analysts jetting around the world to pleasant locales to debate the issues on the conference circuit. International corporate seminars, organized primarily by United States-based firms, became legion. Russell Pipe, a key player in the OECD expert group, launched the journal *Transnational Data and Communications Report,* which instantly became the leading print forum for the discussion, and many other new journals, edited volumes, and authored books soon followed. Governments and TNCs readily doled out the cash and kudos to members of the so-called "TDF mafia" for reports elaborating the range of questions involved. In the United States, the big money was in telling corporate managers that the sky was falling, and that nasty foreigners were going to impose all kinds of horrible regulatory burdens on the "free flow of information." Elsewhere, the tone was more mixed: TNCs based in Europe, Japan, Canada, Australia, and New Zealand were initially less agitated than their American counterparts and preferred quiet, back room accommodations with their home governments to a public brawl. For their part, those governments were concerned about understanding the issues and considering the policy options and had more open minds about what independent analysts with varying viewpoints had to say. And much of what they said pointed to TDF's potential negative effects. A substantial portion of the literature being produced, whether written by TDF's advocates or its critics, posed the problem as "TDF vs. national sovereignty."

Fourth, despite the industrialized countries' desire to address the issues solely amongst themselves, the so-called less-developed countries (LDCs) became involved in the debate. Locked out of the OECD, 37 LDCs took the issues into the Intergovernmental Bureau of Informatics (IBI), where they were joined by France, Spain, and Italy. Originally set up by the United Nations Educational, Scientific and Cultural Organization (UNESCO) in 1951 to promote the use of computers, the IBI became the principal Third World forum on TDF in the late 1970s. Privacy protection was not of great interest to its members. Instead, at a series of conferences held between 1978 and 1984, they consistently expressed the views that TDF was part of a larger grab for economic power by TNCs; that the development of indigenous information technology and services would be squelched by South-North TDF; and that the entirety of the policy problems being identified in the wider international debate boiled down to a multi-faceted threat to national sovereignty, which was explicitly and consistently framed in operational terms. This construction of the problem primarily reflected the LDCs' understanding of TDF's ungovernable properties, and the weaknesses of their own domestic regulatory and industrial capabilities. But it was also influenced by the simultaneous debate going on in UNESCO about the need for a New International Information Order for mass communications and news. From the vantage point of global capitalism's periphery, TNC control of point-to-point data communications and point-to-multipoint mass media were simply two sides of the same coin. In the years to follow, the LDCs' concerns were given further credence by a series of studies conducted by the United Nations Center on Transnational Corporations (UNCTC).

As a result of all these influences, a number of Third World governments advocated national restrictions on TDF, the adoption of industrial policies and transfer of technology programs to build domestic capabilities, and the formulation of an international regulatory regime. For example, at the IBI's Second World Conference on TDF in 1984, the working document proposed as its first regime principles the "Recognition of rights inherent to the sovereignty of States which foresee that [TDF] serve their interests and objectives," and "TDF shall not violate their sovereignty nor their constitutional and legal principles" (IBI, 1984b, pp. 47-48). This sort of talk set off alarm bells in the industrialized countries. Even those which were concerned about TDF did not want the discussion to be "misdirected" by a nationalistic, North-South redistributive agenda based on the transfer of wealth and strong controls that could impact their own TNCs, which were struggling to catch up with the Americans. Instead of forging an alliance with the LDCs, governments in Europe and elsewhere that were leaning toward regulation wanted to devise reformist responses suited to their distinctive local concerns and mixed interests. Hence, the IBI debate and UNCTC research strengthened the resolve of OECD members to quickly work through the issues and preemptively establish "the international consensus."

But on what basis? While TDF's generic properties, such as intangibility and opaqueness, undoubtedly challenged territorial control, it was far less clear how particular types of TDF would impact specific national objectives. To figure this out, Northern governments had to launch intensive research efforts at the national level and in the OECD, as well as to consult the work of independent analysts. Hence, from the late 1970s to the mid-1980s, a range of issues were explored in conferences and publications against the discursive backdrop of the sovereignty framework. The big question, as posed by the Chairman of the OECD's Working Party on Transborder Data Flows, was that "in international law, the sovereignty of a state still refers to the legal powers it has to control national policies and to exercise jurisdiction over a specific tract of territory. Is this still sufficient? Is it necessary to extend the concept to 'informational sovereignty,' and/or 'cultural sovereignty,' and/or 'economic sovereignty'? What are the pragmatic definitions of these terms?" (Robinson, 1985a, p. 27).

INTANGIBLE CHALLENGES TO TERRITORIAL CONTROL

Sociocultural Issues

As noted above, the first issue to generate widespread concern was the *threat to privacy* from flows of personal data. Due to their experience with fascism and other considerations, the Europeans were particularly worried about the impact of corporate practices on privacy.

Data banks may contain information on a person's political and religious affiliations, membership in organizations, magazine subscriptions, sexual preference, medical, financial, and criminal histories, and on and on. Intracorporate TDF about employees was recognized to be a problem if, for example, General Motors executives in Michigan decided to lay off workers in a Spanish plant because they were active in unions or the Communist Party. Moreover, since information about employees and customers is a commodity, its intercorporate sale could lead to additional negative actions by creditors, insurance companies, and so on. Hence, the accumulation and rapid transborder distribution of massive quantities of detailed personal data left citizens exposed to decisions by unacccountable foreign managers who might be insensitive to host country concerns (Beling, 1983; Branscomb, 1986; Freese, 1979; Hondius, 1980; Kirby, 1979; Turn, 1980).

As the debate broadened, many LDCs and a few industrialized countries also became worried about networked information's *cultural construction* and effects on *national identity.* As a top Brazilian official responsible for TDF policy noted, such information "is not neutral. It bears within itself the culture that produced it. The language, in its synthetic and semantic aspects, will receive extraordinary influence from the automatic retrieval systems and information services" (Brizida, 1980, p. 33). And since the majority of online information originated from within the United States or its globally dispersed TNCs, several subissues became apparent. First, TDF deepens *the global spread of English* as the "official" language of business and the professions. Obviously, managerial and staff personnel working for an American-based TNC and engaged in TDF would be compelled to use English. But even independent professionals—French medical researchers, Egyptian economists, Costa Rican administrators, Argentine lawyers, and so forth—might find English necessary if they wanted to access the most advanced, commercially available sources of online information. Second, informational imports involve not only language, but also *intellectual orientations and values.* For example, a Costa Rican administrator responsible for health services who searches American data banks for the latest in managerial wisdom could be persuaded that efficiency and cost containment, triaging among the ill or providing services based on the ability to pay, are viable paths to reform. "Rationalization" according to narrow economic criteria can conflict with universal access, public employment, and other local values and traditions. Hence, TDF may strengthen the linguistic and intellectual incorporation of professionals and elites into a semi-homogeneous and hegemonic foreign culture (Matterlart & Siegelaub, 1979; H. Schiller, 1981; Mowlana, 1986; Ostry, 1979; Wilson & Al-Muhanna, 1985).

Third, this process of incorporation might deepen the divisions between *the information rich and the information poor,* especially within the LDCs. The former could come to identify more with the values and experiences of foreign societies and less with their own. Their cyberspace cosmopolitanism could encourage them to develop or reinforce a class-based disdain for their less-advantaged countrymen who lack access to opportunities in general and informational skills in particular. TDF could even enhance the attractiveness of emigration to the North, thereby accentuating the brain drain. Finally, given the comparative advancement of American information resources, the availability of TDF to elites might *stifle the development of indigenous online cultural products.* As the French Minister of Culture argued, expensive investment and training programs would then be necessary to create attractive local alternatives and prevent the further erosion of national identity (Lang, 1982). All these potential problems led many policymakers and independent analysts to view TDF as a threat to "cultural sovereignty," which a report to the Canadian government defined as "the assurance of viable indigenous cultural expression through a variety of communications and computing media" (Knoppers & Foote, 1982, p. 8). The breadth of this conviction across countries underscores that sovereignty was not understood merely in narrow constitutional terms.

Legal Issues

Since TDF could sidestep national privacy protections, it stood to reason that other legal aspects of territoriality could be threatened. But as the debate shifted to nonpersonal flows, it became clear that existing national and international laws did not address this possibility. Not only would questions of jurisdiction and enforcement need to be addressed, but there were no unambiguous precedents from which to work in doing so. Lawyers would have to piece together new rights and duties from non-TDF court decisions.

The overarching problem was posed by an early and influential Canadian study: TDF was a potential threat to *"information sovereignty"* (Gottlieb, Dalfen, & Katz, 1974). This issue framing was picked up by other analysts around the world who noted that states had the right to determine what information would flow into or out of their territories, and some argued that they should also have some form of semi-proprietary control over it. Regarding the flow of information, the hard law of ITU treaties and soft law of United Nations General Assembly agreements contained some contradictory principles. On the one hand, the ITU's Convention and the UN's 1966 Covenant on Civil and Political Rights recognize states' rights to monitor, interrupt, or terminate transmissions when national security, public order, and morals are at risk; the ITU's Radio Regulations establish the doctrine of prior consent for direct broadcast satellite transmissions; and a 1972 UN Resolution provides some basis for the jamming of unwanted cross-border broadcasts. On the other hand, the ITU Convention, the 1948 UN Universal Declaration on Human Rights, and several other international instruments recognize, with varying degrees of clarity, a right of the public to communicate across borders (Ploman, 1982). Taking advantage of this ambiguity, the United States and its supporters argued that uninhibited "corporate speech" and the "free flow of information" were internationally protected rights (Cate, 1990; Dougan, 1987; Feldman, 1983; Pool & Solomon, 1980b). Nevertheless, most other analysts recognized that international law legitimated the regulation of cross-border flows, even if it did not explicitly invoke the notion of "information sovereignty" (Butler, 1984; Gross, 1979; Novotny, 1980). However, TDF's properties made it difficult to actually do so.

Regarding the claim for some sort of proprietary control over information, the legal situation was less murky. A number of LDCs agreed that information is "a natural resource and that the transborder flow of non-personal data is one of its subsets. The UN Resolution on Permanent Sovereignty over Natural Resources states that sovereignty over natural resources is a permanent and fundamental right of nations" (Adams, 1983, p. 410). They therefore argued that information should be treated as a public good, that states should have the sovereign right to determine who can access and use it in what manner, but that TDF undermined their ability to exercise this right. However, international law clearly did not establish that information was either a public good or a "natural" resource to which states could lay claim, especially since much of it is privately created. This allowed a United States State Department advisor to warn that, "information sovereignty is, or may become, far more pervasive in its interpretation and extension.... The concept... may provide nations who seek a period of neo-isolationism an internationally respected shibboleth for drawing information curtains around themselves" (Eger, 1981, p. 115).

If international law did not provide for a semi-proprietary claim to information in general, what about information pertaining to states' natural resources, which were unambiguously national property? This issue arose most clearly in the case of *remote sensing*. Remote sensing is the use of specialized satellites to monitor conditions above, on, and below the earth's surface. Data on climatological, agricultural, geological, and other physical conditions are gathered and recorded in pictorial or computer-compatible formats. The data are sold to a wide variety of organizations, including governments, research bodies, and TNCs. From the early 1970s to the mid-1980s, the Landsat service of the United States National Aeronautical and Space Administration was the sole commercial provider of remote sensing (Mack, 1990). More recently, new programs such as France's SPOT system have contested Landsat's dominance and broadened the market. One problem is that remote sensing gathers and disseminates information which states may not wish to be divulged. For example, foreign access to such data may affect a government's image regarding ecological issues, as in the cases of African desertification, the Brazilian rain forest, and the Chernobyl disaster. More importantly, the data acquired are sold at a price, which raises questions of competitive access and use. The negotiating positions of Third World commodity producers were said to have been undercut at times, because Northern purchasers of raw materials and agricultural products had better information about their resources than they did. LDCs often lacked the money to purchase and the technical expertise to use sensing data effectively (UNCTC, 1984). Given their dependence on the export of primary products, such inequities could impact bargaining relations and national income. As Cees Hamelink observed, "If a country lacks data about itself—whether because it has no capacity to collect them or because it has no capacity to process them—it lacks pertinent decision-making capacity about its own existence" (Hamelink, 1984, p. 70). Many LDCs therefore argued that such information's unauthorized removal violated their operational sovereignty, and some maintained that their constitutional sovereignty should be extended to cover it and/or the satellite orbital slots from which remote sensing occurs.

If they could not own or control information about their societies in general, did states at least have a legal right of *access to data held abroad?* Did their territorial rights extend outward into the transnational ocean of information in cases when some of it directly contravened their domestic laws and policies? This question first arose under a different label in the early privacy debate. As the Europeans began to consider measures for the TDF of personal information, fears surfaced that countries such as the United States would seek to become "data havens" (Evans, 1981; Fishman, 1980; Pantages, 1978; Tourtellot, 1978). As with banking havens, data havens could offer a permissive regulatory environment for the processing of information and provision of services in order to attract TNC investment at the expense of other countries. What legal recourse would governments have in protecting their citizens if personal data was being transferred to such high-tech Panamas? As the debate moved to nonpersonal flows, the access question was given a different spin by the celebrated Dresser-France affair. In 1982, the Reagan Administration decided that United States-based firms and their subsidiaries could not assist with the construction of the Soviet-European gas pipeline. In compliance, Dresser's American home office chose to cut key TDF links with its French subsidiary, which had contracted to provide equipment for the pipeline. '"We had no choice,' recalled Edward R. Luter, a senior vice president for finance. 'Somebody in Pittsburgh,' where Dresser's data base was then situated, 'flipped the switch, and suddenly Dresser-France was cut off.' Almost immediately, an Australian company terminated a $3 million order with Dresser-France, realizing that without access to the central data base the company was virtually paralyzed" (Sanger, 1983, p. D1). This power play made it clear that dependence on foreign-based information resources could be manipulated for political or economic purposes.

The Dresser affair pointed to another issue as well: *The extraterritorial application of national laws.* The United States was claiming that its own laws took precedence over those of France, which had directed the Dresser subsidiary to fulfill its contract. A similar controversy involved the Bank of Nova Scotia. To prosecute a criminal case, the United States demanded that the Canadian firm's Florida branch provide a print-out of a customer's account record, which was being held in the online computer of its Bahamian branch. But Bahamian banking laws preserve the confidentiality of such records, thereby placing the Canadian firm between competing jurisdictional claims. "If state territorial boundaries are technologically irrelevant to the use and storage of data and information, how can national laws further national objectives without regulating electronic transactions within the territories of other states?" (Robinson, 1985a, p. 27). Many governments feared that the American answer to this question would be a new form of aggressive unilateralism that would assert its jurisdiction within their territories.

The possibility of further conflicts over access and extraterritoriality was underscored by the growing *American effort to control East-West TDF* in the Cold War era. With the expansion of interconnectivity, the Soviet Union and its allies were able at times to acquire software, databases, and other information services from the West over the networks. West German facilities provided the East with access to commercial online services from such firms as Lockheed Dialog, CISI-Wharton, and I.P. Sharpe (Becker, 1989). The International Institute for Applied Systems Analysis (IIASA) in Vienna also provided electronic links in the East-West flow of scientific and technical data (Sebestyen, 1983). The United States argued that national security was one case where the "free flow of information" could legitimately be curtailed (Botein & Noam, 1986). Since other governments did not always share its hard-line view of the "evil empire," they came under strong pressure to submit to the dictates of American laws and foreign policy. The United States pursued a three-pronged attack on East bloc access: First, it applied bilateral pressure on foreign governments to prohibit commercial and scientific TDF. Second, it undertook parallel multilateral initiatives by bringing the issue of information export controls into the Coordinating Committee for East-West Trade Policy; and by demanding that IIASA, which was set up to advance East-West scientific cooperation, cease East-West transfers (MacDonald, 1989).

Third, the United States expanded its own domestic export control laws and demanded that American-based firms, both at home and abroad, comply with the new policy. Jimmy Carter issued a Presidential Directive in 1979 empowering the DOD and the Commerce Department, respectively, to prevent unauthorized access to classified national security-related and unclassified, nonnational security information. In 1984, Ronald Reagan characteristically went much further in a National Security Decision Directive that concentrated responsibility for all systems security issues in the DOD and the NSA; extended their reach to any information they happened to deem "sensitive;" gave them the power to mandate the private use of certain encryption codes; and allotted them broad oversight powers over federal agencies, universities, research institutes, and private businesses. Intelligence agents conducted spot checks at such organizations to urge compliance, and launched other initiatives to limit foreign access to online information, participation in conferences and so on (Berman, 1987; Willard, 1984; Walsh, 1987). All these onerous activities made it clear that the growth of TDF would be accompanied by strident United States demands to toe the Cold War line to the detriment of independent laws and policies.

The issues of access and extraterritoriality involved conscious decisions to employ state power. But what about unintentional disruptions of vital TDF? This was the problem of *systems vulnerability*. The potential fragility of TDF links was first raised in the mid-1970s by the Swedes in connection with the Malmö fire department, which located all its information on local fire hazards and facilities in a General Electric computer in Ohio. As the debate warmed up, attention turned to the broader question: as societies became more and more dependent on computers and TDF in all walks of life, what would happen if systems containing vital information went down? Could the viability of domestic laws and policies be ensured? A widely noted 1977 report to the Swedish military defined vulnerability as:

1. excessive dependency on computers of all types of organizations, especially when inadequate back-up systems or obsolete manual routines exist; 2. unduly high risks of disruption of all aspects of economic and social life through crippling labor disputes, sabotage, terrorism or breakdowns in parts of large systems which affect the entire country; 3. an over-concentration of computer facilities in the major urban areas where physical security programmes are not sufficient to safeguard the critical nature of these installations; and 4. reliance on foreign data resources and processing services which, because they are generally beyond the jurisdiction of national law or control, could threaten the stability of government and industry should interruptions occur.

The concern with vulnerability was raised repeatedly in the years to follow, especially by West European governments.

Relatedly, there was the matter of determining *liability* for errors in transmissions. TDF may cross many networks en route to its final destination, and technical errors may occur at one or more points along the way. When it is difficult to pinpoint the territorial location of a problem, how should liability be apportioned among telecommunications network operators, and/or the information service provider or consumer? Pro-corporate analysts worried that firms could suffer significant financial losses from garbled or failed data transmissions without being able to collect damages. In contrast, some government, and especially those in the Third World, feared that they might be compelled to undertake expensive modernization programs to meet corporate demands for advanced services and thus avoid conflicts with the TNCs on which they relied for jobs, technology transfer, tax income, and so forth.

Another legal problem concerned assigning and protecting *intellectual property rights* for online information. Unlike tangible goods, software, data banks, and other information services are intangible products which can be copied and hence "stolen" without actually removing them from their original location (Pool & Solomon, 1980a). As network interconnectivity spread and individual and corporate hackers became more sophisticated, it was increasingly difficult to limit unauthorized access to online resources. Even in cases where there was no concerted effort to limit access, the rapidly growing range of information available through networks raised the problem that its creators might not be compensated for the transfer and use of their products. National governments varied widely in their development and enforcement of patent and copyright laws, so what was protected in a country of origin might not be in a country to which files are transferred (Reidenberg, 1988). This meant that stabilizing property rights for commodified information would require a coherent collective framework, but international law had not kept pace. As the principal source of online information, the United States strongly favored establishing a legal framework; indeed, intellectual property was one of the few TDF issues it viewed as meriting sustained discussion. Other industrialized countries had somewhat mixed interests, but ultimately supported the basic thrust of the American approach. In contrast, most LDCs remained hostile to establishing strict global intellectual property rights, as they were its most frequent "violators" and would be subject to heavy financial penalties and reduced access to information useful in promoting domestic development.

There was also the growing problem of *computer-related crime.* Among the many questions not well covered by existing laws were technological malfeasance, involving data processing that is defective, inadequate, or not in line with customer specifications; nonfeasance, or the failure to employ appropriate systems; tortfeasance, such as libel or defamation via an online videotext service; and simple theft or manipulation of data banks (Branscomb, 1983). Of particular note was the possibility of *new forms of industrial espionage.* As TNCs put more and more of their sensitive information online for internal use, their competitors had every incentive to try to break into proprietary systems and snoop around. Here too there was something of an international legal void, and many industrialized countries had a common interest in protecting their domestically based companies from theft through the harmonization or mutual recognition of laws. As an Australian judge prominently involved in the OECD dicussion observed,

> Where crimes are constituted of a number of elements, some of which may take place outside domestic jurisdiction by reason of access to international data communications, reforms may be needed to ensure that the legitimate jurisdiction of local courts is not improperly frustrated by technical arguments based on the principle of comity of nations which confines criminal law, as an exercise of sovereignty power, substantially to the sovereign's territory. (OECD, 1986, p. 68)

Again, in contrast, some LDCs feared that they could be the vulnerable targets of legal actions and retaliatory threats.

Finally, perhaps the most fundamental but difficult to evaluate legal problem concerned the *regulation of corporate behavior.* During the course of the TDF debate, most governments retained varying degrees of firm telecommunications regulations on TNCs' networks. Nationally and in the ITU they devised a wide variety of measures restricting somewhat the use and interconnection of private leased circuits, the competitive provision of value-added services to third parties, the resale and sharing of capacity, the attachment of systems to such circuits for the purpose of customizing advanced applications, and so on. But regardless of whether its carriage involved private circuits or public-switched networks, governments had no means of supervising the substantive content of information. Telecommunications regulations affected the access to and capabilities of digital pipes, but not what was "said" within them. Network capacity permitting, corporate users could transmit all kinds of computerized information across borders to instantly shift assets around the globe and reduce tax liabilities, take advantage of exchange rate fluctuations, facilitate transfer pricing and intrafirm trade, bypass "buy domestic" requirements in services industries, and so on. In general, TDF "permits the firm to circumvent government disincentives whether embodied as taxes, rules, interest payment or capital restrictions" (Irwin & Merenda, 1989, p. 334). How then could a state ensure that TNCs did not undertake transactions contrary to its domestic laws and policy objectives? Of course, they could still apply traditional supervisory measures like annual audits at either end of the pipe, but there was reason to worry that such methods would be unable to adequately assess and document any violations of the laws' letter or spirit by huge and globally dispersed TNCs. Here the potential contradictions between a transnational, private, and opaque cyberspace and the territorially bounded nation state were readily apparent to proregulatory forces.

Economic Issues

While many of the legal issues have economic dimensions, a number of more purely economic issues were also identified in the debate. The rise of TDF was understood in the historical context of a broader transformation: the emerging shift to a global information economy. It was recognized that with the increasing centrality of information across the agricultural, manufacturing, and services sectors, those companies and national economies best able to employ the new systems and services could establish dominant positions extending well into the future. This led to concerns which we will group into three categories: TDF's effects on the individual firm, on the nature of global markets and interfirm transactions, and on the nature of information per se.

Beginning at the level of the firm, TNCs' strategies were being redefined around networks and information resources. Large corporate users were elevating the role of information management within their organizational hierarchies, often in specialized departments led by Chief Information Officers. This was especially true of firms in the most information-intensive services industries, such as banking and insurance. For example, American Express was spending half a billion dollars annually on telecommunications and information by the mid-1980s, while Citicorp, owner of the world's largest private network, spent $3.3 billion between 1979 and 1984 (Sauvant, 1986, pp. 105, 110). Huge expenditures were becoming necessary in the increasingly globalized and turbulent business environment of the times, when political instability and other sources of investment risk were growing around the world. TNCs were seeking to cut costs, achieve economies of scale, and otherwise "rationalize" their worldwide activities.

One of the first issues to be identified concerned *the location of corporate decision making*. By radically improving the quality and quantity of information flowing between the head office and geographically dispersed plants and affiliates, TDF made it possible, if not necessary, for TNCs to centralize decision-making activity in the home country (Antonelli, 1981). Layers of local management could be subjected to closer, top-down oversight or even eliminated in light of the viability of continuous real-time monitoring of a firm's entire operations. In such cases, the branches and affiliates might become less responsive to host country objectives regarding production, employment, technology transfer, regulatory compliance, and so on; "the more organizations depend, ultimately, upon flows and networks, the less they are influenced by the social contexts associated with the places of their [physical] location" (Castells, 1989, p. 170). In parallel, TDF might impact *the location of production and other nonmanagerial functions* within a firm. A TNC's far-flung operations could, in effect, be gathered into the same "virtual" neighborhood, thus allowing top managers to identify and eliminate redundant functions and create a streamlined intraorganizational division of labor. This could result in the delocalization of activities that generate jobs, taxable income, and other benefits for the nation state.

Consequently, TDF could also affect *the location, level, and quality of employment*. On its location, a rationalized corporate division of labor might involve sending offshore only menial and poorly paid tasks. For example, "It may be that, within transnational computer-communication systems, less sophisticated data activities (e.g., the mere inputting of data) are located in one set of countries, while the more sophisticated ones are undertaken in another set of countries" (Sauvant, 1986, p. 116). Conversely, the combination of TDF and industrial automation could lead to the onshore repatriation of manufacturing jobs, with only limited final assembly or marketing functions remaining in host countries. Some TNCs have done this to avoid political instability and labor unrest in the LCDs while taking advantage of skilled labor and industrial automation at home. Such moves undermine one of the principal sources of comparative advantage and foreign exchange earnings for the South: cheap labor (Rada, 1984a, 1984b). Some analysts also worried that the possibilities of remote market presence might lead some TNCs to cut back on foreign direct investment in certain industries (Sauvant, 1986). This was especially of concern to LDCs which, while wary of dependence on TNCs, nonetheless needed the capital, jobs, tax, and foreign exchange earnings they can bring. More generally, *national comparative advantage* is increasingly a matter of knowledge engineering, rather than the distribution of natural factor endowments emphasized in trade theory, and the requisite capabilities were highly concentrated in the North.

On the level of employment, companywide integration and automation may mean reductions in the number of workers at both ends of the digital pipe. On its quality, what jobs remain at the wrong end of the pipe may be of a semi-skilled or unskilled nature. For example, United States-based TNCs are increasingly setting simple data entry positions in the Caribbean. Like many network workers, the low-paid woman who performs these tasks are electronically monitored and subjected to substantial stress to maximize key strokes per minute and minimize errors. Needless to say, such technical developments are also a part of larger efforts to expand the surveillance of workers and to bypass or break organized labor (Shaiken, 1984). Computerized speech recognition may further the latter trend, as is exemplified by the current struggle between AT&T and what is left of the Communications Workers of America.

Turning to the level of markets, TDF radically affects the nature of intercorporate commercial transactions. The most obvious impact was *the rise of network-based trade in services*. As the TDF debate expanded in the late 1970s, it began to feed into and overlap with the parallel discussion of services trade taking place in the OECD and other fora. Trade analysts and policymakers in the industrialized world had begun to elaborate the notion that international services transactions could be conceptually treated as trade, and many were advocating that they therefore be brought under the General Agreement on Tariffs and Trade (GATT) regime. Haircutting, construction, restaurants, and many other services require the physical and temporal proximity of buyers and sellers for a transaction to occur. Accordingly, international trade in such services involves the movement across borders of either the supplier or the customer. But with the development of advanced networks and TDF, "it appeared that there was another major means of supply: 'electronic highways' allowing sellers and buyers to remain apart while exchanging information-based services, which could henceforth be separated from their sources, stored in computers, and 'shipped ' across borders (Drake & Nicolaïdis, 1992, p. 48). Computer, advertising, consulting, banking, insurance, and other information-based services could now be disembodied and directly bought and sold in the form of TDF without regard to time and space. Hence, TDF was not simply a matter of intracorporate messages allowing the integration of internal operations. The global network of networks was becoming in itself a huge, multibillion dollar market involving many different industries, one to which old services could be shifted and in which entirely new services could be created.

The networked transportability of informational services can negate *economic borders, boundaries, and barriers to entry*. With TDF, a foreign supplier can be "virtually" present in a country's market without having to be there physically. Since from a technical standpoint, being on the network means being in the market, remote presence raises questions about the traditional division between purely domestic and transnational firms, and perhaps about their differential regulation. Similarly, sectoral boundaries and barriers to entry may lose their weight to the extent that companies redeploy their information resources to cross-enter into proximate activities and markets. For example, corporate users of telecommunications and information like Reuters and Lockheed have become providers of an expanded range of online services to external customers. States cannot effectively monitor such transactions in real time, and are left to put their faith in annual accountings of purchases and sales in order to enforce regulations on the range of informational services industries. As such, TDF is an essential ingredient in the wider globalization process that is integrating national economies more deeply than before.

That TDF and trade in networked services challenges the efficacy of territorial control over national economies is demonstrated clearly in the financial sector. Large banks and other financial institutions are among the heaviest users of TDF, and have been at the forefront of both applications development and the political pressures for global tele-communications and services liberalization. They maintain extensive and very advanced internal private networks, but also use TDF for interfirm transactions (Buyer, 1983; Greguras, 1984; Sellers, 1985; Shrivastava, 1983). Hundreds of banks from around the world have banded together to create closed user group networks such as the Society for Worldwide Interbank Financial Telecommunications (SWIFT), the Clearing House Interbank Payments System (CHIPS), and the Clearing House Automated Payments System (CHAPS). They have created the unregulated, offshore Eurocurrency markets to shoot trillions of dollars around the world, and stock markets are also hooking up via digital pipes. The use of TDF for electronic fund transfers and related purposes has become a key strategic sword, albeit a dual-edged one; for example, as the Chief Economist of American Express notes, "a major investment in technology and systems gave one major US bank a ten-second advantage over other traders, a short but powerful time-gain worth billions of dollars if used properly to react to news ahead of the market" (O'Brien, 1992, p. 9). However, he adds that, "the new information technologies have reduced the barriers to entry into core areas of banking ... The potential new competitors for banks are not just the securities firms entering banking; rather, it is the providers of information technology them-selves, Reuters and Telerate, that are becoming potential competitors" (O'Brien, 1992, p. 14). In short, TDF can support the dominant positions of individual firms, but it may also facilitate expanded cross-entry and competition on a global scale.

Either way, many analysts observed that financial TDF bypasses national regulations and makes constitutional sovereignty irrelevant (Al-Muhanna, 1985; Hamelink, 1982). When progressive or otherwise distasteful governments come to power or the local economy goes sour, investors can now vote with their networks instead of their feet. When stock markets crash, as happened on Wall Street in 1987, the shock waves spread rapidly over the networks to foreign exchanges. And if a currency becomes unattractive, it can be instantly dumped in the currency markets. No less a source than *Business Week* admitted that this was a fly in the ointment.

> The system increases the efficiency of moving cash around the world, and it is this very ease of movement that encourages foreign exchange crises. Moreover, the smooth-running banking system increases the velocity of the money that is careening about the world, raising pressure on the foreign exchange markets. As multinationals and other holders of

big cash hoards race about the Euromarkets seeking protection against a declining dollar, the dollar is pushed down even further. The establishment of a supranational banking system that greases the path of money movements also creates a vicious cycle of currency instability. The very structure of the Eurocurrency markets makes this inevitable. (*Business Week,* 1978, p. 80)

In sum, states lacked the tools to control financial TDF, and in the aggregate such transactions undermined their ability to shape domestic financial conditions and monetary policies.

As with traditional trade in goods, the increasing global accessibility of online services raised the question of *national competitiveness and the location of service production.* Just as intracorporate TDF facilitates the relocation of internal functions, intercorporate TDF allows the procurement of information-based services from interconnected suppliers around the world. Since buying services from thousands of miles away can be as easy as buying them from across the street, which territories in an integrated global economy would be the chosen as the points of origin for lucrative corporate sales? The collapsing of space and time and declining transmission costs mean that corporate customers can choose to purchase the best services from the largest and/or most advanced suppliers, and these were often in the United States. For example, if a Canadian-based bank purchases a database from a firm in California or sends it raw data for processing, Canadian computer service firms correspondingly do not receive the financial stimuli needed to upgrade their operations. Over time, they could become relatively capital starved, less innovative, and less competitive than their American counterparts when bidding for future customers.

This was not an idle concern. A report to the Government of Canada noted that 400 subsidiaries of American TNCs imported $300–350 million worth of computer services into Canada in 1978, and estimated that by 1985 this would mean $1.5 billion of imports and the loss of 23,000 Canadian data processing jobs (Government of Canada, 1978). These numbers were later challenged as being too high, and the government disowned the report, but the basic observation about the squeezing of infant information industries remained valid and was echoed by many other studies. Similar questions were raised about other networked services industries, such as management consulting and banking. National regulations might limit the growth of intangible trade imbalances, but they were not always easy to fully enforce and were in any event being strongly attacked as protectionism by TNCs. Moreover, since access to the best informational services is

critical for companies in every industry and suppliers have no obligation to provide them on a nondiscriminatory basis, the latter's strategic choices may limit the former's ability to compete. And not
surprisingly, "TNCs are not prepared to share such on-line resources of
data supply with their potential domestic competitors in host countries" (Jussawalla & Cheah, 1983, p. 290).

The problem of excessive services imports might also be aggravated
by the growing trend toward *corporate outsourcing*. Corporations
choose varying mixes of two organizational forms: hierarchies, in
which they establish integrated, multidivisional structures to satisfy
all their operational requirements; and markets, in which they cut out
some divisions and functions and rely on external suppliers. Some
economists employ transaction cost theory to try and explain under
what circumstances one or the other option is chosen, and a key
element in the equation is the contractual uncertainties and related
risks of relying on external suppliers. TDF may alter the mix by
reducing such risks, since managers can now maintain ongoing, real-
time linkages beyond the firm's formal boundaries that render such
suppliers "virtual insiders" in the corporate structure (Malone, Yates,
& Benjamin, 1987). In order to downsize and cut costs or simply
procure better services, many companies have reduced or eliminated
their accounting, advertising, data processing, and other divisions and
established networked relationships with specialized suppliers which
may be physically located abroad. In such cases, this deverticalization
or hollowing out of companies increases national trade deficits while
reducing local employment, tax payments, and so on.

Relatedly, TDF facilitates the creation of *new types of networked
relationships* that may not fit under existing conceptual categories and
regulatory policies. For example, the era of the TDF debate coincided
with a growing trend toward flexible intercorporate strategic alliances. To access markets, share risks and research and development
costs, expand product portfolios and economies of scale and scope,
TNCs have formed joint ventures, licensing agreements, management
contracts, shared representative offices, and so forth in which networks are used to maintain the relationships (Mytelka, 1987). Trans-
corporate networks can also be quickly established and disassembled
by particular divisions of companies seeking a joint solution to a given
problem, or between a company and its closest suppliers and
customers.

> The deepening of relationship ... [goes] much beyond exchange of
> products for payment to include 1) interactions *before* the production
> stage to identify products, either existing or to be developed, that would

generate additional value, 2) interactions *during* the production stage to fine tune the product to the needs and possibilities of the customer and producer, and 3) interactions *after* the production stage to facilitate use (training, joint operation), to maintain and service the product, and to identify opportunities for a new round of product development and sales. [Relationships] are increasingly managed through the same technology within the same networks transcending corporate boundaries" (Bressand & Nicolaïdis, 1989, pp. 27-28).

In effect, suppliers and customers may "co-produce" products within the network, thereby challenging regulatory, trade, antitrust, and other policies based on traditional distinctions and identities.

Finally, consider TDF's effects at the level of information itself. As noted above, much of the information being produced and used within networks is *proprietary*, which raises problems for governments seeking clarity about the activities they need to regulate. But the availability of TDF also creates incentives to generate information commodities for sale to networked customers around the world (D. Schiller, 1989). This *commodification of information* raised at least four concerns during the debate. First, *the substantive nature* of the information being bought and sold may pertain to practices contrary to state interests, for example, how to find tax shelters, reduce regulatory vulnerability, streamline the labor force, beat back local competitors, and so forth. Second, *access is on a pay-per basis,* and obviously domestic social groups and companies, especially in the LDCs, may have less ability to pay than large TNCs (Mosco, 1989). Third, some analysts documented a trend toward the *commodification of governmental information* that was formerly provided free to the public (D. Schiller, 1982; H. Schiller, 1981). Particularly in the United States, budgetary problems and ideological shifts led some governments to privatize some types of public information, and the combination of price and TDF might mean that TNCs de facto have greater access to it than citizens.

But the most frequently raised aspect of commodification pertained to the *valuation and taxation* of information and its transfer. Although information consumes an increasing share of corporate resources and is exchanged through networks, it has often not been subjected to taxation. Governments were confronted with a dilemma: On the one hand, it seemed to some, particularly the French, that lucrative TDF transactions should be taxable like any other product. Indeed, where TDF substitutes for traditional activities that were taxed, the failure to do so could even mean a revenue loss. On the other hand, it was often very difficult to establish an independent valuation of information for tax purposes, since its development may involve complex processes which are not easily measured, and its utility to users may exceed the production costs. For example, as computer-enhanced functions are performed in the terminals, switches, and other elements of the networks, information picks up added value at many points in the transmission. Since the majority of TDF appeared to be of an intracorporate nature, efforts to assign values and taxes would be both technically difficult and heatedly opposed by TNCs.

NATIONAL SOVEREIGNTY IN THE GLOBAL INFORMATION ECONOMY

The Empire Strikes Back

Collectively, the potential problems outlined above would seem to constitute a substantial issue area that should have kept analysts and policymakers busy for years to come. But in fact, by the mid-1980s, the majority of them had been eliminated from the international agenda, while most of those that remain are consistent with the corporate demand for unrestricted TDF. To understand how this occurred, it is necessary to examine the power dynamics that came into play as the debate proceeded.

At the outset, the United States laid relatively low in the hope that the storm would just blow over. As the largest providers and users of TDF, American-based TNCs recognized that any strident unilateral efforts on their part to short-circuit the debate could backfire and simply heighten foreign agitation for new regulations. And insofar as privacy protection was the dominant focus until the early 1980s, they were neither threatened by the policies being considered, nor very enthusiastic about being perceived as insensitive to what was clearly a heart-felt concern in Europe. Hence, they contented themselves with establishing consultative committees with the Department of State to fully convey their anxieties to the government, and with expressing fears in the press and on the conference circuit that the legitimate concern for privacy—which of course they shared—might be misappropriated as a tool of trade protectionism.

However, the debate not only failed to blow over, but began in the late 1970s to expand well beyond privacy. All the talk about threats to sovereignty and related national objectives set off alarm bells in the American business community, especially when the subject turned to the intracorporate use of TDF. The specter of governments attempting to devise policies that cut to the heart of their operations forced them to quickly mobilize. The United States government was pressed into service to take a much higher profile and aggressively preemptive stance in both bilateral consultations and multilateral discussions. The Congress held hearings at which dozens of executives decried as "information protectionism" virtually every inconvenience they experienced abroad with telecommunications, and federal agencies began to spew out reports warning of possible American retaliation (U.S. Congress, 1980a, 1980b; NTIA, 1983). State Department officials advanced the view in multilateral fora that "corporate speech" was a human rights issue, in that a multimillion dollar electronic fund transfer was equivilant to calling grandma in the old country. This view was decried by some governments as nonsense (Kirchner, 1982). Clearly, relying on state diplomacy alone would not meet corporate needs, as it would appear to confirm the charge that TDF was a "United States vs. the world" problem. Further, American TNCs were dismayed that foreign companies had maintained a rather somnabulant stance in the hope of a quiet accommodation with their home governments, and had failed to see the storm clouds. If this condition was allowed to persist, American-based firms would be isolated.

Hence, the key to the strategy on TDF, as well as on the wider question of trade in services, was to form multinational business coalitions and present a united front. That would not be easy if the problem was framed solely in terms of free trade, since some foreign service providers might benefit from their governments imposing TDF restrictions in the name of supporting infant industries. Instead, the key was to focus on the *common plight of corporate users*. A user-oriented discourse would emphasize TNCs' collective interest in not only the competitive supply of the best available services, but more importantly, in avoiding restrictions on the internal application of TDF and related systems. Insofar as banks, automobile, airline, and every other large company were users who needed to optimize information management to compete, it would be possible to forge broad and diverse coalitions whose members would press their respective governments to avoid TDF restrictions. It was one thing if General Motors expressed concern to the French government about the policies it was considering, and quite another if Peugot and Renault did the same.

Accordingly, a number of new groups were formed, and existing business organizations established highly visible communications policy committees. Among the most active of these alliances were the International Telecommunications User Group (INTUG), the Association of Data Processing Service Organizations (ADAPSO), the American Federation of Information Processing Societies (AFIPS), the Coalition of Service Industries (CSI), and the International Chamber of Commerce (ICC). Their involvement took several forms: First, they sponsored numerous in-house and contracted studies stressing the economic costs of regulation. A torrent of reports was produced, and prominent spokespersons made the rounds at virtually every conference of the "TDF mafia" (Austin, 1983; Basche, 1984; Business International, 1983; CBEMA, 1982; Diebold, 1980; ICC 1984). Second, representatives became actively involved in domestic policy discussions, working closely with local firms to clarify their interests, and with governments to challenge each and every regulatory initiative they might consider. Third, at the multilateral level, the alliances worked through such organs as the Business and Industry Advisory Committee of the OECD to consistently argue that the entire international business community was aghast at the possibility of "neo-Luddite" policies that would stifle new wealth creation *everywhere*. In an era of painful restructuring, this emphasis on the efficiency costs to the global economy as a whole led many policymakers to believe they had a common interest in avoiding restrictions.

Perhaps these pressure politics would have been less forceful if governments were absolutely certain that new TDF regulations were both viable and necessary. In that case, the corporate pressure could have been written off as an obvious manifestation of narrow self-interest that was contrary to overriding national objectives. But while corporate self-interest was undeniable, the case for strong and comprehensive regulations did not appear to be. One problem concerned the viability and cost of restrictions. Even if they wanted to, there was a widespread sense among governments that it would be technically quite difficult to control TDF TNCs and many independent analysts fed this perception of technological autonomy and inexorability. As the chairman of the OECD's Working Party on TDF noted at a watershed policy symposium in December 1983, many members had been persuaded that

> the technology will foil attempts by governments to exercise any effective degree of monitoring or control over TDF, without extending unacceptably into the area of censorship ... a great deal has been written about the difficulties associated with monitoring or controlling the flow of data between countries: first, because of the wide variety of ways in which the data can be transferred; and second, because traditionally widely different forms of data or information have now become indistinguishable as digital 'bit' streams. (Robinson, 1985a, p. 20)

Of course, TNCs' ability to use systems and services with these properties in the first place was a function of governments' policies and cost/benefit calculations. If they had felt strongly enough about it, they could have attempted to develop technologies for real-time monitoring, required that each transaction be approved in advance, or simply pulled the plug. But policies like these would have outraged the very corporations on which they depend for job creation, economic growth, and so forth. Since "business confidence" is the fundamental source of structural power in a capitalist economy, it is irrelevant that "the ruling class does not rule" (Block, 1977).

Moreover, the case for comprehensive regulations did not appear to be strong enough to merit undertaking such risks. In light of the many issues identified during the debate, this statement might seem non-sensical. *But the fundamental truth is that neither governmental nor independent analysts were able to produce much hard evidence that the anticipated negative effects of TDF actually were occurring at the time.* Why not? Certainly a major factor was that the information about exactly what computerized information flowed through which digital pipes and was used in which corporate decisions and practices was solely the property of the TNCs involved. Naturally, they had little incentive to disclose it to advocates of regulation, their competitors or anyone else. Governments could not compel them to do so through less than heavy-handed measures that would have unleashed even more virulent corporate opposition, and probably would not have been able to enforce full disclosure if they tried. Instead of risking a high-stakes confrontation, the only way to find out how TNCs used TDF was to politely ask them. To that end, both the OECD and the IBI issued voluntary surveys to groups of companies inquiring about TDF usage. TNCs were consulted in the preparation of these surveys, and any intrusive questions were modified or deleted. Even so, the response rates were not very high, and the information obtained unsurprisingly shed little to no light on whether the concerns outlined above were justified (Ergas & Reid, 1985; IBI, 1984b). Some consulting firms conducted multiclient studies that also attempted to survey corporate practice, but the questions asked yielded little more than helpful generalities, such as that managers thought TDF was important to their operations (Basche, 1984; Business International, 1983; Business Roundtable, 1985).

Without detailed information, how could propositions about whether or not corporate TDF actually led to the centralization of decision making, delocalization of production and employment, and so on be assessed? The UNCTC produced several solid studies using the best publicly available data, the general inadequacies of which it repeatedly noted (UNCTC, 1982, 1983a, 1983b, 1984, 1991). Even so, their primary empirical insights were that network nodes and traffic and recorded sales and usage of online services were highly concen-

trated among large TNCs from the industrialized countries, particularly the United States. A few other analysts found similar traffic
trends (Saito, Inose, & Kageyama, 1983). But such data obviously did
not indicate the substantive nature of the transmissions or the
particular corporate decisions and practices involved. And aside from
these works, most of the voluminous TDF literature is necessary
vague on empirical effects. Scores of books and articles were produced
covering the same generalities over and over, that is, TDF could be a
problem, governments are worried about it, some are contemplating
policies, and so on. Without the requisite information, any hypotheses
attributing effects to TDF usage, either for individual firms or in the
aggregate, were empirically untestable. All analysts could do was
extrapolate and guess: given that the technology makes certain
corporate practices possible, they may occur. The answer to Herbert
Schiller's question "Who knows?" remained the same: corporate managers and they were not talking (H. Schiller, 1981).

The mobilization of corporate pressure and the lack of information
put regulatory advocates within governments in an uncomfortable
position. Could they convince either their foreign counterparts or
high-level politicians to take on the TNCs without compelling evidence that this was essential? Could they do so absent support from
unified domestic coalitions strongly favoring regulation? Some labor
unions expressed concern about TDF, but they had no more concrete
evidence than anyone else that the problems experienced by their
members were attributable to TDF per se. At the same time, within
governments, ministries often disagreed about the wisdom of imposing new limitations on business at the same time that global competition was heating up. Between the early and mid-1980s, regulatory
advocates became progressively more isolated from the majority of
policymakers who were deciding either that the case had not been
made, or that while the concerns may be justified, this was a battle
that could not be won, and hence, was not worth fighting.

The End of Territoriality

The primary exception to this pattern was privacy protection. In
Europe, privacy experts had become a vocal and well-organized
multinational group, and governments were willing to impose some
minor restraints on TNCs even in the absence of solid evidence of
abuses. During the 1980s, many industrialized countries adopted new
data protection laws, usually of an omnibus nature, that imposed
limitations on the types of information public and private sector

organizations could gather on citizens. They also established data inspectorates with the power to require advance notification prior to the export of personal data via telecommunications (Burkert, 1981–82; Kirby, 1980; Turn, 1980). One of the biggest controversies was that a few European countries extended protection to both natural and "legal persons," that is, organizations. TNCs and their allies blasted this as protectionism on the grounds that local competitors might demand access to information about them held by larger firms (Grossman, 1982; Maisonrouge, 1981; Rooms & Dexter, 1979). In contrast, corporate opposition has blocked the adoption of a coherent law in the United States, which instead relies on a patchwork of statutes pertaining largely to the public sector (Reidenberg, 1992).

Obviously, the existence of discrepancies between national laws can render any one country's policy meaningless, if information is exported to a data haven. Hence, parallel efforts were devoted to establishing coherent multilateral frameworks. In 1981, the 26-member Council of Europe adopted a convention on privacy and TDF which allows governments to bloc transmissions destined for a nonsignatory country (COE, 1981). It went into force in 1985, and its principles have been incorporated into some national laws. Since a few of its members were not signatories to this Convention, the OECD undertook a parallel initiative designed in large part to woo the United States (Patrick, 1981). The OECD adopted a set of Guidelines in 1981 which laid down broadly similar principles for data gathering and dissemination (Briat, 1985; OECD, 1981). However, in part due to American demands, this accord was a watered down, nonbinding set of objectives with no enforcement mechanism. Accordingly, the United States government launched a public relations campaign to get its TNCs to endorse the Guidelines and demonstrate their good citizenship, and then announced to its counterparts abroad that the problem was now solved. Nevertheless, the Commission of the EC has recently begun to forge ahead with a new and stronger initiative, and has insisted—to American consternation—on establishing privacy as a legitimate grounds for limiting some forms of trade in telecommunications services in the current Uruguay Round negotiations.

How effective are these policies, and how much of a regulatory burden do they actually impose on TNCs? To be sure, there have been a few isolated cases where TNCs were told that they could not export data for processing. For example, the French inspectorate recently prevented Fiat from transmitting files on French employees to Italy, where no effective protections had been established. But on the whole, data protection suffers from its reliance on TNC's willingness to comply. They may not always notify national inspectorates in advance that they plan to export information, which is then comingled in the bitstream with everything else. One need only review the surveys of annual data inspectorate conferences published in *Transnational Data and Communications Report* to see that governments are painfully aware of such limitations, which are now growing with the development of new technologies like integrated services digital networks. As one extensive study summarizes the problem, "The harsh reality is that data protectors run the risk of being only a tiny force of irregulars equipped with pitchforks and hoes waging battle against large technocratic and bureaucratic forces equipped with lasers and nuclear weapons" (Flaherty, 1989, p. 393). Or, for a less metaphorical insight, one can turn to the source. In 1983, a consulting house surveyed 51 American-based TNCs, 34 of which had endorsed the OECD Guidelines. Of the 34, only 10 said they were doing anything at all to comply with European data protection, and top executives of the 10 were completely unaware that their firms had even endorsed the agreement (Business International, 1983).

What about regulations on nonpersonal TDF, which was really the main source of contention? From the late 1970s to the mid-1980s, there was a literal explosion in the number of consulting studies and publications warning of a growing war over TDF. A picture was frequently painted, primarily by Americans, of governments running amuck and imposing all kinds of new restrictions on TNCs. Among the measures being discussed by regulations' advocates and denounced by its opponents were requirements that data processing be undertaken locally employing the equipment and services of national firms; specialized transmission links receive prior approval from PTTs; companies attain authorization for transactions, register them with authorities, or at least notify governments of their intent to import or export certain types of information; and that duplicate copies of important information be retained within the host country in order to preclude access problems. Similarly, postal and customs restrictions could be erected to control the manual movement of hard copies across borders. Writing about these possibilities rapidly became a booming business (Cheah, 1985; Cuadra, 1978; Eger, 1981b; Feldman & Garcia, 1982; Ganley & Ganley, 1982; Jussawalla, 1987; Katzan, 1980; Kirsch, 1983; Novotny, 1982; On-Line Conferences, 1978; Otey, 1982; Pellegrin, 1983; Pollack, 1982; Sanger, 1981; Sardinas & Sawyer, 1983; Seaman, 1981; Sharpe, 1981; Spero, 1982)

But in practice, how widespread were direct restrictions on the types of information that could be transmitted or on its use? Finding actual incidents in this literature of states trying to put strong clamps on TNCs can be a frustrating experience. The Canadian Bank Act of

1980 requires that banks retain duplicate copies of certain records within the country. In 1982, the German Bundepost briefly raised the rates on leased circuits, which TNCs maintained was an attempt to compel them to use local data processing. Mexico clearly declared a requirement for local processing in certain instances, but enforcement is said to have been rather spotty. American-based firms had difficulty accessing the EC's Euronet/Diane information network. These and a few other minor incidents were repeated ad infinitum by free-flow advocates to establish a discursive environment in which states could be depicted as undertaking new and increasingly interventionist policies. But, in fact, they were really a scattered set of marginal impediments which did not cumulatively point to an upward trend in "information protectionism." The only really significant program, which is mentioned in virtually everything written on TDF, was the one adopted by Brazil. Until recently, Brazilian policy required prior approval for transmission links, maintenance in Brazil of duplicate copies of certain databases, and local data processing unless a company's needs could not be met. TNCs feared that this approach would spread, and generally were not amused by a UNCTC study that described the Brazilian model in detail for the benefit of other LDCs (UNCTC, 1983b). For this and other transgressions, the Bush Administration is now demanding that the Center be dismantled.

While direct restrictions were far from rampant, TNCs did nevertheless encounter some indirect problems in meeting all their TDF requirements. These arose not from new restrictions on content, but rather from traditional telecommunications regulations on carriage. As indicated earlier, PTTs imposed a wide array of conditions on the use and interconnection of leased circuits, resale of excess capacity, and so on, and coordinated their efforts in the ITU (Drake, forthcoming-a). In parallel, they set technical standards that limited TNCs' ability to attach specialized equipment to their circuits and to achieve flexible interoperability between such equipment (Drake, forthcoming-b). These practices did diminish the ease, if not the possibility, of advanced information transfer in some cases (Markowski, 1981). However, they were generally not new measures adopted to enforce national objectives regarding TDF. Rather, they were simply monopoly carriers' efforts to maximize traffic and revenues on public-switched networks while limiting competition in value-added transmission services. Nevertheless, TNCs challenged as TDF barriers these negative limitations on their freedom in telecommunications. In parallel, TNCs also attacked as TDF restrictions any positive industrial supports for domestic equipment manufacturers. Both moves proved fruitful, in that by framing such policies as unacceptable impediments to commercial speech and efficiency, they set a propitious discursive context in which to demand not only a stand still on the adoption of new impediments, but also a rollback of existing ones. The furious and preemptive wringing of hands about growing attacks on "free flow" fed into and reinforced the wider liberalization of the global information economy that continues today. In this sense, Brazil may have actually done TNCs a favor.

Finally, we should note the parallel trends in the multilateral policy discussions. After completing the privacy guidelines in 1981, the OECD launched a broader research program on the legal and economic issues. At the outset, attention was to be devoted to questions surrounding intracorporate communications, but very strong opposition from the United States and its corporate allies truncated the effort. For example, a commissioned study in 1981 argued that TDF could lead to centralized decision making and greater specialization of production among subsidiaries and affiliates (Antonelli, 1981). The report was denounced as methodologically unsound, was not released for external distribution, and no follow-up work of a similar nature as pursued. Thereafter, the focus rapidly shifted, at American insistence, to intercorporate trade issues. Here the questions were posed more in terms of how to eliminate barriers to commerce and how to devise network-related trade principles in the run-up to the GATT's current Uruguay Round negotiations (Drake & Nicolaïdis, 1992). By the time of its watershed TDF symposium in December 1983, the political winds had shifted strongly against any elaborate examinations of "controversial" issues, and toward the pursuit of approaches described as "balanced" and "pragmatic." At the symposium, a high-level Canadian representative reflected the new mood, arguing that Canadians "do not wish to create an 'electronic wall' around our country ... [which] would obviously deny to our own industry access to vital information and to new and innovative services, which would weaken its competitive position internationally, and in our own market." And anyway, it would not be "economically feasible to attempt to monitor or control the data crossing our borders in so many different ways—satellite, microwave, cable" (Montgomery, 1985, p. 71). Since Canada had been an influential bridge between the United States and Europe and a source of many critical inquiries, this affirmation of TDF's benefits to domestically based users and the technical difficulties of its regulation was widely viewed as a significant harbinger of a new consensus.

Over the next two years, support for regulations collapsed. Many participants in the Working Party on TDF felt they had spent too much time chasing illusory problems for which there was no hard evidence. Indeed, the group's chairman argued that the TDF term had misdirected their attention, since it "bears little relationship to the range of important issues. It concentrates, inevitably, on the movement of data or information from one country to another. The issues, however, arise not so much from that act of movement or transfer, but in the results of activities which follow from or are directly related to that act" (Robinson, 1985b, p. 272). Moreover, the term "sovereignty" disappeared entirely from the discussion, as participants increasingly concurred with the narrow constitutional use of the term favored by the United States. Attention turned to drafting a list of nonbinding principles that would substitute for what once was expected to be an international regime. The 1985 Declaration on TDF begins by "Acknowledging that computerized data and information now circulate, by and large, freely on an international scale;" continues by "recognizing the growing importance of [TDF] and the benefits that can be derived from [TDF];" as well as "recognizing the Member countries have a common interest in facilitating [TDF], and in reconciling different policy objectives in this field;" and declares members' intentions to "avoid the creation of unjustified barriers to the international exchange of data and information" (OECD, 1985, pp. 2-3). Since 1985, the TDF group has been reformulated to focus on promoting telecommunications liberalization. A few of the old TDF questions get occassional attention in this context, such as privacy, intellectual property, computer crime, and conflicts of law, but the core issues pertaining to corporate practice have been dumped overboard. Moreover, only among privacy specialists does one still find the phrase "TDF" used with much conviction or frequency; everyone else seems to say "information trade."

For its part, the IBI was brought firmly to heel. Internal management problems diminished its stature, and key members like Brazil and France decided the organization no longer suited their needs and quit. What remained was a fairly small group of primarily lower income LDCs that had little chance of adopting and enforcing national policies or an international regime contrary to the mood in the North. By the time of its Second World Conference on TDF in 1984, the hope for global regulations and redistributive measures had been abandoned. As a leading West German diplomat closely involved in TDF issues recalled, the meeting

> clearly demonstrated that many Third World countries are now trying to evolve a more pragmatic and down-to-earth attitude. Such barbed notions as 'informational sovereignty' 'information-poor' or 'self-reliance' were barely heard. Instead there was much talk of interdependence and

practical aid. At the bottom of this is the Third World's apprehension about becoming the big losers in the information revolution. This also accounts for the interest of the more developed Third World countries in concrete projects for the development of specialized electronic archives, bibliographic collections and data banks. (Grewlich, 1985, pp. 64-65)

Since that conference, the IBI has focused its attention on facilitating the LDCs' access to information systems and applications developed primarily by Northern TNCs.

CONCLUSION

Were proregulatory analysts searching for a "solution without a problem?" Does TDF have negative effects on national sociocultural, legal, and economic objectives, or more broadly for sovereignty itself? Maybe yes, maybe no; the debate was abandoned before we found out. The only people who really know how TDF is employed in corporate activities are the users themselves, and they are not talking.

REFERENCES

Adams, J. M. (1983, October). Canada's future TDF policy: Reconciling free flow with national sovereignty. *Transnational Data and Communications Report, 6,* 405-411.

Al-Muhanna, I. (1985, March). *The political economy of information: Transborder data flow and the world's financial system.* Paper presented at the Annual Convention of the International Studies Association, Washington, DC.

Anderla, G., & Petrie, J.H. (1985). The international data market: A background report. In H.P. Gassman (Ed.), *Transborder data flows* (pp. 259-318). Amsterdam: North-Holland.

Antonelli, C. (1981, June 2). *Transborder data flows and international business: A pilot study* (DSTI/ICCP/81.16). Paris: OECD.

Antonelli, C. (1983) *On the diffusion of a major process innovation: International data telecommunications and multinational corporations.* New York: The Rockefeller Foundation.

Austin, R. (1983). *Transborder data flows: The needs of the international business community.* London: Unilever.

Basche, J. R., Jr. (1984). *Regulating international data transmission: The impact on managing international business* New York: The Conference Board.

Becker, J. (1989). Transborder data flow (TDF) between East and West: The case of the Federal Republic of Germany. In J. Becker & T. Szecskö (Eds.), *Europe speaks to Europe: International information flows between Eastern and Western Europe* (pp. 285-295). New York: Pergamon.

Beling, C. T. (1983). Transborder data flows: International privacy protection and the free flow of information. *Boston College International and Comparative Law Review, 6,* 591-622.

Berman, J. L. (1987, June). National security vs. access to computer databases: A new threat to freedom of information. *First Principles, 12,* 1-7.

Block, F. (1977, May-June). The ruling class does not rule: Notes on the Marxist theory of the state. *Socialist Revolution, 33,* 6-28.

Bortnick, J. (1981, Summer). International information flow: The developing world perspective. *Cornell International Law Journal, 14,* 333-353.

Botein, M., & Noam, E. M. (1986). *US restrictions on international data transmission by telecommunications networks.* (Working paper series). (New York: Center for Telecommunications and Information Studies, Graduate School of Business, Columbia University.

Branscomb, A. W. (1986). Global governance of global networks: A survey of transborder data flow in transition. *Vanderbilt Law Review, 36,* 985-1043.

Branscomb, A. W. (1986). Law and culture in the information society. *The Information Society, 4*(4), 279-311.

Branscomb, A. W. (Ed.). (1986). *Toward a law of global networks.* White Plains, NY: Longman.

Bressand, A. (1986). *International division of labor in the emerging global information economy: The need for a new paradigm* (Project Promethee Working Papers). Paris: Promethee.

Bressand, A., Distler, C., and Nicolaïdis, K. (1989). Networks at the heart of the service economy. In A. Bressand & Nicolaïdis (Eds.), *Strategic trends in services: An inquiry into the global service economy* (pp. 17-32). New York: Harper and Row.

Briat, M. (1985). Synthesis report on the application of the guidelines governing the protection of privacy and transborder flows of personal data— Update as of December 1983. In H. P. Gassman (Ed.), *Transborder data flows* (pp. 351-391). Amsterdam: North-Holland.

Brizida, J. de O. (1980). Official Brazilian address. *Transnational Data and Communications Report, 3,* 33.

Brown, L. (1972). *World without borders: The interdependence of nations.* New York: Foreign Policy Association.

Brown, R. W. (1983, May 12-13). International information transfers: A topical survey. In *New developments in international telecommunications policy* (pp. 45-143). Washington, DC: The Federal Communications Bar Association and the International Law Institute of Georgetown University.

Bull, H. (1977). *The anarchical society: A study of order in world politics.* New York: Columbia University Press.

Burkert, H. (1981-82). Institutions of data protection: An attempt at a functional explanation of European national data protection laws. *The Computer/Law Journal, 3,* 167-188.

Business International Corporation. (1983). *Transborder data flows: Issues, barriers and corporate responses.* New York: BIC.

The Business Roundtable. (1985). *International information flow: A plan for action.* New York: BR.

Buss, M. D. J. (1984, May-June). Legislative threats to transborder data flow. *Harvard Business Review,* pp. 111-118.

Butler, R. E. (1984). The international telecommunication union and the formulation of information transfer policy. In J. F. Rada & G. R. Pipe (Eds.), *Communication regulation and international business* (pp. 71-92). Amsterdam: North-Holland.

Buyer, M. (1983, May). Telecommunications and international banking. *Telecommunications,* pp. 44-52.

Castells, M. (1989). *The informational city: Information technology, economic restructuring and the urban-regional process.* Oxford: Basil Blackwell.

Canada, Government of. (1971). *Instant world: A report on telecommunications in Canada.* Ottawa: Information Canada.

Canada, Government of. (1978). *The growth of computer communications in Canada.* Ottawa: Ministry of Supply and Services.

Canada, Government of. (1979). *Report of the Consultative Committee on the implications of telecommunications for Canadian sovereignty: Telecommunications and Canada.* Ottawa: Minister of Supply and Services.

Cate, F. H. (1990, Winter). The first amendment and the international 'free flow' of information. *Virginia Journal of International Law, 30,* 373-420.

Cheah, C. W. (1985, December). An econometric analysis of TDF regulation. *Transnational Data and Communications Report, 7,* 475-479.

Commission of the European Community. (1979, November 26). *European society faced with the challenge of the new information technologies: A community response.* Brussels: CEC, COM 79, 650 Final B.

Computer and Business Equipment Manufacturers Association. (1982, July). *International information flows: The need for flexibility—A CBEMA white paper.* Washington, DC: CBEMA.

Council of Europe. (1981). *Convention for the protection of individuals with regard to automatic processing of personal data.* Strasbourg: COE.

Crawford, M. H. (1980, July). House Hearings on transborder data flows: A reflection. *Information Privacy, 2,* 165-169.

Cuadra, C. A. (1978, June). US-European co-operation and competition in the on-line retrieval services marketplace. *The Information Scientist, 12,* 42-53.

The Diebold Group. (1980). *MIS and communications issues facing multinationals.* New York: Diebold.

Dougan, D. L. (1987, January). An international policy perspective on the information age. *IEEE Communications Magazine, 25,* 18-23.

Drake, W. J. (1984, August-September). Canada-US: Free data services zone? *Transnational Data and Communications Report, 7,* 302-307, 310 & 311.

Drake, W. J. (forthcoming-a). Asymmetric deregulation and the transformation of the international telecommunications regime. In E. M. Noam & G. Pogorel (Eds.), *Asymmetric deregulation: The dynamics of telecommunications policies in Europe and the United States.* Norwood, NJ: Ablex.

Drake, W. J. (forthcoming-b). The transformation of international telecommunications standardization: European and global dimensions. In C. Steinfield, J. Bauer, & L. Caby (Eds.), *Telecommunications in Europe: Changing policies, services and technologies.* Newbury Park: Sage.

Drake, W. J. & Nicolaïdis, K. (1992, Winter). Ideas, interests, and institutionalization: International trade in services' and the Uruguay Round. In P. Haas (Ed.), *Knowledge, Power and International Policy Coordination* (Special Issue of *International Organization), 45,* 37-100.

Eger, J. M. (1981a, March 16). The international information war. *Computerworld,* pp. 103-119.

Eger, J. M. (1981b, Summer). The global phenomenon of teleinformatics: An introduction. *Cornell Journal of International Law, 14,* 203-236.

Ergas, H., & Reid, A. (1985). Transborder data flows in international enterprises: The results of a joint BIAC/OECD survey and interviews with firms. In H. P. Gassman (Ed.), *Transborder data flows* (pp. 213-250) Amsterdam: North-Holland.

Evans, A.C. (1981, Fall). European data protection law. *The American Journal of Comparative Law, 29,* 571-582.

Falk, R., Kratochwil, F., & Mendlovitz, S. (Eds.). (1985). *International law: A contemporary perspective.* Boulder, CO: Westview Press.

Feldman, M. B. (1983, January-February). Commercial speech, TDF and the right to communicate under international law. *Transnational Data and Communications Report, 6,* 51-56.

Feldman, M. B., & Garcia, D. (1982, Winter). National regulation of transborder data flow. *North Carolina Journal of International Law and Commercial Regulation, 7,* 1-25.

Fishman, W. L. (1980, Summer). Introduction to transborder data flows. *Stanford Journal of International Law, 16,* 1-26.

Flaherty, D. H. (1989). *Protecting privacy in surveillance societies: The Federal Republic of Germany, Sweden, France, Canada & the United States.* Chapel Hill: University of North Carolina Press.

Fleiner-Gerster, T., & Meyer, M. A. (1985). New developments in humanitarian law: A challenge to the concept of sovereignty. *International and Comparative Law Quarterly, 34,* 267-283.

Foucault, M. (1970). *The order of things.* New York: Random House.

Freese, J. (1979). *International data flow.* Lund: Student Litteratur.

Ganley, O. J., & Ganley G. (1989). *To inform or control? The new communications networks* (2nd ed.). New York: McGraw-Hill.

Gassman, H. P. (Ed.). (1985). *Transborder data flows: Proceedings of an OECD Conference held December 1983.* Amsterdam: North-Holland.

Gassman, H.P., & Pipe, G. R. (1976). Synthesis report. In Organization for Economic Cooperation and Development (Eds.), *Policy issuesin data protection and privacy: Concepts and perspectives—Proceedings of the OECD Seminar,* 24th to 26th June, 1974 (pp. 12-41). Paris: OECD.

Giddens, A. (1979). *Central problems in social theory: Action, structure and contradiction in social analysis.* Berkeley: The University of California Press.

Gottlieb, A., Dalfen, C., & Katz, K. (1974, April). The transborder transfer of information by communications and computer systems: Issues and approaches to guiding principles. *American Journal of International Law, 68,* 227-257.

Greguras, F. M. (1984, September/October). Impact of transborder data flow restrictions on cash management services. *The World of Banking,* pp. 10-16.

Grewlich, K. W. (1985). Free electronic information and data flows? *German Foreign Affairs Review, 1,* 55-69.

Gross, L. (1979). Some international law aspects of the freedom of information and the right to communicate. In K. Nordenstreng & H. I. Schiller (Eds.), *National sovereignty and international communication* (pp. 195-216). Norwood: Ablex.

Grossman, G. (1982, Spring). Transborder data flow: Separating the privacy interests of individuals and corporations. *Northwestern Journal of International Law and Business, 4,* 1-36.

Haas, E. B. (1964). *Beyond the nation-state: Functionalism and international organization.* Palo Alto: Stanford University Press.

Hamelink, C. J. (1982). *Finance and information: A study of converging interests.* Norwood, NJ: Ablex.

Hamelink, C. J. (1984). *Transnational data flows in the information age.* Lund: Studentlitteratur AB.

Hinsley, F. H. (1986). *Sovereignty* (2nd ed.). Cambridge: Cambridge University Press.

Hondius, F. W. (1980, Summer). Data law in Europe. *Stanford Journal of International Law, 16,* 87-112.

Intergovernmental Bureau of Informatics. (1978). *Strategies and policies on informatics: IBI background documents presented to the intergovernmental conference in Torremolinos (Spain),* August-September 1978. New York: UNIPUB.

Intergovernmental Bureau of Informatics. (1980, October). *World Conference on Transborder Data Flow Policies: Final Proceedings.* Rome: IBI.

Intergovernmental Bureau of Informatics. (1984a). *IBI World Survey of National Policies and Company Practices Concerning Transborder Data Flows.* Rome: IBI.

Intergovernmental Bureau of Informatics. (1984b). *Second World Conference on Transborder Data Flow Policies: Working Document.* Rome: IBI.

International Chamber of Commerce. (1984, December). *Information flows: Analysis of issues for business.* Paris: ICC.

Irwin, M. R., & Merenda, M. J. (1989, December). Corporate networks, privatization and state sovereignty: Pending issues for the 1990s? *Telecommunications Policy, 13,* 329-335.

Jacobson, R. E. (1979, Summer). The hidden agenda: What kind of order? *Journal of Communication, 29,* 149-155.

James, A. (1986). *Sovereign statehood: The basis of international society.* London: Allen and Unwin.

Jussawalla, M., & Cheah, C. W. (1983, December). Emerging constraints on transborder data flows. *Telecommunications Policy, 7,* 285-296.

Jussawalla, M., & Cheah, C. W. (1987). *The calculus of international communications: A study in the political economy of transborder data flows.* Littleton: Libraries Unlimited.

Katzan, H. Jr. (1989). *Multinational computer systems: An introduction to transborder data flow and data regulations.* New York: Van Nostrand Reinhold.

Keeton, G.W. (1939). *National sovereignty and international order.* London: Peace Books.

Keohane, R. O. (1987, May 21-June 3). *Changes in patterns of international cooperation and the valuation of sovereignty.* Paper presented to the American-German Workshop on International Relations Theory, Bad Homburg.

Kirby, M. D. (1979, June). Data protection and law reform. *Computer Networks, 3,* 149-163.

Kirby, M. D. (1980, Summer). Transborder data flows and the 'basic rules' of data privacy. *Stanford Journal of International Law, 16,* 27-66.

Kirchner, J. (1982, January 11). U.S. stance on data flow called 'nonsense'. *Computerworld,* p. 16.

Kirsch, W. (1983). *Transborder data flows: A current review.* London: International Institute of Communications.

Knoppers, J. (1984). Sovereignty and transborder data flows: Some practical and cultural considerations. In Intergovernmental Bureau of Informatics (Eds.), *IBI Second World Conference on Transborder Data Flow Policies: Papers on International Cooperation and Universal Principles on Transborder Data Flows* (pp. 74-105). Rome: IBI.

Knoppers, J., & Foote, J. (1982, September). *Cultural sovereignty and TDF: Online public information retrieval services and the Canadian electronic cultural heritage.* Canada: Inter-Departmental Task Force on Transborder Data Flow, Government of Canada.

Krasner, S. D. (1988, April). Sovereignty: An institutional perspective. *Comparative Political Studies, 21,* 66-94.

Kratochwil, F., with Rohrlich, P., & Mahajan, H. (1985). *Peace and disputed sovereignty: Reflections on conflict over territory.* Lanham: University Press of America.

Lang, J. (1982, December). Culture and economy: The same battle. *Transnational Data and Communications Report, 5,* 407-409.

Leeson, K. W. (1983). *International communications: Blueprint for policy.* Honolulu: East-West Center Communication Institute.

MacDonald, S. (1989). Out of control? US export controls and technological information. In J. Becker & T. Szecskö (Eds.), *Europe speaks to Europe: International information flows between Eastern and Western Europe* (pp. 309-338). New York: Pergamon.

Mack, P. E. (1990). *Viewing the earth: The social construction of the LANDSAT satellite system.* Cambridge, MA: MIT Press.

Madec, A. (1980). *les flux transfrontieres de donees: vers une economie interrnationale de l'information?* Paris: La Documentation Française.

Maisonrouge, J. G. (1981). Regulation of international information flows. *Information Society, 1,* 17-30.

Malone, T. W., Yates, J., & Benjamin, R. I. (1987, June). Electronic markets and electronic hierarchies. *Communications of the ACM, 30,* 484-497.

Markowski, J. R. (1981, Summer). Telecommunications regulations as a barrier to transborder data flow of information. *Cornell International Law Journal, 14,* 287-331.

Matterlart, A., & Siegelaub, S. (1979). *Communication and class struggle, vol. 1: Capitalism, imperialism.* New York: International General.

Montgomery, W. H. (1985). Transborder data flows: Canadian directions. In H. P. Gassman (Ed.), *Transborder data flows* (pp. 71-76). Amsterdam: North-Holland.

Morse, E. L. (1976). *Modernization of international relations.* New York: Free Press.

Mosco, V. (1989). *The Pay-per society: Computers and communications in the informative age.* Norwood, NJ: Ablex.

Mowlana, H. (1986). *Global information and world communication: New frontiers in international relations.* New York: Longman.

Mytelka, L. K. (1987). Knowledge-intensive production and the changing internationalization strategies of multinational firms. In J. A. Caporaso (Ed.), *A changing international division of labor* (pp. 48-70). Boulder: Lynne Rienner.

National Telecommunications and Information Administration. (1983). *Long-Range goals in international telecommunications and information: An outline for United States policy.* Washington, DC: U.S. Government Printing Office.

Nora, S., & Minc, A. (1980). *The computerization of society: A report to the President of France.* Cambridge: MIT Press.

Novotny, E. J. (1980, Summer). Transborder data flows and international law: A framework for policy-oriented inquiry. *Stanford Journal of International Law, 16,* 141-180.

Novotny, E. J. (1982, Winter). Transborder data flow regulation: Technical issues of legal concern. *Computer Law Journal, 3,* 105-124.

Organization for Economic Cooperation and Development. (1981). *Guidelines on the protection of privacy and transborder flows of personal data.* Paris: OECD.

Organization for Economic Cooperation and Development. (1985, April 11). *Declaration on transborder data flows.* (Press/A(85)30. Paris: OECD.

Organization for Economic Cooperation and Development. (1986). *Computer-related crime: Analysis of legal policy.* Paris: OECD.

O'Brien, R. (1992). *Global financial integration: The end of geography.* London: Pinter.

O'Brien, R. C., & Helleiner, G. K. (1980, Autumn). The political economy of information in a changing international economic order. *International Organization, 34,* 455-470.

On-Line Conferences, Ltd. (1978). *Transnational data regulation: Proceedings of the Brussels Conference.* Uxbridge, UK: On-Line.

Ostry, B. (1979, October). *What is the impact of information exchange on cultural and political sovereignty and economic independence?* Paper presented at the 11th Annual Meeting of the Information Industry Association, Washington, DC.

Otey, S. B. (1982, October). Obstructive foreign communications practices: The dilemma of the MNCs. *Transnational Data and Communications Report, 5,* 361-365.

Pantages, A., (1978, November 1). Europe moves toward controlled data flow. *Datamation,* pp. 80-82.

Pantages, A. & Whitehead, J. (1977, September). An international convention on transborder data flow: The need is seeping into the American corporate mind. *Datamation.*

Patrick, H. (1981, Summer). Privacy restrictions on transnational data flows: A comparison of the Council of Europe Draft Convention and OECD Guidelines. *Jurimetrics Journal of Law, Science and Technology,* pp. 405-420.

Pellegrin, J. (1983, August). Transborder data flow: Trickle or torrent? *Satellite Communications,* pp. 80-84.

Pipe, G. R. (1984). International information policy: Evolution of transborder data flow issues. *Telematics and Informatics, 1,* 409-418.

Ploman, E. (Ed.). (1982). *International law governing communications and information.* London: Frances Pinter.

Pollack, A. (1982, April 22). Overcoming data barriers. *New York Times,* p. D2.

Pool, I. de S., & Solomon, R. J. (1980a). Intellectual property and transborder data flows. *Stanford Journal of International Law, 16,* 113-140.

Pool, I. de S., & Solomon, R. J. (1980b). Transborder data flows: Requirements for international co-operation. *Policy Implications of Data Network Developments in the OECD Area* (pp. 79-139). Paris: OECD.

Rada, J. F. (1984a). Advanced technologies and development: Are conventional ideas about comparative advantage obsolete? *Trade and Development: An UNCTAD Review,* No. 5, 275-296.

Rada, J. F. (1984b). Development, telecommunications, and the emerging service economy. *Proceedings of the Second World Conference on Transborder Data Flow Policies, Rome, 26-29 June 1984* (pp. 131-150). Rome: Intergovernmental Bureau of Informatics.

Reidenberg, J. (1988). Information property: Some intellectual property aspects of the global information economy. *Information Age, 10* (1), 3-12.

Reidenberg, J. (1992, March). Privacy in the information economy: A fortress or frontier for individual rights? *Federal Communications Law Review, 44,* 195-243.

Renaud, J.-L. (1986). A conceptual framework for the examination of transborder data flows. *The Information Society, 4*(3), 145-185.

Robinson, P. (1984, May). *Sovereignty and data: Some perspectives.* Paper presented at the conference, "The Information Economy: Its Implications for Canada's Industrial Strategy."

Robinson, P. (1985a). Transborder data flows: An overview of the issues. In H. P. Gassman (Ed.), *Transborder data flows* (pp. 15-29). Amsterdam: North-Holland.

Robinson, P. (1985b, December). Telecommunications, trade and TDF. *Telecommunications Policy, 9,* 310-318.

Robinson, P. (1990, February). TDF issues: Hard choices for governments. *Telecommunications Policy, 14,* 64-70.

Rooms, P. L. P., & Dexter, J. (1979, June). Problems of data protection law for private multinational communications networks. *Computer Networks, 3,* 205-214.

Rosenberg, J. (1990, Summer). A non-realist theory of sovereignty? Giddens' the nation-state and violence. *Millenium: Journal of International Studies, 19,* 249-259.

Ruggie, J. G. (1983). Continuity and transformation in the world polity: Toward a neorealist synthesis. *World Politics, 35,* 261-285.

Saito, T., Inose, H., & Kageyama, S. (1983). A comparative study of the mode of domestic and transborder information flows including data. *Information Economics and Policy, 1,* 75-92.

Sanger, D. E. (1981, August 26). Multinationals worry as countries regulate data crossing borders. *Wall Street Journal,* pp. 1 & 16.

Sanger, D. E. (1983, March). Waging a trade war over data. *New York Times,* (pp. 13). D1, 26-27.

Sardinas, J. L., Jr. & Sawyer, S. M. (1983, November). Transborder data flow regulation and multinational corporations. *Telecommunications,* pp. 59, 60, 62, 102.

Sauvant, K. P. (1984). Transborder data flows: Importance, impact, policies. *Information Services and Uses, 4,* 3-30.

Sauvant, K. P. (1986). *Services and data services: The international politics of transborder data flows.* Boulder, CO: Westview Press.

Schiller, D. (1982). *Telematics and government.* Norwood, NJ: Ablex.

Schiller, D. (1988). How to think about information. In V. Mosco & J. Wasko (Eds.), *The political economy of information* (pp. 27-43). Madison: University of Wisconsin Press.

Schiller, H. I. (1978, Autumn). Computer systems: Power for whom and for what? *Journal of Communication, 28,* 184-193.

Schiller, H. I. (1981). *Who knows: Information in the age of the Fortune 500.* Norwood, NJ: Ablex.

Schiller, H. I. (1982). Sources of opposition to US information supremacy. In J. R. Schement, F. Gutierrez, & M. A. Sirbu, Jr., (Eds.), *Telecommunications policy handbook* (pp. 258-271). New York: Praeger.

Seaman, J. (1981, December). Transborder data flow: Defusing a burning issue. *Computer Decisions*, pp. 58-64.

Sebestyen, I. (1983, February). *Experimental and operational East-West computer connections: The telecommunication hardware and software, datacommunication services, and relevant administrative procedures.* Vienna: International Institute for Applied Systems Analysis.

Sellers, W. O. (1985). Technology and the future of the financial services industry. *Technology in Society, 7,* 1-9.

Shaiken, H. (1984). *Work transformed: Automation and labor in the computer age.* New York: Holt, Rinehart and Winston.

Sharpe, R. (1981, May 28). Data flow: The US takes on Europe. *Computing,* pp 15-16.

Shrivastava, P. (1983, Spring). Strategies for coping with telecommunications technology in the financial services industry. *Columbia Journal of World Business, 18,* 19-25.

Soroos, M. S. (1986). *Beyond Sovereignty.* Columbia: University of South Carolina.

Spero, J. E. (1982, Fall). Information: The policy void. *Foreign Policy, 48,* 139-156.

Stateless Money. (1978, August 21). *Business Week,* pp. 76-80, 85.

Sweden, Government of. (1978). *The vulnerability of the computerized society: Considerations and proposals.* Stockholm: Government of Sweden.

The stateless corporation. (1990, May 14,) *Business Week,* pp. 98-105.

Thomson, J. E., & Krasner, S. D. (1989). Global transactions and the consolidation of sovereignty. In E. O. Czempiel & J. N. Rosenau (Eds.), *Global changes and theoretical challenges: Approaches to world politics for the 1990s* (pp. 192-219). Lexington, MA: Lexington Books.

Tourtellot, J. B. (1978, January-February). A world information war? 'Idealistic' Europeans pushing for international convention. *European Community,* pp. 11-15.

Turn, R. (1980, Summer). Privacy protection and security in transnational data processing systems. *Stanford Journal of International Law, 16,* 67-86.

Turn, R. (Ed.). (1979). *Transborder data flows: Concerns in privacy protection and free flow of information.* Washington, DC: American Federation of Information Processing, Inc.

United Nations Centre on Transnational Corporations. (1982). *Transnational corporations and transborder data flows: A technical paper.* New York: UNIPUB.

United Nations Centre on Transnational Corporations. (1983a). *Transborder data flows: Access to the international on-line data base market.* New York: UNIPUB.

United Nations Centre on Transnational Corporations. (1983b). *Transborder data flows and Brazil.* New York: UNIPUB.

United Nations Centre on Transnational Corporations. (1984). *Transborder data flows: Transnational corporations and remote-sensing data.* New York: UNIPUB.

United Nations Centre on Transnational Corporations. (1991). *Transborder data flows and Mexico.* New York: UNIPUB.

United States Congress, House. (1980). *International data flow.* Hearings before a Subcommittee of the Committee on Government Operations, 96th Congress, 2nd Session, March 10, 13, 27 and April 21.

United States Congress, House. (1980). *International information flow: Forging a new framework.* Thirty-Second Report by the Committee on Government Operations, 96th Congress, 2nd Session, December 11.

Vernon, R. (1971). *Sovereignty at bay.* New York: Basic Books.

Walsh, C. P. (1987). National security controls and transborder flows of technical data. In National Academy of Sciences (Eds.), *Balancing the national interest: U.S. national security export controls and global economic competition* (Working Papers, pp. 136-152). Washington, DC: National Academy Press.

Waltz, K. (1979). *Theory of international politics.* Reading, MA: Addison-Wesley.

Wendt, A. (1992, Spring). Anarchy is what states make of it: The social construction of power politics. *International Organization, 46,* 391-425.

Westin, A. F. & Baker, M. A. *Databanks in a free society: Computers, record-keeping and privacy.* New York: Quadrangle Books.

Wigand, R. T., Shipley, C., & Shipley, D. (1984, Winter). Transborder data flow, informatics, and national policies. *Journal of Communication, 34,* 153-175.

Willard, R. S. (1984). Beyond transborder data flow. *Telematics and Informatics, 1* (4), 419-425.

Wilson, L. J., & Al-Muhanna, I. (1985). The political economy of information: The impact of transborder data flows. *Journal of Peace Research, 22,* 289-301.

NOTES

[1] Keohane (1987) also distinguishes between constitutional and operational sovereignty, but the specific meanings we attach to the terms differ.

[2] Defining the issue as "data" rather than "information" flow was of less consequence. The choice of terms reflected the OECD's initial concerns regarding privacy; the flows in questions, personnel files, were usually in the raw form of medical records, employee absentee records, etc. Retention of the label, "data flows" when the debate subsequently broadened to include a wide range of information was an acknowledged anachronism, but one justified by the requirements of terminological standards and institutional memory. See Pipe (1984).

Chapter 14
The Utilization of International Communications Organizations, 1978–1992

Eileen Mahoney

Historically, telecommunication has been the responsibility of national governmental authorities, whether through public sector service provision or regulation. However, the increasing incorporation of communication and information resources into the transnational corporate economy in the past two decades has prompted efforts to shift control to the private sector. The impact of these policy shifts on decision making in the field of international communications and on the role of international organizations in particular is the focus of this chapter.

Three developments underscore recent conflicts in international communications policymaking. First, telecommunication and information services are indispensable to the transnational business system. They provide the basic infrastructure for global economic activities, and in turn, have become a fast-growing, lucrative economic sector.[1] This operational and commercial reliance upon communication and information resources underpins business demands for deregulation and privatization as "national regulations get in the way of international [corporate] management" (Aronson & Cowhey, 1988, p. 242; see also D. Schiller, 1982).[2]

Yet, the global political economy is comprised of national states. And, the long-standing appreciation of the role of communication in the maintenance of power has been increased, not diminished, by the growing economic significance of communication and information (see Deutsch, 1963). In fact, national governments, for political, economic, technological, and cultural reasons, have generally resisted loss of control over these resources. This political reality was clearly expressed in the well-known French (Nora-Minc) report which stated that "the sovereignty stakes have shifted to control over [telecommunications] networks" (Nora & Minc, 1980).[3]

A third consideration is the nature of communication itself—that is, its inherent requirement for coordination. Effective (i.e., interference-free) international communication necessitates agreements covering technical interconnection and coordinated resource allocation and use. International organizations have been employed to ensure coordination and development of the world's communication systems.

As the conflict between private business interests demanding greater control over communication and the sovereign rights of national telecommunications authorities (e.g., ministries of post, telegraph and telecommunications, PTTs, and regulatory agencies) has intensified, international communications organizations have become the site and subject of political debate.

Throughout the 1970s, two basic issues—namely, policies regarding the flow of information internationally, and policies governing access to and use of necessary natural resources and new technologies—spurred intense debates in international communication organizations. Several policy initiatives—including the call for a New World Information and Communication Order, the Transborder Data Flow (TDF) debate, the prior consent ruling in satellite broadcasting, and a priori planning methods for communication resource use—represented the efforts of a growing number of national states to utilize international communications organizations to formulate policies more in line with their interests. These initiatives critiqued long-standing, Western-supported policies, threatened to regulate transnational business use of communications, *and* challenged American "leadership" in international communications organizations.

This analysis focuses on the efforts of the United States to maintain its ability "to influence the agenda-setting and rule-making process to reflect" its communications "policies and priorities" (United States Congressional Research Service, 1983, p. 1).[4] The United States deserves this attention because of its "power to shape and determine the structures of the global political economy within which other states, their political institutions, their economic enterprises, and (not least) their scientists and other professional people have to operate" (Strange, 1988, pp. 24-25).[5]

The United States has exercised its "structural power" in the development of the postwar international political economy, including in the definition and formation of many of the international organizations understudy (see Preston, Herman, & Schiller, 1989; Finkelstein, 1988; Wood, 1986; Kolko, 1972). However, as American-based transnational businesses seek to overcome the "limitations" of national and international governance, especially in the communication and information sector, the United States has been at the forefront of the drive toward deregulation and privatization. Relatedly, American policies countered the calls for national communication sovereignty of the 1970s by shifting decision making out of multilateral fora and into economic institutions under greater U.S. control.

1978–1986:
REESTABLISHING AMERICAN INFLUENCE IN
INTERNATIONAL COMMUNICATIONS
ORGANIZATIONS

The end of the 1970s and early 1980s witnessed far-reaching political change. The conservative governments elected in England and the United States (i.e., Prime Minister Thatcher and President Reagan) instituted fundamental policy changes (e.g., deregulation and privatization) in the field of communication. Additionally, they individually (and in alliance) pursued unilateralist policies that undercut multilateral and regional negotiations. And, they both reinvigorated the Cold War and concomitant military expenditures. New communication technologies experienced tremendous growth as a result (see Mosco, 1989). These dynamics—deregulation, unilateralism, and militarization—seriously undercut the role of international institutions (see Hughes, 1985–86, pp. 25-48). And, they expressed U.S. structural power in international communication organizations and policies as well.

Two aspects of U.S. international communications policy in the 1980s deserve examination. The United States launched a full-scale policy review of American participation in international organizations. As the largest financial contributor to multilateral fora, this review was generally interpreted as a threat; one that resulted in withdrawal of U.S. support in some instances. The other main direction in American international communications policy was the partial abandonment of the longstanding free flow of information doctrine. Both of these positions were designed to further the general U.S. policies of deregulation and privatization of communications and information resources.

Reviewing U.S. Participation in International Communication Organizations

Emphasis on deregulation and elite decision making (e.g., among "like-minded" advanced countries), if not outright unilateralism, produced growing impatience with international organizations. The American (and subsequent British) withdrawal from UNESCO was a dramatic exercise of unilateralism, and was intended to signal that the United States would not tolerate policies inconsistent with its interests (see *Journal of Communication*, 1987; *Media Development*, 1990). However, UNESCO, in a structural sense, was expendable. The American media, increasingly integrated into the broader corporate economy, supported the U.S. government's decision to withdraw from UNESCO (see Herman & Schiller, in Preston et al., 1989).

This is not to say that there was not opposition to the decision to withdraw. Scientific, cultural, and educational organizations within the U.S. opposed withdrawal, and argued that the U.S. would do better to reform the organization from within (see Coate, 1988). Still, in terms of the overall operation of the international political economy, UNESCO had very little power and could be dismissed as an example.

Access to required communication resources and unrestricted international information flows, however, remained critical issues. The institutions and arrangements involved in these two areas, namely the International Telecommunication Union (ITU) and the organizations that addressed transborder data flow issues, could not be ignored.[6]

U.S. Participation in International Communication Organizations

Following the ITU's World Administrative Radio Conference (WARC) in 1979, where concerted pressure for a priori planning of radio frequencies and satellite orbital slots was registered, the United States faced a real dilemma.[7] Technical coordination of resources use was and remains essential to communication.[8] Therefore, membership in the ITU was not as easily dismissed as in the case of UNESCO.

Two U.S. government reports in the early 1980s discussed the U.S.

predicament. A 1980 Office of Technology Assessment report stated the situation in the following terms: Increasing American use of radio frequencies and satellite orbital slots, alongside of continuing international disparity in access to resources, is leading to disagreements over how the resources should be allocated within the ITU. Third World countries are increasingly capable of influencing ITU decision making, and this will likely have adverse affects on American interests (United States Office of Technology Assessment, 1980, pp. 8-9).

Given these conditions, the report set out three possible options for U.S. relations with the ITU. The United States could withdraw from the ITU, and try to create a smaller, more homogeneous group. Or, the United States could call for abandoning universal suffrage (i.e., one nation, one vote) in ITU decision making, and replace it with weighted voting based on either financial contribution or actual use of resources (United States Office of Technology Assessment, 1980, pp. 18-19).

A congressional report three years later maintained that "the politization trend must be reversed and *the United States and other like-minded major donors must reestablish influence* over the direction of the ITU as an international organization that serves the needs of all its members" (United States Senate, 1983, p. 47; emphasis added). If "unacceptable politization" continues, the report argued that "the United States must have available a fully developed and workable alternative to the ITU" (United States Senate, 1983, p. 47).

Notwithstanding the ironic use of "unacceptable politization," these reports reveal an age-old problem in American policy—that is, the growing use of and dependence upon communications requires coordination (see Smythe, 1957). The diminishing capacity of the United States to control decision making in international communications organizations (i.e., so-called "politization") is only one difficulty. At a more fundamental level, the workings of the transnational business system introduce still additional policy pressures.

These pressures were clearly manifest at the ITU's Space WARC 1985 meeting. Planning methods for use of satellite orbital slots were the subject of this meeting. The press leading up to the meeting called attention to the potential North-South dispute. However, at the meeting the real dilemma issued forth from the competing interests of the advanced market economies themselves. The U.S. push towards deregulation and privatization promised development of new systems that would require access to resources. This would intensify coordination requirements at the same time that U.S. deregulatory policies opposed planning (Mahoney, 1985).

To the extent that the effective operation of international communication systems required a coordinating mechanism, like the ITU, how could it be organized such that its multilateral decision making would not impinge on American interests? Withdrawal of membership or changing the voting procedures, though considered with regard to international organizations in general, was not the direction chosen. Rather, another change in U.S. policy shifted both the terms and the terrain of international communication policy.

Rethinking the Free Flow of Information Doctrine

The most fundamental development in U.S. policy was the decision to abandon, at least partly, the free flow of information. For 40 years, it had been the bulwark of American policy (see Schiller, 1976). Yet, in the 1980s, American decision makers decided it was no longer feasible. Political, economic, and legal limitations of the free-flow doctrine led to this reappraisal.

Calls for rethinking this basic U.S. policy came from policymakers, analysts, and the U.S. private sector. The late Morris Crawford, a career State Department officer, acknowledged the changed political realities. Continued support for the free-flow doctrine, he reported, "found the US deserted even by its staunchest allies" (Crawford, 1980, p. 2). A reassessment of the free-flow doctrine was necessary "in the context of modern communication technologies and their impact on other members of the interdependent world community" (Crawford, 1980, p. 2).

Although Crawford mentions the "world community" as the most powerful, calls for reconsideration of the free flow came from the private sector, and reflected their interests. Despite traditional news and media groups, such as the World Press Freedom Committee, who continued support for the free flow of information on ideological, as well as commercial grounds, the broader operational requirements of the transnational business system prompted the American private sector to call for a more *pragmatic* approach (see Ganley, 1983, p. 346).

Joan Spero, then vice president for international corporate affairs of the American Express Company, was forthright in her analysis. Writing in the influential *Foreign Policy* magazine in 1982, she argued:

> [T]he historical U.S. practice of supporting the free flow of information—
> a philosophical approach grounded in the principles of the U.S. Constitu-
> tion and the U.N. Universal Declaration of Human Rights ... no longer
> enables the United States to defend its interests.... While the free flow
> of information is a compelling position in debates on privacy and freedom
> of the press, this approach is less effective when confronting national

economic prerogatives and aspirations ... [the] free flow of information
is a principle without the leverage necessary to confront barriers to
electronic data flows. The means necessary to enforce the principle are
neither defined in internationally agreed rules nor embodied in any
international organization. (Spero, 1982, pp. 139-140, 149-150)

Expressing the concerns of a wider range of business interests that
was increasingly dependent upon international "electronic data
flows," Spero called for an American policy approach that would halt
the establishment of national telecommunication and transborder
data-flow policies that hindered transnational business.

Additionally, having achieved telecommunications deregulation in
the United States, transnational businesses pressed for similar policy
changes abroad (see D. Schiller, 1982, p. 103). In effect, transnational
companies, in manufacturing as well as services, wanted unrestricted
access to *sophisticated* international telecommunications and information facilities, networks, and markets (D. Schiller, 1982; see also
Organization for Economic Cooperation and Development, 1988, pp.
9-10).

Accordingly, they called for a policy framework that would allow
them to plug their own equipment into existing national networks (at
cost-based prices) and/or to establish unregulated private networks, as
well as grant them "free access and free entry" into foreign telecommunication and information equipment and services markets (D.
Schiller, 1982, p. 123). Thus, the goals of transnational corporate users
of international communications basically advocated the dissolution of
national sovereign control over telecommunications networks. These
objectives extended beyond efficacy of the free-flow doctrine, and
required a new approach.

Development of international trade rules within the General Agreement on Tariffs and Trade (GATT) framework was proposed to replace
the free flow of information. Although communication and commerce
have long been interconnected, this represented a significant shift in
policy. For example, Aronson and Cowhey, who wholeheartedly promote the deregulation and privatization of communication services
and support the use of the GATT to this end, acknowledge that "[t]here
is no inherent economic reason why the GATT should govern telecommunication services" (Aronson & Cowhey, 1988, p. 35). Rather, the
utilization of GATT trade principles for international communication
policymaking represents both the policy objective (i.e., deregulation
and privatization) and the kind of "enforceability" called for by
transnational business.

Redefining communication and information resources as tradeable
commodities shifts not only the terms (from public service to private

property), but also the terrain of policymaking. "Even though the GATT does not possess much telecommunications expertise," it is utilized because it is one of the postwar economic institutions, along with the International Monetary Fund and the World Bank, in which the United States exercises considerable control (see Aronson & Cowhey, 1985). And, as few countries in the world today can ignore the rules by which trade is conducted in the world economy, the outcome can be implemented.[9]

Trade Replaces Free Flow

This shift in American international communication policy, and the redefinition of communications and information resources as trade issues, was echoed in many private sector reports throughout the early 1980s (see The Business Roundtable, 1985). Indeed, there was a flurry of meetings, conferences, and reports organized by the private sector, government agencies, and academics to promote the policy adjustments required by the new *world* information economy (see Sauvant, 1986; Roche, 1987).

Defined in terms of the operational needs and commercial interests of transnational business, the global information economy represented the conceptual framework imposed on policymaking. Despite the concerns raised in international communication debates throughout the 1970s regarding national security, citizen's privacy, cultural identity, social and economic wellbeing—in short, national sovereignty, trade rules for information and communication resources were presented as the policy solution. And, the GATT was promoted as the forum best suited for an information economy (see Feketekuty & Aronson, 1984).

The Politics of Trade

The promotion of the GATT was not a "natural" institutional fit nor the result of "the wisdom" of "an epistemic community" (see Woodrow, 1992; Drake & Nicolaïdis, 1992). Rather, it was an exercise of American structural power in response to changing economic and political realities.[10] As communication and information resources became indispensable to the transnational corporate economy, and as national and international policy debates threatened to restrict business activities, decision making was shifted into more controllable economic institutions.

The transnationalization of the American economy, and the financial and telecommunication sectors in particular, elevated the significance of the "service" industries in the "national" economy. As service providers followed their transnational corporate clients abroad, they encountered both greater needs for information and communication capabilities and more stringent national laws covering foreign services (e.g., banking, telecommunication, etc.) industries. Powerful TNC lobbies called for the global extension of the deregulatory policies adopted in the United States (see Roche, 1987; Sauvant, 1986; D. Schiller, 1982).

Politically, the American adoption of a trade framework was intended to overcome or bypass both the expressions of national sovereignty in the international communication policy debates throughout the 1970s, *and* the entrenched power of the PTTs (and national telecommunications authorities generally). Internationally, the proliferation of international organizations addressing communication and information issues increased the possibility of unwanted policy developments. By redefining the terms of international communication policy to trade, the United States effectively removed meaningful decision making from the multilateral policymaking bodies (Mahoney, 1989).

Indeed, one European diplomat was quoted as saying, "If GATT achieves a services agreement, it will be over the corpses of a dozen international organizations" (Pipe, 1987, pp. 60-61). The impact of the shift towards trade negotiations on international communications organizations has been decisive and will be discussed next.

One organization active in national informatics and international communications policy issues was the Intergovernmental Bureau for Informatics (IBI). The IBI gained the lion's share of its recognition from TDF-related activities. It sponsored two major conferences (one in 1980 and the other in 1984) devoted to TDF and related policy matters. While the 1980 conference and a subsequent IBI survey registered significant support for international and national TDF policy formation, the IBI's 1984 conference yielded no such result. The IBI's leadership, in an effort to placate Western powers, accepted a trade framework for TDF within which it had no mandate (see Mahoney, forthcoming).

Three other UN-affiliated organizations—United Nations Centre on Transnational Corporations (UNCTC), United Nations Conference on Trade and Development (UNCTAD), and ITU—were affected by the push for a trade orientation in communication policy-making.[11] The UNCTC entered international communication policy through its study of the utilization of transborder data flow by transnational corporations (TNC) (United Nations Center on Transnational Corporations, 1981). It began a series of national case studies of the policy implications of TDF and general informatics policy issues. It published the notable Brazilian case study which presented a sophisticated argument in support of their national informatics and telecommunications laws (United Nations Centre on Transnational Corporations, 1983). The UNCTC tried to expand its mandate in the field of TDF, but was thwarted by the United States (see Sauvant, 1986; Mahoney, forthcoming).

UNCTAD, despite its experience in the services sector, and its widespread credibility among the majority of states (i.e., within the Third World), was ignored by those promoting a free-trade framework (Gibbs, 1985, pp. 199-202; see also Williams, 1991; Raghavan, 1990). Throughout the 1980s, UNCTAD produced several studies on "services and development" in order to assist developing countries. However, this body of work, as well as that of analysts in developing countries, has received little or no attention (Gibbs & Mashayekhi, 1988, p. 106).

Although the ITU was not directly involved in the transborder data flow debate, its activities have been greatly affected by the development of a trade framework for international telecommunications. This is discussed at length later on.

Markedly different was the utilization of the 24-member Organization for Economic Cooperation and Development (OECD). It was actively enlisted in promoting a trade framework for telecommunication and information services. The United States first requested that the Trade Section of the OECD study the applicability of trade principles for telecommunications in the early 1970s. Parallel development of American national (i.e., bilateral) trade legislation strengthened the U.S. promotion of a trade approach to telecommunication and information services (see Aronson & Cowhey, 1988, pp. 35-45; Sauvant, 1986).[12]

Once the OECD Information, Computer, Communications Policy division and its Working Group on TDF were established, they issued reports and nonbinding declarations on TDF (Roche, 1987; Sauvant, 1986, pp. 235-245). The initial discussion of the Declaration on Transborder Data Flows within the OECD led one participant to observe critically that "the economic and trade dimensions of these [TDF] issues have squeezed out the human rights, legal and policy aspects" (*Transnational Data Report,* 1982, p. 58). This, it appears, was one of the central objectives. The declaration was designed "to blunt the impact of any transborder data flow proposal advanced by the developing world" (*Chronicle of International Communication,* 1984, p. 5). This precedent laid the foundation for the application of GATT trade principles to international communication.

In sum, most of the international organizations that had engaged in aspects of communications policy analysis and policymaking in the 1970s and early 1980s were hamstrung or excluded by the campaign to apply trade rules to communication and information services.

Rendering the international organizations in communications irrelevant through the promotion of trade alone, however, would not produce the kind of unrestricted operational and investment climate that transnational business wanted. The shifting institutional arrangements called for in the promotion of the GATT were intended to change *national* rules and participants as well.

U.S. deregulation had long targeted national PTTs (see D. Schiller, 1982, pp. 113-122; Aronson & Cowhey, 1988, p. 261). However, domestic industrial, as well as political arrangements bolstered their strength. The imposition of a trade framework attempted to shift the calculus and responsibility of communications policy from national communication authorities (PTTs) to trade ministers. Accordingly, telecommunications would no longer be viewed exclusively within national policy. Rather it would have to be balanced against the interests of other industry, trade, and aid considerations (see Aronson & Cowhey, 1988).

The GATT was not the only instrument involved in restructuring international communications. The United States also engaged in bilateral trade negotiations with Israel, Canada, and Mexico. These initiatives were intended as both a model and threat. The Free Trade Agreement between the United States and Canada, for instance, was utilized to establish the terms for a global agreement (see Mosco, this volume). The implicit threat to those organizations or nations that resisted the trend toward deregulation and privatization was that they would be left behind or "bypassed."

By the mid-1980s, the United States had shifted the terms of international communication policy priorities. The field of international organizations capable of effective communication policy making had been narrowed dramatically. National communications sovereignty was under attack as free trade was promoted in the interests of a transnational corporate information economy.

1986-1992:
TRADE AND INTERNATIONAL COMMUNICATIONS POLICY

A new Round of GATT negotiations was initiated in September 1986 in Montevideo, Uruguay, and was dubbed the Uruguay Round. The United States set out four main principles—namely, national treatment, transparency, nondiscrimination, and market access, for the services negotiations.[13] According to one observer, the primary U.S. objective in the trade negotiations was to gain "greater access to foreign telecom[munications] markets, more investment opportunities, and fewer restrictions on users of information-based services" (Pipe, 1987, pp. 60-61).

Opposition to "Trade in Services" Negotiations

There was significant opposition to including services (e.g., telecommunications and information-based services) in the negotiations. Once more, though under a different guise, basic issues regarding information flows, communication and information resources, and national sovereignty emerged in the negotiations. Developing countries, as well as some in Western Europe and Japan, resisted American pressures to quickly adopt a trade framework. Developing nations clearly believed they had the most to lose.

The greatest concern of Third World countries was "the preponderant role of TNCs in services" (Randhawa, 1987, p. 169). They interpreted TNC pressure for the GATT negotiations as "directed towards dismantling or modifying national regulatory frameworks, [and as such] as a threat to their economies and their sovereignty" (Randhawa, 1987, p. 169).[14] The specific issues concerning developing countries encompassed trade relations, the privatization of information resources, and rules governing foreign investment.

Regarding trade rules, developing countries believed that previous GATT negotiations had not assisted them in securing access to needed markets, while their own economies were forced open. Agreements that had been made (e.g., those covering major export products—tropical fruits, textiles, raw materials—from the Third World) were not kept. And, not unlike in the TDF debate, developing nations argued that they would be unable to develop high-tech sectors within the U.S.-proposed "free trade" environment. At the same time, they have faced growing protectionism in advanced market economies in traditional sectors since the 1970s.

The GATT's "free trade" bias also concerned developing countries as it would facilitate the trend towards privatizing information resources. The United States openly discussed the Uruguay Round as an opportunity to establish and enforce strict patent protection and intellectual property rights (see Sainath, 1992; Raghavan, 1990, pp. 114-141).

Initially, developing countries resisted the inclusion of these issues in the GATT, because they did not view them as "trade" issues, and argued that they were being appropriately addressed in other fora.

However, the United States persisted in proposing "strong enforcement" of patent and intellectual property rights. These stipulations, maintained developing countries, could severely hinder technological and industrial development. For example, some argue they could also put basic medicine beyond the reach of Third World peoples (Sainath, 1992; Kloppenburg, 1991, pp. 14-18).

Foreign investment and the impact of TNCs on host countries was another basic issue raised by developing countries. They viewed the GATT negotiations as a pretext to liberalize rules governing transnational corporate investments. Indeed, given the powerful position of TNCs in the services industries, developing countries considered the weakening of national control over the terms of foreign investment a significant threat of the Uruguay Round negotiations.

In each instance, developing countries believed their capability to manage their economic activities (i.e., to exercise national sovereignty) would be greatly diminished. The result of the Uruguay Round of GATT negotiations, according to one analyst, would be the "recolonization" of Third World (Raghavan, 1990; see also this volume).

In addition to the concerns raised by developing countries, the imposition of a trade framework for services would demand changes in national laws covering such services as banking, insurance, and telecommunications. Service industries have been highly regulated in most countries. They were also viewed as key growth areas in otherwise recession-ridden industrial economies. However, the establishment of a trade framework could undermine national decision making regarding some of the most sensitive national industries.

Once again, Third World states were not the only ones concerned that their sovereignty and development would be limited. Western European countries and Japan showed little enthusiasm for the development of a trade framework.[15] And, the mobilization of the European Economic Community (EEC) in the mid-1980s also introduced another set of dynamics. The development of a common market in telecommunication in Europe became the main objective of the EEC. The impact of this institutional and political development is still unfolding and cannot be fully addressed here. At this point it appears as though political economic integration in telecommunications, especially in the aftermath of the collapse of former East European regimes in 1989, may take some time yet (see Crawford, 1990; Gibbs & Mashayekhi, 1988, p. 89).

While some Third World countries continue to resist certain aspects of the trade negotiations, a unified resistance was inhibited by several factors. First, the choice of venue, that is, the GATT, disadvan taged the developing countries as they had no tradition of cooperation in GATT proceedings (Raghavan, 1990).

Secondly, as Hamelink pointed out, developing countries frequently submit reports to international loan agencies and Western banks. However, national policymakers generally have limited knowledge of (their own, as well as) each others' economies which hindered coordination (see Hamelink, 1983).

Thirdly, many developing countries have different regulatory experiences in their media sectors. For instance, Mattelart discusses the historical deregulation (or no regulation) in Latin American media (Mattelart, 1991, pp. 95-99). In other newly industrializing countries of Southeast Asia, media policy has been more closely articulated with government control. But these countries have been more open to deregulation in the high-tech arena (see Sussman & Lent, 1991).

Relatedly, there were also differences in the character of various national economies and actual levels of development in telecommunication and information-based industries. These contributed to divisions in response to the proposed trade negotiations (see Kihwan, 1986, pp. 37-56).

And finally, within the context of the debt crisis and growing protectionist measures in the advanced market economies, developing countries had little room to maneuver.

These factors were used by the United States in order to undermine or outmaneuver opposition. Aronson and Cowhey report that the United States employed three tactics to overcome resistance to the trade in services negotiations: a public relations campaign to convince others that the United States was not the only one that stood to gain from the negotiations; a carrot and stick approach to developing countries that included consideration of debt renegotiation or punitive bilateral enforcement of American trade legislation; and an effort to avoid unified action by sowing divisions among the developing countries (Aronson & Cowhey, 1988, pp. 43-44).

In the end, the debt, dependence on export earnings and fear of bilateral reprisals, led countries to finally agree to General Negotiations on Services.

The Impact of Trade on International Communication Policy

By the start of the Uruguay Round, the general political environment for international organizations was extremely hostile. The U.S. and the U.K. had withdrawn from UNESCO, the Fortieth Anniversary of the United Nations had met with derision or worse in the Western press and policy circles, and the ITU faced not only the suggestion of alternatives. The actual mobilization of the GATT was a not too subtle warning that the ITU's future was in question (see Aronson & Cowhey, 1988).[16]

The ITU was the only multilateral organization still centrally involved in international communication policy by 1986, and the emphasis on trade was intended to "reform" it. The United States viewed the ITU as a vehicle of "PTT monopolies." Hence, as the ITU pursued its agenda throughout the latter half of the 1980s, it encountered demands for ever greater limits on its mandate, structure, and functions.

That the ITU's mandate was "too broad" became apparent in the preparations for, and actual proceedings of, the ITU's World Administrative Telephone and Telegraph Conference (WATTC) held in Australia in 1988. This major meeting was presented in the press at the time, and continues to be referred to as a "showdown" between those promoting deregulation and privatization, and the PTTs (i.e., national telecommunication authorities) (Cowhey & Aronson, 1991, p. 306).

The agenda of the conference, established by the previous ITU Plenipotentiary in 1982, was to establish "a broad international regulatory framework" for "all existing and foreseen new telecommunications services" (International Telecommunication Union, 1982, pp. 238-239). Conflicts erupted over two basic aspects of this agenda: that is, its temporal and industrial parameters (see Drake, 1988, pp. 218-219).

Basically, the U.S. and U.K., leaders in deregulation, did not want WATTC 88 to develop any stipulations but the most general and liberal possible. They opposed policymaking for "the future," and they did not want the WATTC 88 regulations to apply to service providers other than those providing basic telecommunication services, that is, the PTTs and Recognized Private Operating Agencies (RPOAs). Although preparatory documents for the meeting indicated that a majority of telecommunications administrations agreed that "any entity (administration/PTT, RPOA or other service provider) offering international telecommunication services to the public should be subject to the Regulations," the U.S. and U.K. maintained that new "enhanced" services and the private companies that provide only enhanced services were to remain unregulated (see Gilhooly, 1988).[17]

In order to defuse the debate that ensued, then-ITU Secretary General, Richard Butler proposed a compromise, which "recognized and reaffirmed the push towards competition" in telecommunications services (Cowhey & Aronson, 1991, p. 306). Additionally, it "stressed the duties of national administrations (PTTs) to permit user access to the (public) network, freedom of choice of terminal equipment, and obligation to provide satisfactory quality of services, provide for 'internetworking between services' (Article 4.3 d) and relate pricing to costs" (Cowhey & Aronson, 1991, p. 306). This embrace of the deregulatory agenda of a few (albeit powerful) members weakened the ITU considerably.

Put differently, WATTC 88 "set the stage for a general reform of ITU decision processes" (Cowhey & Aronson, 1991, p. 306). Specifically, efforts to "streamline" the ITU, especially in standards-setting function, were agreed to at WATTC 88 and were pursued in the Plenipotentiary meeting the following year.

At the Nice Plenipotentiary in 1989, the ITU established a High Level Committee to study the ITU. With the cooperation of the new "more liberal-minded" Secretary General, Pekka Tarjanne, the High Level Committee (HLC) has been reviewing the ITU. In the course of its review, the HLC hired an American consulting firm, Booz, Allen and Hamilton, to assess ITU. Curiously, the contracting such a study of a multilateral organization from a company, itself part of the transnational corporate economy and based in a country that has openly criticized the organization, has received little (critical) comment.[18]

The HLC, "with the help of outside consultants," has made several recommendations (Solomon, 1991, p. 374). According to the HLC, "the substantive work of the ITU should be organized in three Sectors, i.e., Development, Standardization and Radiocommunication," that merge and restructure existing ITU working committees (International Telecommunication Union, 1991, p. 5).[19]

Additionally, the HLC recommended the establishment of two "think tanks" to "strengthen" the Secretary General's "key role in strategic planning, management and coordination" (International Telecommunication Union, 1991, p. 5). One would be a "Strategic Policy and Planning Unit," and the other a "Business Advisory Forum through which he can conduct a dialogue with business leaders" (International Telecommunication Union, 1991, p. 5).[20] The HLC's general call for greater private sector involvement in the ITU led one observer to suggest that "there is very much the air of corporate restructuring with a sort of non-executive role for outsiders in this reform package" (Solomon, 1991, p. 374).

Although the HLC recommendations await adoption at the next Plenipotentiary meeting, currently scheduled for Japan in 1994, a quick review of ITU activities offers a good indication of the current role of the organization.

The ITU: Increasing Marginality in
the Telecommunications Market?

Radio communication. In the allocation and registration of radio frequencies and orbital slots, the outcome of the recent World Administrative Radio Conference 1992 (WARC-92) is quite telling. The basic issues at WARC-92, including mobile services, digital audio broadcasting, high-definition television, and new satellite services, pitted the advanced market economies against one another.[21]

Among other issues, Mobile Satellite Services (MSS) allocations were subject to conflicting claims. The Western Europeans for their part are pursuing terrestrial-based systems, and therefore wanted allocations suitable to their needs. In contrast, the United States (and some of its major companies, e.g., Motorola) proposed the use of low earth orbiting (LEO) satellites to provide mobile (telephone) services.

The American LEO mobile satellite services proposal would compete with an international mobile communications system proposed by Inmarsat, the global public consortium that provides maritime and aeronautical communication (see Poe, 1992, p. 7). Additionally, some claim that the planned use of the LEO/MSS (e.g., the Motorola-backed Iridium system) will bypass existing national telecommunication services and take telephone revenues away from local telecommunication authorities. In fact, some viewed the U.S.-proposed use of these resources as impinging on national sovereignty, if not outright "piracy" (*Public Network Europe*, 1992, p. 10).

Alternatively, the United States presented the "prospective" mobile telecommunications services (prospective because none of the services exist) as a "solution" for those countries with weak telecommunications infrastructures. And, it appears as though the Americans were able to garner enough support to outvote the "new European bloc" (*Public Network Europe*, 1992, p. 10; see also McClelland, 1992, p. 6).

Assessing the results of WARC-92, one observer argued that "what distinguished WARC-92 from previous WARCs was the overt presence of the private sector" (Mohan, 1992, p. 6). Another review suggested that "the issues of technology that once would have dominated such (WARC) discussions are being left behind in favor of the wider economic considerations of user groups and prospective market shares" (McClelland, 1992, p. 6).

Possibly because "all the major proposals of big telecommunication powers" were "accepted in full or with minor modifications" at WARC-92, the United States claimed it brought "home the bacon" (Warner, 1992, p. 5). The Chairman of the U.S. delegation, Jan Baran, said "the allocation made by this conference provides sufficient spectrum under technical and regulatory conditions to promote wide open competition" in "new technologies for the 'new world order'" (quoted in *Public Network Europe,* 1992, p. 11). Still, the United States issued a declaration that "reserved the right" to ignore whatever aspects of the Final Acts of WARC-92 the United States found "restrictive" (quoted in *Public Network Europe,* 1992, p. 11).

Thus, communication resource allocation, once a major issue area of developing nations involvement, is now entirely managed by the advanced market economies. According to H.E. Olawale Adeniji Ige, the Nigerian Minister of Transport and Communication, "by and large the countries of the Third World are observers of the technological progress in the advanced world" (quoted in *Public Network Europe,* 1992, p. 10). Another observer suggested that the WARC-92 indicated that the Third World are "more and more becoming passengers when the structures of the future are being discussed and apportioned" (Mohan, 1992, p. 6).

Development. This lack of participation in resource allocation can only negatively affect development efforts, the other main agenda item of the Third World.[22] The ITU's new Telecommunications Development Bureau, like the Centre for Telecommunications Development before it, is likely to have very little "voluntary funding" at its disposal.[23]

One analyst sees the function of the new Bureau as a "main conduit for investment from such sources as the World Bank, the European Investment Bank, the European Bank for Reconstruction and Development, as well as private industry" (Renaud, quoted in Gilhooly, 1991). The *lending* history of such organizations (in telecommunication) does not promise the kind of development that Third World countries have struggled for within the ITU and elsewhere.[24]

More importantly, the entire ITU agenda in "development communication" now reflects the deregulatory, high-tech agenda of transnational business. The ITU's Maitland Commission report of the mid-1980s called for telecommunications in the Third World to be "operated along business lines," and a recent report urges "restructuring of telecommunications in developing countries" (see International Telecommunication Union, 1985, 1991b).[25] And, as will be shown again in the next section on standards, the bulk of the ITU's activities now address the needs of evermore sophisticated telecommunication systems that have little relevance to the basic development needs of developing countries (see Sussman & Lent, 1991).

Standards setting. Finally, standards setting, which has been a main activity of the ITU, deserves brief attention. It is essential to the technical coordination required for interference-free communication, or what is now referred to as "interoperability" of systems (see Savage,

1989, pp. 167-224). However, standards also have enormous economic significance as the establishment of a particular standard generally represents market advantage for those businesses producing or using such technical specifications (see D. Schiller & Fregosa, this volume; see also United States Office of Technology Assessment, 1990).

Rapid technological development, greater private sector involvement in the design and configuration of communication systems, and continuous deregulatory pressures combined to put ITU standards-setting procedures under pressure. Two interrelated developments now threaten ITU preeminence in telecommunication standards making. First, ITU procedures are considered too slow. And second, several alternative national and regional bodies have been created (Besen & Farrell, 1991, p. 311).

The regional standards organizations, including the European Telecommunications Standards Institute (ETSI), the T1 committee of the Exchange Carriers Standards Association of the U.S., and the Telecommunication Technology Committee in Japan, are considered viable alternatives to the ITU for several reasons.

Essentially, the regional standards organizations were designed and created to "speed up" standards making in line with rapid technological and market developments.[26] They are smaller, more "homogenous" groups which leaves them less open to greatly divergent interests. Besen and Farrell maintain that the speed derived from their homogeneity "stems in part from their willingness to exclude those with little market influence" (Besen & Farrell, 1991, p. 321). In the end, their ability to supersede the ITU's standards setting derives from the fact that "their participants have enough authority in the market to ensure that agreements among them can neither be ignored nor seriously disputed" (Besen & Farrell, 1991, p. 320).

Within the ITU, pressures to "reform" standards-making processes have intensified since WATTC 88 and were a central concern of the High Level Committee. The formation of a new Bureau for Standardization is intended to streamline ITU procedures. However, the challenges presented by the regional standards organizations are likely to limit the ITU's role in standards setting. Indeed, Besen and Farrell argue that the ITU may well be reduced to "rubber-stamping" standards set by other organizations (Besen & Farrell, 1991, p. 312).

In each main area of its activities then, the ITU has been marginalized as greater decision-making power is shifted to the private sector. Radio communication resources are being allocated on the basis of "prospective market shares." "Development" is afforded the status of a main ITU sector, but must rely upon "voluntary" private sector funding. And, standards setting has itself become a "competitive marketplace" for various industry and regional groups (Rutkowski, 1991, p. 295).

The extension of market criteria to international communications, the major objective of the U.S. government and its transnational business partners, has resulted in the transformation or elimination of multilateral organizations in the field of communication. Anthony Rutkowski, special advisor to the current and former Secretary of the ITU, sums up these changes thusly: "Regulatory business now goes to the organizations that best support contemporary market-oriented needs" (Rutkowski, 1991, p. 295).[27]

Put slightly different, Garnham argues

> It is in the interest of the controllers of multinational capital to keep nation-states and their citizens in a state of disunity and dysfunctional ignorance unified only by market structures within which such capital can freely flow, while at the same time they develop their own private communications networks. (Garnham, 1986, p. 52)

Market Discipline for Whom?

If we then return to the main "market structure" utilized to marginal-ize international and national communications policymaking, what is happening in the GATT negotiations? Again, this story is still unfolding, but following five years of intense negotiations which the United States has pressured others into, the American telecom-munications industry has decided that it does *not* want a GATT agreement. Just as closure in the services negotiations seemed within reach at the end of 1990, U.S. telecommunications interests, AT&T and MCI in particular, called for a complete reconsideration (*Telecom-munications Reports International,* 1990, pp. 1-2).

Their view, articulated in a letter to the U.S. Trade Representative in August 1990, was that a GATT agreement should not cover basic telecommunication services. Their reason being that the GATT princi-ple of nondiscrimination (i.e., most-favored nation status) would open the U.S. market to foreign competition without guaranteeing entry into foreign markets (*Telecommunications Reports International,* 1990, pp. 1-2). Furthermore, the U.S. telecommunications industry expressed concern that the GATT services agreement could be restrictive of U.S.-based companies as they would become subject to "national treatment" under the laws of foreign countries. (*Telecommunications Reports International,* 1991, p. 9; Preston, 1991).[28]

In short, rather than being a vehicle of liberalization, the GATT principles—discussed for the past six years—would disadvantage U.S.

industry in their view. According to Bev Andrews, director of regulatory policy at Comsat, members of the American telecommunications industry find the draft telecommunications services annexes "unacceptable." They want the U.S. Trade Representative to "get out" of the services negotiations (Andrews, 1991).[29]

Although some still think that an international trade organization would be useful in avoiding "trade wars," others simply expect a rather weak diplomatic statement of intent to bring this round of (services) negotiations to a close (see *The Economist*, 1992; Prestowitz, Tonelson, & Jerome, 1991; Thurow, 1991).

CONCLUSION

Has the GATT been a failure? Hardly! American policy was not about establishing an institution to carry on international communications policymaking, no matter how "liberal." The promotion of the GATT was intended to break down opposition to deregulation and privatization of communications and information resources. It was designed to weaken, if not eliminate, the political institutions, national and international, that stood in the way of transnational corporate use of international communication and information resources. And if no institutional framework, even for trade in international communication results, that may suit well U.S. interests.

The basic goal has been to extend the authority of business interests (not an abstract, neutral "market") to the entire range of communications decision making, nationally and internationally. Political opposition to such efforts in the 1970s led to a moment in which international organizations became potentially influential fora of debate and policy formation. Yet, the power of business interests, greatly assisted by the U.S. government, responded by shifting the terms and the terrain upon which decisions in communication would be taken.

Multilateral organizations involved in international communications have been excluded or greatly weakened by the imposition of trade principles and market criteria in policy matters. While their own internal weaknesses and contradictions are not to be ignored, the restructuring of international communications that has taken place within the past 15 years is not solely the outcome of such factors. Rather, it results primarily from the exercise of American structural power and its ability to organize fundamental decision making in the field of communications beyond national sovereignty.

REFERENCES

Andrews, B. (1991, September 16). Phone interview, Washington, DC.

Aronson, J.D., & Cowhey, P.F. (1988). *When countries talk: International trade in telecommunications services.* Cambridge, MA: Ballinger Publishing Company.

Besen, S.M., & Farrell, J. (1991). The role of the ITU in standardization: Preeminence, impotence or rubber stamp? *Telecommunications Policy, 15,* 311-322.

The Business Roundtable. (1985, January). *International information flow: A plan for action.* New York: The Business Roundtable.

Coate, R.A. (1988). *Unilateralism, ideology and U.S. foreign policy: The United States in and out of UNESCO.* Boulder, CO: Lynne Reiner Publishers Inc.

Communications Systems Worldwide. (1987, November). Why WATTC Matters. London, England. (Reprinted in *Teleclippings,* No. 827, January 11, 1988, p. 4. Geneva: International Telecommunication Union.)

Cowhey, P., & Aronson, J.D. (1991). The ITU in transition. *Telecommunications Policy, 15,* 298-310.

Cox, R.W. (1987). *Production, power and world order: Social Forces in the making of history.* New York: Columbia University Press.

Chronicle of International Communication. (1984, September). Tale of Two Cities. Vol. 5, pp. 1, 5.

Crawford, M. (1980). Toward an information age debate. *Chronicle of International Communication, 1, 2.*

Crawford, M. (1990, July). *The common market for telecommunications and information services.* Cambridge, MA: Program on Information Resources Policy, Harvard University.

Deutsch, K. (1963). *Nationalism and social communication.* New York: Free Press.

Dixon, H. (1992, January 31). Telecommunications: On a Triple Springboard, *Financial Times,* p. 14.

Drake, W.J. (1988). WATTC-88: Restructuring the International Telecommunication Regulations. *Telecommunications Policy, 12,* 217-233.

Drake, W.J., & Nicolaïdis, K. (1992). Ideas, interests, and institutionalization: 'Trade in services' and the Uruguay Round. *International Organization, 46,* 37-100.

Dunkel, A. (1992). Telecomm Services and the Uruguay Round. *Transnational Data and Communications Report, 15.*

Dyson, K., & Humphries, P. (1990). *The political economy of international communications.* London, England: Routledge.

The Economist. (1992, February). After Uruguay: The GATT is worth having for what it is—and even more for what it could become. p. 18.

Eger, J. (1981, March 18). The international information war. *Computer-world/ EXTRA!*

Feketekuty, G., & Aronson, J.D. (1983, November 17-18). *The world information economy.* Paper presented to the Policy Issues in the Canadian-American Information Sector conference, Montreal, Canada.

Finkelstein, L. (Ed.). (1988). *Politics in the United Nations system*. Durham, NC: Duke University Press.

Ganley, O. (1983). Political resolution of communications and information disputes, *Transnational Data Report, VI*, 6.

Garnham, N. (1986). The media and the public sphere. In P. Golding, G. Murdock, & P. Schlesinger (Eds.), *Communicating politics: Mass communications and the political process*. Leicester, England: Leicester University Press.

Gibbs, M. (1985). Continuing the international debate on services. *Journal of World Trade Law, 19* (3), 199-218.

Gibbs, M., & Mashayekhi, M. (1988). Services: Cooperation for development. *Journal of World Trade, 22* (2), 81-108.

Gilhooly, D. (1991, March 18). ITU shake-up urged: High-level group recommends streamlining. *Communications Week International*. Paris, France.

Gilhooly, D. (1988, January). WATTC-88—'Keeping the Luddites at bay.' *Telecommunications* (International ed.). London.

Hamelink, C. (1983). *Finance and information: A study of converging interests*. Norwood, NJ: Ablex.

Hughes, T.L. (1985-86). The twilight of internationalism. *Foreign Policy, 61*, 45-48.

International Telecommunication Union. (1982). *International Telecommunication Convention* (Nairobi). Geneva: International Telecommunication Union

International Telecommunication Union. (1991, April 26). High level Committee to Review the Structure and Functioning of the ITU. *Tomorrow's ITU: The Challenges of Change* (Document 145-E). Geneva: International Telecommunication Union.

International Telecommunication Union. (1991b, May). *Restructuring of telecommunications in developing countries*. Geneva: International Telecommunication Union.

Journal of Communication. (1987). World Forum: The US decision to withdraw from Unesco, p. 37.

Kihwan, K. (1986). Trade negotiations and developing countries in the Asian and Pacific region. *Asian Development Review, 4*(2), 37-56.

Kloppenburg, J., Jr. (1991). No hunting! *Cultural Survival Quarterly, 15* (3).

Kolko, J. G. (1972). *The limits of power: The world and United States foreign policy, 1945–54*. New York: Harper & Row.

Mahoney, E. (1985). Space WARC'85: Negotiating competitive forces. *Journal of Communication, 35* (3).

Mahoney, E. (1989). The Intergovernmental Bureau for Informatics: An international organization within the changing world economy. In V. Mosco & J. Wasko (Eds.), *The political economy of information*. Madison, WI: University of Wisconsin Press.

Mahoney, E. (forthcoming). *Managing the Third World Information Revolution: The IBI, computing and development politics, 1945–1990*. Newbury Park, CA: Sage.

Mattelart, A. (1992). *Advertising international: The privatisation of public space*. London, England: Routledge

McClelland, S. (1992). Working out WARC. *Telecommunications* (International ed.). *26*, 6.

Media Development. (1990). NWICO and the democratisation of communication: One step forward, two steps back. *37*(3), 25-37.

Mohan, V. (1992). WARC-92, Spain. *Intermedia, 20*(2), 5-6.

Mosco, V. (1989). *The pay-per society: Computers and communication in the information age*. Toronto, Canada: Garamond Press.

Nora, S., & Minc, A. (1980). *The computerization of society*. Cambridge, MA: MIT Press.

Organization for Economic Cooperation and Development. (1988). *Trade in telecommunication network-based services*. Paris: Working Party on Telecommunications and Information Services Policy, Directorate for Science, Technology and Industry, OECD DSTI/ICCP/TISP/88.2.

Pipe, G.R. (1987). The ultimate bypass. *Datamation* (International ed.), 60-1–60-9.

Poe, R. (1992, January 20). Spectrum fight. *CommunicationsWeek International*.

Preston, R. (1991, February 4). GATT on rocks. *CommunicationsWeek International*.

Preston, W., Jr., Herman, E.S., & Schiller, H. I. (1989). *Hope and folly: The United States and UNESCO, 1945–1985*. Minneapolis, MN: University of Minnesota Press.

Prestowitz, C.V., Tonelson, A., & Jerome, R.W. (1991, March-April). The last gasp of GATTism. *Harvard Business Review*, pp. 130-139.

Public Network Europe. (1992). Hard WARC, but it was worth it. *2*(4), 10-11.

Raghavan, C. (1990). *Recolonization: GATT, the Uruguay Round, and the Third World*. London, England: Zed Books.

Randhawa, P.S. (1987). Punta del Este and After: Negotiations on trade in services and the Uruguay Round. *Journal of World Trade Law, 21* (4), 163-172.

Roche, E.M. (1987). *The Computer Communications Lobby, the U.S. Department of State Working Group on Transborder Data Flows and Adoption of the O.E.C.D. Guidelines on the Protection of Privacy and Transborder Data Flows of Personal Data*. Unpublished doctoral thesis, Columbia University, New York.

Rutkowski, A. M. (1991). The ITU at the cusp of change. *Telecommunications Policy, 15*, 286-297.

Sainath, P. (1992). *Patent folly: Behind the jargon on intellectual property rights*. Bombay, India: The Indian School of Social Sciences.

Sauvant, K.P. (1986). *International transactions in services: The politics of transborder data flows*. Boulder, CO: Westview Press.

Savage, J.G. (1989). *The politics of international telecommunications regulation*. Boulder, CO: Westview Press.

Schiller, D. (1982). *Telematics and government*. Norwood, NJ: Ablex Publishing.

Schiller, H.I. (1981). *Who knows: Information in the age of the Fortune 500.* Norwood, NJ: Ablex Publishing.

Schiller, H.I. (1976). *Communication and cultural domination.* White Plains, NY: International Arts and Sciences Press, Inc.

Smythe, D. (1957). The structure and policy of electronic communication. *Bulletin of Economic and Business Research, 54,* 75.

Solomon, J. (1991). The ITU is a time of change. *Telecommunications Policy, 15,* (4), 372-375.

Spero, J. (1982, Fall). Information: The foreign policy void. *Foreign Policy,* No. 48.

Sussman, G., & Lent, J. (1991). *Transnational communications: Wiring the Third World.* Newbury Park, CA: Sage Publications.

Telecommunications Reports International. (1990). U.S. coalition aims to exclude basic services from GATT pact, pp. 1-2. Washington, DC: Business Research Publications.

Telecommunications Reports International. (1992). U.S. offers basic service 'MFN' if GATT partners open markets, pp. 15-16. Washington, DC: Business Research Publications.

Thurow, L. (1991). GATT is dead. *Journal of Accountancy,* pp. 27, 29-30.

United Nations Centre on Transnational Corporations. (1990). *Transnational corporations, services and the Uruguay Round.* New York: United Nations Publications.

United Nations Centre on Transnational Corporations. (1983). *Transborder data flows and Brazil.* New York: United Nations Publications.

United Nations Centre on Transnational Corporations. (1981). *Strengthening the negotiating capacity of developing countries. Transnational corporations and transborder data flows: An overview.* New York: United Nations Publications.

United States Congressional Research Service. (1983). *International telecommunications and information policy: Selected issues for the 1980's.* A Report prepared for the Committee on Foreign Relations, United States Senate. Washington, DC: US Government Printing Office.

United States Department of State. (1991, September). *United States participation in the UN: Report by the President to the Congress for the year 1990.* Washington, DC: U.S. Government Printing Office.

United States Department of State. (1990, December). *United States participation in the UN: Report by the President to the Congress for the year 1989.* Washington DC: U.S. Government Printing Office.

United States Department of State. (1988, October). New policy directions: Analysis of the relevance of the trade committee's 'conceptual framework for trade in services' to trade in nonbasic telecommunications network-based services. Submission of the United States to the Committee on Information, computers and Communications Policy of the OECD. Washington, DC: U.S. Department of States, Bureau of International Communications and Information Policy.

United States Office of Technology Assessment. (1990, January). *Critical connections: Communication for the future.* Washington, DC: U.S. Government Printing Office.

United States Office of Technology Assessment. (1980). *Radiofrequency use and management: Impacts from the World Administrative Radio Conference of 1979.* Washington, DC: U.S. Government Printing Office.

United States Senate. (1983, March 11). *Long range goals in international telecommunications and information: An outline for United States policy.* Report for the Committee on Commerce, Science and Transportation of the U.S. Senate. Washington, DC: U.S. Government Printing Office.

Warner, E. (1992, April 6). Motorola, other MSS players evaluate WARC wins and losses. *FCC Week.*

Williams, M. (1991). *Third World cooperation: The group of 77 in UNCTAD.* London, England: Pinter Publishers Ltd.

Wood, R.E. (1986). *From Marshall Plan to debt crisis: Foreign aid and development choices in the world economy.* Berkeley, CA: University of California Press.

Woodrow, R. B. (1991). Tilting toward a trade regime: The ITU and the Uruguay Round services negotiations. *Telecommunications Policy, 15* (4), 323-342.

NOTES

[1] The market in telecommunication services and equipment alone exceeded $400 billion in 1990 (Dixon, 1992, p. 14). In terms of the "services" sector, of which communication plays a vital role as infrastructure and as product, figures exceeding $800 billion in 1991 are authoritatively quoted (see Dunkel, 1992).

[2] Aronson and Cowhey's book was one of the American Enterprise Institute "Trade In Services Series" that advocated deregulation, privatization, and the employment of a trade framework for services. The American Express company paid to have the books distributed free of charge to participants in the services negotiations.

[3] Several national reports (e.g., the Clyne report of Canada, the Brazilian informatics and telecommunication policies and a Japanese industry and trade ministry report which indicated considerable national governmental support for high tech industrial growth) and international and regional meetings throughout the late 1970s and early 1980s, threatened policy developments not in line with American corporate or government interests. Alarmed, members of the American private sector warned of a "coming information war" (Eger, 1981). American government agencies produced reports on "disturbing trends, US interests and the need for action" (U.S. Senate, 1983). (A more complete discussion of these developments may be found in Mahoney, forthcoming.)

[4] Writing in 1983, Jane Bortnick of the Congressional Research Services argued that "our ability to influence the agenda-setting and rule-making process to reflect this Nation's policies and priorities will be critical in determining how the United States fares in maintaining a leadership position" (U.S. Congressional Research Service, 1983, p. 1).

[5] This is the definition of "structural power" provided by Susan Strange (see Strange, 1988, pp. 24-25). In the present study, the ways in which the United States utilizes its

structural power to "shape and determine" the organizations assigned "rule-making" in international communications is a central concern.

⁶ The transborder data flow (TDF) debate followed the movement for a New World Information and Communication Order in the 1970s. However, while the TDF debate raised similar issues regarding the free flow of information, it addresses the much more fundamental electronic data flows. For an analysis of the economic, legal, technological, and cultural issues raised in the TDF debate, see Sauvant 1986; Mahoney, forthcoming.

⁷ Throughout the 1970s, developing countries promoted a priori planning methods for radio frequency and satellite orbital slot allocations in the ITU. Fearful that the resources required for telecommunication and information-based services would be monopolized by advanced countries, they called for equitable planning of resource use. This was a significant challenge to the U.S.-supported "first come, first served" approach to resource allocation.

⁸ The coordination requirements of international communication include: access to required resources, technical interconnection of systems, and standards-setting. The ITU has been the central organization involved in managing these aspects of communication. Therefore, it is subject to the competing interests in international communication.

⁹ P. Sainath underscores this point in his argument that "aid" from the International Monetary Fund and World Bank comprises "no more than five percent of investment for development in the Third World" (Sainath, 1992, p. 10). Whereas, trade is essential to the viability of national economies throughout the world. As Raghavan points out, "it is difficult for any country to close its frontiers and shut itself off from trade with the outside world" (Raghavan, 1990). By situating communication and information resources within the GATT trade negotiations, they become not only bargaining chips in broader negotiations, but the outcome is enforceable.

¹⁰ Aronson and Cowhey indicate the power relations at work as they write: "It is, after all, political institutions, not equilibrium models of the world economy, that decide which priorities will dominate the agenda for liberalizing world trade" (Aronson & Cowhey, 1988, p. 35).

¹¹ These UN-affiliated bodies generally operate in accordance with universal suffrage—that is one nation, one vote. As was indicated in the United States Office of Technology Assessment report discussed above, the principle of one nation, one vote was considered a threat to American "leadership." Indeed, the historical shift of international communications policy issues from multilateral organizations to a trade framework is an attempt to avoid universal suffrage.

¹² Gibbs and Mashayekhi argue that "the developing countries ultimately agreed to participate in the MTN [GATT negotiations] on services to avoid unilateral measures and discriminatory bilateral and regional rules" (Gibbs & Mashayekhi, 1988, p. 90).

¹³ National treatment means that foreign suppliers receive the same treatment as domestic suppliers. Transparency requires that information regarding national regulations be made fully and equally available to all concerned. Nondiscrimination or most-favored nation status assures that foreign suppliers will be treated as favorably as those from whichever third country has the most privileged position. And market access goes beyond national treatment and nondiscrimination insofar as it promotes a foreign suppliers "right of establishment" in another country. This raises complex and sensitive issues of national regulation of foreign investment and the obligations of foreign supplier's to the host country (see United Nations Centre on Transnational Corporations, 1990).

¹⁴ In this regard, it was argued that "TNC's must learn to respect the policy objectives of national laws and regulations, and learn to work within those parameters, rather than seek to undermine them" (Randhawa, 1987, p. 169).

[15] Gibbs argued that many countries finally agreed to the GATT negotiations because they saw "themselves as main targets of the [US] bilateral approach" of American trade legislation, and preferred "to negotiate with the United States in a multilateral context" (Gibbs, 1985, p. 214).

[16] In this regard, Aronson and Cowhey argue that: "Even though the GATT does not possess much telecommunications expertise and it is not perfectly suited to dealing with services, GATT must be able to trump the ITU because its vision and grasp are much broader" (Aronson & Cowhey, 1988, p. 235). Similarly, Pipe quotes one business source as saying, "What we don't get at WATTC [a major ITU meeting], we'll go for in GATT" (Pipe, 1987, pp. 60-68).

[17] Michael Nugent, legal counsel to the American-based Electronic Data Systems, argued that the ITU's preparatory draft represented "the over-reaching expansion of the jurisdiction of ITU regulations over new service providers [and] would lead to ITU dictation of policy to all ITU members," including private companies (*Communications Systems Worldwide*, 1987).

[18] An entire edition of *Telecommunications Policy* was devoted to the International Telecommunication Union in August 1991. In the 10 articles published, all of which addressed aspects of change in the ITU, only one mentioned "outside consultants," and this was in the "Comment" section. It is odd that analyses of the "development" of a multilateral organization comprised of more than 165 national states, as well as private sector members, would not discuss the impact of an American consulting firm's participation. The U.S. government considered it important enough to include in its annual review of participation in international organizations (see U.S. Department of State, 1991, pp. 234-235).

[19] The Standardization sector "should include the work of the International Telegraph and Telephone Consultative Committee (CCITT) and some standardization work currently done by the International Radio Consultative Committee (CCIR)." In the "Development" sector, the work of the Telecommunications Development Bureau and Centre for Telecommunications Development should be combined. And, the Radio communication sector "should include most of the CCIR work and that of the International Frequency Registration Board, and its specialized secretariat." A part-time group is expected to replace the now permanent IFRB (see International Telecommunication Union, 1991, p. 5).

[20] According to the U.S. Department of State, "the US proposal to invite the Secretary General to establish a Business Advisory Forum to promote dialogue with the private sector was endorsed" by the High Level Committee (see U.S. Department of State, 1991, p. 235).

[21] This agenda was in marked contrast to the prior American unwillingness to consider "foreseen new telecommunication services" at the 1988 WATTC meeting as in this instance the US pressed to have "newly identified US needs" considered at WARC 92 (U.S. Department of States, 1991, p. 234).

[22] Previously, planning access to resources was considered essential to development (see Renaud, in Dyson & Humphreys, 1990).

[23] In 1989, the Centre for Telecommunications Development received 18 donations amounting to approximately $2 million (U.S. Department of State, 1990, p. 249).

Regarding the formation of the Bureau for Development of Telecommunications, the U.S. State Department reported the following: "Because an enhanced technical assistance role for the ITU had the overwhelming support of the developing countries, no one spoke against it. However, many countries, including the United States, raised questions about the organization, operations, and financing of the proposed new Bureau. Because these and other questions were not addressed prior to the vote to create the BDT [Bureau for Development of Telecommunications], the United States and 29 other countries abstained. Seventy-three countries voted in favor, with none voting against. Once the creation of the Bureau was approved, the U.S. Delegation took an active role in shaping its mandate" (p. 244).

[24] A recent ITU study on "Restructuring of Telecommunications in Developing Countries," reports "the World Bank with a lending record in the [telecommunication] sector of over 3 billion US$ to more than 50 countries, representing about 1.5% of total World Bank lending, relies increasingly on co-financing arrangements to the effect that 80-90% of total project costs are now on average funded by other external and domestic partners" (International Telecommunication Union, 1991b, p. 16).

[25] This report openly states the kind of "catch-22" developing countries face in contemporary telecommunication development. To wit: "Restructuring may be a precondition for attracting more funds into the [telecommunication] sector, though the bulk of the financial resources will continue to be generated domestically ... Where the restructuring process is half-hearted, unduly slow and thus causing uncertainties, it might even reduce the potential flow of external, especially private, resources. Where restructuring leads to effective financial autonomy [sic] of operations or to a substantial degree of privatization, there would of course be less expectation of still receiving concessional flows from abroad" (International Telecommunication Union, 1991b, p. 46).

In other words, developing countries are encouraged to sacrifice what little national sovereignty that may remain and whatever socioeconomic benefit they may derive from control over telecommunication resources (i.e., "restructure"), in order to receive little or no foreign investment.

[26] Rutkowski reports that "there is just an 18 month window to move a standard from conception to approval. After 18 months it is no longer commercially viable to enter the market ... As a result 'ad hoc' standards forums—which bring an entire cross-section of the industry together to develop a suite of standards in the shortest time possible—have emerged as the most rapidly evolving new form of telecommunication cooperative organization" (Rutkowski, 1991, p. 291).

These industry-based "standards summits" also challenge the ITU's role in standardization.

[27] Following the High Level Committee report, Rutkowski argues that "the ITU's nation-state members must make the hard decisions." It can be argued that the leadership of the ITU has already made the decisions—that is, to promote deregulation and privatization of telecommunications.

[28] The Business Roundtable statement, "International Information Flow: A Plan for Action," cautioned in 1985: "Any international agreement in this area [international information flow] must *not* rely upon the kind of government monitoring and regulation of information flows that we are seeking to avoid" (The Business Roundtable, 1985, pp. 7-8).

[29] A broader critique of the GATT recently emerged in the United States as well. It basically asks why the U.S. bothered with this round of GATT negotiations at all as "GATT is dead" (see Thurow, 1991; Prestowitz et al., 1991).

Chapter 15
Television Marti: "Open Skies" Over the South*

Laurien Alexandre

There is in America a nation that due to geographic morality, has proclaimed its right to crown itself ruler of the continent ... that it is entitled to all of North America and that its imperial right should be acknowledged South from the isthmus.
  —Jose Marti, 1889

America's ideas are powerful; and through the power of communication, we can share them with the world.
  —George Bush, 1990

The potential for crossborder television to be used by the North as the high-frequency battering ram of low-intensity warfare against countries of the South has never been greater. Global realignments and technological breakthroughs have combined to create previously unimagined possibilities for cultural intervention. Recent history is replete with examples of the South's vulnerability to the political might and cultural omnipotence of its powerful northern neighbors. It is in the context of this history that the United States government has embarked on a cross-border television operation without precedent, pure media adventurism that breaks all the rules. Far from being an

*A version of this chapter was published in *Media, Culture, and Society*, Vol. 14, No. 4, October 1992, pp. 523–540.

isolated episode of media foreign policy, Television Marti is a harbinger of things to come in the skies over the South.

Television Marti, the official daily transmission of the United
States Information Agency (USIA), broadcasts directly into another
nation, Cuba, without prior consent or consultation. The signal is
transmitted on frequencies allocated for Cuba's domestic use and
could, if unjammed, be received by ordinary television sets in the
homes of Havana and three other western provinces. The International
Telecommunications Union (ITU) has ruled TV Marti in violation of
global communications regulations. Despite that decision and the
opposition voiced by one of the most powerful and conservative
domestic lobbies, the National Association of Broadcasters (NAB), the
project was congressionally approved for a 4-month test in 1989 and as
a yearly $16 million project in August 1990. Faced with this opposition,
President George Bush reminded the audience at NAB's 1990 annual
conference of their patriotic duty: "Before we are business men and
women," said the President, "we are Americans. Americans have
always stood for free speech and we always will. To stand for TV Marti
is to stand for freedom" (Bush, 1990). Cuba, considering TV Marti an
illegal transmission in violation of its sovereign borders, has interfered with the incoming signal, at a fraction of the cost of transmission
itself, by strategically situating antennas, boats, airborne helicopters
and mobile land units.

As consistent and illustrative as TV Marti is with three decades of
White House actions and attitudes towards Cuba, it is equally as
consistent with U.S. approaches to international communications
policy and multilateral commitments. The United States insists on its
unbridled right to broadcast where, when, and to whom it wants, and
by whatever medium it chooses, regardless of regulation and without
consultation. Washington finds its authority to beam media messages
anywhere at anytime in its novel interpretation of international
telecommunications regulations, in its transnationalization of the
First Amendment, which precludes limitations on broadcasting, and
in the primacy of the doctrine of the free flow of information. Its
intractable opposition to regulation of transnational media and information systems allows, of course, for the maintenance and expansion
of cultural and political preeminence, even in times of eclipsing
economic hegemony.

Whether or not developing countries can effectively exercise their
right, it is within their authority as sovereign states to control their
land, sea, and airspace and to lawfully protect these tangible and
atmospheric borders from unwanted interventions of any kind, be they
mercenary forces by air or ideologically charged consumerist mes-

sages by airwaves. Territorial sovereignty, cultural integrity, eco-
nomic/political self-determination, and in this case, a strong dose of
Cuban pride, are at the heart of the controversy over the case of TV
Marti.

At the core of the conflict is a fundamental clash between national
sovereignty, communications technology, and U.S. ideology. In the
process of exploring the nature of that clash, this chapter will
specifically examine several areas of relevant international communications law: those concerning cross-border radio [television] broadcasting and the notion of harmful interference, and those concerning
direct television broadcast via satellite and its applicability to this
precedent-setting case. Significant differences over interpretations of
relevant international principles and multilateral agreements will be
discussed. A brief examination of antecedents to this current media
operation will be set within the context of regional broadcasting
accords and widespread regional opposition to TV Marti. Finally, the
chapter will consider the case of TV Marti as a reflection of current
U.S. approaches to multilaterialism and global information strategies,
and as a harbinger of a new era of government external broadcasting,
one which moves beyond shortwave radio to the transmission of
television signals across borders. Whether by balloon or satellite, the
United States has proclaimed its entitlement to open skies over the
countries of the South.

INTERNATIONAL LAW AS IF NATIONS MATTERED

Portraying TV Marti as a struggle between the free flow of information on the one hand, and stifling government control on the other, as
the White House and American media seem predisposed to do, serves
several functions: first, it omits the political motives of the sender
nation; second, it dismisses the sovereign rights of the receiver
country; and, third, it patently ignores existing international norms
relevant to the regulation of crossborder broadcasting, thereby divert-
ing attention away from the blatant disregard of these standards by
the United States.

Global telecommunications law rests on the basic premise that all
states have the sovereign authority to regulate their own telecommunications system. This "information sovereignty" includes the right
to develop a national communications infrastructure, the right to
participate as an equal in international information relations, and the
obligation to respect the information sovereignty of other nations. This
notion (information sovereignty) converges with the right of self-

determination, the freedom to determine economic, social, and cultural development without external interference. Accordingly, every nation, no matter how small or poor, deserves the protection of cultural patrimony without the invasion of unwanted values imposed by a more powerful communicating nation. In other words, Cuba has as much right to determine its cultural and telecommunication order as does the United States, and both countries have the warranted expectation to be free from outside intervention with their respective communications systems.

Inadmissibility of Interference

By anybody's rules, interference is unacceptable behavior. The critical question, of course, is what constitutes informational interference.

The *U.N. Declaration of inadmissibility of intervention and interference in the internal affairs of other states* asserts, "No state has the right to intervene in any form for any reason whatsoever in the internal affairs of another." The principles of noninterference include the following: (a) "the sovereign and inalienable right of states to freely determine their own political, economic, cultural and social systems ... without outside intervention, interference, coercion, subversion or threat in any form whatsoever," and (b) "the sovereign and inalienable right ... to have free access to information and to develop fully, without interference, their own system of information and mass media and to use their media in order to promote their political, social, economic and cultural interests and aspirations based, *inter alia*, on the relevant articles of the Universal *Declaration of Human Rights*" (Powell, 1985, pp. 74, 274).

Similarly, the 1980 resolution from the U.N. General Assembly stresses that it "strongly condemns any violation of the U.N. Charter, particularly of its principles of sovereignty, political independence and territorial integrity ... in accordance with their political, economic, social and ideological aspirations ... by the use of military force or intervention and interference or by more subtle and insidious means of subversion and destabilization, or *by any form of political, economic, military, psychological, financial or ideological pressure*" (Powell, 1985, p. 89; emphasis added).

Finally, the *Declaration On the Principles of International Law Concerning Friendly Relations and Cooperation Among States in Accordance with the Charter* (1970), among many other documents, bars "all forms of interference or attempted threats ... against [a state's] political, economic and cultural elements." This principle implies a prohibition of foreign broadcasts that attempt to change another country's governing system or try to foment discontent and incite unrest.

Recognizing a nation's sovereign right to freedom from ideological intervention in its cultural, territorial, and political system has everything to do with the case of Television Marti. According to the *Declaration of Inadmissibility of Intervention and Interference,* it is "the duty of a state to refrain from any action or attempt in whatever form or under whatever pretext to destabilize or to undermine the stability of another state or any of its institutions" (Powell, 1985, p. 276). Organized, financed and implemented by the United States government, TV Marti is a politically motivated media enterprise that holds these international standards of nonintervention in disregard.

The International Telecommunications Union: The 1982 Convention and Nonconformity

While an in-depth study of specific international communications law and TV Marti could justifiably examine hundreds of documents from those already mentioned to the 1906 International Radio Telegraphy Convention to the 1936 Geneva Convention Concerning the Use of Radio Broadcasting in the Cause of Peace to myriad documents concerning liability law, space law, and culture and education law, perhaps the document most relevant to crossborder broadcasting is the 1982 International Telecommunications Convention and corresponding regulations of the International Telecommunications Union (ITU).

Found in the 1982 Convention are the threefold cornerstones of international communications regulation—to protect sovereign rights, promote international cooperation, and guarantee freedom of information. The preamble recognizes "the sovereign right of each nation to regulate its telecommunications system" as well as the "growing importance of telecommunications for the preservation of peace and the sovereign and economic development of all countries."

Of the many specifications and regulations within the 1982 Convention, several seem particularly relevant to the case of TV Marti. Regulation No. 2665 prohibits the establishment of stations broadcasting from boats, ships, or other flying objects, in water or by air, that are outside of national territory. Although TV Marti's balloon is technically located in U.S. airspace, given its characteristics, and the spirit in which the regulation was written, the applicability of this regulation can be raised. Regulation No. 2666 regulates *television* frequencies so as not to cross borders. "In principle, the power of the stations which utilize frequencies 5060kHz to 41 mHz [TV] should not exceed the power necessary to assure a national service of good quality *within the limits of the country*." Additionally, "all technical means shall be used to reduce to the maximum extent practicable, radiation over the territory of other countries *unless an agreement has been reached previously*" (Powell, 1985, p. 166; emphasis added).

In essence, certain frequency bands are limited to domestic service: While shortwave frequencies (HF) can and are used for external broadcasting, such as Voice of America and Radio Havana, as well as for domestic systems in a few countries, mediumwave (AM) and television (VHF) frequencies have historically been considered solely for domestic use *within* a nation's own borders. TV Marti intentionally broadcasts television signals beyond U.S. borders into another country on frequencies that have been "vested" by the ITU to that host country for its own use. By so doing, the U.S. government is asserting that it is permissible and desirable to broadcast television across borders in a fashion similar to that which has transpired for decades with short-wave radio. However, no such global consensus has been reached regarding external television crossborder broadcasting and the polarized debates over guidelines for direct broadcast satellites indicates the sharp divisions over the nature, use, and regulation of crossborder television transmissions.

In April 1990, the ITU's International Frequency Registration Board (IFRB) ruled that "the establishment of this broadcasting station [TV Marti], considering its location, relative power, high antenna height, and the given antenna directivity is, in the view of the board *not in compliance* with the intent and spirit of No. 2666 of the Radio Regulations ... Therefore, the board concludes that the operation of this station is in contravention of No. 2666 of the Radio Regulation." The ITU, however, has no sanctionary power and must depend upon the voluntary acceptance of its decisions by the world community.

In this case, the United States rejects the IFRB's ruling. The President's Report to Congress on TV Marti Test Broadcasts to Cuba (released 27 July 1990) stated: "The United States disputes the IFRB's interpretation of this regulation because many countries broadcast across borders. We believe that the IFRB argument is flawed and that the Board is acting beyond its scope of authority" (p. 6).

This rejection must be placed within the broader context of the U.S. government's disapproval of the Union's current character, which, according to the National Telecommunications and Information Administration, has "continued to drift from its traditional role of dealing with technical aspects" (in Sterling, 1984, NTIA, p. 39). In fact, the U.S. government charts ITU's "politicization" in much the same way that it politically villified UNESCO. According to one NTIA document, ITU's politicization, although beginning in 1965 rose to prominence in 1973 when the organization became "consumed by overheated debates over membership [South Africa's] and other political issues, not radio frequency management" (in Sterling, 1984, pp. 118-120). The ITU was chastized for passing a 1979 resolution "sponsored by a block of developing countries to guarantee equitable access to the geostationary orbit" and later, in 1982, when amendments to the ITU constitution expanded the organization's purposes. This expansion ultimately took institutional shape at the 1989 Nice Plenipotentiary with the creation of the ITU's new International Telecommunications and Development Bureau, a decision which was opposed by many developed countries.

George Codding, Jr., has noted recently that "As [developing countries] have risen over the years and have made their ability to organize and articulate their demands, [so too] the influence of developing countries in ITU affairs has continued to increase" (Codding, 1990, p. 140). The fact that the United States considered withdrawing from the organization because of an "extraordinary degree of politicization" (NTIA, in Sterling, 1984, p. 36) must be viewed in this light. Disregard for the ITU's ruling and denial of its authority are consistent with other United States initiatives to undermine multilateral decision making and to bypass forms of international oversight which might restrict its access to worldwide telecommunications markets.

The United States believes it has been judged unfairly in the case of TV Marti. However, the IFRB's ruling was made on the basis of technical obligations and not political partisanship. Nevertheless, the State Department charges that, when Radio Regulation No. 2666 states "*in principle* the power of stations should not exceed that necessary for good quality national use," it is allowing for exceptions and TV Marti is one such permissible exception to the rule (D. Schrumm, telephone interview, May 16, 1990). Additionally, the U.S. argues that hundreds of non-shortwave stations (AM and TV) are already being used for international crossborder broadcasting, despite the prohibition. That a number of countries, including both the United States and Cuba, use mediumwave (AM) frequencies is true. But to use existent infractions as justification for greater violations seems a questionable legal maneuver.

The issue of nonconformity is of particular significance. Earlier versions of the "Broadcasting to Cuba Bill" stated the importance of operating the station consistent with international law and not contravening obligations of the United States to international law. The final version (SF963; 1989, July 14) states, "The transmissions must be consistent with international law." If the ITU decision were to be accepted, the U.S. would be obliged to cease TV Marti transmissions, not only because of multilateral conventions, but also under congressional mandates. Otherwise, the United States would have to acknowledge its violation of international norms and regulations. The only other option, and the one ultimately chosen, was to declare the decision itself illegitimate and to accuse the ITU of acting beyond its authority.

Recognition of this nonconformity is important for Cuba. As early as the 1938 International Convention Concerning the Use of Broadcasting in the Cause of Peace, multilateral documents expressed the right of nations to prevent broadcasts from being used in a prejudicial manner and condoned a nation's right to stop without delay broadcasting within its territories "of any transmission which to the detriment of good international understanding is of such a character as to incite the population of any territory to acts incompatible with the internal order or the security of a territory" (Nordenstreng, 1984, p. 196). The premise and aspiration of freedom of information cannot be used to disseminate information media contrary to international law. Media that violate such laws are operating to the detriment of good international understanding. Ian Brownlie, professor of international law at Oxford University, noted: "States need not submit to subversion … but may take all possible counter-measures on their territory and commit acts of lawful reprisal.…Thus jamming of propaganda broadcasts would be lawful reprisal" (Brownlie, 1963, p. 435).

Cuba has, indeed, taken countermeasures and effectively jammed the broadcasts. Although the USIA projected that approximately 28% of the households in Havana and the three Western provinces could view TV Marti, the General Accounting Office reported that the USIA's results were flawed, because they were based on incorrect methodology and sampling techniques. Moreover, the U.S. Interests Section (located in Havana) reported that less than 1% of Cubans had been able to view TV Marti during the test period (GAO, 1990).

Although the U.S. government, mainstream media, free flow advocates, and popular public opinion have been quick to criticize Cuba's jamming of TV Marti as an illegal act, which reflects the restrictiveness of a closed society, the abovementioned 1938 international convention notes a nation's right, *under certain conditions,* to engage in legal behavior to stop broadcasting into its territory, especially if, as in this case, the transmission has been declared in violation of international standards of broadcasting conduct between nations.

Interference in Unoccupied Space

A major element of the TV Marti controversy rests with the notion of *interference*—what it is and when it is considered harmful. Article 35 of the 1982 ITU Convention states that "all stations must be established and operated in such a manner as not to cause harmful interference to the radio services or communications of other Members."

Washington upholds TV Marti's interference innocence on the grounds that Cuba's Channel 13 (on which Marti is transmitted), although fully registered with the ITU as a daily 24-hour Cuban station, has been unoccupied. According to the State Department, Cuba's vested right to Channel 13 is "only on paper" (D. Schrumm, telephone interview, May 16, 1990). Apparently, an unoccupied channel anywhere at anytime is for anybody's taking, especially if the taker has the technological ability, financial capability, and political motivation to do so.

Washington also bases its right on the fact that the operating hours of TV Marti (3:00 a.m.—6:00 a.m.) have been selected so as to avoid harmful interference with regular programming. If Cuba were to occupy Channel 13 with a signal, any signal, during TV Marti's hours, the United States would be in clear violation of this interference prohibition. In fact, during one of TV Marti's test-period broadcasts, the U.S. government knocked a speech by Fidel Castro off the air. Cuba grieved its case to the ITU. The U.S. expressed its regrets and abstained from broadcasting on the following night.

"Harmful interference" could, however, be addressed conceptually as well as in strict radiofrequency terms. Only the most technically circumscribed interpretation concludes that "harmful interference" refers only to the actual transmission of one signal on top of an already existent ITU-registered *and* occupied frequency. An interpretation of interference that incorporates notions of information sovereignty and the right of nonintervention might conclude that interference includes broadcasting by a foreign (and in this case antagonistic) power with programming reflecting different cultural and political values into an unwilling receiver nation on that nation's domestic television channel without prior consultation and in nonconformity with international convention.

The notion of *harmful* is obviously problematic, difficult to define, and virtually impossible to regulate. However, the concept of harmful—be it psychological, cultural, political—merits discussion when a foreign power broadcasts unwanted television signals directly into the homes of another nation. The U.N. Secretariat in a 1984 study on state responsibility relative to the consequences of acts wrote, "Activities causing injuries beyond the territorial jurisdiction or control of the acting state vary. They may include use of air space, nuclear activities, industrial activities, conservation and utilization of economically important resources, *and even communications and broadcasting*" (Taishoff, 1987, p. 53; emphasis added). The Secretariat's analysis continued, "Non-material harm refers to moral or qualitative harm, for example, a blow to the dignity or respect of a state, such as *broadcasting materials into another state which are inconsistent with its internal order and territorial integrity*" (p. 67; emphasis added).

Since *harm*—damage for which a broadcasting sender nation might be held liable—has been defined as, among other things, "loss of life, personal injury or other impairment to health," and since the World Health Organization defines *health* as "a state of complete physical, mental and social well-being," it could be theoretically argued that the effects of television, from seditious to subliminal transmissions, affect overall well-being. Although establishing criteria to identify and remedy harmful activities is problematic, it is important to note that many countries, from the North like Canada and from the South like Mexico, capitalist like France or socialist like Cuba, have voiced concern over the potentially deleterious effects of uncontrolled foreign broadcasts. To forget this fact would be to ignore the concerns of countries vulnerable to the broadcasting whims of their neighbors, friend or foe alike.

Ultimately, the issue of "harmful" must be based both on the direct and indirect effects of the programming, which are difficult to correlate and determine, and on the intent of the broadcasts. It must be assumed, with history as our guide, that the U.S. government's intended purpose in broadcasting to Cuba is not to stabilize Cuba's socialist system or encourage the Cuban people's allegiance to their present leaders. One need only turn to classics on U.S. government psychological operations, as well as the stated intentions of U.S. government radio broadcasting to Cuba, to assess the purposes. In *Strategic Psychological Operations and American Foreign Policy,* authors Holt and Van de Velde state: "The distinctive nature of the psychological instrument of statecraft derives from the fact that it attempts to influence the behavior of foreign states, not by manipulating objects in the material world, but by affecting the manner in which the world is perceived and interpreted" (1960, p. 24). If TV Marti is engaged in "the systematic attempt through mass communication media to influence and manipulate the thinking and behavior of target audiences in the interests of an organized ideological group" (Howell, 1986, p. 236), then it is engaged in state propaganda. One wonders why else the United States government would be spending 16 million taxpayer dollars annually if not to influence the thinking of the Cuban people in a manner consistent with Washington's interests.

Innumberable U.N. documents address the issue of propaganda. Baseline was set by the 1947 U.N. General Assembly that unanimously adopted a resolution condemning all forms of propaganda designed to provoke or encourage any threat to peace, breach of the peace or act of agression (Nordenstreng, 1984, p. 169).

There can be little doubt that TV Marti, and its sponsor the United States government, hope to affect the way Cubans see the world and perceive their leader. The originating document proposing TV Marti's predecessor, Radio Marti, illuminates these motives. Said the 1980 proposal, formulated by the Council for Inter-American Security's Santa Fe Committee on New Inter-American Policy for the 1980s, "The establishment of Radio Free Cuba under open U.S. government sponsorship, [which] will beam objective information to the Cuban people that, among other things, details Havana's unholy alliance with Moscow. If the propaganda war fails, a war of national liberation against Castro must be launched" (Alexandre, 1989, p. 141).

In his testimony before the House Foreign Affairs Committee, American University professor William LeoGrande noted, "We should not fail to mention, however remote, that Radio Marti may be part of a wider effort aimed at overthrowing the Cuban government by force of arms.... One cannot dismiss the possibility that Radio Marti is intended to play the same role as Radio Swan [CIA radio] was two decades ago" (Frederick, 1986, p. 37).

Although no such publicly released report concerning TV Marti is available (the author has been denied access to potentially similar documentation requested under the Freedom of Information Act), the Bush Administration's intent can be gleaned from other sources. After the Sandinista election loss to a war-weary population after 10 years of U.S.-sponsored low-intensity warfare, and after the December 1989 U.S. invasion of Panama, Vice President Dan Quayle referred to Fidel Castro as "the last problem in the hemisphere." Deputy assistant secretary for Inter-American Affairs, Michael Kozak, told the House Foreign Affairs Committee in August 1989 that Cuba is "a threat to peace and security in our hemisphere" (Kozak, 1989). And State Department spokeswoman Margaret Tutwiler said, after Panama and the Sandinista defeat, "It's two down and one to go." The United States has virtually molded the hemisphere in its own image; how fitting for our mass-mediated age that the last battle is now partially waged with a high-frequency invasion of television signals.

Outer Space Regulations and an Aerostat Balloon Named Fat Albert

Regulations concerning direct television broadcasts via satellite also seems to provide regulatory guidelines and standards applicable to the unusual case of direct broadcast television via balloon. TV Marti's technology is unique: It uplinks from Washington to the SpaceNet 2 satellite, which then downlinks to Florida; then the signal is relayed up to the land-cabled aerostat (Fat Albert), which is tethered some 14,000 ft above land and from which the signal is then beamed to Havana. Although not technically transmitted via a direct broadcast satellite (DBS), the essence of TV Marti's transmission is identical: It enables a foreign power with access to sophisticated, costly technology to broadcast directly into another country, bypassing any form of sovereign authority exercised by the host nation. Given DBS's potentially interventionist capabilities, it has been suggested at numerous international forums that prohibitions be enacted to bar cross-border DBS by one state into another without explicit prior consent, or at least consultation, of the governments concerned.

Given the lack of precise demarcation between airspace that falls under the sovereign authority of a nation state and outer space, which is open to the use of all for peaceful purposes, it is unclear under which basis Marti's aerostat activities should be judged. It is probable that in the future, the aerostat will be substituted by a satellite and thus the norms of outer space would be more clearly applicable. The 1967 *Outer Space Treaty,* to which both Cuba and the United States are signatories, obligates all states to direct the use of outer space for the welfare of all peoples and to contribute to the consolidation of friendly relations between countries and peoples. The *Draft Principles On the Use Of Outer Space,* designed to serve as recommendations on program content, restrict broadcasts "aimed at interfering in domestic affairs of other states," prohibiting broadcasts that "undermine the foundations of local civilization, culture, way of life, traditions or language."

The principle involved in the debate over direct broadcasts and prior consent is relatively simple: In order to broadcast into another country via satellite, the sender nation accepts responsibility to seek beforehand the consent of the receiving country. As early as 1972 the United States position on DBS marked its isolation in the world. By a vote of 102 to 1 (with the United States as the lone "nay" vote), the U.N. General Assembly called upon its Committee on the Peaceful Uses of Outer Space to elaborate DBS regulatory principles. A U.N. Resolution in November 1982 banning DBS transmissions across international frontiers without obtaining prior consent of the receiving nation's government passed with a vote of 88 to 15, with 11 abstaining. It was solidly opposed by the Western nations (Howell, 1986, p. 269).

The United States and other Western nations equate prior consent with prior restraint. "Any principle requiring that broadcasts must obtain the consent of a foreign government," said one U.S. delegate to the United Nations' debates, "would violate U.S. obligations towards both the broadcaster and the intended audience; it would also violate Article 19 of the Universal Declaration of Human Rights and the right to freedom of expression" (Taishoff, 1987, p. 138). Yet Article 1 of the U.N. General Assembly Resolution 37/92 (1982), indicates that "the activities in the sphere of direct television via satellite must be realized in such a way that they are compatible with the sovereign rights of nations, with the principle of nonintervention as well as the right of each individual to seek, receive and impart information and ideas. Articles 6, 10, 13 and 14 of the resolution exhort transmitting states to collaborate with the receiver state and in the case of initiating television transmissions, to meet and sign agreements. U.N. Resolution 37/92 clearly states that an international television broadcast satellite service shall only be established after a state is notified, after consultation if requested, and *in conformity with relevant instruments of the International Telecommunications Union* and in accordance with these principles" (Powell, 1985, p. 168).

TV Marti is a direct television broadcast from outside a nation's borders; however, by a fluke of technology and geography, it need not transmit from outer space. TV Marti breaks the spirit if not the letter of these conventions.

THE PRINCIPLE OF THE MATTER

At the heart of the case of TV Marti is the fundamental clash between communications technology, national sovereignty, and the U.S. perception that it can, in the words of Cuban poet Jose Marti, "crown itself ruler of the continent." For the United States, TV Marti is a case of "free flow" being obstructed by a government opposed to democractic principles. From this perspective, the U.S. believes it has the right to broadcast wherever, however and to whomever it chooses. In the case of

TV Marti, the standard charge is that Cuba's claims of territorial and cultural integrity are smokescreens masking a dictatorship's fear of change.

For nations of the South, however, the notion of free flow untempered by considerations of national sovereignty is problematic, to say the least. "There is talk about freedom of information," wrote one Colombian delegate to the U.N., "but those that advocate it forget that such freedom applies not only to the broadcasting but also ... to the reception and to the content of the message" (Taishoff, 1987, p. 138).

Whereas Washington upholds TV Marti as an example of free flow, Cuba considers the transmission an electronic aggression violating its sovereign borders, interfering with its domestic telecommunications systems and, not unrelatedly, insulting its national hero. Said Cuban President Fidel Castro in a March 1990 press conference, "The equivalent of TV Marti is if we developed a new trash can and named it George Washington." Although U.S. sit-coms and MTV International are of questionable intellectual quality, Cuba's contention is not with TV Marti's programs themselves but with the principle. "The issue," said vice-president of Cuban television, Gary Gonzalez, "is not with the content. The issue is not accepting what you are being forced to accept" (*Export TV,* 1990). In other words, the principle is sovereignty and noninterference, not "Kate and Allie."

In this clash, the United States employs Article 19 of the Universal Declaration of Human Rights (1948) to justify and defend its international communications policies and practices. The article provides that "everyone has the right to freedom of opinion and expression; this right includes freedom to hold opinions without interference and to seek, receive and impart information and ideas through any media regardless of frontiers." In fact, this precise language can be found in the 1990 congressional legislation approving broadcasting to Cuba: "The United States government supports the right of the Cuban people to seek, receive and impart information by any medium regardless of frontiers" (Television Broadcasting to Cuba Act, 1989, p. 80).

However, employing Article 19 to defend TV Marti is specious. Firstly, the Universal Declaration establishes the right of individuals to freely express their opinions. Whether this right is meant to cover government propaganda is as questionable as whether the U.S. First Amendment is designed to protect corporate speech. And, just as corporate speech has become a central component of domestic cultural and economic life, "free flow" has become its embodiment at the global level.

Secondly, freedom of speech is always an abridged freedom, never an absolute. The same Universal Declaration imposes limits on the exercise of this freedom when, for example, that exercise puts into danger public order and society's well-being. The 1966 International Convenant on Civil and Political Rights complements Article 19 with Paragraph 3, which observes that the right to free expression implies duties and responsibilities. Moreover, both documents determine in no case can this right be exercised contrary to the principles of the United Nations Charter and other documents that specify sovereign equality, nonintervention, and the responsibility to contribute to the consolidation of peace and international understanding.

Additionally, employing Article 19 to justify TV Marti is especially questionable given the nature of U.S.–Cuba relations. Whether or not Cuba's communications system is as free and uncensored as many U.S. and Cuban citizens would like it to be, adherence to the doctrine of "free flow of information" can hardly be asserted while a 30-year U.S.-imposed blockade has restricted the movement of ideas, information, and travel—as well as dollars—into and out of that island.

Additionally, the application of "free flow" currently practiced by Washington is contradictory. On the one hand, TV Marti, a one-way, government-financed media enterprise, is clothed in the protective robe of the free flow of information. On the other hand, that same government has denied ABC network permission to broadcast live from Havana during the 1991 Pan-American Games, saying that electronic transmissions are not "informational materials" and, therefore, are not protected by a 1989 congressional amendment freeing information from the stranglehold restrictions of the embargo. It is unclear how TV Marti's electronic transmissions can be considered "informational" whereas ABC's are not. Obviously, there are other intervening variables which undermine consistent adherence to a multidirectional free flow of information. Among these other factors, the doctrine's selective application reflects decades-old U.S. foreign media policies in this hemisphere and practices toward Cuba.

MEDIA POLITICS IN THE HEMISPHERE

While perhaps unusual in its technology, TV Marti is not an anomaly to U.S. media politics in the volatile region. According to Herbert Schiller, the underlying direction of U.S. international information policy since World War II has been to contain worldwide changes that interfere with the vital needs of transnational corporatism and its attendant systems (Schiller, 1989, pp. 287-288). In particular, socialism and national independence movements throughout the hemisphere have been unrelentingly delegitimized through every communication media and information technology at the disposal of government and corporate centers. One need only recall the documented efforts against Salvador Allende's Unidad Popular or against Nicaragua's Sandinistas to understand the power of this media intervention.

As early as the mid-1940s, the United States had developed communications practices and policies in Latin America and the Caribbean designed to complement and enhance its economic, military, and political control of the region and to control political resistance. In those areas where private media interests were successful in penetrating the nations, such as film and advertising, the government lent assistance; in the areas where private interests were not successful, such as shortwave radio, the government stepped in and undertook media activities (Fejes, 1983, p. 25). In conjunction with Kennedy's Alliance for Progress, for example, the U.S. government augmented shortwave broadcasting to the region, and since then, the Voice of America has been transmitting throughout the continent.

Antecedents to an Electronic Bay of Pigs

Employing government television in the media war to contain worldwide changes, especially socialist and national liberation movements, has an interesting history, one as long as that of television itself. In 1950, Senator Karl Mundt proposed the creation of an agency for televising government propaganda, "Vision of America," to complement the Voice of America radio (MacDonald, 1985, p. 18). Under the Eisenhower Administration, the USIA recognized the critical role that government-produced TV played in the struggle for "the hearts and minds" of the world. Between fiscal 1955 and 1957, USIA funds for production and placement of video programs on foreign stations skyrocketed from $376,000 to $5.9 million. This latter figure represented one-quarter of the USIA budget for radio-TV operations (MacDonald, 1985, p. 66). In reviewing USIA's assistance for television broadcasting in 1956, VOA Deputy Director Robert Button said, "If I ever saw anything that could lick the communists on their own front this is it" (Barnow, 1970, p. 112).

Crossborder television broadcasting to Cuba exemplifies this media foreign policy. In the early 1960s, the United States Information Agency (USIA) in conjunction with the Department of Defense explored the idea of beaming television from the top-secret "Blue Eagle" plane (H. Ryan, telephone interview, April 6, 1990). In 1962 the USIA's Edward R. Murrow elaborated a plan to broadcast into Cuba using two DC-6s flying at 18,000 feet, but the idea was rejected as too risky and extreme. The television concept reappeared during the Carter presidency, but given that Administration's desire to establish better relations with Cuba, the proposal to transmit from Key West using an unoccupied Cuban channel was dismissed (*Teleagresion III*, 1990, p. 14). When the television idea finally reappeared during the Reagan/Bush Administration, lobbied forward to receptive White House ears by the inordinately powerful Cuban-American conservative community, it was merely the culmination of decades of interest, by both Democratic and Republican administrations, to harness television as an electronic technique of unsettlement and destablization. Said scholar R. Hernandez in *U.S.-Cuban Relations in the 1990s,* "TV Marti, while formulated by conservatives, coexists within the old liberal strategy of influencing Cuban socialism 'from the inside' and, indeed, with the policy of changing the present Cuban system" (Hernandez, 1989, p. 50).

Television Marti is one more media payback for socialist Cuba's audacity to survive in the backyard of the United States. Throughout the 30 years of assassination attempts, an economic blockade, and invasionary mercenary forces, broadcasting—from the CIA's Radio Swan to commercial radio stations beaming their advertising jingles the short 90 miles—has played a significant role in the U.S. efforts against the island.

While a seemingly novel idea, television broadcasting to Cuba is, therefore, not a particularly new one. The interest has long been present, but now the current conjuncture of circumstances is ripe for this venture: the communications technology is easily available to wealthy countries like the United States; the celebratory domestic climate welcomes efforts to do away with "the last problem in the hemisphere"; and the changes in the former Soviet Union insure that no significant force will join in Cuba's defense while, in the broader context, the global realignment insures that no significant force will stand up for Third World sovereignty. Regional neighbors to the north and south of the United States, however, have voiced strong concern over this media project and the precedent which it is establishing in this hemisphere.

Regional Broadcasting:
Goat Glands for North American Impotence

The Americas is a region inundated with media. Recent UNESCO figures (see Table 1) indicate the plethora of radio and television broadcasting taking place.

Table 1.   UNESCO Broadcasting Figures

Country	Radios per 1,000 (1986)	TVs per 1,000 (1986)	VCRs (% of TV households)
Argentina	645	214	7.3
Brazil	365	76	15.0
Chile	335	164	5.0
Colombia	153	102	39.2
Costa Rica	263	79	9.5
Cuba	335	202	—
El Salvador	349	70	8.7
Haiti	30	3.7	—
Jamaica	400	105	—
Mexico	297	117	19.4
Panama	184	161	43.0
Peru	247	84	37.8
Venezuela	425	141	38.8

From *UNESCO World Communications Report*, (1989)

There is a great need for nations of the Americas to regulate this flood of frequencies and act in each other's mutual benefit. Regional treaties governing AM, FM, and television broadcasting have been entered into over many decades. Regional agreements concerning AM broadcasting cover the widest territory, because long-distance sky-wave propagation affects the scattered islands of the Caribbean as well as the two common-border nations, Canada and Mexico. Canadian stations within 400 kilometers of the U.S.–Canada borders, for example, are mutually regulated; with Mexico, the limit is 400 kilometers for VHF and 320 for UHF. Agreements on FM and television have also been reached with Canada and Mexico.

Through 1981, regional radio broadcasts were regulated under the North American Regional Broadcast Accord (NARBA, 1937–1938), signed by the United States, Canada, Mexico, Cuba, the Bahamas, and the Dominican Republic (which never ratified it). Dividing up 107 channels of the AM band, the United States received 24 unduplicated clear channels and 19 shared; Cuba ended up with one unduplicated and one shared (with Canada) to serve the entire 700-mile island (Frederick, 1986, p. 32).

In an interesting twist of historic irony, the NARBA was born out of the *U.S. interest* in protecting its sovereign borders from broadcasts entering its territory from Mexico. Specifically, during the 1930s a mid-West quack doctor began advertising his goat gland implant surgery as a fix for American male impotence via pirate radio originating in Mexico. In the process, while perhaps aiding male virility, he alienated the American Medical Association and the Federal Radio Commission (Nichols, 1989).

The U.S., considering the doctor a menace to public health and the pirate station (and its imitators) a violation of American sovereign airwaves, urged Mexico and other regional neighbors into negotiations, and in 1937–1938, they met in Havana. Although Mexico immediately closed down the pirate stations, the U.S. did not ratify the accords until 1960, when unfolding events in Cuba sparked increased interest in protecting U.S. borders from unwanted Cuban broadcasts. Despite ratification, the U.S. almost immediately began disobeying the treaty with the CIA's Radio Swan.

In fact, charges of deliberate interference and violation of the NARBA have been voiced by both sides over the years. Since 1981 when Cuba abrogated the treaty, no regional accords regulate broadcasting across their borders. The announcement of Radio Marti in September 1981, and a clash over frequency changes at the ITU Regional Administrative Radio Conference on Medium Frequency Broadcasting in the Western Hemisphere, wrecked these efforts at regional good faith accords (Frederick, 1986, p. 33). As a result, Radio, and now TV, Marti transmit over a sea of unregulated airwaves.

Regional broadcasting associations have voiced their disapproval over the TV Marti project, expressing concern that it is intrusive, not only to Cuba, but to their own domestic stations. In a 1989 letter to NAB, the Caribbean Broadcasting Union, covering 19 countries and 29 radio and television stations, stated that "We view as potentially harmful any system that would promote signal interference for both existing as well as proposed systems .... Our understanding is that it is proposed that TV Marti transmit on a number of frequencies allocated to Channels 2–13. Some of our members will suffer direct interference to their local services .... [TV Marti] may ultimately prove counterproductive to otherwise helpful efforts on the part of the United States to promote greater exchange of information within the Caribbean region" (Holder, 1989). The executive committees of the Canadian and Mexican Associations of Broadcasters also expressed concerns that TV Marti "poses a substantial threat to radio and TV services in North and Central America" (*NAB News*, 1988).

At the time of the reactivated immigration agreement in 1987 (after the interruption resulting from Cuba's response to Radio Marti), Cuba and the United States agreed to continue discussion over crossborder radio transmissions on non-shortwave frequencies. They affirmed that discussions were needed on two major problems—interference and Radio Marti—and that solutions were to be in *strict conformity* with international radio law.

With the appearance of TV Marti, both issues not only still remain unresolved, but their resolution is even less likely. The long history of broadcasting interference between these two countries, some resulting from unintentional spillage due to geography and some due to intentional intrusion, continues. Florida broadcasters have complained of Cuba interference with their stations, and, in some cases, the FCC has granted permission to increase their power as a countermeasure. And, Cuban stations, even those far into the interior of the island, have been drowned out by the United States. One Cuban media scholar argues that "the U.S. AM system is engineered such that it solves some of its incompatibility between its own stations (especially nighttime) ... by beaming its signal to the South (to Cuba) so as to accommodate more stations in the U.S." (Frederick, 1986, p. 34).

Since the beginning of the mid-1980s, Cuba has also consistently indicated its interest in resolving the Radio Marti problem based on the principle of reciprocity. One Cuban proposal has been to arrange for Cuba to broadcast on mediumwave to the United States using several domestic clear channel frequencies that could cover the entire continental United States (Rowles, 1989, pp. 288-289). For a number of reasons including the paucity of clear channels in the U.S., the domestic opposition of American broadcasters and an ideological antipathy to Cuba's interests, the U.S. opposed this possibility. Radio and TV Marti demonstrate disregard for regional concerns, and they pursue a path of media confrontationism instead of negotiation as the broadcasting strategy for the future.

LESSONS WHICH INFORM THE FUTURE

While TV Marti tells us much about the worsening state of U.S.–Cuba affairs and regional relations in the early 1990s, it also provides an important case study of current U.S. approaches to global information policies, international agreements, and multilateral organizations. In doing so, it also offers clues about the future of U.S. government broadcasting.

In the case of TV Marti, the United States government has categorically dismissed the ruling by the ITU, the multilateral organization designated with the task and authority to regulate worldwide broadcasting. Additionally, Washington has chosen to ignore the opinions of neighboring nations, which are unable to exert enough pressure on the U.S. to sway its foreign policies and practices. Noted the July 1990 Presidential Report to Congress on the TV Marti Test Period, "International and bilateral reaction to TV Marti has not resulted in any demonstrable harm to U.S. foreign policy" (p. 6). It is left unstated what would have constituted sufficient demonstrable harm. The United States has acted in a unilateral fashion, using media in ways antithetical to international cooperation and friendly relations between nations. It has "crowned itself ruler of the continent" and assumed its perogative to exploit the open skies of the Caribbean.

In many ways, the United States finds unilateral or bilateral action the most efficient in its pursuit of its transnationalized goals of integrated information networks and open media skies. Said media scholar Chin-Chuan Lee, "The United States has opted to shift its commitment away from universalism and broad-multilateralism towards bilaterialsm or limited multilateralism which it can control" (1989, p. 86).

Not unrelatedly, it is in multilateral bodies, such as UNESCO and the ITU, that Third World countries have had some small successes in conference diplomacy. Undermining those organizations is one way to insure that the Third World loses a vital forum for the articulation of its grievances. A case in point, of course, is the U.S. withdrawal from UNESCO. The withdrawal appears to have significantly weakened UNESCO's commitment to the call for a New International Information and Communications Order (NIICO). The 1988 5-year plan omitted NIICO, focusing exclusively on improving Third World communications capabilities rather than on, for example, limiting transnational media. Even that, however, failed to satisfy the Bush Administration, which refused to rejoin the organization. The State Department's Bolton report noted, "There are built-in factors which invite and encourage the type of politicization in which extraneous issues creep into, or even dominate, debates" (*Newsletter of AUU*, 1990, p. 1). The built-in factors, it must be assumed, are the 120-odd nations of the Third World and their stubborn insistence on national sovereignty. Washington wants "à la carte" participation in U.N. projects, paying only for those dishes it likes and rejecting those, such as the IFRB ruling, which are not to its liking.

The prerogative to assert its right by broadcasting television directly into another nation against international regulations and regardless of regional considerations also provides the context and the clues for the future of U.S. government external media. In his classic 1982 text, *International Radio Broadcasting: Limits of the Limitless Medium,* Donald Browne argues that the potential development of international television, especially DBS, will not essentially redirect external radio because the mainstays of shortwave—news, commentary, music—have little to fear from visual adaptations (p. 347). The global popularity of MTV International and music videos casts some doubt on his earlier projections. Nevertheless, it remains that short-wave radio does an effective job of broadcasting cheaply, and in many regions of the world, it will continue to be the West's medium of choice.

However, in some parts of the world, the days of shortwave radio broadcasting are numbered. Particularly in Eastern Europe and Latin America, high television receivership indicates a new future for external broadcasting. A still-classified 1990 National Security Council working paper on the future of government media recommends merging the nation's shortwave radio systems—Radio Free Europe/Radio Liberty with the Voice of America, an idea which had been discussed in previous decades but dismissed partially because of RFE/RL's past history with the CIA from which the VOA had assiduously tried to disassociate itself. And, a 1990 report by the U.S. Advisory Commission on Public Diplomacy notes, "Rapidly declining shortwave listenership in parts of Eastern Europe will require diversified signal delivery systems.... local medium wave and FM stations, additional satellite distribution of English and language service direct broadcasts ... VOA should also give greater emphasis to its examination of Direct Broadcast Satellite technology" (*Public Diplomacy,* 1990, p. 12).

The USIA's tremendous interest in using broadcast satellites as a means of enhancing coverage of its shortwave radio service and of supplementing it with transnational television transmissions is an indicator of this trend. The USIA entered the world of foreign television via satellite in 1983 by initiating a weekly 30-minute news feed *TV Satellite File* to broadcasters in other countries. The VOA has, for a number of years, used satellites to improve the quality of range of its signals, especially to Latin America. And the USIA's Worldnet uses a global hookup of five satellites and a dozen earth stations capable of two-way video broadcasts. Indeed, satellite communication is in the U.S. government's plans for external broadcasting and TV Marti is merely the tip of the proverbial iceberg.

For the Third World in general, and the Caribbean region in specific, satellite broadcasting portends a dismal future. The recent proliferation of satellite broadcasting has exacerbated imbalanced information flows with the Caribbean being the hardest hit. According to one 1990 study, Caribbean dependency on imported television in the four nationally owned television services of Jamaica, Barbados, Antigua, and Trinidad-Tobago has increased by 8.5%, from 78.5% of programming in 1975 to 87% in 1987 (Brown, 1990, p. 12). In fact, the Caribbean is the most media-penetrated region in the world. In the first place, the islands are small and poor. They cannot afford to support quality domestic television and radio productions. So some island governments simply set up satellite dishes to receive U.S.-based programs and then rebroadcast these over a local TV channel.

In a telling plea about the unhealthy state of broadcasting in the region, the secretary general of the Caribbean Broadcasting Union wrote,

> To a large extent, electronic media is supposed to mirror the community which it serves. On a typical day in the life of a Caribbean TV station, I may see CNN International Hour, "Popeye," "Price Is Right," "The A-Team," "Miss Marple," "Miami Vice," "Dallas," "Crazy Like a Fox," "the Jimmy Swaggert Ministry" and ESPN sports. We have a Cadillac mentality in a bicycle economy....Where, I ask, and certainly not rhetorically, is my community in all that? (Rudder, 1986, p. 122)

One example of what happens when communications come from outside the culture is the situation in Grenada. The island had a local TV station for 10 years prior to the U.S. invasion. In 1986 the U.S. government offered to bring "Discovery TV," a U.S. satellite-fed system to Grenada "to aid in development" (Fore, 1990, pp. 102-103). The system that arrived was privately owned by a U.S. corporation, and the new manager was a North American. The "studio" that was constructed for the Grenadians had a single camera and a few tape recorders. There was no serious effort to provide local programming at all. Coverage of the rest of the Caribbean was also nonexistent. In fact, the famous annual Tobago Festival can be seen on television worldwide but not in Grenada, just a few miles away.

Cuba is not the "last problem" in the hemisphere, especially given the external debt, hyperinflation, mercenary forces, drug trafficking, and endemic poverty which are ravaging the peoples of the region; it is, however, the last hold-out to a "free flow" of endless American sitcoms, MTV, game shows, and commercials. Ironically, under the cloak of free choice, TV Marti forces its message on its target. In the battle for the skies of the South, TV Marti wages high-frequency war against those who resist. Far from being an isolated case of media adventurism, TV Marti is a harbinger of things to come.

REFERENCES

Alexandre, L. (1989). *The Voice of America: From detente to the Reagan Doctrine.* Norwood, NJ: Ablex.

Barnow, E. (1970). *The image empire.* New York: Oxford University Press.

Brenner, P. (1988, September 22). Testimony before the subcommittee on Western Hemisphere Affairs, Committee on Foreign Affairs, House of Representatives.

Brown, A. (1990). Effects of the New World Information and Communications Order on Caribbean media. In S. Windor & W. Suderland (Eds.), *Mass media and the Caribbean*. New York: Gordon and Breach.

Browne, D. (1982). *International radio broadcasting: The limits of the limitless medium*. New York: Praeger.

Brownlie, I. (1963). *International law and the use of force by states*. Oxford: Oxford University Press.

Bush, G. (1990, April 2). Remarks to the National Association of Broadcasters. Office of the White House Press Secretary.

Codding, G., Jr. (1990). The Nice ITU Plenipotentiary conference. *Telecommunications Policy, 14(2)*, 139-149.

Dominguez, J., & Hernandez, R. (Eds.). (1989). *U.S.-Cuba relations in the 1990s*. Boulder, CO: Westview Press.

Export TV: Anatomy of an electronic invasion. (1980). Independent video distributed by the Center for Cuban Studies, New York.

Fejes, F. (1983, November). *The U.S. in Third World communications: Latin America, 1990-1945* (Journalism monographs, No. 86). Columbia: College of Journalism.

Fore, W. (1990). *Mythmakers: Gospel, culture and the media*. New York: Friendship Press.

Frederick, H. (1986). *Cuban-American radio wars*. Norwood, NJ: Ablex.

General Accounting Office. (1990, August 9). Letter from the GAO, National Security and International Affairs Division to Honorable John D. Dingell, Chairman, Subcommittee on Oversight and Investigations, Committee on Energy and Commerce, House of Representatives. B-240007.

Hernandez, R. (1989). Cuba and the United States: Political values and interests in a changing international system. In J. Dominquez & R. Hernandez (Eds.), *U.S.-Cuban relations in the 1990s* (pp. 35-61). Boulder, CO: Westview Press.

Holder, T. (1989, March 20). *Caribbean broadcasters express concern over proposed operation of TV Marti: Letter to NAB*. Washington, DC: National Association of Broadcasters.

Holt, R., & Van de Velde, R. (1960). *Strategic psychological operations and American foreign policy*. Chicago: University of Chicago Press.

Howell, W.J. (1986). *World broadcasting in the age of satellite*. Norwood, NJ: Ablex.

Kozak, M. (1989, August 2). *Cuba: A threat to peace and security in our hemisphere* (Current Policy No. 1204). Washington, DC: Department of State, Bureau of Public Affairs.

Lee, C. (1989). The politics of international communication: Changing the rules of the game. *Gazette, 44* (2), 75-91.

MacDonald, J.F. (1985). *Television and the red menace: The video road to Vietnam*. New York: Praeger.

NAB News. (1988). Broadcasters of the U.S., Canada, Mexico unite on common social, economic and technical issues. Washington, DC: National Association of Broadcasters.

Newsletter of Americans for the Universality of UNESCO. (1990, June). Vol. 6, No. 2. Washington, DC: Americans for the Universality of UNESCO.

Nichols, J. (1989, November). Remarks made at the conference, "Cuba and the 1990s," St. Mary's University, Halifax, Nova Scotia.

Nordenstreng, K. (1984). *The Mass Media Declaration of UNESCO.* Norwood, NJ: Ablex.

Powell, J. (1985). *International broadcasting by satellite: Issues of regulation, barriers to communication.* Westport, CT: Quorum Books.

Public diplomacy in a new Europe. (1990, May). Washington, DC: U.S. Advisory Commission on Public Diplomacy.

President's Report to Congress on TV Marti test broadcasts to Cuba. (1990, July). Washington, DC: Office of the White House Press Secretary.

Rowles, J. (1989). Dialogue or denial: The uses of international law in U.S.-Cuban relations. In J. Dominguez & R. Hernandez (Eds.), *U.S.-Cuban relations in the 1990s* (pp. 281-305). Boulder, CO: Westview Press.

Rudder, M. (1986, October 28). Broadcasting, step child or blood relative? In *Telecommunications for development: Exploring new strategies—An international forum* (Proceedings sponsored by INTELSAT). Washington, DC: International Telecommunications Satellite Organization.

Schiller, H. (1989). Privatization and transnationalization of culture. In I. Angus & S. Jhally (Eds.), *Cultural politics in contemporary America* (pp. 317-332). New York: Routledge.

Sterling, C. (Ed.). (1984). *International telecommunications and information policy* (including NTIA Report). Washington, DC: Communications Press.

Taishoff, M.N. (1987). *State responsibility and the direct broadcast satellite.* London: Frances Pinter.

Teleagresion III. (1990). Havana, Cuba: Editorial Jose Marti.

Television Broadcasting to Cuba Act (H.R. 1487). (1989). Senate. 101 Congress, 1st session.

World Communication Report. (1989). Paris: UNESCO.

PART V
Emerging Perspectives

Chapter 16
Globalism and National Sovereignty

Cees J. Hamelink

In 1979 Kaarle Nordenstreng and Herbert I. Schiller edited the predecessor of the present book. They decided to take national sovereignty as the crucial concept for the analysis of basic contemporary issues in international communication.[1]

This was a relevant and legitimate choice since, particularly in the multilateral political negotiations of the 1970s, the concept was emphatically present in twofold meaning: as object of grave concern, and as policy principle.

CONCERN

The concern about the integrity of national sovereignty emerged with the aggressive proliferation of Western technology and cultural products that began in the 1950s and accelerated throughout the 1960s.

Throughout debates and studies on international communication a regular feature became the recurrent anxiety that the existing realities of oligopolistically controlled communication flows did erode the decision-making capacity of national governments. This concern was expressed in the context of the problems related to the North/South information imbalances, the social impact of advanced information and communication technologies, and the new controversies surrounding the phenomenon of transborder data flows. As Herbert I. Schiller observed, "a combination of modern communication technologies have been developed, installed, and are operating, which ignore and bypass national decision making" (Schiller, 1981, p. 112).

These technologies did create advantages for a privileged few, and "At the same time as these technologies reinforce the TNCs and assist the integration of capitalist enterprise worldwide, they also serve to weaken the authority of the national state, which is unable to cope with the tremendous economic and technological power of these transnational structures formalistically operating under their domain" (p. 112).

The literature on remote resources sensing provided convincing illustrations of the concern about erosion of autonomous political decision making by national governments. "Internationally, the very basis of national sovereignty, for a majority of states, is threatened" (Schiller, 1984, p. 99). The concentration of data-processing facilities in only a few countries, the export of data relevant to resource allocation, and the foreign control over data storage were seen as contributory to a serious diminishing of sovereignty in essential processes of national decision making. The reasoning behind the concern was that, if a country lacks data about itself, it in fact lacks pertinent decision-making capacity about its own existence. If a foreign entity possesses the data and the resulting information/knowledge, decision-making capacity is extraterritorially located and national sovereignty subverted. "This can result in a national self-perception of impotence, an inability to effect one's vital choices, and the effective erosion of one's political sovereignty" (Gotlieb, Dalfen, & Katz, 1974, p. 247).

The concern about national sovereignty became also of pivotal importance during the 1970s in the multilateral negotiations on the standards for direct satellite broadcasting. As Carl Q. Christol (1982, p. 609) observed, "The degree to which sovereign concerns for national interest have been elevated in discussion of direct television broadcasting activity is quite noteworthy."

The DBS negotiations were characterized by the collision between the proponents of an unqualified free flow liberty and those parties arguing for limitations on program contents as barriers to the erosion of state sovereignty. The latter states were, for example, concerned that DBS would involve broadcasts "which might hurt the national sentiments of the people of a country" (United Nations Doc. A/AC.105/66, August 12, 1969, p.7).

The unsolicited beaming of broadcast signals was seen as a threat to the sovereignty of receiving nations if such signals were conducive to social unrest or did constitute interference in the internal affairs of states.

PRINCIPLE

Throughout the U.N. debates on space communications state sovereignty has been the fundamental principle. For example the United Nations Committee on the Peaceful Uses of Outer Space (COPUOS) has claimed that DBS activities would have to be developed on the basis of respect for sovereignty (Taishoff, 1987, p. 178).

Sovereignty also has been a recurrent issue in multilateral instruments addressing the preservation and development of cultural values. Several of these affirm "the sovereign right of each state to formulate and implement in accordance with its own conditions and national requirements, the policies and measures conducive to the enhancement of its cultural values and national heritage" (Preamble, United Nations General Assembly Resolution 3148, 1973, on the Preservation and Further Development of Cultural Values).

In the debates about the New International Information Order several fora and participants stressed the role of the sovereignty principle. For example, the fourth meeting of the Intergovernmental Council for Coordination of Information among Non-Aligned Countries (Baghdad, June 7, 1980) resolved that the NIIO is based on the fundamental principles of international law, notably self-determination of peoples, sovereign equality of States, and noninterference in internal affairs of other States. According to the resolution this recognition of national sovereignty as policy principle implies the recognition of the right of every nation to develop its own independent information system and to protect its national sovereignty and cultural identity.

REVIEW

Taking a fresh look at the contemporary issues in international communication, the concept of national sovereignty is in need of some critical review.

Today the basic issues of international communication have to be analyzed against the background of social processes that are most adequately described as "globalization" processes. This calls into question the adequacy of the conventional conceptual tools applied to the analysis of international communication.

- The social theory that was basic to the study of the junction of national sovereignty and international communication did operate from the nation-state/society-state as unit of analysis.
- The concept of national sovereignty is firmly rooted in a tradition of international relations theory in which the nation-state is fundamental.
- International communication studies have a similar background and perceive their object of study primarily as inter-nation-state communications.

Today's accelerated globalization processes, however, confront the analyst with cultural developments and communication processes that transcend the frame of reference applied to interstate relations, intercultural communications, or national cultures. If, for example, current developments raise the issue of the globalization of culture, it is questionable whether the problem of a "global culture" can be understood with the concepts that are essential to the understanding of national culture. Can the conceptual oppositions (e.g., homogeneity versus heterogeneity) that were frames of references for comprehending culture within the state-society serve the analysis when cultural processes are now projected onto the globe? (These formulations are borrowed from Featherstone, 1990).

This is important since conceptual tools have both descriptive and normative functions. The choice of concepts, such as national sovereignty and international communication, not only aims to provide descriptive categories for the comprehension of social phenomena, it also offers a normative definition of how we want these phenomena perceived.[2]

A review of the concept of national sovereignty in the context of globalization is particularly pertinent, since globalization processes are by no means monolithic. They follow different routes leading to different destinations. Global integration takes different forms that serve different social interests. Consequently, we have to discuss how the concept of national sovereignty relates to the distinct modalities of global integration.

THE DISCOURSE OF "GLOBALISM"

The prefix *global* has become ubiquitous. It pervades academic, commercial, and political discourse.

Global challenges are caused by such phenomena as global warming. The so-called *greenhouse effect* causes global climatic change, as the Report of the World Commission on Environment and Development (1987) warned. The same report recommended that a Global Risks Assessment Program should be established.

In December 1988 the George Washington University Conference on the Global Economy took place to explore the emerging global economic order. The papers of the conference were presented in a special issue of the periodical *Futures,* and guest-editor William E. Halal (1989, p. 555) wrote in his preface, "A new global order is emerging, with a vengeance."

In July 1989, the magazine TIME calls the International Monetary Fund "the top cop of global finance." This suggests the global nature of contemporary financial institutions and markets.

The *Fortune* issue of May 21, 1990 states that "the hunt for the global manager is on. From Amsterdam to Yokohama, recruiters are looking for a new breed of multilingual, multifaceted executive who can map strategy for the whole world."

The May 14, 1990 front cover of *Business Week* announces the stateless corporation. According to the magazine, the multinational of the 1970s is obsolete. A new type of company is evolving: the global company. "It does research wherever necessary, develops products in several countries, promotes key executives regardless of nationality, and has even shareholders on three continents. As world markets consolidate further, the trend will accelerate."

By 1992 U.K.'s Cable & Wireless intends to have its second private transatlantic cable—PTAT 2—enter into service. PTAT2 is part of a series of transoceanic fiber-optic cables that should create a new infrastructure for international communication: the *global digital highway,* as the periodical *Telecommunications* calls it.

In advertising globalism is the dominant wisdom. Only global advertising, it is suggested, can provide the adequate response to the increasing global operations of advertisers. The "one-stop shop agency" is emerging that can package commercial messages in global symbols: one advertisement for the whole world. The general expectation is that global advertising is business only for global ad firms and their global clients.

It is quite common parlance to acknowledge that Marshall McLuhan's *global village* prophecy has become reality, and that satellites and optical fibers have made the world a smaller place.

There are striking commonalities in this globalist discourse. There is generally a positive ring to the use of the word *global.* It connotes esteemed values such as one world, coming together, commonness, familiarity, and sharing.

There is also an unmistaken reference to progress and advancement of human civilization. As William E. Halal (1989, p. 561) writes, "the long evolution of civilization may be leading to some climactic phase."

The discourse suggests a progressive historical trend from primitive tribes, to cities, to nations, to superpowers. This historical trajectory will soon reach "the next logical stage of human progress: a coherent, manageable, unified global order that works—One World" (p. 561).

GLOBALISM: HOW GLOBAL IS GLOBAL?

The prefix *global* suggests a condition in which its related noun (an institution, an activity, an attitude) affects most if not all human beings and stretches out to all parts of the globe. This begs the question how global *global* really is? Taking a close look at contemporary realities, it would seem that the pretense of globalism is not necessarily in step with the world as it is.

Today's world is certainly still a long way from conducting financial business in a global currency or governing through a global government.

What is referred to as global communications is virtually the transnational proliferation of mass-market advertising and electronic entertainment produced by a few megacompanies. The fundamental shift in superpower relations has yielded an unprecedented confidence in global security. Yet most public funds across the globe are still spent rather on national military security than on the global security of sustainable development.[3]

The world's citizens have hardly begun to address the problems of the global coexistence of races and cultures. In reality the potentially explosive multiethnic encounter on the municipal level has not even been satisfactorily resolved. What is generously termed the *global economy* would rather seem the *economies of few* OECD member states and newly industrializing countries.

When the magazine *Business Week* writes about "The Global Race in Innovation," it really equates *global* with the consortium that comprises the U.S., Japan, Europe, and Asia's four tigers (Korea, Taiwan, Singapore, and Hong Kong) (*Business Week*, June 25, 1990). And as with so many other "global" events, the majority of the world's population is not included.

This does not mean that there would be no demonstrations of global reverberations in which all parts of the globe are vulnerable to acts performed by some. The ecological risks provide the classical example. The environment seems to be the unique area where there is a genuine search for global solutions under way and where a level of global consciousness would seem to be emerging.

The discourse of globalism does suggest rather strongly that such global consciousness is on the march in a grand way. On the one hand it could be argued that the over 3,000 nuclear free zones across the globe, the over 4,000 active nongovernmental organizations involved in world problems, the growth of international tourism and the increased media exposure of large audiences in many parts of the world, are an indication of a proliferating global understanding.

On the other hand, it could be argued that global consciousness would have to go way beyond these laudable activities and should include:

- an awareness that local events have global consequences;
- an understanding of the political roots of global problems;
- a sensitivity to the need of global solidarity;
- an acceptance and mutual recognition of sociocultural differences;
- a perception of the needs of the global community as more important than those of the local community.

In this broad sense global consciousness is constructed on the three levels of values, knowledge and interests.

Global consciousness implies a choice for such humanist values as responsibility, cooperation, compassion, diversity, equality, and participation. In the real world, however, there are formidable bureaucratic standards and technological constraints militating against this choice. Business conglomerates, state apparatuses, and fundamentalist religious movements across the globe are very energetically promoting a very different set of values.

Global consciousness implies knowledge about the world that is different from what today's mass media and educational systems offer.

Our educational systems pose formidable obstacles because of the highly specialized, fragmented, piecemeal approaches to knowledge. Our current university systems go a long way discouraging any unconventional, multidisciplinary exploration. Multidisciplinarity, which would be prerequisite to any attempt at global understanding and knowledge, remains an adhortation in numerous academic memoranda. In reality, most universities do not train students to speak the language of sciences other than those they study.

The mass media are equally ill-equipped to enhance global consciousness. They commonly stress the priority of the local over the global, deal with problems in isolation and as incidents, leave whole parts of the globe outside their audience's reach, and report in superficial, often biased, if not racist, ways about foreign peoples and their cultures.

Global consciousness implies that people see mutual recognition on a global scale as in their interest. In the real world there would seem a tendency to rather strengthen local consciousness (the in-group orientation) than developing global consciousness. In most local societies the out-group orientation is probably limited to the occasional diner in exotic places. As the "stranger" bias and stereotype does often serve the social function of justifying existing social inequities, this tendency is only likely to grow more intensely, as in many societies the insecurities related to unemployment, income distribution, corruption, and crime rates aggravate further.

As long as local societies do not manage to establish sufficient levels of security for their citizens, it is illusory to expect that these perceive global consciousness as serving their interests.

As long as many people see the immediate interests of housing, safe neighborhoods, sufficient education, and jobs threatened by an influx of political refugees and migrant labor, they are likely to suspect that forms of global solidarity distract from the resolution of their most pressing problems. Anyway, it would seem that, as people are themselves insecure, they are reluctant to trust "strangers" and to accept the diversity of tastes and lifestyles as beneficial.

Common globalism discourse also suggests the emergence of a global culture. The worldwide proliferation of standardized food, clothing, music, and TV drama, and the spread of Anglo-Saxon business style and linguistic convention, create the impression of an unprecedented cultural homogenization. Yet, in spite of the McDonaldization of the world, there remain forcefully distinct cultural entities to which the manifold interethnic conflicts are ever so many dramatic testimonies. There is certainly an increase in cultural contacts and more cultural movements that go beyond national boundaries, but this does not yet bring about a global culture. Although more people may have become more cosmopolitan than ever before, this does not yet create a collectively shared cosmopolitan consciousness. For a long time to come, it will be difficult, if not downright impossible, to provide the world's citizens with a historically and spatially located world culture they can identify with. A remarkable feature of globalism is that it completely bypasses the fact the world is very starkly divided and fractured on many counts.

Highly visible fissures are present in the growing economic disparities between both the North and the South and between different social groups within countries. The global society of globalist discourse is in fact a world "in which a privileged few coexist in uneasy truce with a majority of dispossessed" (Sagasti, 1990, p. 419).

Even the pretense of a global dialogue that searches for global justice and equality has been shattered. North–South negotiations on fundamental changes in the world economic system have been aborted. Current trade negotiations, such as in the Uruguay Round, "have been called by the North, with an agenda designed to further its global interests. They have been imposed by the North on the South" (The South Commission, 1990, p. 216).

DIVERGENT VALUE SYSTEM

It also needs to be recognized that there is worldwide a clear divergence of value systems. World society is by no means a homogenous entity. There are noteworthy upsurges in ethnic politics, communalism, and nationalism. Nationalist minorities in Romania and Turkey, and most dramatically, the different nationalities in former Soviet Union and Yugoslavia, have become very active and militant. As, for example, Hungary proposes autonomy for the Hungarian minorities in Romania, the Romanians insist on their territorial sovereignty.

For most of these nationalist actors local autonomy and state sovereignty take precedence over global integration. There is obviously also the rise of religious fundamentalism as a very divisive force. Interestingly enough, fundamentalism partly derives its strength from the resistance against movements towards global integration. "The resistance, or perhaps better, the digestion of globalization in various parts of the contemporary world has given rise to movements informed by the conservative religious option: political mobilization as service (performance) of the religious faith" (Beyer, 1990, p. 390)

Increasingly, also the ethical questions involved in many of the world's most pressing problems (in health, population, ecology, drugs abuse, or law enforcement) show that the meaning of global is very limited indeed. We have very little knowledge about which values and norms may be perceived as universally valid in all cultures. The proclamation of human rights to be universal does not in reality grant those standards global legitimacy. The globalist discourse seems to suggest a universal moral consensus that simply does not exist. The intellectual debate continues to have difficulties in transcending the unproductive universalist versus relativist positions (for a helpful critique of this debate, see Renteln, 1990).

Globalism would also seem to agree with Francis Fukuyama (1989) that our history has ended. "What we may be witnessing is...the end of mankind's ideological evolution and the emergence of Western liberal democracy (capitalism) as the final form of human government." It needs to be asked against this facile position whether the historical conflict between different ideologies really did end? Has the conflict between private profit and equitable welfare really been resolved?

Globalism entertains the unqualified assumption that current social processes lead inevitably to global integration. As William Halal (1989, p. 555) writes, "Until recently the very idea that the Earth would be integrated into a single whole was so monumental that it was almost universally regarded as radical, unworkable, or utopian. Now a unified planet suddenly seems possible."

This would seem to neglect that the same forces propelling the globalization processes may lead to integration as well as disintegration, and that both integration and disintegration may be perceived by those affected as legitimate or illegitimate. As globalization processes are steered by the intent to create a homogeneous pattern in which divergent values and norms merge, the forces that engineer this integration can also unleash strong disintegrating tendencies. The effort to impose homogeneity can lead to great disorder and uncontrollable tensions can be the result if everyone is to be squeezed in a common mold. An aggressive form of disintegration can evolve as the value system that dominates the globalization process is refused. This form is found in those fundamentalist movements that reject the modern world and in turn attempt to impose their spiritual globalism on the whole world.

Disintegration can also be sought in order to protect the independence of weaker units in the globalization process. It can be that such units first need to seek autonomy in order to survive asymmetrical interdependencies.

The existence of greater interdependence does not necessarily merge nations into larger units, as globalism seems to assume. Since interdependencies are often asymmetrical, a growing number of global transactions may equally well create more cooperation as more competition and conflict.

The intensification of contacts across the globe may lead to more cultural competition, as Anthony Smith (1990, p. 185) emphasizes: "The cultures themselves have been thrown into conflict, as communities in their struggle for political rights and recognition have drawn upon their cultural resources—music, literature, the arts and crafts, dress, food and so on—to make their mark in the wider political arena, regionally and internationally, and continue to do so by the use of comparative statistics, prestige projects, tourism and the like. These are veritable 'cultural wars', which underline the polycentric nature of our interdependent world."

The reflections above all seem to point to the conclusion that the descriptive use of the prefix *global* is very inadequate and indeed highly misleading.

GLOBALIZATION PROCESSES

Since the use of the concept *global* as a descriptive category lacks precision and relevance, it would seem more useful to apply the concept of *globalization processes*. This means that whereas it is not analytically helpful to talk about *global culture,* for example, it serves the purpose of our comprehension of contemporary reality to refer to the process of *cultural globalization.*

This concept reflects that although no integrated, unified global culture may exist at present, there are certainly observable processes of cultural development that transcend inter-nation-state relations.

Globalization does not ignore the proliferation of Western, commercially packaged cultural products and the aggressive marketing of a consumerist lifestyle, but it also allows to accept that non-Western values are by no means extinct and that an impressive volume of local customs and standards is very much alive around the globe. For the sake of analytical precision globalization has to be seen as distinct from *internationalization* or *transnationalization.*

Internationalization refers to transactions involving two or more national units, usually bilaterally or regionally or between actors with specific shared interests. Internationalization evolved in response to the grossly devastating implications of nationalist ideologies preceding the second world war. The concept is firmly based in nation-state thinking. Yet it also expresses the strongly felt need for solidarity among nations. Internationalist thinking was essential to the movements supporting the demands for a new international economic order and a new international information order.

Transnationalization refers to transactions across national borders that are directed from one central national location and in which essential decision making remains firmly centralized in spite of levels of local autonomy. Transnationalization implies the aggressive proliferation of one preferred definition of reality as the legitimate universal model.

Globalization describes the social process of transition to a condition in which transactions affect most citizens of world society. Globalization refers to "becoming global": a process of social transformation.

Although it can be argued, as Robertson (1990, p. 26) does, that globalization has been taking off since the 1870s, there are many signs of an accelerated process in more recent times.

There are undeniably globalization processes at work today.

They are observable, for example, in trade and finance. Increasingly, local military conflicts open the possibility of global implications.

There are developments towards global exchanges in education and tourism, and to a lesser extent in science and technology. More companies are involved in across-the-globe management and production.

Global standard-setting instruments are emerging, as in the case of the Law of the Seas.[4]

There are trends towards cultural activities spanning the globe. The communications industry is affected by globalization as it continues to extend its activities geographically, develops into an oligopoly of few global media companies, and as many of its corporations are reaching toward "statelessness." Some examples are given in Table 1.

The driving forces of the globalization processes:

1. Technological innovations, especially in the field of informatics, telecommunications and their convergence have largely facilitated

Table 1.   The stateless communication corporations.

Company	Nationality	Sales 1989 in billion $	% outside home country
Philips	Netherlands	30.0	94.0
Reuters	UK	1.9	80.0
Bertelsmann	GER	6.7	68.0
Sony	Japan	16.3	66.0
IBM	US	62.7	59.0
NCR	US	6.0	58.9
Digital	US	12.7	54.0
Xerox	US	12.4	54.0
Hewlett Packard	US	11.9	53.0
Siemens	GER	36.3	51.0
Time-Warner	US	10.8	23.0
Disney	US	4.8	20.0

processes of globalization. In fact, one could argue that communication/information technologies provide the essential infrastructure for global transactions.

2. Important incentives for globalization stem from concerns about military security and deterioration of the environment. The need to survive is a powerful force to address problems on a global scale.

3. Particularly in the field of human rights there has been a growing understanding that elementary justice for all depends upon the realization of global solidarity. Globalization is indeed driven by the force of such ideas as "Injustice anywhere is a threat to justice everywhere" (Martin Luther King Jr.). In the realm of ideas also, the acceptance of the notion of the common heritage of humankind (e.g., outer space, the oceans, Antarctica) has reinforced globalization.

4. Financial markets. It is likely that the growth of global financial markets in the 1970s triggered off the acceleration of globalization processes. This was reinforced by the rapid proliferation of offshore financial markets and the global circulation of vast amounts of money outside the jurisdiction of national authorities.

5. The enormous growth of trade. Sweeping reductions in costs of air travel and shipping have facilitated phenomenal expansion of cross-border trading. In the process, not only has the volume of trade enormously increased, but its character has also changed considerably. The steeply rising costs of developing new technologies and new products "put firms under intense pressure to expand their shares of global markets in order to amortise the huge fixed costs involved. One result has been to increase pressures on firms to take a global approach to sales (e.g. through global brand-names and global advertising), thereby reinforcing globalisation of markets" (OECD, 1989, p. 24).

The new global approach has meant that corporate strategies focus increasingly on global delivery systems, corporate interconnections networks and electronic markets. "Rather than just shipping goods across borders, they are seeking customized, in-depth interactions with clients, suppliers and partners, through an expanding gamut of networking strategies, many of which have a strong information and advanced communication content" (Bressand, 1990, p. 58).

Exports and foreign investments in the conventional sense are increasingly replaced by networking arrangements with local delivery systems. Transactions are conducted through TDF computer communication networks. A wide variety of corporate networks has been created in the past two decades.

6.   Politics. The politics of deregulation and privatization that became
the decisive policy tools over the past decade in many countries
provided additional impetus to globalization. The establishment of
global corporate information networks has been greatly supported
by the deregulation of telecommunications in the U.S.A. and
several European Community member countries.

MONISM VERSUS PLURALISM

A decisive feature of current processes of globalization is their *monist*
orientations. The monist mode of global integration seeks to impose on
a global scale its preferred, autocentric value system and refuses to
accept the reality of a polycentric cultural space. The monist mode is
found among those entrepreneurial globalists who seek the
unobstructed trading of their goods and services around the globe and
the creation of a globally integrated market in which the same product
can be made available globally. It is guided by the belief that
entrepreneurial efficiency and effectiveness demand a global reach,
and perceives its interests optimally served if its preferred socioeconomic standards are replicated across the globe.

Monist globalism represents an imperial interest in the creation of
a coherent set of values and norms, discouraging divergent norms, and
perceiving deviance from its standards as a threat to stability.

This mode of globalism is also found in those fundamentalist
religious movements that seek the global proliferation of their idio-
syncratic definition of reality, which is perceived as exclusively valid.
These movements demand global loyalty to the standards of conduct
they believe to be essential for humankind and are ready to impose
those standards aggressively on everyone. Their missionary zeal is
guided by the manichean perspective of a world divided into *them*
versus *us*. These spiritual imperialists are found in Christianity,
Islam, Judaism, and Hinduism. Their "Holy Terror" "seeks to impose
a supreme set of religious beliefs and social values on every individual.
Internationally, it targets other faiths and cultures for subjugation"
(Conway & Siegelman, 1984, p. 386).

Against the monist trend in globalization a *pluralist* globalism is
beginning to emerge among those social movements that seek to
develop a "civil society" on a global scale. The search for a world civil
society is actively conducted by those groups that place global security
over national security, that aim at global cooperation in tackling
problems related to drug abuse or AIDS, and that see the protection of
human rights as a global mandate.

The pluralist mode of global integration aspires to accommodate the multipolarity of current world society. Pluralism departs from the recognition of diversity and seeks consensus on values which can be shared across the globe.

Pluralist globalism is guided by the belief that the future of civil society depends upon a global ethical consensus, i.e., the insight that, while cultural diversity is maintained, basic values can be shared by all citizens of the world. This modality of globalism represents a cooperative and multifaceted form of integration in which it is understood that genuine global cooperation can only be achieved on the basis of the recognition of diverse sets of values.

Pluralist globalism proposes that universal human rights can only be global if world society genuinely seeks the moral convergence in cultural diversity.

NATIONAL SOVEREIGNTY

The accelerated processes of globalization raise new questions about the exercise of national sovereignty. These questions have to be studied in the light of the observation that globalization processes are predominantly guided by "monist" interests. On the surface it would appear that current developments towards global integration do indeed undermine the sovereignty of the nation-state.

In fact, globalization processes propelled by transborder finance flows, offshore electronic markets, and worldwide marketing of cultural products are affecting the decision-making powers of individual states, as most observers would agree.

As the Brundtland Commission observed, "Increasing ecological and economic interdependence presents challenges to current concepts of national sovereignty" (*Sustainable Development*, 1990, p. 59). And as a representative of the "stateless corporations," Unisys Chairman Blumenthal, says, "I wouldn't say the nation-state is dead...but the sovereignty has been greatly circumscribed...even for a country as large as the U.S." (*Business Week*, May 14, 1990, p. 59).

Against these observations, however, one could propose the following considerations.

Despite the far-reaching regional economic integration of the European Community member states, the sovereign state is still the basic unit of European politics.

The conception of national sovereignty in which states treat their nationals as they see fit is still powerful, in spite of the recognition of universal human rights.

Current international politics is still strongly based on a state-centric system in spite of the increasingly essential role of nonstate actors.

Across the globe national interests (basically elite interests) continue to successfully claim resources for security needs rather than for human needs. Around the world state security manages to be better guaranteed than civil security.

The most serious attack on nation-state sovereignty would appear to originate with the most powerful protagonists of globalism, the transnational corporations. The reality is, however, more complex and ambivalent. Precisely, these corporations tend to benefit from the maintenance of strong nation-states. There are certainly contentions between states and TNCs, but as Mel Gurtov (1988, p. 31) observes, "these conflicts should not obscure their overall symbiotic relationship."

National sovereignty helps the TNCs to avoid the creation of genuine supranational regulatory institutions that might control their restrictive business practices.

TNCs need national governments to guarantee safe investment environments, to create market opportunities through foreign aid or to promote the trade of their "national" companies through their diplomatic missions. They may also benefit from supportive national regulation on technical standards, patent and trademark protection, or acquisitions and mergers. Governments furthermore provide important markets through purchases in defense and information/communication sectors. Much corporate R&D also depends upon the provision of public finances.

Tran Van Dinh and Rosemary Porter (1986, p. 125) strongly argue that the independent nation-state and international capital should be seen as interdependent. For example, "international capital is at its most cost efficient if it separates itself from responsibility for the expense of reproducing the system (i.e. education, child care, health, and subsistence economies) and relies upon the nation-states and the people themselves to provide these services."

By and large, then, it would seem that current globalization processes leave the exercise of national sovereignty unhampered. It is even arguable that the currently dominant form of global integration operates largely through the continued existence of strong independent nation-states that conveniently serve the maintenance of an asymmetrical world society.

At this point of the analysis it needs to be remembered that the concept of national sovereignty is firmly rooted in the realist paradigm of international relations. It conceives the world as a state-centric system and in extending nation-state based power politics to the interstate arena aspires to the maintenance of the status quo or maximally to system reform rather than to fundamental transformation of world society.

This state-centric conception justifies state sovereignty commonly with the reference to the "national" interest. However, "in any political system, the 'national interest' usually defines the political-economic priorities of an elite—that set of interests which it decides national power ought to promote" (Gurtov, 1988, p. 14). In the political reality of most states, sovereignty is indeed claimed in the service of the bureaucratic, military and corporate elites, and usually not in the interest of citizens.

The 1970s debate on a new international information order (NIIO) was seriously impaired by its exclusive reliance on this state-centric paradigm. This incapacitated the debate to search for solutions to cross-border communication problems that transcended the existing system and to take serious account of the numerous nonstate actors that had become essential forces in international politics. As a result the NIIO debate never explicitly promoted the notion that the effective protection of international human rights (pertinent to information matters) would never be guaranteed under the conventional nation-state-centric system. This would demand more than cooperation and equity in communication between states and would require a devolution of state power both in the sense of the acceptance of supranational authorities (world courts of justice, for example) and the recognition of active nonstate actors (for example citizen's human rights movements across the globe).[5]

The realist paradigm tends to gloss over the internal dimension of state sovereignty. It focuses mainly on the external dimensions of nation-state protection against external claims and limitation of liberty of action in view of the sovereignty of other states.

However, the outwardly sovereign state tends to appropriate also sovereign control over its citizens. This is the characteristically Hobbesian vision in which only the absolute sovereignty of the state (the Leviathan) can control the eternal civil strife.[6]

This ignores that state sovereignty represents more than the emancipation from the powers of emperors, popes, and nobility. The development of legitimate sovereign states went together with the development of egalitarianism in which subjects became citizens. The

French revolution and the American revolution gave birth to both independent nation-states as well as to citizens with basic civil rights. As a matter of fact the French revolution recognized the primacy of the people's sovereignty.

From the above one could conclude that national sovereignty in its conventional, one-dimensional version is not likely to be threatened by current processes of globalization. The key actors in today's international relations, the states and the transnational corporations, do benefit from their mutual reinforcement of the state-centric system.

The forces steering the predominantly "monist" modality of globalization stand to benefit most with states that may be externally limited in power, but that maintain a good measure of sovereign control over their citizens.

What does seem to be rather at stake in a serious way in the sovereignty of the world's citizens: their autonomy in expressing divergent persuasions and lifestyles. Citizen sovereignty is today equally threatened by the political mechanisms of the modern state and the economic tools of transnational capital.

Against this threat, global citizenship needs to be protected by citizens themselves, by a self-organizing civil society that transcends national borders and defends a pluralist globalism against state and market.[7]

CITIZEN SOVEREIGNTY AND GLOBAL COMMUNICATION

If one accepts a pluralist globalism as the preferred normative position, national sovereignty as policy principle would have to be superseded by the concept of citizen sovereignty. This would, however, not imply, at this point in time, the complete rejection of national sovereignty, as it would still be urgent to grant a level of protection to the weaker states in a highly unequal world.[8]

As a result of the conceptual shift a key question for the debate on international communication would then be how to design a global communications system "as if citizens mattered." In other words what are the political conditions for global communications to serve civil society on a global scale?

A pluralist world demands a global communication order that transcends interstate relations, facilitates communication flows as if people mattered, and contributes to the realization of global civil society.

Three critical policy principles should guide the design of this global communication order.

Citizen Sovereignty

This would imply the recognition of a civil communication space not interfered with by state commerce. This is urgent in view of the increasing commercialization of communication spaces and cultural production in many countries. The public sphere is increasingly eroded or fully equated with state-controlled activity. For citizens to exercise their sovereign right to citizenship, civil society needs its own space.

Representation and Redress

Presently the interests of the largest group of users of global communications (the small users) are not represented in multilateral negotiations. This is remarkable, since these negotiations commonly claim to ultimately benefit all the world's citizens. Not only should form of civil representation be sought and implemented; there should also be mechanisms designed through which citizens can seek redress in case communication wrongs are inflicted upon them.

These may range from misleading information to the refusal of free expression and to unfair tariffing.

Social Accountability

A remarkable feature of today's cross-border communications is the lack of accountability. Whatever the errors, failures, or distortions, no participating party accepts any responsibility. This is particularly problematic as the dominant means of social communication inflict harm and injustice upon their clients by misinforming them, by distorting their realities, by invading their privacies, by refusing to listen to them, by keeping them ignorant, ripping them off, and then denying all liability.

SUMMARY

Today's prevailing globalist discourse does not provide a sufficiently precise description of present world-society. Inadequate as the notion *global* may be, however, there are far-reaching processes of economic, political, and cultural globalization at work. By and large these processes are guided by a "monist" mode of global integration. The interests steering this mode of globalization are in fact no serious threat to the conventional one-dimensional exercise of national sovereignty. What is really at stake in current globalization is a pervasive threat to the exercise of autonomous citizenship. To counter this threat the development of a pluralist mode of global integration is required.

In the realization of this normative position, the conventional concepts of national sovereignty and international communication are inadequate. Their basis in the realist, state-centric paradigm of international relations collides with the recognition of the sovereignty of citizens. Pluralist globalism demands a global communication order that supports the creation of a global civil society.

This requires forms of social communication that acknowledge public accountability and operate on the basis of an equitable sharing of communication resources. This can only be achieved by an unprecedented emancipatory political activity on the part of citizens of all nations.

It remains to be seen whether this activity can be generated against technoutopias, nonstop distractions, disinformation gluts, and holy terror as these proliferate to all citizens of the world society.

REFERENCES

Albrow, M, & King, E. (Eds.). (1990). *Globalization, knowledge and society.* London: Sage.

Alger, C. (1984). Effective participation in world society: Some implications of the Columbus Study. In M. Banks (Ed.), *Conflict in world society. A new perspective on international relations* (pp. 131–145). Brighton, UK: Wheatsheaf Books.

Beyer, P. F. (1990). Religion in global society. In M. Featherstone (Ed.), *Global culture, nationalism, globalization, and modernity* (pp. 373–395). London: Sage.

Bressand, A., Distler, C., & Nicolaïdis, K. (1989). Networks at the heart of the service economy. In A. Bressand & K. Nicolaïdis (Eds.), *Strategic trends in services. An inquiry into the global service economy* (pp. 17–32). New York: Harper & Row Publishers.

Bressand, A. (1990). Beyond interdependence: 1992 as a global challenge. *International Affairs, 66* (1), 47–65.

Brundtland Commission (The World Commission on Environment and Development). (1987). *Our common future.* Oxford: Oxford University Press.

Christol, C. Q. (1982). *The modern international law of outer space.* New York: Pergamon Press.

Conway, F., & Siegelman, J. (1984). *Holy terror. The fundamentalist war on America's freedoms in religion, politics and our private lives.* New York: Dell.

Featherstone, M. (Ed.) (1990). *Global culture. Nationalism, globalization and modernity.* London: Sage.

Fukuyama, F. (1989). *The end of history.* New York: The Free Press.

Goodwin, G. L. (1978). Theories of international relations: The normative and policy dimensions. In T. Taylor (Ed.), *Approaches and theory in international relations* (pp. 280–304). New York: Longman.

Gottlieb, A., Dalfen, C., & Katz, K. (1974). The transborder transfer of information by communications and computer systems. *The American Journal of International Law, 68*(2), 227–257.

Groom, A. J. R., & Heraclides, A. (1985). Integration and disintegration. In M. Light & A. J. R. Groom (Eds.), *International relations. A handbook of current theory* (pp. 174–193). London: Frances Pinter.

Gross, L. (1979). Some international law aspects of the freedom of information and the right to communicate. In K. Nordenstreng & H. I. Schiller (Eds.), *National sovereignty and international communication* (pp. 195–216). Norwood: Ablex.

Gurtov, M. (1988). *Global politics in the human interest.* London: Lynne Rienner.

Halal, W. E. (1989). A unified planet suddenly seems possible. In *Futures, 21(6),* 555–561.

Heller, A. (1988). On *formal democracy.* In J. Keane (Ed.), *Civil society and the state* (pp. 129–145). London: Verso.

Heller, J. (1988). *Picture this.* New York: Ballantine Books.

Henderson, H. (1989). Mutual development. Towards new criteria and indicators. *Futures, 21*(6), 571–584.

Hodges, M. (1978). Integration theory. In T. Taylor (Ed.), *Approaches and theory in international relations* (pp. 237–256). New York: Longman.

Marien, M. (1989). Driving forces and barriers to a sustainable global economy. *Futures, 21*(6), 563–570.

Mitchell, C. R. (1984). World society as cobweb. States, actors and systemic processes. In M. Banks (Ed.), *Conflict in world society* (pp. 59–72). Brighton, OK: Wheatsheaf Books.

Mitchell, J. M. (1986). *International cultural relations.* London: Allen & Unwin.

OECD Development Centre. (1989). *Programme of research, 1990–1992.* Paris: Author.

Partsch, K. J. (1982). Fundamental principles of human rights: Self-determination, equality and non-discrimination. In K. Vasak (Ed.), *The international dimensions of human rights* (Vol. I, pp. 61–86). Westport, CT: Greenwood Press.

Rangarajan, L. N. (1985). *The limitation of conflict.* London: Croom Helm.

Renteln, A. D. (1990). *International human rights. Universalism versus relativism.* London: Sage.

Robertson, R. (1990). Mapping the global condition: Globalization as the central concept. In M. Featherstone (Ed.), *Global culture, nationalism, globalization, and modernity* (p. 15–30). London: Sage.

Sagasti, F. R. (1990). International cooperation in a fractured global order. *Futures, 22*(4), 417–421.

Schiller, H. I. (1981). *Who knows: Information in the age of the Fortune 500.* Norwood, NJ: Ablex.

Schiller, H. I. (1984). *Information and the crisis economy.* Norwood, NJ: Ablex.

Schiller, H. I. (1989). *Culture Inc. The corporate takeover of public expression.* New York: Oxford University Press.

Schiller, H. I. (1990). The global commercialization of culture. *Directions, 4*(1), 1–4.

Sid-Ahmed, M. (1990). The coming global civilization. *IFDA Dossier, 77,* 89–92.

Smith, A. D. (1990). Towards a global culture? In M. Featherstone (Ed.), *Global culture, nationalism, globalization, and modernity* (pp. 171–191). London: Sage.

The South Commission. (1990). *The challenge to the South.* Oxford: Oxford University Press.

Steinberger, H. (1987). Sovereignty. In R. Bernhardt (Ed.), *Encyclopedia of public international law* (pp. 397–418). Amsterdam: North-Holland.

Sustainable development. Guide to the report of the world commission on environment and development. (1990). Geneva: The Center for Our Common Future.

Taishoff, M. N. (1987). *State responsibility and the direct broadcast satellite.* London: Frances Pinter.

Van Dinh T., & Porter, R. (1986). Is the concept of national sovereignty outdated? In J. Becker, G. Hedebro, L. Paldan (Eds.), *Communication and domination* (pp. 120–128). Norwood: Ablex.

NOTES

[1] In the preface to *National Sovereignty and International Communication* (1979) Kaarle Nordenstreng and Herbert I. Schiller write: "It seems to us that the concept of national sovereignty will increasingly emerge as a point of reflection for the most fundamental issues of international communication." In fact, the earlier reader preceding the present publication focused on the basic contemporary issues of international communication with the concept of national sovereignty as "the springboard for a unifying perspective" (p. xiv).

[2] The significance of such choices can be demonstrated if one were to propose to switch the concept *development* for the concept of *empowerment.*

[3] Some US $900 billion is spent annually for military security against, some US $46 billion for the security of sustainable development. Data from the Worldwatch Institute, Henderson (1989, p. 582).

[4] See Gurtov (1988, p. 180): "The Law of the Sea Treaty, signed by 119 nations in 1982, established and important globalist principle—that the planet's undersea wealth is the common heritage of mankind.

[5] It needs to be observed here that it was logical that the NIIO issue was addressed in realist discourse. It would have been very difficult to mobilize support within the multilateral system for the demands had realist language not been employed.

[6] One cannot escape the impression that states by and large perceive of their own citizens as their worst enemies and as more threatening than other states. As Joseph Heller comments on the leaders of the Soviet Union and the United States, "Leaders in both places never seemed to hate each other as much as they hated members of their own populations who differed with them" (Heller, 1988, p. 90).

[7] It should be observed that it is not sufficient to stress the bipolarity of state and society. Civil society also needs protection against those corporate legal entities that control large parts of national and international economies and global cultural production. The tendency to include these actors in civil society reflects the successful lobby of industrial conglomerates to be seen as private citizens. Recent trends in U.S. and West-European jurisdiction that grant corporate entities the status of private citizen imply the extension of free speech protection to forms of commercial speech. As the corporations take over more means and places of public expression (in the performing arts, the museums, the mass media, and the shopping malls), public space needs defended against both commercial raiders and the state. The takeover of public space by commercial interests is well documented and analyzed by Schiller (1989).

[8] Sid-Ahmed (1990, p. 91): "In fact, the question of curtailing national sovereignty raised a still more important question, namely, that of depriving weaker states of prerogatives which protect them from stronger states in a world still marked by uneven development.... Obviously, I could not accept the principle of placing constraints on national sovereignty at a time certain peoples of the Third World, such as the Palestinians, are still suffering from the non-recognition of this right."

Chapter 17
New Global Order and Cultural Ecology

Hamid Mowlana

The last decades of the 20th century have had the vibrations of earthquake about them. The world shuddered. It was neither an "end of ideology" (Bell, 1960), a convergence between capitalism and socialism as sociologist Daniel Bell had predicted, nor "the end of history," (Fukuyama, 1989), an unabashed victory of economic and political liberalism, as political analyst of the American conservative wing, Francis Fukuyama, had explained. Simply, history cracked open; the quest for new ideologies began. New leaders and followers came darting out, with dark surprises for some and the light of hope for others. American politics, Islamic culture, Japanese technology—to cite a few—ventured into new and experimental regions: uplands of new enlightenments, some people thought, and quagmires of the id. The years were also pivotal. They produced vivid "theaters" of operations: Vietnam, Iran, Lebanon, Afghanistan, Nicaragua, Panama, Chile, China, South Africa, Kuwait, Iraq, and, of course, Eastern Europe and the Soviet Union, not to mention the developments from Kashmir to Algeria and from Northern Ireland to South Africa. A spirit of change seemed to pervade the political, economic, and cultural climates of the world.

QUEST FOR A NEW CULTURAL ORDER

It is precisely in this environment that cultural forces have come into play globally. As international relations expand into a multitude of diverse interests and structures, ranging from military to political, from economic to cultural spheres, the question of communication ecology, and the environment in which a new structure is taking its roots, occupies a prominent role. The growth in recent years of both fora and literature in the area of ethical and moral dimensions of international relations illustrates the centrality of value systems and the attention given to the symbolic environment created by information technology. The ideological, religious, and spiritual struggles of the last 10 years highlight both the urgency and depth of cultural clashes in international relations (see Mowlana & Wilson, 1990; Van Dinh; 1987, Smythe, 1981; Shari-ati, 1980; Walker, 1984; Said, 1978; Chay, 1990; Mattelart, 1990; Schiller, 1990).

Embedded in the rhetoric and conduct of international politics over this period is convincing evidence of the interlocking of ideology and technology, and with this a direct or indirect call on the part of individuals and even nation states for a new information ecology with culture at its center. Nowhere is this better illustrated than by looking at the events in the Middle East and the United States involvement in that part of the world over the last several decades. For example, while in 1991 the strategy of "information dominance" (Mowlana, 1990a) and high technology enabled the United States to gain victory over the secular and aggressive regime of Iraq, in 1979 Washington's persistent effort to keep the Shah of Iran in power and to prevent the Islamic revolution was indeed unsuccessful. Thus, any discussion of a new world order must take into account the broader ecological/communication context as well as the diversities of global culture. What are the sources of legitimacy and authority in contemporary global politics and how embedded are these sources in current institutional arrangements of national and international relations? What methods of accountability can be instituted to insure the defense of the global public interest and the world society at large? Will the new world order be introduced internationally in such a way that developing countries become increasingly dependent?

Long before Canadian Marshall McLuhan's phrase *the global village* became popular, American Wendell Willkie, with an enthusiasm touched off by modern air transport, popularized the phrase *one world*. The complex feelings and ideas now generally associated with these phrases, however, were not originally Willkie's or McLuhan's discourse. These phrases have a long history.

The fact that the world is one in astronomical or technological senses, as a single planet located in the gravitational field of a definite star, is not of political, economic, and cultural importance. Historical geography depends upon an Einsteinian rather than a Newtonian function. Despite technological and scientific development, including the tremendous growth of communication and information hardware/software over the last several decades, the large majority of residents of this global village live in undignified conditions of illiteracy, disease, hunger, unemployment, and malnutrition and still are deprived of the basic tools of modern communication and knowledge. The irony is well-captured by an Indian writer:

> If there were 100 residents in this global village, only one would get the opportunity for education beyond school level, 70 would be unable to read and write. Over 50 would be suffering from malnutrition, and over 80 would live in substandard housing. Six of the 100 would hold off the entire income of the village. How would these six live in peace with their neighbours without arming themselves to the teeth and supplying arms to those willing to fight their side? (Vilanilam 1989, p. 171)

One of the most crucial questions that faces them with the coming of the so-called *information explosion* and *information society* is the ultimate control of information processing and technology in the contemporary electronic age and the gradual disappearance of oral or traditional culture that has been a major resistance force in the face of cultural domination. The concept of secular society was introduced into the complex life of Islamic lands at the time when the forces of resistance were at a minimum. With the new awareness, and the degree of mobilization and cultural resurgence that we have witnessed during the last decades in Islamic communities around the world, the introduction of the information revolution and the entry into the information society seem to land on rocky soil.

The crucial question for the Islamic societies is whether the emerging global information communication community is a moral and ethical community or just another stage in the unfolding pictures of the transformation in which the West is the center and the Islamic world the periphery. Throughout Islamic history, especially in the early centuries, information was not a commodity but a moral and ethical imperative. Is information society a kind of "network community" in which a new rationalism is likely to impose a policy of radical instrumentation under which social problems will be treated as technical problems and citizens will be replaced by experts? Will the new technologies of information encourage the centralization of decision making and the fragmentation of society leading to the replacement of forms of community life with an exasperated individualism? Is information society in a position to produce qualitative changes in traditional forms of communication and eventually to transform social structures, and will such new structures require new ethics? Thus, it seems that the discourse and concepts of global order now at the center of world politics both celebrate the arrival of a new communication ecology and hold the key to greater information control.

THE INFORMATION SOCIETY PARADIGM

I shall begin this analysis with the question whether the global information community now emerging will facilitate or impede the social use of information of the Islamic community. The answer lies in examining the elements of the so-called information society, which is central to the dominant model of economic, political, social, and cultural activities of the United States and a number of other countries. It also calls for an examination of the broader conception of social life that underlines the Islamic model community and the state.

At the center of the controversy are two visions of society, the Information Society Paradigm and the Islamic Community Paradigm. On the intellectual and philosophical levels, the philosophy and theory of information and communication have replaced transcendental discourse as the prime concern of philosophical reflection in the west. On the practical and policy levels, the Information Society Paradigm in the West has come to portray the ideology of neomodernism, postmodernism, or postindustrialism without abandoning the capitalist economic and social systems that continue to characterize its core. Thus, the Information Society Paradigm is presented as "the realization of society that brings about a general flourishing state of human intellectual creativity, instead of affluent material consumption" (Masuda, 1981, p. 3). According to this assertion, the relationship between the state, the society, and the individual will be determined by the production of information value and not material value. Thus, information society, as it is argued, will bring about the transformation of society into a completely new type of human society. Some of the characteristics of the Information Society Paradigm, according to its proponents are "spirit of globalism," "the satisfaction of achieved goals," "participatory democracy," "realization of time value," "voluntary community," and a "synergetic economy" (pp. 31–33). Furthermore, we are told that such an information society is based on services; therefore, it is a game between persons (see Bell, 1973). What counts is information. The central person is the professional who is educated and trained to provide the kinds of skills the information society requires. The information society also is supposed to be a supersecular knowledge society based on the nation-state system.

THE ISLAMIC COMMUNITY PARADIGM

In a number of fundamental ways, the notion of the Information Society Paradigm and the emerging global information community runs counter to the basic conception of Islamic community and a number of principal tenets of Islam. More specifically as it relates to the central questions posed in this chapter, four areas of inquiry are fundamental to the understanding of the Islamic Community Paradigm and its experience with the West. These are: (a) the world view of *tawhid*, (b) the sociology of knowledge, (c) the integration of personality, and (d) the meaning of society and the state.

The World View of *Tawhid*

The Islamic Community Paradigm is the paradigm of the revelation and not the paradigm of information. It is Islam and the theory of *tawhid* (the unity of God, human beings, and universe) that determines the parameters of information, and not the other way around. In the world of natural and transcendental orders, it is the latter that a Muslim looks to for the values by which to control the direction of the former; therefore, information and knowledge are not value free but have normative, ethical, and moral imperatives. The world view of *tawhid* provides meaning, spirit, and aim to life and commits the individual to an ethic of action. In short, it is the eternal principle of *tawhid* that regulates the Islamic Community Paradigm and does not allow itself to be subservient, in whole or in part, to any other paradigm.

Thus, from the perspective of Islam the science paradigm, developed largely as a result of the industrial revolution, and the information paradigm, now promoted to depict the postindustrial societies, both are partial and in the state of change. A major dualism and contradiction created in the Islamic countries over the last 100 years was precisely the fact that the Western science paradigm was imported and presented as a dominant force to guide the processes of economic and social development. Now, the Information Society Paradigm is being echoed as the realization of society that brings about a general flourishing of human intellectual activity and spiritualism. Why should the Islamic communities wait for the coming of this information paradigm to bring about spiritualism when the world view of Islam is founded on spiritualism and human activities in the first place with its elaborate legal, judicial, and ethical principle?

The Sociology of Knowledge

The contemporary information revolution that underlines the Information Society Paradigm should not be portrayed as a unique phenomenon in human civilization, nor should it be treated as a separate phenomenon from the Islamic Community Paradigm. As I have argued elsewhere, in all three stages of technological and societal development—agricultural, industrial, and now the postindustrial—information has been the central and most pervasive and common element in their development processes (Mowlana, 1986, pp. 166–173). Information in the form of skill and knowledge preceded capital formation and, in many ways, characterized all three stages. If we accept this assumption, it simply means that information and knowledge are not the exclusive property of industrialized societies.

Indeed, the Islamic Community Paradigm was responsible for the information and scientific revolution that characterized the medieval ages. What is known as a dark age of the medieval period in Western history was a golden age in the Islamic community, which stretched from Indonesia and the Pacific in the east to Spain and the Atlantic coast in the west, from central Asia and the Himalayas in the north to the southern African nations and the Indian Ocean. Islamic community and civilization in Spain were, during the middle ages, a source of worldwide progress in information and science. While Europe was passing through a phase of ignorance, the schools of Cordoba and Granada became the centers of light for the continent. When the ancient classical thought was buried in the darkness of monasteries, the Islamic scholars, philosophers, and scientists were producing a variety of knowledge in Central Asian cities of Bukhara and Samarkand and in the metropolitan libraries of the Middle East from Ray in Iran to Baghdad in Iraq. The knowledge acquired not only was exponential in nature but also was molded into technology such as mechanics and agriculture.

The orientation of Islam toward temporal life in this period was highly significant, and it left a deep impression on the course of information science and technology. The fundamental difference between the Greek culture of the classic period and the Islamic culture of the medieval time lay in the fact that, while the Greek mind was riveted on the study of mankind only, the Islamic culture encouraged its scientists to study the whole universe. Thus, the scientific and information age that marked the development of Islam between 700 and 1300 witnessed, not only the spiritual earnings, but also the temporal, and with them came the enormous contribution of Islam to such areas as mathematics, astronomy, chemistry, biology, medicine, as well as those in philosophy, literature, history, geography, demography, politics, sociology, and economics. The Muslims, therefore, developed interests in interstate relations and international problems and, as a consequence, a great appreciation for knowledge and power.

The concept of the unity of God and the brotherhood of mankind—the two fundamental concepts within the theory of *tawhid*—gave sustenance to the knowledge and scientific inquiry of this period (for example, see Mutahhari, 1985, 1986). The concept of the unity of man knocked down the geographical barriers and racial and linguistic walls which had been promoted earlier. The Greeks systematized, generalized, and theorized about knowledge, but the systematic investigation and scientific methods, prolonged observation, and measurement belonged to the Islamic era of information and knowledge. What we know as modern science arose in Europe as a result of this new spirit of inquiry which was introduced by Muslim scientists to Europe before the period of the Renaissance. This is an important point for the appreciation of Islamic culture and characteristic of the information/science era that transferred the static quality of the classical Greek to one of the dynamic universe in terms of the infinite in space and time. Islam underlined reason and experience put emphasis on nature and history as sources of human knowledge.

In the realm of information, Islam regards both self and world as sources of knowledge. The method of observation and experiment, the scientific method of induction, emphasis on sense perception as a source of knowledge, all belong to this period of information and scientific revolution in Islamic history. Indeed, had it not been for the fall of Cordoba and the sack of Baghdad and Ray at the hands of foreign invaders in the 12th and 13th centuries, Europe would not have had to wait three centuries to see the dawn of its scientific renaissance.[1]

The scope of this information and scientific revolution has been recognized by many historians in the West and is well summarized in the words of Briffault:

> For although there is not a single aspect of European growth in which the decisive influence of Islamic culture is not traceable, nowhere is it so clear and momentous as in the genesis of that power which constitutes the permanent distinctive force of the modern world, and the supreme source of its victory—natural science and the scientific spirit. (Briffault, 1938; quoted in Igbal, 1982/1986, p. 130)

Information was not neutral but a social and cultural entity. Its conversion into knowledge, its pursuance and understanding in religion, social, and natural sciences necessitated the study of linguistic, grammatical, and even speculative fields. The speculative aspect of this knowledge, especially in the matter of beliefs, was responsible for the development of the science of *Kalam* (scholastic) and the discipline of *Tasawwuf* (mysticism/spiritualism). At the same time in its comprehensive character, legal science or *Figh,* developed among Muslims, and, along with that, biographical dictionaries, which were one of the characteristics of the era.

Al Farabi (870–950), Alpharbius of Latin scholastics, known as the second Socrates, made original contributions to the fields of ontology, cosmology, rational psychology, and political economy. The great Christian scholastics Albert the Great and St. Thomas Aquinas acknowledged their indebtedness to him in the development of their own works. His views are extremely close to those of Spencer and Rousseau in political theory. His treatises on the "Opinion of the People of the Ideal city" and "Political Economy" resemble the Hobbesian law of nature, Rousseau's theory of social contract, and the Nietzchean principle of "will to power."

Al Bairuni (973–1014), the father of geodesy, was a great scientist, mathematician, astronomer, and historian who searched into every branch of human knowledge. His theory of the universe, his work on cosmogony, calendar, and chronology, his critique on Aristotle's Theory of Moving Cause (in which Bairuni advanced the notion of a dynamic and changing world), all these made the 11th century the "Age of Bairuni." His travel to India and his monumental work on the subcontinent is only one example of the emphasis given to data gathering and information by the Muslim scholars of the medieval period. He emphasized the importance of the *akhbar wa rawayat,* or information, news, and traditions, in understanding the international relations of the time and the propagation of knowledge "to speak truth."

Al Ghazali (1058–1111) was one of the greatest and most original thinkers of all time. In reviewing his work, one finds traces of ideas and theories that later became Descartes' method of doubt, Hume's skepticism, Kant's criticism of pure reason, and the spiritual empiricism of a number of philosophers of modern times. He doubted the evidence of sense perception and for the first time advanced the notion that there is no necessity to any causal connection. As Hume had found out centuries later, and as Al Ghazali argued extensively that what we call causality is mere "following upon" and repetition, leading us to conclude that a cause is usually followed by its effect. His works began to be translated as early as middle of the 12th century, first in Latin and later in Hebrew.[2]

The Islamic Community Paradigm also was responsible for the production of hundreds of great literary and creative works in poetry, symbolism, and mysticism by such giants of history as Ibn Arabi, Mowlana Rumi, Hafiz, Sa'di, Nizami, and Attar. All of these were important works in the expansion of Islamic *Weltanschaung,* including a communication and information world view that has yet to be examined and explored fully. They are not simply the literary and poetic interpretation of Islamic values but also have significant sociocultural and psychonormative dimensions that characterized the Islamic society.

Unlike the Roman and Persian empires, which had to rely on military and administrative machineries to hold the various nationalities together, the early Islamic state had the unique advantage of having in its possession the Divine Book—the *Quar'an*—and the Divine Law—the *Shari'ah*—which eliminated national political boundaries and accelerated the process of physical and social mobilities across the vast Islamic land. Exchange of goods and services, as well as the dissemination of information and science within the Islamic model of community, needed communication. This led to the establishment of new postal, transportation and navigation networks as well as publication of geographical guides and maps detailed in historico-economic descriptions of each place, with the names of cities and towns arranged alphabetically. The time and place of daily postal services in each town was announced in advance by governors so that both official and private letters could be dispatched in time from such destinations as Egypt to Central Asia. The calendar created by Umar Khyyam outdistanced by far any other scientific calendar including that of the Gregorian period. Muslim mariners established navigational networks stretching from Basrah in Iraq to the coasts of China. Today, words such as *arsenal, cable, monsoon, douane,* and *tariff,* which are all of Arabic origin, are testimony to the communication and information age that characterized Islamic history during the medieval period.

Acquisition of knowledge is one of the highest values in Islam. However, it was the conception of society as an integrated whole within the Islamic Community Paradigm that directed the course of information and scientific revolutions of the middle ages in Islamic civilization, and not the nationalistic, economic, political, or corporate interests. In Islam, the ideal and the real, that is, the social policy and information, should not be developed separately since they are not irreconcilable opposing forces.

Stagnation in the Islamic world over the last five centuries began precisely when the internal forces in terms of dynastic disorders and conflict, and external forces in terms of colonialism, began the process of disintegration. The demarcation between Islamic and modern science, on the one hand, and adrift toward luxury, materialism, and metaphysics on the other, set the Islamic community into decline. Thus, Islamic thought on science and the arts remained practically stationary. The process of dependence on Western science and technology began to take its course. Impressed by the new round of scientific and industrial revolutions in Europe, weakened by the division of the community into smaller units, fearful of the rise of the "new order," the rulers of the Islamic world began to embrace the Western models of development making themselves subservient societies under the rising international economic and political systems. The rise of "orientalism," complicated by the dependence established on the Westernized education system, produced a class of intellectuals and modern bureaucrats whose political leadership helped to accelerate and legitimize this process of disintegration and disunity.

The Integration of Personality

The Information Society Paradigm is based on secularism, while the Islamic Community Paradigm is founded on a religiopolitical, socioeconomic, and cultural system based on an elaborate legal code and jurisprudence. The *ullamas,* as scholars of the Islamic religious sciences, especially jurisprudence, are unlike the information experts and intellectual class of secular societies, whose tasks center around economics, politics, and law alone, and unlike the priesthood class of Christianity, who are preoccupied with theological questions alone. The *ullamas* or scholars of Islam are considered *marja-i-taqlid* (source of practices), whose authoritative guidance is followed in matters of Islamic polity, law, economics, and culture.

Thus, secularism becomes alien to Islamic social and political thought when it attempts to separate religion from politics, ideas from matter, and rationality from cosmic vision. Islam views all these as an integrative whole. Consequently, Western secularism was not welcomed into the Islamic communities and did not develop into a positive virtue because it symbolized the atheism and materialism of the West—a process of materialism in which technologies, methodologies, and ideologies were imported from Europe and later America.

The Islamic conception of secular (versus religious) life is difficult to describe, since there is no demarcation between properly political and other kinds of institutions. Islam encompasses all aspects of social and political life and formulated norms of conduct. Since, fundamentally, there is no separation between religion and politics in Islam, the Islamic community has never constituted, either in theory or in practice, a theocracy, as was the case with Christianity in Europe. The term *theocracy* is both improper and paradoxical in Islamic history, because the heads of state in Islamic communities have never been religious chiefs alone as occurs in the Christian tradition. Moreover, a priestly class has never governed Muslim societies, since the concept of church is an institution foreign to Islam. No intermediary exists between the individual and God in Islam, and no person or organ has the authority to modify, amend, or complete the divine law, the *Quran*, and the *Sunnah*, the tradition.

The French Revolution gave rise to political and philosophical dimensions of modern secularism when it replaced the regime controlled by the Christian Church. In contrast, the Islamic Revolution in Iran was the end of the secular monarchy promoting Western models of development and the rise of an Islamic state based on the authority of Revelation and the Quran. Whereas the execution of Louis XVI symbolized the death of sacred monarchy and the rise of secular polity in France, the removal of the Shah marked the death of the secular *taghut,* or oppressor, and the reappearance of spiritual and temporal power in Iran. "Modernization" movements in Islamic societies over the last century have failed because they were unable to elaborate coherent doctrine based on the unity of spiritual and temporal powers. In the Islamic Community Paradigm these two forces are inseparable.

The Meaning of Society and the State

The Islamic notion of community, or *ummah,* has no equivalent in either Western thought or historical experience. *Ummah* is conceived in a universal context and is not subject to territorial, linguistic, racial, and nationalistic limitations. Thus, the Islamic Community Paradigm is not based solely on either politicoeconomic or communication-information foundations. The community is a universal society and polity whose membership includes the widest possible variety of nationalities and ethnic groups but whose commitment to Islam as a faith and ideology binds them to a specific social order. Sovereignty belongs to God and not to the state, ruler, or people. Therefore, the concept of *ummah* is not synonymous with "the people," or "the nation," or "the state," which are the vocabulary of modern international relations and are determined by communication grids, information flows, geography, language and history or the combination of these.

It was the concept of *ummah* that for centuries guided the Islamic state from the time of the Prophet, and made it a world power. The border of such a community is determined by Islamic beliefs and values and not by geographical, political, and treaty boundaries. This paradigm supports the notion of nationality but rejects the concept of nationalism. It acknowledges and respects diversity but it emphasizes unity. Thus, the Islam "Community Paradigm" runs counter to the nation-state system, which characterizes the current global political system. This includes the Muslim lands that are divided into small political entities unable and unwilling to mobilize their economic, cultural, natural, and human resources under a unified Islamic state.

There is a misconception in the West and among the general public that Islam is only a religion. The division of the world into sacred and profane, religious and secular, priesthood and laity, does not exist in Islam. The separation of politics from ethics, and politics from economics, is all unnatural under the Islamic Community Paradigm. Islam is a total life system and, hence, the Islamic *ummah* provides guidance for the conduct of human activity. Only a small section of the Islamic law deals with rituals and personal ethics; the large part concerns social order. Unlike in the West, where religion is a private affair for the citizen, in Islam religion is a public affair. Whereas in liberalism the political and communication sovereignty stands for the sovereignty of persons, the sovereignty in the Islamic community stands for the sovereignty of Islamic principles.

Similarly, the notion of *fundamentalism* or *fundamentalist* so often used in the Western media discourse has no place in the Islamic dictionary. Unlike the case in Christianity, there was no historical separation between religion and the state in Islam and thus no "fundamentalism" or "reformation," and if attempts were made by the late modernizers to do this, the process never succeeded. Thus, Islamic socioreligious ethics not only encompassed a person wholly but also shaped the conduct of the individual in general. In short, whereas modern ethics in the West became predominately social in nature, in Islamic societies that power remained social as well as religious.

It is precisely here that the Information Society Paradigm and the Islamic Community Paradigm have philosophic and strategic conflict, and this conflict has a cultural base and information-cultural consequences. For example, ever since the Islamic Revolution in Iran in 1979, the term *Islamic fundamentalists* has been created and used in the European and American mass media primarily in reference to the militant resistance of those in the Islamic world, especially the *Shi'a,* who strictly oppose the interventionist policies of the West in their lands in all forms. The Saudis, who are *Sunnie Wahhabies,* are not mentioned as "fundamentalists" in the Western media presumably because the Saudis are "moderate" and have close ties to the West.

In sum, the nation-state system has divided the Islamic *ummah* into smaller parts, a process of disintegration and political frontierism that emerged in the early part of this century. The failure of the ruling elites of the Islamic countries to challenge the dominant political and economic paradigms which have laid the foundation of the existing world order has slowed down the grass-roots polity characterizing the Islamic Community Paradigm. The Islamic state was founded by the prophet in 622 A.D. in Medinah. The political culture and the constitution which cultivated this state kept Islam as a world power until the end of World War I, despite the internal turmoil and division created within the larger Islamic law. The Islamic *ummah,* now divided into various states, is being confronted with a new order that has its base in modern information and communication technologies. Will the new order bring communities closer together, or will it tend to atomize relationships which are already precarious?

For centuries, the Islamic culture maintained a fine balance between oral and print cultures and between interpersonal and intermedia communication (see Mowlana, 1989, 1990b,c). The print and electronic culture, primarily in the West, helped to concentrate power in the hands of a few and to contribute to the centralization of the state apparatus and corporate monopoly. On the contrary, the oral mode of communication in Islamic societies helped to decentralize and diffuse the power of the state and economic interests and establish a counterbalance of authority in the hands of those who were grounded in oral tradition. The individuals maintained their ability to communicate within their own community and beyond, despite the influence of state propaganda and modern institutions. The resurgence of Islam and the political and revolutionary movements within the Islamic countries, led by traditional authorities and institutions such as the *ullama,* are only one example of the potential use of oral culture and its confrontation with modernism inherited in mediated electronic cultures. Today, the information needs of many countries are manipulated primarily by market interests and the media, and by the dominant global powers, and not necessarily by the articulation of the genuine needs of individuals, groups, and societies.

Social justice and economic order are at the heart of the Islamic Community Paradigm and so are the notions of globalization and interdependency. What is presented as a discourse of globalization today is a kind of "complex interdependency," a process of "networking," which brings interconnectedness in the sphere of economic, financial, natural resources, and technologies without generating a

meaningful cultural framework which characterizes the community. In the West among the early examples of such writers were Hugo Grotius and Immanuel Kant (Grotius, 1939; Kant, 1957). Grotius is commonly know as the founder of Western international law, and Kant as the first cosmopolitan thinker. Although from different perspectives, and with different aims in mind, both personalities wish to assign a liberal morality to international relation: Grotius on the basis of the "natural law" of states, and Kant, on the basis of individual human rights; however, both emphasized their thinking from the perspective of the nation-state system.

From the Marxist and the neo-Marxist points of view, globalization was nothing more than the expansion of capitalism as a "world system." Through this process, different national units are assigned different roles in a global division of labor. However, as Wallerstein, one of the proponents of this thesis, explains, while the states are no longer regarded as the units of analysis, nevertheless, they keep playing a very crucial role in maintaining the global status quo which features a privileged core of states against one exploited periphery (Wallerstein, 1974, 1980, 1990).

And who are among the periphery side of this equation? Notably, the more than one billion Muslim people who constitute one-fourth of the world's population. Who will assume responsibility for maintaining contact with this large population and for establishing communication between individuals and the *ummah*'s larger institutions? In the medieval ages and later, the provisions of the Islamic Law, known as *Shari'ah,* made it possible for industrial and agricultural goods of non-Islamic nations to move freely into and out of the Islamic territories. Globalism was as much a fact of international trade of this early time as it was of cultural, educational, and social consciousness of the Muslim world. Indeed, the Islamic Community Paradigm created the first comprehensive welfare system, abolished frontier custom houses, and encouraged truly free trade. Today, the Islamic countries, with their vast and rich natural resources, capital, and potential geopolitical and strategic locations, are incorporated into a global order that contributes to their fragmentation and not to their integration into a unified community.

DARK SURPRISES OR LIGHT OF HOPE

What emerges from these historical developments in regards to both the Information Society Paradigm and the Islamic Community Paradigm are the two cultural ecological systems that account for a multitude of economic, political, and social factors. This larger cultural ecological sphere will determine the parameter of actions as well as the possibility of convergence or even of dominance of one paradigm over the other. Furthermore, the lack of comprehension or the neglect of this broad cultural framework is responsible for much of the inability to understand, explain, or even predict the social and political movements of our time.

Contemporary global events took many American and European international relations experts and social scientists by surprise. In a pattern well established immediately after World War II, millions of dollars were spent on social science research to learn just how the political and communication systems worked in such lands as the Soviet Union, Eastern Europe, and the Middle East. Yet, in the spring of 1989, almost no one in the West entertained, let alone predicted, the unraveling of the communist regimes, the fall of the Berlin wall, and the unification of Germany. The "experts" in academia, the government, and the media were wrong: The third rise of Germany in this century was heading for a supposedly "different" ending than its precedents in 1914 and 1939. The Russians, Czechs, Poles, and Rumanians were indeed successful in attempting to challenge their political institutions. Simulation models, game theories, and bargaining and decision-making texts so dearly memorized by graduate students and admired by their teachers were of little help to explain these phenomena. A few scholars and observers who had predicted these developments were either ignored or put aside.

A decade earlier, virtually no one in the West foretold the resurgence of Islam and its consequences in the Middle East and around the world. The Islamic Revolution in Iran was perhaps the greatest imbroglio and embarrassment social science research and methodology had suffered in some time. Practically no one in main stream social science, the government, or the media could have guessed that Mohammad Reza Pahlavi, the Shah of Iran and close friend of the West, would be overthrown by Ayatollah Ruhollah Imam Khomeini, a man then relatively unknown to the West (Mowlana, 1986, pp.175–176). If the resilence of the Iranian people to withstand the 8 years of war imposed by Iraq surprised observers, the alignment of the West and the conservative states of the Persian Gulf with Saddam Hussein of Iraq in the 1980s, and their realignment against him following his subsequent invasion of Kuwait in the 1990s, were indeed astonishing.

What went wrong? Why did the observers neither prophesy nor delineate the communication, political, and cultural landscapes that prevail today? Was this because they paid too much heed to those elements in modern life which characterize formal institutions and

formal ideologies? Or did they simply misconstrue the processes of social change taking place in our time? Were they misled by their cultural bias and the pattern of discourse which had dominated their social interactions? How critical were their "critical" methodologies?

Elsewhere, I have tried to demonstrate that the economic determinism schools of thought and the geopolitical power-oriented traditions of "realist" phase of international relations all have certain commonalities:

- They share a power-driven notion of international relations that is either political or economic or both;
- they are state-centric in that they believe in the notion of the nation-state as a "political" state;
- they make communication and cultural factors subservient to political, economic, and technological superstructures;
- they tend to classify social relations as well as international relations with natural and biological science, and
- they tend to study and measure what is measurable, observable, and tangible.

These fundamental assumptions make it impossible to separate some of the world's most distinct activities, which are not in a simple feedback relationship to politics, work, and production. Global politics and its sources of power not only include tangible resources and their allocations, such as economics, military, and natural resources, but also less measurable and little understood elements which I have labeled as *intangible resources*. These include belief and value systems, communication, and knowledge. Both tangible and intangible resources can be defined in terms of control over particular base values and the flow of information in society or in international systems, reflecting the ability to act and to affect outcome. Thus, the transformation of power is comprised of two dimensions: the *access* to necessary resources to act, and the *ability* and *will* to convert these sources into actions. Power configurations in national and global systems involve more than just the reallocation of economic, political, and technological bases. These involve multidimensional factors with authority, legitimacy, and will playing crucial roles.

Indeed, in the closing decade of the 20th century, there were some reflections among the group called "strategic thinkers" that there must be more to international relations than simple military-diplomatic situations. They were realizing that the world they had known for four decades, since World War II, could not go on forever. With such global development and its molecular ferment of popular movement and immanent relation between capital and information, we had entered the plain of chaotic digital transformation in which human beings, real estate, social relations, and international politics now were converted into a complex and uncertain world. The unpredictability of international events, and insecurity dominating the major powers, are one side of the coin; the other in the increasing capacity of smaller nations to mobilize their populations and resources to challenge the old order and demand a new. The implosive collapse of the state-machine in which it becomes sucked into its own black-hole rationality through electronic and bureaucratic techniques is only one symptom of this phenomenon; the erosion of the legitimacy of the nation-state system in all its ideological forms is another.

The political-economic division of this planet into three distinct worlds was never scientific, and its reconceptualization into a single world is proving to be no better. The Third World is divided, as the Persian Gulf War and other events proved; the Second World and the Soviet Union have unraveled, and America and the rest of the First World are becoming increasingly irrelevant for the rest. To appreciate the transformation and the complexity of global politics, a communication and cultural perspective is indeed needed.

THE ECOLOGICAL DIMENSIONS OF
INTERNATIONAL RELATIONS

It now seems more imperative than ever to discuss global tension, not only in terms of explicitly economic, geopolitical, and military structures, but also equally in the context of cultural communication and information struggles. To suggest that culture and communication are crucial for analyses of international relations is not to view these areas as exclusive territories of the idealist approach to world politics that so often characterized the Wilsonian era of international politics and the more normative discourse of war and peace literature which followed the years immediately after the first and second World Wars. The post-Cold War era, I believe, will bring the cultural dimensions of world politics to its most prominent position.

For one, the reductionism of the conservative school of realpolitique, and that of radical political economy, which dominated the scholarly and policy fields for over four decades, proved incomplete in answering the many questions regarding developments around the world. Furthermore, the epistemological tradition of research, in which the realm of ideas was separated from that of matter, was not only historically specific to the tradition of Western philosophy and science

but also created a dualism which impeded the formulation of concepts and theories of a practical nature. Most important of all, the erosion of state legitimacy, and the political development that followed the events of Eastern Europe and the Soviet Union, combined with the economic crisis in the West and challenges emanating from non-Western culture, made the "inevitable" conduct of human affairs by the Western powers more problematic.

Today, as the West moves toward the Information Society Paradigm, the conceptions of justice, derived from civil society by the intellectual elites of the 19th and 20th centuries, have run into trouble. On the international level, the conventional argument was popularized that, if one wanted peace, one should prepare for war. The systems of autonomous nation states had little sense of community but strove for power and divergent interests under pluralism. For much of humankind, on national and international levels, culture became increasingly something that arrived in cans. Indeed, a contradiction developed between nationalism of the small powers and integration of the big powers. Thus, hegemony in the name of universalism was asserted by the big powers as small nations struggled against domination. Both realism and historical materialism directed attention to conflict. On the national and societal level, the line between civil rights and state rights became blurred.

Elsewhere, I have argued that the process of information and technological innovations, as it relates to communication between human beings and their environment and among peoples and nations, can be explained under what could be termed *the unitary theory of communication as ecology* (see Mowlana, forthcoming). I use the term *ecology* here in a broad sense to include all the symbolic environments in which human and technological communication takes place.

Thus, the major dimensions of this ecological terrain include the following: (a) ecology of goods and commodities, such as industrial and manufacturing items; (b) ecology of services, which includes banking, insurance, education; (c) ecology of warfare, meaning all the military and security hardware, software and the infrastructure therein; (d) ecology of information encompassing such processes as cultural industries and mass media; (e) ecology of habitat comprising such areas as demography, housing, physical environment, and pollution; and (f) ecology of ethics and morality referring to specific normative discourse such as religion, mores, laws, and social contracts (see Figure 1).

These six ecological terrains are not spatial but relational and integrative—that is, not only do we interact with these environments as separate and one-to-one bases, but also the interactions of all these

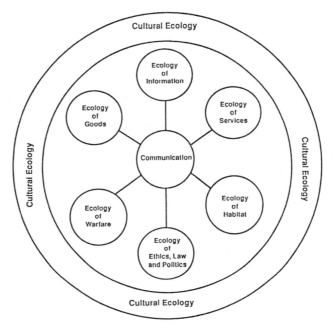

Figure 1. Unitary Model of Communication as Cultural Ecology: The order in which the six ecological dimensions are shown is not fixed and static, but rather dynamic and interchangeable.

six with each other and with human beings in an integrative form characterize the unique aspect of our civilization. Hence, our cultural, economic, and political environments cannot be understood completely unless we turn our attention to this unitary phenomenon in terms of communication and culture. Thus, our notion of self, society, and universe is very much shaped by this ecological view and the way we perceive language, literacy, arts, sciences, and, in short, reality.

Our world view under such an integrated ecological perspective is shaped by at least three distinct actors and participants: (a) the state, (b) groups and institutions, and (c) individuals. For example, the linkage between ecology of goods and commodities with that of ecology of services has created an environment of international economic and financial complex. In the same way, the network of ecology of goods and commodities, when intersected with the ecology of warfare produces the so called military industrial complex.

International propaganda and political discourse are as much the result of the linkages between ecology of warfare and the ecology of information as the mass media and cultural industry complex are in major part the result of ecology of information and those of ethics and morality, etc. Take, for example, the integrative nature of the meaning of such phrases as *democracy* or *individual rights,* with that of automotive industry. Here the automobile is not only the means of transportation and mobility, and even prestige and wealth, but also, in a very quintessential way, is perceived as the individual's freedom of action as well as rights.

In the same manner, ecology terrains are created when military is linked to security, private space to public space, data to knowledge, dependency to interdependency, and progress to decay. The dualism as well as simplification and mystification in contemporary international politics, at least since World War II, can be well illustrated by the relations and the discourse of the great powers in such reductive terms as capitalism versus socialism, liberalism versus authoritarianism, dependency versus interdependence, and internationalism versus nationalism.

CONCLUSION

Two major developments now characterize the state of international communication and international relations as we approach the 21st century. First, a new global order based on The Information Society Paradigm has been in the making. It is the new order of the advanced industrialized nations which has evolved as a result of a number of economic, political, and technological developments (see Mowlana, 1991). The world also is witnessing a second development—a desire and, indeed, a quest for a new cultural order which goes beyond the simple notion of communication and information. The quest for The Islamic Community Paradigm is a manifestation of such a development. This new discourse, which has a potential for a major international and worldwide debate, makes communication and information concepts subservient to the broader notion of culture and social ecology.[3] The assumption that the global information and communication structure can or should be altered to a new form without first explaining that form and its cultural ecology is indeed premature.

Although "issue definition" such as trade, monetary systems, population growth, disarmament, food, environmental problems, security, war, and peace will remain the areas of negotiation, cooperation, and conflict among and between the nation states and institutions, it is the nature, direction, and development of the images and realities of the grand culture ecology discussed here that will determine the parameters of global actors and participants. It will be the source and determinants of power transformation as well of the future struggles within the international system. While the super-powers speak a similar language about the new world order, they do not mean to distribute and equalize power, but to seek national and international stability at the top of the global hierarchy with inequality of power below. The present dominant cultural ecology through its international communication network and intellectual-cultural power is determined to keep the centrality of the United States and a few European powers at the top in political, military, and economic affairs that necessitates inequality below in such cultural systems as Islam and others in the South.

The Eastern socialist systems are crumbling, but the alternative models for them are not clear; yet the centrality of the North is being increased as secular transcontinental Europe and North America form a cultural ecology over the southern half of this world. As the economic and political power of the former Soviet Union declines and as the former Eastern bloc nations are incorporated into the global market economy, the centuries-old cultural ties between Europe and America are bound to find new alliances and common ground. This is not simply a matter of economics and technology but has its roots in epistemological, ontological, linguistic, and cultural experience of the past. The East versus West Cold War may be over, but the South versus North Cold War is an emerging system. The demands for a new world order by the North and the demands for change and redistribution of resources and power by the South have cultural contexts and stem from different notions of politics and culture.

Today, the states are no longer the sole political and economic actors in the world. National elite structures, transnational institutions, and other groups to a large degree exert similar (parallel, if not identical) influence over the international system and its cultural ecology. It is precisely here that the relationship between political strategy and culture becomes evident. As the dominant powers monopolize the ability to create the norms and institutions of the international economic and political systems, the so-called *retribalized* and *nomadic* politics of other cultures in the form of states, institutions, and groups will be released in response to submerged cultural tendencies in changing societies.

REFERENCES

Arnold, T., & Guillaurne, A. (1960). *The legacy of Islam*. New York: Oxford University Press.

Bell, D. (1960). *The end of ideology*. New York: Free Press.

Bell, D. (1973). *The coming of post-industrial society*. New York: Basic Books.

Briffault, R. (1938). The making of humanity. In A.M. Iqbal, *The reconstruction of religious thought in Islam* (p. 130). Lahore, Pakistan: S.H. Muhammad Ashraf.

Chay, J. (Ed.). (1990). *Culture and international relations*. New York: Praeger.

Fukuyama, F. (1989, Summer). The end of history. *The National Interest*, 3–18.

Grotius, H. (1939). *The law of war and peace: Selections from De Jurebelli et Pacis* (W.S.M. Knight, Trans.). London: Peace Book.

Grunebaum, G. E., von. (1953). *Medieval Islam: A study of cultural orientation* (2nd ed.). Chicago, IL: University of Chicago Press.

Holt, P.M., Lambton, A.K.S., & Lewis, B. (Eds.). (1970). *The Cambridge history of Islam, Vol. 2*. London: Cambridge University Press.

Kant, I. (1957). *Perpetual peace*. New York: MacMillan.

Khaldun, I. (1967). *The mugaddimah (An introduction to history)* (F. Rosenthal, Trans.). London: Routledge & Kegan Paul.

Kohmeini, I. (1981). *Islam and revolution: Writings and declaration of Imam Khomeini* (H. Algar, Trans.). Berkeley, CA: Mizan.

MacDonald, D.B. (1903). *Development of Muslim theology, jurisprudence, and constitutional theory*. London: Routledge & Sons.

Masuda, Y. (1981). *Information society as post industrial society* (pp. 3, 31–33). Bethesda, MD: World Future Society.

Mattelart, A., (1990). *Communication and class struggle, 3: New historical subjects*. New York: International General.

Mizra, M.R., & Siddiqi, M.I. (1986). *Muslim contribution to science*. Lahore, Pakistan: Kazi.

Mowlana, H. (1979). Technology versus tradition: Communication in the Iranian revolution. *Journal of Communication, 29*(3), 107–112.

Mowlana, H. (1986). *Global information and world communication: New frontiers in international relations* (pp. 166–173, 175–176). White Plains, NY: Longman.

Mowlana, H. (1989). Communication and cultural settings: An Islamic perspective. *The Bulletin of the Institute for Communication Research, 33*, 1–21.

Mowlana, H. (1990). Objectives and aims of tabligh from the Islamic viewpoint: Toward a theory of communication and ethics. In M.J. Pelaez (Ed.), *Papers in comparative political science, Vol. XVI* (pp. 4627–4642). Malaga & Barcelona: University of Malaga Press.

Mowlana, H. (1990). Communication, ethics, and the Islamic tradition. In T.W. Cooper, C.G. Christians, F.F. Plude, & R.A. White (Eds.), *Communication ethics and global change* (pp. 137–146). White Plains, NY: Longman.

Mowlana, H. (1990). Geopolitics of communications and strategic aspects of the Persian Gulf. *The Iranian Journal of International Affairs, 11*(1), 85–106.

Mowlana, H. (1993). From technology to culture. In G. Gerbner, H. Mowlana, & K. Nordenstreng (Eds.), *The global media debate: Its rise, fall, and renewal*. Norwood, NJ: Ablex.

Mowlana, H. (forthcoming). Civil society, information society, and Islamic society: A comparative perspective. In S. Splichal, A. Calabrese, & C. Sparks (Ed.), *Information society and civil society: An international* dialogue on the changing world order. West Lafayette, IN: Purdue University Press.

Mowlana, H., & Wilson, L.J. (1990). The passing of modernity: Communication and the transformation of society. White Plains, NY: Longman.

Mutahhari, A.M. (1985). Fundamentals of Islamic thought: God, man, and the universe (R. Campbell, Trans.). Berkeley, CA: Mizan.

Mutahhari, A.M. (1986). Social and historical change: An Islamic perspective (R. Campbell, Trans.). Berkeley, CA: Mizan

Said, E. (1978). Orientalism. New York: Vintage.

Said, H., & Zahid, A. (1981). Al-Biruni: His times, life, and works. Karachi, Pakistan: Hamdard Foundation.

Sarton, G. (1950). Introduction to the history of science, Vols. I-III. Baltimore, MD: Williams & Wilkens.

Schiller, H.I. (1990). Culture, Inc. New York: Oxford.

Shari-ati, A. (1980). Marxism and other western fallacies (R. Campbell, Trans.). Berkeley, CA: Mizan.

Smythe, D.W. (1981). Dependency road: Communications, capitalism, consciousness, and Canada. Norwood, NJ: Ablex.

Toynbee, A. (1946). A study of history, Vol. III (p. 332). London: Oxford University Press.

Van Dinh, T. (1987). Independence, liberation, revolution: An approach to the understanding of the third world. Norwood, NJ: Ablex.

Vilanilam, J.V. (1989). Reporting a revolution: The Iranian revolution and the NWICO debate (pp. 171–173). New Delhi: Sage.

Walker, R.B.J. (Ed.). (1984). Culture, ideology, world order. Boulder, CO: Westview.

Wallerstein, I. (1980/1974). The modern world system, Vols. I & III. New York: Academic

Wallerstein, I. (1990). Culture as the ideological battleground of the modern world system. Theory, Culture, and Society, 7, 31–55.

Wickens, C.M. (Ed.). (1952). Avicenna: Scientist and philosopher, A millenary symposium. London: Luzac.

NOTES

[1] Al Khawarizmi (780–850) was the founder of modern algebra, whose contribution moved the theory of a static universe to one of a dynamic universe. His work was used in European universities as the principal mathematical text until the 16th century, with great influence on the works of Leonardo Filionacci of Pisa, Master Jacob of Florence, and even of Leonardo da Vinci. Razi, known to the West as Rhazes, (865–925) was one of the founding fathers of medicine. His great medical work on medicine, especially his research on small pox and measles, were printed at least 40 times in the period from 1498 to 1868 as major texts in European universities. Ibn Sina, known in the West as Avicenna (980–1037) and as one of the great thinkers and medical scholars in history, gave both experience and reason a share in the formulation and growth of the data of the

scientists. Not only were his medical books the texts in Europe until modern times, but his contribution to logic, philosophy, psychology, and metaphysics also anticipated some of the foremost views of Descartes, Kant, and even those of Bergson. *Al Haitham* (965–1039) was a renowned physicist and one of the greatest investigators of optics and communication science of all time. His research and refraction of light passing from one medium to another laid the foundation for the training of the late scientists of Western Europe. *Al Kindi* (803–873), the first Muslim philosopher, brought science and philosophy together. His application of quantitative methods to medicine brought him very close to propounding the Weber-Fechner Law and won him a word of praise from Roger Bacon, who, along with Witelo and others five centuries later, were influenced by him in their scientific and methodological works. He was one of the early pioneers in the theory of knowledge.

  ² *Ibn Bajjah* (1106–38) known as Avempace or Avenpace in Latin and English, was a celebrated Muslim philosopher from the Iberian peninsula who traveled in Spain and North Africa. He dealt mainly with the question of ethics and, like the Hegelians, he believed that thought is man's highest function, but, like Platonists, he added that perceptual experience of the particulars, as opposed to purely conceptual experiences of the universals, are deceptive. *Ibn Tufayl* (1110–1185), known as Abubacer, was a Spanish Muslim philosopher, physician, mathematician, and poet whose work was translated into Hebrew as early as 1349 and into most of the European languages. The German philosopher Leibniz (1646–1716) studied Ibn Tufayl's work through the Latin edition and had a very high estimation of him. It is reported that his celebrated philosophical romance Hayy Ibn Yaqzan (The Living One, Son of the vigilant) was the central idea of the famous novel Robinson Crusoe, written in 1719, and was borrowed by Daniel Defoe. *Ibn Rushd,* or *Averroes* in Latin (1126–1198), was a great thinker whose work represented the most complete analysis of Aristotle at the time. He has been called the Commentator in Dante's *Divine Comedy* because Ibn Rushd was considered the greatest commentator of Aristotle's work. *Ibn Khaldun* (1332–1406) was a Muslim thinker and historian who has been called the father of sociology and demography. His economic analysis of social organization produced the first scientific and theoretical work on population, development, group dynamics, and his monumental work, called *Mugaddimah* (The Introduction), laid the ground for his observation of the role of state, communication, and propaganda in history. According to Arnold Toynbee, Ibn Khaldun "in the *Mugaddamah* to his *Universal History*...has conceived and formulated a philosophy of history which is undoubtedly the greatest work of its kind that has ever yet been created by any time or place (Toynbee, 1946, p.332). The views of sociologists like Spengler, Danilevsky, Sorokin, Kroeber, and Ogburn are in conformity with Ibn Khaldun's work.

Chapter 18
Rethinking the Agenda
of International Law

Richard Falk

INTERNATIONAL LAW IN THE CRUCIBLE
OF POST-COLD WAR HISTORY

The development of international law over the centuries discloses a pattern. Law has functioned mainly as an instrument on behalf of leading territorial states. Over the centuries international law has at various times rationalized and legalized colonial conquest, overseas intervention to protect capital, and unequal trade relations. In recent decades it has dropped the formal pretension that the system operates on behalf of "civilized" values, a code expression for the West that in practice has defied the humanistic intent of such values at every critical juncture. International law now purports to be global in conception and reach, and is not always any longer invoked by the North against the South. In practice, distinctions based on the hierarchy of North/South relations persist, perhaps nowhere more manifestly than in relation to the development and possession of nuclear weapons.[1]

International law reflects the complexity, contradictory possibilities, shifting interests and values, and fragmented structure of international political and economic reality. Often cynics have been too quick to dismiss international law as either an ineffectual plaything of states or as their oppressive instrument, while enthusiasts have been too ready to assume that law can remake politics and economics. As the background reality shifts, as new social forces emerge, as the tactics relied upon by those seeking change become more transnational, the role and potential of international law also shifts away from its almost exclusively statist origins. Also, as the practicalities of self-interest and survival become intertwined at regional and global levels, the pressures mount at the level of the state to evolve more appropriate frameworks for regulation and coordination. In particular, there are tensions mounting between state and market, between state and nature, and between state and civil society that will shape the evolution of international law in the years ahead. To gain some appreciation of the dimensions of this struggle between opposed possibilities, we consider several illustrative settings.

The Sandinista Innovation

Perhaps the Nicaragua initiative deserves to be highlighted. The Sandinista government, victimized by Contra violence and by extensive covert operations under the auspices of the CIA, appealed to the International Court of Justice back in 1983, claiming violations of its sovereign rights under international law. One needs to step back from the controversy to appreciate its innovative character. Here was a tiny, poor, left state taking the time and trouble to appeal to the World Court, an institution long identified with the historic traditions of the Western experience. What did Nicaragua hope to achieve? Was it so naive as to suppose the World Court would defy geopolitical realities? And if, miraculously, the Court decided in favor of Nicaragua, did those misguided priests and Marxists in Managua really believe that the power wielders in Washington would drop their interventionary policies in deference to the opinions of the jurists in The Hague?

The outcome validated both the innovators and the cynics, revealing, in the process the double-edged sword that international law has become, is becoming. Those that favored the initiative, especially Nicaragua's idealistic Foreign Minister, Michel d'Escoto, can take comfort in the outcome of the legal proceedings, and moved on from the courtroom triumph to persuading the Non-Aligned Movement to take the further initiative in urging the United Nations to proclaim the 1990s to be The Decade of International Law.[2]

The World Court held clearly, by a large majority, that Nicaragua's sovereign rights were being fundamentally violated by a series of U.S. activities, including mining harbors, intruding on Nicaraguan territory, financing and guiding Contra operations. But the U.S. leadership can also feel vindicated. After all, it persisted with the Contra operations and can take some credit for the outcome of the 1990 elections that drove the Sandinistas from power. Furthermore, defying the World Court decision produced hardly a ripple of protest and concern, either at home or abroad, even by those who claimed to be opposed to helping the Contras on substantive grounds. And in the United Nations itself, the silence was deafening; the organization was quick to turn the other cheek when the defiant member happened to be the leading dues-payer and superpower, and to overlook its own charter that calls for Security Council enforcement of World Court decisions that are repudiated by the losing side. And, most surprisingly, perhaps, respected international law scholars, especially in the United States, devoted their energies to a criticism of the decision while generally ignoring the duty to comply (cf. literature on case, Franck, AJIL symposium).

The Gulf War

The Gulf War of 1991 illustrates another side of the complex situation of international law in relation to emerging trends. Truly, Saddam Hussein, as leader of Iraq, challenged the most basic legal norm by the outright invasion and annexation of Kuwait, a member of the United Nations and a sovereign state. To protect weak states against aggression was definitely the main objective of the United Nations, allegedly thwarted for decades by the paralyzing tensions of the Cold War. Now, then, was the testing time for the idea of collective security in the face of aggression. The League of Nations had failed such tests in the 1930s, most vividly by its inability to heed Ethiopia's appeal for help in the face of fascist Italy's aggression; this failure of collective security has been widely understood as a step along the way to World War II.

For George Bush to speak about "a new world order" during the early phases of the Gulf Crisis made rhetorical sense, and as it turned out, only rhetorical sense. To convert the Security Council into a legitimating source for unrestricted warfare by an American-dominated coalition stretched the relevant legal provisions of the Charter beyond the limits of credible interpretation: first, by the refusal to exhaust peaceful alternatives to war (that is, sanctions, negotiations, containment); second, by authorizing recourse to war without a clear delineation of the mission (that is, withdrawal from Iraq) and without procedures for supervision and accountability (that is, Chapter VII of the Charter or at the very least some improvised equivalent that safeguarded the collective and world community character of what was done after January 15, 1991). The end result was the perceived and actual use of the United Nations for an exercise in war making, itself "aggressive" in the double sense of not being either clearly "necessary" or "proportional" to Iraqi wrongdoing (that is, adding the objective of destroying Iraq's war-threatening capability to that of obtaining its withdrawal).[3]

Without entering the debate about the overall effects of the Gulf War, the jurisprudential moment is clear. Even rather mainstream commentary has reacted subsequently to the abuse of the United Nations by proposals designed to ensure somewhat greater constitutional fidelity in future collective security undertakings by the Security Council. Of course, if such efforts to contain geopolitical forces by reference to international law succeeds, the short-run effect will likely be to weaken the perceived capacity of the United Nations and other international institutional arenas. After the adverse judgment in the Nicaragua case, the United States withdrew its acceptance of compulsory jurisdiction from the Court. If the Security Council had frustrated the White House game plan in the Gulf, there is little doubt that the United States, in conjunction with its coalition partners, would have acted on its own mandate, claiming of course the backing of international law. The effect of such an undertaking would have been clarifying, exposing the response for what it was, as geopolitically motivated. Fewer illusions would have been fashioned.[4] Acting outside the UN would have reminded the world of the continuing impotence of the United Nations even after the Cold War. This dilemma of choosing between pure statism and fig leaf internationalism arises from the unwillingness of geopolitical elites to let go of the instruments of legitimation and the inability of more progressively oriented political forces to exert sufficient influence in media and institutional arenas.[5] The result is the subordination of international law, in its most crucial aspects bearing on the use of force, to geopolitics.

BCCI

The Bank of Credit and Commerce International (BCCI) scandal, although not yet unraveled, dramatically illustrates a further dimension of the weakness of international law and the related vulnerability of people and weak societies to economic wrongdoing of mammoth proportions. This globally constituted banking operation, territorially rooted for purely opportunistic reasons (that is, to minimize regulatory scrutiny) in Luxembourg and Cayman Islands, but operating in at least 59 countries, included among its depositors many ordinary persons, charitable organizations, as well as notorious terrorist groups (e.g., Save the Children, Abu Nidal) (for background, see *The Sunday Times of London*, July 21, 1991, pp. 1, 20). The initial banking rationale of BCCI, apparently carried out in practice to some extent, was to bolster Third World financial resources by establishing a powerful global banking institution that would be willing and able to extend loans and credit to non-Western borrowers, especially in the North. In practice, BCCI was widely used to launder drug money, by illicit arms dealers, by the CIA to hide arms purchases and transfers of assets, and by a variety of influential actors, precisely because it fell so far outside the web of regulatory effectiveness, which at its most, is more or less associated with the territorial domain.[6]

What is illustrated in vivid form by BCCI is the extent to which the global economy operates in a normative vacuum; what effective regulation exists is territorially situated in leading industrial states, with the borders of the country of principal registry respected rather scrupulously. Illicit banking can hide in the havens of the North, further insulated by hiring prominent lawyers and appointing elite figures to its directorate, in a manner that illicit drug dealing generally cannot. This is partly for class reasons (that is, the drug lords are outsiders, whereas the bankers belong to the very best social clubs) and partly for geographic reasons (that is, drug operations are centered in the South, a setting in which intervention in internal affairs is an option—Noriega, Panama, whereas banking operations, despite the BCCI partial exception, are centered in the North). The point here is that, even as compared to the use of force or human rights, the evolution of international law responsive to the predatory operations of global capital and the transnational corporation is rudimentary and totally unsatisfactory.

Antarctica

Not all that happens in international life bears witness to the weakness of international law. The safeguarding of Antarctica is illustrative of constructive potentialities. Antarctica has been protected against sovereign appropriation and military and most commercial uses by a broad lawmaking treaty that entered into force in 1959. Although the vast continent is buried beneath a thick sheet of ice, its development could have been far more destructive. Several countries, including Argentina and Chile, continue to regard Antarctica as part of their vision of territorial expansion. The treaty was a compromise, suspending sovereign claims, fostering cooperative scientific uses, and showing that a cooperative regime can persist among countries otherwise hostile (both the U.S. and USSR remained active during the Cold War). Some have claimed that the Antarctica Treaty System comes as close to world government as the planet has ever known.

Problems have emerged over the course of the last decade: at their root is the belief that valuable minerals (especially oil and gas) are situated in Antarctica's waters; this concern has led Third World countries to attack the ATS as an exclusive rich country's club and for environmental NGOs to mount a transnational campaign to have Antarctica constituted as a world park, forever beyond commercial and resource exploitation. There are two stages of the evolution of ATS that each disclose positive features of the international legal order:

Phase One—no minerals in sight, but a treaty prevented fragmenting Antarctica into separate sovereign slices forever beyond the reach of effective regulation on behalf of the general human interest; arguably, these positive results were attainable because neither strategic nor economic interests were at issue, and cooperation for scientific inquiry was well established; also, that the principal claimant states were in the South, making internationalization an ingenious means to keep control effectively in the North.

Phase Two—the mineral factor emerges, bringing both commercial pressures to bear by way of transnational corporations and environmental concerns to mount under the initiative of a coalition of NGOs backed by a militant segment of public opinion in key treaty countries. Certainly, Greenpeace and the Cousteau Society exhibited their capacity to perform as political actors in the arenas of decision, their experts being accorded a real role in policymaking arenas on the future of Antarctica.

Although the outcome of Phase Two remains in some doubt, the compromise recently reached at a 1991 meeting in Madrid of parties to the treaty seems definitely inclined in favor of environmental forces. At present, a treaty on minerals development, itself weighted during negotiations to take impressive account of environmental factors, has been shelved in favor of a 50-year moratorium on minerals development that has been formally adopted by ATS procedures. Skeptics can still argue that environmentalists won out only because the prospects for valuable commercial exploitation were so poor, but part of what diminished these prospects was the expensive regulatory burdens that were to be attached to any serious effort to explore and develop the mineral resources. The experience with Antarctica shows that in some situations the mobilization of transnational democratic forces can effectively challenge statism and even the dispositions of geopolitics. Of course, it is necessary to put Antarctica in the perspective created by the other three instances examined here.

The Rushdie Fatwa

When Ayatollah Khomeini issued his notorious *fatwa* decreeing death to Salman Rushdie for his authorship of *The Satanic Verses*, a new kind of limit condition was disclosed. Rushdie, living in Great Britain, had written a work of literature that was fully within his legal rights, and for which he received critical praise and financial reward. In the Moslem world the novel was viewed as an assault on Islam, an act of both apostasy and blasphemy on Rushdie's part, giving a plausibility, rooted in the Koran, to the *fatwa*. The impact has been enormous— Rushdie has been forced to live underground in the presence of security guards provided by the British government; in July 1991, in separate incidents, his Italian publisher was stabbed and his Japanese translator was assassinated.

> Kalim Siddiqi, Director of the Muslim Institute in London, writes, "*The Satanic Verses* is the eye of the global storm raging between two views of the world and the future of mankind—the religious and the secular. This conflict cannot be settled in terms of the 'national' laws of one or more nation-states...there are no frontiers of time or space. The outcome of this controversy may well determine the outcome of history itself. The *fatwa*, and the West's response to it, have rended (sic) the nation-state obsolete." (Calligurgus 1991, p. 3).

Two important developments, bearing on the future of international law are evident:

* the globalization of communication
* the interpenetration of cultures

In the face of these developments, the traditional allocation of territorial supremacy has indeed become obsolete. Devout Muslims are sufficiently dispersed in the world and borders permeable, that there is no safe haven for Rushdie and those associated with the publication of the book. The challenge posed is formidable, especially as compromise seems out of the question (for instance, allowing publication in the West, but forbidding distribution and translation elsewhere). Perhaps no Muslim leader will in the future imitate Khomeini's *fatwa* and no writer dare publish again a work so disrespectful of Islam. What is revealed in the interim, however, is the impotence of the state, with all of its capabilities, to uphold elemental security within its territory, not of borders against an enemy state, but of an individual resident and of a highly valued end (freedom of expression).

Globalization means vulnerability, first of all, to images. Britain's inability to insulate Rushdie is an extreme instance of a wider reality, the spread of cultural images in a world of antagonistic cultures, not geographically separable. International law cannot address these challenges in any conventional manner, that is, by positing standards, procedures, sanctions. Perhaps, cross-cultural dialogue can work toward a position of greater mutual respect and tolerance over time, but the point here is that the world is confronted with a new kind of profound challenge, a response to which it has not even started to fashion.

Conclusions

Several diagnostic conclusions emerge. First of all, international law as currently operating does not protect elemental human concerns about peace, justice, or environmental protection. Secondly, the rules, doctrines, and institutions that compose the international legal order are largely controlled by the same geopolitical forces that control the world economy, the world communications structure, and world political life. Thirdly, these geopolitical forces are located in the capitalist North, especially so in the aftermath of the Cold War. Fourthly, the prospects for reorienting international law around the well-being of the peoples of the world depends on strengthening global civil society, as well as shaping and strengthening democratizing tendencies on all levels of social organization, from the family to the world. Fifthly, developments in the context of environmental protection and human rights suggest that the exertion of far greater influence on the processes and structures of international law is a tenable, and essential, project for progressive politics at this time.

International law now functions more ambiguously than ever before, at the interface of antagonistic political tendencies. It continues to reflect geopolitical structures, but it also can be credibly invoked on behalf of a wide range of countermoves in the global arena. The reality of international law in relation to emancipatory goals has become inherently ambiguous, and must be assessed on a case by case basis. Because of the close links between hegemonic media, capital, and state power, there is a constant danger that the emancipatory roles of international law will remain virtually occluded from public consciousness, which would itself deprive democratizing forces in the world of a crucial instrument in the overall symbolic struggle to control the heights of legitimation. The ascendancy of information, and the electronic manipulation of symbolic reality in the domains of global capital and relative state power, assigns a corresponding importance to the politics of legitimacy. The strengthening of international law to satisfy the needs and aspirations of the peoples of the world, not the holders of capital and state power, should definitely be included among the priority goals of those committed to the potentialities of global civil society based on widely shared values.

WHICH NEW WORLD ORDER?

A mood of American arrogance can be associated with Fukuyama's absurdly naive contention that, with the collapse of state socialism, there emerged a final consensus on the level of ideas that market-oriented constitutionalism was the only legitimate foundation for politics.[7] Bush's enthusiastic claim to generate "the new world order" out of the Gulf Crisis extended such pretensions, carrying with it the insistence that whatever arrangement for global governance emerged after the bipolar certitudes of the Cold War years would necessarily be inscribed with the emblazoned inscription "Made in the USA." Only months later, even Bush himself seems to have forgotten his own legitimizing rhetoric, undoubtedly to avoid calling attention to the outcome of the Gulf War and to let slip the implicit promise to build the United Nations into the central organ of global security.

The apparent fate of the phrase "the new world order" is revealing. As with so much of mainstream politics, language is appropriated for the sake of a transitory image suitable to the moment. When the moment passes, the image disappears, slips back into the electronic memory, conceivably to be retrieved if a future occasion should require. This short lifespan of "the new world order" is one of the strongest confirmations that ours is indeed a postmodern politics.

And yet there is bound to be *a* new world order. There exists an obvious need to adjust to the collapse of the geopolitical structures and attitudes that had taken shape since 1945, and were organized around the strategic and ideological presuppositions of bipolarity, containment, and deterrence. The absence of any consensus about a post-Cold War world is suggested by the Pentagon's announcement that the change in East–West relations has enabled war plans to focus on 7,000 strategic targets in the former Soviet Union rather than the previous 10,000, implying that the former Soviet threat persists in a massive, if slightly moderated form (*International Herald Tribune*, July 22, 1991, p. 1). Conceptual schemes fade away slower than the pattern of relationships that gave rise to them; it is just as hard to adjust to the loss of the Soviet Union as a strategic rival as it is to admit that the new rivalry is likely to focus on the tripolar relations among Japan, Europe, and the United States.

The most likely repatterning of geopolitics in the years ahead is likely to involve the globalizing pressures of capital and media, on the one side, and of environmental decay and transnational democratization on the other. In other words, the new world order is likely to be constituted by the complex tensions between *globalization from above and globalization from below*. The territorial state is likely to be bypassed increasingly by both sets of forces, making the Fukuyama/ Bush view of the future particularly inapropos. There are a number of developments pointing in the globalizing direction: the regionalization of sovereignty in Europe; the formation of three gigantic trading blocs in the North; the globalization of business and banking; the rise of ethnic politics as an alternative to the modernist "nation-state"; the obvious need for global policy in the coming decades on the discharge of greenhouse gasses, consumptive patterns, and population growth (Brown, 1991). Other issues of global concern also challenge the viability of the sovereign state—drugs, terrorism, refugees, mass migration, disease. And finally, the growth of a global popular culture erodes the significance of political boundaries; music, clothes, heroes and heroines, fast food are shared throughout the global market by youth attracted to logos, sound rhythms, and life styles originating mainly in the United States.[8]

It is not easy to fit international law into this emergent repatterning of geopolitics. The BCCI is paradigmatic of the new type of reality, manifesting the complicity and the impotence of statist politics in relation to global economic crime of the most gross variety; in this regard, it is "poetic justice" that both the CIA and Abu Nidal should be linked as depositors. International law, evolving as an instrument of statist politics, must adapt in radical fashion or die. The adaptive possibilities were illustrated in different ways by Nicaragua's recourse to the World Court and by the effective militancy of the transnational environmental movement in the struggle to save Antarctica from the mineral developers. The main card left in the hands of the statists is war, and it is often a trump, as illustrated by the way it was played to resolve the Gulf Crisis. Can international law help devalue this card at this time?

Powerful states, especially in democratically organized states, have been playing a double game when it comes to war. The most powerful of these states, the United States, has attempted both to lead the fight against the legitimacy of unilateral war making while retaining warmaking discretion for itself.[9] In some situations, leaders of states have been held criminally accountable for violating international law, for committing crimes of states. The Nuremberg Principles, if rigorously applied, would effectively remove the warmaking card. The United States government is susceptible to law-oriented initiatives designed to restrict war making at the state level, provided such initiatives have strong democratic backing, a condition that cannot be taken for granted. One discouraging feature of the Gulf War was the popularity of the battlefield victory, making the President temporarily larger than life, converting the commanding generals into instant presidential nominees, and producing victory parades that exhibited a jingoist ethos as at the core of the American experience of democracy. What is suggested, at the very least, is that democratic constraints will not abate war making if the political culture has itself become militarist, racist, and paranoid; a deeper political pedagogy dedicated to peace is needed if the war system is to be challenged by law, ethics, and a democratic polity.

Such developments can only occur in the course of building a genuine collective security system in the United Nations, reorienting military capabilities of states to territorial defense, and establishing a procedure of courts and enforcement on the global level that could assert its authority *within* territory. The recitation of such conditions suggests the remoteness of such a transformation of geopolitics.

What can be done is to have the nascent structures of global civil society increasingly appropriate international law as part of the struggle to insinuate democratizing values into the processes and structures of globalization. In this regard, when the Stockholm Initiative on Global Security and Governance, a body of eminent persons including heads of state, diplomats, and policy influentials, issues a report *Common Responsibility in the 1990's* calling for more accountability and supervision by the Security Council and a stronger global network of regulation in the common interest of humanity, there is disclosed a cleavage in statist ranks. This cleavage acquires greater importance when it is coupled with the growing strength and sophistication of the transnational social movements in the areas of environment, human rights, and peace. Part of this sophistication is expressed by making use of international law as if it were a resource of global civil society, and not just part of the repertoire of statist diplomacy. It is worth noting that the most serious attempt to bring together responsible governmental officials to discuss the gaps in the environmental law of war was organized by Greenpeace (London Geneva V Conference; see also excellent background paper by Greenpeace Staff, W. Arkin, & others, "On Impact.")

It is also notable to observe the silence of international law when it comes to the Rushdie affair.

A PROVISIONAL ASSESSMENT

It is difficult to assess prospects at this stage. In the immediate future, an infatuation with the market is likely to prevail at both governmental and popular levels. Such an infatuation could generate some significant global lawmaking, especially if state and market forces in the North perceive their own legitimacy as requiring such bolstering. The regulatory effects generated by the BCCI revelations should be monitored closely from this perspective.

Similarly, it is crucial to notice what sorts of lawmaking responses are fashioned for the array of environmental challenges. The treaty framework that has emerged in relation to ozone depletion is far more impressive than what has occurred in relation to the threat of global warming, acid rain, and ocean pollution. The explanation of such differences is revealing. There exists a strong scientific consensus with respect to ozone depletion that encompasses both cause and cure. Inexpensive substitutes for the coolant chemicals that produce ozone depletion have been commercially developed by leading companies supportive of the shifts. Governments, that is, taxpayers, have agreed to bear the adjustment costs for the shift in the South, and the amounts involved are small. None of these conditions pertain in relation to the other environmental problems of global scope. Adjustment costs involve major shifts in life style (e.g., giving up unrestricted use of private transportation based on the internal combustion engine) and challenge major industries with huge capital investments. Whether transnational environmentalism can overcome the reluctance of market and state to make suitable adjustments seems doubtful at this stage.

The United Nations is another critical arena for assessment. The state, as exemplified by hegemonic designs, is extremely unlikely to give up effective control over warmaking when its other capabilities are being eroded by globalization from above and below. Arguably, war is obsolete in the North, but it continues to be a robust social institution in the South and in North/South relations. Militarist institutions and societal attitudes remain strong in leading states, and seem unlikely to be seriously challenged in the years ahead. As such, the contentions made by the United States during the Gulf Crisis that the time had come to make collective security effective under UN auspices are likely to fade quickly. A more likely prospect is for the United States to oppose even modest UN reforms giving the

Secretary General more independent authority in world crisis and improving the accountability of security undertakings of the UN in relation to the Charter and its membership. That is, the geopolitical side of statism is likely to hold tenaciously to its warmaking discretion during this period in which other functions of the state are being diminished.

The outlook for international law is mixed. It has been argued here that it will be increasingly important for progressive political actors to appropriate international law for their reformist and transformative projects. In the first instance, this is a matter of changing perceptions, overcoming the illusion that somehow law belongs to governments rather than to civil society. Some useful innovations have been challenging this still widely held view. The Permanent Peoples Tribunal, organized from Rome, has for almost 20 years been claiming the authority to apply international law—the rights of peoples—as against governments and international institutions. Their proceedings have included a highly critical judgment against the IMF for its imposition of "conditionality" on many of the economies of the South, condemning such policies and structures as "illegal."

Three progressive projects seem of utmost importance for the development of international law in this period: the strengthening of global civil society, including the appreciation of the degree to which its visions of a better world can and must make use of law as an instrument of struggle and change; the remaking of political culture by affirming human rights, repudiating war and warmaking, and fulfilling ecological imperatives; and the fuller realization that the future viability of international law depends on its capacity to achieve legitimacy in the main constitutive cultures of the world, thereby stressing the relevance of intercultural dialogue and intracultural self-reflective criticism.

REFERENCES

Calligurgus, A. (1991). *The revenge of history.* Cambridge: Polity.

NOTES

[1] Israel, as belonging to the North, is allowed nuclear weapons, but countries like Pakistan, Iraq are not; the Islamic South is viewed with strongest bias; NPT reflects this dual structure even if not framed in such a manner.

[2] A major feature of the original NAM resolution calling for the Decade stressed the desirability of including all governments to agree in advance to settle disputes by recourse to the Court; the originality of this initiative can only be appreciated against the background of Third World hostility toward international law, with a particular skepticism about the Court, strongly held by all left governments that regarded the institution as an expression of Western values.

[3] Note that, under the cover of "collective security," the very dangerous and entirely "illegal" doctrine of "preventive war" was implemented; self-defense and repudiating "appeasement" as justifying arguments were deliberately confused with taking the occasion to eliminate an alleged growing future danger to regional security interests, in Iraq's case linked to the contention of its emergence a few years hence as a nuclear power; it is also relevant that prior to the war, both domestic and international support was primarily mobilized around the collective security/withdrawal theme, but that, during and after the war, the dominant motif was the destruction of Iraq's war-threatening capability; one of the many defects of Security Council Resolution 678 was that it was open to this broader interpretation.

[4] Liberal public opinion was confused about the Gulf War, partly because it was a UN war and they had waited decades for the UN to be used in such a serious manner.

[5] Democracy is not enough even if it is operative in giving assent to policy, as the political culture fostered by capitalism and materialism has made war by the strong against the weak popular, especially if the leader of the weak can be portrayed as evil and menacing; in these respects, Saddam Hussein fulfilled all the requirements to uphold the myth of the good war for democratic society, and reaching back for the Hitler analogy was not farfetched despite the arresting differences.

[6] But the Savings and Loan scandal suggests that the same regulatory lapses can occur within the territory of a supposedly well-governed constitutional democracy.

[7] To dismiss socialist prospects is premature—see Calligurgus, 1991; to dismiss a green postmaterialist alternative to the market is premature—see Dobson; and to proclaim the death of the political imagination at a time of planetary overload is a form of pessimism that makes Schopenhauer appear pollyannish about the human future.

[8] It is the packaging of popular culture, not precision-guided missiles and market forms, that gives the U.S. what purchase it has on shaping the future.

[9] Parallel with nuclear weapons—retain option, while disallowing to others.

Chapter 19
Toward the Universal
Interactive Neighborhood

Leonard R. Sussman

"WE'RE ALL CONNECTED"—NOT YET, BUT SOON

At Homa Bay on the shore of Lake Victoria in Kenya, East Africa, an experiment in "small" communication began a decade ago. A cholera epidemic sparked the creation of a simple community radio station to transmit information about good hygiene. There was virtually no other public communication system. Nairobi's central radio transmitter was too distant. Homa Bay FM (frequency modulation) radio was set up for less than $25,000. It is now possible to assemble a 10-watt transmitter for $950, and secure a turntable, mixer, microphones, and software for $6,000. That modest sum enables community radio to transmit news, music, and educational programs to tens of thousands of formerly isolated people within a range of 30 miles (Allard, 1990).

Small FM radio stations have been created in Ghana, Sri Lanka, Cape Verde, St. Lucia (Caribbean), Bhutan, Maldives, Tonga, Niue, and the Philippines. In some places FM radio provides the major information source for an island community or, as in the Mahaweli region of Sri Lanka, for residents in a newly settled region. Even electricity is not needed for broadcasting or receiving. At little additional expense, solar energy is the power source in some areas. Broadcast receivers cost about $30 for a family or group. Indeed, it is possible to place the entire FM radio transmitter in a medium-sized suitcase, raise a small antenna, and instantly broadcast a good quality radio program.

Similarly portable television transmitters—flyways—have been used to send pictures and sound from high in the Himalayas, via satellite, to living rooms worldwide. On the smaller scale, low-power television has the same potential for community service as FM radio. It can reach 25 miles on a few thousand watts at far less cost than present commercial TV. While commercial broadcast networks, affiliates, and newspaper chains in the United States were becoming more dominant in the 1980s, the number of low-power TV outlets in the U.S. increased eight-fold. From 1988 to 1990, the number of low-power stations nearly doubled to 809. The Federal Communications Commission expects as many as 4,000 by the end of the 'nineties.

Radio and television are but two of the "small" technologies destined to alter the mode of communication in the poorest as well as richest societies. Ultimately—soon in some places, later in others—everyone, everywhere will be online. This universalization of communication networks will become far more than a "global village"—a universal interactive neighborhood.

But is communication development likely to follow a straight-line projection from *here* (state monopolization of communication power in many places and commercial domination of the media in other places) to *there* (democratization of the vastly enlarged network of networks, with real opportunities for personal interaction)?

In the past, technological developments surprised the forecasters. Some impact could be foreseen, but not without major unanticipated results. The mass production of the automobile foretold greater mobility, but forecasters did not envision dramatically changed social mores, clogged city streets, mushrooming suburbs, fouled air, and new related industries.

Political consequences are no less difficult to predict. Fearful rulers bring new industrial or agricultural processes under their control. The same leaders often coopt new communications tools. They are inclined to regard the "small" communications technologies as threats to central authority. The FM radio transmitter set in a suitcase and the flyway TV transmitting to a satellite may be seen by rulers as Cold-War-style spying equipment, or tools to subvert authoritarian control.

How, then, can the advantages of small commtech ever be realized in places where they are most needed?

And how can similar advantages of small media provide the

diversity of ownership and pluralism of content which are threatened in politically democratic states with high-intensity market drives tending toward domination of the media by fewer owners?

THE UNIVERSAL CONNECTION

"We're All Connected" is taken from the advertising song of the New York Telephone Company (NYNEX). The telephone is more than a metaphor for global interconnectedness. The worldwide phone system is the largest integrated machine ever built. There are slightly more than a half-billion telephones in the world for 5.3 billion people (World Media Handbook, 1990). Fully 80% of the world's telephones are in only 10 countries of North America and Europe where 750 million people reside. Thirty percent of the phones are in the United States. Several American cities have more phones than people. Yet 200,000 households in isolated rural areas of the U.S. are without phone service. The developing world has 12% of the phones for 2.8 billion people. These statistics reflect not only an inability to make the heartwarming family calls the NYNEX television commercials depict. Indeed, social scientists and others have long neglected the role of the telephone as a generator of extensive social and political change. For that reason, the International Telecommunications Union (ITU) is determined to see that, by the early years of the next century, every citizen on the planet will be within easy reach of a telephone. Not everyone would have a personal phone, but even the remotest tribe, village, or outlying province would have a common phone which anyone could use.

The telephone, as all communicating devices, is at once a stimulant to economic development and dependent on such development for the expansion of the communication systems. Yet in the decade 1973–1983 developing countries spent $211.5 billion on military imports rather than on communications and other primary development tools (Arms Control and Disarmament Agency, 1985, p.89).

The telephone is more than a conversation piece. It is the lifeline to the new world of communication technologies. That, I have called the coming age of ISDN—the linking of everyone, everywhere, to the Integrated Systems of Digital Networks (Sussman, 1989–1990). By using mainly telephone lines and cable systems linked to computer terminals, the ISDN systems will carry news and information, pictures and sound; encyclopedic, archival, and data files; scientific and vocational supports; agricultural and industrial developments; and banking and marketing services direct to home and office.

Tied to these systems will be the "small" technologies: fax, recorder, copier, VCR, cassette player, television, and radio. The community FM radio, described above, can be added to the network. This would relay the news, information, and music of the most isolated hinterland to the capital city and the world beyond.

Most important, these linkages would be interactive. They could enable the receiver to respond to the sender in real time. The global networking of networks will be accomplished by using satellites and fibre optic cable. Each year, both systems become more accessible and less costly. A portable TV satellite uplink used by a U. S. television network (CBS) broadcast from Kuwait City in 1991 even before the smoke of combat cleared, and while all electric power on the ground was still blacked out. Home viewers, worldwide, needed only telephone and cable links to receive instantaneous reports and pictures from the embattled area.

The Persian Gulf war also demonstrated, even limitedly, the first truly international television news reporting. Cable News Network (CNN) enters homes and offices in more than 105 countries. Although based in the U. S. (Atlanta), CNN is partly interactive in its programming. It carries video from all countries to which it delivers words and images, under contract. Iraq permitted CNN to broadcast from Baghdad when other Western journalists were expelled. This raised criticism of CNN in the U.S. for continuing to broadcast with a censor at the reporter's elbow, and under strict Iraqi controls. Western news media, meanwhile, complained that the U.S. Central Command in Saudi Arabia restricted access of journalists to military news and censored outgoing reports.

Were reports from Baghdad "subversive" of the UN coalition's war effort, while U.S. press controls were "patriotic"? However one responds, such questions will arise increasingly in the age of ISDN. The mixture of large and small communication systems, all tied to the global network, is bound to cause political discomfort in some places. Indeed, such linkages will challenge the individual citizen as never before. Once all manner of news and information is available at the touch of the terminal keyboard, verifiable fact will be mixed with misinformation and disinformation. Public education in the uses of communication will be urgently needed.

POLITICAL USES

Education in the political and social implications of publicly communicated messages will be as diverse as the 170-odd national governments. No government anywhere precludes efforts to manage the news about itself. There is, however, a broad spectrum of the degree of government influence over domestic (and in some cases foreign) news and information. Fully 28% of the countries own or control all mass media and determine the content of all important messages. There is no formal channel for dissent or difference. Another 30% of the countries allow *some* pluralism in ownership and diversity of views expressed in the mass media. Generally, however, these governments exert economic or political influences, or threaten repercussions from unwanted reportage. The 42% of countries with the most permissive news media policies permit the sharpest, most vocal dissent from governmental activities. Many of these countries reserve all or most of their communication systems for private ownership. Other nations in the most free group are increasingly privatizing their communication facilities. Even in the most free group, however, governments use sophisticated methods to persuade journalists to favor Administration policies (Sussman, 1992).

The small communication technologies—fax, the copier used as printer, cassette, FM radio, VCR, recorder, telephone—are ready-made tools for the dissenters in highly restricted societies; indeed, for activists intent on revolutionizing their polities. These technologies provide an alternative means of mass communication.

Cassettes taped in France by the Ayatollah Khomeini and smuggled into Iran undermined the Shah and established a Shiite government in 1978.

Aboriginal people in Australia use VCRs to record meetings and present their land-rights case in places far distant from where they live.

Before the 1989 revolution, Poland's Solidarity underground used radio, copiers, and VCRs to harass and even substitute for the official communication systems. Occasionally, moving sentences carried Solidarity messages beneath the video on official Polish television.

Using copiers, Hungarian underground writers produced more books each year than the state publishers.

Panama's journalists, fleeing after General Noriega shut down opposition newspapers, produced daily new reports from Florida, sent by fax and published by copiers in the writers' homeland.

During the occupation of Kuwait in 1991 the resistance used cellular telephones to tell the world of conditions in the beleaguered country.

In mid-1980s, even before Soviet glasnost took hold, the automatic-dial telephone—bypassing the censors—opened the USSR to international people-to-people contacts.

Most dramatic, the policy of glasnost in the former Soviet Union was based on a fundamental perception and decision. That is: Any modernizing society must be transformed into a self-supporting country, and that is possible only if information machines are massively introduced. People trained to operate computers and their associated information links, however, must learn to face and make intelligent choices. It is a short step to citizens making real choices in the lives of their families and their country. Diversity and choice becomes the norm. This undermines a highly restrictive, centrally controlled society. Inside the Soviet Union fax machines were appearing, unofficial publications mushroomed, and cross-border contacts greatly increased. Political reversals also occurred. The news media were temporarily reined in and freed again, but stringent Stalinist controls are not likely to return. In the longer term—30 to 40 years—new communication technologies are more likely to democratize Russia and the other former Soviet republics, as other countries. Intelligent machines make possible, not only access to vast banks of information, but the capability to interact with a sender. This opens news, information, and opinion flows from the center to the periphery, and the reverse, and—most important—from the periphery to the periphery, without passing through central authority. That is democratization-by-information-machine; developing the *universal interactive neighborhood*.

AN ORWELLIAN NIGHTMARE

Will the dream of a universal interactive neighborhood, a spur to political democratization on a global scale, be realized in the age of ISDN—the networking of networks—or will these same communication networks strengthen central controls in authoritarian as well as democratic societies? Indeed, will George Orwell's *1984* become the nightmarish pattern for 2034?

Clearly, political will is needed to deploy intelligent machines and assure freedom for citizens to use the new media freely. Dissenters in politically restrictive societies may use small commtech to undermine controls on both the machines and the polity. It is clear even in the most isolated parts of the world that far better lifestyles are possible. Cross-border radio, travelers, and a new generation free of old shibboleths is coming to know that ideas—even revolutionary ideas—are needed to spur social and political development. The new idea-machines are increasingly within reach as central authorities act to end generations of stagnation.

Commtech will thus provide public enlightenment even as it works to alter the system of governance. In India, an independent news report on video cassette has been a popular alternative to the state-run radio and TV channels. The Asian community in London is a heavy user of Indian films, distributed on video cassettes. In developing countries, whether politically restrictive or not, small commtech can provide a flow of indigenous news, information, and other cultural elements. For three decades, more than 100 countries in the Non-Aligned Movement have criticized the major transnational news and cultural media for transmitting mainly Western news and cultural products. In many NAM countries the Ministers of Information or Culture are the actual purchasers of Western films, cassettes, and news services. While deprecating these products, the ministers explain that their own countries cannot afford to produce alternative materials.

That rationale is passing as less expensive equipment becomes available. Indeed, developing countries have created international news and information agencies, several transnational television services, and cassette and film studios dedicated to Third World subjects. All of these channels together are small in comparison with the major global services originating in the North. Most of these Third World channels are still owned or strongly influenced by the respective governments. Citizens of these countries await the democratization, *domestically,* which their leaders have demanded for themselves, as *nations,* on the world communication stage.

The key to both sets of aspirations—the citizen's need to use information machines with diverse, interactive possibilities, and the government's desire to have its national views and culture accessible around the world—is the networking of networks through ISDN. How can the NYNEX slogan, "We're All Connected," be made globally operational?

Political will, differently exhibited in each country, is the key to ISDN. This is most obvious in presently restrictive societies. They must open their wholly owned or controlled media to diverse views, even if ownership remains centrally controlled. They must also permit the small commtech, especially the telephone, to become accessible to all citizens. The domestic networks thus formed can be linked by telephone or satellite to the transnational systems. The smaller countries and cultures, particularly minority cultures in all societies, should be carefully allocated time and space on the larger networks. In some places this may require the concentration of cultural anthropologists to ensure the display or retention of indigenous music, dance, and literature as well as current news and views. Such cultural artifacts disappear in developing countries even without competition from transnational media. New commtech tends to impose its own cultural impact quite apart from specific extranational or extracultural competition. In the hands of sensitive professionals, the new media are quite capable of enhancing the values of older indigenous cultural forms.

Where is the point of connection with the global flow?

The widespread linkage of ISDN will create an interest, call it a market, in the global community for representations from even the most isolated societies. Indeed, the least known places and peoples are likely to be watched with some new-found interest on greatly expanded television channels worldwide. There will be upwards of 100 channels from which the average viewer can choose. That is not to say that every Third World leader who wants an international audience will always be heard. But it is likely that every country will be accessible on the home screen with some frequency.[1] The diversity of programming from each country will depend largely on the liberality of the leaders in permitting their own people to display their innate diversity. There will be TV channels in the developed countries which feature such diversity. Today, Cable News Network (CNN) provides an example through "World Report." This features reports from a dozen countries, each telecast as prepared by the indigenous reporter.[2] CNN, which reaches more than 80% of American households and many more millions in other countries, will soon be challenged by a European, multilingual, round-the-clock TV news consortium. There is thus likely to be competition for the best servicing of news, information, and culture, including that originating in Third World countries.

COMPETITION AS MOTOR

Competition is the core of the economic system in the homelands of the major international news and culture purveyors: the United States, the United Kingdom, and France. Free enterprise accompanies political freedoms. Broad freedom of expression with minimal governmental regulation generates the opportunity and motivation to maximize control of print, broadcast, and other cultural channels. Such nongovernmental, commercial controls generate power—information power convertible into political power—as well as financial gains. In the United States a few newspaper chains are steadily absorbing independent newspapers. The Times Warner merger in 1989 created the world's largest information conglomerate. Several non-Britishers now run most of the national newspapers in the United Kingdom. Japanese buyers control a major share of American film production and the bulk of the U.S. recording libraries. The European Community plans to legislate protection for EC cultural products, thereby diminishing the flow of film from Hollywood.

Despite these symptoms of giantism, steps to inspire massive competition are beginning to surface in the United States. The first is juridical recognition that the new communication technologies have created new modes of public expression. Cable television is not merely a carrier of other producers' programs. Cable news and entertainment are now produced just for cable audiences. Cable systems, therefore, are as entitled to protection under the U.S. Constitution's First Amendment as have been newspapers, radio, and traditional television. Similarly, the telephone companies have the most pervasive lines into homes and offices nationwide. The telecos could transmit, not only other peoples' messages—the traditional "carrier" service of telecos—but originate news and information services as well. Should not telecos be permitted to perform such services and gain protection for them under the First Amendment?

This is the dynamic battleground of the immediate future. To confer First Amendment rights on telecos and cable would place them in direct competition with one another and with newspapers and radio/television networks. Indeed, a further breakdown, is likely of the present large purveyors of ideas. For several years, the audience for nightly network news has diminished. Cable news and news programs of local channels appear to have won a significant share of the audience. A continuing decline in network news is predicted by industry specialists. Even the information giants face severe competition. Competition driven by financial objectives can lead to diversified reportage and cultural products, particularly if the public discriminates in supporting one purveyor over another. The fact that there may be cross-representation on the corporate boards of the large communication media has rarely resulted in demonstrable interference in the content of print or broadcast news.

In the maze of new communication technologies tied to ISD networks there will likely be a new role for government. Since 1934 the federal government has licensed radio and later television to assure orderly use of the limited space on the broadcast spectrum. To avoid interfering with the broadcaster's freedom under the First Amendment, the government rarely exercised even its limited right to assure fairness or equal access in the content of programs. The regulators, though, have limited the number of radios or television channels owned by a national network. The government also limited the cross-ownership of newspapers and broadcasters.

The threat of cross-ownership will become quickly apparent as ISDN permits the linkage of many new, diverse systems of information purveyance. Precaution will be needed in international as well as domestic communications. The promise of ISDN to citizens of the developing world, after decade-long debates at UNESCO and elsewhere, is clear: the cry for some new information order can, finally, be answered in the direct applicability of new networking to the needs of small, poor, nonindustrialized nations. But in domestic and international communications the human rights of the citizen—the right to diverse information—should become an operative guide to governmental action. This may mean, ironically, more governmental regulation in free societies , to avert monopolization; and much less governmental control in less-than-free societies to permit citizens to exercise free choice as a function of economic development.

REFERENCES

Allard, M. (1990, December). Radios Communautaires: l'antenne est à vous. *Unesco Sources,* 9. (Allard is the engineer-designer who installed FM radio systems in many countries as part of Unesco's program, begun in 1980, to develop community radio.)

Sussman, L. R. (1989–1990). *Power, the press and the technology of freedom: the coming age of ISDN.* New York: Freedom House.

Sussman, L. R., (1992, January-February), Censors retreat—except in the Gulf including table, News media control by countries. *Freedom Review,* p. 56.

World media handbook. (1990). New York: United Nations, 1990, The world almanac, (1990) New York: Pharos Books.

U.S. Arms Control and Disarmament Agency. (1985). *World military expenditures and arms transfers.* Washington, DC: Author.

NOTES

[1] The International Channel, a U.S. cable service, carries multilingual programming to ethnic groups. Programs are in Japanese, Chinese Korean, Filipino,, Vietnamese and Cambodian, Hindi, French, Portuguese, Farsi, Armenian, Arabic, and Hebrew were to be added.

[2] For the first time since the 1959 revolution, Cuban television has carried a new program by a private company—CNN's World Report.

Chapter 20
New Technologies in Political Campaigns

Robert G. Meadow

Modern politics is at a crossroads where new technologies intersect with more traditional methods of political campaigning. On the level of electoral politics, these new technologies have the potential to change, or already rapidly are changing, how voters are informed about candidates and issues, the organization of political campaigns, the role of political consultants and professionals, and the day-to-day activities of political parties and interest groups. We are entering the era of high-tech politics.

In the past decade, as the techniques of addressing voters have begun to employ the new communication technologies, a new breed of "international" political consultants has arisen, exporting American methods of electioneering and election technologies to nations ranging from Panama to Poland. Some practitioners see unlimited virtue in the new technologies, suggesting that they enhance public participation and have democratized the practice of politics. Yet such unqualified exuberance of the high-tech political world may not be warranted when we take a closer look at the distribution and control of the new technology.

On the level of democratic theory and practice, these new technologies are altering the relationships between the governors and the governed and are raising new questions of campaign communication, public policy, and, perhaps most significantly, the nature of political competition.

IDENTIFYING THE NEW TECHNOLOGIES

The new technologies of political campaigning are not really "new" technologies, but are technologies which have developed from the merger of computers and telecommunications. Occasionally there are new inventions, like the fax machine or the home videocassette recorder/player, but for the most part, the new technologies in politics are in reality new applications for technologies that have developed over the past decade, including microcomputers, interactive cable television, satellite transmissions and laser printing.

1. Cable Television —Cable television is hardly a new technology. Having been with us for 30 years, it would more appropriately be called middle-aged technology. Although most cable television is used for viewing an expanded menu of entertainment programming, there have been five developments with explicit political implications.

First, as more and more households subscribe to cable systems, the share of the audience for traditional network entertainment programming has been declining. Since 1980, for example, the share of households viewing network programming has declined from about 90% of the viewing audience to approximately 62%, due in part to the ever-expanding percentage of households with cable television. This means that some percentage of the electorate may not be reached by traditional broadcast political advertising, necessitating an expansion of other means of voter communications. At the same time, the expansion of the cable television audience means a decreasing common exposure of voters to broadcast political advertising. Political ads for national candidates, traditionally broadcast over network television, *defined* the campaign between 1964 and 1988, and most voters would have a common experience of voter information. But with cable fragmenting the audience, the commonality of experience of the televised election is declining. Moreover, fragmented audiences may receive *different* messages as ads are tailored to the diverse cable markets, with ads narrowly targeted to seniors, sports fans, home shoppers, rerun fanatics, or others who have withdrawn from common broadcasting into their specialized cable world. How can print journalists, who have come to recognize the importance of the televised campaigns, possibly cover the media campaign when there is no single media campaign, but a series of fragmented messages which are virtually impossible to find, let alone subject to "truth box" scrutiny?

Second, with the expanded capacity of many cable systems to 128 or more channels, cable operators are constantly seeking additional programming to fill channels. Elected officials (about 50% of those in Congress) are producing their own "Washington Report" programming and providing it to cable operators, enabling incumbents to bypass traditional media gatekeepers, access constituents directly, and reinforce the trend toward permanent, ongoing campaigning among incumbents. Although news media have not always presented a critical perspective on the proclamations of public officials, editors have never before been completely bypassed on broadcast media as they now are on many "Washington Report" programs. In short, cable now allows officeholders to engage in propaganda programming unchecked by regulation and unedited by media gatekeepers.

Third, the legal status of cable television is constantly evolving, with continuing uncertainty as to whether cable television should be governed by the rules and principles established for broadcast television (such as fairness and equal time) or by the practices established for print media. The final decisions will have important implications for the growth of cable as a significant campaign technology. As cable proponents argue (even when they have monopoly franchises) that the print model of "plenty" and a lack of scarcity should apply, outside public access channels (with political shows sandwiched in between electronic crystal ball readers, poets, and amateur theater), there rarely are opportunities for those dissenting from mainstream political values.

Fourth, there are a number of systems (reaching about 1 million households) with two-way or interactive capability. Although initially extolled as one of the major virtues of cable, the electronic town meeting has been a rarity, relegated to experimental status. Widespread "teledemocracy" or "electronic democracy," with voters at home casting advisory ballots after viewing or participating in town meetings or hearings or candidate debates, has not changed the level of policy debate. Indeed, the major result of interactive capability has been candidates testing campaign positions by instantaneous feedback of viewers turning dials toward "approve" or "disapprove" meters when a candidate gives a speech. The result is that candidates hone their speeches to make the perfect electronic "pitch" by removing from their standard stump speech the phrases that generate "disapproval," and pandering to audiences with slogans and phraseology which generates strong "approval" ratings on the interactive systems.

In many ways, interactive systems have not enhanced democratic participation, but have oversimplified democratic processes by reducing complex policy questions to "yes" or "no." There is little discussion of who formulates the questions or who is the designated spokesperson for the respective positions. Rather than being truly *interactive,* many of the systems are really *feedback* systems. Moreover, these systems create the myth of political dialogue while working to the contrary. Feedback technologies such as *telepolls* (where viewers or listeners *pay* to call a 900 number connected to an automated answering system which tallies "yes" or "no" votes) purport to present results of a "survey" when in fact these systems result in self-selected callers who are willing or able to pay (wealthy Republicans?) to register their viewpoint, while those with limited resources (working-class Democrats?) are unable to pay to register their perspectives.

In general, the most widespread uses of electronic democracy through interactive cable have been electronic "gong shows," where debaters are electronically cut off when a majority of viewers has had enough. Experiments in teledemocracy have had mixed results, with success limited by the interest of voters. Most problematic have been concerns over equality of access to the means of participation as well as questions surrounding the responsibility for setting the teledemocratic agenda and posing questions in a format suitable for electronic voting. Will the interactive technologies be dominated by a few, technologically sophisticated participants? Will a spiral of silence emerge in which dissenters, not seeing wide support for their views, remain silent and are discouraged from expressing their views in the public forums?

Finally, the availability of the Cable Satellite Public Affairs Network (CSPAN), with its cablecasting of legislative proceedings, provides political junkies with the ability to continuously monitor incumbents, and a video record of statements on the floor. Already the Republican National Committee is taping and indexing the proceedings to provide instant access to CSPAN broadcasts for subsequent use in political campaigns. And unlike the *Congressional Record,* videos on file cannot be "amended" before they are broadcast, thus making gaffes a permanent part of the record.

2. Videocassette Players —Videocassette player sales mushroomed dramatically after 1983, and are now found in over 80% of the voting households in the United States. Increasingly, they are being harnessed by political candidates.

First, videocassette technology has affected politics, as has cable, by drawing audiences from broadcast television and political advertising. But increasingly videocassettes are being produced for political candidates for three purposes. First, at least a few well-funded campaigns have distributed videocassettes to homes as political direct mail—a sort of electronic potholder. Although most candidates struggle to have their direct mail pieces read, the novelty of a videocassette arriving in the mail would undoubtedly prompt many a voter to view the tape. Political videotape duplicating services can provide thousands of cassettes for direct mail similar to printed direct mail.

Again, these messages on videotape are *private* messages, not accessible broadly as are broadcast advertisements. Candidates and ballot proposition committees can fragment the audience, sending different, privatized messages to voter groups out of the view of public scrutiny. And the legal status of these messages, including disclaimers or identification of the sponsor, is not yet clear.

A second use of videocassettes is for providing video endorsements and messages at private campaign functions. Fund-raising events in particular have employed videotaped "personal" messages from the President or governor endorsing a local candidate. And tapes have been used as gift premiums to thank campaign contributors. A president can spend an afternoon in the White House basement and record hundreds of "private" endorsements on videotape enhancing the political advantage of selected candidates.

3. Teleconferencing —Teleconferencing, in particular video conferencing (using voice and video connections to link two or more ground facilities, usually via satellite) is also being used increasingly in statewide and national campaigns.

Teleconferencing allows candidates to "meet" with various groups personally without travelling to meet those groups. Thus, a candidate can stay in a studio all day yet "attend" meetings with a dozen or more groups scheduled for a half-hour exclusive videoconference with the candidate, groups whose size, influence, or geographic inaccessibility might otherwise not warrant a full meeting with the candidate. On the one hand, teleconferencing may provide access to candidates for groups that would otherwise be too small to justify the time required of the candidate. On the other hand, teleconferencing enables a candidate to avoid public, spontaneous campaigning and the give-and-take of a live audience, and minimizes the opportunity of a candidate to learn through personal interaction and extensive travel.

The capacity of candidates to expand their travels through satellite hookups has been demonstrated in several political campaigns, many of which have full-time teleconference coordinators. Candidates have announced their campaigns with teleconference hookups that allowed virtually any local newscaster across the country to electronically attend the campaign kickoff press conference and ask "exclusive" interview questions of the candidate, while he remained in a single studio.

Although, on the surface, this again suggests that new technology can enhance the openness and access of a campaign, the reality may be different. In particular the emphasis on *local* news media outlets works to the advantage of the national politician. Local journalists unfamiliar with national politics may ask "soft" questions and look for local angles to the story. Unlike national network correspondents who routinely interact with national political figures, local news personnel have little experience, and experience substantial status and prestige gaps, with the national politicians. The result is that candidates remain unchallenged in the interviews and use the teleconference as "free" advertising for the campaign.

As one example, in opening his 1986 campaign for reelection, California governor George Deukmejian scheduled a 5:30 p.m. news conference, hoping that local news stations would "go live" with the announcement, and hinting that he might take questions from local news anchors who used the teleconferencing capabilities available at the announcement.

4. Electronic Mail —Electronic mail consists of electronically transmitted messages that are computer addressed and sorted and stored until the receiver accesses them. Unlike ordinary mail, transmission is instantaneous. Both the sender and receiver must be linked on a computer network to send and receive mail. Although the use of electronic mail is limited, already there are pilot projects in Congress to enable home computer users to communicate directly with their members of Congress, and vice versa. In addition, the immediacy of electronic mail makes it possible to deliver, at least to computer users, direct mail at literally the last moment as voters are sent messages right up until the time they vote.

A variety of interest groups have established electronic mail *network alert systems,* where members are notified of pending legislation affecting the group and urged to contact representatives with messages supporting or opposing the position. The immediacy of responses can overwhelm decision makers before slower, more traditional communications arrive.

Electronic mail is one of the many technologies that has the *potential* to enhance participation but in reality may limit participation to those who are computer literate and who have (usually paid) access to computer bulletin boards. The ability of computer users to send multiple messages far outpaces the ability of those using traditional communication to send multiple messages. In addition, electronic mail may be subject to the censorship of the electronic mail provider. Recently, for example the Prodigy system (a joint IBM-Sears venture) cut off service to those who protested rate increases on the electronic mail system and who tried to organize other system users to mobilize against the system operators.

5. Electronic Databases —Electronic databases are proprietary collections of abstracts, statutes, legal cases, news service clippings, public data, and other records electronically accessible to subscribers. Although online databases have been used commercially in the legal and technical fields for some time, increasingly they are used for political purposes. Nationally, *Congressional Quarterly's* (CQ) Washington Alert Service, Legi-Tech, and, in New York and 11 other states, the Legislative Retrieval System or its equivalent provide information to subscribers. Included in these data bases are texts of bills introduced to the legislature, the status of the bills, calendars, agendas, and hearing schedules. In addition, Legi-Tech provides information on campaign contributions and spending by registered lobbyists, while the CQ database includes role call votes, interest group ratings, and biographical information on legislators, features which are valuable in campaign fund raising and opposition research.

Although most of the information in the databases is available through other means, the cost of electronic bases (from $200 to $5,000 initial fee, plus monthly fees from $20 to $600, plus hourly charges for use) limits access to them to large commercial enterprises, consultants, and lobbyists. At times the speed of transmission provides an important time advantage; information on the CQ database is available 3 days before the printed copy of the Weekly Report is delivered in the mail.

The electronic political databases raise some of the same issues that are being raised with respect to the general privatization of archival material in terms of costs, access, and their ultimately replacing freely available information on legislative and political process.

6. Political Databases —As more and more local registrars of voting computerize their records of registered voters, candidates are building proprietary files of voters derived from computerized official lists, and using these proprietary files to target voter communications. Typically, a candidate (or consultant) will purchase a computer list of registered voters (or even create such lists by keypunching registration rolls) containing only name, address, date of registration, and age, and "enhance" the list by matching the list with other computerized lists such as homeowners, union members, political party members, vehicle owners, ethnic name "dictionaries," and telephone numbers. In addition, information may be added to the file based on telephone or personal canvassing. The result is a proprietary database that has, not only a name and address, but information that enables the candidate to target messages based on one or more variables in the file, such as union member households with Hispanic surnames or Democrats who own two or more vehicles, or homeowners in houses with assessed values over $100,000. Thus, voters receive one or more of hundreds or thousands of combinations of variables in highly targeted or even personalized (see laser printers below) messages addressing their interests. The targeted groups are usually identified through political polling.

Perhaps more than any other new campaign technology, the construction of political databases has offended voters. While proponents of political databases management suggest that in a mass society and in a world of mass, undifferentiated political messages, it is important to touch individual voters with messages that address their unique concerns, opponents have suggested that targeting and fragmenting the audience is yet another way for candidates to disguise their ideology.

Targeting through political database management can allow a candidate to send one message to a group of voters with a certain demographic or ideological profile, and a second—perhaps contradictory—message to another group of voters. Since the messages are largely "private" in the form of direct mail, voters and opponents may be unaware of the differences between the messages they receive and those received by others. Although it is rare for candidates to send completely contradictory messages (e.g., proabortion to one group of voters, antiabortion to another), it is commonly the case that one group of voters will be aware of some of a candidate's positions, while another group of voters is completely unaware of that position and instead has heard about still other issues about which they are presumably interested.

Another major criticism of targeting through political databases is that it deindividualizes the voter, compelling him or her to become part of a "group" based on stereotypic qualities. Although voters may have individual issue concerns and preferences, simply because they are "Hispanic" or "over 65," or perhaps "Hispanic *and* over 65," they are presumed to care about the issues and will respond similar to those who are similarly demographically situated.

Finally, demographic targeting through the manipulation of databases may create categories of individual voters that may be based on ethnic, racial or other stereotyping. Voters who live in a certain geographic area may be assumed to be a member of a certain ethnic group or be classified by their sexual preference. Rather than provide individual messages, the result is messages based on an assumed homogeneity of interests.

7. Laser Printers —In conjunction with political databases, high-speed laser printers are capable of producing individual messages at the speed of a high-speed photocopying machine or small printing press, form several hundred to over ten thousand pieces per hour. Laser printed products may range from "personal" letters, with the message based on variables selected from the political database, to "slate" cards in which the names of endorsed candidates for various offices appear in mailings only to voters residing in the appropriate geographic area, to absentee ballot applications that are already filled out by the laser printer, awaiting only the signature of the recipient. Laser printing enables political databases to be used efficiently in the preparation of highly targeted mail.

Slate mail in particular has been problematic for many voters and candidates. Slate mail is created by individual political consultants, some of whom have no particular political loyalty. Candidates are virtually compelled to buy a space on the mailer out of fear that the opposing candidate will appear on the mailer instead. For candidates in low-visibility elections or for ballot proposition committees with no other voter communication, the slate mailers become all important. Voters often are unaware that the slate mailers, decorated with the political party symbols of a donkey (sent to Democrats only) or elephant (Republicans only), are not official party mailings. Indeed, based on ability to pay, strange configurations of slate mail appear. Republicans may be mailed a slate mailer with a picture of a Republican president, yet find the names of Democrats for some low-visibility offices, or Democrats may find that they should vote "yes" on a slate mailer containing ballot measure "suggested votes" even though the measures are opposed by the party leadership. In essence, there is substantial outright deception made possible by the laser printer and political databases that enable the production of literally thousands of combinations of versions of slate mailers.

8. Personal Computers —Personal computers, and software developed for them, have dominated much of the discussion concerning the use of new technologies in political campaigns. Even small campaigns for local office with very limited resources may have access to technology for the manipulation of lists, preparation of financial disclosure reports, demographic targeting of voters, personalizing direct mail, campaign budgeting, scheduling, and so forth as a result of the development of political software packages marketed by a dozen vendors.

Virtually all campaign software packages are divided into three modules, which enable campaign managers (often the candidate himself or herself) to manage lists (of supporters, donors, volunteers), budget (account for campaign funds raised and spent, and comply with campaign disclosure laws through the use of political-oriented spreadsheet calculation programs and report writers), and target voters through analysis of previous election returns. Other enhancements in the programs enable managers to write news releases in the proper form, schedule campaign activities, conduct amateur polls, or process and send data to and from larger computer files.

Personal computers with communications devices allow campaign workers and offices to communicate electronically in a local area network with terminals at various headquarters locations, the incumbent office, and candidate's and campaign manager's homes. In addition, personal computers allow subsets of large databases to be downloaded for manipulation. For example, all information on a particular precinct can be electronically sent from a large database, and information resulting from intensive phoning or precinct walking can be incorporated into a database through the personal computer.

Despite the widespread availability of software packages to enable candidates to manage their own campaign, these packages are useful only at the lowest election level. Other campaigns still rely on campaign professionals. Indeed, the myth that an unknown and underfinanced candidate can compete with the better financed, professionally managed candidates is one of the difficulties that campaign software and hardware have created. Candidates and voters may feel that anyone can run for office with these tools, yet the hardware simply is not sufficient to compete with large, mainframe computer systems and databases.

9. Electronic News-Gathering Equipment —The miniaturization of videotape equipment, and the development of portable ground stations to transmit, have enabled large campaigns to produce their own "news" shows daily during campaigns. Typically, the candidate is followed by a videotape crew with portable equipment throughout the day, the tape edited, and available for immediate broadcast. National and statewide campaigns broadcast the day's campaign activities in selected state or media markets.

Some observers have argued that even national politics is becoming more localized as a result of microwave transmission equipment. This technology allows even local television broadcasters covering an incumbent or a campaign to have a presence in Washington, or, on the floor of a political convention, to give a "local" twist to news. And traditionally, local news is generally positive, thus favoring the incumbent.

10. Telephone —New high-tech uses of the telephone are playing increasingly important roles in political campaigning beyond the traditional telephone bank boiler room staffed by volunteers. As a result of innovations developed largely for commercial telemarketing operations, automated dialing equipment makes it possible to dial tens of thousands of numbers daily to deliver taped campaign messages without human operators (where permitted by law). In addition, new equipment makes it possible to call voters and ask them if they would like to hear a message from the candidate on any of a variety of issues. A tape prerecorded by the candidate is then played for the voter, who hears an almost personal message. Finally, touch-tone telephones are being used to canvass voters automatically. Voters are asked to touch a phone button to indicate support or opposition to a candidate, and the results are fed directly into a political database described earlier.

Systems available to automatically record incoming calls have led to the development of the *telepoll,* where viewers or listeners call into a news organization to register support or opposition to a question. Such instant data, however unscientific, often are treated as if they were valid, leading campaigners to use countermeasures such as automatic redialers to register dozens of "votes" and skew the results favorably.

CULTURAL LIMITS AND THE NEW TECHNOLOGIES

The importance of new technologies of political campaigning depends in part on whether or not the technologies will alter the process of political campaigning, and, more importantly, whether they ultimately enhance or limit democracy and public participation. Thus far, there is little evidence that the new technologies are democracy enhancing; indeed, the opposite may be the case.

The ability of the new technologies to significantly alter campaigning is limited by the cultural, economic, legal, and political environments in which they are applied. Voters have come to see the campaign process as a highly ritualized courtship between themselves and the candidates. Voters expect to be wooed by candidates who come to their door, phone them, and solicit their votes through the mails or through telephone pitches. The culture of campaigning welcomes new methods for delivering these messages as we have shifted from billboards and posters to radio to television to highly targeted print and electronic mail, but the ritual of contact remains the same. In the past, voters may have expected a potholder or campaign favor from a campaigner; now they may come to expect a videocassette brought to them courtesy of the candidate. Regardless of the technology, voters expect to be contacted. To be sure, the methods and efficiency of addressing the specific voter and touching him or her with a personal and meaningful message might change in the shift from broad- to narrowcast messages, but the process is constant. But do these new technologies represent an "enhancement" of democracy?

Another cultural limit to the political applications of the new technologies is the willingness of voters to adapt to, and be more than passive recipients of, the products of the new technologies. Even if the hardware of electronic democracy were in place, some voters would prefer to vote the old-fashioned way. What becomes of those who are swept away in the tide of technological "progress?" Just as automatic teller machines are not used by those who are intimidated and confused by them, there will be voters who are reluctant to participate in any form of teledemocracy that robs them of the ritual of going to the polls to vote.

The one area where new technologies have made significant inroads into the culture of campaigning is through the rise of a class of professional campaigners. And few people suggest that the new campaign technocrats have any interest in enhancing participation. The opposite generally is true, as candidates seek to limit campaign messages only to supporters and persuadable undecided voters.

Candidates, and to some extent voters, expect campaigns to be professionally managed. The rise of popularly expressed cynicism about the motives of candidates probably is linked to the "slick" campaigning that has permeated even local elections, and may well be tied to the replacement of the citizen/public servant with the professional "politician" who is employed as a public official as a permanent career.

Economic issues of the new technologies are inevitably intertwined with the participatory questions. First, the costs of new technologies are still prohibitive for many candidates. It is important to note that the new technologies have not *replaced* the aging ones, they are used to *supplement* them. The result is ever-increasing costs of campaigning.

Even as candidates discount the efficacy of some forms of voter communication, they are reluctant to discard them as new ones emerge. Candidates in contested elections can never be too sure of victory, and they cannot afford to be wrong about a decision to discard an outmoded technology.

The development of databases and the mainframe computers they require, videoconference facility rentals, or the use of automated dialing equipment is simply prohibitive for small campaigns. Even political software for personal computers is expensive to small campaigns and grassroots organizers. From the perspective of the voter, the hardware required to participate in politics electronically is prohibitive. Most households do not even have access to CSPAN on cable systems, and only a small minority have access to an interactive cable system. Even commercial services such as electronic home banking services and teletext/videotex systems have failed to prove viable because there are so few subscribers. In short, most voters simply will not be plugged into any high-tech system for the foreseeable future. Even when "most" voters are hooked into the electronic political network, the issue of what is to be done about those who cannot afford to be part of the network must be addressed. Will teledemocracy terminals be provided to the poor, the institutionalized, and the geographically isolated? This is unlikely, because of the enormous costs involved.

The legal status of many of the new technologies also may serve to constrain their ability to enhance democracy. Are these technologies to be treated as common carriers, open to all who seek to use them at a reasonable fee, or are they private facilities that may be made available on a more discretionary basis? Will municipalities continue to have the power to establish service monopolies or to compel cable systems to provide public access channels? The legal status of these technologies with respect to political campaigning is at best uncertain.

Finally, there are political limits to the spread of new technology. Candidates who wish to maintain or develop an image as populist candidates often seek large numbers of unskilled volunteers. Yet technology-intensive campaigns require faster unskilled volunteers, and more highly skilled equipment operators, or no volunteers at all. Volunteers may find that the tasks to which they are accustomed (folding, stuffing, hand addressing, etc.) are not needed. Volunteers may also simply become alienated from campaigns that become more and more professionalized because of the need for high-technology specialists.

Candidates and elected officials who recognize that organized economic interest groups are most likely to acquire technology first may, for political reasons, be reluctant to abandon older methods of communication or initiate new ones. For example, an electronic mailing employed instead of a printed newsletter would reach only a very limited segment of the constituency, and responses would come from group members easily mobilized by prosperous interest groups.

A third political factor is that candidates who have become accustomed to the current candidate-based campaign made possible by television-dependent campaigns may be reluctant to become dependent upon the resources of the national or state parties which are often required to launch high-technology campaigns.

Finally, candidates and public officials may be unwilling to abandon the time-honored methods of political deliberation and decision making. The interactive technologies capable of tapping the immediate responses of constituents can, as some have argued, lead, not to national town meetings, but to national mob rule. Candidates who are subject to an interactive electronic thumbs-up or thumbs-down following a campaign debate, for example, may be unwilling to debate. And among office holders, some decisions require that public officials act, not solely as delegates instructed by constituents constantly watching and prepared to instruct them on every move, but as representatives entrusted with making the right choice. And, in the Madisonian tradition of deliberation and judgment, officials may require time to deliberate and think unswayed by instant electronic feedback. Incumbents as well may resist the new technologies as they realize the temptation these technologies hold for turning their offices into permanent reelection campaigns rather than offices of public service.

NEW TECHNOLOGIES AND POLITICAL COMPETITION

With so many new technologies available to political campaigners, surely there will be significant alterations in the dominant patterns of campaigning for office, and in some political institutions themselves. The new technologies simultaneously make it possible to manipulate candidate images for individual constituencies, yet provide mechanisms for candidates to converse with and respond to voters.

First, there can be little doubt that there will continue to be an increasing professionalization of political campaigning. Although the personal computer no doubt will raise the level of sophistication of the very smallest and most localized amateur campaigns, until personal computers with communications capabilities are widely distributed throughout the population, their relevance to the ability of ordinary voters to research candidates or send or receive electronic mail will be limited because of economic reasons. In addition, political interest in the United States is limited. Regardless of the amount of information made available, voters with the ordinary concerns of earning a living, raising the kids, or repairing the family car simply will not spend their leisure playing politics.

However, the overall result of technological developments will be that high-tech experts will be more central in political campaigns. Just as survey researchers, media specialists and general campaign consultants have become central campaign figures, specialists in harnessing the new technologies will become important members of the campaign teams. As candidates for the past 20 years have learned to play to the cameras, candidates will emerge who will play to the computer. The make-up specialist will be less and less important than the database manager in the campaign of the future. The result is likely to be a reduction of political competition as classes of political "haves"—those with access to newer technologies—are more success-ful than the political "have-nots" who are unable or unwilling to harness the new methods of campaigning.

Second, even as the cost of specific technologies declines, the demands for increasingly sophisticated capabilities will continue to push the cost of campaigning upwards. Thus, the relationship between money and political success is unlikely to change as a result of the newer technologies. Even as computing costs decline, and as the new technologies have the capacity to reduce costs of time, travel, and so forth, the new technologies cost real dollars. Moreover, the costs of reducing information costs are borne by the campaigners and pro-ducers of information, not by consumers of information. The result is higher campaign budgets.

Third, there will continue to be a tension between the recent trend of candidates to be independent of their political parties, and the need for party support to develop campaign essentials such as a sophisti-cated database. As an example, the rise of CSPAN would suggest that it is in a candidate's interest to demonstrate independence and appeal to voters rather than to party leaders. However, coping with the development costs of preparing political databases and maintaining them are enormous tasks that require ongoing party and organization efforts. Candidates who develop their own databases, of course, may maintain independence; candidates who lack those resources may be subject to greater party discipline.

Fourth, the new technologies make the "permanent campaign" even more of a reality. Electronic mail makes it possible to send narrowly targeted constituency newsletters at a fraction of the cost of printed ones. Cable programming makes it possible to bypass news gatekeepers and access constituents directly and routinely. The need to continue to update political databases will make every political contact a potential input to the database. Interactive cable systems may make it possible for constituents to routinely voice their preferences to public officials. But at present, since interactive capabilities are limited, most information resulting from the new technologies continues to flow from the top down, from leader to constituent, rather than vice versa.

The question of whether or not voters *want* interactive political capabilities is far from resolved. Another factor is that the relatively easy mobilization of constituencies through videoconferencing and electronic mail can lead to a rise in single-issue political constituencies ready to overwhelm decision makers with a flood of information at a moment's notice. Grassroots lobbying through rapidly mobilized constituencies is becoming a tool of special interests. In anticipation of this, candidates soon may be addressing their constituents, not as voters concerned with a common good, but as single-issue voters where interests are determined through database analysis. Direct mail specialists have demonstrated considerable success with recruiting and mobilizing voters. Already there is concern that the instantaneous *articulation* of concerns is replacing the slower *aggregation* of interests.

Ultimately, there are a few key dimensions of communication to consider when pondering the long-term consequences of the new technologies for voter communication: will there be more information, will it be disseminated broadly, will it be sent quickly, will it be interactive, and will it be centralized?

Although the answers to these are not certain, there are some hints that not all the consequences of the new technologies will be positive. For the first question, it is not clear that there will be more information available to each citizen. Although the total volume may increase, the targeting of messages may well result in voters having more information about some issues, and less information about others. If voters are "targeted" as interested in a single issue, communication on solely that issue may be targeted to them. The result is a potentially fragmented electorate, with little commonality in their interests, and an increasingly parochial viewpoint on politics.

Perhaps more problematic is that the proliferation of media outlets containing nonpolitical programming will enable the electorate to completely escape from politics and the inadvertent exposure afforded when the programming options (i.e., the networks) were limited. With highly specialized cable programming, it is possible to escape news and public affairs programming completely.

A seventh issue is that, increasingly, the technology is capable of bypassing the traditional mass media and directly accessing voters. Thus, candidates may no longer strive for moderation of rhetoric, knowing they are in the public spotlight with their messages. There already is ample evidence that private messages—phone pitches and direct mail "hit" pieces, are far more strident and ideological than mass media messages.

Finally, the new technologies raise questions of communications public policy with respect to new technologies. The vocabulary of *fairness* or *reasonable access* or *equal time* developed for broadcasting, to insure robust debate and political competition, may not apply to the new technologies. Will voters have the right to be removed from proprietary databases? Will candidates have access to common carrier technologies they cannot afford to lease at market rates if these technologies become the most common method of political communication? And surely we must ask ourselves whether or not, as the older technologies become less important, regulation of them will be eliminated. If that becomes the case, there may well be no guidelines at all to enhance political competition.

PART VI
Postscripts

Sovereignty and Beyond

Kaarle Nordenstreng

In 1979, when the predecessor of this book appeared, there were 150 nation states in the world, customarily divided into the "first" (capitalist West), "second" (socialist East) and "third" (developing South). By the end of 1992, the number of sovereign nations (UN members) has risen to over 180, but the neat division into three worlds is gone. Meanwhile, regional superstates are taking shape, notably in Europe (European Community/Union) and North America (USA, Canada, Mexico). The world has undergone a drastic change, with geopolitical transformations as graphically outlined by Galtung in Chapter 2.

PARADOX

The turmoil has turned national sovereignty into a paradoxical issue. On the one hand, with the new nations—following the dissolution of the Soviet Union, Yugoslavia, and Czechoslovakia— sovereignty seems to be an ever *more* valid factor in the contemporary world. On the other hand, with the economic and cultural integration— prompted by new communication technologies—sovereignty seems to be a less and *less* significant factor. Moreover, there is a paradox concerning the social and political role of sovereignty: It serves *both* as a shield protecting people's authentic interests against foreign domination *and* as an instrument of people's repression by national elites.

It is only recently that national sovereignty has been widely seen as such a paradox; as late as the 1970s it was still taken more or less for granted. Today, in the 1990s, we may even conclude— as suggested by most authors of this volume, beginning with Frank in Chapter 1—that the customary concept of sovereignty should be seriously questioned. In this line, political scientists and international lawyers have begun to challenge the cornerstone of their disciplines, using titles such as "the decline of sovereignty" (Rosas, 1993) and even "the end of sovereignty" (Camilleri & Falk, 1992). To be sure, the concept of sovereignty has not become completely obsolete or 'academic'; it still remains a vital issue in the real world as well as in scholarship about the world. Thus the concept is under revision but not under extinction.

HISTORY

At this stage it is important to put the concept of national sovereignty into historical perspective. As pointed out by Drake in Chapter 13, it dates back to the post-medieval era, with landmarks such as the Peace of Augsburg in 1555 and the Peace of Westphalia in 1648 giving rise to the notion of nation state, accompanied by a horizontal system of sovereign and equal states (each having a vertical inner power structure). This 'modern' notion of nation state coincided with the emergence of capitalism; it was preceded by the 'classic' notion of an international system under a feudal order, made up of small entities dominated by the Catholic Church. The 'modern' notion was based on the idea of a natural law common to humankind *(jus gentium)*, instead of a divine law administered by the Pope. Nations were understood as sovereign actors which do not surrender to any outside power—neither divine nor secular.

This paradigm of international relations rested on the principle of anarchy—the Hobbesian view that international order is to be maintained only by the states, each pursuing her selfish interests. The corresponding 'realistic' school of international relations has survived until our time, as has the parallel 'idealistic' school which emphasizes international cooperation and multilateralism but is still based on the same principle of anarchy, with national sovereignty as a central concept.

Actually, the 'modern' notion of an international system made up of sovereign states has remained the dominant paradigm over several centuries, unchallenged even by such turning points as the French (bourgeois) Revolution and the Russian (socialist) Revolution. For example, the novelties of democracy and human rights introduced with the Enlightenment—whereby all people have inalienable citizen's rights and all political power rests ultimately with the people—did not lead to a revision of the national sovereignty concept. The idea of people's sovereignty over society was limited to the governance of one nation state at a time, while the concept of national sovereignty was separately applied to the international system. On the other hand, some ideas of the Enlightenment—such as the universality of human rights and the common good of humankind which all freedoms were supposed to serve—did pose a challenge to national sovereignty, but this challenge was suppressed by other considerations with greater political weight.

Today the history of ideas has once more reached a turning point—not so much because of the ideas themselves but ultimately because of the changing realities in the world. We may see a shift to a third stage in the evolution of the concept of state, as outlined by Rosas (1993):

	Feudal State	Capitalist state	Civic state
Legal structure	monism	dualism	pluralism
Organization	fragmented	centralized	decentralized
Legal sources	natural law contract	laws, private contracts	plurality, including reason & justice
Ideology	authority	freedom	equality
Administration of violence	private armies	standing state armies	police

Such a sweeping view also suggests that after the 'classic' and 'modern' notions of the international system a third one is emerging. And if one follows the reasoning of Hamelink, Mowlana, and Falk (Chapters 16–18), the cornerstone of this new paradigm is no longer national sovereignty but rather, *global civil society.*

REFERENCES

Camilleri, J., & Falk, J. (1992). *The end of sovereignty? The politics of a shrinking and fragmenting world.* Aldershot, England: Edward Elgar.

Rosas, A. (1993). The decline of sovereignty: Legal perspectives. In J. Iivonen (Ed.), *The future of the nation state in Europe.* Aldershot, England: Edward Elgar.

The Context of Our Work*

Herbert I. Schiller

What then, are the distinctive features of this post-Cold War era which we have entered so recently? Its characteristics are many but I will limit myself to those few I regard most significant.

HISTORY CONTINUES

However obvious it may be to state it, the historical process continues. We are not in some ultimate stage of development in which the institutions and practices that structure our world have reached their final refinement. As will be evident in what follows, it is necessary to be fully and constantly aware of this reality if we are not to be locked into archaic formulas and apprehensive modes of thought. Already new demands are being placed on our understanding, and these can only intensify as the social conditions now present mature and unfold. This understood, the implications of the overarching features of the age can better be appreciated.

THE NEW ALIGNMENT OF GLOBAL POWER

It is now evident the global system that has prevailed since the end of the Second World War, lasting nearly half a century, is in transition.

---

* This was the opening address delivered at the 8th National Congress of the French Association of Information Science and Communication, in Lille, France, May 21, 1992.

The American global primacy is coming to an end. Not all at once and, as will be noted later, not in all respects, but unmistakable all the same. However the United States' Secretary of State may designate the new situation—"collective engagement" is his term, "we led, we had partners and together we succeeded" (Friedman, 1992, p. 1)—the reality is a diminution of U.S. unitary power.

Who will seize that power remains to be determined. Yet, whoever does achieve it, fully or partially, one fundamental condition will not have changed. This is the stratification of the global community into the "haves" and the "have nots," with possibly one new preeminent "have." Much like the typical coup, the top changes, but the bottom remains where it was with all its attendant difficulties. The United Nations Program on Development recently reported the continuing growth in the gap between the rich and the poor countries. It noted that while the South had 80% of the world's population it undertook only 4% of the research and had less than 5% of the global stock of computers. Additionally, from 1983 to 1989, a net transfer of wealth amounting to $242 billion flowed from the South to the North (Fottorino, 1992, p. 1).

For this reason, the admonition that history continues is actually another means of calling attention to the unresolved, and overriding, issue of global disparity. What we can take for granted in our work and studies is that the struggle for domination of the global system will be matched by an equally strenuous, though less acknowledged, effort on the part of the presently unfavored. The question of acknowledgment introduces the second distinctive characteristic of these times. In exploring who acknowledges and who is not acknowledged, we come to the ever more central subject of media-informational control.

ASCENDANCY OF THE MEDIA-CULTURAL SECTOR

From the time when Marshall McLuhan began to embroider his media theories in the 1950s, increasing attention has been given to the role of media and information flows. It is now commonplace, yet accurate, to regard the media/informational sector in a developed economy as a crucial component of the economic, political, and cultural landscape.

Information flows now determine the site and regulate the processes of industrial production. They facilitate global financial transactions and allow capital flows either to accelerate or sometimes to dry up. Media practices now govern the electoral process (at least in the United States), and a national campaign without television and a variety of ancillary services, such as opinion polling, advertising, and public relations, is literally unthinkable.

All of these developments, seemingly, are the outcome of the new technologies that have been installed in recent decades, notably television, satellites, computers and cable. Yet what may be even more striking than the capabilities of this advanced instrumentation are two interrelated social features that direct its utilization. One is the ongoing and accelerating process of consolidation and concentration in what may be termed the cultural industries. The other is the near total appropriation (again, most advanced in the United States) of this powerful technological infrastructure for the marketing and commercial needs of the national and transnational business system.

Huge private structures now preside over the publishing, radio, television, film, recording, and entertainment fields. Time-Warner, for example, a $20 billion cultural conglomerate includes in its holdings film, recording, television, cable, and book publishing. There are a couple of dozen similar, if not so vast, aggregates based in Europe, North America, Japan, and elsewhere. In a few years only a handful of media combines are expected to survive and dominate the global terrain.

These integrated cultural colossi have become the educators and guardians of the social realm. They select, or exclude, the stories and songs, the images and words that create individual and group consciousness and identity. They do this for commercial gain, and this in itself produces grave distortions. However, they have also become so entwined with the industrial engines of the market that increasingly all spheres of human existence are subject to the intrusion of commercial values.

How this works need not detain us here, though it is instructive to observe how what is regarded as exclusively an entertainment—Euro-Disney—is a "cultural" enterprise totally embodying, and serving, general corporate objectives. For example, the giant food processing company, Nestlé, has been a major promoter of Euro-Disney, "staging contests across Europe that are intended to publicize the opening of the theme park.... In the Netherlands, contests and promotions involve 2,500 stores, representing 90% of total Dutch grocery sales" (Browning, 1992, p. B6).

The promotions, *The Wall Street Journal* reports, included newspaper inserts, stories in children's magazines, live broadcasts on leading European TV stations, and sales pitches to children between cartoons on TV programs. In short, a cultural industries' conglomerate, in tandem with other major players in the corporate sector, can saturate human consciousness with its messages, the most important of which, clearly, is: CONSUME.

There are other messages as well. In all the industrialized societies, the print mass media are firmly in the hands of a few corporate enterprises. When the Labour Party in Britain lost its fourth successive election in April 1992, the first comment by the party's leader, Neil Kinnock was: "the Conservative-supporting press has enabled the Tory Party to win yet again when the Conservative Party could not have secured victory for itself on the basis of its record, its program or its character. (Whitney, 1992, p. 1). Perhaps this is overstated, but would not other labor and social democratic parties in Europe and elsewhere have similar frustrating experiences?

What these new capabilities and practices mean for such traditional areas of communication research as media effects, the marketplace of ideas (the ideas of the market place?), free speech, the use of language, and so on, are worthy subjects for study. The very notion, for example, of what constitutes free speech in a privatized and corporately dominated society may have to be recast.

One conclusion needs no additional substantiation. The control of the informational/cultural sphere, nationally and internationally, along with military and economic strength, confers hegemonic power. It is therefore either naive or disingenuous for the chief executive officer of the Walt Disney Company to assert, in a recent interview in *Le Monde,* that "l'imperialisme americain est mort. Nous ne sommes meme plus capables d'exporter des voitures ou de l'acier, la seule chose qui nous reste, ce sont nos produits culturels"[5] (*Le Monde,* 1991, p. 2). Why so modest a view of the value of cultural products, from the chief executive of a company exclusively engaged in their output?

Actually, the current condition of American imperialism despite the view of Walt Disney Company's chief deserves more than passing comment. To this we now turn briefly.

THE UNITED STATES IN THE NEW WORLD ORDER

As has already been noted, the United States' world position has suffered serious erosion in recent years. How far the slide will go and how global power will be reconfigured are still obscure. But the impact domestically of this realignment of global authority cannot fail to be immense. Ordinarily, this should not unduly concern those living elsewhere. When Britain, for example, found its world position downgraded at the end of World War II, unpalatable as it may have been to some privileged sections of the population, the impact hardly disturbed the international scene. It is not likely that the American decline will be so tranquil, either at home, or in its effect abroad.

The United States, even when slumping, possesses nearly a $6 trillion economy, almost one-sixth of which is engaged in international trade. The American military machine remains the largest on earth, and its dispositions, nuclear and otherwise, continue to be global. And, not least, American information (news and data services), pop culture (film, TV, music, theme parks), and the English language itself continue to dominate the world's cultural space, either directly or by imitation.

Yet, this powerful system is in a profound crisis which gives no sign of moderating or disappearing. While the current economic slump may be overcome, the structural imbalances in the economy are deepening. Amongst a wealth of recent statistics, it is reported that "by 1989, the top 1 percent, or 834,000 households with about $5.7 trillion of net worth, was worth more than the bottom 90 percent of Americans—84 million households, with about $4.8 trillion in net worth (Nasar, 1992, p. 1) Other figures show that the real income level of the majority of Americans is lower today than it was 20 years ago. Here too, the inequality factor turns up. The income of the top brackets has jumped startlingly in the same period.

At the same time, the basic physical infrastructure of the country has deteriorated. Highways, bridges, underground city facilities, housing, and a multitude of socially needed installations require renovation, to say nothing of expansion. The list of unattended problems could be almost unlimitedly extended.

These conditions are widely experienced and well known, though not everyone draws the same conclusions from them. Yet, if this is true of physical structures, what can be said about the general social condition? A number of recent developments illuminate what is producing the anger, mistrust, and disenchantment of sizable groups of people and an increasing number of coercive practices of state and corporate authorities.

There is general agreement that the electoral process and representative government itself are functioning poorly. More elected representatives than ever before are resigning. In the recent highly publicized Democratic primaries held in early 1992, in which Bill Clinton was chosen as the Democratic candidate to oppose President Bush, "only 12.3 percent of those eligible have voted" (Hinds, 1992, p. 3).

In the Republican primaries in the same period, a Ku Klux Klanner and an extreme rightwing conservative, though coming nowhere near to winning, nevertheless, in the latter's case, obtained considerable support.

Meanwhile, capital punishment has been resumed with the benign approval of the Supreme Court; organized labor, as a consequence of governmentally supported corporate use of "replacement workers"—

scabs who are given the jobs of the striking workers—is being effectively denied the right to strike; the right to abortion is imminently threatened; and racist actions (including a rising anti-Japanese sentiment) are multiplying. The rage of African-Americans, expressed in Los Angeles and other American cities not long ago, suggests the dimension of the mounting crisis. No less indicative is the rising demand among a significant portion of the white population for stern "law and order" measures—otherwise put, a no-nonsense repression.

INTERPRETATIONS

What to make of all this? Are these temporary aberrations uncomfortable, but unlikely to be longlasting? The customary expectation would be that the healthy forces of democracy would sooner or later set things right. In his most recent book, one of the most perceptive and senior interpreters of the American economy, John Kenneth Galbraith (1992) takes up this matter. His conclusions are sobering indeed. Galbraith concludes that there is no longer a "full democracy" in the United States. There is instead a "culture of contentment" which is comprised of a majority of those who vote. These have no desire to change the conditions under which, in the short run, they thrive. The State, which in Galbraith's estimate is the only force capable of remedying the structural imbalances in the country, has been made suspect by the very groups who now direct national policy. The state's most important instrument, fiscal policy—the use of taxes and the budget—also has been, in effect, abandoned.

The culture of contentment, it is hardly necessary to add, is by no means limited to the American electorate. It is thriving as well in Western Europe and a few other privileged enclaves around the world.

Not surprisingly, there are other interpretations. One view that has been given extraordinary publicity and attention, first in the conservative and then in the mainstream American media, is that of Francis Fukuyama (1992). He sees recent developments—the collapse of communism, in particular—as the triumph of liberal democracy, of both its economic component, the free market, and its political component, liberty and pluralism. An alternative systemic model, according to Fukuyama, is unimaginable.

But as we have noted, the condition of liberal democracy in the United States and elsewhere, is exceedingly tenuous. Whether it can withstand "the not inconsiderable likelihood of an eventual shock," that Galbraith (1992, p. 183) foresees, is uncertain at best. Predicting the political evolution of the United States, or anywhere else for that matter, at this point is foolhardy. But the likelihood of growing turmoil and the emergence of coercive States to combat it are no longer dismissible fantasies.

When a society such as the United States, with such enormous resources and capabilities, moves away from its historical principles, however inadequately implemented they may have been in the past, and lurches toward large-scale irrationality, it cannot be of indifference to the world and especially to those who have the obligation to chart and analyze political, social, and cultural messages.

Some years ago, a well-known American communications scholar wrote about the "passing of the dominant paradigm" (Rogers, 1976). By that he meant that the theory of communication and development associated with Daniel Lerner and Wilbur Schramm, and dominant in international thinking in the early post-World War II years, was no longer applicable. Today it may be necessary to include several other revered doctrines in the obsolete file before we can begin to think about creating a more humane world. The danger of the bureaucratized state has been amply demonstrated in the 20th century. Our task today may be to focus attention on the cultural and political consequences of the gargantuan private economic structures that now direct the global (mis)allocation of resources and the cultural and political pollution that results therefrom.

REFERENCES

Browning, E. S. (1992, April 1). Helping hands promote Euro-Disney. *The Wall Street Journal*, p. B6.

Fottorino, E. (1992, April 25). Le gouffre Nord-Sud. *Le Monde*, p. 1.

Friedman, T. (1992, April 22). *International Herald Tribune*, p. 1.

Fukuyama, F. (1992). *The end of history and the last man.* New York: The Free Press.

Galbraith, J. K. (1992). *The culture of contentment.* Boston: Houghton-Mifflin.

Hinds, M. de. (1992, April 25–26). Clinton can't beat Bush, democratic governor asserts. *International Herald Tribune*, p. 3.

Le Monde. (1992, April 15). p. 2.

Nasar, S. (1992, April 22). The bucks have it: America's richest made a killing in the '80s. *International Herald Tribune*, p. 1.

Rogers, E. (1976). The passing of the dominant paradigm. *Communication Research*, 3, 213–240.

Whitney, C. R. (1992, April 14). Quitting Kinnock blames Tory press for defeat. *International Herald Tribune*, p. 1.

Author Index

Subject Index